1888	Amateur Athletic Union (AAU) founded.
	Invention of the "safety" bicycle.
1889	Walter Camp's first "All-America" team was selected.
1891	Dr. James Naismith invented basketball at YMCA in Springfield, Massachusetts.
1893	Volleyball (known as "faustball") invented by W.C. Morgan in Massachusetts.
	Jockey Club created.
1895	First basketball game between two colleges played, Minnesota State School of Mines and Hamline College (with nine players on each side).
	First automobile race sponsored by the Chicago *Times-Herald*.
	William R. Hearst began the first sport section in a newspaper.
	Volleyball imported to America.
	James Smart, president of Purdue, facilitated formation of first intercollegiate athletic conference (later to become the "Big Ten").
1896	Modern Olympics reinstituted by Pierre de Coubertin.
1897	First modern intercollegiate basketball game between Yale and Penn (five players per side).
1900	Davis Cup tennis competition inaugurated.
	Women made their Olympic debut (Paris).
	Penn State becomes first school to offer athletic scholarships.
	American League for professional baseball, formed.
1902	First Rose Bowl Game (Michigan-49, Stanford-0).
1903	First baseball "World Series" (Boston beat Pittsburgh).
	New York Public School Athletic League formed.
1905	Eighteen deaths attributed to college and high school football caused Theodore Roosevelt to summon football representatives to White House.
	Intercollegiate Athletic Association (forerunner of NCAA) founded.
1907	Cycle racing began on the Isle of Mann off the coast of Scotland.
1908	Jack Johnson became first black heavyweight boxing champion.
1910	H. Steinitzer's *Sport und Kultur* (first sport and society book).
1911	First Indianapolis 500.
	Henry McDonald became first black professional football player.
1912	Ohio State became tenth member to join the "Big Ten."
1916	American Tennis Association founded by and for black players.
	Fritz Pollard became first black All-America football player.
	Olympic Games cancelled because of World War I.
1917	National Hockey League (NHL) founded in Canada.
1919	Baseball's Chicago Black Sox scandal.
	First coaches' journal, *Athletic Journal,* published.
1920	Beginning of "Golden Age of Sport."
	National Football League (NFL) founded when 11 teams were granted charters.
1921	KDKA, Pittsburgh, broadcast baseball games and fights.
	First radio station broadcast of the World Series results.
	Judge Kenesaw Mountain Landis became professional baseball's first commissioner.
1922	Supreme court decision in *Federal Baseball Club of Baltimore* vs. *National League* made baseball exempt from Sherman Antitrust Law of 1890.
	First black head coach in NFL, Fritz Pollard, Hammond Pros.
1923	White House Conference on women's athletics.
1925	Gertrude Ederle became first female to swim the English Channel.
1927	Harlem Globetrotters organized by Abe Saperstein in Chicago.
1928	Females permitted to participate in Olympic track and field events for the first time.
1929	Carnegie investigation of men's intercollegiate athletics.
1930	Rens (black professional) basketball team formed.
1932	Babe Didrikson "swept" LA Olympics.
1934	Men's collegiate basketball tournament, Madison Square Garden.
1935	Roller derby invented.
	First major league night baseball game, Pittsburgh played Cincinnati in Cincinnati.
1936	Jesse Owens wins four gold medals in Berlin Olympics.
1938	National Basketball League was organized.

A Sociological Perspective of Sport

FOURTH EDITION

Wilbert Marcellus Leonard II

Illinois State University

Macmillan Publishing Company
New York

Maxwell Macmillan Canada
Toronto

Maxwell Macmillan International
New York   Oxford   Singapore   Sydney

Cover Photos/Art: Yale Crew, Kentucky Derby, Althea Gibson, and
 Jesse Owens, courtesy of UPI/Bettman;
 Joan Benoit © M.Y./LPI, 1984.
Editor: Ann Castel
Production Editor: Sheryl Glicker Langner
Art Coordinator: Peter Robison
Photo Editor: Anne Vega
Text Designer: Jill E. Bonar
Cover Designer: Russ Maselli
Production Buyer: Patricia A. Tonneman

This book was set in Galliard by Compset, Inc. and was printed and bound by Book Press, Inc., a Quebecor America Book Group Company. The cover was printed by New England Book Components.

Macmillan Publishing Company
866 Third Avenue
New York, NY 10022

Macmillan Publishing Company is part of the
Maxwell Communication Group of Companies.

Maxwell Macmillan Canada, Inc.
1200 Eglinton Avenue East, Suite 200
Don Mills, Ontario M3C 3N1

Library of Congress Cataloging-in-Publication Data
Leonard, Wilbert Marcellus.
    A sociological perspective of sport / Wilbert Marcellus Leonard
  II.—4th ed.
      p.   cm.
    Includes bibliographical references and index.
    ISBN 0-02-369871-3
    1. Sports—United States—Sociological aspects.   I. Title.
  GV706.5.L465   1993
  306.4'83'0973—dc20   92-28102
                                                               CIP

Printing: 1   2   3   4   5   6   7   8   9   Year: 3   4   5   6   7

Photo credits: pp. 1, 29, 73, 139, 171, 329, 365, 385, 407 courtesy McLean County Historical Society; p. 47 courtesy Photo Archive 3M Italy; pp. 103, 203, 245, 283, 439 courtesy Illinois State University.

Preface

My purpose in writing this and the previous three editions of *A Sociological Perspective of Sport* was to contribute to the expanding field of sport studies by invoking a *sociological perspective* and demonstrating its utility in understanding sport in society. Prior to the 1970s, sport as a social institution had been generally ignored by academicians. Although analysts and observers of the social scene have peered into the world of sport, historically this literature has been characterized by journalistic and anecdotal accounts; there have been relatively few concerted efforts to collect empirical data, formulate and test hypotheses, and build theoretical explanations. I attempt to bridge this gap by adopting a consistent sociological framework for comprehending the social world of sport.

Of the numerous themes reflected in this book, three provide a central focus: (1) sport is a *social institution* and can be described, investigated, and analyzed as any other social institution (e.g., marriage, family, politics, economy, religion), (2) sport is a *microcosm* of the larger society—a social phenomenon that provides important clues about the nature of society, and it can be neither isolated nor insulated from broader social currents, and (3) there exist numerous *institutional interconnections* among the basic institutions of a society, and changes in one sphere reverberate into others because of their systemic connections.

To understand sport sociologically, I have chosen several pivotal sociological concepts—*culture, social organization, socialization, deviance, social stratification, prejudice, discrimination, majority/minority groups, social institutions, collective behavior, mass media,* and *institutional interrelationships*—as foci for writing and discussion. Their usefulness and application to sport as a social phenomenon are amply demonstrated.

Chapter titles and headings are organized around key sociological concepts. In general, the sequence of chapters proceeds from a broad "macro" to a more narrow "micro" view. Chapter 1 lays the foundation for a sociological perspective of sport by defining and illustrating critical sociological and sport concepts. Chapter 2 briefly surveys the history of sport in America, its diversity, and its social impact. Following these two chapters the sociological threads are made apparent in successive chapters dealing with sport and: culture, social organization, socialization, social deviance, social stratification, race, gender, education, economics, religion, politics, the mass media, and collective behavior and social change. The book concludes with a brief summary and discussion (Chapter 16).

To make the book pedagogically sound, I have employed a generic organization: Each chapter begins with an introductory section which serves to locate the contents within the proper sociological context. Major issues, concerns, and queries are raised that are dealt with in the chapter proper. Similarly, each chapter concludes with a succinct summary of what has been discussed. A section of Key Concepts are distillations of the major conceptual tools used to describe and explain the essential concerns of the chapter. Endnotes in each chapter serve to refine a point, elaborate a meaningful matter, and/or provide a valuable supplement to the text proper.

Since sport lends itself to many inherently interesting illustrations, each chapter contains a variety of supplementary and complementary matter such as tables, figures, illustrations, and vignettes. According to reviews, the vignettes are perceived as positive features of the earlier editions. The raison d'etre of these "literary sketches" is to stimulate and motivate students' interests in sport and society. Many of the vignettes have been gleaned from the popular press and, although not necessarily sociological in nature, provide alternative vantage points for examining the sport-society linkages. Some of them provide a humanistic vis-à-vis an empirical view of sport and reinforce theoretical materials wtih concrete illustrations. It is hoped that they serve as stimulating adjuncts for creating and maintaining student interest in the course material.

This text has been specifically designed for audiences in the sociology of sport regardless of whether the course is taught under the auspices of the sociology or physical education department. I have attempted to clearly define, illustrate, and apply all relevant concepts and terms. In addition to adoption for sport sociology courses, this text could also be used in courses such as sport and society, sport and culture, the study of social institutions, and American society. It can and has been used at both the undergraduate and graduate levels.

Various individuals have directly and/or indirectly aided me in writing this text. I am indebted to my editor, Ann Castel, my production editor, Sheryl Langner, and my copy editor, Luanne Dreyer-Elliott. I appreciate the contribution of Patricia J. Murphy, who originally researched and wrote the chapter on sport and gender. My colleagues—Bill Tolone, Shailer Thomas, Ray Schmitt, and Bob Walsh—provided valuable insights and kept me abreast of significant sport occurrences during the writing of the manuscript.

I am particularly grateful to the following reviewers of the manuscript, who provided valuable comments: Richard A. Clower, Western Maryland College; Joyce Graening, University of Arkansas; Marvin R. Gray, Ball State University; and Dana D. Brooks, Western Virginia University.

Finally, I would like to acknowledge Tracy Ellman, Neil White, Jeff Smith, Steve Bivens, Janis Billington, Terri Chesebrough, and Mickey McCombs for a variety of clerical, typing, editorial, and potpourri assistance.

The creation of a book is not an isolated individual effort. Several other important individuals provided assistance. Without their support, cooperation, and sacrifice, this task would have been nearly insurmountable. I thank them for this and many other reasons. The final "beauty" of writing this text resides in the fact that one of my lifelong loves, interests, and activities—sports—could be fashioned into a professional contribution.

W.M.L., II

Contents

1

Introduction to the Sociology of Sport

I always turn to the sports page first. The sports page records people's accomplishments; the front page has nothing but man's failures. EARL WARREN

Sports is the toy department of human life. JIMMY CANNON

Although major controversies have rocked the North American sporting world, the social significance of **sport** in American society remains unparalleled.[1] (Throughout this text I frequently use the term *sport* rather than *sports*. The generic noun *sport* refers to sports in a collective sense rather than to specific activities such as football, baseball, basketball, or tennis.) Boyle aptly declared:

> Sport permeates any number of levels of contemporary society and it touches upon and deeply influences such disparate elements as status, race relations, business life, automotive design, clothing styles, the concept of the hero, language, and ethical values. For better or worse, it gives form and substance to much in American life. . . .[2]

Americans are sportophiles, but Americans are not unique in the excitement, enthusiasm, dedication, and fanaticism that participation and spectator sports engender. A similar sport fervor can be observed in other parts of the world, and it is easy to demonstrate the pervasiveness and penetration of sport in society. The time, money, energy, and emotion invested in sport implies that our games are more than frivolous, carefree, and inconsequential activities.

Billions of dollars are spent annually by those who promote, participate in, and watch sporting activities, and an exorbitant amount is wagered on sport events. This is an astronomical sum to spend on something related to play. It is not uncommon to hear critics complaining about the extravagant amount of money spent on sport, especially when it is compared with the amounts spent on education, health care, or social welfare. Sport, as will be shown, is a growth industry.

Professional athletes have earnings far exceeding those of public officials, teachers, physicians, lawyers, dentists, clergy, business leaders, or scientists. Sports news often receives at least as much coverage as news about business, culture, and public affairs. Sport programs are a top priority in the budgets of many municipalities. Those who support sport as a valuable institution argue that its programs improve physical and emotional health, promote esprit de corps, and build character. Some also claim that it instills national identity, encourages social teamwork, and fosters patriotism, nationalism, and even religious piety. Critics, on the other hand, deride sport as being a kind of drug—a sedative—that distracts people from the more serious issues in life.

Recently, sport buffs have debated the merits and demerits of sport. Allegations of academic improprieties, student-athlete misconduct, sport monopolies, indictments, illicit betting, point shavings, recruiting scandals, and salary disputes have begun to penetrate deeply and stir discontent. The sport strikes of the 1980s and the more recent machinations of our college sport system—some of which have been acted on by the reform measures instituted during the 1991 National Collegiate Athletic Association (NCAA) convention by college presidents and the Knight Commission—have prompted increasing numbers to adopt a more critical and less condoning approach to the institution of sport.

Sociologists are quick to point out that social reality is not always what it appears to be, what people say it is, or what is officially proclaimed. Social reality is like the onion—it has multiple layers that must be peeled back if its multifaceted nature is to be exposed. Sociologist Peter Berger captured this notion when he wrote:

> The sociological frame of reference, with its built-in procedure of looking for levels of reality other than those given in the official interpretation of society, carries with it a

logical imperative to unmask the pretensions and the propaganda by which men [sic] cloak their actions with each other.[3]

In this book, you are provided a broad perspective of sport in society. We will examine some difficult-to-see realities and uncover a few fictions and falsehoods—some overly romanticized myths or cruel hoaxes—about sport. One primary goal is to facilitate your literacy of sport in contemporary society, an achievement eclipsing a mere knowledge of names, places, trivia, or statistics. According to Beisser, sports have been shrouded in a mystique:

> We prefer not to know too much about what we treasure. . . . This is the prevailing attitude of Americans toward their love affair with sports. But in sports, unless more than the surface is explored, men can become slaves, entrapped instead of (exercising) free will.[4]

Alas, this infatuation with sport is showing serious signs of crumbling—avarice, greed, violence, mayhem, injury, and courtroom scenes are becoming more prevalent. These modern scenarios are becoming a cancer in the mind of the beholder. Concern over sport, however, is not of recent vintage: "Sports nowadays have deteriorated to the extent that they represent a painful thorn in the hearts of all of us who truly love them" said Philostatus, circa 200 A.D. In later chapters, the causes and consequences of the dissolution of our romantic attachment to sport will be explored.

In this first chapter, we lay the foundation for a sociological perspective of sport by examining the social significance of sport in society. We briefly look at the relationships between sport and several other prominent social phenomena—economics, family, politics, popular culture, and the mass media; consider sport as a concept (and how it differs from play and game); discuss some of the contributions of the social and behavioral sciences to our knowledge of sport; and explore three major theories about sport in society.

☐ SOME BRIEF OBSERVATIONS OF THE SOCIAL SIGNIFICANCE OF SPORT

Sport permeates virtually every social institution in society. The ubiquity of sport is evidenced by news coverage, sports equipment sales, financial expenditures, the number of participants and spectators, and its penetration into popular culture (movies, books, leisure, comic strips, and everyday conversation).

Sports are among the most popular leisure activities in America today. Personal experience and impersonal statistics add substance to this statement. For many of us, our indoctrination in sport began early in life—in the elementary grades or, perhaps, even earlier. For males, and more recently for females, participation in organized sporting activities begins in Little Leagues, pony leagues, Babe Ruth leagues, American Legion baseball, or the like. Few of us immersed as youngsters in this sport milieu escaped the hobby of collecting and trading bubble gum cards or exchanging sport trivia. While disengagement from active participation takes its toll as one grows older, many adults still find sport significant, even though they may have curtailed active participation and adopted a spectator's role.

Spectatorship and Participation

Our appetite for sports appears to be nearly insatiable. Americans and other nationalities (although empirical data for other countries are more scarce) appear to be more interested in sports, as both spectators and participants, than ever before. Consider **spectatorship** first.

The data in Table 1.1 afford empirical confirmation of this assertion. Data of this sort are enlightening but rarely inspiring. The following observation by Murray Ross has more dramatic impact:

> Spectator sport is entertainment. . . . There is an element of vicarious pleasure in watching good athletes perform.
>
> One often sees oneself, Walter Mitty-ish, making a tough set point in tennis, flooring a world champion, dancing through the opposition in a local soccer match, or scoring thirty points in a crucial basketball game. In addition to the fantasy of participation there is something more to spectator sports. . . . They are integral parts of one's culture.[5]

Fred Exley, the "ultimate fan," echoes this view as he reflects on the authenticity provided him by the institutional demands inherent within the social world of sport.

> Why did football bring me so to life? I can't say precisely. Part of it was my feeling that football was an island of directness in a world of circumspection. In football a man was asked to do a difficult and brutal job, and he either did it or got out. There was nothing rhetorical or vague about it; I chose to believe that it was not unlike the jobs which all men, in some sunnier past, had been called upon to do. It smacked of something old, something traditional, something unclouded by legerdemain and subterfuge. It has that kind of power over me, drawing me back with the force of something known, scarcely remembered, elusive as integrity—perhaps it was no more than the force of a forgotten childhood. Whatever it was, I gave myself up to the Giants utterly. The recompense I gained was the feeling of being alive.[6]

TABLE 1.1 Number of spectators at major sports events for 1990		
	Sports Events	*Number of Spectators*
	Thoroughbred racing	69,551,000
	Major league baseball	55,661,000
	Auto racing	49,000,000*
	College football	36,406,000
	Greyhound racing	33,818,000
	College basketball	33,020,000 (men's)
		3,576,000 (women's)
	Professional football	17,399,000
	Professional basketball	16,586,000
	Minor league baseball	13,000,000*
	Professional hockey	12,579,000
	Jai Alai	5,227,000
	Soccer	3,229,000*
	Professional boxing	3,000,000*

*1982 figures.

SOURCE: *Statistical Abstract of the United States* (Washington, DC: U.S. Bureau of the Census, 1991), p. 36.

TABLE 1.2 Participation in sports activities, 1990

Sports Activity	Number
Swimming*†	70,489,000
Exercise walking*†	66,558,000
Bicycle riding*	56,941,000
Fishing (fresh and salt water)	52,331,000
Camping	46,514,000
Bowling	40,810,000
Exercising (with equipment)	31,476,000
Basketball	26,182,000
Aerobic exercising*	25,108,000
Running/jogging	24,803,000
Volleyball	25,071,000
Hiking	23,516,000
Golf	23,156,000
Softball	22,092,000
Tennis	18,844,000
Hunting	17,715,000
Skiing (alpine and cross-country)	15,940,000
Baseball	15,406,000
Calisthenics*	15,141,000
Football	14,728,000
Target shooting	12,607,000
Backpacking	11,357,000
Soccer	11,168,000
Racquetball	8,244,000

*More women than men

†More below than above median household income participate

SOURCE: *Statistical Abstract of the United States* (Washington, DC: U.S. Bureau of the Census, 1991), p. 238.

Participation in sports, like spectatorship, has soared. Table 1.2 documents this growth. More than 15 million people participate in swimming, exercise walking, bicycling, fishing, camping, and bowling. An estimated one half of the U.S. population participates in various sporting activities regularly.

The Economic Impact of Sport

Sport is big business—a multibillion dollar industry. The gross national sports product is estimated to be $50 billion. Athletes' salaries are sky-high. Television contracts alone, which provide the lifeline for many professional and amateur teams, cost billions of dollars. Advertising costs for the Super Bowl exceed $1.7 million per minute. University teams participating in some postseason bowl games (Rose, Orange, Cotton, and Sugar) are rewarded with multi-million-dollar rebates (more than $6 million per team in the 1991 Rose Bowl). Sports betting is in the billions of dollars. The scope of sports betting in the United States is staggering. In the mid-1980s, illegal sports betting amounted to around $70 billion! Professional football alone had wagers estimated to be in the $50 billion range, with the Super Bowl often being the single event with the largest number of bettors and the most dollars wagered. Horse and dog racing used to garner about 85% of sports betting. This is not surprising, insofar as horse and dog betting are legal in three fourths of all states and legal sports betting exists in a single state—Nevada. Today, however, informed reports suggest that these percentages may be flip-flopped. The economic impact of sport is awesome and will be discussed more fully in Chapter 11.

Sport and Politics

Many **political** figures have aligned themselves with sport and have done so with good reason. Because the average person can identify easily with the tugs of war that take place in sports, politicians find analogies between political life and sporting life useful and thus make such analogies frequently to accomplish political goals as well as to initiate changes in the sport institution. For example, midway through the 1905 football season, President Theodore Roosevelt became the catalyst for important changes in intercollegiate football. After viewing a picture of a badly mauled Swarthmore College football player, Roosevelt threatened to abolish the game if remedial steps were not taken to modify its most objectionable aspects. His influence also had great impact on the institution of the forward pass and formation of the Intercollegiate Athletic Association, the forerunner of the NCAA. Former President Richard M. Nixon was so fond of his "number one sports fan" label that he did not hesitate to call teams and coaches. Years ago Penn State fans were in an uproar when he declared the University of Texas football team "number one," when both teams had identical records and bowl games to play. Former President Gerald R. Ford, a former football player at the University of Michigan, wrote an article for *Sports Illustrated* praising sport competition. John F. Kennedy used *Sports Illustrated* as a forum to warn Americans that they were becoming physically soft and lackadaisical and stressed the importance of physical fitness, claiming that it provided the foundation for the vitality of a nation. Both Ronald Reagan and George Bush invited successful athletic teams to the White House to publicly proclaim their prowess.

Other political figures, such as former President Lyndon B. Johnson and General Douglas MacArthur, had been asked to help settle disputes between the Amateur Athletic Union (AAU) and the NCAA, and even the Supreme Court has made decisions about situations wrought by sport. Furthermore, the Congress has been the ultimate authority for determining the makeup of the U.S. Olympic teams as well as for determining exemptions from federal antitrust legislation. Congress has also been instrumental in the formulation of blackout policies, the composition and interpretation of Title IX (no education program receiving federal funds can discriminate on the basis of sex), media decisions and deliberations, and the determination of travel visas for U.S. Olympic teams.

Sport has also played a role, sometimes an undesirable one, in international sporting events. Sport is used as a political tool in the Olympic Games. Critics have argued that the intrusion of politics into sport has "bastardized" the sport ethic.[7] Politics have infused sport at the state and local levels as well. The 1991 Fiesta Bowl, spurred by a dispute over a holiday honoring the late civil rights leader Martin Luther King, Jr., planned a tribute to civil rights during its half-time entertainment. In short, sport and politics have been and continue to be intricately entwined, and this interaction will be discussed more fully in Chapter 12.

Popular Culture and Sport

Many expressions coined in sport have filtered into nonsport contexts. Sport idioms and figures of speech such as laying the ground rules, low blow, foul play, jumping the gun, bush league, game plan, cheap shot, dirty pool, toss up, touch base, out-of-bounds, score, hit, spoilsport, go to bat, pinch hit, struck out, out in left field, ballpark figure, not in the same ballpark, hit below the belt, and the like have become a daily part of our semantic life-styles. For example, during the Persian Gulf War, it was common for military leaders and politicians to talk about combat strategies as if they were talking about a game plan for an upcoming sport contest. Even electronic chalkboards with diagrams were part of the daily military briefings. When the war terminated, Norman Schwarzkopf, commander in chief of the allied forces, said:

> . . . the allied strategy was very much like a football play, in which the air campaign set up the conditions for the running game to succeed. . . . Once we had taken out his [Saddam Hussein's] eyes, we did what could best be described as the "Hail Mary" play in football. . . [8]   .

Finally, when concern surfaced over what appeared to be faulty assessment of Iraqi power, Representative Henry Hyde (R–IL) responded (to the charges that Iraqi military capability was overestimated): "Every football coach does that . . . it's not cynical, just good strategy." [9] Is it any surprise that a Pentagon-approved video about the Persian Gulf War was being made by National Football League (NFL) filmmakers?

Sport and the Mass Media

Sport coverage by the mass media (television, radio, public cinema, newspapers, and magazines) has become a mainstay of daily life. In fact, our appetite for televised sports appears to be bottomless. On network television alone, not to mention exclusive cable service, sporting events occupy about 15% of all telecasts. In 1988, network sport events numbered 453, and ESPN (cable) sporting events soared to 723. This skyrocketing is particularly striking because a decade earlier these numbers were 341 and 158, respectively. Similarly, the media have influenced such changes as night baseball, Monday and Thursday night football, and the relocation of franchises. The media even influence the timing, the place, and the manner of play.

The creator of the television epic "Civil War" was given $1 million in seed money by Public Broadcasting Service (PBS) and the Corporation for Public Broadcasting to produce a series on the history of baseball to be ready by the 1993 World Series. The 1993 program will treat baseball as being equal to the Civil War in its importance to American history. Similarly, a full-length film entitled *Heaven Is a Playground,* based on a book by Rick Telander, was released in the spring of 1991.

Books, theatrical performances, and movies with sport themes have been appearing in steadily increasing numbers. In 1991, for example, during Black History Month, the Chicago Theatre Company produced a play entitled *Mr. Rickey Calls a Meeting,* a script focusing on Rickey's historic decision to sign Jackie Robinson to a major league contract. The intricacies of sport have been reported in memoirs by such former athletes as Hank Aaron (*I Had a Hammer*), Jim Bouton (*Ball Four*), Jack Tatum (*The Assassin*), Dave Schultz (*The Hammer*), Jerry Kramer (*Instant Replay* and *Distant Replay*), Dave Meggyesy (*Out of Their League*), Gary Shaw (*Meat on the Hoof*), Peter Gent (*North Dallas Forty*), and Dan Jenkins (*Semi-Tough*). Other muckraking books and exposés focusing on sport have been written by George Plimpton (*Paper Lion* and *The Bogey Man*); David Wolf (*Foul!*); Curt Flood (*The Way It Is*); Roger Kahn (*The Boys of Summer*); Johnny Sample (*Confessions of a Dirty Ball Player*); Robert Vare (*Buckeye, A Study of Coach Woody Hayes and the Ohio State Football Machine*); and Martin Ralbovsky (*Destiny's Darlings: A World Championship Little League Team Twenty Years Later*). Sports also have provided settings and themes for such famous writers as James Michener, Zane Grey, Ernest Hemingway, Norman Mailer, John Updike, and Ernest Thayer.

Although historically, sport films have not been winners, a number of recent ones—*Rocky* (and *Rocky II, III, IV, V*), *Heaven Can Wait, Field of Dreams, Major League, The Natural, Bad News Bears, Slapshot, Hoosiers, Wildcats, Raging Bull, Johnny B. Goode, Karate Kid, Days of Thunder, Chariots of Fire, Personal Best, Bull Durham, White Men Can't Jump,* and *The Babe*—have done well, in some cases grossing over $100 million. Motion pictures have captured sport themes and reflected the cultural values and heroes of our times. According to Loy, McPherson, and Kenyon,[10]

> Generally, the movies have depicted or used sport as an autobiography of a particular hero or anti-hero; . . . as an analysis of a subculture with structure, rules, roles, and function; . . . as a comment on the ethics of sport that attempts to raise social consciousness; . . . or as a background or subtheme in advancing the main theme or plot of a movie. . . .

The symbiotic relationship between sport and the media will be covered more fully in Chapter 13. The preceding observations support the fact that sport is a prominent feature of society, particularly of North American society. To ignore it is to ignore one of the most significant and pervasive aspects of North American social life. Edwards has suggested that if America has a religion, it is sport.[11]

❑ SPORT AS A CONCEPT

Concepts are the essence of scientific and everyday communication.[12] They are words or symbols that typically represent an object (e.g., a person) or a property of an object (e.g., intelligence). Concepts are abstract generalizations based on perceptual or conceptual experience. All disciplines employ a special vocabulary—jargon—that functions to identify matters, issues, and ideas of central concern. My goal is not to overly burden you with jargon; instead, it is to clearly identify the fundamental ideas for understanding sport in society and society in sport.

What Is Sport?

The meaning of sport, like love, marital success, time, life, sex, satisfaction, or religiosity, is self-evident until we attempt to define it unambiguously. Each of these terms is an idea—technically a concept—that undoubtedly means something to each of us. Although one may have a casual understanding of these terms, such understanding is often too general and imprecise for effective communication. Academicians are not afforded the luxury of using vague, sloppy, or ill-defined terms. Hence, **conceptualization**—the mental operation that permits a scientist to determine the precise meanings of concepts—is necessary.

Generally speaking, sport is not a precisely delineated concept. For example, the concepts *sport* and *game* are often used interchangeably. Few would argue that checkers is a sport and similarly, few would consider boxing a game. The line of demarcation between these two kinetic activities is fairly clear-cut; but what about orienteering, skydiving, bridge, judo, rock climbing, bungee jumping, wallyball, and poker? While the physical skill factor is paramount in distinguishing sports from games, there are linguistic exceptions. Although both ballet and modern dance require high levels of physical skill, they are cataloged as performing arts.[13] Professional wrestling, on the other hand, is clearly a form of entertainment akin to show business, but it also requires physical prowess. Finally, reports in the mass media discuss various "sporting" activities, such as chess and rifle shooting, which in the strict sense of the term are dubious. In short, sport is not easily distinguished from other closely related terms by the layperson, even though social scientists have achieved some general consensus on its meaning (see the interactionists approach to the meaning of sport later in this chapter).

Ideal Types

In defining the terms *play, game,* and *sport,* a technique—the **ideal type**—developed by pioneering sociologist Max Weber will be enlisted. Weber (1864–1920) argued that an understanding of the social world is enhanced by the construction of conceptual models or mental constructs to analyze social phenomena. Here, the term *ideal* carries no connotation of importance or value (e.g., better or worse); rather, it refers to a concept constructed from the "pure" characteristics of the phenomenon under investigation. The term also does not imply a direct correspondence with the real world. For example, the trilogy of play, game, and sport can be thought of as a set of ideal types that can be used to describe fundamental principles, even though none of them adequately describes a specific type of physical activity. Ideal types are like statistical or mathematical models (e.g., the normal curve) that present a perfect "picture" of what should result when certain criteria are met.

Because of the conceptual morass surrounding sport and sport-related notions, some general distinctions need to be made concerning the three related terms of *play, game,* and *sport.* Because they have a cumulative property, we begin with the basic notion of play.

Play.   Roger Caillois advanced five distinguishing characteristics of **play.**[14] First, play is *free*; individuals choose to engage in particular activities, and the duration of their engagement in them is also a matter of voluntary choice. *Separateness,* the second feature, refers to limitations in space and time. Unlike sport, play is not restricted to specific spatial milieus (e.g., bullrings, gymnasiums, golf courses, arenas, stadiums, courts, field houses, or swimming pools); and play is not restricted to specific time intervals (e.g., quarters, halves, rounds, or periods). Third, play is *uncertain*—the course, end result, or outcome cannot be predetermined. Such indeterminacy often contributes to the excitement and anticipation of play activity. Fourth, play is *unproductive* or *nonutilitarian* in both process and product. *Unproductive* here means that the outcome does not result in the creation of material artifacts, and nonutilitarian implies that the purpose of the activity is simply the activity itself. Finally, play may contain a *make-believe* component; that is, the participant adopts a role temporarily but does not identify with this role outside of the space–time confines of the activity. In summary, Edwards defines play as "a voluntary and distinct activity carried out within arbitrary boundaries in space and time, separate from daily roles, concerns, and influences and having no seriousness, purpose, meaning, or goals for the actor beyond those emerging within the boundaries and context of the play act itself."[15] Similarly, according to Talamini and Page, play is voluntary activity characterized by minimal rules and spontaneity, and is viewed by players and nonplayers as non-work."[16] Pure play is difficult to identify, although children's mimicry, role playing and pretending capture the notion.

Game.   **Game** can be contrasted with play. A game is nonseparate in that the goals for participating originate outside the game itself. One may participate for prestige, recognition, status, or a combination of reasons. Moreover, a game is structured on the basis of rules, formal or informal, by which its players must abide. Finally, a game is characterized by a seriousness—winning—and is collective in character. A game is not free in that its rules define when the event is terminated, and its perceived seriousness frequently begets preparation. Edwards defines a game as "an activity manifest in physical and/or mental effort, governed by formal or informal rules, and having as participants opposing actors who are part of or who represent collectivities that want to achieve a specific goal that has value beyond the context of the game situation, that is, prestige, recognition, influence. . . ."[17] According to Talamini and Page, "Games are rulebound and competitive; they are won or lost by skill or luck or both."[18]

Caillois devised a fourfold classification of games. *Competition ("agon"),* the first, includes games in which contestants attempt to establish mental or physical superiority over rivals within the rules of the game.[19] Football, baseball, hockey, chess, and billiards are examples. The second type, *chance ("alea"),* refers to events like coin tossing, card playing, dice rolling, or roulette in which luck or fate are more important than ability or skill. *Mimicry* or *pretense* constitutes the third bracket and refers to activities in which children and adults participate as part of their socialization experience. For example, young children love to role play as mother, father, cowboy, astronaut, rock singer, or athlete. Adults, too, are fond of masquerading, especially at Halloween or during Mardi Gras. The fourth and final rubric is *vertigo ("ilinx"),* which includes those experiences in which one transcends or loses a sense of self (e.g., dancing, jogging, skiing, meditating, acrobatics, swimming, or mountain climbing). Roger Bannister's emotional experience in breaking the four-minute mile nicely captures the vertigo type of game:

> I had a moment of mixed joy and anguish, when my mind took over. It raced well ahead of my body and drew my body compellingly forward. I felt that the moment of a lifetime

had come. There was no pain, only a great unity of movement and aim. The world seemed to stand still, or did not exist. . . . I felt at that moment that it was my chance to do one thing supremely well. I drove on, impelled by a combination of fear and pride.[20]

These game categories are not mutually exclusive but intermix and overlap. Caillois describes a continuum of game forms that spans childlike activity, which he calls *"paideia"* and which is characterized by spontaneous, reckless, and turbulent activity, to more regulated or highly disciplined activity (e.g., professional football), which he calls *"ludus."*

Sport. Etymologically, the word *sport* derives from the Latin root *desporto,* meaning "to carry away." This historical origin implies diversion from instrumental (economic and utilitarian) routines and suggests recreation afforded through leisure pursuits. Howard Cosell captured this theme when he wrote:

> Once upon a time, the legend had it, there was a world that remained separate and apart from all others, a privileged sanctuary from real life. . . . The sports establishment, the commissioners, the owners, the leagues, the National Collegiate Athletic Association— would have us believe the legend. Their unceasing chant is that sport is escapism, pure and simple; that people have enough daily problems to cope with in a complex, divided, and even tormented society; and that the relief provided by sports is essential to the maintenance of . . . mental and emotional equilibrium.[21]

For many present-day serious participants, however, the meaning of sport poses a striking contrast to this root meaning. According to Coakley, three variables are helpful in defining sport:[22] (a) the types of activities involved, (b) the structure of the context in which the activities take place, and (c) the participants' orientations.

Type of Activities Involved.   According to Edwards, as one transits from play to sport, the following transformations occur:

1. Activity becomes less subject to individual prerogative, with spontaneity severely diminished.
2. Formal rules and structural role and position relationships and responsibilities within the activity assume predominance.
3. Separation from the rigors and pressures of daily life becomes less prevalent.
4. Individual liability and responsibility for the quality and character of . . . behavior during the course of the activity is heightened.
5. The relevance of the outcome of the activity and the individual's role in it extends to groups and collectivities that do not participate directly in the act.
6. Goals become diverse, complex, and more related to values emanating from outside of the context of the activity.
7. The activity consumes a great proportion of the individual's time and attention due to the need for preparation and the degree of seriousness involved in the act.
8. The emphasis upon physical and mental extension beyond the limits of refreshment or interest in the act assumes increasing dominance.[23]

Sport may be thought of as a special type of game requiring physical competition (against other players, the clock, or impersonal foes such as Mount Everest or the English Channel).

The Structure of the Context in which the Activities Take Place.   Sport is conceptualized as a special type of game or contest. The essence of sport lies in its patterned and regulated form. Through the social process of institutionalization—the formalizing and standardizing of activities—sport is regulated. Rules constitute the major element in the institutionalization of sport. Each participant must perform according to the rules of the game; that is, all participants are constrained by external rules that they impose on themselves and have imposed by officials.

The Participants' Orientation.   Motivations of sport participants usually reflect a combination of **intrinsic** and **extrinsic** considerations. Activities that are engaged in for no apparent external rewards are intrinsically motivated; when external rewards are the catalyst for activities, they are extrinsically motivated. These different motivating forces can be captured in the orientation of **amateur** and **professional** athletes. The term *amateur* stems from the Latin word for love and refers to sport participants who play for intrinsic rewards. In reality, many amateurs and professionals are motivated by a combination of these factors, although one may be more important than the other. The reason for this is simple; if motivation were based solely on intrinsic rewards, the activity would become, by definition, some variant of play; if motivation were based exclusively on extrinsic rewards, the activity would become, by definition, some form of work.[24] In reality, however, a dynamic balance between these two motivating forces often exists.

According to Jerry May of the U.S. Olympic Sports Psychology Advisory Panel, "Most world-class athletes have developed . . . 'internal' as well as 'external' rewards or incentives. The external goals are important, but to excel, an athlete must receive satisfaction from within and basically like himself to consistently achieve." Olympic gold medalist Carl Lewis said:

> I have a talent to do certain things and the desire to be the best I can be. Doing well is determined by how I compete with myself, not with my competitors . . . I like the challenge, whether it's to set world records, to change the events I compete in, or to come back and do the same things with an improved performance to try to equal or surpass personal bests.[25]

With some primary distinctions among play, game, and sport elaborated, several caveats are in order. First, the defining characteristics of each are ideal-typical. Problems of categorizing a particular activity still remain, because many sporting activities are not "pure." For illustration, Little League sports have the basic elements of their professional counterparts but are clearly distinguishable. In our everyday activities, some degree of play is typically found in our work and, often, some degree of work permeates our play. Remember, too, there are different conceptions of sport. For example, Luschen defines sport as institutionalized competitive physical activity located on a continuum between work and play.[26] This is diagrammatically depicted in Figure 1.1. Two distinguishing features of sport emerging from Luschen's definition are: (a) the activity is physical and excludes activities of a sedentary nature (e.g., chess, cards, or checkers), (b) the emphasis on the agonistic, or competitive (competition literally means "seeking together"), aspect is central.

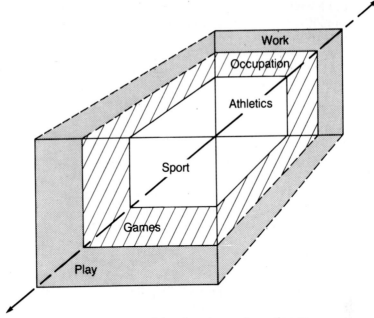

FIGURE 1.1   A scheme for conceptualizing the play-work continuum
SOURCE: Adapted from John Loy, Barry McPherson, and Gerald Kenyon, *Sport and Social Systems* (Reading, MA: Addison-Wesley, 1978), p. 23.

Others, notably Slusher, have maintained that sport is indefinable:

> The parallel between religion and sport might not be so far-fetched as one might think. As a result of mystical commitments sport and religion open the way towards the acceptance and actualization of being. A partial answer is now uncovered to our obvious difficulty in defining sport. Basically, sport, like religion, defies definition. In a manner it goes beyond definitive terminology. Neither has substance which can be identified. In a sense both sport and religion are beyond essence.[27]

Edwards formally defined sport as:

> Activities having formally recorded histories and traditions, stressing physical exertion through competition within limits set in explicit and formal rules governing role and position relationships, and carried out by actors who represent or who are part of formally organized associations having the goal of achieving valued tangibles or intangibles through defeating opposing groups.[28]

☐ SPORT IN THE SOCIAL AND BEHAVIORAL SCIENCES

Many disciplines—sociology, history, psychology, economics, anthropology, and physical education, among others—have contributed to our fund of knowledge about sport in society. Not surprisingly, many of them center on different aspects of the nature of sport. These different perspectives, often stemming from different interests, goals, values, and/or occupations, filter our interpretations of situations and events. Consider a college football game. A businessperson courting a client may consider the contest an auspicious setting for carrying on business transactions. Law enforcement personnel may focus on the potential disruption of law and order and the necessity of restoring it if mayhem broke out. An economist might see the game as a financial transfusion for the fiscal well-being of the community. Finally, a sociologist might be predisposed to notice the different groups represented, such as fraternities/sororities, couples, families, visitor/home team fans. Let us examine, however, the nature of sport from a purely sociological perspective, the theoretical orientation of this book.

Sociology, a behavioral science, is the study of human social life. Social life is broad and encompassing; so is the discipline of sociology. In fact, few fields have such scope. According to the American Sociological Association, "Sociology's subject matter ranges from the intimate family to the hostile mob, from crime to religion, from the divisions of race and social class to the shared beliefs of a common culture, from the sociology of work to the sociology of sport."[29] Social behavior can be studied from a variety of viewpoints—not just the sociological. Furthermore, perspectives should not be construed as good or bad, better or worse, right or wrong, but merely as different. All perspectives or orientations contribute to understanding human social behavior. To see the different facets of sport as a social phenomenon, we will approach it, on some occasions, from other than a sociological viewpoint.

Defining Sociology and Sociologists

Of the many conceptions of sociology, one that is heuristic in the present context defines *sociology* as the scientific study of social structures and social processes. By *scientific* is meant the orderly, empirically based, and systematic quest for reliable and valid social facts. Reliance on authority, tradition, common sense, and intuition are relegated to a secondary position, and the canons of science—objectivity, precision, empirical verification, operationalization, and conceptualization, among others—occupy the front stage. **Social structures** refer to organizations of people within a web of social relationships. Social structures range in size from a dyad (e.g., a player and coach), to a small group (e.g., a basketball or football team), to an entire institutional complex (e.g., sport as a social institution). Different types of social structures will be discussed more fully in Chapter 4.

The dynamic component of sport in society is social process. **Social processes** are the repetitive and reoccurring interactional patterns characterizing individual and group transactions. Some social processes relevant to an understanding of sport include institutionalization, industrialization, commercialization, bureaucratization, socialization, urbanization, collective behavior, mass communication, conflict, and social change. These and other social processes help to explain the development, maintenance, and change within the sport institution. In brief, sport sociology can be considered the scientific study of social structures and social processes in the sport domain.

Sociologists are professionals who typically hold a doctorate, study social life in a disciplined manner, and engage in three primary activities: (a) teaching, (b) research, and (c) administration. They are employed frequently at institutions of higher learning, although nonacademic employment is also a viable option for those formally trained in sociology. Because sociology embraces such an expansive social territory, sociologists tend to specialize in subareas such as family, social psychology, statistics, methodology, law, occupations, social gerontology, and/or the sociology of sport. Regardless of specialization, the sociologist, as Berger sees it:

> . . . is someone concerned with understanding society in a disciplined way. The nature of this discipline is scientific. This means that what the sociologist finds and says about the social phenomena he studies occurs within a certain rather strictly defined frame of reference. One of the main characteristics of this scientific frame of reference is that operations are bound by certain rules of evidence. As a scientist, the sociologist tries to be objective, to control his personal preferences and prejudices, to perceive clearly rather than to judge normatively. . . . Nor does the sociologist claim that his frame of reference is the only one within which society can be looked at. For that matter, very few scientists in any field would claim today that one should look at the world only scientifically.[30]

Wedding Sociology and Sport

The **sociology of sport** represents an application of sociological concepts, particularly those of social structure and social process, theories—functionalism, conflict, and interactionism—and methodologies—survey research, case studies, and observational inquiries—to the phenomenon of sport. From the sociological perspective, we can describe, explain, and analyze sport as an element of the social order. The sociological perspective of society is a special form of consciousness that sometimes makes us strangers in a familiar world. This vantage point allows us to see the familiar and taken-for-granted world in a fresh and somewhat novel light. Sociological discovery is culture shock—an anthropological term describing the impact of a foreign culture on a visitor—minus geographical displacement.[31]

What Is a Sociological Perspective of Sport?

I suspect that many of you are reading this book because of your curiosity and interest in sports. (I, too, became involved in sport academically—i.e., with teaching, writing, and researching—for the same reasons.) I also suspect that you have pondered, "What is a sociology of sport?" Perhaps you think that sports are sports. Sports are sports, but when analyzed in greater detail, we find that sports can be studied from multiple perspectives—the psychology of sport, the history of sport, the physiology of sport, the philosophy of sport, and the anthropology of sport, to name a few of the more popular ones. Sport, then, like many other facets of our experience in the world, can be examined, dissected, and understood from a variety of viewpoints. Because much of this book looks at sport through the eyes of a sociologist, let's consider briefly how and why sport is a sociological matter.

Sport is, intrinsically, a social phenomenon. Many sporting events take place in a social context involving opposing teams or players or both, spectators, officials, coaches, trainers, and so forth. Furthermore, sporting events are socially defined; their goals, objectives, and means (rules are arrived at through consensus, e.g., at NCAA conventions) and become formalized and institutionalized. Different sports tend to develop unique subcultures, encompassing norms, values, and language (argot).

Sports also display a pattern of social organization among participants, officiating agents, and even fans (e.g., contrast the etiquette of football and tennis spectators). Finally, sociological variables such as ethnicity, race, sex, and social class influence participation and spectatorship. In summary, sport can be analyzed and comprehended using a sociological lens. A sociological perspective of sport is not the only vantage point or, necessarily, the best one from which to examine the world of sport; however, it provides one with a distinct conceptual tool for critically analyzing one pervasive component of contemporary society.[32]

Based on Edwards's[33] definition of sport, the sociological significance of sport includes the following elements: it (a) is characterized by relatively persistent patterns of social organization; (b) occurs within a formal organization comprised of teams, leagues, divisions, coaches, commissioners, sponsors, formalized recruitment and personnel replacement practices, rule books, and regulatory agencies; (c) is serious competition in which outcomes are not predetermined; and (d) emphasizes physical skill. Hence, the gamut of rules, roles, statuses, relationships, beliefs, values, and behaviors constitute sport as a social institution.

SOCIOLOGICAL THEORIES OF THE RELATIONSHIP BETWEEN SPORT AND SOCIETY

Although various definitions of theory exist, a *theory* is an explanation of the existence and operation of some phenomenon. For example, an object tossed in the air will drop to the ground. We explain the object's behavior by resorting to the law (or theory) of gravity. Three major theoretical approaches that shed sociological light on sport are **structural functionalism, conflict theory,** and **symbolic interactionism,** and each of these will be used to help explain sport. First, consider the following question: Why do competing theories exist for analyzing sport? I will frame and answer this query with an analogy. There is an apocryphal story about an Indian raja who wanted to know what an elephant was like. He convened a group of blind men, took them to an elephant stable, had each feel the elephant, and finally asked them what the elephant was like. When asked, one man said a horn (he had felt the tusk), a second said a broom (he had felt the tail), a third said a wall (he had felt the leg). Which explanation is correct? Each is, although only partially so. What one explains, therefore, depends on one's vantage point or position. Analogously, competing theories of sport exist because of the different perspectives or viewpoints possible. Like the blind men's description of the elephant, these theories are only partially correct, not all encompassing. The moral of the blind men and the elephant parable is that reality, be it social or physical, is not fixed, permanent, immutable, or universally agreed on. Everyone does not see the world in the same way. Sociology offers a particular perspective on society and social behavior—a viewpoint somewhat different from that of the psychologist, economist, biologist, physical educator, or theologian. The purpose of discussing structural functionalism and conflict theory is to present two macroscopic perspectives of the sport–society relationship (symbolic interactionism is a microscopic view). *Macrotheories* focus on large social structures (or groups), whereas *microtheories* focus on smaller social structures (or groups).

Structural Functionalism

Structure and function are the key illuminating concepts from this vantage point. By analogy, *structures* can be thought of as bodily components of a biological organism, and *functions* can be equated to the purposes of these structures. Hence, the lungs are the structure while respiration is their function; the stomach is the structure and digestion is the function. This theory's focus in sociology is on social structures—not physical structures—such as families, clubs, groups, organizations, dyads and the like, and their functions or contributions to the larger society.

According to structural functionalists, societies consist of interrelated and interdependent institutions (family, sport, education, religion, polity, economy), each of which contributes to overall social stability. Like a biological organism in which the heart, lungs, kidneys, and the like must function properly if the organism is to remain viable, the parts of society must also operate in concert. This parallel is commonly known as the *organic analogy* (i.e., society as an organism), a "rough" metaphor assisting the understanding of functionalism. Functionalism focuses more on equilibrium than social change and, consequently, analyzes societal components in terms of their role in maintaining social homeostasis.

According to Dahrendorf, functionalism assumes the following:[34]

1. Every society is a relatively persisting configuration of elements.
2. Every society is a well-integrated configuration of elements.
3. Every element in a society contributes to its functioning.
4. Every society rests on the consensus of its members.

Several fundamental concepts within the functionalist domain are significant in comprehending sport.[35] **Eufunctions** are practices contributing to and facilitating adjustment and adaptation. In sport, many eufunctions are incorporated into the "dominant sports creed" (see Chapter 3), whereby sport participation apparently performs a host of individual functions (e.g., builds character, cultivates self-discipline, prepares one for competition in life, and promotes physical and mental fitness) and social functions (e.g., reinforces social cohesion through nationalism and strengthens traditional religious beliefs). Few would dispute that these functions are generally desirable.

Dysfunctions refer to practices that disrupt the social order. Excessive violence, cheating, substance abuse, gambling, brutality, hyped commercialism, aggression, and ruthless competition have undesirable ramifications. The infamous "Soccer War" between Honduras and El Salvador was stimulated by excessive on-field violence that "spilled over," causing a severance of diplomatic and commercial relations between the two nations. Similarly, player-against-player and fan-against-player violence have become problems in high school, collegiate, and professional settings.[36] The Vince Lombardi ethic—winning is not the most important thing; it is the only thing—has filtered down into colleges and high schools and is partially responsible for questionable recruiting tactics. Another illustration of a dysfunctional feature of sport is its commercialization. Not only have the media influenced the place, playing, and timing of sport contests (see Chapter 13), but also the sport "spirit" has been relegated to a position of secondary importance.

Functionalists also distinguish between **manifest and latent functions**. The former are apparent, agreed on, anticipated, and generally recognized, whereas the latter are frequently covert, unintended, unanticipated, and unrecognized. A manifest function of sport is the belief that it affords individuals from lower class backgrounds but with highly developed physical skills a channel for upward **social mobility**—a chance to better oneself in the manner of the Horatio Alger rags-to-riches stories. A latent function is the perpetuation of myths regarding the ease of individual social advancement through sport achievements, when the statistical odds of such success are miniscule.

Sport journalist Robert Lipsyte vividly captures the distinction between manifest and latent functions.[37] The following commentary highlights the notion of manifest functions and eufunctions:

> For the past one hundred years most Americans have believed that playing and watching competitive games are not only healthful activities, but represent a positive force on our national psyche. In sports, they believe children will learn courage and self-control, old people will find blissful nostalgia, and families will discover new ways to communicate among themselves. Rich and poor, black and white, educated and unskilled, we will all find a unifying language. The melting pot may be a myth, but we will all come together in the ballpark.

On the other hand, Lipsyte's following statement is indicative of a latent (and dysfunctional) feature of sport:

> Even for ballgames, these values, with their implicit definitions of manhood, courage, and success, are not necessarily in the individual's best interests. But for daily life they tend to create a dangerous and grotesque web of ethics and attitudes, an amorphous infrastructure that acts to contain our energies, divert our passions, and socialize us for work or war or depression.[38]

The controversial *Proposition 48* (the rule requiring a certain grade-point average and/or standardized test score) can also be examined with these concepts. The manifest function is to enhance the likelihood that athletes will graduate from college and thereby mitigate some of the charges of exploitation; the latent function is that it disproportionately affects the opportunities of minority athletes to matriculate.

Social system is another crucial concept in functional analysis. It highlights the systemic relations among individuals, groups, and institutions. The elements of society are interrelated, and alterations in one sphere may have repercussions in others. Examples of the social system's interconnectedness are legion. According to Snyder and Spreitzer, the institution of leisure and sport fills a need for exercise, tension release, diversion, and entertainment.

> The institution of sport is linked with other social institutions in a web of mutually reinforcing exchange relationships:
>
> 1. *The family.* Sport socializes children and provides a source of family recreation. In return, the family provides a source of players, parental encouragement, and financial support through transportation, fees, and equipment.
> 2. *Education.* Sport is a source of school spirit and cohesion, an outlet for adolescent energy, and it provides insulation against delinquency. In return, education legiti-

mates sport through trophies, rallies, and assemblies, and provides a training ground for elite athletes.

3. *The Economy.* Sport provides spin-off dollars for restaurants, bars, hotels, and transportation; profits for television, radio, and newspapers; profits for manufacturers of team emblems. In return, corporations support sport (by buying blocks of season tickets for example), and manufacturers of products with team emblems pay back royalties.

4. *The Polity.* Sport reinforces patriotism and civil religion at sports events through flag raising, color guards, and the national anthem. It also reinforces political values through the athletic creed. In return, sport is protected by antitrust exemptions, favorable tax laws, and government subsidies to stadiums. And many political leaders endorse sports.

5. *Religion.* Sport uses team chaplains and prayer chapels, and reinforces traditional morality through the athletic creed. There also exist evangelical organizations of Christian athletes. In return, churches sponsor athletic leagues, and reinforce sports through the use of athletic metaphors in sermons and religious writings.[39]

How Functionalism Helps Us Understand Sport.   According to functionalists, societies have needs—called *functional imperatives*—that must be satisfied. Social institutions, including sport, help meet and satisfy these societal needs. According to Gruneau, sport assists in meeting these needs in the following manner:[40]

1. Sport reflects a constellation of values, ideas of what are important and desirable, that are commonly shared by many members of society. Such value consensus promotes integration and a common perspective.

2. Sport operates to make the stratification of society more explicit. This is accomplished in two ways: (a) athletic performance facilitates generating status and recognition (through media publicity, scholarships, drafts); (b) it is sometimes used to display status and conspicuous consumption (through participation in the so-called "country-club" sports).

3. Sport provides an avenue for upward social mobility through lucrative salaries, endorsements, and later after one's sport career has terminated, access to jobs (particularly those involving public relations).

Conflict Theory

Since the mid-1960s, functionalism's popularity as the dominant sociological paradigm has waned. Critics asserted that its emphasis on equilibrium was essentially conservative and that modern societies are in a state of perpetual and rapid sociocultural change. Conflict theorists address the causes and consequences of conflict and speculate about its function, resolution, and regulation. Conflict theorists maintain that what may be dysfunctional for one group may be functional for another.[41] Illustratively, artificial turf is valuable to owners because it can be kept aesthetically pleasing for telecasting; but to players it is considered the root of new injuries and has increased some of the old ones.

Conflict theory focuses on the social processes producing instability, disruption, disorganization, disharmony, tension, and conflict. Although conflict theory has a long history, two proponents have been Karl Marx (1818–1883) and Ralf Dahrendorf (1929–). From the conflict perspective (also known as *radical* and *dialectic theory*), the concepts of *power* (the extent to which the will of an individual or group can be imposed on others) and *conflict* (a social process characterized by the competition between individuals and/or groups for the same goals) are the critical analytical tools. Following Marx's lead, the history of societies is one of class struggle between owners and workers, the powerful and the powerless, the dominators and the dominated. Capitalistic societies, accordingly, comprise two social categories: (a) the bourgeoisie, those well-heeled persons who own the means of production, and (b) the proletariat, the common workers who sell their labor to the capitalistic entrepreneurs. Marx hypothesized that the two classes, because of their divergent economic interests, develop polarized class consciousnesses. These antagonistic world views are a necessary prelude to class conflict, and class conflict is endemic to all vertically structured societies. Noted columnist George F. Will, in commenting on the 1982 football players' strike, captured the Marxist position on sport when he wrote: "The class struggle between labor and capital is heating up. . . . [t]he proletariat whose trade union is the National Football League Players Association may next be seen on picket lines."[42] The paradox of professional sport's economics is that it is an island of socialism surrounded by a (formal) sea of capitalism. In short, Marx viewed social conflict in terms of the relentless struggle between social classes over property and production.

Dahrendorf sees the unequal distribution of power and authority as the bedrock of social conflict. Those with power and authority have vested interests in maintaining the status quo, while those without these resources attempt to alter it. Hence, conflict is endemic to the very fabric of society. According to Dahrendorf, conflict theory is based on the following premises:[43]

1. Every society is subjected at every moment to change; social change is omnipresent.
2. Every society experiences at every moment social conflict; social conflict is omnipresent.
3. Every element in a society contributes to its change.
4. Every society rests on the constraint of some of its members by others.

Hoch, a scathing critic of the contemporary sport establishment, has advanced the following statement and model to underscore the exploitation of sport by the power elite: "The character and scale of sports today is the child of monopoly capitalism. . . . So throughout the sports industry under capitalism, control is exercised, not by the consumers (fans), nor by the producers (players), but by the owners of capital. It is they who decide whether or not to stage their spectacles and when, where, and how to do so."[44]

$$scarcity \rightarrow competition \rightarrow elitism$$
$$\rightarrow racism$$
$$\rightarrow sexism$$
$$\rightarrow nationalism$$

How Conflict Theory Helps Us Understand Sport. Whereas functionalists tend to view sport positively, conflict theorists see it as a tool of oppression—an instrument through which the powerful manipulate, exploit, and coerce those with less clout. Gruneau summarizes the conflict perspective, as revealed through Marxist analysis, as follows:[45]

1. Sport must be examined within the context of the material conditions of capitalistic societies.
2. Sport is correlated with social class; social classes emerge from differences in power, prestige, and wealth.
3. A bourgeois ideology is reflected in sport, i.e., it is rational, utilitarian, meritocratic, and mobility oriented.
4. Professional sport is alienating. It produces a "false consciousness" undermining social revolution.
5. An equalitarian sport can only exist in societies that are democratically controlled, especially in the economic arena. It is highly unlikely that competitive sport can exist in a classless and egalitarian society because the essence of sport is not equalitarian.

Sport as an Opiate. Conflict theorists view sport as a social institution wherein those occupying positions of power (the elite) coerce, cajole, control, and dominate the workers (in this case, the athletes directly and fans indirectly). Marx's much quoted edict, "Religion is the opiate of the masses," can be reworded as "Sport is the opiate of the masses." Opium, from which opiates are derived, is a narcotic that eases pain and produces euphoria. Marx referred to religion as an opiate, because he believed it reduced the frustration and pain of the sometimes meaningless work-a-day world; moreover, he believed that it provided the working masses with hope for a better life . . . in the hereafter. Some see sport as operating in much the same fashion, as a diversion and temporary fix from the harsh realities of everyday living.[46] The notion of sport as an opiate is richly captured in Lipsyte's observation:

> On the day the Steelers clinched their second straight Super Bowl appearance, the streets of Pittsburgh were suddenly thronged with people jabbing their forefingers at a wintry sky and screaming, "We're number one, we're number one!" It didn't seem to matter that day that the teachers were still on strike in Pittsburgh, that there had been no public education in the city for weeks, that millions of lives were feeling dislocation and damage; the Steelers—hyped as a mythic extension of the city— had won to show the world that the Iron City was "OK, Jack", and deserved to be plugged into the national happy news network. For the moment, at least, it was a hero city of super people.

Those cries of "we're number one," from major league cities and from high school gyms, have been described lately by social scientists as symptoms of the growing need of Americans to identify with tangible and respected organizations; the increasing fragmentation of American life has made sports fandom a hook to hang onto.

> More and more commentators have begun describing spectator sports as "the opiate of the people," as the "modern bread and circuses" and as the nation's "real religion" (while describing religion as America's real spectator sport), as if it were a . . . phenomenon, sprung fullblown from the swollen coffers of the television networks, instead of a logical progression in the growing cultural importance of sports as a shaper of ethics, values and definitions.[47]

Professional Athletes as Economic Commodities.   Webster's dictionary defines a commodity as "an article of trade or commerce. . . ." **Professional** athletes as commodities? Granted, most of us are familiar with the concept in other contexts—commodities budgets, stocks and bonds, brokers, and the like. Mass media publications (Vignette 1.1) carry news about sports transactions just like the Dow Jones averages, stocks and commodities exchanges. To conflict theorists, professional athletes have been (and continue to be, although less so) economic commodities, akin to chattel and traditionally mired in peonage. This argument is supported by scrutinizing several features of corporate sport (e.g., the player reserve system, the option system, the college draft, and the determinants of salaries). In addition, sport uses a mechanistic imagery as revealed in the slang used to describe athletes—metaphors such as "he's revving up," "she's burning up the track," "he has wheels," "she's running out of steam," and facsimiles.[48]

In summary, functionalism and conflict theory are two highly regarded macrosociological perspectives for viewing the relationship between sport and society. There are other perspectives, but rather than provide an exhaustive inventory of theories, let me demonstrate the manner in which one popular microtheory deals with sport as a social phenomenon.

Symbolic Interactionism

The *interactionist* perspective, sometimes thought of as an interpretative mode to differentiate it from the preceding structural perspectives in sociology, is the intellectual heir of Max Weber. Weber underscored the significance of comprehending the world from the subjective point of view. The method that accomplishes this is *"verstehen"*, a German word meaning understanding behavior from the actor's vantage point. Sociologist W. I. Thomas also captured this notion in his concept "definition of the situation." It's not necessarily objective reality that is "true" but what people believe to be true that is real in its consequences. Much nonrational behavior can be understood only by considering the actor's subjective meanings. Interactionists are notably concerned with the meanings and interpretations that individuals apply to social acts. Herbert Blumer, who coined and championed this view of human social life, succinctly describes its fundamental assumptions:

> The term "symbolic interaction" refers . . . to the peculiar and distinctive character of interaction as it takes place between human beings. The peculiarity consists in the fact that human beings interpret or "define" each other's actions instead of merely reacting to each other's actions. Their "response" is not made directly to the actions of one another but instead is based upon the meaning which they attach to such actions. Thus, human interaction is mediated by the use of symbols, by interpretation, or by ascertaining meaning of one another's actions. This mediation is equivalent to inserting a process of interpretation between stimulus and response in the case of human behavior.[49]

Figure 1.2 captures the important notion that one's response to an event is affected by the subjective meaning or interpretation of the event to the responding individual. The notion that social reality isn't fixed but depends on social definition is captured in the contrasting descriptions of the *same* acts in the sport world:[50]

> On our side, a guy is "colorful." On their side, a "hotdog."
> Our team is "resourceful." Theirs is "lucky."

☐ VIGNETTE 1.1

Professional Athletes as Economic Commodities

The purchase of professional athletes resembles the sale of other items in the marketplace. The marketplace is often crowded, but the following chart, although dated (adapted from *USA Today*), highlights the market value (as a result of interviews with player agents and NFL general managers) of several NFL quarterbacks.

Quarterback/ NFL Club	1985 Salary ($)	Likely Market Value
Marc Wilson, Raiders	800,000	No. 2 draft pick, or starter and middle-round pick
Richard Todd, Saints	650,000	No. 4 pick
Vince Ferragamo, Packers	550,000	Free-agent type

Quarterback/ NFL Club	1985 Salary ($)	Likely Market Value
Steve Bartkowski, none	475,999	Free-agent type
Steve Grogan, Patriots	450,000	No. 4 or 5
Joe Theismann, Redskins	405,000	Free-agent type
Jim Zorn, Packers	375,000	Middle-round pick
Gary Hogeboom, Cowboys	325,000	No. 3 pick
Dave Wilson, Saints	240,000	No. 3 pick
Steve DeBerg, Bucs	350,000	No. 4 pick or low-round pick

SOURCE: *USA Today* (26 March 1986), p. 5C.

☐

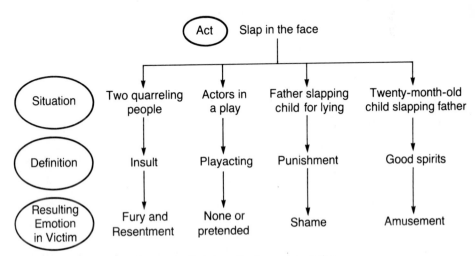

FIGURE 1.2 Illustrating the symbolic interactionism perspective
SOURCE: Alfred Lindesmith, Anselm Strauss, and Norman Denzin, *Social Psychology,* 4th ed. (New York: Holt, Rinehart and Winston, 1975), p. 213.

Our guys are "trusted associates." Theirs, henchmen.

Our team gives rewards. Theirs, bribes.

Our team plays spirited football. Theirs gets all the breaks.

Our guy is confident. Theirs is an egotist.

Sport as Symbol.   The idea of social symbol emerges from interactionism theory in sociology and social psychology. This tradition was promoted by George Herbert Mead, Charles Horton Cooley, and William Issac Thomas. According to interactionists, objects and events have no intrinsic meanings; instead, they are defined and refined by individuals in society. Humans reside in both a physical and symbolic world. A **symbol** is something that represents something else. Physical "things," events, persons, and behaviors have no intrinsic meaning; instead, they are defined and redefined by individuals in society. Contemporary interactionists, building on the leads of Mead, Cooley, and Thomas, continue to take seriously the observation that individuals interact in a world of "manufactured" objects and symbols. Kuhn emphasizes, for instance, that "in the broadest sense, a social object refers to any distinguishable aspect of social reality."[51] People never exclusively experience the "givens of nature." Virtually everything that individuals focus their covert or overt attention on is a symbol; even death, a gesture (see Figure 1.2), a ring, gender, and natural resources are symbols. Language, and the words it comprises, is an especially important symbolic system to the interactionist.

Sport is also an object. Its meaning is socially constructed and emerges from the human capacity to create and manipulate symbols. Consequently, one way of determining the meaning of sport is to consider what it means to persons in the everyday world. However, with few exceptions, sport has not been conceptualized in this manner. To the extent that the meaning of sport has been considered, it has been looked at from the "viewpoint of the scientist." But interactionist Norman Denzin stressed that "the sociologist must operate between multiple worlds when engaging in research—the everyday worlds of the subjects and the world of his or her own sociological perspective."[52] Persons in the everyday world will not provide a scientific view of sport. The everyday world differs from the world of the scientist. But the scientist must consider the meanings of sport that reside in the everyday world if a scientific determination of the nature of sport is to be made. The following investigations delineate the meaning of sport in contemporary America from the interactionist position.

The meaning of a concept such as sport is socially constructed and results from the ability of humans to create, use, and manipulate significant symbols. Sport is a social symbol, and one way to understand it is to ask people what it means to them.[53] Following this school of thought, Stone asked a sample of 562 Minneapolis residents to list the activities they associated with the word *sport*.[54] He discovered more than 2,600 activities connected with the term and an arithmetic mean of 4.6 responses. Of those questioned, sport as a spectator activity was primarily associated with football (73%), baseball (67%), and basketball (43%). While most responses were conventional, such atypical activities as sex, movies, woodworking, and relaxing were also mentioned.

Leonard and Schmitt replicated and extended Stone's seminal inquiry.[55] The three most frequent sports mentioned in their study were football, basketball, and baseball.

☐ VIGNETTE 1.2

Some Significant Questions Addressed by the Dominant Sociological Theories

Functionalism

- How are sport and the social institutions of marriage and the family, economy, polity, education, and religion interrelated?
- In what ways does sport promote, reinforce, and reflect social values, social norms, social statuses, and social roles?
- How does sport perform an integrative function in society?
- In what manner does sport reinforce the status quo or act as a catalyst for social change?

Conflict Theory

- How is sport exploitative?
- How might minority group members achieve greater power and influence in society?

- How does sport serve the needs of the dominant group, that is, what are the mechanics of cultural hegemony?
- How does sport promote or deter sociocultural change?

Interactionism

- How do sport experiences reflect subjective definitions of the situation?
- How does one's self-perception of athletic ability affect sport performances?
- How do sport participants and spectators manage their impressions?
- What are the emergent meanings of sport?

SOURCE: Eldon Snyder and Elmer Spreitzer, *Social Aspects of Sport* (Englewood Cliffs, NJ: Prentice-Hall, 1989), p. 14.

☐

These activities were mentioned by 86%, 85%, and 76% of the subjects, respectively. The three highest ranking sports—football, basketball, and baseball—were also the three highest ranking activities in Stone's study. Baseball, however, ranked second in Stone's research.[56] Further, 11 of the 13 activities reported by Stone were found among Leonard and Schmitt's top 20. These common sport activities were football, basketball, baseball, swimming, tennis, ice hockey, golf, snow skiing, wrestling, bowling, and boxing. Stone's report also included fishing and hunting—popular sports in Minnesota. The activities mentioned in Leonard and Schmitt's study but not reported in Stone's were track and field activities, volleyball, soccer, gymnastics, badminton, softball, ice skating, rugby, and handball. Comparing the similarities and differences between Stone's and Leonard and Schmitt's studies is interesting because their samples were distinct (gainfully employed adults in the former and college students in the latter).

The important sociological perspectives just elaborated commence with different assumptions, raise different questions (Vignette 1.2), and often arrive at different conclusions. This variability may be unsettling; however, this is not unusual. For example, in the highly developed science of physics, light is sometimes regarded as continuous waves;

sometimes as particles. Useful insights have been gained with these apparently competing theoretical models and have been integrated in quantum physics.

Consequences of Different Theoretical Perspectives

Some consequences of these different analytical lenses can now be advanced. Let us use a college football game as the stimulus event. From a functionalist perspective, football could be viewed as socially valuable, having positive consequences for participants, the community, and the larger society. It could be considered a channel through which young adults are socialized into the traditional male role, emphasizing strength, toughness, and endurance. Moreover, it could be seen as reinforcing the Protestant ethic of hard work and effort, paying off in dividends of success and also providing lower class youth with an escalator for enhancing their status in life and providing fans and players a legitimized setting for discharging pent-up frustrations and hostilities. In brief, functional theorists, while not denying negative features of the social system, tend to view the social world in more positive images.

Conflict theorists could define the college football scene differently. To them, it could be thought of as a manipulative ploy to divert the attention, time, and energy of youth from more meaningful activities and, perhaps, could be seen as a conspiracy for diverting lower socioeconomic status youth from the real channel of vertical social mobility—education. It could produce what Marx dubbed "false consciousness," a belief to which one adheres and that is, objectively, counterproductive. Conflict theorists view college football as dehumanizing and decadent, camouflaging class conflict and perpetuating existing social injustices. While not denying positive features of the event, conflict theorists tend to be more critical of established practices.

Symbolic interactionists would hone in on the meanings and definitions the participants in the college football parties attach to the event and surrounding circumstances. Do spectators define it as a substitute for war, a means of achieving catharsis, a social occasion? Do participants see it as an avenue for gaining notoriety, a means for financing their college education, as preprofessional training? Interactionists consider the dual world of social life, that of the scientists and that of the everyday actors. The two viewpoints are both relevant to an understanding of sport and society.

❑ SUMMARY

The pervasiveness of sport is indicated by the number of participants and spectators in various sporting events as well as the interconnections between sport and economics, politics, popular culture, and the mass media. Sport is defined as a concept and is distinguished from two closely related activities—play and game. Three characteristics to be considered in defining sport are (a) the types of activities involved, (b) the structure of the context in which the activities take place, and (c) the participants' orientations. *Sociology* is defined as the scientific study of social life; and sociologists, as individuals who study human social life in a disciplined manner. Like other scholars, sociologists specialize in various subareas, the sociology of sport being one of the most recent subfields to emerge within the mother discipline. Three theoretical approaches in the discipline of sociology are structural functionalism, conflict theory, and symbolic interactionism.

☐ KEY CONCEPTS

Sport
Spectatorship
Participation
Political functions of sport
Conceptualization
Ideal type
Play
Game
Amateur
Professional
Intrinsic rewards
Extrinsic rewards
Sociology

Social structures
Social processes
Sociology of sport
Structural functionalism
Conflict theory
Symbolic interactionism
Eufunction
Dysfunction
Social mobility
Manifest function
Latent function
Social system
Symbol

☐ ENDNOTES

1. Some of the observations that follow appeared in Craig Pearson, *Sports in American Life* (Columbus, OH: Xerox Publications, 1974). Special permission granted, Xerox Education Publications, 1974, Xerox Corp.
2. ROBERT BOYLE, *Sport-Mirror of American Life* (Boston: Little, Brown, 1963), pp. 3–4.
3. PETER L. BERGER, *Invitation to Sociology* (Garden City, NY: Doubleday, 1963), p. 38.
4. ARNOLD BEISSER, *The Madness in Sports* (New York: Appleton-Century-Crofts, 1967), p. 227.
5. MURRAY ROSS, "Football Red and Baseball Green," *The Study of Society*, ed. Peter I. Rose (New York: Random House, 1977), pp. 111–112.
6. FRED EXLEY, *A Fan's Notes* (New York: Random House, 1968), p. 8.
7. JOHN C. POOLEY & ARTHUR V. WEBSTER, "Sport and Politics: Power Play," *Sport Sociology*, eds. A. Yiannakis, T.D. McIntyre, M.J. Melnick, & D.P. Hart (Dubuque, IA: Kendall/Hunt, 1976), pp. 35–42.
   JOHN P. McMURTY, "A Case for Killing the Olympics," *Sport Sociology*, eds. A. Yiannakis, T.D. McIntyre, M.J. Melnick, & D.P. Hart (Dubuque, IA: Kendall/Hunt, 1976), pp. 51–55.
8. *Chicago Tribune* (28 February, 1991), p. 1, (1 March 1991), p. 6.
9. *Ibid.*
10. JOHN W. LOY, BARRY D. McPHERSON, & GERALD KENYON, *Sport and Social Systems: A Guide to the Analysis, Problems, and Literature* (Reading, MA: Addison-Wesley, 1973), p. 320.
11. HARRY EDWARDS, *Sociology of Sport* (Homewood, IL: Dorsey, 1973), p. 90.
12. The term *concept* refers to a phenomenon that has a direct empirical referent (e.g., a dog, football, or baseball). Some concepts are more abstract in that they represent other concepts. Such sociological notions as culture, value, norm, and social organization have no immediate empirical referents and are called *constructs*. The social science literature, however, is not always consistent in such usage.
13. RONALD W. SMITH & FREDERICK W. PRESTON, *Sociology: An Introduction* (New York: St. Martin's Press, 1977), p. 427.
14. ROGER CAILLOIS, *Man, Play and Games* (New York: The Free Press, 1961).
    Op. cit.,[10] pp. 5–8.
15. *Op. cit.*,[11] p. 49.
16. JOHN T. TALAMINI & CHARLES H. PAGE, eds., *Sport and Society: An Anthology* (Boston: Little, Brown, 1973), p. 43.
17. *Op. cit.*,[11] p. 55.
18. *Op. cit.*,[16] p. 43.
19. ROGER CAILLOIS, "The Structure and Classification of Games," *Diogenes* 12 (Winter, 1955), pp. 62–75.
20. ROGER BANNISTER, *The Four Minute Mile* (New York: Dodd, Mead, 1957), pp. 11–12.

21. HOWARD COSELL, "Sports and Good-bye to All That," *The New York Times,* 5 April 1971, p. 33.

22. JAY J. COAKLEY, *Sport in Society: Issues and Controversies* (St. Louis: C.V. Mosby, 1990), p. 9.

23. *Op. cit.,*[11] p. 59.

24. *Op. cit.,*[22] pp. 10–11.

25. *The Pantagraph* [Bloomington-Normal, IL], (17 October 1985), p. C3.

26. GUNTHER LUSCHEN, "On Sociology of Sport: General Orientation and Its Trend in the Literature," *The Scientific View of Sport*, eds. O. Grupe, D. Kurz, & J. Teipel (Heidelberg: Springer-Verlag, 1972), p. 141.

27. HOWARD S. SLUSHER, *Men, Sport and Existence: A Critical Analysis* (Philadelphia: Lea & Febiger, 1967), p. 141.

28. *Op. cit.,*[11] pp. 57–58.

29. "Careers in Sociology" (Washington, DC: American Sociological Association, 1977), p. 3.

30. *Op. cit.,*[3] pp. 16–17.

31. *Ibid.*

32. GEORGE RITZER, KENNETH C.W. KAMMEYER, & NORMAN R. YETMAN, *Sociology* (Needham, MA: Allyn & Bacon, 1979), p. 510.

33. HOWARD L. NIXON, II, *Sport and Social Organization* (Indianapolis: Bobbs-Merrill, 1976), p. 3.

34. RALF DAHRENDORF, "Toward a Theory of Social Conflict," *Social Change*, eds. E. Etzioni-Halevy & A. Etzioni (New York: Basic Books, 1973), p. 103.

35. ROBERT K. MERTON, *Social Theory and Social Structure* (Glencoe, IL: The Free Press, 1957).

36. Documentation of violence between fan and player as a major problem in high school, collegiate, and professional settings is interestingly provided in several *Sports Illustrated* articles. See the three-part series on brutality in football, vol. 49 (14 August 1978), pp. 68–82 (21 August 1978), pp. 32–56 (28 August 1978), pp. 30–41.

37. ROBERT LIPSYTE, "Sportsworld," *Sport in Contemporary Society,* ed. D. Stanley Eitzen (New York: St. Martin's Press, 1984), p. 3.

38. *Ibid.*

39. SNYDER SPREITZER, cited in Robert Hagedorn, *Sociology* (Dubuque, IA: William C. Brown, 1983), p. 357.

40. R.S. GRUNEAU, "Sport, Social Differentiation, and Social Inequality," *Sport and Social Order,* eds. D. Ball & J. Loy (Reading, MA: Addison-Wesley, 1975), p. 142.

41. LEWIS COSER, *Continuities in the Study of Social Conflict* (New York: The Free Press, 1967). Ralf Dahrendorf, *Class and Class Conflict in Industrial Society* (Stanford University Press, 1959).

42. GEORGE F. WILL, "Football Profits Up for Grab," *The Pantagraph,* (21 January 1982), p. A8.

43. *Op. cit.,*[34] p. 103.

44. PAUL HOCH, *Rip Off The Big Game* (Garden City, NY: Anchor Books, 1972), p. 202.

45. *Op. cit.,*[40] pp. 136–137.

46. STEVEN K. FIGLER, *Sport and Play in American Life* (Philadelphia: W.B. Saunders, 1981), pp. 38–40.

47. ROBERT LIPSYTE, "There's No Escape From Impact of Sports," *The Pantagraph* (19 March 1978), p. D20.

48. ELDON SNYDER & ELMER SPREITZER, *Social Aspects of Sport* (Englewood Cliffs, NJ: Prentice-Hall, 1989), pp. 174–175.

49. HERBERT BLUMER, "Society as Symbolic Interaction," *Human Behavior and Social Processes: An Interactionist Approach*, ed. Arnold Rose (Boston: Houghton Mifflin, 1962), p. 180.

50. JIM MURRAY, "Vocabulary Takes on a Ruddy-Faced Look," *Rocky Mountain News,* (9 December 1976), p. 150.

51. MANFORD H. KUHN, "Social Object" *A Dictionary of the Social Sciences,* ed. Julius Gould & William L. Kolb (New York: Free Press, 1964), pp. 659–660.

52. NORMAN K. DENZIN, *The Research Act* (New York: McGraw-Hill, 1978).

53. For a fuller treatment of symbolic interactionism, see Jerome G. Manis & Bernard H. Melzer, *Symbolic Interaction* (Needham, MA: Allyn & Bacon, 1978).

54. GREGORY P. STONE, "Some Meanings of American Sport: An Extended View," *Aspects of Contemporary Sport Sociology: Proceedings of C.I.C. Symposium on the Sociology of Sport*, ed. G.S. Kenyon (Chicago: The Athletic Institute, 1979), pp. 5–27.

55. WILBERT M. LEONARD II, & RAYMOND L. SCHMITT, "The Meaning of Sport to the Subject," *Journal of Sport Behavior* 10 (2), 1987, pp. 103–118.

56. *Op. cit.,*[54]

2

A Brief History of
American Sport

Sports nowadays have deteriorated to the extent that they represent a painful thorn in the hearts of all of us who truly love them.   PHILOSTATUS, 200 A.D.

A review of the social structures, social processes and social history affecting the rise of sport in America could easily fill several volumes. Here, a synopsis of some of the more significant factors in its development is offered. For instructional purposes, this chronology will be divided into five overlapping time frames: (1) 1600–1700, (2) 1700–1800, (3) 1800–1850, (4) 1850–1918, and (5) 1919–present.[1]

❏ 1600–1700

The tentacles of American sport reach back to the colonial period. The settling of Jamestown, Virginia (13 May 1607), the first permanent settlement in America, and the founding of Plymouth, Massachusetts (21 December 1620), the colony of our Pilgrim forbearers, provide points of departure. Although life was less barren and monotonous than traditional accounts sometimes have us believe, these early settlements, particularly New England, placed strong restrictions on play, game, and sport.[2] In the early 1600s, for example, bowling on the lawn green was prohibited in Jamestown, Virginia, and about the same time, Governor Endicott cut down Merry Mount's maypole. Two interconnected factors were primarily responsible for such prohibitions: (1) the harsh demands for survival (i.e., the threat of starvation wrought by the unpredictable and unfamiliar wilderness as well as the forays by the Indians) necessitated perpetual work, leaving little time, energy, or opportunity for recreation, and (2) the strong religious regulations "in detestation of idleness" and "mispense of time."[3]

Puritanism, a social movement emerging within England's established Anglican church, originated in the late sixteenth century and embraced a variety of groups including the Congregationalists and Presbyterians. Puritans were dissenters from the Church of England (the Anglican Church) and, dismayed by the crumbling of the church orthodoxy, desired to purify and reform some of its doctrines and practices. Dissatisfied with both church and state in England, the Puritans began emigrating to the New World, where they hoped to form God-fearing utopian-like communities. The Pilgrims were the first to arrive in 1620, but the mass migration of this group did not begin until 1629, and by 1640, some 20,000 people had settled in the northeast.

The Puritans' official displeasure with sports was multifaceted. They opposed all ceremonies and rituals that, in their view, misdirected the spiritual relationship between humankind and God. They also had a social class bias in their condemnation of worldly pleasure. Having emerged from the lower social classes—poor, hard working, and struggling to enhance their social position—they resented the amusements that the wealthy, more leisured groups enjoyed. Hence, these two influences—spiritual reform and economic envy—cannot be completely disentangled in understanding the Puritan influence on early American society and sport.[4]

In 1618, two years before the Pilgrims set sail on the *Mayflower* for the New World, King James I, head of the Anglican Church, countered the Puritan ideology with a declaration in *The Book of Sports* that read:

> . . . that after the end of Divine Service, our good people be not disturbed, letted, or discouraged from any lawful recreation; Such as dancing, either men or women, Archeries for men, leaping, vaulting, or other harmless Recreation, nor from having of May-

games, Whitson Ales, and Morris-dances, and the setting up of Maypoles and other sports therewith used. . . . But withall We doe accompt still as prohibited all unlawful games to be used upon Sundayes onely, as Beare and Bull-baiting, interludes, and at times in the meaner sort of people by Law prohibited, Bowling.[5]

When the Puritans achieved hegemony in Great Britain in 1643, the House of Commons ordered *The Book of Sports* to be burned publicly in major cities by the hangmen.

In New England, the wayfaring Puritans were equally intolerant of many forms of entertainment. Having sought religious asylum, they were determined to leave no trace of worldliness (Although the middle-class Puritan disdain for physical activities held sway, the English royalist tradition was favorable toward sports and gaming.) The Puritan contempt for sports began to wane in the latter half of the nineteenth century. Thomas Hughes's publications of *Tom Brown's Schooldays* in the mid-1800s provided moral justification for sport's role as a socializing agent. For the most part, such a theology was functional. When conditions no longer demanded such asceticism, however, fissures began to appear, even though Puritanism's sway continued. The tavern became the site of social gatherings, and drunkenness became a social problem. Even at the peak of Puritan orthodoxy, however, people engaged in sport and recreation, despite official condemnation. For example, hunting and fishing, because of their instrumental connection with work and survival, were popular. On the other hand, the upper classes were already engaging in horse racing. In fact, the turf (i.e., horse racing) has the longest continuous history of any sport in America. As early as 1660, when the first horse race was held on Long Island, New York, wealthy men from the Massachusetts Bay Colony were entering their horses in equestrian events.

Attitudes toward sport were not homogeneous, but varied according to geographical region.[6] New England settlers were the most adamant in their condemnation. The Middle Atlantic states did not display the same degree of intolerance. The southern states, with a single-crop economy and a more favorable climate, revealed a more permissive attitude. Because many plantation owners were parishioners in the liberal Anglican Church (or other tolerant groups), games and recreation were generally not scorned. Religious restrictions were markedly less effective on the frontier. Gambling on horse races, cockfights, and bearbaiting was widespread. The popularity of fistfights, wrestling, and rifle shooting was paralleled by the roughness and brutality of these activities. The most popular sport, however, was horse racing.

Despite the varied religious condemnation of play, game, and sport, the sport spirit was not completely smothered. The tavern became a social center where drinking (sometimes competitively), cards, billiards, bowling, and rifle and pistol shooting provided lively competition and entertainment. In colonial Williamsburg, Virginia, the three most popular "sports" were horse racing, cockfighting, and dancing.[7]

1700–1800

In the larger settlements of the 1700s, sports such as running and swimming were suspected of being health hazards! At the same time, however, recreational and work activities were semiformalized through the institution of the **bee.** The term *bee* has been subject to alternative interpretations. Some believe it referred to the convening of people to engage in social and utilitarian activities in a manner characteristic of bees; others maintain it has no connection with the insect. In any event, bees in early America were popular ways to raise barns, quilt, husk corn, or perform other chores. The worklike bees were typically followed by recreational activities (e.g., dancing, eating, wrestling, and other contests).

Benjamin Franklin (1706–1790), an early advocate of physical fitness, wrote essays praising the benefits of sport. In 1743, he wrote:

> The first drudgery of settling new colonies, which confines the attention of people to mere necessities, is now pretty well over; and there are many in every province in circumstances that set them at ease, and afford leisure to cultivate the higher Arts. . . .[8]

But Franklin was not a proponent of sheer frivolousness and insisted that leisure time be used constructively. He also drew an analogy between life and games when he wrote, "Life is a kind of game, in which we have points to gain and competitors or adversaries to contend with. . . . You must not, when you have gained a victory, use any triumphing or insulting expressions, nor show too much pleasure. . . .[9] A wide range of sporting festivities surfaced during this epoch—walking races, hopping and leaping contests, throwing axes, turkey shoots, gander pulling and quoits (a rudimentary form of horseshoes). In most cases, winners received prizes or cash or both, and drinking and gambling often accompanied such bouts.

In 1732, the first sport social club, the Schuylkill Fishing Company, was organized in Philadelphia, and it was followed later by the formation of a fox-hunting club in Gloucester City, New Jersey, in 1776; a golf club, in Charleston, South Carolina; and a cricket club in New York City in the late 1700s. Most of these organizations, however, remained removed from the common person. The commoner was predominately confined to spectating at boxing matches, bullbaiting, bearbaiting, and cockfighting contests. Although these latter events were part of the rural American tradition, they quickly became commercialized at hotels, inns, and taverns.

Collegiate sports during this period were still only in their infancy and characterized by brutality. Students at some Ivy League schools engaged in wrestling and prototype football games, but these contests were generally so destructive that college officials discouraged them. In 1787, the Princeton faculty banned them because they were deemed ungentlemanly, excessively rough, and of dubious personal and social worth.

During this century, American society was primarily agrarian (about 90% of the people were engaged in agriculture), and the population was geographically dispersed. Furthermore, because transportation was crude and slow, many people spent their entire lives within a 25-mile radius of their birthplace.[10]

Engaging in sports, recreation, and other secular activities on Sunday was officially tabooed by the **blue laws,** given this name because they were printed on blue paper in New Haven, Connecticut, in 1781. These statutes restricted many sports and pastimes but did not forbid activities with utilitarian overtones, such as hunting and fishing. While the blue laws continued officially well into the present century, enforcement of them grew lax. Today, commercialized Sunday sport is as popular as attending church and synagogue and may even capture a larger audience.

◻ 1800–1850

While attitudes toward sport and recreation during this antebellum period (i.e., the pre-Civil War years) reflected ambivalence, mass media reports and distinguished personalities began to endorse the benefits of sport engagement. Tom Molyneux, a black slave, is reported to have won his freedom by defeating a fellow slave. He received a modicum of news coverage in 1811, when he traveled to London to defend his informal heavyweight boxing crown against Tom Cribb, the English champion. This heralded fight lasted 44 grueling rounds, and although Molyneux was defeated, and never returned to the States after that, the *Times* of London reported him to be a promising pugilist. Reporting this event enhanced sport interests. By 1830, boxing clubs in New York, Philadelphia, and Washington, DC offered instruction in "the art of self-defense" or "the manly science of pugilism."

Newspapers and periodicals applauded this sport expansion and kindled interest in other forms of participation. Soon footracing tracks, the English game of fives (a forerunner of handball), and racquets (a game of fives played with paddles) gained wide popularity. Ninepins and skittles (both variations of bowling) became popular. By the late 1820s, classes in swimming and archery were being taught in Boston and Philadelphia.

For the most part, however, the elitist orientation of sport participation maintained its grip. Sport participation and spectatorship correlated with social class. Veblen argued that the availability of leisure time was indicative of high social status and interest in sport smacked of "conspicuous consumption."[11] Prosperous men, not women or men of modest financial means, occupied the front stage of sport participation. For example, a group of Philadelphia gentlemen organized in 1831 a town ball (baseball) club, which was a refined version of one-old-cat, and fourteen years later, the Knickerbocker Club played a more sophisticated version of the game that was destined to become America's national pastime.[12]

The elitist orientation of sport participation at this time is depicted in Seymour's account of the Knickerbocker Club:

> It was primarily a social club with a distinctly exclusive flavor—somewhat similar to what country clubs represented in the 1920s and 1930s, before they became popular with the middle class in general. . . . To the Knickerbockers a ball game was a vehicle for genteel amateur recreation and polite social intercourse rather than a hard fought contest for victory.[13]

Another memorable illustration of the chasm between elite and folk sport resides in the tennis championship tournament at the posh country club—the Casino Club—in Newport, Rhode Island. Only those of the upper crust could participate and/or spectate the tournament. In fact, so exclusive and snobbish was this club that President Chester A. Arthur had been denied admittance because of his suspect social standing!

Wealthy individuals sponsored numerous sporting events (e.g., rowing, sailing, and footracing), which were attended by large numbers of spectators from all social classes. A rowboat race in 1824 drew 50,000 spectators and a footrace attracted 29,000. The fervor over horse racing and betting is illustrated in Stephen Foster's

(1826–1864) song "Camptown Races," the first popular song based on a sporting theme, which ends with, "I'll bet my money on da bob-tail nag, somebody bet on da bay."

Rader reports that, as the population and wealth of the United States grew, a gentry (i.e., elite) and hoi polloi (i.e., common people) style of recreation emerged.[14]

1850–1918

The development of modern sport accelerated between the Civil War (1861–1865) and World War I (1914–1918). During this time, **industrialization** coupled with the loosening of religious restrictions revolutionized the life-styles of the populace; at last sport had come to be viewed positively, and as Paxson noted, sport became a "safety valve," a theme that continues to this day, for people deprived of the freedom of frontier life and the opportunities it offered.[15] Unlike America's agrarian era, when recreation revolved primarily around the family, the movement toward urban living shifted the recreational function to secondary institutions.[16]

Because camp life was filled with games, notably baseball, the return of Civil War veterans hastened expansion of the sport. By 1868, baseball had become so popular that admission fees were charged, and in 1869, all members of the Cincinnati Red Stockings were playing for season salaries ranging between $500 and $1,400. Popularity, combined with the profit motive, stimulated the formation of the first continuous baseball league, the National League, in 1876. Sport became more businesslike, as control shifted from players to managers and club owners. By 1800, team owners had instituted reserve clauses restricting players' career movements. Despite attempts by players and other owners to start new leagues, the formation of the American League in 1900 was the only one that proved viable. In 1903, factions warring over players and cities in the two professional baseball organizations agreed to authorize and play a World Series.[17]

The post-Civil War years witnessed growing concern over amateur and professional issues. Prosperous and genteel men of the New York City Athletic Club helped organize the National Association of Amateur Athletes of America in 1868, which in 1888, became the AAU (Amateur Athletic Union).

Intercollegiate athletics began to blossom during this period. The first collegiate competition took place between rowing crews of Harvard and Yale in 1852. The first collegiate baseball game was played in 1859 between Amherst and Williams; the first collegiate football game was considered to be played in 1869 between Rutgers and Princeton, although they actually played soccer. It was in 1874 that football, as we know it, was played between McGill and Harvard. The first modern intercollegiate basketball game was played in 1897 between Yale and Penn. Regatta competitions, often featuring track meets as side events, became commonplace.

Intercollegiate sport gained a foothold in higher education during the 1870s and 1880s. The popularity of football, which Walter Camp promoted, maintained an aristocratic flavor, because college students were generally from the upper classes. By the turn of the century, however, football had become a national sport with mass appeal crossing social class boundaries.[18] Football's development, however, was more problematic, because it was a game dominated by ruthless violence and fierce partisan loyalties. In 1885, the faculty of Harvard banned football because of its violent mayhem. News about both the abuses of the game (i.e., brutality, injuries, and even deaths) and the use of players who were not even enrolled at the college—"trampathletes" or "ringers"—reached the White House. These events contributed to the purely recreational aspect of sport becoming secondary to formalized competition.[19]

Preparatory schools soon organized after the collegiate model. The New York Public School Athletic League in 1903 sanctioned competition for high school students in track, football, baseball, basketball, soccer, cross-country, swimming, ice-skating, roller-skating, and rifle shooting.

In 1896, the Frenchman Pierre de Coubertin (1863–1937) reinstituted the modern Olympics after a period of dormancy spanning 1500 years. His actions were motivated by a belief that England's, and to a lesser extent Germany's, emergence as a world power was promoted by integrating sport and education.[20]

During this time, sport took on a more formalized appearance, and national championships were held in numerous activities: chess (1857), billiards (1859), rifle shooting (1871), archery (1870), croquet (1879), bicycling (1880), canoeing (1880), horsemanship (1883), fencing (1891), golf (1894), bowling (1895), handball (1897), logrolling or birling (1898), skiing (1904), and lawn bowling (1915).

Women, too, became active participants, albeit slowly—first in croquet, then in lawn tennis (which was imported from Bermuda in 1875), roller-skating, bicycling, and golf. The bicycle, known as the "high wheeler" because its front wheel was as much as five feet in diameter, was exhibited at the Centennial Exposition in Philadelphia in 1876. It "liberated" women by providing them with greater mobility and brought about changes in their clothing (skirts and dresses were replaced by bloomers). Regarding Olympic competition, women made their debut in Paris in 1900, but their participation was limited to tennis and golf. Twenty-eight years later, they were permitted to participate in track-and-field events.

Newspapers, starting with the *New York Journal* in 1895, began to cover such "games" as polo, lacrosse, squash, volleyball, field hockey, basketball, and water polo. Also in 1895, the *Chicago Times-Herald* promoted the first auto race as a publicity stunt.

The first superstars were those created by sport journalists. The conquests of John L. Sullivan, heavyweight boxer, both inside and outside the ring, made the front page, and he was even boosted as a candidate for Congress. Walter Camp's selection of All-Americans, which started in 1889, placed outstanding college athletes in the limelight. Similarly, U.S. newspapers heralded the nation's "victory" in the 1896 Olympics in Athens, where students from Harvard and Yale captured nine of twelve gold medals. Jack Johnson, the first black heavyweight boxing champion in 1908; Eleanora Sears, the first well-known female athlete who was accomplished in swimming, tennis, golf, boating, and auto racing; and Jim Thorpe, who was hailed as the greatest athlete in the world after winning both the pentathlon and decathlon gold medals in the 1912 Stockholm Olympics, were famous sport personalities who received favorable media recognition.

❏ 1919–PRESENT

The years between 1919 and 1930 have been lauded as the "Golden Age" of sport.[21] Three social factors seem responsible for the upsurge during this period of professional and amateur sport: (a) affluence, (b) the increased availability and use of the automobile in people's lives, and (c) the newspaper industry. America's sportsmania was also invigorated by more leisure time, increasing numbers of amateur and professional sport organizations, advances in technology, dramatic publicity and promotion, and greater possibilities of fame, fortune, and money.[22] In 1924, Fordham University took in over $500,000 dollars in football gate receipts. In 1926, Stanford University received nearly $200,000 from its intercollegiate sport program; in 1927, Ohio State University grossed nearly $276,000. During this time, the athlete emerged as a national hero—a celebrity.

The gallery of "Golden Age" sport personalities included the following household names: Babe Ruth (baseball); Jack Dempsey, Gene Tunney, and Joe Louis (boxing); Bill Tilden (tennis); John Weismueller (swimming); Red Grange, George Halas, and Knute Rockne (football); Cliff Hagen and Bobby Jones (golf); and Tommy Hitchcock (polo). Female athletes also became famous. In 1925, Helen Wills Moody became a tennis world favorite. Mildred (Babe) Didrikson Zaharias became perhaps the most versatile athlete of all times; she was accomplished in running, hurdling, javelin throwing, high jumping, swimming, diving, golf, baseball, basketball, billiards, and rifle shooting. Also in 1925, Gertrude Ederle won fame as the first woman to swim the English Channel. Sonja Henie became one of the richest sport heroes of all time (she earned in excess of $40 million) after winning three consecutive Olympic gold medals in figure skating and later entering show business and producing her own Hollywood Ice Revue.

Black professional athletes broke (actually "rebroke" as you will see in Chapter 8) the color bar in the late 1940s when Brooklyn Dodgers owner Branch Rickey signed Jackie Robinson to a professional baseball contract. In amateur sports, Jesse Owens won four gold medals in the 1936 "Nazi" Olympics. Although blacks had been stellar boxers previously, only during the past three decades has their proportionate makeup in certain team sports exceeded their percentage makeup of the total population. Because much of the discussion in later chapters will analyze sport after Robinson's monumental entry, this brief synopsis of America's sporting heritage ends here.

From the 1920s to today, sport has become an increasingly pervasive feature of society. It permeates virtually all educational levels and has drifted increasingly into social agencies, private clubs, industry, religious organizations, and business. The last generation has witnessed two significant developments in sport that were considered briefly in Chapter 1 and will be examined more fully in later chapters: (a) the growth of amateur and professional spectator sports and (b) the soaring interest in mass participation.[23] The time line presented on the inside front and back covers of this book chronicles some significant sport events from 776 B.C. to the present.

❏ CHARACTERISTICS OF MODERN SPORT

Modern sport, says Guttmann, contrasts with primitive, ancient, and medieval sport in several ways.[24] Today sport is characterized by (a) *secularism,* or an emphasis on

TABLE 2.1   Characteristics of sports during various time periods

	Primitive Sports	Greek Sports (1000 to 100 B.C.)	Roman Sports (100 B.C. to 500 A.D.)	Medieval Sports (500 A.D. to 1300 A.D.)	Modern Sports (1800 A.D. on)
Secularism	+ and −	+ and −	+ and −	+ and −	+
Equality	−	+ and −	+ and −	−	+
Specialization	−	+	+	−	+
Rationalization	−	+	+	−	+
Bureaucracy	−	+ and −	+	−	+
Quantification	−	−	+ and −	−	+
Records	−	−	−	−	+

KEY: + = yes; − = no.

SOURCE: Allen Guttmann, *From Ritual to Record* (New York: Columbia University Press, 1978), p. 54.

material (i.e., economic) and social (i.e., prestige) success; (b) *equality of opportunity*, for those of different sexes, races, ethnicities, social classes; (c) *role specialization*, (e.g., the designated hitter); (d) *bureaucratic formal organization* (e.g., NFL, NCAA, AAU, IOC [International Olympic Committee]); (e) *quantification;* and (f) the *quest for record breaking*. This configuration of traits dovetails with Weber's notion of rationalization and demystification in which some of the wonder and awe of life are lost. Table 2.1 contrasts modern sport with sport at other historical time periods.

☐ HOW SOCIOLOGICAL THEORIES EXPLAIN THE RISE OF SPORT

The two dominant macrotheories in sociology provide different interpretations for the development of sport. Taking the lead from their primary intellectual father, Karl Marx, conflict theorists contend that those who control the wealth of the society ("bourgeoisie") ultimately control the society. Those who are controlled, the masses (or "proletariat") are little more than hapless pawns buffeted by the whims of the ruling class. According to Marxist-oriented Paul Hoch, "The character and scale of sports today is the child of monopoly capitalism."[25] In short, their answer to the query "Why is there sport?" is because the ruling class finds it profitable; the masses can be hoodwinked into liking it, and it diverts the common workers from focusing on their unenviable plight.[26] The conflict theorists' interpretation of the rise of sport illustrates the concept of **cultural hegemony** (the dominance of a particular view on various cultural practices).

Functionalists have a different explanation for the emergence of sports. To them, sport satisfies an underlying need, albeit biological and/or cultural in origin. The reason for sport, according to this perspective, is that it reflects the manifestation of an underlying universal urge or need for physical re-creation, and through sport this need is partially satiated. Sport fulfills human and social needs in a similar way to how the economy, family, religion, polity, and education—the primary social institutions—satisfy other "needs" of humans in society.

☐ INDUSTRIALIZATION, URBANIZATION, AND MASS COMMUNICATION

Three social processes—**industrialization, urbanization,** and **mass communication**—have been catalysts in the development of American sport. These processes are sufficiently important to warrant separate discussion.

Technology and Sport

The application of scientific knowledge and the tools employed in the production of goods and services is known as **technology.** Technology includes both the know-how and wherewithal of a society. Technological developments in agriculture and industry (i.e., industrialization), transportation, and communication have been instrumental in the growth of American sport.

Betts provides an excellent summary of the impact of technology on the development of sport:

> Technological developments in the latter half of the nineteenth century transformed the social habits of the Western World, and sport was but one of many institutions which felt their full impact. Fashions, foods, journalism, home appliances, commercialized entertainment, architecture, and city planning were only a few of the facets of life which underwent rapid change as transportation and communication were revolutionized and as new materials were made available. . . .
>
> The first symptoms of the impact of invention on nineteenth century sport are to be found in the steamboat of the ante-bellum era. An intensification of interest in horse racing during the 1820s and 1830s was only a prelude to the sporting excitement over yachting, prize fighting, rowing, running, cricket, and baseball of the 1840s and 1850s. By this time the railroad was opening up new opportunities for hunters, anglers, and athletic teams, and it was the railroad of all the inventions of the century which gave the greatest impetus to the intercommunity rivalries in sport. The telegraph and the penny press opened the gates to a rising tide of sporting journalism; the sewing machine and the factory system revolutionized the manufacturing of sporting goods; the electric light and rapid transit further demonstrated the impact of electrification; inventions like the Kodak camera, the motion picture, and the pneumatic tire stimulated various fields of sport; and the bicycle and automobile gave additional evidence to the effect of the transportation revolution on the sporting impulse of the latter half of the century. Toward the end of the century the rapidity with which one invention followed another demonstrated the increasingly close relationship of technology and social change. No one can deny the significance of sportsmen, athletes, journalists and pioneers in many organizations, and no one can disregard the multiple forces transforming the social scene. *The technological revolution is not the sole determining factor in the rise of sport, but to ignore its influence would result only in a more or less superficial understanding of the history of one of the prominent social institutions of modern America.*[27]

Industrialization

Industrialization is a stage of social and technological development characterized by mass production of goods in factories that employ power-driven machinery and a specialized division of labor. Such societal changes began in England between 1760 and 1860.[28] The growth of sports was greatly facilitated by certain technical advances—in particular, the development of transportation and communication facilities and the birth of electronics. Developments such as these were spawned by industrialization.

The factory system was one of the socially significant offshoots of the Industrial Revolution. The textile industry was the first to feel its impact, largely as a result of the invention of the sewing machine by Elias Howe (1819–1867). The introduction of the sewing machine caused a dramatic change in the production of clothes, shoes, and leather goods; and the impact on sport of newly created products was considerable. For example, the modern baseball era began around 1920 with the introduction of the "jack-rabbit" ball, a ball made from stronger and stouter Australian yarn. Because this ball was wound and sewn tighter, it traveled farther and bounced higher and quicker when hit. Babe Ruth's home runs doubled from 29 to 58 and correlated with this change. Previously, during the "deadball era" (1900–1919), fans saw about one homer every four games. During the modern baseball era (1920–1945), which featured only daytime play, spectators saw almost two per game. The number of home runs had multiplied eight times![29] The vulcanization of rubber in the 1830s by Charles Goodyear improved the elasticity and resiliency of rubber balls in the 1840s and tennis and golf balls later in the century. Also, with the improvement in production techniques, not only did sport equipment become "better" but it also became standardized in size, shape, and weight. In 1876, Albert Spalding was manufacturing athletic goods, and by the turn of the century, he and his brothers were nationally known and recognized as one of the leaders in sports equipment production.

The impact of this technological revolution on sport was felt in three major areas: (a) transportation, (b) communication, and (c) facilities and equipment.[30]

Transportation

The effect of technological discoveries on **transportation** was monumental. During the colonial era, transportation was slow and cumbersome. Movement from one locality to another was restricted to travel on foot, horse, or water. During the early 1800s, the swiftest form of locomotion was the steamboat, the development of which depended on the invention of the steam engine. When Robert Fulton (1776–1815) built the first steamboat, the Clermont, it took over 24 hours to complete a 159-mile journey up the Hudson River. Steamboats carried horses to various cities located along the major waterways, but this was still a relatively slow mode of transportation and inadequate for transporting participants and spectators (for horse races and prize fights) to places not situated along the navigable waterways.

The smelting of iron set the stage for steel production used to build the rapidly expanding railroad system and greatly facilitated movement of persons and goods. Thus, even the railroads made their contribution to the development of organized sport. Before the Civil War, the railroad had nurtured Americans' interest in horse racing by transporting both horses and crowds from track to track. Similarly, participants and spectators for boxing and footraces could also be carried to the site of the event by the railroads. In many areas, prize fighting was prohibited, which necessitated scheduling such events in more remote areas. The railroad provided the means of transportation.

Both collegiate and professional sport benefited from the growth of the railroad networks. For example, the first intercollegiate athletic event—a crew race between Harvard and Yale at Lake Winnipesaukee, New Hampshire, in 1852—greatly fueled the sporting spirit by using a promotional gimmick: Participants received an expense-paid, two-week train vacation, which provided free publicity to the railroad in the areas serviced by the company. Similarly, the first intercollegiate football game (soccer, actually) between Rutgers and Princeton in 1869 was attended by students transported by train to the playing site. Professional baseball also took advantage of the expanding railroad system, and teams tended to locate close to the railways to ensure easier access to the burgeoning metropolises.

During the nineteenth century, the steamboat and railroad were among the most significant technological developments contributing to the rise of sport. But it was the internal combustion engine that revolutionized transportation during the twentieth century. Both the automobile, invented by Henry Ford (1863–1947), and the airplane, invented by Wilbur (1867–1912) and Orville Wright (1871–1948), were descendants of the internal combustion engine. While auto racing eventually developed into a sport of its own (the first Indianapolis 500 was held in 1911), the automobile is most notable for assisting travel to ski resorts, beaches, golf courses, tennis courts, and sporting events whenever people had the desire, time, and money. While airplane races have never been particularly popular sporting events, air travel enables teams to travel to virtually any location for sporting contests. Hence, interregional and international sport competition is commonplace today.

Communication

The improvements in transportation were paralleled in communication. The invention of the telegraph—the electric device for transmitting messages or signals over a distance through wires—by Samuel F.B. Morse (1791–1872) around 1844 was instrumental in transmitting sport information, and most newspaper offices were soon equipped with telegraph installations. During the 1850s, it was not uncommon for the outcomes of various sporting events—prizefights, horse races, and regattas—to be reported via telegraph. About the same time, the printing press was being improved, and literacy rates were rising.[31] Both the telegraph and printing press contributed to catapulting sport journalism into the limelight.

The advent of reporting international sports came with the laying (ca. 1858 and 1866) of the transatlantic cable by Cyrus Field (1810–1892). The last quarter of the nineteenth century saw perhaps the most revolutionary of all inventions. The invention of the telephone by Alexander Graham Bell (1847–1922) enabled the transmission of the human voice over wide geographical distances. The newspaper industry and its sports departments reaped enormous benefits from the introduction of the telephone.[32] Technological inventions such as these helped to fan the fires of sport journalism.

Mass communication, another social process, is the transmission of a message via the mass media to a spatially dispersed audience. The printed newspaper—the press—became an important agent of sport development around 1830. Much later, radio (1920) and particularly television (1940s) became almost synonymous with sport. Today, television is so significant in the financial picture of sport that some believe it has become the lifeblood of sports, an issue explored in Chapters 11 and 13.

The growth of sport is not the consequence of a single factor. Modern technology, however, notably television, has greatly accelerated this growth. One classic example is the fledgling American Football League (AFL) in the early 1960s. NBC signed a contract with the league to stave off a financial disaster caused by faltering franchises.

Other Technological Inventions

Other technological apparatuses that influenced the course of sport included the still camera (which provided pictures for programs, newspapers and periodicals); photography; motion pictures; and the incandescent lightbulb; which was invented by Thomas A. Edison in 1879. Before the invention of the lightbulb, sporting events were confined to the daylight hours. Shortly after its invention, however, various sporting events—prizefights, walking contests, horse shows, wrestling matches, and basketball games—could be played during nighttime hours. Madison Square Garden in New York City was staging sport events at night in the mid-1880s; having been completely electrified by 1885.[33] Before the Garden's electrification, gas lights had been used and, in 1883, John L. Sullivan and Herbert Slade fought in a crowded arena filled with a mixture of gaslight fumes and tobacco smoke. As the fight continued, legend has it that the boxers became elusive figures in a cloud of smoke.

Outdoor sports, notably baseball, did not use artificial light to any great extent until the 1930s. While night baseball was being played in various minor league localities, such as Des Moines and Wichita, the first major-league night baseball game—between Cincinnati and Pittsburgh in Cincinnati—was not played until 1935. Although the Negro leagues had experimented with artificial illumination, night baseball in the major leagues did not become entrenched until the 1940s. In fact, Wrigley Field, the home of the Chicago Cubs, did not capitulate until the late 1980s. On 9 August 1946, for the first time in major-league history, every scheduled game was played at night. One correlate of night baseball has been a general lowering of batting averages; although another plausible reason for the general reduction may be the expansion of franchises, tending to dilute the quality of teams.[34]

Urbanization

Urbanization refers to two different but interrelated social processes: (1) the migration of people from rural to urban areas, and the resulting concentration of the population in metropolises, and (2) the impact of urban styles, values, and cultural patterns on life in all areas.[35] We will focus on the first of these two processes. Transformations in communication, transportation, industrialization, and other technological advances hastened the migration of people to urban centers.[36]

The first population concentrations sprang up around seaports associated with transportation and merchandising. Many early cities developed around the transportation nexuses (e.g., Boston, New York, and New Orleans—harbor cities, Buffalo—a canal city, and Omaha—a railroad center). Because industry tended to concentrate around transshipment areas (e.g., Chicago and New York), the factory system was a stimulant in creating large urban centers.[37]

At the time of the American Revolution (1775–1783), only about 5% of the 3.5 million people in the United States lived in urban areas. By 1860, the rapid growth and concentration of the population in urban centers and the drudgery of routinized, mechanical work created a demand for recreational outlets. According to Betts, "ur-

banization brought forth the need for commercialized spectator sports, while industrialization gradually provided the standard of living and leisure time so vital to the
support of all forms of recreation."[38] In 1890, about 35% of a population that then
numbered 62 million had been urbanized. During the early twentieth century, 50%
of the U.S. population was urbanized, and by 1990, over 75% of the more than 250
million people in the United States lived in urban settings.

Some early cities—New York, Louisville, New Orleans, Boston, Chicago, and
St. Louis—became hubs of organized sport. Betts summarizes the impact of the city
on sport as follows: "Urban areas encouraged sport through better transportation
facilities, a growing leisure class, and the greater ease with which leagues and teams
could be organized."[39]

In summary, urbanization, a correlate of industrialization, refers to both *how* and
where people live. Professional teams tended to organize in large metropolitan areas
because their potential market—ticket purchasers, advertisers, and food franchises—
looked promising. Even today, the size of a market area is one of the most crucial
factors determining the location and success of professional sport franchises as well
as athletes' salaries.

❑ A BRIEF CHRONOLOGY OF SPORT SOCIOLOGY

The sociology of sport is a relatively recent addition to the social sciences.[40] Such
newness inevitably bestows growing pains on the upstart field, the scope and content
are ill-defined, and consensus is lacking as to the emphasis and direction it should
take.

Historically, the triad of play, game, and sport has occupied a niche in the scholarly
writings of classic sociologists. Sociological pioneers such as Max Weber, George Sim-
mel (1858–1918), William Graham Sumner (1840–1910), George Herbert Mead
(1863–1931), and Thorstein Veblen (1857–1929) highlighted the trilogy's role in
society and social relations. Out of Germany during the first quarter of this century
came the first textbooks devoted to the study of sport as a social phenomenon. Steinitzer's *Sport und Kultur*[41] explained the connections between sport and culture, and
Risse's *Soziologie des Sports*[42] examined sport using the tools of sociological theory and
methodology. These initial treatises failed to stimulate much interest in the sociological study of sport; the next major publication (Cozens and Stumpf's *Sports in American Life*) did not appear until 1953.[43] Further, much of this writing remained
fragmented and unsystematic until recently. An article by Kenyon and Loy in the mid-
1960s stimulated scholarly concern about sport as a social phenomenon.[44]

Riley surveyed the academic specialities of members of the American Sociological
Association (ASA) in 1950 and 1959.[45] So few designated sociology of sport as an
area of specialization that a separate category was not warranted; instead, those practicing in this subfield were placed under a miscellaneous rubric. Even as late as 1970
only 0.7% of sociologists claimed as their area of study leisure, sports, recreations, or
arts (a category that includes more than sport sociology) and ranked 30 out of 33 in
terms of membership.

Indications that this area of specialization is coming of age can be found in advanced degree programs in the field, publication of scholarly journals disseminating theoretical and empirical literature, and professional conventions, workshops, and seminars. In 1990 about 31 universities offered postgraduate sociology degrees in leisure, sports, and recreation, and approximately 150 ASA members indicated this tripartite division as an area of academic interest. These curricula tend to be interdisciplinary. The seminal journal in the field was the *International Review of Sport Sociology* (1966), followed by the *Sport Sociology Bulletin* (now called *Review of Sport and Leisure*), the *Journal of Sport and Social Issues,* the *Journal of Sport Behavior,* and *Sociology of Sport Journal*. The first session on sport sociology at the ASA meetings took place in 1971, and several regional and international associations (e.g., Midwest Sociological Society, North Central Sociological Association, and the International Sociological Association) have also devoted sessions to the topic. Finally, the North American Society for the Sociology of Sport (NASSS) held its first annual convention in Denver in 1980.

Several factors thwarted the growth of sport sociology. First, philosopher Weiss traced the benign neglect of sport research to Aristotle, who apparently shunned sports as too common and mundane to be worth serious consideration:

> Aristotle wrote brilliantly and extensively on logic, physics, biology, psychology, economics, politics, ethics, art, metaphysics, and rhetoric, but he says hardly a word about either history or religion, and nothing at all about sport. Since he was taken to be "the master of those who know" his positions became paradigmatic for most of the thinkers who followed, even when they explicitly repudiated his particular claims. . . . The fact that these subjects are studied today by economists, psychologists, and sociologists has not yet sufficed to free them from many a philosopher's suspicion that they are low-grade subjects, not worthy of being pursued by men of large vision.[46]

A second reason for this neglect may be the prejudgment that sport implies physical rather than social behavior. Social scientists have shied away from areas believed to be devoid of social interaction. Third, sociology has been notorious for its amoeba-like tendency to subdivide into numerous content areas. Hence, sociologists have been reluctant to further this proliferation. Fourth, sports-related interests have not occupied the same level of prestige as sociological theory, methodology, statistics, and other substantive areas. Some believe it is part of children's but not adults' activities. In this regard, Dunning has speculated that the hesitancy of social scientists to study sport may reflect a Protestant ethic orientation that considers play, game, and sport as frivolous topics unworthy of serious inquiry.[47] A fifth reason is that role models in sport sociology have been in short supply. Because outstanding academic figures have been lacking, the opportunity to follow in the footsteps of established scholars has been slight. In view of the suspect research that has characterized this specialty, we have little difficulty understanding why the field has been slow in attracting new practitioners.[48] In 1987 MacAloon characterized the sociology of sport as intellectually and politically suspect, containing research that was diffuse and narrow and theory typified by sameness, not asking penetrating and meaningful sociological questions, and making occasional conceptual *faux pas*.[49] Finally, sport, games, and recreation were, until fairly recently, privileges enjoyed only by the elite. Today, however, they constitute a mass phenomenon.

☐ SUMMARY

The emergence of modern sport is the product of many events, social forces, inventions, and people. The taproot of American sport extends back to the colonization of America. During the colonial period, orthodox Puritan theology coupled with harsh demands for survival restricted the settlers' quest for recreation and amusement. Nonetheless, the sporting spirit survived the century, and its intensity varied according to geographical region. From 1700 to 1800, a diverse assortment of sporting festivities surfaced. Various sport social clubs were founded, but a few collegiate sports, particularly the rudimentary forms of football, were discouraged because of their brutal character. Between 1800 and 1850, newspapers and periodicals began to celebrate the sport trend, which kindled interest in other forms of participation sports. Just the same, the elitist tradition in participation sports continued to prevail. Between the Civil War and World War I (1850–1918), developments in modern sport accelerated. Intercollegiate sporting events were inaugurated, and national championships in many sports were instituted. From 1919 to 1930, during America's "Golden Age" of sports, affluence, the increased popularity and significance of the automobile, and the newspaper industry stimulated the growth of collegiate and professional sport. From the 1920s to today, sport has become an increasingly pervasive feature of society. Three social forces—*industrialization, urbanization,* and *mass communication*—have been instrumental in the development of American sport. In examining the chronology of sport sociology, we considered why its development has been somewhat retarded.

☐ KEY CONCEPTS

Puritanism   Urbanization
Bee   Mass Communication
Blue Laws   Technology
Industrialization   Transportation
Cultural Hegemony

☐ ENDNOTES

1. This chronology and some of the following observations are gleaned from Craig Pearson, *Sports in American Life* (Columbus, OH: Xerox Publication, 1974). Special permission granted, Xerox Education Publications, 1974, Xerox Corp.
   GEORGE H. SAGE, *Sport and American Society* (Reading, MA: Addison-Wesley, 1974), pp. 61–103.

2. JOHN BETTS, *America's Sporting Heritage: 1850–1950* (Reading, MA: Addison-Wesley, 1974), p. 4.

3. FOSTER RHEA DULLES, *A History of Recreation: America Learns to Play* (New York: Appleton-Century-Crofts, 1965).

4. *Ibid.*

5. KING JAMES I, *The Book of Sports* (London, England, 1618).

6. *Op. cit.*,[3] Chapter 1.
7. WILLIAM C. EWING, *Sports of Colonial Williamsburg* (Richmond, VA: The Dietz Press, 1937), p. 1.
8. *Op. cit.*,[1] p. 27.
9. *Ibid.*, pp. 27–28.
10. C.W. HACKENSMITH, *History of Physical Education* (New York: Harper & Row, 1966), p. 343.
11. THORSTEIN VEBLEN, *The Theory of the Leisure Class* (New York: Penguin, 1967, original work published 1899).
12. The origin of baseball remains controversial. Some, like A.G. Spalding, a fine pitcher of his day and the founder of a sporting goods company that bears his name, contended that baseball was uniquely American. On the other hand, Henry Chadwick, the inventor of the box score and an acknowledged authority on baseball, maintained that baseball evolved from "rounders," a girl's game played in the British Isles before Spalding was born. Although Abner Doubleday is often credited with inventing the game, he himself never claimed that achievement.
13. HAROLD SEYMOUR, *Baseball* (New York: Oxford University Press, 1959), p. 15.
14. BENJAMIN G. RADER, *American Sports* (Englewood Cliffs, NJ: Prentice-Hall, 1990).
15. FREDERIC L. PAXSON, "The Rise of Sport," *The Mississippi Valley Historical Review* 4 (1917), pp. 144–168.
16. Typically, family pastimes grew into organizations and competitions, and then often became profit-makers for manufacturers or promoters of public contests. A.G. Spalding, a professional baseball stalwart, co-founded the National Baseball League, promoted a sporting goods business, and sponsored many athletic contests and sports awards. HARRY EDWARDS, *Sociology of Sport* (Homewood, IL: Dorsey Press, 1973), p. 25.
17. PAUL HOCH, *Rip Off: The Big Game* (Garden City, NY: Anchor Books, 1972).
18. *Op. cit.*,[2] pp. 15–19.
19. DR. JAMES NAISMITH, inventor of basketball in 1891, echoed this sentiment when he declared that adults as well as children preferred contests over sheer physical exercise. Gymnastics had been promoted by the YMCAs by 1860 and the turner (*Turnverein*) societies of German immigrants, but it never became particularly popular.
20. JAMES A. MICHENER, *Sports in America* (New York: Random House, 1976).
21. JOHN DURANT, *Pictorial History of American Sports* (New York: A.S. Barnes, 1952).
22. *Op. cit.*,[15] p. 33.
23. D. STANLEY EITZEN & GEORGE H. SAGE, *Sociology of American Sport* (Dubuque, IA: William C. Brown, 1978), pp. 29–30.
24. ALLEN GUTTMANN, *From Ritual to Record* (New York: Columbia University Press, 1978), p. 54.
25. *Op cit.*,[17] p. 39.
26. TIMOTHY J. CURRY & ROBERT M. JIOBU, *Sports: A Social Perspective* (Englewood Cliffs, NJ: Prentice-Hall, 1984), p. 25.
27. JOHN BETTS, "The Technological Revolution and the Rise of Sport," *Mississippi Valley Historical Review* 40 (September 1953), p. 256.
28. *Encyclopedia of Sociology* (Guilford, CT: Dushkin Publishing Group, 1991), pp. 142–143.
29. MIN S. YEE & DONALD K. WRIGHT, *The Sports Book* (New York: Holt, Rinehart, & Winston, 1975), pp. 14–15.
30. Some of these observations are gleaned from Eitzen & Sage, *Sociology of American Sport, op. cit.*,[23]
31. FREDERICK W. COZENS & FLORENCE SCOVIL STUMPF, *Sports in American Life* (Chicago: University of Chicago Press, 1953).
Op. cit.,[23] pp. 34–39.
32. *Encyclopedia of American History* (Guilford, CT: Dushkin, 1973).
33. *Op. cit.*,[23] pp. 39–41.
34. *Op. cit.*,[29] p. 15.
Op. cit.,[23] pp. 39–41.
35. *Op. cit.*,[28] p. 301.
36. *Op. cit.*,[2] pp. 173–213, 308–325.
37. *Op. cit.*,[32] pp. 29–30.
38. *Op. cit.*,[27] p. 232.
39. *Ibid.*, p. 30.
40. This brief chronology of sport sociology neglects the contributions of physical educators and Canadians. For their contributions, see John W. Loy, "An Exploratory Analysis of the Scholarly Productivity of North American Based Sport Sociologists," paper presented at the IX World Congress of Sociology ISA, Uppsala, Sweden, 14–19 August 1978.

41. H. STEINITZER, *Sport und Kultur* (Munich, Germany, 1910). Cited in Harold J. Vanderzwaag & Thomas J. Sheehan, *Introduction to Sport Studies* (Dubuque, IA: William C. Brown, 1978), p. 180.

42. H. RISSE, *Soziologie des Sports* (Berlin, Germany, 1921). Cited in Harold J. Vanderzwaag & Thomas J. Sheehan, *Introduction to Sport Studies* (Dubuque, IA: William C. Brown, 1978), p. 180.

43. FREDERICK W. COZENS & FLORENCE SCOVIL STUMPF, *Sports in American Life* (Chicago: University of Chicago Press, 1953).

44. GERALD S. KENYON & JOHN W. LOY, "Toward a Sociology of Sport," *Journal of Health, Physical Education and Recreation* 36 (1965), pp. 24–25, 68–69.

45. MATILDA RILEY, "Membership in the ASA, 1950–1959," *American Sociological Review* 25 (1960), pp. 914–926.

    GEORGE H. SAGE, *Sport and American Society* (Reading, MA: Addison-Wesley, 1974).

46. PAUL WEISS, *Sport: A Philosophical Inquiry* (Carbondale, IL: Southern Illinois University Press, 1969), p. 5.

47. ERIC DUNNING, "Notes on Some Conceptual and Theoretical Problems in the Sociology of Sport," *International Review of Sport Sociology* 2 (1967), pp. 143–153.

48. In reviewing the status of sport sociology, Eldon E. Snyder and Elmer Spreitzer, "The Sociology of Sport: An Overview," *The Sociological Quarterly* 15 (Autumn 1974) pp. 467–487, acknowledge the increasing sophistication of research in sport sociology. They see it as shaking off its "lumpen image." Eldon E. Snyder & Elmer Spreitzer, *Social Aspects of Sport* (Englewood Cliffs, NJ: Prentice-Hall, 1989).

49. JOHN J. MACALOON, "An Observer's View of Sport Sociology," *Sociology of Sport Journal* 4 (1987), pp. 103–115.

3

Sport and Culture

The Battle of Waterloo was won on the playing fields of Eton.

THE DUKE OF WELLINGTON

True sport is always a duel, a duel with nature, with one's own fear, with one's own fatigue, a duel in which the body and the mind are strengthened.

YEVGENY YEVTUSHENKO

Sociology, as a scientific endeavor, commences with two basic observations: (a) humans are *social* animals and (b) human behavior exhibits *repetitive* and *recurrent* patterns. Humans, of course, are not the only social creatures. Other species, such as ants, bees, geese, and elephants, to name a few, display sociability and social organization. However, it is generally believed that most of the predictability of nonhumans stems from genetically based mechanisms, thereby limiting the variability in their respective social orders. The way of life of humans stems primarily from learned behavior patterns and thus displays variation. The concepts of *culture* and *social organization* are vital in explaining and understanding these observations. According to Blau and Scott,[1] the influence of social conditions can be divided into two categories: (a) the structure of social relations in a group or collectivity (i.e., the network of social relations in which people are enmeshed, sometimes called the *social structure* or *social organization;* discussed in Chapter 4) and (b) the common ideas, beliefs, practices, and perspectives that societal members share and that, in turn, provide "blueprints" for their behavior (i.e., the *culture;* discussed in this chapter).

This and the following chapter demonstrate how two reciprocal and fundamental sociological concepts—culture and social organization—facilitate our understanding of sport and society. The two notions are meaningfully discussed in tandem since patterns of social organization are possible only through societal members' sharing cultural symbols. Without common understandings, social life would well be a helter-skelter phenomenon. It is through the common agreements that people have and share that social order results. One link between culture and social organization is found in the concept of *social role,* which refers to the rights, duties, and obligations expected of persons who occupy *social statuses.* Of course, individuals neither automatically nor uniformly enact their social roles. Through *social interaction,* role behavior typically takes on both "traditional" and emergent features. Social interaction based on social roles produces the patterned regularities we call *social structure.* Following is an elaboration on the linkages between culture and social organization. Figure 3.1 provides a schematic representation of the "bridges" between culture and social structure that will become clearer as the chapter unfolds.

The concept of culture is as fundamental in understanding human social behavior as the concept of gravity is in physics, or disease is in medicine, or evolution is in biology. In fact, it is so pervasive that it is easy to be unaware of its influence on our thoughts, feelings, and behaviors. A proverbial story suggests that the last thing fish would be aware of would be the water in which they swim. As famed anthropologist Ralph Linton mused:

> It has been said that the last thing which a dweller in the deep sea would discover would be water. He would become conscious of its existence only if some accident brought him to the surface and introduced him to air.[2]

In a less dramatic fashion, humans everywhere are immersed in a culture. Because it is second nature, becoming cognizant of the manner in which it channels our attitudes, emotions, and actions takes special effort. As Berger has observed, "the fascination of sociology lies in the fact that its perspective makes us see in a new light the very world in which we have lived all our lives."[3] *Homo sapiens,* throughout most of their history, have been only vaguely aware of the existence of culture. The ability to

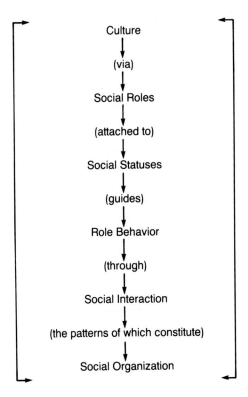

Figure 3.1 The connections between culture and social organization

SOURCE: Adapted from Jon M. Shepard, *Sociology,* 2nd ed. (St. Paul: West, 1984), p. 109.

Culture

(via)

Social Roles

(attached to)

Social Statuses

(guides)

Role Behavior

(through)

Social Interaction

(the patterns of which constitute)

Social Organization

"see" the influence of one's culture calls for a degree of objectivity rarely, if ever, fully achieved.

☐ CULTURE

Unlike other living creatures, humans possess few (some say none) genetically based mechanisms that invariably channel behavior in predetermined ways. Instead, humans' phenomenal learning capacity enables them to adapt to and/or to modify their behaviors and/or environments. These learned "designs for living" are subsequently transmitted to future generations and fall under the sociological heading of "culture." Understanding how culture penetrates our very being goes a long way in helping us understand human social life.

Culture is the "changing patterns of learned behavior and the products of learned behavior (including attitudes, values, knowledge, and material objects) that are shared by and transmitted among members of society," according to John Cuber.[4] Whereas laypeople tend to connote the term *culture* with refinement, social etiquette, or niceness and manners, social scientists use the term in a nonevaluative sense. Instead of only some people having culture ("highbrow"), all people have, or more appropriately learn, culture, although their "tastes" may differ in content. Culture may also be thought of as the way of life of a social group, the distinctive features—values, norms, and institutions—that characterize it.

Culture can be partitioned into material and nonmaterial modes. **Material culture** includes tangible objects such as sports arenas, velodromes, natatoriums, baseballs, bats, tennis rackets, nets, hockey sticks, uniforms, gloves, goggles, footwear, turnstiles, skis, "exploding" scoreboards, and the like. Many of these physical artifacts are products of technology. In sport, one of the more captivating examples of material culture is the stadium. Michener[5] maintains that architectural creations have symbolic significance transcending their utility: first, came the "Age of Pyramids"; then, the "Age of Temples"; followed in subsequent chronological order by the "Age of Cathedrals, Bridges, Railroad Stations, Skyscrapers, Traffic circles, Airports, and Shopping Centers"; and today we live in the "Age of the Stadium." The keen observer of the sport scene is familiar with the construction of multimillion-dollar sport palaces, such as the Skydome in Toronto (at a cost of one-half billion dollars), Superdome in New Orleans, the Astrodome in Houston, the Omni in Atlanta, the Harry S. Truman Sports Complex in Kansas City, Hackensack Meadows in New Jersey, and with the refurbishing of existing stadiums, such as Yankee Stadium in New York City and Soldier Field in Chicago.

Nonmaterial, or **ideational, culture** consists of intangibles. Common nonmaterial cultural elements that have been identified include symbols, attitudes, beliefs, language, values, and norms. *Norms,* or social expectations, vary in their social importance. *Mores* (singular, *mos*) are supported by strong sanctions, whereas *folkways,* or customary behaviors, are less subject to such responses. Illustratively, the incest taboo is a mos, whereas wearing matching socks is a folkway. Let us examine the significance of social values in understanding sport in society and society in sport.

❏ CULTURE AND VALUES

Values are conceptions of what is desirable; they are the underlying assumptions by which individual and social goals are chosen. Our own and others' behaviors are evaluated in terms of these beliefs. People will ordinarily expend great energy to achieve those features of social life that they deem important and worthwhile.

One of the recurring themes in the sport sociology literature is that sport can be viewed as a **microcosm** of the larger society. As a social institution, it can neither isolate nor insulate itself from broader social currents. Well-known sportscaster and writer Howard Cosell promotes this perspective.

> . . . Sport is a reflection of the society, that it is human life in microcosm, that within it the maladies of the society, that some athletes drink, that some athletes do take drugs, that there is racism in sport, that the sports establishment is quite capable of defying the public interest, and that in this contemporary civilization sport does invade sociology, economics, law, and politics.[6]

The nature of sport—its organization, values, goals, functions, and structure—provides revealing clues about society. Sport infiltrates and mirrors many levels of society (see Boyle's quotation on p. 1). Voigt,[7] for example, suggests that American baseball's evolution from a loosely organized to a bureaucratic structure reflected the socioeconomic changes occurring in the larger society. Similarly, Riesman and Denney[8] traced the transition of rugby into American football and noted that the process of change was consistent with the dominant American ethos. In much the same vein, Nixon notes:

> One could interpret the introduction of running, the minimum yardage rule, mass play, and the forward pass as responses to the need of American spectators for constant excitement and visible action. The emergence of clear, standardized, formal rules could be seen as a result of the increasing diversity of the social backgrounds of participants in football. This expansion of participation, which was consistent with American democratic ideology, demanded formalization of the rules to prevent differences of opinion that informal collegiate, class, or local interpretations could produce. The rationalization of the game could be viewed as a partial outcome of the capitalistic emphasis on productive efficiency in American society . . . the sports arena will accommodate itself and its culture to the rules and themes embodied in the broader culture of the society . . . the culture of sport and the process of sports socialization bear some important similarities to the patterns of culture and socialization in the broader societal context.[9]

Hence, there is reason to argue that the institution of sport provides a means for expressing the core values of a society. Edwards summarized this theme succinctly when he wrote:

> Sport . . . has primary functions in disseminating and reinforcing the values regulating behavior and goal attainment and determining acceptable solutions to problems in the secular sphere of life. . . . This channeling affects not only perspectives on sport, but . . . affects and aids in regulating perceptions of life in general.[10]

❑ VALUES IN AMERICAN SOCIETY

If sport is a microcosm of society, we would expect it to reflect and transmit some of the primary motifs prevailing in the larger culture. Since one of the distinguishing elements of a culture is its value system, consider the major value orientations of American society and assess the correspondence between these values and the values perpetuated in the sport realm. Sociologist Robin Williams identifies the following values as characteristic of American society:[11]

1. Achievement and success
2. Activity and work
3. Moral orientation
4. Humanitarianism
5. Efficiency and practicality
6. Progress
7. Material comfort
8. Equality
9. Freedom
10. Conformity
11. Science and rationality
12. Nationalism and patriotism
13. Democracy

14. Individualism

15. Racism and group-superiority themes

Several caveats regarding these value orientations merit attention. First, some of these values stand in paradoxical contrast to others (e.g., individualism vs. conformity; and racism and group-superiority themes vs. freedom, equality, and democracy). Second, although these values may receive much lip service, they may not be reflected in actual behavior. This is not unique. Disparities between ideal and real culture preside in all societies. For example, most Americans endorse the value of equality; yet, in practice, some act as if certain individuals and groups are "more equal" than others. Slusher captures the paradox well:

> Grantland Rice was noble, but wrong, when he indicated that they remember you for "how you played the game." They remember you for sixty-one home runs, 9.1 seconds in the 100-yard dash, 10-foot vaults, four-minute miles, and over one-hundred stolen bases. Mr. Durocher, in saying that "nice guys finish last" might have been right, but that is only because he confused values with placement.[12]

Finally, specific subgroups in a society may not pay homage to official mainstream values. In short, deviations from core values are not uncommon and may vary from one societal segment to another.

❑ VALUES IN SPORT

Does the Public View Sport in a Positive Light?   Yes

Is sport defined in positive terms? Do the values expressed in sport operate as eufunctions? Spreitzer and Snyder's research provides some answers.[13] They asked a sample of 500 residents in a Midwestern metropolis what they thought the consequences of sport were. Of those surveyed, 90% believed sport was of value because it taught self-discipline, 80% felt it cultivated fair play, and about 70% believed sport nurtured respect for authority and good citizenship. Both men and women had generally similar value perceptions. The sex differences that emerged "revolved around a tendency for females to emphasize the social control functions of sport (that is, to teach discipline and respect for authority), while the males were more likely to emphasize the value of sports as a means of relaxation and diversion from the tensions of the day."[14] As equality of sport opportunities increases, male and female attitudes may converge even more in the future. Since evidence suggests that sports are perceived in positive terms, let's examine the specific values attributed to sport.

The Dominant American Sport Creed: The Ideology of Sport

Harry Edwards has enumerated the social values attributed to sport in what he calls the **dominant American sport creed**.[15] He culled statements of opinion, belief, and principle from newspapers, magazines, and athletic journals for the light they shed on the presumed benefits of sports. Using content analysis methodology, Edwards grouped the themes emerging from his analysis under seven basic rubrics reflecting the reoccurring value orientations in sport: (1) character building, (2) discipline,

(3) competition, (4) physical fitness, (5) mental fitness, (6) religiosity, and (7) nationalism.

Character Building.   The most common virtue attributed to sport participation is probably **character building.** Character, in this context, refers to sport's contribution in nurturing the development of socially desirable personality traits such as integrity, responsibility, wholesomeness, maturity, honesty, dependability, and cleanliness. A historically important example illustrates. During the latter 1960s and early 1970s, beards and long hair were volatile male symbols in both collegiate and professional circles. The symbolic importance of this adornment can hardly be underestimated. Long hair, beards, mustaches, and headbands had been trademarks of the counter-culture—a *subculture* that became known for explicit defiance of mainstream or estab-lishment values. The juxtaposition of long hair (a symbol of defiance) with athletics (an institution valued for its character-building and conformist qualities) was incon-gruous.

Where did the idea that sports build character originate? Tutko and Bruns pro-posed three sources.[16] First, former amateur athletes who have achieved success out-side the sport realm (e.g., in politics or business) are fond of testifying to the positive influence of their earlier sport experiences on their subsequent successes. In other words, the road to the boardroom leads through the locker room. Second, individuals who make their livelihood at sports (e.g., athletic directors, coaches, and athletes) banter the alleged positive functions of sports. Third, prominent national leaders and those on the banquet circuit frequently use sport metaphors in their speeches and exhortations. In short, the notion that sports build character is "manufactured," sus-tained, and reinforced by individuals of social prominence.

To some, the character-building function of sports is poppycock. Sportswriter John R. Tunis once wrote:

> The Great Sports Myth . . . is a fiction sustained and built up by . . . the news-gatherers . . . who tell us that competitive sport is . . . character-building. . . . Why not stop talking about the noble purposes which sports fulfill and take them for what they are? . . . let us cease the elevation of [sport] to the level of religion.[17]

Former professional football player John Brodie said,

> Sport is one of the few activities in which many Americans spend a great deal of time developing their potentialities. It influences character, I think, as much as our schools and churches do. But, even so, it falls far below what it could be.[18]

Finally, when Robert Maynard Hutchins was president of the University of Chi-cago, he persuaded the trustees of the school to abolish football in 1939 by arguing that education should be character-building, and football wasn't.

Discipline.   Some contemporary social critics insist that today's youth lack **disci-pline,** which in this context means obedience to authority. Those critics claim that such an undesirable tendency stems from overpermissive socialization. According to the sport ethic, participation in athletics generates self-discipline and social control. The asceticism of the Protestant ethic is clearly evident in the importance attached to self-discipline. Woody Hayes, the curmudgeonish former football coach at Ohio

State, was perennially fond of talking about the need to cultivate discipline in student athletes and how football accomplished that mission.

Obedience to authority is a prevalent standard even in professional sports. Former baseball superstar Reggie Jackson, who refused to follow the manager's orders, was suspended for five days during the late 1970s and early 1980s. Similarly, the Cincinnati Reds, under Sparky Anderson's helm, imposed a restrictive code on facial and head hair. Players were forbidden to wear mustaches and beards or to have hair longer than a predetermined length. Even today, dress and hair codes exist in sports, as illustrated by superstar Don Mattingly's benching for refusing to have his hair cut during the summer of 1991. Strict obedience to authority can and does have dire consequences (see Vignette 3.1 for a tragic account of overdiscipline). Take the case of Bob Hayes, a former receiver for the Dallas Cowboys. In the spring of 1979, he was found guilty of selling narcotics to an undercover agent. After psychological examination, Hayes' psychiatrist declared:

> Bob Hayes is a victim of his own existence as a celebrity . . . he is emotionally incapacitated . . . he has a difficult time sustaining himself as a person of value . . . he has a need to be liked . . . he lived a life as a person under discipline, controlled and managed . . . he didn't learn any social skills.[19]

Former all-professional wide receiver George Sauer[20] had this to say about sport and self discipline:

> It's interesting to go back and listen to the people on the high school level talk about sport programs and how they develop a kid's self-discipline and responsibility. I think the give-away that most of this stuff being preached on the lower level is a lie is that when you get to college and professional levels, the coaches still treat you as an adolescent. They know damn well that you were never given a chance to become responsible or self-disciplined. Even in the pros you are told when to go to bed, when to turn your lights off, when to wake up, when to eat, and what to eat.

Competition. Another view of the value of sport is, in essence, Darwinian. Life is a struggle that only the fittest survive. Accordingly, sport participation prepares one for the competitive nature of living. Sport advocates suggest that it cultivates fortitude, perseverance, and courage—desirable traits, by our society's definition. According to Douglas MacArthur (1880–1964), sport's competitive spirit develops tomorrow's leaders by "preparing young men for their roles as the future custodians of the Republic."[21] When Gerald Ford was Vice President, he also lauded the social significance of sport **competition:**

> Broadly speaking, outside of a national character and an educated society, there are few things more important to a country's growth and well-being than competitive athletics. If it is a cliché to say athletics build character as well as muscle, then I subscribe to the cliché. It has been said, too, that we are losing our competitive spirit in this country, the thing that made us great, the guts of the free-enterprise system. I don't agree with that; the competitive urge is deep-rooted in the American character. I do wonder sometimes if we are adjusting to the times, or if we have been spoiled by them.[22]

American games are highly competitive. Measures are usually taken to ensure that one contesting party (team or individual) emerges victorious. The American people

□ VIGNETTE 3.1

When Discipline Becomes Your Epitaph

On November 21, 1977, Bob Vorhies, a Virginia Tech freshman halfback, collapsed and died approximately an hour after he was administered punishment drills. This brutal drill went as follows: "Ten 50-yard sprints, with both the sprint and the return to the starting line to be completed in thirty seconds; fifty pushups; fifty sit-ups; two 100-yard bear crawls, in which the player "runs" on his hands and feet without allowing his knees to touch the ground; four other 100-yard runs of various kinds, and an indeterminable number of laps around the field."

The punishment was for a minor drinking incident in Vorhies' dormitory room the previous Saturday following Tech's victory over Wake Forest, a game in which Vorhies gained twelve yards in his first, and only, collegiate carry.

There are quite a few unusual aspects surrounding Vorhies' death. First, the university administration seemed to sweep the case under a rug. Of the 1,500 people attending the funeral, no one came on behalf of Virginia Tech. The coaches did send flowers, but not one member of the alumni club sent even a note.

Second, the assistant coach who issued the punishment did not administer it. Another assistant coach put Vorhies through the paces. He is now coaching at a Virginia high school and refuses to discuss the case.

The only other witness, a fieldhouse janitor, says Vorhies fell several times in exhaustion. A local sheriff saw Vorhies having difficulty breathing just after the drill, but said he recovered soon and returned to his dormitory.

Dr. David W. Oxley, the county coroner, announced Vorhies had died of cardiac arrhythmia, a disturbance of the heartbeat. Oxley said, "There was probably some relationship between the drill and Vorhies' death, but there was no way to prove it."

A grand jury "found no basis to conclude that anyone acted in bad faith, or with a disregard for the safety and health of Robert Vorhies, or deliberately caused him any harm."

However, the strangest twist to this morbid affair was the fact that Bob Vorhies was probably one of the most disciplined athletes you could ever meet. He wanted more than anything else to be a major running back and he worked hard to reach that goal. "Most players would have dreaded the drills, but Vorhies joked about the prospect." A friend recalls, "he'd do the punishment to the letter. There was nothing a coach could do to make him quit." Another teammate said, "Bob never took any drugs, so everybody knew it wasn't that. People were saying they must have run him pretty hard. Bob was in pretty good shape. He didn't die easily."

It is pointless to make Vorhies out to be more in death than he was in life. Many of his teammates were puzzled because Bob never paid much attention to a secret in running punishment drills called "sucking wind early." One player says "you act like you're tired in the beginning so they won't run you so hard." It is a shame that discipline became Bob Vorhies' epitaph!

SOURCE: William Taff, "A Teen's Brutal Run-to Death," *Chicago Tribune,* 19 February 1978.

□

are generally dissatisfied with ties, draws, or stalemates. To circumvent this possibility, sporting contests frequently climax in sudden deaths, overtimes, extra innings, World Series, Super Bowls, and championship playoffs.

Why is competition such an important motif in our culture?[23] Although no definitive answers exist, several explanations have been advanced. Many individuals engage in competitive behavior, not only in sports but in business, academics, and interpersonal relations. Why, then, is competition a ubiquitous phenomenon? Several possibilities exist. When individuals seek goals in which there can be only a single or few winners (e.g., only one person can win the gold medal in an Olympic sprint, only one team can win the World Series or the Super Bowl, and only one driver can win the Indianapolis 500), competitive behavior is unavoidable. Not only sports, but many varieties of games are structured in this fashion. Hence, one answer to why we compete is that the nature of contests compels individuals to perform competitively.

A second tenable explanation derives from the simple fact that competition produces excitement among participants. Whether participating in sports, games, plays, dances, or facsimiles, there is a certain thrill obtained from the process. In brief, people compete because it excites them. However, research also shows that competition is not positively perceived under certain circumstances and, in fact, may be deliberately avoided (e.g., aversive sport socialization and success phobia).

A third reason for the near-universality of competition stems from a formulation in social psychology known as **social comparison.** *Social comparison theory* suggests that individuals engage in an activity to compare themselves with others. In athletics, we obviously learn a great deal about our own abilities by comparing our performances with others. Without competing with others, directly or indirectly, how would we know whether we were a good swimmer, a good jogger, or a good boxer? In other words, one possible explanation is that competitive activity provides us with valuable information about our talents and competencies. Social psychologists Baron and Byrne offer this conclusion:

> Findings . . . suggest that, in many cases, individuals . . . compete with others in order to accomplish social comparison. That is, when they are uncertain about their abilities on some task, they seek to gain such information by engaging in competitive behavior. To the extent this is actually the case, competition may often stem from a source we might not at first expect: our desire to gain fuller and more valid knowledge about ourselves.[24]

In the same vein, Jane Frederick has said, "What else but sports gives you an absolute measurement of where you stand and how much you've progressed?"

Physical Fitness.   Physically healthy and fit bodies are often, not always, the result of athletic participation. Americans subscribe to the virtue of **physical fitness.** Even the late John F. Kennedy (1917–1963) admonished Americans for becoming "soft" and "out of shape." Many sporting activities require limbering and stretching exercises and calisthenics that develop and maintain muscle tone. Some sports and exercise regimens not only firm the muscles and make the body look good but also induce positive changes in the cardiovascular system, reduce cholesterol and triglyceride levels in the blood, bring about weight loss by increasing caloric expenditure, lower blood pressure readings, redistribute body fat, and diminish stress.[25]

Much confusion surrounding physical fitness stems from different implications of the term because people often have different meanings in mind. To some, fitness means big muscles or a beautiful body. To others, it means suppleness. To still others, it means how strong you are, how far and how fast you can run, or how many push-ups or laps you can do. Exercise physiologists identify three different kinds of fitness: (a) muscular, (b) skeletal, and (c) cardiovascular. Calisthenics (e.g., push-ups and sit-ups) and weight lifting designed to strengthen and tone your muscles lead to **muscular fitness. Skeletal fitness** primarily implies flexibility and is developed by stretching exercises. **Cardiovascular fitness** refers to the strength and health of your cardiovascular system.

Exercises can also be conveniently divided into two types: (a) **aerobic** (with oxygen) and (b) **anaerobic** (without oxygen). Examples of anaerobic exercise include weight lifting, stretching, and isometrics. They do little to improve your ability to use oxygen. Aerobic exercises, on the other hand, improve your body's ability to take in and transport oxygen to its tissues. Common aerobic exercises include running, bicycling, and swimming.

A common misconception must be dispelled. To some extent, most physical fitness exercises affect the muscular, skeletal, and cardiovascular systems, but to varying degrees. For example, yoga primarily affects the skeletal system, but it also conditions the muscles and heart to lesser degrees.

The physical fitness mania has reached epidemic proportions. The physical exercise that accompanies organized and recreational sporting activities is lauded for its physiological and psychological benefits. Exercise is advocated as an adjunct to both psychological and medical therapy. Enthusiasts claim that exercise slows down the aging process and produces a natural high.

Physician George Sheehan, a modern guru of physical fitness, believes that exercise has a disease-preventative component and is a valuable form of therapy. Unlike some, Sheehan has been reluctant to claim that aerobic exercises will automatically reduce the likelihood of disease. In extolling its virtues, Sheehan sees running as a means of exercising the mind as well as the body and calls it a form of play.

Other health researchers have accumulated data indicating that exercise can delay the aging process. According to research conducted at Washington University, "preliminary results show that keeping in shape may help cut the aging process in half for the important cardiovascular and respiratory systems."[26] One of the best indicators of an individual's physical fitness and exercise ability is aerobic capacity and functioning. Medical researchers suggest this capacity decreases about 8% every ten years after age twenty-five. One study, however, discovered that oxygen capacity declined by 4% for older men who continued to be engaged actively in physical exercise. Hence, the empirical data suggest that continued physical exercise may mitigate some of the usual concomitants of aging.

Vigorous physical exercise has also been linked to the production of narcotic-like substances, called *endorphins,* which produce a natural sense of euphoria. Researchers have discovered that intensive aerobic exercise increased dramatically the production of these chemical compounds. These compounds induce a natural high and, at the same time, help the body control pain. Such studies lend credence to the addictive character of physical exertion. In fact, fitness buffs sometimes complain of suffering withdrawal symptoms after missing a workout.

Mental Fitness.   Benjamin Franklin aptly said, "Games lubricate the body and the mind." **Mental fitness,** often presumed to have direct educational benefits, is another frequently mentioned manifestation of sport participation. Many believe that sports not only prepare the body but also prepare the mind for doing battle in the labor market. Former college wrestling coach George Girardi has attested to the role of athletics in cultivating mental toughness.[27]

> Wrestling is a sport where a kid gets to take a look at himself and find his limitations both mentally and physically. I know that as an employer, I would hire the athlete before the nonathlete if they had the same skills and abilities. The ones that make it in college are the ones that are mentally tough. You try to get the kid to believe in himself and he's got to want to put in the time. The ones that aren't mentally tough fall by the wayside.

A slogan formerly adopted by Illinois State University's basketball program evokes this notion well: Locker rooms, banners, towels, and even uniforms were labeled with *MTXE,* an acronym for the phrase "*M*ental *T*oughness and *E*xtra *E*ffort"—the coach's formula for victory.

Religiosity.   Sport and religion have been interfaced for centuries. In the beginning, sport contained elements characteristic of a religious cult and served as a preparation for life. In writing on the origins of sport, Brasch said; "I was amazed . . . to discover how greatly religion and even humble clergymen, have influenced sports. It is a fact that many modern sports descend from ancient religious rites."[28] When the first recorded Olympic Games were convened in 776 B.C., delegations from all over the Greek world met to honor a dozen revered guests—the twelve greater gods of the Greek pantheon spearheaded by Zeus. These gods were thought to inhabit Mount Olympus, which overlooked the alluvial plain on which the stadium was constructed. For the gods' satisfactions, they also engaged in oratory, poetry, religious pageants, and music.

During the present century, there are numerous indications of a close relationship between sport and religion. Today sport is a form of civil religion, a topic explored more fully in Chapter 13.

Nationalism.   Athletes, particularly Olympic ones, are often billed as ambassadors of goodwill. Sports reinforce **nationalism** and patriotism, forms of **ethnocentrism.**[29] *Ethnocentrism* is the practice of judging alien cultural practices by the standards of one's own culture. Hence, others' behavior is frequently judged to be unnatural, wrong, or bizarre, while one's own is judged natural, right, and proper. In early 1991, some sports left no doubt where they stood on patriotism as it applied to the United States' involvement in the Persian Gulf War:

• At the National Basketball Association (NBA) All-Star Game, miniature American flags were handed out to those in attendance, and the President spoke about our involvement in the Middle East before the tipoff. The players wore flags sewn onto their uniforms and Most-Valuable Player (MVP) Charles Barkley held a postgame interview on national TV adorned in a camouflage cap with "Desert Storm" written on it.

- Players participating in the 1990 World Series wore flags on their uniforms, and Cincinnati Reds Owner Marge Schott thanked our troops in the Middle East for defending truth and justice.
- The backs of National Football League (NFL) helmets, even before the Super Bowl, were adorned with flags.

Additionally, when George Foreman strutted around the ring after winning the Olympic heavyweight boxing championship in Mexico City in 1968, Americans were ecstatic. He toted a miniature American flag, a cultural symbol glorifying the United States. On the other hand, when track stars Tommie Smith and John Carlos gave the black power salute on the victory podium during the same Olympic Games, many Americans looked on with consternation, contempt, and disbelief, and the duo was banned for life from future Olympic competition.

In 1938, Joe Louis, an American, and Max Schmeling, a German, fought for the world heavyweight championship. The "Brown Bomber," as Louis was popularly dubbed, was twenty-four years old and had been fighting professionally for four years. During this time, he had lost only one previous bout—to Schmeling in 1936, and boxing analysts did not predict victory in the rematch. At the time, nationalistic and racial overtones were highly significant. Adolf Hitler (1889–1945) had reached his height of power in Germany, and the United States was becoming seriously alarmed by his proclamations that a master race of "perfect" Germans (the Aryans) was destined to rule the world. Schmeling was explicit in his disdain for blacks and referred to Louis as a "stupid black amateur." On a hot, humid night (22 June 1938) Louis knocked out Schmeling in about two minutes of a legendary first round amidst the screams of some 70,000 while millions of others listened to the abrupt climax on their radios.[30]

In summary, we have examined seven basic categories of value orientations traditionally associated with American sport. Edwards even sees this dominant American sport creed in ideological terms, that is, as a set of beliefs aimed at convincing people of the virtues of sport.[31] But, like other social institutions, sport is neither immune from the distortions of self-praise nor free from exaggerations by the media. The problem is one of balance—balancing out the myths against the realities.

Winning?

Ironically, winning is not an explicit value mentioned by Edwards in the dominant American sport creed. Is winning not important? Obviously, it is. In fact, many sport critics argue that the Lombardian ethic ("Winning is not everything—it's the only thing") is the dominant goal in sport. At the professional level, there is no denying the importance of winning, as the following observations by professional coaches George Allen and Don Shula explicitly express: "Winning is living. . . . Everytime you win, you're reborn; when you lose, you die a little" [Allen]; "No one ever learns anything by losing" [Shula].[32] Los Angeles Lakers former coach Pat Riley has said,

"There are only two things in this league, winning and misery. And the Lakers don't want to be miserable." Even at the high school level, the emphasis on winning is obvious in sport slogans such as:[33]

A quitter never wins, a winner never quits.
Never be willing to be second best.
The greatest aim in life is to succeed.
Win by as many points as possible.

To appreciate our culture's emphasis on winning, it may be necessary to travel to a foreign culture so as to have a yardstick for comparison. Dean Smith, basketball coach at the University of North Carolina, after an extended sojourn outside the United States remarked, "Our American culture is far more competitive than any other culture I have observed. . . . We toast 'winners'—whether it is in business or athletics—regardless of the methods used to become a winner."[34] Finally, "Winning is like drinking salt water. It's never satiable. I'm trying to save sports from the lunatics who believe that winning is the only reason for playing," says Tom Tutko.

CROSS-CULTURAL DIFFERENCES: SPORT AS A MIRROR OF DOMINANT SOCIETAL VALUES

American sport values overlap with the general value orientations in American society. But if sport is universally a microcosm, it is necessary to demonstrate this claim in other cultural complexes. A body of literature demonstrates that the nature of sport is conditioned by ideological, political, and economic social forces. For example, there exist nationally "indigenous" sports—football in the United States, sumo wrestling in Japan, cricket in Britain, and the martial arts in the Orient. Furthermore, when a sport "migrates" from its original culture, modifications and adjustments typically ensue, as illustrated in football and taketak.

First, consider the **Human Relations Area Files**, an international data archive. It contains ethnographic (*ethnography* is a branch of anthropology concerned with describing dominant aspects of a culture) information on various topics pertaining to over 200 societies. These data permit social scientists to engage in cross-cultural research in many areas. Consider some of the comparative inquiries in sport.

Sport and game, as demonstrated in Chapter 1, are not synonymous concepts. Anthropological investigators have advanced three game classification categories:[35] (a) **games of strategy**, (b) **games of chance**, and (c) **games of physical skill**. Zurcher and Meadow[36] correlated Mexico's national sport, bullfighting, with the country's socialization practices. According to those authors, the national sport and the Mexican family both reflect cultural themes of "death, dominance, personal relationships, respect, fear, hatred for authority," and passive–aggressive character structures. Recently, the sport of bullfighting has undergone some changes as a result of protests over its inhumane treatment of animals and excessive violence and destruction. Zurcher and Meadow suggest that the changes in the sport paralleled recent alterations in the "macho" (virility) complex in Mexican culture and the decline of authoritarianism in the Mexican family. In short, changes in sport and the larger society tend to reinforce each other.

Another cross-cultural variation illustrating the manner in which games and cultural values mutually reflect each other is taketak, a game resembling bowling and played by the Tangu of New Guinea. **Taketak** is described by Light and Keller as a game

> . . . played with a top that has been fashioned from a dried fruit and with two groups of coconut stakes that are driven into the ground (more or less like bowling pins). The players divide into two teams. Members of the first team take turns throwing the top into the batch of stakes; every stake the top hits is removed. Then the second team steps to the line and tosses the top into their batch of stakes. The object of the game, surprisingly, is not to knock over as many stakes as possible. Rather, the game continues until both teams have removed the same number of stakes. Winning is completely irrelevant.[37]

The nature, rules, and objectives of taketak reflect the dominant value—*equivalence*—of the Tangu culture. The idea of defeating opposing parties through competition disturbs them, because they believe winning fosters ill will and contempt among the participants. Not surprisingly, when Europeans introduced the competitive game of soccer to the Tangu, the rules were modified so that the object of the game was for the two "opposing" sides to score an identical number of goals!

The manner in which dominant cultural values influence the character of sport is also illustrated by Ruth Benedict's ethnographic observations of a "model" Zuni Indian runner:[38]

> The ideal man in Zuni is a person of dignity and affability who has never tried to lead, and who has never called forth comment from his neighbors. Any conflict, even though all right is on his side, is held against him. Even in contests of skill like their foot races, if a man wins habitually he is debarred from running. They are interested in a game that a number can play with even chances, and an outstanding runner spoils the game: they will have none of him.

Apparently, then, the Zuni emphasize participation over competition in their contests, and those individuals who stand "above" the rest of the field are victims of social rebuke.

A final example of the way in which a society's sports mirror or reflect the dominant cultural ethos is found in a provocative essay by Murray Ross, who argues that sports' appeal derives from an archetypal, mythical essence.[39] In his view, fans enjoy sporting contests because they are able to temporarily live out fantasies in an imaginary world created through vicarious identification with the players. He applies this approach to two American sports: baseball and football.

Baseball is a pastoral sport best illustrated by examining its spatial organization and use of time. Structurally, the defensive arrangement of the positions fans out from the battery, to the infield, and finally to the outfield. Ross implies that the intensity and frequency of action is analogous to the transition of the United States from a rural to an urban society. He notes a similarity between the intensive interaction between the battery and urban society and compares the lesser interaction in the outfield with rural society. The meaning of time is also of social significance. Baseball games have no time limit, when a tie occurs at the end of regulation play, the game goes into extra innings and continues until one of the competing teams scores more runs, after each has been given the same opportunities. Viewed in this context, baseball can be seen as an attempt to escape the rigid time consciousness dominating our work-a-day world. In Ross's words, "Baseball evokes for us a past which may never have been ours, but which we believe was, and certainly that is enough. . . . But now the . . . dream is no longer our preeminent national pastime and now its myth is being replaced by another more appropriate to the new realities (and fantasies) of our time."[40]

It is football that has become the cynosure of our new fantasies. Whereas baseball embodies a pastoral myth, football embodies a heroic one. To Ross, football players, unlike baseball players, take on a larger-than-life or superhuman dimension. Although many of us are capable of performing the feats of baseball players (i.e., hitting a ball, fielding it, and so forth), few of us can seriously entertain the notion of participating in football without being injured or humiliated. Football is a contest of collective brutal activity. Baseball requires coordination and teamwork, but to a different degree than football. Furthermore, football is a game closely entwined with modern technology—the armor (i.e., uniforms, helmets, and padding), the synthetic turf, and the like. Football, says Ross, is the sport for our times:

> Football's collective pattern is . . . one aspect of the way in which it seems to echo our contemporary environment. The game, like our society, can be thought of as a cluster of people living under great tension in a state of perpetual flux. . . . Football metaphysically yokes heroic action and technology to suggest that they are mutually supportive.[41]

Football, unlike baseball, has strong jingoistic overtones. For example, the object of football is to "infiltrate the opponent's territory," whereas the object of baseball is to get "home." The militaristic nature of football can be clearly inferred from such widely used phrases as "ground attack," "air attack," "fighting in the trenches," "blitz," "the bomb," and "trap." Woody Hayes was fond of planning his game strategy like a military general and, on numerous occasions, spoke of one of his favorite military idols—General George Patton.

In conclusion, baseball provides us with a metaphor of what our society once was, whereas football is more analogous to what our society has become. Both sports tell us something about the nature of our society and the evolution of our national pastime. What can we say of the future? Despite the strong traditions of these two sports, a new national pastime—perhaps soccer—may emerge. In any event, sport and society have been and continue to be reciprocally interconnected.

In summary, sports tend both to change with and to promote the values of the culture as a whole. A heuristic contemporary illustration is found in Vignette 3.2, which highlights baseball in Japan. Note how the differences between American and Japanese baseball reflect dominant value orientations in the two societies. Curry and Jiobu describe how Japanese baseball mirrors Japanese culture:

> Japanese managers are mostly concerned with their team's sense of harmony. Japanese managers make decisions via conferences with coaches and key players—a sharing of authority unprecedented in the United States (and which causes the Japanese game to last much longer than the American game). Japanese managers never get fired for losing. They are given "leaves of absence" to contemplate their team's problems while an "interim" replacement "temporarily" takes over—permanently. Japanese players never hire agents and rarely negotiate for higher salaries; that would imply that one has placed himself ahead of the team. Japanese players do not display temper over "bad" calls; that would destroy the harmony of the game and show disrespect. Japanese players do not

□   VIGNETTE 3.2

Baseball in Japan: A Case Study

Baseball in Japan is an example of the ways cultural differences affect a particular sport.

Japanese baseball is distinctive in a number of ways that Americans would find quaint. For example, the annual game of musical chairs wherein managers are "replaced" is foreign to Japan; managers are rarely fired, and when they are, a ritual is used to permit face saving. Also, in Japan baseball games can end in a tie, whereas in most North American sports the emphasis is on a definite winner and loser through rules that provide for a tie breaker. Moreover, in Japan the manager and players emphasize the collective goal of winning the pennant even at the expense of individual careers. A manager may call on a star pitcher, therefore, whenever a game is critical. Star pitchers are also used for relief work, which commonly results in only two days of rest between starts. Such heavy use no doubt shortens careers. In a 1958

Japanese series, for example, one pitcher worked in six of the seven games, and he once won 42 games in a single season, but his career ended when he was 26.

To the American observer, Japanese baseball seems authoritarian and highly ritualized; really, however, Japanese baseball simply reflects traditional Japanese values. Individualism and egotism are highly stigmatized in Japan: salary disputes, asking for individual exemptions from team policies, temper tantrums, moodiness, complaining, clubhouse lawyers, attacking the umpire, criticizing the manager, mouthing off to the media, bad-mouthing teammates, violation of training rules, fist fights—these things are just not done.

SOURCE: Robert Hagedorn, ed., *Sociology* (Dubuque, Iowa: William C. Brown, 1983), p. 359. This Vignette was written by Elmer Spreitzer and Eldon E. Snyder.

□

skip workouts [and] Japanese teams are notorious for their dedication to physical fitness.[42]

If contradictions and paradoxes exist in sport values, it is probably because similar inconsistencies exist in the larger culture as well.

Cultural differences in sport socialization also help us understand Asian-Americans' generational conflicts. Berler reports how difficult it is for Asian American high schoolers to receive parental support for participation in basketball.[43] Because of the value attributed to education, not sport, parents are much more interested in and supportive of academic pursuits. It's not the parents' insensitivity, but their own cultural conditioning that relegates sports to a subordinate position.

□   SPORT HEROES REFLECT DOMINANT CULTURAL VALUES

Societies commonly project and personify their cultural ideals into specific "people-types." Cultural heroes or heroic archetypes manifest typically the major value orientations and symbols that a society holds in high regard. Earlier, we discovered that values provide directives and motivation for action; hence, it is predictable that cultural heroes, individuals who personify such values, become objects of admiration and emulation. Smith believes that heroes function to maintain the social structure by perpetuating societal values and norms and, in doing so, contribute to social solidarity.[44]

Hero worship in sport is common, and its manifestations are multitudinous. Consider the number of sports enthusiasts seeking autographs, acquiring and memorizing sport statistics, reading sports feature stories, collecting and trading cards picturing sport personalities, attending publicity events, and making pilgrimages to sports memorials (in Canton, Ohio, and Cooperstown, New York). The nature of the **sport hero** in the United States has changed throughout the twentieth century, and these changes mirror significant alterations in dominant cultural values.

Frank Merriwell, a fictional baseball player, was probably the best-known sport figure and appeared in comic books between 1896 and 1914. Merriwell was an all-American lad. He was gentlemanly, well-educated, brave, handsome, wealthy, admired, clean-living, and a superb athlete. As Boyle has observed, "Frank Merriwell in the words of his creator, Gilbert Patten, stood for truth, faith, justice, the triumph of right, mother, home, friendship, loyalty, patriotism, the love of alma mater, duty, sacrifice, retribution, and strength of soul as well as body."[45] During this time, many sport heroes were associated with skills of strength, especially boxers like John L. Sullivan, James J. Corbett, and Louis Cyr.

When Merriwell disappeared from popular culture, he was replaced by new idols. With technological advances during the 1920s and 1930s, heroes of strength were superseded by heroes of persistence, finesse, and guile. The new celebrities, men like Jesse Owens, Red Grange, Babe Ruth, and Johnny Weismueller, reflected a change in cultural values.

During the early 1940s, the civilian heroes of the previous era were replaced by those with military connections. Ted Williams, a baseball player and ex-Marine fighter pilot, and Felix "Doc" Blanchard and Glenn Davis, football standouts at West Point, were catapulted to fame. Maurice Richard, even though he refused military service, surfaced as a Canadian hockey star idol.

The 1950s and 1960s saw football emerge as a source of adulation. Smith has said, "It was a sport for the times, the highly complex organization, specialization, and division of labor in the game coincided with exactly the key characteristics of highly industrialized society. The sport heroes were the equivalent of business executives."[46] Quarterbacks Johnny Unitas and Bart Starr epitomized this breed, and Vince Lombardi gained popular acclaim. The New York Yankees, Boston Celtics, Green Bay Packers, and Montreal Canadiens—efficient and conservative commercial entities—were glamorized (somewhat similar to the 1980s).

With the social protest movements of the 1960s and early 1970s, the nature of the sport celebrity changed to accommodate the change in society's social atmosphere. Such sports personalities as Joe Namath, Derek Sanderson, Dick Allen, Dave Meggyesy, Jim Bouton, Muhammad Ali, and Duane Thomas presented an antiestablishment-type image that was more in tune with the times. Sport commentator and writer Robert Lipsyte[47] wrote:

> Sports is an unsparing mirror of our life and fantasies. Nowhere is this easier to see than in sports' choice of its super heroes. The Gold-Plated Age of American sports, that mid-sixties to late seventies era of instant legends and sudden millionaires and overnight

bankrupts was dominated by the images of three celebrity athletes whose impact on the nation's psyche was as deep and significant as their effect on the games they played.

Joe Namath, Billie Jean King, and Muhammad Ali were supreme performers at their peaks . . . but each had something more. Call it magnetism or sex appeal or charisma, it allowed people to use them as extensions of their hopes and daydreams, as living symbols of the ultimate.

Today's sport heroes include Michael Jordon, Joe Montana, and Bo Jackson, among others.

☐ IMMORTALITY VIA SPORT

The social significance of the values of "achievement and success" that Williams (see section entitled "Values in American Society") identifies can be witnessed by considering athletes' concerns about how their sport performances will be remembered even after their death, a notion referred to as **symbolic immortality.** Sociologists and sociologically oriented self-theorists have failed to consider the postself, the concern of the person with the presentation of his or her self in history.

Schmitt and Leonard explored the mass media to discover the processes through which individuals attempted to leave their footprints, so to speak, on the sands of time through the sport act.[48] Outstanding accomplishments, such as Hank Aaron's record of 755 home runs, Don Larson's perfect World Series game, and Nadia Comaneci's incomparable gymnastics score are one route to immortality. The social world of sport facilitates the postself by providing occasions, settings, and mechanisms through which sport participants can be remembered, eulogized, and endeared. The social world of sport is an arena in which to consider the postself because self-glorification and temporality are dominant and interrelated features of this world. Heroes and history represent the very essence of sport; there are beginnings, but there is also continuity. The social world of sport, largely through its emphasis on the values of achievement and success, records, and communication, facilitates the postself.

Lifton contends that five traditional modes, or vehicles, for attaining symbolic immortality have characterized human history. The *biological* mode is epitomized by family continuity and entails an "imagery of an endless chain of biological attachment." The *theological* mode concerns the idea of life after death or, more significantly, "the idea of release from profane life to existence on a higher plane." One mode is linked to nature itself, "the perception that the natural environment around us, limitless in space and time, will remain." Another mode, *experiential transcendance,* is a state so intense that in it time and death disappear." The *creative* mode reflects immortality that is attained through one's creative works or deeds. Within the social world of sport, the creative mode is the primary vehicle through which athletes seek to "leave their mark," and it is their athletic accomplishments and failures that become etched in the collective memory of sports.[49]

Recognition Through Awards and Commemorative Devices

The postself requires that one's acts be recognized and remembered. Individuals have to feel that their acts were "worth doing." The social world of sport (hereafter, "SWOS") gives more awards, prizes, and honors than almost any other social world.

Certain athletic awards involve a commemorative quality. The Baseball Hall of Fame, the National Football Hall of Fame, and the Basketball Hall of Fame encourage fans to eulogize and remember the greats of yesterday. Such monuments are established within the broader community and at athletic sites. Examples include Paul "Bear" Bryant Park, Wayne "Woody" Hayes Drive, Jesse Owens Plaza, Steve Garvey High School, Joe Louis Sports Arena, Amos Alonzo Stagg Bowl, Kinnick Stadium, Ryan (after Nolan) Expressway, Comisky Park, Hancock Stadium, and Lambeau Field. Participants are also honored through the naming of prestigious accolades after sport celebrities (e.g., the Heisman Trophy, the Outland, Davy O'Brien, Butkus, Doak Walker, and Unitas Awards, the Jim Thorpe Trophy, the Lombardi Award), the issuing of commemorative stamps (e.g., the 1983 stamps honoring Jackie Robinson, Bobby Jones, and Babe Zaharias), and the retiring of uniform numbers (e.g., Babe Ruth's "Number 3").

Creative Mode of Athletic Achievement

The anchoring of the postself in time through the sport act was an object of reflection and communication for athletes in various sports. The athletes themselves anticipated and sought a place in sport history, reflected on their progress, and expressed concern when they failed to achieve the progress they desired. They understood that their postselves were contingent on their athletic accomplishments, a form of creative immortality. Cindy Nicholas, a swimmer, predicted that if she executed the three-way, "nobody can bring out a history book and point to someone else who did it first."[50] Jim Valvano, ex-basketball coach at North Carolina State, worried that, "I hadn't made my own mark."[51] George Raveling, college basketball coach, seemed unconcerned about his postself in sport, but admitted, "I want it to say on my tombstone . . . that I was a team player."[52] Beth Daniel, a professional golfer, concluded, "If I were to quit golf today, I would go down in history as nothing."[53] Eamonn Coghlan said, after setting an indoor mile record, "What I accomplished here today was something that can't be taken away. . . ."[54] Brooks Robinson, the baseball player, said, "Being inducted into the Hall of Fame, is, well, it means immortality."[55]

Audiences, too, comment on the athletes' postselves; coaches, laypersons, journalists, telecasters, broadcasters, and peers talk and write about their accomplishments. After the Blitz made their United States Football League (USFL) debut, coach George Allen said, "You were part of history today. . . . Savor this moment. History."[56] Jerry Kramer stressed that, after twenty-five years, fans still remember the famous block he made in the Green Bay-Dallas championship game.[57] Sport analysts recognize that Bobby Thomson,[58] Phil Mahre,[59] and Jack Nicklaus and Tom Watson[60] have "left their mark" in baseball, skiing, and golf, respectively.

Negative Role Identity

Athletes and their audiences are aware that failure as well as success is remembered in the SWOS. The sociological processes that foster the postself in history can engrave it in a favorable or an unfavorable light. The SWOS "assures at least some modicum of failures.[61] Sport participants do not want to be remembered for their negative achievements. Roger La Francois, who informed the official scorer that a passed ball charged to him in the fifteenth inning had actually been a wild pitch, said, "I didn't want to be remembered for a passed ball in the longest game in history."[62]

As with other forms of stigma, negative experiences in sport have the capacity to obliterate positive accomplishments. Hewitt said, "In general, it can be said that the establishment of a deviant identity tends to negate all or most other possible identities in the eyes of those others for whom the label in question is treated as especially grave."[63] Bruce Sutter, a relief pitcher, observed that although Willie Wilson had a super year, the only thing anybody remembers is that he struck out a lot in the World Series.[64] Sport analysts have concluded that striking a player, a "grandstanding play," a catching error in the 1981 World Series have mitigated the contributions of Woody Hayes, Dave Smith, and Mickey Owen, respectively, and have tarnished their positive role identities in the SWOS. Probably the most well-known contemporary athlete whose stellar performances are overshadowed by dubious activities is Pete Rose. Despite his acknowledged feats on the field, his qualifying for membership in the Baseball Hall of Fame received vitriolic pro and con arguments, and ultimately, Rose was barred from the Hall of Fame.

Although clear evidence indicating that fans literally identify with the athlete's postself is not readily available, this does remain a distinct possibility. Exley, a rabid Giants fan, recognized "how I had tried to content myself with reverie" in the sport world while struggling to be successful in the writer's world.[65] Cialdini and his colleagues did not consider the postself but they present convincing evidence that fans "bask in the reflected glory" of athletes and teams, concluding that: "Through their simple connections with sport teams, the personal images of fans are at stake when their teams take the field. The team's victories and defeats are reacted to as personal successes and failures."[66] Another investigation found that 28% of 1,252 adult Americans said they sometimes, often, or always fantasize that they are the competing athletes when watching their favorite sport.[67] Complete emotional unity is required if the person is to be immortalized through another's acts.

Collective Memory as Locus of the Postself

Although certain formal sport acts become anchored in the athlete's very emotional being, some athletic performances are also etched in the collective memory of the SWOS. The collective memory is public and sharable. A social world in which achievement and multiple communication channels are so dominant is uniquely equipped to preserve its past. One wonders if Joe Louis, Red Grange, and the Four Horsemen will ever be forgotten. There are different collective memories, but the "resemblances are paramount."[68] Numerous features of the SWOS retain its collective memory, but five seem most crucial.

First, "Our memory of the past is preserved mainly by means of chronicling, the direct recording of events and their sequence."[69] Sport records and the media fulfill this function. Second, physical objects renew the memory of past events by serving as emotional reminders.[70] Individual and collective monuments, athletic sites, slogans, bumper stickers, pennants, T shirts, and other artifacts preserve the collective memory in the SWOS. Third, the collective memory is continued by awards and commemorative devices in the SWOS. Fourth, the recurrent character of formal sport acts provides occasions for the selective reconstruction of collective memories. It is this recurrency that best exemplifies the selective "calling out" of past events. Media descriptions of the 1984 Olympics, for example, frequently entailed discussions of previous Olympics, but—for whatever reasons—only a few of many possibilities were relived. Fifth, social worlds and subsocial worlds write and rewrite collective memories, with periods and personages being reassessed. Although accounts are given for failures in sport, and sport acts are negotiable, the possibility of a mythical past being created in the contemporary SWOS is probably not as possible as it is in other worlds. The sport act is too public—too clearly anchored in history. It took seventy years, for instance, for the regilding of the legend of Jim Thorpe. The fact that Thorpe had violated his amateur standing could not readily be disputed.[71]

Evidence of the collective memory as well as other processes involved in fostering and experiencing the postself were present at the 1984 Olympics (Table 3.1). Al-

TABLE 3.1 Evidence of postself at 1984 Summer Olympic Games

Fostering the Postself	
Opportunity for Role Support:	"They have added spice to the Olympic Games—athletes who distinguish themselves with outstanding performances, who leave their mark on the Games. Los Angeles will be no exception . . ." (*Adidas News* 1984).
Engrossment through Participation and Communication:	"At a moment like this, the Olympics sweeps over everything in its path" (Axthelm 1984).
Comparison through Measurement and Records:	"His [Jesse Owens'] name went into the language. His marks went on stone. Pretenders came and went. . . . An upstart named Carl Lewis has finally overtaken the legend" (Murray 1984).
Recognition through Awards and Commemorative Devices:	"I [Lewis] have four gold medals. That's something nobody can take away" (AP news release 1984).
Experiencing the Postself	
Creative Mode of Athletic Achievement:	Lewis "takes great comfort in knowing he will never die" (Smith 1984, p. 39).
Negative Role Identity:	"There's no way to escape this place if I [Tiina Lillak] get second" (Moore 1984, p. 314).
Expansiveness:	"If Klaus wins at the Olympics . . . he will put Caldaro on the map . . ." (Pileggi 1984, p. 459).
Deep Emotion:	"When I [Tracie Ruiz] got out there and looked into the stands, the energy from the audience filled my entire body and it was a very easy swim for me. I've never felt like that before" (*USA Today* 1984b).
Collective Memory:	"Debate over Decker's 3,000-meter race will afford these Games a kind of immortality . . ." (Leerhsen et al. 1984, p. 16).

SOURCE: Raymond L. Schmitt and Wilbert M. Leonard, II, "Immortalizing the Self through Sport," *American Journal of Sociology* 5 (March 1986), p. 1102. Used with permission of the University of Chicago Press.

though the Olympics entailed numerous competitions, the facts that (a) this evidence pertains to a single point in time and (b) the Olympics are the apex of amateur athletic achievement further confirm the premise that the social organization of sport anchors the self in time and history.

❏ SUMMARY

Culture is the changing patterns of learned behavior and the products of learned behavior that are socially shared by and transmitted among members of society or the way of life of a social group, the distinctive patterns—values, norms, institutions—that distinguish it from others. Culture can be dissected into two modes: (a) *Material culture* includes tangible artifacts, and (b) *nonmaterial culture* includes intangibles, such as values, attitudes, norms, and beliefs. The *dominant American sport creed* advanced by Edwards demonstrates the social values or the conceptions of what is desirable that are attributed to sport. The *ideology of sport* espoused by the sport creed include (a) character building, (b) discipline, (c) competition, (d) physical fitness, (e) mental fitness, (f) religiosity, and (g) nationalism. Although winning is not explicitly mentioned in the sport creed, there is sufficient evidence to suggest that it is a value of importance in sport and in life in general. Linkages exist between sport values and cultural values, and cross-cultural illustrations of sport behavior in Mexico, in New Guinea, among the Zuni Indians, and in the United States support this claim. Sport heroes reflect dominant cultural values, and the changing image of the popular sport hero from the turn of the century to the present demonstrates the manner in which sport heroes and cultural values tend to change in parallel fashion.

❏ KEY CONCEPTS

Culture
Material Culture
Nonmaterial, Ideational, Culture
Values
Microcosm
Dominant American Sport Creed
Character Building
Discipline
Competition
Social Comparison
Physical Fitness
Muscular Fitness
Skeletal Fitness

Cardiovascular Fitness
Aerobic
Anaerobic
Mental Fitness
Nationalism
Ethnocentrism
Human Relations Area Files
Games of Strategy
Games of Chance
Games of Physical Skill
Taketak
Sport Hero
Symbolic Immortality

❏ ENDNOTES

1. PETER M. BLAU & W. RICHARD SCOTT, *Formal Organization* (San Francisco: Chandler, 1962), p. 2.

2. RALPH LINTON, *The Cultural Background of Personality* (East Norwalk, CT: Appleton-Century-Crofts, 1945), p. 125.

3. PETER L. BERGER, *Invitation to Sociology* (Garden City, NY: Doubleday, 1963), p. 21.

4. JOHN F. CUBER, *Sociology* (East Norwalk, CT: Appleton-Century-Crofts, 1968), p. 76.

5. JAMES A. MICHENER, *Sports in America* (New York: Random House, 1976), p. 338.

6. HOWARD COSELL, "Sports and Good-bye to All That," *The New York Times* (5 April 1971), p. 9.

7. DAVID Q. VOIGT, "Reflections on Diamonds: American Baseball and American Culture," *Journal of History* 1 (May 1974), pp. 3–25.

8. DAVID RIESMAN & REUEL DENNEY, "Football in America: A Study of Cultural Diffusion," *American Quarterly* 3 (1951), pp. 309–319.

9. HOWARD L. NIXON, II, *Sport and Social Organization* (Indianapolis: Bobbs-Merrill, 1976), p. 14.

10. HARRY EDWARDS, *Sociology of Sport* (Homewood, IL: Dorsey Press, 1973), p. 90.

11. ROBIN M. WILLIAMS, JR., *American Society: A Sociological Interpretation*, 3rd ed. (New York: Alfred A. Knopf, 1970), pp. 454–500.

12. HOWARD S. SLUSHER, *Man, Sport, and Existence: A Critical Analysis* (Philadelphia: Lea & Febiger, 1967).

13. ELMER SPREITZER & ELDON E. SNYDER, "The Psychosocial Functions of Sport as Perceived by the General Population," *International Review of Sport Sociology* 10 (1975), pp. 87–93.

14. ELDON E. SNYDER & ELMER SPREITZER, *Social Aspects of Sport* (Englewood Cliffs, NJ: Prentice-Hall, 1978), p. 28.

15. *Op. cit.,*[10] pp. 63–69, Appendix A.

16. THOMAS TUTKO & WILLIAM BRUNS, "Sports Don't Build Character—They Build Characters," *Sport in Contemporary Society,* ed. D. Stanley Eitzen (New York: St. Martin's Press, 1979), pp. 232–237.

17. JOHN R. TUNIS, cited in *ibid.,* p. 232.

18. *Ibid.,* p. 233.

19. DENNE H. FREEMAN, AP sportswriter.

20. *Op. cit.,*[16] p. 233.

21. *Op. cit.,*[10] p. 121.

22. GERALD R. FORD (with John Underwood), "In Defense of the Competitive Urge," *Sports Illustrated* (8 July 1974), p. 17.

23. ROBERT A. BARON & DONN BYRNE, *Social Psychology* (Boston: Allyn & Bacon, 1981), pp. 376–377.

24. *Ibid.,* p. 377.

25. KENNETH H. COOPER, *Aerobics* (New York: M. Evans, 1968).

26. "Keeping in Shape Slows Aging Process, *The Barnesboro Star* (29 August, 1979), p. B4.

27. Interview with George Girardi, *The Daily Vidette* [Illinois State University] (16 November 1981), p. 12.

28. RUDOLPH BRASCH, *How Did Sports Begin?* (New York: David McKay, 1970), p. x.

29. *Encyclopedia of Sociology* (Guilford, CT: Dushkin, 1991), p. 107.

30. JACK ORR, "The Black Boxer: Exclusion and Ascendance" *Sport and Society*, eds. John T. Talamini & Charles H. Page (Boston: Little, Brown, 1973), pp. 240–261.

31. *Op. cit.,*[10] pp. 367–375.

32. D. STANLEY EITZEN & GEORGE H. SAGE, *Sociology of American Sport* (Dubuque, IA: William C. Brown, 1978), pp. 66–67.

33. ELDON E. SNYDER, "Athletic Dressing Room Slogans as Folklore: A Means of Socialization," *International Review of Sport Sociology* 7 (1972), pp. 89–102.

34. JAY J. COAKLEY, *Sport in Society* (St. Louis: C.V. Mosby, 1990), p. 66.

35. JOHN ROBERTS, J. MALCOLM, & ROBERT R. BUSH, "Games in Culture," *American Anthropologist* 61 (August 1959), pp. 597–605.
BRIAN SUTTON-SMITH, JOHN ROBERTS, & ROBERT M. KOZELKA, "Game Involvement in Adults," *The Journal of Social Psychology* 60 (June 1963), pp. 15–30.
ELDON SNYDER & ELMER SPREITZER, *Social Aspects of Sport* (Englewood Cliffs, NJ: Prentice-Hall, 1978).

36. LOUIS ZURCHER & ARNOLD MEADOW, "On Bullfights and Baseball: An Example of Interaction of Social Institutions," *Sport: Readings From a Sociological Perspective,* ed. Eric Dunning (Toronto: University of Toronto Press, 1972). *Op. cit.*[9] pp. 14–15.

37. DONALD LIGHT, JR., & SUZANNE KELLER, *Sociology* (New York: Alfred A. Knopf, 1975), p. 74.

38. RUTH BENEDICT, *Patterns of Culture* (New York: Mentor Books, 1934), p. 95.

39. MURRAY ROSS, "Football Red and Baseball Green," *The Study of Society,* ed. Peter I. Rose (New York: Random House, 1977), pp. 111–119.

40. *Ibid.,* p. 114.

41. *Ibid.*, p. 117.

42. TIMOTHY J. CURRY & ROBERT M. JIOBU, *Sports: A Social Perspective* (Englewood Cliffs, NJ: Prentice-Hall, 1984), p. 46.

43. BERLER, cited in *Chicago Tribune* (24 February 1991), Section 2, p. 17.

44. GARY SMITH, "The Sport Hero: An Endangered Species," *Quest* XIX (January, 1973), pp. 59–70.

45. ROBERT BOYLE, *Sport—Mirror of American Life* (Boston: Little, Brown, 1963), p. 242.

46. *Op. cit.*,⁴⁴ p. 62.

47. ROBERT LIPSYTE, "Sports: Instant Legends and Super Heroes," copyright 1977 by the Regents of the University of California. The quote was excerpted from "Popular Culture: Mirror of American Life." Reprinted by permission, p. 1.

48. RAYMOND L. SCHMITT & WILBERT M. LEONARD, II, "Immortalizing the Self Through Sport," *American Journal of Sociology*, 91, no. 5 (1986), pp. 1088–1111.

49. R.J. LIFTON. *The Life of the Self* (New York: Simon & Schuster, 1976).

50. S. PILEGGI. "Channeling Her Energies," *Sports Illustrated* 55 (10 August 1981), pp. 30–35.

51. AP News Release. "Valvano: State 'Home'," *South Bend Tribune* (31 March 1983), p. 37.

52. M. ISAACSON, "Raveling's Jokes Belie Serious Man," *The Daily Iowan* [Iowa City, IA] (6 April 1983), p. 1-A.

53. B. MCDERMOTT, "The Game Is Her Life and Only Love," *Sports Illustrated* (2 February 1981), pp. 34–39.

54. UPI News Release. "Coghlan Sets Mile Record," *The Daily Vidette,* (1 March 1983), p. 11.

55. AP News Release. "Hall Inducting Four Today," *The Pantagraph,* [Bloomington-Normal, IL] (31 July 1983), p. C7.

56. B. VERDI, "History May Lurk Amid the Humbug," *Chicago Tribune* (7 March 1983), pp. 4-1, 6.

57. E. KAPLAN, "The Legend of Vince Lombardi," *Family Weekly* (30 January 1983) pp. 8, 10.

58. J. DREES & J. C. MULLEN. *Where Is He Now?* (Middle Village, NY: Jonathan David, 1973).

59. J. HUSAR, "Phil Mahre's Alone on Top of the Hill," *Chicago Tribune* (9 March 1983) pp. 3–4.

60. D. JENKINS, "An Upside-Down Game," *Sports Illustrated* 25 (28 November 1966), pp. 22–27.

61. D.W. BALL, "Failure in Sport," *American Sociological Review* 41 (1976) pp. 726–739.

62. J. KIRSHENBAUM, "Scorecard," *Sports Illustrated* 24 (14 February 1966), p. 35.

63. J.P. HEWITT, *Self and Society* (Boston: Allyn & Bacon, 1984).

64. K. HIERONYMUS, "Cardinals Stop in Town," *Daily Vidette* (3 February 1983) p. 12.

65. F. EXLEY, *A Fan's Notes.* (New York: Random House, 1968).

66. R.B. CIALDINI, R.J. BORDEN, A. THORNE, M.R. WALKER, S. FREEMAN, & L.R. SLOAN, "Basking in Reflected Glory: Three (Football) Field Studies," *Social Psychology of the Self-Concept,* eds. M. Rosenberg & H. B. Kaplan. (Arlington Heights, IL: Harlan Davidson, 1982), pp. 88–101.

67. *The Miller Lite Report on American Attitudes Toward Sports.* (Milwaukee, WI: Miller Brewing, 1983).

68. B. SCHWARTZ, "The Social Context of Commemoration: A Study in Collective Memory," *Social Forces* 61 (1982) pp. 374–402.

69. *Ibid.*

70. R.L. SCHMITT, "Embodied Identities: Breasts as Emotional Reminders," *Studies in Symbolic Interaction,* ed. N.K. Denzin (Greenwich, CT: JAI Press), pp. 229–289.

71. J. MCCALLUM, "The Regilding of a Legend," *Sports Illustrated* 57 (25 October 1982), pp. 48–49, 52–54, 56, 63–65.

4

Sport and Social Organization

Whoever wants to know the heart and mind of America had better learn baseball. JACQUES BARZUN

Figure 4.1 displays baseball's basic defensive alignment and serves as a simple graphic metaphor of the concept of **social organization.** Each player has specific tasks to perform under particular circumstances (e.g., the pitcher hurls the ball; the catcher flashes signals to the pitcher, catches the ball after it is delivered, and covers first or third base under certain circumstances; the first baseman covers first base to receive throws from other fielders and so forth). To win, or at least enhance the probability of winning, each player must know what, when, how, and where to act in proper conjunction with the other players' activities. When all players properly coordinate their specialized duties, we call their collective efforts *teamwork*. Analogously, this is what is implied by *social organization*—an overarching strategy or plan that is known and implemented by all participants. Without an orderly blueprint, social activity would be chaotic.[1]

In addition to patterned or coordinated activity, several key characteristics of social organization apply to sport teams as well as to society in general. First, baseball teams have a goal—namely, winning; and members of society tend to share common goals and values also. Typically such goals cannot be realized without others' cooperation. Second, baseball teams must play according to a set of formalized rules, which can also be said for societal members. When a player breaks these rules, the team or player or both may be penalized via suspensions and/or fines and the like. For example, a pitcher doctoring the ball with a forbidden "foreign substance" may be either warned or removed from the game. Similarly, in the game of life, an income-tax evader may be fined or sentenced to a correctional facility or both. Third, each position in baseball has certain responsibilities and rights. If these are not carried out, sanctions of various sorts may be applied. Finally, those who perform spectacularly are rewarded socially (with prestige and praise) and/or materially (with financial remuneration). In summary, the concept of social organization refers to the interconnected rules, positions,

FIGURE 4.1 Baseball's social structure

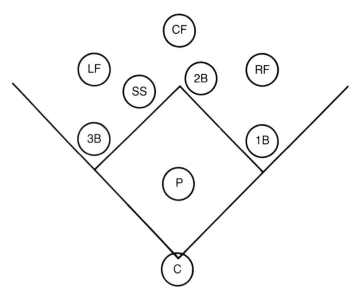

☐ VIGNETTE 4.1

Sport Contests, Social Integration, and Suicide

Sociologist Émile Durkheim spent much of his scholarly life theorizing and conducting research on the role that integration or social solidarity played in the lives of societal members. His well-known study of suicide—that it varies inversely with the extent to which individuals are integrated in society—is a starting point for some recent sport-related inquiries. Phillips and Feldman have argued that the structural integration of individuals in society may be heightened during major public holidays, such as Christmas, Thanksgiving, and the Fourth of July, and that such social bonds may deter suicide in comparison to times when these social bonds may be attenuated. This phenomenon, that is, the reduction in suicide during major ceremonial events, has been dubbed a "suicide dip." Curtis, Loy, and Karnilowicz explored a related research query, namely, "Are suicide rates lower before and during two sport ceremonial hol-idays (the finale of the World Series and Super Bowl Sunday)?" They discovered that for both sport ceremonial holidays and civil holidays suicides are comparatively lower before and during and comparatively higher following them. Although the findings were not pronounced during the sport ceremonies, the direction of the findings was consistent with Durkheim's proposition that sport holidays enhance social integration and, correspondingly, lessen the incidence of suicides.

SOURCES: James Curtis, John Loy, and Wally Karnilowicz, "A Comparison of Suicide-Dip Effects of Major Sport Events and Civil Holidays," *Sociology of Sport Journal* 3, no. 1 (1986), pp. 1–14. Émile Durkheim, *Suicide: A Study in Sociology*, trans. J. A. Spaulding & G. Simpson (New York: Free Press, 1951). David Phillips and Kenneth Feldman, "A Dip in Deaths Before Ceremonial Occasions: Some Relationships Between Social Integration and Mortality," *American Sociological Review* 38 (1973), pp. 678–696.

☐

roles, and relationships that constitute the activities of a social group, be it a sport team or society. Social organization may be thought of as the process through which social life becomes recurrent, predictable, patterned, and orderly and has some latent consequences, as revealed in Vignette 4.1.

Consider the 1992 Oakland Athletics. The A's baseball aficionados know that the personnel of this team differed radically from that which won three consecutive World Series (1972, 1973, and 1974). Their manager was no longer Dick Williams, and key players (namely, Catfish Hunter, Joe Rudi, Sal Bando, Rollie Fingers, and Reggie Jackson) had retired; yet, in spite of this player turnover, the basic social organization of the club remained essentially the same. From year to year, there is typically a slightly different lineup of players, which is due to trades, free-agent acquisitions, injuries, retirements, and promotions of minor-league hopefuls. As in the past, the front office and management made new policies (or stressed the old) and instituted changes. No one would deny that the Oakland Athletics remained a recognizable entity despite the personnel changes. The social relationships among management and players, players and coaches, and so on were still identifiable. Even though the individuals composing the team changed, the general social organizational nature of the baseball club remained similar and therefore analyzable and predictable.[2]

The relative enduring quality of the Athletics' teams was its social organization. The team then and today is recognizable and familiar because all categories of persons—players, coaches, and manager—knew, in general, what was expected of them with respect to their duties, obligations, and rights.

LEVELS OF SOCIAL ORGANIZATION: INTERPERSONAL, GROUP, AND SOCIETAL

Sociologists find it helpful to distinguish three **levels of social organization:** (a) interpersonal, (b) group, and (c) societal.[3] These echelons move from the concrete to the abstract. The **interpersonal** level, the most elementary social bond, refers to social relationships existing between two persons sharing some kind of role relationship with each other. In sport, such relationships could be those between player and coach, fan and player, or manager and front office president. The **group** level refers to interactions that occur between groups, such as the negotiations between the National Football League (NFL) Players' Association and the team owners (i.e., labor vs. management). The most abstract organizational level, the **societal**, refers to the structure of social relations in society as a whole. At this level, sport can be conceived of as a social institution comprising associations, organizations, and groups that organize, administer, and regulate human activity in the context of sport. Included at this level are sporting goods manufacturers, sport clubs, athletic teams, sport regulatory and governing bodies, and the mass media.[4]

SPORT ORGANIZATIONS AS ASSOCIATIONS

Association and *formal organization* are synonymous concepts. The former term, instead of the latter, is used to minimize confusion with the sociological concept of *social organization,* a term whose meaning has much broader connotations than presently applicable. An *association* is a special-purpose group constructed deliberately to pursue specific objectives, goals, and/or values such as profit, public service, entertainment, or any combination of these. Considering the number, size, and influence of organizations in the modern world, as well as their pervasive effects on people's lives, social scientists sometimes descriptively use the phrase *organizational society* when referring to the postindustrial period (a stage of social and economic development when the principal economic activity is "services" depending on specific knowledge).

Sport Associations

Sport can be understood from an organizational perspective; for example, Vignette 4.2 demonstrates how research on sport organizations has many beneficial effects. A brief chronology of baseball ownership will prove enlightening. Originally, professional teams were owned by the players.[5] The players determined when, where, who, and how they would play as well as how the team's revenue would be distributed. Apparently, the players liked this arrangement, because it remained effectual until the latter half of the nineteenth century. Before the formation of the National League in 1876, professional baseball players moved freely from one team to another, depending greatly on where they commanded the largest salaries. Baseball's success and growth,

Sport as a Natural Laboratory

A cardinal methodological principle is that when two or more units, groups, situations, or conditions are compared, it is imperative that the objects being contrasted be as identical as possible. Otherwise, false relations—what are technically called *spurious correlations*—may be inappropriately established. When such diverse circumstances exist, the validity of the study often is questionable. Sport leagues are excellent for testing organizational theories and principles since many salient factors can be controlled, sometimes with little conscious effort. Let me explain.

Suppose two associations are compared. If they differ in size, complexity, and other factors, it is virtually impossible to make a legitimate comparison and conclusion. The advantage of testing organizational theories in sport resides in the fact that a variety of variables are held constant and thus can be ruled out (controlled or held constant to use the research vernacular) as possible explanations for the phenomenon being studied.

Suppose we're interested in the relationship between the degree of autonomy granted coaching staffs (the independent variable) and success (the dependent variable), that is, winning, in the NFL. Operationally, autonomy is assessed by making an informed subjective judgment on the degree to which owners and front offices avoid meddling in coaching affairs and winning is determined by calculating the winning percentage. By confining the analysis to professional football, several significant confounding factors are eliminated as possible explanations. The following factors are held constant: (1) size of units since each team is limited to the same number of players, (2) the player draft, premised on providing all teams with a similar chance of selecting the most talented athletes, (3) amount received from the media insofar as television revenue is concerned, since all teams are guaranteed the same amount regardless of their records, and (4) success or failure (as measured by wins and losses), is an unambiguous de-

termination. Hence, one of the few factors that varies across teams is the management's intrusion or lack of intrusion into the coaching decisions.

Fans who complain about front office and owner intrusion are indirectly supporting the *decentralization hypothesis* (the dispersal of authority from a few central administrators to those directly involved in a particular activity) and the importance of "management by objectives" approach. This hypothesis in sport says leave the crucial game decisions to the coaches and have top-level management decide to hire or fire them on the basis of their success. So long as all parties agree on the firm's goals, this approach to management science is sensible.

Stark found a correlation of +.60 between winning and coaching autonomy. This means the tendency is that the more freedom granted the coach (conversely, the less meddling), the more success the team has. Stark discovered that of the ten teams that went to the Super Bowl between 1980 and 1984, six scored highest on the autonomy measure and the other four scored next to the highest on a four-point autonomy scale. Obviously, there are always exceptions to the rule: Super Bowl XX (1986) teams—Chicago Bears and New England Patriots—both received a 1 rating (0 = least autonomy and 3 = most autonomy). A correlation of +.60 is not perfect (±1.0 is), but it is a significant positive correlation that supports the decentralization and management by objectives doctrines.

In summary, sport often provides a pure natural laboratory for testing research propositions because many critical factors are standardized. The example cited here is not an infallible test of organizational theory, but it does provide one with a sense of the facility with which hypotheses can be tested in such settings.

SOURCE: Rodney Stark, "Organization and the National Football League," *Demonstrating Sociology* (Belmont, CA: Wadsworth, 1985), pp. 190–193.

■

however, presented problems that ultimately sowed the seeds of organizational change.

As payrolls expanded, as the need for more than part-time administration of the programs grew, and as the cost of equipment and facilities spiraled, the players reluctantly permitted owners and front offices to administer their off-the-field business affairs. The players neither fancied their loss of control nor appreciated the strings attached to their contracts. It was about 1880 that owners insisted on players' signing contracts that contained reserve clauses, giving owners virtual unilateral control over the players' destinies.

When the American League was formed in 1900, there was a brief respite, during which players could choose between the two leagues. This meant that owners in each of the leagues had to bid competitively for players. The owners soon realized that the situation was not suited to their best financial interests, so they conspired not to hire each others' players. This usurpation of the player's right to self-determination relegated the players to a powerless bargaining position. This set of historical developments provides the backdrop against which the contemporary structure of sport can be pictured, and we will examine these developments more closely in Chapter 11.

Sport franchises today are *associations*—special-purpose groups—seeking to make profits while providing entertainment. They are formal organizations, colloquially referred to as *bureaucracies*. Like other bureaucratic structures, in their ideal form, they possess the following characteristics: (a) a division of labor specifying the job description for each position and producing an unambiguous chain of command among the hierarchy of positions, (b) a rationalization of the operations and impersonal relations among the positions that enables the objectives of the organization to be implemented, (c) an impersonal application of the rules without regard for person or circumstance, and (d) routinization of tasks that makes specific individuals replaceable.[6] Amateur sport organizations (e.g., the Amateur Athletic Union [AAU], the National Collegiate Athletic Association [NCAA], the National Association of Intercollegiate Athletics, the International Olympic Committee, and the United States Olympic Committee) and professional sport organizations (e.g., the Professional Golf Association, the Ladies' Professional Golf Association, the NFL, and the NFL Players' Association) are bureaucratic structures in sport that exist at both the national and international level.

Formal Structure

The official organizational chart, i.e., the **formal structure** of a football team, shown in Figure 4.2, highlights some of the bureaucratic characteristics of a professional football team. Note the hierarchical "power" arrangement with the head coach at the top and players at the bottom. Those at the top are generally in a position to wield influence on those below. The professional baseball and football strikes of the 1980s altered, to some extent, some of the traditional power arrangements between players and owners.

Each position in the organization is specialized with a set of rules and regulations— a job description—specifying what each incumbent is and is not required to do. The players, for example, cannot fire the coach, but the owner can. The coach, on the other hand, can decide who should play the various positions and when, as well as

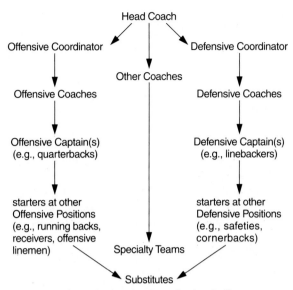

FIGURE 4.2   A glimpse of the formal organization of a football team

the special teams. A system of rules such as dress codes or curfews designates attitudinal and behavioral prescriptions and proscriptions. Finally, the structure is impersonal in that the decisions—hiring, releasing, suspending, or trading—are made, theoretically, for the greater good of the organization.

Informal Structure

The nature of bureaucracy being discussed is "ideal-typical," which is to say that, in theory, these characteristics and operations apply. In practice, however, they do not always mesh neatly with locker-room realities. Bureaucracy has another face, what sociologists call the **informal structure,** or *informal organization*. This informal structure, which fulfills some of the needs that the formal organization cannot meet, takes the form of behavior patterns that develop when persistent problems are confronted. Certain issues that inevitably give rise to an informal organization are lag, the gap between abstract and concrete operations; generality and abstractness of regulations, which in individual cases may be bent, modified, or even suspended; and the impersonality and dehumanization that goes against the social grain. In the film *Fighting Back,* one catches a glimpse of the informal organization. Rocky Blier received special treatment and consideration from Steelers' owner Art Rooney. Had the formal structure been operating impersonally, Blier might never have played professional football.

☐ SPORT AS A SOCIAL INSTITUTION

To explain sport as a **social institution,** we may refer to the two dominant macrosociological theories discussed previously. Here, we will elaborate on the functionalist perspective. Just as human survival depends on the continuous operation of certain vital functions, societies, too, have tasks or activities that must be performed if they are to exist and flourish. This biological metaphor, aptly referred to as the **organic model of society,** pictures society as an organism with certain needs. According to the structural functionalists,[7] society has five needs—called *functional imperatives*—that must be satisfied: (a) *pattern maintenance* refers to the societal need for value socialization by which social patterns are maintained and perpetuated; (b) *tension management* refers to the societal need for regulating tension, conflict, and hostility in a socially acceptable manner and for maintaining social equilibrium; (c) *integration* is the need for societal solidarity, stability, and cohesiveness, (d) *goal attainment* is the means by which societal values are translated into goals to guide day-to-day behavior; and (e) *adaptation* refers to the societal need to adjust to both the social and physical environment. The institutions of society, including sport, help meet and satisfy these societal needs. When individual and societal needs are adequately met, the organism (i.e., society) maintains a state of equilibrium or homeostasis (see the discussion of functionalism in Chapter 1). Conversely, when such needs are not adequately served, disequilibrium results.

 The life-sustaining societal tasks are performed by the *social institutions,*[8] cultural patterns organized around the essential needs of individuals in society (see Table 4.1). The five fundamental social institutions are: (a) economy, (b) marriage and family, (c) education, (d) polity, and (e) religion. Social institutions can be classified in terms of their major functions. The functions of the economy are the production, distri-

TABLE 4.1   The distinguishing characteristics of some major social institutions

	Some Statuses/Roles	Some Value(s) Embodied	Some Societal Needs Met
Family	Mother, father, child, grandparent, aunt, uncle	Fidelity	Socialization, maintenance position placement, legitimation
Economy	Entrepreneur, cashier/ accountant, nurse, teacher, coal miner	Free enterprise	Production, distribution, consumption of goods and services
Polity	President, supreme court justice, senator, mayor, congressperson	Justice	Protection of citizens' inalienable rights
Education	Principal, teacher, custodian, cleric, student	Knowledge	Transmission of cultural heritage to the young
Religion	Pope, bishop, minister, rabbi, Sunday school teacher, parishioner	Belief in a supernatural	Social solidarity via common beliefs and practices
Sport	Coach, trainer, athlete	Competition, character building, health	Recreation, catharsis

bution, and consumption of goods and services. The functions of marriage and family are reproduction, socialization, legitimation, and position maintenance of children. Education is responsible for formally transmitting the cultural heritage. The polity establishes laws and protects the citizenry. Religion is the vehicle through which humans relate to the supernatural.

What are the functions of sport? Like other social institutions, sport does not have a single nor, necessarily, a unique function, and its multiple functions are not independent from other institutions.

Social Functions of Sport

Sport performs numerous eufunctions for spectators, participants, and society.[9] On the surface, sport is a form of recreation and diversion for participants and spectators. It is also a source of physical fitness and stress reduction as well as a means of status display, particularly when considering the cost of fashion clothing for jogging and skiing. Finally, in a capitalistic society oriented toward the profit motive, sport can promote the interests of investors and entrepreneurs. Spectator sports, according to Spinrad,[10] accomplish a variety of functions such as hero lionization, exchanging folklore, and inundation with facts, figures, and statistics. Sport is also a mass spectacle that can provide fantasy and psychic adventure. Acknowledging their global categorizations, Stevenson and Nixon[11] elaborate five social functions of sport: (a) socioemotional, (b) integrative, (c) political, (d) social mobility, and (e) socialization.

The *socioemotional function* refers to sport's effect on the social and psychological states of individuals and has three interrelated dimensions: (a) The cathartic function, rooted in psychoanalytical thought, views sports as a physical form in which frustration, conflict, anxiety, tension, and aggression can be expressed in socially acceptable ways. Spinrad writes: "unlike most popular culture involvements it [sport] is a viable escape, partly because the experiences suggest a caricature of so many unstated features of regular societal processes. The result is a respite, a small-scale catharsis."[12] Later, we will see that the cathartic function of sport is highly dubious in light of scientifically valid studies. (b) In a mobile society like the United States, sport may engender feelings of belonging, an esprit de corps, a sense of camaraderie, and may facilitate social networking. (c) The third division of the socioemotional function of sport is ritualistic. According to Figler, "Sport seasons and the championships that punctuate them flow regularly through our lives."[13]

Perennial events like the Kentucky Derby, the Indianapolis 500, the World Series, and Super Bowl are examples, as was the playing of the entire slate of NFL games on 24 November 1963, John F. Kennedy's national day of mourning. Sporting events continued through many international conflicts including Korea, Vietnam, Grenada, and Panama. During the Persian Gulf War, while some voices were raised against the telecasting of playoff games and even the Super Bowl, there was strong public opinion that the events should proceed for the apparent psychological boost they would provide during the crisis. Other examples include the playing of the NCAA basketball championship when then President Ronald Reagan had survived an assassination attempt. So, too, was the playing of the 1989 Super Bowl while the neighborhoods of Miami were burning following a riot and Super Bowl XXV in Tampa during the potential for terrorist activities during the tensions of the Persian Gulf War. Events such as these can provide psychological anchoring and security in a chaotic and rapidly changing world.

Sport's *integrative function* focuses on the coalescing of isolated individuals into a "cohesive" group with a common perspective. Participants, as well as spectators, may be molded into a common network. Depending on the scope of the competition, participants may be woven into an in-group on the basis of a team, school, city, region, or country. The opponent becomes the out-group, with the consequence that the bonds of belonging and friendship are facilitated among the members of the in-group. Sociologists have documented the in-group cohesion produced by out-group competition. At virtually all levels of sport competition and in all sports, teams (as well as individuals) have archrivals. Such rivalries tend to breed bipartisan sport fans who strongly identify with "their" team. Team "worship" manifests itself in symbolic integration through banners, patches, clothing, blankets, and other facsimiles bearing the name of one's sport devotion.

The *political function* refers to sport's use as a tool to demonstrate power. Despite the belief that sports should be free of politics, ample evidence shows that the two are not independent of each other. One may wonder why nations with little political clout and meager per capita incomes allocate relatively large sums of money to sports. The answer, in part, is that countries perceive the production of superior athletes as indicative of national character and the strength of their political and economic systems. Examples of the infusion of politics into sport is the United States' boycott of the 1980 Moscow Olympics and the U.S.S.R.'s reciprocation at the 1984 Los Angeles Olympics. In 1980, the United States protested the Soviet Union's invasion of Afghanistan by refusing to send its athletes to Russia. While former President Carter's administration was dubious about the withdrawal of Soviet troops, it believed that such a boycott would have detrimental effects on the Soviet economy and undermine the international prestige that would have resulted from the staging of the Olympic Games there.

Sport's *mobility function* centers on sport as a status escalator. Accordingly, sport is seen by some as a pipeline out of the ghetto, barrio, or "wrong side of the tracks" for ethnic minorities. It is not, however, a particularly good mobility channel, because, for example, of the 550,000 young men who played high school basketball in the late 1980s, less than 1% could expect someday to play in the National Basketball Association (NBA).

The *socialization function* refers to the manner in which individuals are conditioned to be socially viable members of society. Stevenson and Nixon note that in Western society "sports . . . are believed to socialize participants towards such desirable social values and personality characteristics as leadership, cooperation, respect for rules, sportsmanship, self-control, achievement drive, a collective orientation, respect for opponents, and a negative attitude toward racism."[14] These self-proclaimed virtues sound auspicious but the problem remains that these goals are frequently not realized. In Chapter 5, we critically address the issue of how well sport seems to achieve this function by examining research relating to sport socialization.

In summary, sport appears to perform at least five social functions (see Vignette 4.3 for a typically nonidentified function of sport). The categories are neither exhaustive nor mutually exclusive. They do, however, provide a tentative conceptual

☐ VIGNETTE 4.3

Creative Symbolic Immortality through Sport

Raymond L. Schmitt in his study of symbolic immortality in ordinary contexts within the American society has pointed out that athletes are able to "leave their marks" through their accomplishments in sports. Symbolic immortality involves an attempt on the part of individuals to be remembered after their deaths. Immortality can be achieved through creative deeds and the institution of sport provides ample opportunity for persons to be recognized and remembered for their successes.

Schmitt provides four excerpts from the mass media to support his contention. The first excerpt involves the golfers, Jack Nicklaus and Tom Watson. The second and third excerpts are unusual in that they refer to animals. These "animals," however, actually become sport participants when they are entered in sport competition. The two excerpts show that Americans even attribute immortality to animals. The final excerpt is an extraordinary example of creative symbolic immortality in the sport world because it illustrates the competitiveness that can occur in this area. Amos Alonzo Stagg's son is concerned about the "memory of his father" and wants Paul "Bear" Bryant to "earn his place in history."

- Jack Nicklaus and Tom Watson: "Somewhere on the granite it says: 'Their name liveth forever more.' Well, if theirs (Jack Nicklaus and Tom Watson) doesn't, there's not a kidney left in a pie in Ayrshire."
- Bruce Hamilton's Champion Frog: "'Last Chance' takes leap into immortality."

- Also Rans in 1978 Kentucky Derby: "Although Affirmed and Alydar are the only real threats to win this race, the rest of the horses will always be remembered for simply being in the Kentucky Derby."
- Amos Alonzo Stagg: "Amos Alonzo Stagg Jr., has petitioned the NCAA to immediately recount the number of career football victories of his father, the legendary coach. If successful, he insists, this would push Alabama's Coach Bear Bryant further back into second place in the all-time standings and 'make him earn his place in history. . . . I (Amos Alonzo Stagg Jr.) expressed my sentiments to the coach (Bear Bryant) . . . explaining my concern for the memory of my father.'"

Schmitt's effort is important for sport sociologists because it directs attention to a previously overlooked *function* of sports. Sport participation is functional for individuals and societies because it helps people to accept their own mortality. On the other hand, the main theme of Schmitt's research is that the modes of symbolic immortality inhibit Americans' realization of the danger of nuclear war. In this respect, sporting and other creative activities are *dysfunctional* for the society because they direct attention away from the possibility of nuclear annihilation.

SOURCE: Raymond L. Schmitt, "Symbolic Immortality in Ordinary Contexts: Impediments to the Nuclear Era," OMEGA 13 (1982–83), pp. 95–116.

☐

map facilitating an understanding of structural functionalism, particularly the ways in which sport provides services (and sometimes disservices) to the individual and society.

Two additional functions of sport other than those just discussed—integrative, political, mobility, and socialization—are (a) a value receptacle and (b) a safety valve. The *value receptacle* function refers to the way in which values are mirrored by a particular institution, in this case, sport. When carefully investigated, sport can be seen to reflect and reinforce the values that society holds important. In this regard, sport is a microcosm of society. Just the same, the relationship between sport and society is not one-way, because within sport, values and norms may be generated and/or negotiated and reverberate back to the larger society. In methodological terms, while society is typically construed as the independent variable in the causal flow, sport may also be viewed as the independent variable.

The *safety valve* function of sport implies that athletics provide an arena in which overt acts of hostility, violence, and aggression are permitted. Sport thus becomes a socially accepted channel for the expression, catharsis, and displacement of pent-up feelings that might otherwise disrupt the dynamic balance of society. In this latter statement, one of the dominant theoretical paradigms in sport sociology is, again, made explicit. As we saw in Chapter 1, functionalism has, historically, been given conceptual priority over conflict theory.

Institutions ordinarily develop in one of two ways. They are either *crescive*, emerging naturally and spontaneously in the routine course of social interaction, or *enacted*, deliberately and concertedly formed. Both of these developmental processes have occurred within the sport institution. The primordial intercollegiate sports had a crescive flavor to them. The fragmented collegiate sports existing between 1850 and 1875 were created by students; college administrators and faculties neither oversaw nor were particularly interested in students' leisure-time activities. Later, when the problematic and/or commercial and prestige-generating potential of sport became more apparent, administrators took specific steps to control intercollegiate athletics. Television has been instrumental in the creation of *trash sports*, with created events such as *Super Sports, Challenge of the Sexes, Battle of the Network Stars, American Gladiators,* and *Super Teams* that fit into this new genre. Other sports that have been deliberately enacted include snowmobiling, superstar competition, roller derby, demolition derby, and box lacrosse. The reason for such enactments often is derived from the anticipated profit-making and/or the promotional potential of the sport.

Institutionalization of Sport

Sport, today, is institutionalized. *Institutionalization,* a social process, refers to procedures becoming organized, systematized, and stabilized. Organization denotes a delineation of positions, roles, and role relationships; *systematization* indicates the specification of tasks and duties to be performed by the role incumbents; and *stabilization* refers to the tendency of the structures and processes to exist beyond the lifetimes of individual participants. Sport as a social institution may be thought of as an intricate system of social relationships or a network of statuses and roles (e.g., athlete, coach, manager, athletic director, cheerleader, and owner) that embody ultimate values people hold in common (the dominant American sport creed) and satisfy certain

TABLE 4.2   A partial list of social positions in the institution of sport

Professional athlete	Cheerleader
Superstar	Band member
Starter	Alumni
Substitute	Owner
Captain	Sport equipment wholesaler
Coach	Sport equipment retailer
Manager	Concessionaire
Physician	Fan
Trainer	Spectator
Athletic director	Timekeeper
Referee	Scorekeeper
Umpire	Statistician
Line judge	Public address announcer
Field judge	Television, press, and radio reporter

societal needs. Table 4.2 presents a partial list of the positions embodied in the institution of sport.

KEY SOCIOLOGICAL CONCEPTS FOR UNDERSTANDING THE SOCIAL ORGANIZATION OF SPORT

Social Structure

Virtually all phenomena have a set of interrelated parts called a "structure." A domed stadium, like other "buildings," possesses a structure—a ceiling, walls, floor, and the like. While all domed stadiums have the same generic parts, they nevertheless may vary in style, contents, and materials used in their construction. Molecules have a structure (consider the differences between water (H_2O) and hydrogen peroxide (H_2O_2); rocks have a structure (e.g., igneous, metamorphic, sedimentary); and social creatures (human as well as infrahuman) have a structure. Two of the most important ingredients of human *social structures* are social statuses (or social positions) and social roles.

Social Position (Social Status) and Social Role

To better understand the individual's place in a social institution, one must appreciate two sociological concepts: (1) **social position (or social status)** and **social role.** A *social position* is the niche one occupies in a group or society. Most often these positions are occupational (e.g., teacher, physician, lawyer, professional athlete) or kinship based (e.g., mother, father, brother, sister, aunt, uncle). A *social role*, on the other hand, is the behavior expected, required, or anticipated from the occupant of a social position. Returning to our baseball analogy, the nine individuals on the team occupy nine different statuses, and each has a somewhat unique role to play. Pitchers have one role, shortstops another, and so on. **Social norms**—the expectations that the larger society or subgroups within a society have for the position-holder's rights and duties—govern social roles. William Shakespeare evoked the concept of role in the following lines of his play *As You Like It:*

> All the world's a stage
> And all the men and women merely players:
> They have their exits and their entrances;
> And one man in his time plays many parts

Sociologists use the term *role* to refer to the behavioral expectations or actual behavior of occupants of social positions. For illustrative purposes, consider the role of the professional athlete. The general public, fans, teammates, and coaches expect (although *demand* might be the more appropriate term in some cases) certain behavior from an individual playing this role. These expectations may include performing at certain competency levels, practicing regularly, dressing and conducting oneself appropriately, and maintaining good mental and physical conditions through exercise and proper nutrition. Additionally, during the course of athletic competition, the athlete will be expected to abide by the rules of the game, display good sportsmanship, play hard, and so forth.

Having considered some of the athletes' duties, let us turn now to their rights. Assuming the athletes meet the obligations, they may be treated as celebrities by media reporters, other sport personnel, and autograph seekers. If athletes are not treated fairly, they may feel slighted and choose to ignore some of their responsibilities. The public's negative reaction to Olympic medalists Tommy Smith and John Carlos at the 1968 Mexico City Olympics stemmed from their willful flaunting of role obligations. The black gloved hands they raised at the winner's podium during the playing of the "Star Spangled Banner" called attention to racial inequality in the United States. Their gestures were unwelcomed and unappreciated by United States Olympic Committee (USOC) personnel and television viewers.

Role Set

The position-role schema implies that roles are reciprocal, complementary, or relational in nature. In other words, the rights and obligations accorded any social position (e.g., father) are always related to other positions (e.g., mother, child, and grandparent). The role of the player, then, is not isolated from the roles of manager, coach, owner, or even fan. Figure 4.3 is a schemata of the partial **role-set** of a college student-athlete. The reciprocal nature of roles testifies to the importance of social relationships in human conduct.

The flow of social interaction does not always proceed smoothly and orderly. Sometimes players refuse to follow the rules. Richie Allen, Thomas Henderson, Joe Namath, Derek Sanderson, Jimmy Connors, Muhammad Ali, and John McEnroe had notorious reputations for deviating from their official duties. Such individuals are referred to as **deviants** (a topic more fully discussed in Chapter 6), which is the generic name given to persons who depart, usually significantly, from social expectations. What happens in such cases?

First, roles are not straitjackets; rather, they define a *range* of acceptable behaviors. Hence, some leeway is permitted. Second, star performers frequently accrue "idiosyncrasy credits."[15] That is, if their performances are superior to the rest, they are allowed

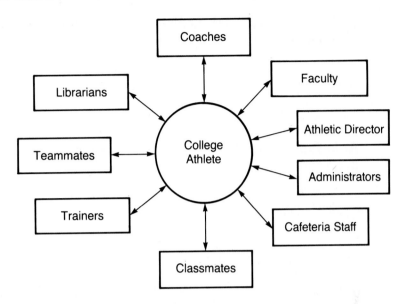

Within the social structure called the "university," the role of "student-athlete" is systemically connected with a cluster of other roles. Note the relational, complementary, or reciprocal nature of roles.

FIGURE 4.3   A schemata of the role-set associated with the college student-athlete

a greater range of departure from the norms. However, the case of Pete Rose is testimony to "idiosyncrasy credits" not always being attached to stellar athletic performers. The all-time hit leader had his reputation severely tarnished by betting on baseball games, income tax evasion, and a lifetime suspension from the game. Baseball's Hall of Fame directors declared that any player ruled permanently ineligible is permanently ineligible for the Hall of Fame. (Fifteen players have been permanently banned in the more than 100 years of baseball.) Too much deviation (e.g., Woody Hayes's slugging a Clemson player during the 1978 Gator Bowl) and by too many individuals (e.g., the "Athletic Revolution" of the late 1960s) threatens the system's stability and existence. In such cases, measures are taken to remove the offending elements (e.g., Hayes's dismissal). However, given the value of winning in American society, the mechanisms of reform and change may be slow to operate. In fact, one coach has been quoted as saying, "They'll fire you for not winning before they'll fire you for cheating." Curry and Jiobu raise the query (apropos Hayes),

> How can a winning coach survive a career filled with so many incidents? The reason is simple: winning is highly prized, and winning coaches are few in number, so the winning coach can do just about whatever he wants. By winning he eliminates the major reason for which he might be fired. And in the course of winning year after year, he accumulates so much charisma, power, adulation, and support that he becomes politically unassailable. Firing a winning coach would cause a communitywide, perhaps even statewide or nationwide, controversy and trauma, a reaction few administrators dare to face.[16]

Third, roles are negotiated. Rarely do two people perform the same role identically. Although the essayist Henry David Thoreau claimed in *Walden* that an individual may walk to the beat of a different drummer, or, in other words, may be somewhat independent of normative social expectations, sociologists are dubious as to the extent and frequency with which this phenomenon can occur without serious repercussions. For society to function in an orderly manner, there must be social consensus; otherwise, "anomie" or normlessness will prevail.

Role Repertoire, Role Conflict, and Role Strain

Each individual in society plays several roles and occupies several positions. The athlete typically holds other positions (e.g., father or mother, husband or wife, son or daughter, uncle or aunt, brother-in-law, or a combination of these). Typically, one of these positions is the most important one, a notion giving rise to the concept of *master status*. The master status refers to the position that is most salient to the individual, and some of its consequences are considered in the following discussion. For each of these positions, there are social norms dictating the nature of the interaction with specific other positions. This multiplicity of positions and roles is called a **role repertoire.** In the course of acting out the various roles we play, we often face an impasse; that is, sometimes the expectations of different roles or even the same role are inconsistent. Sociologists use the concept of **role strain** when incompatible demands stem from a *single* status and the concept of **role conflict** when the incompatible demands stem from *multiple* statuses. Consider the manager's role, for example. Managers are expected to make decisions, cultivate a respect for authority and rules, and discipline their players. They are also expected to be sensitive to the needs and idiosyncrasies of their players. Not infrequently, these two sets of expectations conflict with one another. In the course of role behavior, the coach may be subject to pressures and strains arising out of conflicting expectations from the status of coach, a phenomenon known as *role strain*.

An illustration of *role conflict* is that of the so-called student-athlete. The appellation "student-athlete" directly intimates the two roles that are likely to conflict. The student role includes such behaviors as attending classes, studying for examinations, writing term papers, and the like. The athlete role includes such behaviors as practicing one's sport, attending "chalk talk" sessions, and viewing game films (in certain sports). The problem is that time and energy are finite and often require adaptation and adjustment. Not surprisingly, at major universities, one's athlete role often takes priority over one's student role. Adler and Adler,[17] reporting on their participant observation study of a basketball program at a big-time school write:

> . . . the athletes received greater reinforcement for athletic performance than for academic performance. No one closely monitored their academic behavior, but they were carefully watched at games, practices, booster functions, and on road trips. The celebrity and social status they derived from the media, boosters, and fans brought them immediate gratification, which the academic realm, with its emphasis on future rewards, could not offer. . . . Given the paucity of contact with the faculty, the lack of reinforcement within the academic realm, and the omnipresence of the coaches, media, fans, and boosters, who provided both positive and negative feedback on daily athletic performance, it be-

came easier for athletes to turn away from academics and concentrate their efforts on sport.

Empirical evidence of role conflict and role strain in sport is equivocal. Leonard surveyed basketball players in three different NCAA divisions and reports that the subjective acknowledgement of role conflict among student athletes was not prevalent.[18] Decker reports on a study of role conflict among teachers–coaches at small colleges.[19] After administering a role-conflict scale, she concluded that such individuals typically experience only small amounts of role conflict. Sage studied high school athletic teachers–coaches and discovered a significant amount of role strain—often resulting from too many demands and too little time—among these individuals.[20]

Ascribed and Achieved Positions

Positions in society may be either ascribed or achieved, although positions often reflect a combination. **Ascribed positions** are secured involuntarily and based on attributes over which the individual has little or no control. For example, sex, age, race, and ethnicity are social categories to which all of us belong through no choice of our own. We do not choose to be male, white, age forty-eight, or a WASP. **Achieved positions** are those over which we have some control and are secured voluntarily. We may choose to be a doctor rather than a lawyer, a ditch digger rather than a sociologist. Attaining professional athlete status is generally considered to be an achieved position, although both ascribed and achieved features have facilitating or inhibiting influences. Certain physical, physiological, and genetic factors of an "ascribed" nature are extremely important in achieving certain positions. For example, short and stout individuals are unlikely to appear on professional basketball rosters and, similarly, weak and frail individuals are unlikely to do well in football, hockey, or boxing.

Of the several social positions listed in Table 4.2, we isolate one—that of the professional athlete—for further discussion of the sociological concepts introduced in this chapter. The aim is to demonstrate how sociological conceptualizations facilitate understanding the social world of sport.

THE PROFESSIONAL ATHLETE

According to the *Random House College Dictionary* (1973), an athlete is a person trained to compete in contests involving physical agility, stamina, or strength. Of course, athletes do not form a homogeneous group. There are many different "types" of athletes: male–female; white–nonwhite; and grade school–high school–collegiate–professional. These latter considerations are significant when discussing the athlete's role, because athletes are differentially affected by the level at which they perform. For instance, sandlot players have skills, expectations, and motivations for playing that differ from those of professional athletes (see the discussion of the distinguishing characteristics of sport, game, and play in Chapter 1).

Today's professional athlete is a cherished idol, subject to adulation but often not well understood. Take a moment and mentally note the characteristics and traits you attribute to athletes. Does a certain stereotyped image emerge?

Literary Depictions of the Athlete

According to Umphlett, American fiction conveys a three-sided image of the male athlete.[21] First, the fictional stereotype suggests that the athlete is antiurban and striving for a life closer to nature. Former professional basketball player Bill Walton epitomizes this image. Second, the stereotype portrays the athlete as sexist and incapable of maintaining meaningful intimate relationships—Johnny Bench, formerly of the Cincinnati Reds, as described in the following news brief, seems to conform to this characterization:[22]

> On his wedding night, Johnny Bench played ping-pong with his best man. . . . Vicki Chesser [Bench's wife at the time] said when she received an offer to pose in the nude for *Hustler* Magazine for $25,000 Bench told her, "Why not, it's good money."
> She said the incident proved to her that Bench wanted a "whore in the bedroom," not a wife, and that he had "no respect for any woman and probably for any man."

Finally, this stereotype depicts the athlete as a victim of prolonged adolescence, clinging to poignant memories of bygone days of glory and unable to grapple with adult problems, issues, responsibilities, and concerns. Some former players have experienced emotional, social, and/or economic crises after their disengagement from active sport participation. Several excerpts from literary works capture this facet. Michener, for example, wrote:

> The fact that success in athletics does not always mean success in business or life provides Philip Roth in *Goodbye, Columbus* and Irwin Shaw in "The Eighty-Yard Run" with a convenient means for satirical expression. We discover that Roth's Ron Patimkin and Shaw's Christian Darling as ex-college athletes are unable to involve themselves with the realities of life. Instead, they continue to live in the idealized world of "the game"; consequently their lives exemplify still another theme in modern literature—the search for maturity.
> Like a child, he cannot see himself in relationship to his environment, and in this socalled innocent state is compelled to relate everything to his own egocentered world. The result is lack of self-awareness and a failure in communication, not only in marriage but in social dealings as well. The only real world for him is, and always will be, we recognize, the world of the game.[23]

The thesis advanced by the stereotypic vision of the athlete is that sports provide a vehicle for ascending to greatness, which is then followed by a precipitous descent into social, economic, and psychological oblivion. Here are two vivid accounts of this process from real life:

- Former San Diego second baseman Alan Wiggins was forced out of baseball in 1987 because of drug problems and died in January 1991 at the age of 32. He had deserted his wife and three children. Pneumonia, tuberculosis and other medical complications were listed as the causes of death.
- Bill Madlock, winner of four batting titles, charged that his agent Steve Greenberg had defrauded him by investing money in speculative deals. Not only did Madlock find that he was broke, but the IRS claimed he owed $700,000 in back taxes. Madlock sold his home, many of his possessions, and was jobless in February 1991.

(Greenberg had gone from agent to No. 2 man in baseball by serving as Fay Vincent's deputy assistant.)

In short, the social, psychological, and economic gains achieved through sport are often quickly wiped out when (generally) short careers terminate. The public's attention is usually riveted on those athletes who stand out: football players Jimmy Brown, Roger Staubach, and Joe Namath; baseball players Willie Mays, Pete Rose, Reggie Jackson, Jim Palmer, and Mickey Mantle; golfers Jack Nicklaus and Arnold Palmer; hockey player Bobby Orr and Bobby Hull; boxers Joe Louis, Sugar Ray Leonard, and Muhammad Ali; and tennis players Jimmy Connors, Chris Evert Lloyd, and Billie Jean King. Only when the *career patterns* of typical participants within a sport are carefully examined is the full truth disclosed. Let us proceed with a *scientific* rather than fictional account of select professional sports and athletes.

Scientific Depictions of the Athlete: Individual Sports

Participants in individual sports—boxing, horse racing, wrestling, auto racing, bowling, golf, tennis—typically confront a distinct set of considerations when transiting to the professionals. In individual sports, participants must secure their own financial backing, and concerns transcend the paying of expenses because they must have access to the field of competition, whether it consists of matches, contests, events, tournaments, or meets. For example, boxers and wrestlers need sponsors and agents; sports car racers need to be recognized by other participants; and bowlers, golfers, and tennis players must maintain their memberships in professional organizations and/or sometimes await special invitations.

Boxing.   The classic example of problems and exploitation faced by individual athletes is boxing. Boxers, who typically come from lower socioeconomic backgrounds (as do soccer players in South America),[24] inevitably require a sponsor, in addition to a trainer and manager, to meet the financial costs of their training and travel. Such external financial support has greatly reduced the prize monies received by even recognized champions and contenders. Boxers have negotiated contracts that give the bulk of their purse money to their sponsors. Studies of boxers have shown that relatively few have maintained a professional career or save money, and many have been exploited. Investigations of boxers, originally called pugilists, consistently show that boxers emerge from the lower social classes. Weinberg and Arond's research documents this.[25] In both 1909 and 1916, Irish and German surnames (Table 4.3) were most prominent in the boxing world. In 1928, these two ethnic groups were supplanted by boxers of Jewish and Italian descent. From 1948 to the present, blacks and Latinos have dominated the ring. Although the data indicate that boxing has appealed to ethnic minorities occupying lower rungs of the social stratification ladder (see Chapter 7 for a definition and discussion), boxing has been a major avenue of social mobility for a relatively small number of minority group members. Weinberg and Arond offer convincing evidence that vertical mobility, or movement up the social-class ladder (socially and economically) via boxing is more apparent than real. After analyzing the careers of 90 former boxing champions who earned more than $100,000 when that sum was substantial and taxes modest, they found that virtually

TABLE 4.3 Prominence of race in ethnic boxers for select years

Year	Rank Order of Importance		
	1	2	3
1909	Irish	German	English
1916	Irish	German	Italian
1928	Jewish	Italian	Irish
1936	Italian	Irish	Jewish
1948	Black	Italian	Mexican
1970	Black	Mexican	
1985	Black	Latino	

SOURCE: Adapted from S. Kirson Weinberg and Henry Arond, "The Occupational Culture of the Boxer," *American Journal of Sociology,* 58 (March 1952), pp. 460–469.

none of the former champions had substantial jobs—they were working in bars and taverns or as unskilled laborers (e.g., movie house ticket takers, bookies, janitors, gas station attendants, and the like). Furthermore, regardless of period (1938 or 1950) the majority of fighters (more than 90%) were restricted to local and preliminary bouts, which are generally poor paying and less socially significant, and only a small minority (less than 10%) received recognition as national contenders (Table 4.4).

Consider the fate of several heavyweight boxing champions.[26] Four recent ex-champs are dead. Rocky Marciano was killed in a plane crash in 1969, Sonny Liston died of a drug overdose in 1970, and Ezzard Charles succumbed to "Lou Gehrig's disease." Consider also the biography of Joe Louis, who captured the heavyweight crown from James J. Braddock in 1937 and successfully defended his title twenty-five times and scored twenty-one knockouts. Although he earned $5 million during his reign, ill-advised business ventures, a costly divorce, and a tendency to live lavishly left him in debt. By 1956, he owed $1.25 million in taxes. In 1970, his family committed him to a psychiatric hospital, and he had to learn to walk again after suffering a stroke that followed a heart attack. The memorable "Brown Bomber" finally died of cardiac arrest in the spring of 1981.

Jersey Joe Walcott beat Ezzard Charles for the title in 1951. Fourteen months later, after being knocked out by Marciano, he retired. Today he lives in New Jersey and has gained acclaim as a community organizer for handicapped and retarded children.

TABLE 4.4 Career patterns of boxers, 1938 and 1950

Year	National Recognition	Local and Preliminary Fighters	Number Studied
1950	7%	93%	1,831
1938	9%	91%	107

SOURCE: Adapted from S. Kirson Weinberg and Henry Arond, "The Occupational Culture of the Boxer," *American Journal of Sociology,* 58 (March 1952), p. 465.

Walcott, who proclaimed he never earned a purse larger than $300 during his first fifteen years of boxing, concedes that some of his later winnings "could have been better invested."

Ingemar Johansson was driven out of Sweden by high taxes after his fight with Floyd Patterson. After retiring in 1963, he dabbled in real estate and the restaurant business before moving to Florida. Since retiring he says: "I haven't done anything, really. I am like a used-car dealer; I stick my nose in everything I can make a profit on."

Other surviving champions like Floyd Patterson, Joe Frazier, George Foreman, Muhammad Ali, and Larry Holmes appear to have fared reasonably well. Patterson claims he has achieved what he's always been searching for—"peace of mind." Frazier invested his money wisely and suffers no financial problems. George Foreman, after losing to Jimmy Young, became a religious convert and prepared himself for spiritual work and waged a comeback at 40–plus. Muhammad Ali, after several unsuccessful bids to deny "father time," continues to be economically comfortable (although he suffers from tremors associated with being hit in the head), as is Larry Holmes (see Vignette 7.2).

Golf.   When golf buffs think of professional golf personalities, Arnold Palmer, Jack Nicklaus, Tom Watson, Nancy Lopez, and Kathy Whitworth come to mind. During their prime, these athletes have won lucrative prize money, but what many golf fans fail to realize is that many others—the "rabbits," or those who haven't made it—live from hand to mouth in a relentless struggle for a chance at the big time. Let's briefly consider these less glamorous players and their lives.[27]

About 420 golfers are on the Professional Golf Association (PGA) tour. In 1990, the leading male and female money winners, Jose Maria Olazabal and Beth Daniel, made $1,633,640 and $863,578, respectively. But, for the male players, 190 players (or 45%) earned nothing, and about the same percentage did not earn enough money to even cover their expenses. Gaining a slot on the tour is not easy. Most players gain admittance through the Tour Qualifying School in Pinehurst, North Carolina. Although there are lectures on finance, tournament etiquette, and rules, the school is not a school in the traditional sense of books, classroom lectures, and written exams. Instead, the school provides on-the-job training: PGA official Jack Stirling describes the process by which golfers reach the qualifying school: "Most players . . . learn the game as preteens, play all through high school and college, then practice in earnest. The ideal training process means hitting about 600 balls a day. That means . . . swinging a club every 45 to 60 seconds and doing it for four hours in the morning, breaking for lunch, then another four hours in the afternoon—day after day. All the while . . . analyzing . . . grip, . . . swing, . . . stance." Of the golfers who gain a slot on the tour, most have to qualify for each tournament. The number of golfers competing in weekly tournaments varies according to the number of daylight hours. During daylight savings time, about 156 compete, during standard time about 144. The deck is stacked against the substar players, because it is customary for the top players to have the first opportunity to secure these spots, and sometimes as few as five spots are available for qualifiers. It is the "rabbits"—the journeymen players—who are most prone to travel each week from one tournament to another around the country. Stirling says, "It is a demanding life . . . Monday is for qualifying, Tuesday is the practice round, Wednesday is the pro-am, Thursday through Sunday, the tournament—that is, if he [sic] makes it."[28]

Golf, like other sports, presents a constant challenge. Since the big winners are the ones most clearly remembered, it is necessary to debunk the myths of glamour and money to catch a glimpse of what truly typifies the sport.

Scientific Depictions of the Athlete: Team Sports

The idolization of professional athletes frequently culminates with baseball, basketball, and football players. Empirical data reveal a relatively short professional career for most. Statistics show that the average playing career in major league baseball and football is about five years.[29] This means that most players: (1) retire before age 30 and (2) often do not play long enough to qualify for a pension. The evidence apropos whether the athlete will be economically, if not psychologically and socially, downwardly mobile (Vignette 4.4 reports on some of the adjustment issues following "retirement" from professional football) is equivocal.

The short duration of most careers in baseball, basketball, and football is often only vaguely acknowledged by the public, because it is the players who play for a decade or two who are locked in the public's mind. Similarly, it is the highly paid and widely publicized athletes who remind us of the bountiful rewards associated with professional sport. Money is not all since psychological and social status factors also play significant roles in a player's decision to go or remain professional. Jerry Kramer, the ex-all-pro offensive lineman of the Green Bay Packers, described his feelings about this social loss:

> Giving up football is giving up . . . the hero's role. I worry about that, I wonder how much I'll miss being recognized, being congratulated, being idolized. For years, as an offensive lineman, I worked in relative obscurity, but with the block against Jethro Pugh and with the success of *Instant Replay,* I became as well known as a running back. I was recognized in restaurants, on the golf course, in the streets, and I loved the strange taste of recognition.
>
> I know that the fan's memory is not long, that my name will fade quickly, that in a few years I'll sink back into anonymity. I have to wonder how I'll react to that. . . . You get spoiled being a celebrity. . . . I was pursued just enough to keep my ego well fed. I hope I don't need that ego gratification to survive, but I just don't know. I won't know for a few years.[30]

Talamini's investigation of the retirement patterns of major league baseball players paints a more auspicious picture.[31] Focusing on the occupational prestige of the jobs filled by ex-baseball players, he discovered that nearly three fourths of them were working in high-prestige occupations. Only 42% of the ex-players were in positions completely separated from the sports world; nearly 60% were within the social world of sport (e.g., within baseball itself, teacher–coach, athletic director, recreational director, sports information director, etc.). He reports that "contrary to the tragic theme in drama and literature, most ex-ballplayers were working in comfortable occupations with a middle class lifestyle."

Disengagement from Sport

Sportswriter Myslenski describes professional athletes as "rookies at reality" and professional sports as an adult Disneyland where needs, whims, fancies, and idiosyncrasies are taken care of, if not catered to.[32] But the fairyland eventually ends and the harsh realities begin. Some athletes found the transition from professional sports to the "real" world too difficult.

- There was the story of former Kansas City All Pro Jim Tyrer, who was a leader and pillar of strength when he starred for the great Chief teams in the late '60s and early '70s; in September 1980, five years after his retirement, he took a .38-caliber pistol, killed his wife and himself, and left four children as orphans.
- There was former DePaul star Bill Robinzine, who went on to a seven-year career in the NBA; in September, 1982, shortly after realizing that his career was over, he drove his car into a garage, shut the door and—his engine idling—fell into a sleep from which he never awoke.
- There was former Southern Cal All-American pitcher Bruce Gardner, who later failed in his attempt to make the Los Angeles Dodgers; he went home, collected all the awards he had won, rode to Southern Cal's field, ritualistically arranged his awards around the pitcher's mound, then stood in the middle of them and blew his brains out.
- There were the well-documented stories of former Super Bowl stars Bob Hayes and Mercury Morris, who ended up in jail on drug-related charges, and the less publicized story of former Packer great Lionel Aldridge, who went from being a star for Vince Lombardi to a life of living in street missions.[33]

Consequences of Sport Disengagement: Some Empirical Studies

Andreano hypothesized that athletes feel "a direct and psychic association with the legendary players of the past; they are part of American history and therefore above the din of the average person who works for a weekly or hourly wage."[34] This proposition, however, did not meet with scientific support. Charnofsky tested these hypotheses by asking major-league baseball players how they viewed their role.[35] Contrary to Andreano's thesis, they did not see themselves distinct from the average worker and did not identify with the bucolic tradition of the greats of yesteryear. In fact, while still acknowledging their extraordinary physical skills and celebrity status, they saw themselves as similar to the average worker in values, intelligence, and personality. Moreover, money ranked considerably above the fun, challenge, prestige, and love of the game. Players perceived their jobs as exciting yet marred by undesirable job-related characteristics such as traveling, separation from families, and job insecurity.

Kiersh[36] interviewed fifty-five ex-baseball players and provided a picture of both positive and negative aspects of their retirement from the sport role. Among the positive aspects of having a baseball career were the following:

1. Travel
2. Upward mobility (apparently, economic and social)

☐ VIGNETTE 4.4

Life after Football
Pro Players Learn too Late the Value
of a College Degree

In the silent stadium, brooms push aside the litter left by this season's reverent football fans—the empty cups, ragged pompoms, and crumpled programs.

The fans will be back next autumn. They'll cheer passes caught and goalline stands and talk of the rookies who promise to make the team better than ever.

Except for the stat books and trivia quizzes, the fans have forgotten yesterday's heroes.

William E. Lide doesn't forget. As a fan and former professional football player, he's seen too many lifelong dreams fumbled away after only a year or two in the pros.

It's broken some players, the glory days replaced by alcohol, drugs, or a life of unfulfilled promise.

But there are survivors, too.

A Pleasant Dream Turns Bitter

As an Ohio State doctoral student in physical education, Lide interviewed 28 athletes who spent one to four years in professional football. He wanted to find out just what it means to be told you're not good enough to make the squad again. After almost 20 years of training, 20 years of being a hero, the game's finally over for good.

Most were bitter when they learned they'd been cut. Some still are.

But their bitterness is that of the man wakened from a pleasant dream. Why can't the dream last a bit longer? Why won't it return?

Some take longer than others to wake up.

John (a pseudonym) is now 34, married, a vice principal with an advanced degree, and a salary in excess of $25,000 a year. He's adjusted, but he

recalled the bitterness he felt when he got his walking papers after three years as a lineman.

Coming Back from the End of the World

"I felt like it was the end of the world. I had no degree. I'd made no other preparations. I looked at football as being an end in itself," he said.

John made the transition. Others weren't so lucky. They didn't recover so quickly from forced retirement.

"It was a 'hellacious' feeling. I wasn't ready. I was unprepared, concerned about my financial state. They cut me during mid-season, and I was injured when they did it," said Ron (a pseudonym). "I changed after being cut. My head wasn't on straight."

After four years as a professional running back, Ron's now serving a prison term for robbery.

The dream had already soured for some by the time they were injured or cut from the team.

A 24-year-old financial planner who spent about 15 years training for a career as a professional running back was injured and cut after his first season. He recalled his relief at being out of professional athletics.

"I had enough of pro sports. I was so very happy when it was all over. I enjoyed it, but I made almost an immediate transition because I knew what the game was all about. I didn't place all my faith in it," he said.

Some former Ohio State football players who had longer than average careers in pro ball support Lide's findings.

Doug Van Horn, a former Ohio State lineman who spent 14 years as a pro, said he, too, "missed it terribly" after deciding for himself that the 1979 season would be his last.

"There are other things in life. You can't play that game forever," Van Horn said.

The transition from professional ranks to civilian takes preparation, Nick Roman said. Roman, who graduated from Ohio State in 1980, spent six years with the Cincinnati Bengals and the Cleveland Browns.

A Business— Not Personal—Decision

"If you don't prepare yourself, it is a hell of a separation. A lot depends on if you have family to help you," the former defensive end said.

Many players feel hurt or bitter, Roman said, because they consider being cut a personal attack.

"It's just a business decision. It's nothing personal," said Roman, who also made his own decision to leave the game.

Many of Ohio State's players have been fortunate that ability and good health kept them in the game longer than the average career. Some say extra time gave them a chance to mature, get a clearer picture of what professional football meant to them.

However, researcher Lide found that athletes who had played three to four years were more bitter than those who had played only one or two years. Perhaps this is because the three-to-four-year veteran felt he had invested more of himself, trusted more, without an adequate return, Lide said.

A Big Ego Trip

"Those who expressed bitterness and disappointment seemed to feel cheated because of the dedication and love for the game they had identified with for a long time," Lide said.

Professional football was the glorious life they had been promised by parents, friends, coaches, and television commercials.

"We have idolized them, praised them, and congratulated them," the researcher said. "The athletic career gives the athletes new status in society. The lifestyle is unique—unusual working hours, travel, and a public image unlike the ordinary individual."

"Rookies come into professional football, and it's a big ego trip," Van Horn said. "They're put on a pedestal, and everybody does cater to them."

The situation was quite different for William Willis, a 1944 Ohio State All-American. Joining the Cleveland Browns in 1946, Willis became one of the first black players in modern football.

When the Roar of the Crowd Stops

Today's players should learn to disregard much of what is said about them, said Willis, now director of the Ohio Youth Commission.

Fan worship is "unfair only if the athlete makes it unfair, only if the athlete believes everything said about him, and becomes dependent on the 'roar of the crowd,' so to speak," Willis said.

The roar quiets and the pedestal crumbles quickly when the athlete is let go.

Friends who came easy for the professional athlete are gone. "People surround themselves with athletes because of the success factor of the individual," one former player said. "But most of my real friends were not and are not in athletics."

While most of the athletes said they had enjoyed the praise and recognition from family and friends during their school days, they said they "cared very little or not at all as to how others perceived them when they were forced to retire," Lide said.

Most didn't want to discuss their pro careers with others outside of sports because "it wasn't important anymore." Outsiders just couldn't understand.

Did the Marriages Die with the Glory?

Surprisingly, Lide found that four of five marriages remained stable after some period of adjustment.

"Playing professional football made our marriage stronger," said Phil (a pseudonym). "It gave us a better life—the opportunity to travel."

"However, it did make us realize, when I was cut, what a fantasy world we were living in," said the 32-year-old recreation specialist who spent four years as a receiver. "Pressure was placed on the marriage. We're just now really feeling married again."

But some wives didn't like the transition their husbands made from professional athlete to civilian. "I was caught by a 'glory girl' from a different background. When the glory died, so did the marriage," a former receiver said.

The social adjustment many former pro football players make is often aggravated by financial problems.

Easy Come, Easy Go?

"A lot of players are foolish with their money in the beginning, because they think it's going to be there all the time," Roman said.

Football players just don't make as much during the first few years as fans think they do, Lide said. Few of the 320 rookies who get a shot at the pros each year earn big bonuses. Fewer will play long enough to be eligible for pension plans.

More than half the athletes Lide talked with said they barely made enough during their short careers to live for six months to a year.

One athlete admitted, "I had only my house to show for my money. I thought I would play for years."

Few professional athletes plan for the days when the football is set aside, Lide said. One survey of NFL athletes states that only 40% make plans for a second career, and not all of these act on their plans while playing.

'Look Past Today'

"Football's a great life while it lasts, but you have to prepare," Van Horn said. "It's tough to tell these guys, 'Hey, look past today.'"

As one former pro said while examining his career options, "Everything I have always done has been with a ball."

It's hard for players to take an honest view of their finances and emotions when they've finally made it to the pro ranks, an opportunity that most have dreamed of since their days at the neighborhood playground.

"Rookies come in and it seems like a lot of money is being spent unnecessarily," Archie Griffin said. "But this is what they've always dreamed of, and they want to live that dream. They'll settle down in a year or two if they get the chance."

Griffin, who managed to earn a bachelor's degree in business a quarter early, along with his two Heisman trophies, said a college degree was his first goal at Ohio State.

"Professional football was something I thought was a bonus. I was looking at football as a means of getting a college education," Griffin said.

His elder brothers and parents, among others, stressed the importance of the degree, Griffin said. "Coach (Woody) Hayes always said that if you didn't get a degree you were cheating yourself."

But many players also understand that a college diploma is no assurance of a job or decent salary. More blacks than whites in Lide's survey earned bachelor's degrees, but athletes who are white averaged $27,818, while blacks made about $10,000 less.

Working at a second career while playing professional sports can be difficult, Lide said. Summer work is possible, but even then, time restrictions and team commitments can hinder dual careers.

Planning for Life After Football

Griffin said he still has plans of attending law school, but his pro football career leaves little time for that. Roman worked summers to build his brokerage business, and Van Horn opened a New York area restaurant toward the end of his football career.

Van Horn urges players to work as much as possible between seasons so they have work experience when their playing days are over.

"These guys will go into an employer one day and tell him they ran the ball 500 times and gained

5,000 yards, and the employer will say, "So what,'" the ex-lineman said.

Both the NFL and the Players Association have recognized the need to help players. Workshops are now conducted on planning for life after football. But Lide said these are typically aimed at the player who makes it through more than four years, enough playing time to become part of the pension system.

Although two thirds of those Lide talked with had completed their college degrees, it's estimated that only one in three professional football players earned a diploma.

Most of the players considered college a stepping stone to the pros and didn't want to take any chances.

"I went to college to play ball, not to get an education," said one former player. "I adjusted my schedule around football, hoping to get a shot at pro ball. I didn't want anything to get in the way."

Get a Degree, Pros Advise

More than half of those Lide interviewed said they didn't consider a degree important while they were in school. But nearly all said they would recommend that today's athletes complete work for a diploma.

"Those who succeed at a second career are usually those who have learned to be good at something other than football," Lide said.

"Coaches need 'to pound into the athletes' that football is only one part of life," he said. "The public shouldn't be afraid to take a closer, more honest look at sports," Lide added.

"We have a love affair with sports. It's like a beautiful woman. No one wants to acknowledge the wrong side or ills of sports," Lide said.

In his own case, Lide was prepared when an injury cut short his football days. "I had alternatives. I came out of college with the degree that I'm using now. I used football to enhance my career rather than detract from it," said Lide.

SOURCE: Ginny Halloran, *OSU QUEST* [Columbus, OH] 3, no. 5 (1981), pp. 6–7.

3. Mental improvement
4. Fame
5. Fan adulation
6. Esprit-de-corps and camaraderie with teammates
7. Excitement
8. Fun
9. Being on a winning team
10. Comfortable standard of living
11. Pension (e.g., after five years in the major leagues, a player can collect $12,360, $17,364, and $45,000 at age 45, 50, and 62, respectively, and a ten-year veteran can collect $24,708, $34,728, and $90,000, respectively, at these same age junctures)
12. Playing with star players
13. Learning valuable lessons about life that can be adapted to nonsport contexts

Among the negative features were

1. Clubhouse rivalries and jealousies
2. Politics
3. Too much travel away from family

4. Fan abuse

5. Too conservative

6. Being traded or treated like chattel

Finally, when the fifty-five ex-players were asked why they retired, most indicated (62%) that they were beyond their prime, and 15% and 11% mentioned sport injuries and strained relations with front office and/or coaching staff, respectively. Less than 10% (in each of the categories) responded that retirement decisions stemmed from family reasons, being forced out, and substance abuse problems.

Curtis and Ennis's study of the consequences of former elite hockey players' exodus from the game failed to support the thesis that disengagement from sport leads to "stress-induced negative consequences."[37] Life satisfaction, employment, and marital status were not negatively affected by the players' departures from the game. In short, the select scientific evidence reported herein suggests that the evidence regarding disengagement from sports is neither uniform nor clear-cut. It does suggest that one cannot make blanket statements such as sport retirement leads to social, psychological, and economic oblivion.

When discussing the social organization of professional athletics, one becomes aware of the importance of the level of performance under consideration. A limitation in the present discussion is that minorities, women, youth, high school, and collegiate athletes have not been systematically accounted for. These "types" are examined in Chapter 8 (minorities), Chapter 9 (women), Chapter 5 (youth), and Chapter 10 (high school and college).

❑ SUMMARY

Social organization is the way in which human conduct is patterned, regulated, and organized as a result of social conditions. Two key sociological concepts that help us understand the individual's place in the social organization are *social position* (the niche one occupies in the larger society) and *social role* (the expected, required, and/or anticipated behavior associated with a social position). Positions in society are either obtained voluntarily (*achieved*) or "thrust" on the individual (*ascribed*). Individuals often occupy more than a single position and play more than a single role; hence, the concepts of *role repertoire* and *role set* are used to explain the multiplicity of positions and roles. Finally, when individuals experience different and contradictory behavioral expectations, they may experience *role strain* (within a single role) and *role conflict* (between different roles). The various levels of social organization—interpersonal, group, and societal—were defined and discussed within a sport context. Sport organizations are essentially *associations* or special purpose groups deliberately constructed to seek specific objectives, goals, and values. Sport constitutes a *social institution*, a system of social relationships or a network of positions and roles (e.g., athlete, coach, manager, athletic director, and cheerleader) that embodies the ultimate values (i.e., the dominant American sport creed) people hold in common. Value receptacle and safety valve are two key functions characteristic of the institution of sport along with the socioemotional, integrative, political, social mobility, and socialization functions. Finally, we selectively examined one of the social positions that exist in sport—that of the professional athlete.

☐ KEY CONCEPTS

Social Organization	Social Position (Social Status)
Levels of Social Organization	Social Role
Interpersonal	Social Norms
Group	Role Set
Societal	Deviants
Association	Role Repertoire
Formal Structure	Role Strain
Informal Structure	Role Conflict
Social Institution	Ascribed Position
Organic Model of Society	Achieved Position

☐ ENDNOTES

1. MELVIN L. DEFLEUR, WILLIAM V. D'ANTONIO, & LOIS B. DEFLEUR, *Sociology: Human Society* (Glenview, IL: Scott, Foresman, 1981), pp. 56–58.
   REECE MCGEE et al., *Sociology* (Hinsdale, IL: Dryden, 1977), p. 133.
2. *Ibid.*
3. LEONARD BROOM & PHILIP SELZNICK, *Sociology* (New York: Harper & Row, 1968), pp. 15–16.
4. JOHN W. LOY, "The Nature of Sport: A Definitional Effort," *Sport, Culture, and Society*, ed. John W. Loy & Gerald S. Kenyon (New York: Macmillan, 1968), pp. 56–71.
5. PAUL HOCH, *Rip Off: The Big Game* (Garden City, NY: Anchor Books, 1972).
6. *Encyclopedia of Sociology* (Guilford, CT: Dushkin, 1974), p. 30.
7. JAY J. COAKLEY, *Sport in Society* (St. Louis: C.V. Mosby, 1990), pp. 22–26.
8. MAVIS H. BIESANZ & JOHN BIESANZ, *Introduction to Sociology* (Englewood Cliffs, NJ: Prentice-Hall, 1973).
9. C.L. STEVENSON & J.E. NIXON, "A Conceptual Scheme of the Social Functions of Sport," *Sportwissenschaft* 2 (1972), pp. 119–132.
10. WILLIAM SPINRAD, "The Functions of Spectator Sports," in G. Luschen & G. Sage, *Handbook of Social Science of Sport* (Champaign, IL: Stipes, 1981).
11. *Op. cit.*[9]
12. *Op. cit.,*[10] p. 363.
13. STEVEN K. FIGLER, *Sport and Play in American Life* (Philadelphia: W.B. Saunders, 1981), p. 20.
14. *Op. cit.,*[9]
15. EDWIN P. HOLLANDER, "Conformity, Status, and Idiosyncrasy Credit," *Psychological Review* 65 (1968), pp. 117–127.
16. TIMOTHY CURRY & ROBERT JIOBU, *Sports* (Englewood Cliffs, NJ: Prentice-Hall, 1985), p. 123.
17. PETER ADLER & PATRICIA ADLER, "From Idealism to Pragmatic Detachment," *Sociology of Education* 58 (1985), pp. 241–250.
18. WILBERT M. LEONARD, II, "Exploitation in Collegiate Sport: The Views of Basketball Players in NCAA Divisions I, II, and III," *Journal of Sport Behavior*, 9, no. 1 (1986), pp. 11–30.
19. JUNE I. DECKER, "Role Conflict of Teachers/Coaches in Small Colleges," *Sociology of Sport Journal* 3, no. 4 (1986), pp. 356–365.
20. GEORGE H. SAGE, "The Social World of High School Athletic Coaches: Multiple Role Demands and Their Consequences," *Sociology of Sport Journal* 4, no. 3 (1987), pp. 213–228.
21. WILEY LEE UMPHLETT, *The Sporting Myth and the American Experience: Studies in Contemporary Fiction* (Lewisburg, PA: Bucknell University Press, 1975), p. 225.
22. *Daily Vidette* (3 March 1977), p. 8.
23. JAMES A. MICHENER, *Sports in America* (New York: Random House, 1976), pp. 225–226. Reprinted with permission.
24. JANET LEVER, "Soccer as a Brazilian Way of Life," *Games, Sport, and Power,* ed. Gregory P. Stone (New Brunswick, NJ: Transaction, 1972),

pp. 36–43. Lever's study of professional Brazilian soccer players also revealed that the social and economic gains wrought by sport were short-lived.

25. D. KIRSON WEINBERG & HENRY AROND, "The Occupational Culture of the Boxer," *American Journal of Sociology* 57 (1952), pp. 460–469. ORR, *The Black Athlete: His Story in American History* (New York: Lion Press, 1969).

26. "Where Are the Ex-Champs Now?" *Time* 27 (February 1978), p. 79.

27. ARLENE GARBETT, "Pro Golf's Rabbits: The Guys Who Haven't Made It," *Family Weekly* 19 (February 1978), p. 19.

28. *Ibid.*

29. WILBERT M. LEONARD, II, "Mortality Ratios of Professional Baseball Players and Managers (1876–1973): "An Investigation in the Sociology of Sport," *Journal of Sport Behavior* 6 (1983), pp. 117–129.

30. JERRY KRAMER, *Farewell to Football* (New York: Thomas T. Crowell, 1969), pp. 9–10.

31. JOHN T. TALAMINI, "After the Cheering Stopped: Retirement Patterns of Major League Baseball Players," *Free Inquiry in Creative Sociology*, 17, no. 2. (1989), pp. 175–178.

32. SKIP MYSLENSKI, "Rookies at Reality," *The Chicago Tribune Magazine* (19 January 1986), pp. 8–11, 19–22.

33. *Ibid.*

34. RALPH ANDREANO, *No Joy in Mudville* (Cambridge, MA: Schnekman, 1965), p. 144.

35. HAROLD CHARNOFSKY, "The Major League Professional Baseball Player: Self-Conceptions versus the Popular Image," *International Review of Sport Sociology* 3 (1968), pp. 39–53.

36. E. KIERSH, *Where Have You Gone, Vince Dimaggio?* (New York: Bantam), 1983.

37. JAMES CURTIS & RICHARD ENNIS, "Negative Consequences of Leaving Competitive Sport: Comparative Findings for Former Elite-Level Hockey Players," *Sociology of Sport Journal* 5, no. 2 (1988), pp. 87–106.

5

Sport and Socialization

Sports do not build character, they reveal it.   HEYWOOD BROUN

The path to the boardroom leads through the locker room.   DAVID RIESMAN

Americans of every walk of life increasingly recognize the potential values of sports as a promoter of the democratic spirit. . . . Fair play demands that all who partici-pate in the context must abide by the rules, and in sports the competitor is most sharply confronted with this necessity.   JOHN BETTS

Socialization is the general process through which humans learn their culture and become participating members of society. Various socializing agents and social processes fashion the immature biological being (i.e., "naked ape") into a "mature" social being. The process is a kind of social metamorphosis, from which we infer that what is human is due to the acquisitions persons make as a consequence of their interactions with significant others in their social environment. Socialization can be viewed from two different perspectives: (a) the transmission of nonmaterial or ideational culture (values, beliefs, attitudes, and norms) and (b) the development of self.[1] Although much of the literature focuses on socialization during the formative years, it is an experience that endures a lifetime and entails the interplay of biological, psychological, and social forces.

It is not uncommon for someone to be called a "natural athlete." Malamud aptly describes the prowess of the "born" baseball player in this passage from his novel *The Natural:*

> Roy took everything they aimed at him. He seemed to know the soft, hard and bumpy places in the field and just how high a ball would bounce on them. From the flags on the stadium roof he noted the way the wind would blow the ball, and he was quick at fishing it out of the tricky undercurrents on the ground. Not sun, shadow, nor smoke-haze bothered him, and when a ball was knocked against the wall he estimated the angle of rebound and speared it as if its course had been plotted on a chart. He was good at gauging slices and knew when to charge the pill to save time on the throw. . . . He stood at the plate lean and loose, right-handed with an open stance, knees relaxed and shoulders squared. The bat he held in a curious position, lifted slightly above his head as if he prepared to beat a rattlesnake to death, but it didn't harm his smooth stride into the pitch, nor the easy way he met the ball and splashed it out with a flick of the wrists. The pitchers tried something different every time he came up, sliders, sinkers, knucklers, but he swung and connected, spraying them to all fields. He was . . . a natural.[2]

Social scientists maintain that any role—physician, college professor, athlete, assembly line worker, or dentist—necessitates the acquisition of appropriate emotional, social, cognitive, perceptual, and behavioral skills. The notion of a natural or "born" athlete is misleading because it belies the fact that individuals must learn a host of social, psychological and kinetic movements associated with a particular physical activity. Typically, an individual is referred to as a "natural" if he or she possesses the "tools" or motor skills (i.e., coordination, agility, speed, strength, power, and stamina) enabling one to perform sport feats with relative ease. Studies have shown that while the possession of specific physical characteristics is essential to an athlete, so, too, is the acquisition of relevant psychosocial characteristics. To illustrate, Carlson's study of the socialization of elite tennis players in Sweden provides some interesting and significant observations that contribute to participation in sport.[3] Although the sample sizes were small, the study used an experimental group, the top five male and female Swedish players, and a control group, players with junior ranking matched with the elite group on age and sex. Carlson found that between the ages of 12 and 14 both groups were about equal, but after puberty they began to diverge. What is of particular interest is that who became a world-class tennis player and who did not could not be predicted on the basis of ability or talent alone. According to Carlson, "Personal qualifications and early life experiences in combination with social structures, tradition of sport, and tennis culture all worked together in an optimal way, particularly the local club environment and the players' relationships to coaches."

The idea of the "natural athlete" is remniscent of a tireless debate that burned in the social sciences from the middle of the last century until fairly recently. At issue was whether our social behavior (e.g., athletic savvy) was the result of "nature" (heredity) or "nurture" (socialization). Today, in hindsight, we realize the "either–or" debate was virtually futile because a dynamic interaction between heredity and environment appears to produce our unique selves and social behaviors.

A helpful scheme for comprehending the complexities of the social learning process called socialization has been proposed by McNeil.[4] His scheme contains three categories: (a) the *individual dimensions* of socialization, (b) the *agents* of socialization, and (c) the general and specific *acquisitions* or learned consequences. For our purpose, this model, which applies to socialization in general, will be adapted to the learning of sport roles, values, skills, and attitudes. In this chapter, we examine two facets of sport socialization: (a) **socialization into sport** and (b) **socialization via sport.**

◻ SOCIALIZATION INTO SPORT

Of the array of socializing agents (Figure 5.1), the individual will selectively experience a few, the significance and impact of which may vary across persons and across time. The social stimuli with the most telling impact are **significant others** or **reference groups,** those individuals or groups whose attitudes, values, and behaviors contribute decisively to the formation of one's own attitudes, values, and behaviors. Regardless of our relationships with significant others (e.g., with parents, peers, siblings, relatives, coaches, and teachers), the same social learning mechanisms are in operation. Although there are several theoretical perspectives from which to examine the process of acquiring social roles (e.g., psychoanalytic, cognitive-developmental),

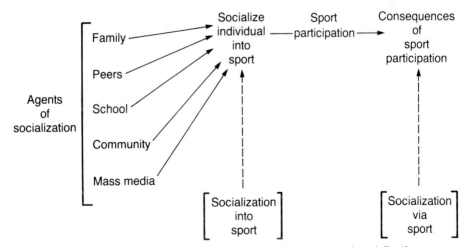

FIGURE 5.1   A model for conceptualizing socialization into sport and socialization via sport

social learning theory is particularly applicable to an understanding of the attainment of sport roles.

Social Learning Theory

Learning, broadly speaking, is the change in behavior resulting from experience. **Social learning theory** focuses on the acquisition and performance of social behaviors.[5] Three features of this approach—(a) **reinforcement,** (b) **coaching,**[6] and (c) **observational learning**—can be adapted to the learning of sport roles.

Reinforcement.   Reinforcement highlights the impact of sanctions—reward and punishment—on the acquisition and performance of social roles. For most of us, our parents were the initial socializing agents. Later in life, siblings, peers, teachers, and coaches become increasingly important. These socializing agents dispensed or withheld rewards and punishments. Basically, behavior that is positively reinforced or rewarded tends to be repeated (known in psychology as the *law of effect*), and behavior that is negatively reinforced or punished tends to be inhibited. Behavior patterns that are neither rewarded nor punished tend to be extinguished.[7]

Parents teach children, sometimes in a subtle, reflexive, and selective fashion, to acquire what they believe is appropriate sex role behavior. For example, past traditions have dictated that young boys be shrouded with toy soldiers, trucks, doctor's kits, footballs, soccer balls, baseballs, and bats, whereas young girls are given dolls, toy kitchens, and nurse's uniforms. Hence, some of the basic differences in the learning of social roles can be traced to differential social sanctions, social experiences, and social expectations. Direct rewards and punishments influence the kinds of behavior learned and performed. In addition to controlling reinforcement contingencies, parents provide verbal and nonverbal messages about what is expected and socially desirable.

Coaching.   *Coaching* is the deliberate teaching of the "socializee" by the "socializer." Parents fond of sports frequently coach their children how to perform specific athletic feats. This direct tutelage has at least three primary effects on children: (a) they come to know the range of behaviors their teacher thinks appropriate, (b) they acquire new skills and responses, and (c) they often exhibit greater motivation as a result of the rewards extended to them.[8]

One important factor in coaching is the issuing of challenges or dares. When children accept a challenge, they commit themselves to act in a particular manner. When the challenge is successfully met, the child gains recognition and reward and often becomes more committed and motivated to perform the behavior.

Observational Learning

While coaching entails a *direct* approach to role learning, not all behavior is acquired in this fashion. *Observational learning* refers to the learning and performance of tasks resulting from merely observing another's behavior and then acting accordingly. In essence, the simple observation of another's behavior may produce a disposition to behave similarly.

Bandura,[9] a proponent of *observational learning* or *modeling,* proposes that the following effects result from exposure to models: (a) Novel response patterns may be acquired (e.g., learning how to hold a baseball bat, golf club, or tennis racket); (b) existing responses may be strengthened or weakened by attending to the consequences of such behavior (e.g., line drives are more likely to be hit when the bat is held in a certain way, when a particular stance is taken, and when the batter swings at certain pitches); and (c) certain types of stimuli are distinguished from others (e.g., preponderance of blacks playing outfield positions in baseball today is attributed by some to the relative abundance of role models at those positions when blacks first entered professional baseball).[10] Blacks apparently distinguished between those positions available (outfielder) and those unavailable (catcher) to them. Similarly, women's historical lack of participation in sport can, in part, be attributed to the scarcity of role models and rewarding sport experiences. In summary, exposure to models can teach new behavioral skills, provide information about the probable outcome of engaging in a certain act, and generate knowledge about various situations.

Agents of Sport Socialization

Because socialization is the process through which the learning of skills, traits, dispositions, values, and attitudes for the performance of roles occurs, it is apparent that someone or something must initiate the process. The entities responsible for such transmission include a myriad of individuals, groups, and institutions.[11] Here we examine the influence of some significant **agents of sport socialization.**

The Family.   Because socialization begins at birth, an important part of the process occurs within the **family**-kinship unit. The nuclear and extended family's importance in the acquisition of any role and skill, particularly those learned early in life, is widely recognized. This early learning may be the result of direct teaching, for example, when a father, mother, or older sibling deliberately teaches a youngster a particular sport skill. Or it may be the consequence of role modeling, for example, when a parent or older sibling participates in sport with a child's knowledge of it. The fact that a statistically disproportionate number of former athletes (Bonds, Griffey, McKay, Doby, Cassidy, Murtaugh, Berra, Salem, Basset, Shula, Howe, and Rote) have children who are or have been athletes themselves may be explained, in part, by the models the parents provided. Vignette 5.1 explores some of the reasons why father–son professional baseball players have been relatively abundant.

The family's location in the social matrix of society—its social class mooring, structure, and patterning of activities—affects socialization in general and sport socialization in particular.[12] Because social class is determined by education, occupation, and income, it is not surprising that some sports such as golf and tennis have traditionally drawn their constituency from higher social classes, while others, like basketball, boxing, football, and baseball, have drawn on the lower social classes. In summarizing the family's influence on sport socialization, Loy, McPherson, and Kenyon conclude: The family as an institution is intimately related to sport in a variety of ways. The family serves as a socializing agent for the learning of sport roles . . . it provides a structure from which ascribed and achieved attributes impinge on an individual in a

☐   **VIGNETTE 5.1**

"The Natural Choice"

How important is familial influence in sport social-ization? Considering professional baseball exclu-sively, the sons of former major league baseball players are 50 times more likely to become profes-sional baseball players than the sons of fathers who were not pros! This was the finding of econ-omist David N. Laband and Bernard F. Lentz. Sport socialization, like socialization in other spheres, is affected by multiple factors. Included in this cadre would be a child's desire for approval (what the psychologists call positive reinforce-ment), genetic makeup (i.e., "nature"), the impact of the parent as a role model and teacher, and the parent's ability to facilitate entry into the profes-sion. According to Laband and Lentz, in 1980 1,147 athletes spent some time in the major leagues. Forty-seven (or 4%) of the total were sons of former major leaguers. On the surface this statistic doesn't appear striking. However, it gains monumental sociological significance when con-sidering that the 1980 census indicated some 29 million males were between the ages of 20 and 34 (which includes the prime baseball playing years). In other words, the probability of a male between 20 and 34 playing major league baseball in 1980 was about 1,147/29,000,000 or .00004.

Illustratively, some well-known father-son pro-fessional baseball names include Ripken (Cal Jr. and Cal Sr.), Law (Vance and Vern), Bell (Buddy and Gus), Kennedy (Terry and Bob), Boone (Bob and Ray), Stenhouse (Mike and Dave), Schofield (Dick Jr. and Dick Sr.), Kunkel (Jeff and Bill), Berra (Dale and Yogi), Trout (Steve and Dizzy), Skinner (Joel and Bob), Francona (Terry and Tito), and Vir-gil (Ozzie and Ossie). According to the research-ers, a primary reason why this occurs is based on economic theory—"the availability of valuable hu-man capital from their parents." According to La-band and Lentz:

Probably the most important type of human capital transferred from baseball fathers to sons is accu-rate information transmitted early and often. Fa-thers who make it to the major leagues, especially if they are good enough to last for a few years, learn a lot about how to be a better ball player—every-thing from batting stances and fielding to how to pace themselves during the grueling 162 game season. The earlier in his career a player learns these things, the greater chance he has to refine his abilities. He can work on a throwing or batting style until it becomes almost unconscious action. The children of doctors or plumbers, laborers or dentists may not pick up some of these tips until they reach college or even later, and then they must struggle to master these new skills.

Obviously the theory propounded is one stress-ing the valuable role of the social environment and early as well as later learning experiences. During the summer of 1985 as Pete Rose began his final conquest of Ty Cobb's hit record, his son Pete was often shown watching on. Perhaps he will some-day be a major league baseball player. The re-searchers make a provocative statement, "As baseball becomes big business, with personal contracts worth millions, we may start seeing fam-ily dynasties much like we now see in oil and pub-lishing."

In April 1987 *Sports Illustrated* reported that there were 67 sons (and one grandson) of former major leaguers playing professional baseball. Ap-parently one player, Casey Candaele of the Mon-treal Expos, had a *mother* who played for the All-American Girls Baseball League in the 1940s.

SOURCE: David N. Laband and Bernard F. Lentz, "The Natu-ral Choice," *Psychology Today* (August 1985), pp. 37–39, 42–43. Julian and Stan Javier, "Fathers and Sons," *Sports Illus-trated* (6 April 1987), pp. 62–73.

☐

sport system, and it uses sport as an expressive microcosm of the larger society in its attempt to socialize children.[13]

The family's importance in socialization stems from the fact that it provides the context within which infants are exposed first to such cultural products as values, norms, beliefs, and knowledge. Its monumental impact on us is almost frighteningly described by Wilson:

> . . . when [the child enters the human group] he is quite at the mercy of parents and siblings. They determine both what and when he shall eat and wear, when he shall sleep and wake, what he shall think and feel, how he shall express his thoughts and feelings (what language he shall speak and how he shall do it), what his political and religious commitments shall be, what sort of vocation he shall aspire to. Not that parents are ogres. They give what they have to give; their own limited knowledge, their prejudices and passions. There is no alternative to this giving of themselves, nor for the receiver is there any option.[14]

The Peer Group.   During adolescence, the parental-kinship influence is typically subordinate to the **peer group.** During the teen years, the reference group for many youths switches from their family-kinship unit to age cohorts (i.e., companions of the same age), although this transformation is affected by such factors as social class background, relationships within the family, and the importance attached to the youth or teenage subculture. The powerful socializing force of the peer group is highlighted in Axthelm's book, *The City Game,* in which he describes how playground basketball in Harlem captures the interest, motivation, and energy of working and lower class black youth—a phenomenon duplicated in other metropolises across the country.[15] In summarizing peer group influence on sport socialization, Loy, McPherson, and Kenyon suggest:

> There is little question . . . that peer pressure operates to influence sport-related facets of our lifestyle. During childhood, peer groups are found in the immediate neighborhood and tend to be somewhat similar in values to the individual; during the adolescent years, peer groups (youth subcultures) are located within the high school and therefore may include individuals with different values and interests; and during adulthood, influential peer groups are normally comprised of peers at the place of employment, providing an even greater likelihood of there being diversity in interests and values concerning sport. However, despite this influence throughout the life cycle, it is still not possible to determine whether an individual selects a peer group to "fit" with their previously established life style or whether an individual can experience dramatic changes in life style because of the influence of the peer group.[16]

The School.   Most **schools** have physical education classes and intramural and interscholastic athletic programs that provide sport experiences for young people (See Chapter 10 for a more thorough discussion of the relationship between education and sport). Mass education and mandatory gym classes have enabled many to learn the fundamentals of a variety of sporting activities. Loy, McPherson, and Kenyon summarize the influence of the school on sport socialization as follows: "The school, along with the family and peer group, is an influential institution in the process of sport role socialization. However, like other social systems, the role of the educational system in the process varies by sport, by roles within sports, by sex, and stage in the life cycle."[17]

The Community.   Many **communities** sponsor sport programs for males and females. Thus, the availability of sport opportunities—what is sometimes called the *opportunity structure*—is an important variable when considering socialization into sport. Baseball is one of the oldest and most highly developed programs, and many are familiar with Little Leagues, Ban Johnson, Pony Leagues, Babe Ruth Leagues, and American Legion baseball. Add to this compendium Pop Warner football programs, Bittie basketball, youth hockey leagues, track, soccer, and swimming clubs, and one easily senses that community-sponsored sport programs provide important opportunities for the socialization of youth into sport. We examine some of the effects of youth sport programs later in this chapter. Surveys indicate that in excess of 25 million youngsters participate in organized sport programs. In summarizing the influence of community youth sport programs, Eitzen writes:

> The involvement of boys, and increasingly girls, in adult-supervised sport is characteristic of contemporary American society. About two million boys, age 8–14, play Little League baseball or its community equivalent; about one million boys play in organized tackle football leagues outside of school; some 5,200 hockey teams exist for youngsters age 9–12; and organized golf and bowling involve 1.2 million juniors. This wide participation in adult-sponsored sports activities is a phenomenon of the past twenty-five or thirty years. There are at least two reasons for this recent surge in organized children's sports. Foremost is the belief held by most adults that sports participation has positive consequences for youth.[18]

The Mass Media.   The **mass media**—instruments of communication reaching large audiences (generally) without direct communication between sender and receiver—can play a dramatic role in sport socialization. Through sport exposure via television, radio, and the press, many youngsters become acquainted with sports and are exposed to sport heroes, who function as role models.[19]

Are athletes considered good role models by parents? According to *The Miller Lite Report,*[20] 75% of Americans believe that athletes are good role models for children, and about 60% believe athletes are often the best role models children can emulate! Not surprisingly, these statistics are even higher for sport fans (vs. nonfans) and for those who make a living from sports (e.g., coaches vs. the general public). Many young men and boys and, increasingly, young women and girls can name the top teams and players in various sports. Moreover, sport celebrities are among the most endeared idols of contemporary youth. In summarizing the influence of the mass media, Hoch wrote:

> This brings us to that other main socializer for consumption—the mass media. As Marshall McLuhan has obliquely pointed out in his book *Understanding Media,* almost all news, views, and entertainment heard over the media are essentially advertisements for the consumption-oriented way of life favored by media advertisers and owners. Sports news, for one, has never really been much more than a bit of razzamatazz for promotional purposes, and the bribery of the media-men by professional promoters has long been institutionalized.[21]

In Chapter 13, we will examine more intensively the role of the mass media in sport. For now, suffice it to say that the media are a major socializing agent in contemporary society; they socialize one to participate in as well as consume sport.

While the family, peer group, school, community, and mass media do not exhaust the sport-socializing agents in our society, they are among the most profound influences on young people.[22] A person not affected by sports during his or her formative years is rare indeed. In reviewing sport-socialization studies, Kenyon and McPherson concluded that sport participation is an outgrowth of early involvement with sports, rewarding and successful sport experiences, positive encouragement from significant others, and accessibility to adequate facilities and instruction.[23] Shepard captures socialization via sport by noting the role of various socializing agents, including sport, in the following way:

> The family, school, peer groups, and mass media are the major agencies of socialization during childhood and adolescence, but they are not the only ones. Although the church does not have the same degree of influence in all societies, it can affect the moral outlook of young people even in secular societies like the United States. Traditionally, athletic teams have taught young boys to compete, win and lose, cooperate with others, and handle their dislike of some peers. Girls are being increasingly exposed to these experiences as they participate in sports from grade school through college. Other potentially significant agencies of socialization are youth organizations such as the Cub Scouts, Girl Scouts, and YMCA.[24]

Factors Contributing to Participation in Sport

Kenyon and Grogg[25] studied antecedent factors important to the socialization of athletes at the University of Wisconsin. Two of the outcomes of this investigation merit attention: (a) Of the many possible socializing agents—such as parents, siblings, relatives, male and female friends, classroom teachers, school coaches, school counselors, nonschool personnel, and others—parents emerged as the most significant socializing agents. Furthermore, their influence was slightly greater at the high school and collegiate levels than during the pre-high school period. (b) The influence of the agents of socialization varied according to the particular sport that athletes participated in during their pre-high school years.

Not surprisingly, researchers found that adult sport participation for both sexes could be traced back to rewarding childhood experiences. Data secured from *The Miller Lite Report*[26] are significant in this context. First, 62% of the sample indicated that their children participated in organized sports. The reason for this high level of participation reflects the nature of the sport socialization process:

1. 75% of American parents encourage (always or often) their children to engage in sports.
2. Only 6% encourage their children to spend less time playing sports.

Spreitzer and Snyder have advanced the following causal model to explain sport involvement: [27]

Parental Interest in Sport → Parental Encouragement for Sport → Offspring's Participation in Sport → Offspring's Perceived Ability in Sports → Adult Participation in Sports.

American society provides multiple opportunities for sport-socializing experiences, and numerous studies attest to the central role occupied by sport in the youth culture.[28] According to some,[29] the motivation for sports participation is affected by (a) socioeconomic factors, (b) the prestige and power of socializing agents, and (c) the perceived opportunity structure. As important as these factors are, they are insufficient to explain socialization into sport. To this list must be added substantive psychological and physical factors, although these will not receive much emphasis in the present discussion.

The preceding conceptual framework for explaining sport socialization appears to be most pertinent to white male Americans. There is evidence that among females of all races and among males of minority races sport socialization processes do not conform to this model. For example, Snyder and Spreitzer found that parental sport interests (particularly the father's) positively correlated with sport involvement for both male and female children.[30] For other types of involvement—reading, talking, and watching—the sport interests of the opposite-sex parent loomed more significant. The inquiry suggested the need for separate analysis of male and female sport-socializing experiences. Bischoff found that male college athletes perceived the family as more influential than either peers or coaches in their sport socialization.[31] Female high school athletes found peers more influential than coaches or family members; however, female college athletes found coaches (both male and female) as important. Sport socialization for minority groups, especially blacks, also differs. Sailes's data indicate that black and white males have dissimilar sport socialization experiences.[32] He found that whites were influenced to a greater degree than blacks by their parents, whereas blacks were significantly influenced by others outside the family; sport opportunities (facilities and programs) were more widely available to whites than blacks; blacks showed greater interest in sport and had predominately black role models, whereas whites had less interest in sports and role models of both races, but the impact of these models was less important.

Types of Sport Involvement: A Typology

Sport involvement varies along such dimensions as degree, frequency, duration, intensity, and kind.[33] Two broad involvement categories—**primary** and **secondary**—can be further divided into direct and indirect types. *Primary involvement* refers to direct participation (formally prescribed roles) in either the athletic contest itself or related supporting activities. Primary involvement may be further partitioned into direct and indirect types. For example, consider a football game. The most obvious role is that of the players (e.g., quarterback, end, tackle). These roles involve direct primary involvement. Nevertheless, other roles are vital to the staging of the contest, namely, coach, official, trainer, physician, scorekeeper, timekeeper, public address announcer, telecaster, broadcaster, cheerleader, band member, and the like. These roles reflect indirect primary involvement and consist of primary activities other than those engaged in by the athletic participants.

Secondary involvement comprises a residual category encompassing activities not qualifying as primary in nature. Direct secondary involvement includes the roles of financial controllers such as professional club owners, promoters, alumni, members of athletic committees, regulators, and administrators (e.g., rules committees, governing bodies, and athletic directors), and entrepreneurs (e.g., sport equipment manufacturers, retailers, concessionaires). The spectators of sporting events fall into the category of indirect secondary involvement.

In short, there are different categories of sport involvement and the previously mentioned scheme attempts to classify some of the identifiable social positions in sport (see Table 4.1); a person may fall into different categories of involvement at different times.

Kenyon distinguishes three categories of sport involvement:[34] (a) **Behavioral involvement** includes active (participant in sport) and passive (sport watching and sports talk, perusal of the sports page, or subscribing to sport journals) modes. (b) **Affective involvement**[35] refers to a person's feelings and emotions about sport (whether they are deemed cathartic, a waste of time, satisfactory, or unsatisfactory). (c) **Cognitive involvement**[36] refers to a person's knowledge about sport—its rules, personalities, and so forth. Importantly, involvement in sport can be other than behavioral; it can also be cognitive or affective. Although these dimensions are likely to be mutually reinforcing, they can be differentiated for analytical purposes.

The Fan

The potential fan is generally socialized into sport at a young age. The word *fan* first appeared in 1682 and was spelled either *fann* or *phann*. Originally, it was short for *fanatic* and meant a person with an extreme or unreasonable enthusiasm or zeal. In 1899, it first appeared in an American dictionary and was defined as meaning "an enthusiast, originally of sport." *Sportnik* has also been used for fan. It is not uncommon for parents to purchase sport paraphernalia—stuffed footballs, miniature basketballs, toy baseballs and bats, sweatsuits, jackets, and caps bearing their favorite team's insignia and name—as gifts for infants and children. As children mature, they are frequently provided with more appropriate accouterments of various sports—plastic bats, small rubber footballs, basketballs, cheerleading outfits, roller skates, and the like. After exposure to sport stimuli since birth, the motives for fan involvement take on different forms. Two personal functions performed by sport (other than those considered earlier) for fans are relevant here:[37] (a) It engenders a feeling of belonging and social identification, and (b) it provides a socially acceptable outlet for the catharsis of hostile and aggressive feelings. Research has shown that the rowdyism of British soccer fans is indeed a catharsis but certainly not in a socially acceptable manner. In commenting on the hooliganism of British soccer fans, Thomas writes: "They [the British soccer fans] come from depressed neighborhoods here, from childhood, violence is the currency of daily life, where men prize street smartness and the capacity to drink and fight. For these men . . . fighting is one of the few sources of excitement, meaning and status available. . . . what you have in this country [England] is the transposition of New York or Chicago street gangs into a football contest."[38] Not everyone agrees with these functions, and a reading of Vignette 5.2 suggests some professional differences of opinion.

Beisser has argued that sport enthusiasm stems from the nature of mass society and the secondary forms of social interaction conditioned by it.[39] He contends that the increasing prevalence of impersonal forms of social interaction (which is due in part to family ties being extenuated and to an increase in geographical mobility); affective

☐ VIGNETTE 5.2

Football's Effect on Fans: Some Experts' Views

BY SHEILA MORAN, TIMES STAFF WRITER

For 20 years, Ralph Richmond has gone dove hunting on Sept. 1, opening day of the season. This year, there was a conflict: the Rams vs. San Diego.

A season ticket-holder for 30 years, Richmond wrote the Rams demanding to know "what idiot in your organization" was responsible for the scheduling.

"Now you people have forced me to charter an airplane from the Imperial Valley to fly back to Los Angeles to see you play the Chargers," Richmond wrote.

Jack Teele, a club executive, wrote to explain that the scheduling allowed fans to have the long Labor Day weekend free.

Richmond finally changed his mind about chartering a plane because "it's just too much of a hassle." He skipped the dove hunting and instead drove the 80 miles from Redlands with his wife, Luella, to see the game.

"I hunt ducks all winter long," Richmond said, "and I can go dove hunting the whole month of September."

Richmond is a football fan, one of millions who attend pro and college games each autumn. Their attachment to the sport and its mystique—and the ways they manifest it—has prompted studies and analyses by psychologists and other students of the human condition. They don't always agree.

Some experts say watching a football game is a catharsis; that by witnessing the violence on the field a fan rids himself of his aggressions. Others say it's the other way around; that a guy is more likely to belt his wife after watching a football game. Still others say that football is one thing for one person and something else for another.

Dr. William Beausay, president of the Ohio-based Academy for the Psychology of Sports In-

ternational interviewed 800 football fans in a study four years ago that also included auto racing and wrestling addicts.

"We were curious about why people would want to go to an auto racing event and watch people get killed," he said. "From there, we went into football, and from football into wrestling."

A clinical psychologist and professor at Bowling Green State University, Beausay concluded that watching a football game was "far more therapeutic than six months of psychotherapy for a lot of neurotic people."

"You feel spent after watching a game, like after taking a shower," he said.

Beausay said the football fans were questioned at Ohio State and Michigan games and at a Detroit-Chicago pro contest. Some of the questions included "items we lifted from a psychological test to measure hostility and tolerance, impulsivity and self-discipline.

"The women tended to be tolerant; the men, hostile and aggressive. The same trend showed in auto racing, but in wrestling, which is the best example in sports of fans venting hostility, the men and women were identical psychologically."

In football, he said, about 70% of the women most enjoyed the esthetics—the colors of the uniforms, the half time ceremonies, the fashions worn by other women.

"There was no significant difference between the women at the pro game and the college games," Beausay said.

"We discovered that about one-fifth of the men were what we call technicians. They loved the strategy, the tactics, the playing style. Of the other 80%, 55% were hostile and, of those, half would be further agitated through watching the game and the other half would feel satisfied. The remaining 25% were the guys with the flasks in their pockets who didn't care who won. They were just out with the gang."

The football fans also were asked if they "got into trouble" after the game. Of the more than 50 who did, 35 said they got a traffic ticket. Others said they got into a fight about the game with someone in their own group.

Fan hostility tends to be higher if the home team loses. And it increases with the temperature.

"If the Jets played the Rams and the Jets won, your highways outside the Coliseum wouldn't be safe for an hour," Beausay said.

"Football ranks fourth on the Academy's Sports Violence Index, behind hockey, rugby, and auto racing," Beausay said.

"Baseball fans are much more docile. There are many more technicians. Whether a team gets beat or not isn't that much of an issue. And one of the things that kills basketball is that they have games every day. The teams are smaller and there are more of them than in football, so the loyalty is more diffused."

Dr. Jeffrey Goldstein, a Temple University psychology professor, surveyed 150 male spectators before and after the 1969 Army–Navy game in Philadelphia and concluded that watching football—or any contact sport—increases spectator hostility, regardless of which team wins.

As a control for the experiment, Goldstein asked the same questions of male spectators at the Army–Navy gymnastics meet, where there was no body contact. The statistics indicated that hostility did not significantly increase over the meet, he said.

Anthropologist Christie W. Kiefer of UC San Francisco leans toward the opposite viewpoint: that football has a cathartic effect.

"If a viewer feels really frustrated, maybe watching a game could provoke him to violence. But if a person is basically civilized that won't happen," he said.

Kiefer regards football as a "ritual of renewal" that can make a fan feel better. He compares it to ancient Greek dramas designed to "cleanse the soul."

"When I go to a game, I come out feeling good. I often get a lift. I think most people do because you get rid of frustrations. You feel closer to your fellow Americans; more tied in.

"Americans are not encouraged to show their emotions in public. If you yell and curse on the street you'd be hauled to the looney bin. You can do things in a football stadium you can't do on the street."

Kiefer said many societies have rituals in which people gather in large groups and experience an emotional high.

Japan, he said, has "an emotionally repressed society like ours, and the national male ritual there is to periodically go out and get drunk together. Once drunk, anything goes. They sing, cry and tell sad stories. A football game is like that."

Women are sometimes involved in the rituals, Kiefer said, and in Japan are allowed to show their emotions more than men.

Dr. Stuart Miller, a Maryland psychology professor and Baltimore Colts fan, said that the effect of football on spectator violence is an open question, but most evidence supports the theory that watching a violent sport stimulates rather than quiets aggressions.

In a study of 400 students at Towson State College, where he teaches, Miller said no differences were noted between male and female hostility.

"One thing that did come out was that female fans tended to be sensation seekers—the sort of individuals who sought out novelty, variety, unpredictability, risk," he said.

Dr. S. Harvard Kaufman, a Seattle psychiatrist and sports fan, believes violence is part of football's spectator appeal. An even bigger part, he said, is the escape from boredom and daily routine.

"People are looking for some excitement outside of themselves and want to grab onto something. People are looking for heroes.

"Football is bang-bang, clashing miniwars," Kaufman said. "The players don't get killed but they practically do. Indoor stadiums take away the excitement. There's no wind to deal with, and no rain, so the ball doesn't slip out of the players' hands. It's too predictable. It's like you know what they're going to do on third down."

"Football stimulates action, sex. Most players are sexually active after a game. All kinds of people are attracted to football. The nicest woman you ever met can look at the players sexually and have a helluva time. The beer drinker can yell and holler while the players get hurt instead of him."

In his book "The Madness in Sports," Dr. Theodore Beisser, a Los Angeles psychiatrist, said that watching any sport can fulfill psychic needs. The fan, he said, "can project onto the players the whole gamut of his emotions as they enact the competitive drama. In sports, unlike the theater, all things are possible in any role with which the spectator may identify, for there is no script. The outcome is always in doubt; as long as it continues, the game can still be won."

Beisser added: "Regression, the return to simpler and more elemental stages of adjustment, is acceptable within the matrix of sports watching. Grown men carry banners or wear hats denoting their favorites. In the same way youngsters emulate their idols. . . . Regression, if controlled, tends to refurbish the individual for return to the monotony of his daily life."

According to Beisser, Los Angeles fans are different from those in other cities. Los Angeles is a melting pot of transplants, a "fluid, centerless mass." "It's not surprising," he said, that "the citizens seek, sometimes desperately, groups they can identify with."

While ardent supporters, Rams fans are "less antagonistic toward visiting teams than fans in other cities," said the Rams' Teele who has at-

tended games in every NFL city except Tampa. "That could be because so many of our fans used to live somewhere else."

He rates Philadelphia fans as the most hostile. He said Ram players are told to keep their helmets on while they're on the bench in Philadelphia because "the fans throw golf balls and you can get clobbered."

From their seat near the 50-yard line, Tom Pierce, a stockbroker from Tarzana, and his wife, Jan, watched intently as the Rams and the Philadelphia Eagles matched running games on the field below.

"If the Rams win, I feel great," Pierce said. "If they lose, it's a long drive home."

He likes the game, he said, because it's more exciting than other sports.

"If you watch the last five minutes of a basketball game, you've seen it all," Pierce said. "And baseball puts you to sleep, it's so slow."

For Marvin Simmons, a Los Angeles county probation officer, football is "like a chess game. There are a lot of intricate plays and it's fast moving. That's why I like it."

For other fans, such as a Beverly Hills management consultant in her 30s who asked that her name not be used, football is "an outlet. You can yell and scream."

The sport offers social benefits too.

"I became interested in football in college at UCLA," the businesswoman said. "The best-looking men were either playing the game or they liked it a lot."

SOURCE: *Los Angeles Times,* copyright 1977 (21 September 1977), reprinted by permission.

---

neutrality (in other words, emotional blandness); and social isolation of individuals force a search for more permanent roots through which a sense of belonging, social anchoring, and purpose can be nurtured. Additionally, fans' zeal emerges from a desire to share experiences with others.

Schafer has rhetorically asked: Why do fans give their energy and interest to athletics to the extent they do? and proposed the following three-part explanation:[40] (a)

Normative social influence indicates what is important, what should be done, where interest should lie, and so forth. This reasoning is circular, yet valid. Because success breeds success, one might argue that because sports are popular, many people participate in and identify with them; hence, many people emulate and idolize sport figures, and consequently, sports are popular. Fans' interest in sport becomes a preoccupation, because of the snowballing effects of its initial popularity. (b) Sports provide a sense of belonging and identification with a social group beyond the immediate family or kinship unit. The affiliative motive for becoming a fan may be of considerable motivational significance. (c) Team identification may represent an extension of the self, but this identification is double-edged; when one's team wins, one's self-feelings are enhanced; when it loses, one's self-feelings are strained. Although not typical, a Denver Bronco fan left a suicide note in which he expressed consternation about the Broncos fumbling and a Florida cab driver shot himself after missing Hank Aaron's record-breaking home run.

The effects of team identification on self-feeling have received empirical corroboration and is referred to as "BIRG"—*basking in reflected glory.*[41] Cialdini and colleagues discovered that at big-time college football schools, students were more prone to wear their school's paraphernalia (logo sweatshirts, T-shirts, jackets, caps, etc.) on the Monday following a victory, particularly an important one, than one following a loss or tie. Apparently, the students wanted to link themselves with successful models via the principle of association. The "BIRG" phenomenon refers to the tendency to flaunt positive associations and hide negative ones, because the former positively influences how we and our audiences feel, perceive, and act, and the latter often produces the converse. Fandom may be explained in psychological terms by invoking the reference group concept. Hastorf and Cantril's study of reactions to a football contest between Princeton and Dartmouth fits nicely into this framework (see Chapter 14).[42] These social psychologists hypothesized that loyalty to one's team—in this case study, either to Princeton or Dartmouth—affected perceptions of what took place during the football contest between the two schools. As the results unequivocally demonstrate, students perceived the game differently; moreover, the game was viewed through a filter of identification with their alma mater.

Mann studied fans' reactions to a series of games in the South Australian Football League.[43] (In Australia, football is the game North Americans call *soccer.*) Mann hypothesized that dedicated fans attribute defeat to external factors (e.g., poor playing conditions, referee partiality and oversights, bad luck, and poor sportsmanship on the part of the opposition), or to factors other than poor play on the part of their preferred team (internal factors). To empirically test this hypothesis, Mann interviewed spectators as they departed from a game, and the results proved consistent with the hypothesis that "fans of the losing team judged that their team received fewer 'free kicks,' was the victim of 'dirty play,' and had less 'luck,' than did fans of the opposing team or nonpartisan spectators." According to Mann, the reaction of the Dartmouth students in Hastorf and Cantril's study[44] was a classic case of rationalization, because Princeton had been victorious over their school.

While these explanations for fan involvement appear to have face validity, two conspicuous questions remain unanswered: Why and how does sport fulfill these needs? Why are fans predominately males rather than females? Edwards's provocative thesis is of interest:

> As an institution having primarily socialization and value maintenance functions, sport affords the fan an opportunity to reaffirm the established values and beliefs defining acceptable means and solutions to central problems in the secular realm of everyday societal life. But this fact does not stand alone; particular patterns of values are expressed through certain intrinsic features of sports activities; in combination, the two aspects explain not only fan enthusiasm but sport's predominately male following. Sports events are unrehearsed, they involve exceptional performances in a situation characterized by a degree of uncertainty and a lack of total control, and they epitomize competition for scarce values—prestige, status, self adequacy, and other socially relevant rewards.[45]

In other words, Edwards argues that the typical worker cannot control all the myriad forces affecting his life, and work is characterized by striving for scarce resources. Sport reaffirms the viability of the values the fan must accept in the instrumental pursuits necessitated by the work-a-day world. Thus, sports have personal significance to the fan insofar as they reflect and reinforce the values, beliefs, and ideologies existing in other institutional spheres, particularly the economic.

Psychologically, there appears to be more to spectator sports for the fan than the mere enjoyment of witnessing an event. A study reported by the International Society of Sports Psychology[46] concluded that the intensity of the emotional response indicates that sports mean more to the fan than many people realize. The satisfaction that the fan experiences at the end of each game, of seeing a conflict settled (regardless of which team wins), compensates for the permanent conflicts in the fan's own life. This vicarious conflict resolution may be one of the most important psychosocial contributions of sport to our culture.

Finally, according to Melnick, there currently exists a dearth of scientific research on sports fans and, of course, without them, many games would be for naught. He suggests seven schemes that may be found helpful in the study of fandom:[47]

1. Spectatorship in a sociohistorical perspective
2. Sport consumption patterns
3. Spectatorship in popular culture
4. Economic aspects of sport spectatorship
5. The psychology of the sports fan
6. Functions and dysfunctions of sport spectatorship
7. Spectator violence in sport

SOCIALIZATION VIA SPORT

Physical activities and games are essential elements in the socialization process, according to the famed social theorist George H. Mead:

> The game is . . . an illustration of the situation out of which the organized personality arises. Insofar as the child does take the attitude of the other and allows that attitude of the other to determine the things he is doing with reference to a common end, [the child] is becoming an organized member of society. The child is taking over the morale of the society and is becoming an essential member of it.[48]

According to the values espoused in the dominant American sport creed, sport involvement produces desirable consequences and outcomes or eufunctions. Illustratively, it is presumed to build character, teach discipline, prepare one for life's competitions, facilitate moral development and good citizenship, and cultivate desirable personality traits. Does scientific research bear out these admirable and lofty claims?

Webb's data support the position that the value placed on winning is enhanced and correlated with the institutionalization of athletic activity.[49] Using a quasi-longitudinal research design (i.e., studying a variable at different points in time to determine change or stability), random samples of students in grades 3, 6, 8, 10, and 12 in Battle Creek, Michigan, were drawn. The students ($N > 1,200$) were asked to rank the relative importance of three principles: (a) to play as well as you can (called "skill"); (b) to beat your opponent (called "victory"); and (c) to play fairly (called "fairness"). Webb discovered a positive association between grade level and importance attached to winning; as year in school increased, so, too, did the importance attached to beating one's opponent. In other words, as students progressed through formal schooling channels, their attitudes became more professional and achievement oriented (i.e., skill and the importance of victory were more salient than fun or fair play). Of course, correlational data do not permit a causal interpretation; because two factors go together or covary does not necessarily mean that one causes the other.

Mantel and Vander Velden,[50] whose research corroborated Webb's, contend that sports function as cultural models and hypothesized that the professionalization of attitude toward play (operationalized, as in Webb's study, by having subjects rank the importance of "skill," "victory," and "fairness") was related to participation in organized athletics. Only preadolescent males were studied, thereby eliminating the confounding influences that correlate with age (recall that Webb used several age–grade cohorts.) The sample of 133 subjects was divided into two groups: (a) an experimental group ($n = 73$), whose members had participated in baseball or football for a minimum of two years in either a Boy's Club or Catholic Youth Organization (CYO); and (b) a control group ($n = 60$), whose members had never participated in organized athletics. Mantel and Vander Velden found empirical support for their hypothesis. Professionalization of attitude toward sport covaried with participation in organized sport (Table 5.1), and, conversely, nonparticipants ranked fairness more

TABLE 5.1   Skill or victory responses among participants and nonparticipants

Rank Skill or Victory	Participants		Nonparticipants	
	n	%	*n*	%
1	39	53	20	33
0	34	47	40	67
	73	100	60	100
	$\chi^2 = 5.39$	$p < .05$	$C = .20$	

SOURCE: R.C. Mantel and L.V. Velden, "The Relationship Between the Professionalization of Attitude Toward Play of Preadolescent Boys and Participation in Organized Sport," Third Annual Symposium on the Sociology of Sport, Waterloo, Ontario, Canada (August 1971).

important than participants (Table 5.2). Whereas participants ranked skill and victory as most important, nonparticipants stressed fairness. Despite these associations, the specific mechanisms accounting for this relationship were not isolated. Although sport is a socializing agent, it is but one of several institutions shaping attitudes, behaviors, and values.

Richardson's[51] study of male physical education majors ($N = 233$) suggested that positive attitudes toward sportsmanship and fair play are *not* the result of involvement in organized collegiate sports. After dividing his sample into letter and nonletter winners, Richardson discovered that monogram recipients expressed lower regard for sportsmanship than nonmonogram winners and that football players in comparison to other sport participants had the lowest scores of all. Apparently, sport involvement did not generate the desirable attitudes of fair play and sportsmanship alluded to in the sport creed.

The major benefits of sport involvement are widely believed to be health, character development, and training for the competitive environment of the adult world. However, empirical evidence challenges these alleged functions. "Sports do not build character, they reveal it," according to Heywood Broun. In the context of sport socialization, we must ask "Do sports develop character and personality?" On some test batteries, athletes have scored higher than nonathletes on measures of self-discipline and other traits. The unanswered riddle, however, is whether sports produce these effects or whether the athlete enters athletic competition with these traits intact or with a predisposition to develop them. In commenting on the self-selection factor, Coakley wrote:

Allow me to illustrate this point by using a reference to physical rather than character traits. If we had data to clearly indicate that participants in sport were stronger, faster, and more coordinated than nonparticipants, would it be reasonable to conclude that the strength, speed, and coordination of participants were acquired as a result of their involvement in sport? Obviously . . . not. It is rather clear that youngsters with certain physical attributes will be attracted to sport, and, once involved, it is likely that they will be continually encouraged by peers, parents, and coaches. It should also be obvious that youngsters who lack strength, speed and coordination may never try out for an organized team. . . . Those possessing the desired traits will probably stay involved and further develop those attributes through continued participation. This does not mean that sport participation has no effect on the development of physical attributes, but it does mean

TABLE 5.2 Fair responses among participants and nonparticipants

Rank Fair	Participants		Nonparticipants	
	n	%	n	%
1	34	47	40	67
2	29	40	18	30
3	10	14	2	3
	73	101	60	100
	$\chi^2 = 7.19$	$p < .05$	$C = .23$	

SOURCE: R.C. Mantel and L.V. Velden, "The Relationship Between the Professionalization of Attitude Toward Play of Preadolescent Boys and Participation in Organized Sport," Third Annual Symposium on The Sociology of Sport, Waterloo, Ontario, Canada (August 1971).

that the effects of sport participation are likely to be limited to a select group of individuals who are physically predisposed to that development.[52]

Sport psychologists Ogilvie and Tutko maintain that some undesirable traits are characteristic of "athletes who survive the high attrition rate associated with sport competition. . . . Competition doesn't seem to build character, and it is possible that competition doesn't even require much more than a minimally integrated personality."[53] Some athletes have achieved success despite severe personality disorders. Ogilvie and Tutko wrote:

> We know from our work hundreds of outstanding competitors who possess strong character formation that complements higher motor skills. . . . But we found athletes who possessed so few strong character traits that it was difficult on the basis of personality to account for their success. . . . There were gold medal Olympic winners in Mexico and Japan whom we would classify as over-compensatory greats. Only magnificent physical gifts enabled them to overcome constant tension, anxiety, and self-doubt. They are unhappy, and when the talent ages and fades, they become derelicts. . . .[54]

Another negative syndrome of sport participation documented by Ogilvie and Tutko is **success phobia**—the anxiety, fear, and apprehension aroused by anticipated success. Track athletes, for but one example, who break records in practice but not in meets and athletes who "choke" at crucial times are cases in point. Examination of the personal and social histories of success phobics reveals two major precipitating factors: (1) phobic athletes feel they will "kill" their competitors by beating them, and (2) phobic athletes feel they will not be able to live up to the expectations of significant others that have accrued as a result of prior stellar performances. The following poignant case history of one success phobic was gleaned from their files: The father of one success-phobic athlete spent many hours coaching and teaching his son a particular sport skill. As part of the training, the father would compete with his son and win repeatedly because of his superior size, strength, and speed. However, the athlete was informed that he was improving rapidly and would soon be able to compete more equally with Dad. A few years later, when the son could consistently defeat his father, Dad became disturbed and, as a consequence, overly critical of his son's play. Training became punishment, and verbal rewards were few and exhortations many. The boy's pressure was eased only when Dad beat him—only then were his social and emotional needs met. Hence, this success-phobic athlete pretended to go all out to beat his father but relinquished because of his need for social recognition, reward, love, intimacy, and acceptance. The conflict over winning and being punished soon gave way to losing and being loved, a pattern that followed the athlete into his college sport involvement.

In summary, the preponderance of evidence does *not* unequivocally support the presumed positive consequences of sport presented in the dominant American sport creed. We question whether the Battle of Waterloo was won on the playing fields of Eton, as the Duke of Wellington is reported to have uttered. Orlick nicely balances the socialization functions of sport:

> For every positive psychological or social outcome in sports, there are possible negative outcomes. For example, sports can offer a child group membership or group exclusion, acceptance or rejection, positive feedback or negative feedback, a sense of accomplish-

ment or a sense of failure, evidence of self-worth or lack of evidence of self-worth. Likewise, sports can develop cooperation and concern for others, but they can also develop intense rivalry and complete lack of concern for others.[55]

Are Sport Experiences Generalizable?

Social scientists often ask "Does an experience—skills, techniques, values, attitudes, or motivation—transfer beyond the specific context in which it was acquired?" In sport, the question can be phrased as follows: "Does socialization via sports develop generalized role skills or merely the ability to play specific roles in specific contexts?" Advocates of physical education and sport programs frequently claim that a host of positive traits result from athletic participation and then carry over to other contexts. As we have seen, the dominant American sport creed promotes this view.

Theoretically, socialization involves interactions between individuals and their significant others (e.g., parents, siblings, girlfriends, boyfriends, peers, coaches, and teachers). These significant others, or reference groups, are the audiences for which we play. Social psychologists claim that reference groups serve *two* functions: They (a) provide a frame of reference for guiding our behavior—providing norms, values, and behavioral blueprints—and (b) serve as standards against which to judge or evaluate ourselves.[56]

According to Snyder, sociological literature suggests that attitudes and behaviors learned in specific contexts (e.g., sport activities) may *not* carry over to more general settings (e.g., the family, school, and work).[57] The research suggests that such transference occurs only when situations are similar.

Because humans do not automatically absorb social influences through osmosis, *five* variables—what Snyder calls "dimensions of social interaction"—crucial to socialization experiences have been forwarded. The first is the *degree* (i.e., the frequency, intensity, and duration) of involvement. Consider the differences between members of the first team in a varsity program and participants in a required physical education class, an intramural event, or sandlot game. Because the commitments, motivations, and goals of these participants vary, the development of role traits will likely be a function of their degree of involvement.

The second factor is whether the participation is *voluntary* or *involuntary*. Although it seems reasonable to conclude that free choice is valuable to general role learning, a branch of social psychological theory, cognitive dissonance, might argue that forced compliance may also have some beneficial end results.[58]

The third factor affecting socialization is the *nature of the socialization relationship*. More specifically, one might reasonably expect different outcomes when comparing instrumental versus expressive social interaction. Some sport researchers have advanced the notion that blacks who have been reared in matriarchal families are superior athletes because the coach becomes a surrogate father—an expressive social relationship.[59] Instrumental relationships, on the other hand, provide a means to a desired end without the same emotional overtones between interacting parties.

The prestige and power of the *socializer* is the fourth factor. As we know from socialization in general, prestigious, powerful, and emotionally significant persons generally have more influence on the socializee than their counterparts.

The fifth key variable includes the *personal and social characteristics of the participant*. Not only is the participant's actual skill level important but so, too, is the perception of that skill. How persons define their skill may sometimes be as important as their actual skill level, because self-perception (i.e., the self as a social object according to interactionists) motivates present and future behaviors. The social characteristics of participants—their social class, race, and ethnicity—mediate present participation and the adoption of future diffuse roles. The aborted 1968 Olympic Games boycott can be viewed as a struggle between conflicting loyalties. Black athletes had to decide whether or not they were willing to forego individual recognition to protest racist practices in American society.

In summary, whether traits, skills, and values learned in a specific milieu will or will not carry over to other contexts depends on several dimensions of social interaction that mediate the specific and general contexts.

❑ ORGANIZED YOUTH SPORT PROGRAMS

One of the most significant and earliest sport socialization experiences occurs during youth. Youth sport programs have been maligned in recent years. Despite the equivocal research findings regarding the effects of youth sport, one thing is certain—few of those involved take a disinterested and neutral stance. In one camp are the disillusioned cynics; in the other are the staunch supporters. Cynics and supporters alike, however, are concerned with the psychological, social, and physical effects of organized sports. In this section, we consider some issues in youth sport as they pertain to early sport socialization experiences.

Although youth sport programs are not new, the number of participants has reached record proportions. Youth programs have existed since the turn of the century. For the first quarter of the twentieth century, the school took an active role in organizing, administering, promoting, and endorsing youth sport endeavors. During the 1930s, the school's support of youth programs waned because of criticisms of athletic elitism and charges that competition had negative consequences. The void created by the school's deemphasis of these extracurricular activities was filled by social service agencies (e.g., the YMCA and the YWCA) and various boys' and girls' clubs. The economic climate produced by industrialization and child labor practices was a major impetus behind the development of this movement. The goal was to provide adolescents with wholesome social, physical, and psychological stimulation.[60]

Today, youth sport programs have become integral components of Western society. It is estimated that, between the ages of 6 and 16, approximately 25 million youngsters participate in formalized sport programs (e.g., baseball, soccer, hockey, basketball, swimming, football, gymnastics, tennis, and other sports). What is remarkable and unprecedented is that there are sport leagues for children who have barely entered the primary grades. Given the large number of youth sport programs and participants, two timely questions arise: What are the consequences? What is learned via sports?

Many have strong opinions as to the value of competitive sports. Some of these beliefs are based on personal experiences; others are not. Sport has become an important regulating institution in North America, and competitive sport has existed in virtually every culture throughout history. Many children are exposed to organized competitive sport early in life, and their successes and failures may either enhance or jeopardize their self-concepts. Because youth sport is institutionalized, we examine select literature concerning some of its social, physical, and psychological effects on children.

Beneficial Consequences of Youth Sport Programs

When the youth sport movement was conceived and initially enacted, it was presumed that sport involvement would facilitate the development of desirable personality and social characteristics. Accordingly, the initial objectives of such programs included the development of wholesome personalities; the building of physical fitness (i.e., strength, agility, coordination, and stamina); the appreciation of sportsmanship and fair play; the creation of socially redeeming experiences that stimulate cooperation with others (teamwork); and cultivation of leadership skills.[61]

Theoretically, there are a variety of potentially positive outcomes of organized sport competition. There are opportunities to practice and develop specific sport skills and apply them in actual game situations. Sports participation can develop physical fitness, nurture cognitive skills such as making quick decisions under pressure, encourage strategy planning, and provide an understanding of the body and the mechanical and physical principles of movement. In the affective domain, there lies much concern and controversy. Proponents claim that competitive sports help develop sound body images leading to positive self-concepts, independence, favorable attitudes toward physical activity and to life itself, self-identity, strong character, and sound morals and provide challenges in which children can experience success and achievement. On the other hand, some claim that the structure of competition or the way in which it is handled, or both, not only defeats these realizations but actually has negative repercussions.

Unfortunately, there is not an abundance of concrete research evidence to back up either opinion. Dickey found no significant differences in social and personal adjustment between competitors and noncompetitors in Little League baseball, either before or after the season.[62] Maul and Thomas found no significant differences in self-concepts of third-graders—both participants and nonparticipants—in community gymnastics.[63] Based on these and other findings, Ash concluded that there are few or no personality differences between participants in organized athletics and nonparticipants between the ages of eight and sixteen.[64] Because personality profiles of participants differ from those of nonparticipants after age sixteen, Ash maintains that those who continue to compete do so as a result of self-selection processes. In reviewing the empirical findings regarding the social benefits of sport participation, Stevenson concluded that neither positive nor negative attitudes and values appeared to result from such engagement.[65] Recall Mantel and Vander Velden's study that found a correlation between the age of participant and the value placed on victory and success (vs. fair play); younger participants seemed to value fair play, whereas older participants considered success (wins and losses and performance) more important.

Questionable and/or Negative Consequences of Youth Sport Programs

In this section, we examine the five following areas in youth sports in terms of their socialization consequences: (a) win–loss emphasis, (b) cutting, (c) differential maturity levels, (d) adult intrusion, and (e) psychological effects. These are among the most important issues connected with organized youth sport programs.

Win–Loss Emphasis.

"Winning isn't everything, it's the only thing."—Vince Lombardi

"Defeat is worse than death because you have to live with defeat."—Bill Musselman

"Nice guys finish last."—Leo Durocher

"Winning isn't all that matters. I don't care how many games you win, it's how many championships you win that counts."—Ed McCluskey

These familiar quotes,[66] reflecting the **win–loss emphasis,** were made by coaches involved in pressure-cooker sport; men who were required to win if they wished to retain their jobs and who valued winning as a primary goal. Professionals are held in high esteem and widely publicized in the media. The danger is that both children and adults may idolize and emulate these sports figures and imitate not only their actions but endorse their philosophies as well. These heroes are or were involved in the big business of dollars and of winning, and they applied their philosophies and methods to players who chose to participate. Parents and youth coaches sometimes reflect these attitudes—sometimes called the **professional model of youth sports**—without giving serious thought to the psychological, social, and physical needs of children. Children need to learn skills in an environment that provides intrinsic rewards. They should not need to singlemindedly strive for winning records.

Winning, for most, is more satisfying than losing and typically is the immediate, short-term goal of many sport contests. Winning is often thought to be a bad word in the context of youth sport, but it need not be. There is nothing wrong with winning in one sense; the lessons of life are replete with victories and defeats. However, children need to learn to enjoy the *process* of sports participation. This encompasses mastering body skills like running, jumping, throwing, hitting, catching, and kicking a ball. Children's abilities to perform these psychomotor tasks depend on their physical, social, and intellectual stage of development. Early maturers will excel in these activities, but slow maturers may be labeled by others and themselves as unathletic. A serious danger in highly competitive organized sports is that they encourage children to become superstars, thus relegating the slow, uncoordinated, or awkward to the sidelines. As a consequence, some children fail to learn to enjoy and participate in sports, and these same children often become the adult spectators and non-participants[67] in their later years and/or sport misanthrops.

Winning can be viewed as secondary to the process of developing fundamental skills and exercising them to the best of one's ability. Winning does not prove that one is a better person, only that one performed better. Conversely, losing does not make one a lesser person. Unfortunately, when sports become highly organized under adult supervision, winning and losing are often placed in a perspective that causes children to suffer. As Michener exhorts, "The evil . . . begins with adults who desperately want to win championships. They use children, often not their own, to achieve this dream, and in doing so, pervert the normal experience of youth."[68]

Winning often becomes more important than the game itself or, more disheartening, than the children involved. When this occurs, many deleterious practices may surface. Young athletes with lesser abilities do not receive adequate attention, coaches and parents chastise their children for making mistakes, cheating and rule breaking become commonplace, and the fun of playing sports becomes work. When winning overshadows the game itself, it becomes a source of personal evaluation that supersedes the game. There are feelings of success for the winner and failure for the loser. Although one often hears, as Grantland Rice uttered, that it's not whether you win or lose, but how you play the game, our society, in fact, places high value on achievement and success. In Western sport, *winning* is synonymous with *success*. After investing much time and energy in preparation for a tournament or big meet, individuals allow winning to acquire an increased importance. As children attain higher levels of performance and move into more competitive contests, reasons for participating other than winning often fall by the wayside.

What is **competition** and what are its socialization consequences in youth sport? According to Martens "Competition consists of activities directed . . . toward meeting a standard or achieving a goal in which performance by a person or by his [sic] group is compared and evaluated relative to that of selected other persons or groups."[69] Rausch and colleagues studied whether competitive games increased participants' aggression.[70] Boys between the ages of ten and twelve were observed in their natural environment; 89% of their interactions were deemed friendly. But when engaged in a competitive game, 42% of their acts were judged unfriendly. Rausch et al. concluded that, "the situation sets a tone influencing the likelihood that certain acts will occur, and competitive situations make unfriendly behavior highly probable."[71]

Children, as well as adults, often base their self-evaluations on their athletic performances. Roberts' study of 200 Little League baseball players revealed that consistent winners attributed winning to their high ability (and failed to see that ability was affected by occasional losses).[72] Consistent losers attributed their losing to limited ability and felt that the game's outcome was beyond their control. Therefore, they would be unlikely to respond to repeated failures with effort and determination and would be more likely to quit the sport.[73] The reason is that motivation to engage in an activity is affected by the actor's perception of the probability of success. When success is seen as likely, motivation is high; when success is seen as unlikely, motivation is low. Orlick and Botterill[74] discovered that many of the dropouts (Vignette 5.3) from competitive teams quit because of the emphasis on competition, little playing time, and/or because their experiences were not successful or rewarding.[75]

The essential nature of our sports produces more losers than winners. In a gymnastics meet, there may be 50 contestants competing but only one winner. In a swimming meet, typically, only one has the best time. The structure of organized sports contributes to this list of losers. There are elimination tournaments, playoffs, championships, all-star teams, and rewards that stress improvement, good sportsmanship, and hard work. The overjustification hypothesis proposed by Greene and Lepper states that when children receive an expected external reward for participation in phys-

☐ VIGNETTE 5.3

Some Reasons Why Children Quit Youth Sports

Sport psychologist Rainer Martens has advanced the following reasons for children relinquishing their sports participation. Assuredly, these are not all the reasons; however, they do appear to cover some of the basic causes of attrition in youth sport programs.

1. *Not Getting to Play*—Some children spend much effort and time in practicing a sport only to sit on the bench for a game or even an entire season. Orlick's survey indicated that 90% of the males questioned would rather *play* on a losing team than sit on the bench on a winning team. Since playing is more highly valued than winning, children who do not play may drop out.

2. *Negative Reinforcement*—Children are involved in the learning of sport skills, and miscues are an important part of the learning process. Consistent with learning theory, negative reinforcement and criticism may only dissuade them from further participation.

3. *Mismatching*—When children are mismatched in terms of size, the smaller ones are often constantly defeated and fear physical, social, and/or psychological harm.

4. *Psychological Stress*—When parents, coaches, or peers demand more of children than they are capable of giving, stress may result, which causes the sport experience to be unpleasant.

5. *Failure*—Repeated failure causes anxiety, decreased motivation, and a devalued self-concept. Children who fail, or even think they will fail, probably will not enjoy the activity and will terminate it.

6. *Overorganization*—Fun is the primary purpose for engaging in sports. When the fun is removed by highly organized and regimental practices, a major incentive for participation is gone.

SOURCE: Rainer Martens, "The Uniqueness of the Youth Athlete: Psychological Considerations," *American Journal of Sports Medicine*, 8, no. 5 (1980), pp. 382–383.

☐

ical activity, the reward "overjustifies" the behavior.[76] As a result, children define participation as a means to the goal of acquiring the expected reward.

Because competition is highly structured, games and sports are geared for the success of only a few, only the more talented children experience continued success. Ordinarily, failure to achieve some success discourages participation and eventually leads to discontinuation of the activity. The trend is for players to disengage from organized sport as they grow older. Statistics from the Canadian Amateur Hockey Association show that of the 600,000 players registered, 53% were under age twelve, 35% were between the ages of twelve and fifteen, and 11% were over fifteen.[77] To some degree, it would be expected that a smaller percentage of children participate in sports as they grow older, because of changing interests and increased opportunities in other areas (music, art, drama, and so forth). However, these children may not have their needs met through sport competition.

Cutting. Not every child, or adult for that matter, needs a physical conditioning regimen that produces the proverbial Charles Atlas or Arnold Schwartzenegger physique. Just the same, the acquisition and cultivation of sport skills can teach a child some valuable psychomotor skills like running, jumping, skipping, throwing, eye–hand coordination, and how to apply the right amount of force to move an object. A sport program can contribute to good muscle tone, proper posture, strong and healthy bones and joints, as well as stamina and endurance. With these positive physical consequences of sport participation in mind, it is indeed ironic that children are frequently eliminated from sport competition. Why are children cut?

Eliminating children from participation is a serious matter; in fact, some contend that it is the most critical problem in children's sports.[78] Sometimes youth are removed for unintentional reasons while, other times, their elimination is deliberate. Coaches may provide the impetus for a child's termination of a sport; sometimes it might be significant others in the child's social environment such as parents or relatives; other times it might be the child's choice.

Sometimes children are eliminated inadvertently. The unskilled players may not receive much attention in practice and then collect splinters on the bench during the season. Girls may be poked fun at for participating, and coaches may chastise players for making mistakes. Whatever the reason, the result is that children may feel unworthy or unwanted and experience failure. The values of sports should be extended to all children who want to participate. According to Martens, "It is ridiculous to promote participation on one hand, and then to cut interested individuals from the team or to any way limit their participation."[79] Since all children can benefit from learning sport skills, there is reason to encourage them because they will generally improve, regardless of their skill level. Many of the children who lose interest early will later become inactive, and maybe cynical, adults.

Cutting, whether intentional or not, may be viewed as an example of **aversive sport socialization,** a process that deters individuals from future sport participation. Not only can this process produce immediate physical, social, and psychological stress, but it can also produce a long-term spiral of negative repercussions. Orlick and Botterill have written:

> The process of cutting is a vicious circle for the one who doesn't make it. He [sic] is cut because he is not good enough to make it and is consequently given no opportunity to practice on a regular basis so that he can become good enough to make it—so he is rejected again the following year. We not only are doing an injustice to the individual but also are cutting our own sporting throats. Twenty years later, these cut individuals do not support our programs. We have firmly entrenched in them a negative feeling about sport. The least that this negative feeling will do is to relegate these people to the role of spectators, which is bad enough in itself.[80]

Being rejected in sports at a young age can produce a sense of total rejection, a perfidious denial of one's self-worth. This is particularly true for males for which sport is a functional equivalent to a rite of passage and indeed a source of popularity and social recognition. Moreover, it may well condition one's future sport interests, perspectives, and behaviors as well.

Maturity Levels.   Another reason that children may experience failure and frustration in sports stems from differential **maturity levels.** Many organized youth sports are structured into age-graded hierarchies. There may be significant differences in size and strength among children of the same age, and even greater differences when children's ages range over several years. From the ages of about ten to sixteen years, the diversity of individual differences in physical structure is greater than at any other time in life. There could be a difference of sixty months in the skeletal age for two boys of the same chronological age. Martens claims: "For two boys, both 13 years old, one could have a skeletal age typical for boys aged 10 and the other for boys aged 15. These same boys may vary as much as 15 inches in height and 90 pounds in weight."[81] In sports, where size makes a difference, those who are small or late in maturing are not likely to be successful, even if their skill level is high. Therefore, to enhance a child's chances for success, levels should be determined by maturity sorting rather than by chronological age. Although skeletal age is the most accurate indicant of maturity, it would be impractical to implement. Maturity sorting is done according to size (age, height, weight) and skill ability in those sports in which the opponent is another person or team and the competition is direct. Age ranges could be limited to reduce size variations. It should be remembered that the purpose of the sport is to have fun and to learn skills within the structured setting at levels of performance appropriate to the participant.

Understanding the significant effect of chronological age on sport performance also requires recognition of a hidden dimension that overzealous adults may inadvertently forget: Children, from a maturational standpoint, are not always capable of performing sport maneuvers designed for adults. Consider batting in baseball. The individual's ability to track a ball with the eyes from the pitcher to the catcher influences batting prowess, which is obvious. What is not as obvious is a point raised in the following observation by Pascoe: "Up to age six, children can track a ball only as it moves horizontally. From six to seven and a half, they can track a ball that's moving vertically or horizontally, but if it's moving in an arc they probably won't be able to follow it visually until they are eight or nine and a half."[82] Typically, children must reach a certain level of physical maturity before they can successfully perform certain psychomotor tasks. By analogy, bowel training is virtually impossible before a child learns to control the sphincter muscles. To expect such a feat before a certain level of maturity is achieved can produce undue psychological stress.

Of equal concern is the fact the physical damage can occur when youngsters model their actions on those of mature adults. Adult pitchers are capable of throwing curve balls, to use a familiar example, without damaging their arms or elbows (although there are even cases of professional athletes who have incurred such damage). X-rays reveal that throwing certain pitches or excessive pitching can permanently damage a child's arm and elbow. The empirical evidence on this matter is, however, equivocal. One study did not find more elbow problems among former Little League players than among nonplayers.[83] Although opinions on this matter vary, it is wise to recommend that children who have not yet reached middle adolescence avoid throwing certain pitches. In youth football, there is concern with certain practices that can produce knee and neck injuries. One medical research team believes that certain blocking and tackling techniques can have a "shearing effect" on bones not fully matured.[84] Even though the possibilities of physical damage from sports participation have generated varying contentions, it makes good sense to protect young children from situations and conditions that may jeopardize their growing bodies and activities later in life. Another pragmatic consideration of youth sport is the inclusion of parallel or "house" leagues. These programs are for the slow-maturing or physically underdeveloped child or for those juveniles who prefer sport experiences with a mild competitive ambience. These seem to be significant adjuncts to the more competitive programs.

Adult Intrusion.   Sport, as discussed in Chapter 1, may be conceptualized as a type of game in which the physical skill factor is paramount. Devereux nostalgically and critically asked the question "What has happened to the culture of children's games in America?"[85] In reflecting on his own childhood games—red rover, capture the flag, blind man's bluff, and leapfrog—he recalls the spontaneity with which they were executed. These games, says Devereux, were characterized by modest levels of competition and organization. Present-day youth sport programs stand in striking contrast: They are highly organized and can even foster cutthroat behaviors. According to Figler, "This greater level of organization and the control necessarily taken over by adults in order to achieve this organization are the main factors that distinguish youth sport from childhood play and games."[86] Consider the following situation as reported by Pascoe:

> The West Springfield (Massachusetts) Hockey Association was having another championship season last winter. But in the locker room it was civil war. Some of the players had quit and their parents were consulting lawyers about the terms of the youngsters' releases, which allowed them to play for other teams. What was at stake? Athletic scholarships? A chance to play with the pros? Nothing like that. This was Pee Wee hockey, and the players were only eight to ten years old. Some of their parents were simply miffed that their sons had been assigned to the scrub team instead of the first string.[87]

Undoubtedly, the West Springfield parents were extreme in their reactions, but their zeal for youth sports is not atypical. Competitive youth sport has become serious business. From the first organized youth sports program, Little League Baseball (established in 1939), parents have spearheaded the formation of a wide assortment of juvenile athletic programs and such programs are available for children as young as six.

Adult influence has been discussed in terms of the win–loss emphasis. However, adults are also the ones who organize, finance, and administer the sport programs for children. Therefore, adult values, expectations, and standards are sometimes imposed on the children who participate. Most involved adults (administrators, coaches, and parents) are probably truly interested in providing redeeming experiences for children through sports activities. Nobody wants to be a bad parent or coach. The team parents from my son's soccer team showed great enthusiasm and support for the players, before, during, and after the games. This is not always the case, however, and codes of ethics for youth sport programs are commonplace. To read about competitive sport and children is to read many horror stories about parents' and coaches' attitudes and behaviors.[88] There are accounts of how coaches drill their players mercilessly, expect them to practice and play like adults, taunt them if they are afraid, call them names, tell the poorly skilled to stay home during important games, punish their miscues with extra running, and encourage them to cheat. There are also stories about parents who are overly critical, who get into fights with the umpires, who scream obscenities at the players, who will not talk to their children after a loss, and who gain a position on the team for their child by rewarding the coach in some way. Four hypotheses for why adults dominate children's sports have been proposed by McPherson:[89]

1. Parents and coaches who have dull and unexciting lives become involved "to receive gratification and prestige" through the sport medium.
2. Parents and coaches are involved to "vicariously experience success" that eludes them in the adult world.
3. Parents are involved to facilitate "the attainment of career aspirations" that they hold for their children in the sport world.
4. Parents are involved to ensure that the sport experience is a healthy one and to protect their child from "coaches who have a win-at-all-costs philosophy."

When the suspect parental motivations occur, there are many losers—the parents, the coaches, and the children.

Some evidence shows that the win-at-all-costs ethic has permeated some youth sport programs. This perspective has, on occasions, cast an ugly shadow on children's athletics. Consider the case of Craig Blum, a 5-foot, 7 1/2-inch, 122-pound fourteen-year-old. For more than a week, he had been on a crash diet to reduce his weight to 116 pounds so that he could qualify for an age–weight-graded football league. To reduce his weight to the required level, he had drastically diminished his caloric intake by drinking only liquids three days before the weigh-in, by using a sauna, and by taking water pills (which contain caffeine and ammonium chloride) that were administered by his coach. Like many drugs, this one—known as Aqua Ban—was viewed differently by medical authorities. Some believed it was harmless; others thought it could produce intestinal irritation and was risky for individuals with liver disorders. Shortly thereafter, an editorial appeared in the *Washington Star.*[90] Gene Rovello, Blum's coach, was called "a local symbol of a sad phenomenon: The American habit of ingesting pills and relying on drugs of every sort to remedy problems." The editorial continued with the following warning: "If the use of medication is common in youth athletics, parents who are not captive to the notion of winning at any cost had better insert themselves into an appalling situation with urgency." Such accounts of Pee Wee pill-poppers is testimony to a sport philosophy that seems out of bounds.

Here's another case in point. This one combines the winning-at-all-costs ethic with adult intrusion. An investigation of the Thirty-sixth Annual Soap Box Derby (Akron, Ohio) revealed that one of the young participants was driving a vehicle carrying a strong electric magnet hidden in the nose of the car. When activated, the magnet would follow the backward fall of the iron plate, making the car spring forward a little faster than a competitor's car. The official Derby rules mandated that youngsters (between the ages of eleven and fifteen) could build their own cars at a maximum cost of $75 and that the cars should coast unaided down a macadam track called Derby Downs. The boy's uncle, Robert Lange, Sr., who was primarily responsible for this unethical maneuver, admitted to a host of improper and illegal acts, including testing the racer in a wind tunnel to ensure that it was aerodynamically sound, inserting the magnet, and spending thousands of dollars in its production and testing. Lange, when interviewed, was not particularly penitent about his misdeed and rationalized his behavior by saying:

It is common knowledge that eleven-year-olds cannot build winning racers. That was why there were adult professional builders who build cars for sale to participants or race the cars themselves with young, lightweight drivers who are known as chauffeurs.

After seeing my nephew work hundreds of hours to build his own car, knowing that he would be competing . . . against professionally built cars, and against cars that would be equipped with a magnetic nose, I determined that he should build and install a magnetic nose so as to be competitive. I knew that this was a violation of the official . . . rules and consider it now to be a serious mistake in judgment.[91]

Sport sociologist Jonathan Brower offered these sobering comments:

Laws exist to protect children at work and school, but their "play" as governed by adults goes unchecked. Playground ball is a pressure-packed thing for boys. For good athletes it may be fun. At least they can tolerate it, but for boys who are not good athletes and who try to please their managers and parents, it's a matter of tension.

Parents get too caught up in the win ethic. One father proudly told a friend, "My kid doesn't care about sportsmanship. He says winning is what's important." This thirst for victory and its accompanying competitiveness was far stronger among managers and coaches than players.[92]

Psychological Injury.   In some youth sport settings, children may be subject to intense emotional stress or **psychological injury** caused by fear and anxiety, concern about physical safety, and doubts about performances and outcomes. This anxiety may emerge if children are ignored, chastized, or made to feel that they are no good. Scanlan and Passer's study of preadolescent boy soccer players showed that losing players evidenced more postgame anxiety than winning players.[93] Children who experience anxiety in sport competition may try to avoid failure by shying away from active participation, by developing excuses, or by refusing to try new things. Orlick found that 75% of nonparticipating children thought they were not good enough to make the team but would go out for a team if they thought they would be accepted.[94] Two situational factors that determine the amount of threat perceived are the ratio of success to failure and the amount of attention focused on the children as they perform.[95] Children's attitudes and feelings in sport are affected by the perspectives offered by the people who are important to them; namely, their families, teachers, coaches, and peers.

From a social psychological perspective, we can understand the manner in which a child forms a self-concept in sport competition by drawing on the lead of Charles Horton Cooley.[96] Cooley's formulation, the **looking-glass self theory,** proposes the following processes in the development of self-evaluation: (a) imagining how we appear to others, (b) imagining how the others are evaluating us, and (c) forming an impression of who we are. Youngsters pick up various cues—smiles, frowns, back pats, words of praise or condemnation, and so forth—that provide the raw material for their own self-evaluations. Such cues are provided by coaches, parents, teammates, peers, and others who are significant to the individual's self-assessment. If children pick up negative vibrations from their significant others—whether such impressions are real or imagined—they will not likely receive the reinforcement necessary to continue a particular endeavor. Hence, the self-fulfilling prophecy may come into play. In the same vein, Jane Frederick has said, "What else but sports gives you an absolute measurement of where you stand and how much you've progressed?" Again, it must be underscored that the negative consequences of sport participation appear to be more probable when the professional model of youth sport is imposed on children's organized games.

One of the psychological (although it has physical aspects as well) consequences of youth sport has been described by Figler as the **Little League Syndrome**.[97] He argues that this malady has three forms: (a) *washout,* (b) *burnout,* and (c) *superstar.* Youngsters who lack the physical skills may be criticized and discouraged in blatant or subtle ways; regardless, the net outcome is the same—the child assiduously avoids sport competition for fear of failure. At an early age, these youngsters are "washed up." John Palmer, a member of the 1954 Little League world championship team, describes his experience. In 1955, Palmer graduated to the Babe Ruth League because of his age and had to try out for the team. After the tryout, he was told by the coach to look in the local paper for a roster of players who made the clubs.

> So one morning, sure enough the paper comes, and the team rosters are in it; I look through all of the names, and my name wasn't there. I was mortified. I didn't make the team! . . . I said to myself, "This is really ridiculous." I don't remember ever feeling so betrayed in my life; like here I was a twelve year old, playing left field on a team that won it all, and now, at thirteen, I'm not good enough to make a team. That finished me with baseball. I was thirteen years old, and I was washed up.
>
> All through high school, I had this feeling that I wasn't going to commit myself to anything unless somebody committed himself to me first; I wasn't going to risk getting let down again.[98]

The *burnout syndrome* is manifest in those young athletes who have experienced too many excesses (i.e., practice, criticism, success, or failure), too quickly, and often too early in life. Joey Jay, the first Little League ballplayer to make the transition to the majors, captured the burnout concept when he said, "Our team went all the way to the 1948 Little League World Series and our shortstop had his picture in *Life* magazine. By the time that boy entered high school, he had lost all interest in baseball."[99] Apparently, the excesses of early sport competition prompted the boy's decision to forego further sports participation.

The *superstar malady* has been described as an excessively competitive attitude and behavior that is manifested by constant comparisons of one's performance with the performances of others and by the continual need of approval from others. Such an attitude can lead to serious psychological pressure, as was demonstrated by one of "destiny's darlings." A team from Schenectady, New York, won the Little League baseball championship in 1954. Twenty years later, Ralbovsky interviewed members of this team for their perceptions of their youth sport experience. Jim Barbieri poignantly recalled his feelings:

> Those games weren't fun; there was no fun to it at all. The pressure was unbelievable; you know, if I was ever going to get an ulcer, I would have gotten it then. . . . It was especially tough because we lost the year before; we had this additional pressure on us to make sure we don't blow the thing again. All that pressure, I think, gave us this killer instinct; . . . the only way to insure that we would win was for us to go out there and be as mean and as ruthless as we could; . . . we had a job to do, we had a mission to accomplish, and nobody, nobody, was going to prevent us from doing it.[100]

❑ SUMMARY

Socialization refers to the processes through which a biological organism is fashioned into an adult social being. Sport roles require learning just as other roles do. To explain socialization into sport, we considered *social learning theory*. How individuals acquire and perform social roles is the focus of this conceptual approach, which has three features of particular significance to sport: (a) *reinforcement,* (b) *coaching,* and (c) *observational learning*. We considered various agents of sport socialization, such as family, peer group, school, community, and mass media, and examined factors contributing to participation in sport and characterizing sport involvement. Sport involvement may be behavioral, affective, or cognitive, or some combination of the three. Because much sport involvement is of a secondary nature, we explored the role of the fan and some of the personal functions of fandom. To explain socialization via sport, we analyzed the values expressed in the dominant American sport creed and discovered that the available evidence does not consistently support the traditional claims that sports invariably produce desirable traits.

One of the most significant and earliest sport socialization experiences, *organized youth sport programs,* have been maligned in recent years. Five controversies within these organizations were addressed: (a) the *win–loss emphasis,* (b) *cutting,* (c) *differential maturity levels,* (d) *adult influences,* and (e) *psychological injury*. Not all juvenile sport programs stress winning, but when the professional model is imposed on youth programs, numerous undesirable consequences may result. Cutting, or eliminating children from sport programs, can be a serious problem, and those cut may experience *aversive sport socialization* experiences, which later condition their future sport interests, perspectives, and behaviors. The child's maturity level is a significant variable that affects a participant's experience of success or failure. The role of adults is preeminent in organized youth sport programs, because adults typically organize, finance, and administer these programs. Expecting too much from a youngster at an early age can and has produced various forms of psychological damage, as is evidenced by *Little League syndrome*.

❑ KEY CONCEPTS

Socialization
Socialization into Sports
Socialization via Sports
Significant Others (Reference Groups)
Social Learning Theory:
  Reinforcement
  Coaching
  Observational Learning (Modeling)
Agents of Sport Socialization:
  Family
  Peer Group
  School
  Community
  Mass Media

Types of Involvement in Sports:
  Primary
  Secondary
  Behavioral
  Affective
  Cognitive
Normative Social Influence
Success Phobia
Professional Model of Youth Sports
Win–Loss Emphasis
Competition
Cutting
Aversive Sport Socialization
Maturity Levels

Adult Influence
Psychological Injury

Looking-Glass Self Theory
Little League Syndrome

☐ ENDNOTES

1. LEONARD BROOM & PHILIP SELZNICK, *Sociology* (New York: Harper & Row, 1968), p. 84.

2. BERNARD MALAMUD, *The Natural* (New York: Farrar, Straus, Giroux, 1961), pp. 66–67. Reprinted with permission.

3. ROLF CARLSON, "The Socialization of Elite Tennis Players in Sweden: An Analysis of the Players' Backgrounds and Development," *Sociology of Sport Journal* 5, no. 3 (1988) pp. 241–256.

4. ELTON McNEIL, *Human Socialization* (Belmont, CA: Brooks/Cole, 1969).

5. LAWRENCE SEVERY, J.C. BRIGHAM, & BARRY R. SCHLENKER, *A Contemporary Introduction to Social Psychology* (New York: McGraw-Hill, 1976), pp. 134–175.

6. *Coaching* in this context means direct teaching.

7. B.F. SKINNER, *Contingencies of Reinforcement* (East Norwalk, CT: Appleton-Century-Crofts, 1969).

8. A. STRAUSS, *Role Theory: Concepts and Research* (New York: Wiley, 1966).

9. ALBERT BANDURA, *Social Learning Theory* (Morristown, NJ: General Learning Press, 1971).

10. JONATHAN J. BROWER, "The Racial Basis of the Division of Labor Among Players in the National Football League as a Function of Stereotypes." Paper presented at the annual meeting of the Pacific Sociological Association, Portland OR, 1972.

11. Implicit in this research is the idea that the general value orientations of the larger culture are distilled into the normative structure of society and, through socialization, become imparted to and internalized by individuals. Agents and agencies of socialization are vitally important in this socialization process.

12. HOWARD L. NIXON, II, "Sport, Socialization, and Youth: Some Proposed Research Directions," *Review of Sport and Leisure* 1 (Fall, 1976), pp. 45–61.

13. JOHN W. LOY, BARRY D. McPHERSON, & GERALD KENYON, *Sport and Social Systems: A Guide to the Analysis, Problems and Literature* (Reading, MA: Addison-Wesley, 1978), p. 226.

14. EVERITT K. WILSON, *Sociology: Rules, Roles, and Relationships* (Homewood, IL: Dorsey Press, 1966), p. 92.

15. PETE AXTHELM, *The City Game* (New York: Harper & Row, 1970).

16. *Op. cit.,*[13] p. 238.

17. *Ibid.,* p. 229.

18. D. STANLEY EITZEN, *Sport in Contemporary Society* (New York: St. Martin's, 1979), p. 115.

19. GERALD S. KENYON & BARRY D. McPHERSON, "Becoming Involved in Physical Activity and Sport: A Process of Socialization," *Physical Activity: Human Growth and Development,* ed. G.L. Rarick (New York: Academic Press, 1973), pp. 303–332.
    JOHN W. LOY, JR. & ALAN INGHAM, "Play, Games, and Sport in the Psychosocial Development of Children and Youth," *Physical Activity: Human Growth and Development,* ed. G.L. Rarick (New York: Academic Press, 1973), pp. 257–302.
    GEORGE H. SAGE, "Socialization and Sport," *Sport and American Society: Selected Readings,* ed. G. Sage (Reading, MA: Addison-Wesley, 1974), pp. 162–172.

20. *The Miller Lite Report on American Attitudes Toward Sports* (Milwaukee: Miller Brewing Company, 1983), p. 62.

21. PAUL HOCH, *Rip Off: The Big Game* (Garden City, NY: Anchor Books, 1972), p. 137.

22. ELDON E. SNYDER, "Athletic Dressing Room Slogans as Folklore: A Means of Socialization," *International Review of Sport Sociology* 7 (1972), pp. 89–102. Snyder has demonstrated that athletic dressing room slogans are a means of socializing sport participants.

23. KENYON & McPHERSON, *op. cit.*[19]

24. JON M. SHEPARD, *Sociology* (St. Paul: West, 1984), p. 164.

25. GERALD S. KENYON & TOM M. GROGG, *Contemporary Psychology of Sport: Proceedings of*

the Second International Congress of Psychology (Chicago: The Athletic Institute, 1970).

26. *Op. cit.*,[20] p. 42.

27. ELMER SPREITZER & ELDON E. SNYDER, "Socialization into Sport: An Exploratory Analysis," *Research Quarterly* 47 (May 1976), pp. 238–245.

28. ROBERT LYND & HELEN LYND, *Middletown* (New York: Harcourt, Brace, 1919).
A.B. HOLLINGSHEAD, *Elmtown's Youth* (New York: John Wiley, 1949).
C. WAYNE GORDON, *The Social System of the High School* (Glencoe, IL: Free Press, 1957).
JAMES S. COLEMAN, "Athletics in High School," *Annals of the American Academy of Political & Social Science* 338 (1961), pp. 33–43.

29. A. WOHL & E. PUDELKIEWICS, "Theoretical and Methodological Assumptions of Research on the Processes of Involvement in Sport and Sport Socialization," *International Review of Sport Sociology* 7 (1972), pp. 69–84;
GERALD S. KENYON & BARRY D. MC-PHERSON, "An Approach to the Study of Sport Socialization," *International Review of Sport Sociology* 1, no. 9 (1974), pp.127–139.

30. ELDON E. SNYDER & ELMER A. SPREITZER, "Family Influence and Involvement in Sports," *Research Quarterly* 44 (1973), pp. 249–255.

31. JUDITH BISCHOFF, "Influence of Significant Others in the Sports Participation of Female and Male Athletes." Paper presented at North American Sociology of Sport Society, Boston, 6–10 November 1985.

32. GARY SAILES, "Sport Socialization Comparisons Among Black and White Male Athletes and Non-athletes." Paper presented at North American Sociology of Sport Society, Boston, 6–10 November 1985.

33. GERALD S. KENYON, "Sport Involvement: A Conceptual Go and and Some Consequences Thereof," *Aspects of Contemporary Sport Sociology*, ed. G.S. Kenyon (Chicago: The Athletic Institute, 1969).
HARRY EDWARDS, *Sociology of Sport* (Homewood, IL: Dorsey Press, 1973).
Op. cit.,[12] pp. 46–47.

34. KENYON, *op. cit.*[33]

35. SNYDER & SPREITZER, "Orientations Toward Work and Leisure as Predictors of Sports Involvement, *Research Quarterly* 45 (1974), pp.

398–406. Snyder and Spreitzer used three items to measure affective involvement: (1) "Sports are a way for me to relax," (2) "Sports are a waste of time," and (3) "I receive little satisfaction from sports."

36. *Ibid.* Snyder and Spreitzer measured this variable by having respondents match sport personalities with their appropriate sport.

37. EDWARDS, *op. cit.*,[33] pp. 238–239.

38. JO THOMAS, "British Soccer Fan: Why So Warlike?" *The New York Times* (31 May 1985), p. 5.

39. ARNOLD BEISSER, *The Madness in Sports* (East Norwalk, CT: Appleton-Century-Crofts, 1967), p. 126.

40. WALTER E. SCHAFER, "Some Sources and Consequences of Interscholastic Athletics, *Sociology of Sport,* ed. G.S. Kenyon (Chicago: The Athletic Institute, 1969), p. 33.

41. R.B. CIALDINI, R.J. BORDEN, A. THORNE, M.R. WALKER, S. FREEMAN, & L.R. SLOAN, "Basking in Reflected Glory: Three (Football) Field Studies," *Social Psychology of the Self-Concept,* eds. M. Rosenberg & H.B. Kaplan. (Arlington Heights, IL: Harlan Davidson, 1982), pp. 88–101.

42. ALBERT H. HASTORF & HADLEY CANTRIL, "They Saw a Game: A Case Study," *Journal of Abnormal and Social Psychology* 48 (1954), pp. 129–134.

43. MANN, cited in Edwin P. Hollander, *Social Psychology* (New York: Oxford, 1976), p. 25.

44. *Op. cit.*[42]

45. EDWARDS, *op. cit.*,[33] pp. 243–247.

46. JOHN E. GIBSON, "Sport Fans," *Family Weekly* (26 April 1981), p. 29.

47. MERRILL J. MELNICK, "The Sports Fan: A Teaching Guide and Bibliography," *Sociology of Sport Journal* 6, no. 2 (1989), pp. 167–175.

48. GEORGE H. MEAD, *Mind, Self, and Society* (Chicago: University of Chicago Press, 1934), pp. 154, 159.

49. HARRY WEBB, "Professionalization of Attitudes Toward Play Among Adolescents," *Aspects of Contemporary Sport Sociology,* ed. G.S. Kenyon (Chicago: The Athletic Institute, 1969), pp. 161–178.

50. RICHARD C. MANTEL & LEE VANDER VELDEN, "The Relationship Between the Professionalization of Attitude Toward Play of Preadoles-

cent Boys and Participation in Organized Sport," *Sport and American Society: Selected Readings,* ed. G. Sage (Reading, MA: Addison-Wesley, 1974), pp. 172–178.

51. DEANE E. RICHARDSON, "Ethical Conduct in Sport Situations," *National College Physical Education Association for Men Proceedings* 66 (1962), pp. 98–103.

52. JAY J. COAKLEY, *Sport in Society: Issues and Controversies* (St. Louis, MO: C.V. Mosby, 1978), p. 107.

53. BRUCE C. OGILVIE & THOMAS A. TUTKO, "Sport: If You Want to Build Character, Try Something Else," *Psychology Today* (October 1971), pp. 61–63.

54. *Ibid.,* p. 62.

55. TERRY ORLICK, "The Sports Environment, A Capacity to Enhance, A Capacity to Destroy." Paper presented at the Sixth Canadian Symposium of Psycho-Motor Learning and Sports Psychology, 1974.

56. H. KELLEY, "Two Functions of Reference Groups," *Readings in Social Psychology,* eds. G. Swanson, T. Newcomb, & E. Hartley (New York: Holt, Rinehart, & Winston, 1952).

57. ELDON E. SNYDER, "Aspects of Socialization in Sports and Physical Education," *Quest* 14 (June 1970), pp. 1–7.

58. LEON FESTINGER, *A Theory of Cognitive Dissonance* (New York: Harper & Row, 1957).

59. *Op. cit.*[32]

60. STEPHEN K. FIGLER, *Sport and Play in American Life* (Philadelphia: W.B. Saunders, 1981), pp. 79–105.

61. *Ibid.*

62. DICKEY, cited in *Children in Sport: Contemporary Anthology,* eds. Richard Magill, Michael J. Ash, & Frank L. Smoll (Champaign, IL: Human Kinetics, 1978).

63. MAUL AND THOMAS, cited in *Children in Sport: Contemporary Anthology,* eds. Richard Magill, Michael J. Ash, & Frank L. Smoll (Champaign, IL: Human Kinetics, 1978), pp. 149–157.

64. MICHAEL J. ASH, "The Role of Research in Children's Competitive Athletics," in *Children in Sport: Contemporary Anthology,* eds. Richard Magill, Michael J. Ash, & Frank L. Smoll (Champaign, IL: Human Kinetics, 1978), p. 180.

65. CHRISTOPHER L. STEVENSON, "Socialization Effects Participation in Sport: A Critical Review of the Research," *Research Quarterly* 44 (1975), pp. 287–301.

66. JAMES MICHENER, *Sports in America* (New York: Fawcett-Crest Books, Random House, 1976), p. 520.

67. ELIZABETH JEAN PASCOE, "How Sports Can Hurt Your Child," *McCall's* (May 1978), pp. 49–50.

68. *Op. cit.,*[66] p. 152.

69. RAINER MARTENS, *Joy and Sadness in Children's Sports* (Champaign, IL: Human Kinetics, 1978), p. 82.

70. RAUSCH, cited in *Children in Sport: Contemporary Anthology.*

71. D.M. GELFAND & D.P. HARTMANN, "Some Detrimental Effects of Competitive Sports on Children's Behavior," *Children in Sport: Contemporary Anthology,* eds. Richard Magill, Michael J. Ash, & Frank L. Smoll (Champaign, IL: Human Kinetics, 1978), p. 167.

72. ROBERTS, cited in Thomas, *op. cit.,*[63] p. 152.

73. JERRY J. THOMAS, "Attribution Theory and Motivation Through Reward: Practical Implications for Children's Sports," *Children in Sport: Contemporary Anthology,* eds. Richard Magill, Michael J. Ash, & Frank L. Smoll (Champaign, IL: Human Kinetics, 1978), p. 152.

74. TERRY ORLICK & CAL BOTTERILL, *Every Kid Can Win* (Chicago: Nelson-Hall, 1975).

75. BARRY D. MCPHERSON, "The Child in Competitive Sport: Influence of the Social Milieu," in *Children in Sport: Contemporary Anthology,* eds. Richard Magill, Michael J. Ash, & Frank L. Smoll (Champaign, IL: Human Kinetics, 1978), p. 237.

76. GREENE & LEPPER, cited in *op. cit.,*[73] pp. 152–153.

77. *Op. cit.,*[69] p. 145.

78. *Op. cit.,*[74]

79. *Op. cit.,*[69] p. 146.

80. ORLICK & BOTTERILL, "Every Kid Can Win," in *Sport Sociology: Contemporary Themes,* eds. A. Yiannakis, (T.D. McIntyre, M.J. Melnick, & D.P. Hart. (Dubuque, IA: Kendall/Hunt, 1979), p. 141.

81. RAINER MARTENS, "The Uniqueness of the Youth Athlete: Psychological Considerations,"

American Journal of Sports Medicine 8, no. 5 (1980), pp. 382–383.

82. *Op. cit.,*[67] pp. 49–50.

83. R. FRANCIS et al., "Little League Elbow: A Decade Later," *The Physican and Sportsmedicine* 6 (1978), pp. 88–94. Cited in Figler, *op. cit.,*[60] p. 86. According to the Department of Health and Human Services, the injury rate to youth (5 to 17 years old) was 33% in the mid-1970s.

84. D. JACKSON et al., "Injury Prediction in the Young Athlete," *American Journal of Sports Medicine,* 6 (1978) pp. 6–14. Cited in Figler, *op. cit.,*[60] p. 86.

85. EDWARD C. DEVEREUX, "Backyard Versus Little League Baseball: Observations on the Impoverishment of Children's Games in Contemporary America," in *Sport Sociology: Contemporary Themes,* eds. A. Yiannakis, T.D. McIntyre, M.J. Melnick, & D.P. Hart (Dubuque, IA: Kendall/Hunt, 1979), pp. 123–129.

86. *Op. cit.,*[60] p. 85.

87. *Op. cit.,*[67] p. 49–50.

88. JOHN UNDERWOOD, "Taking the Fun Out of Games," *Sports Illustrated* (11 November 1975), pp. 87–98.

89. *Op. cit.,*[75] p. 232.

90. MICHAEL J. KAUFMAN & JOSEPH POPPER, "Pee Wee Pill Poppers," *Sport in Contemporary Society,* ed. D. Stanley Eitzen (New York: St. Martin's, 1979), p. 151.

91. RICHARD WOODLEY, "How to Win the Soap Box Derby: In Which Craftsmanship Abets the Passion for Success to Produce a Tale of Moral Confusion," in *Sport in Contemporary Society,* ed. D. Stanley Eitzen (New York: St. Martin's, 1979), pp. 136–148.

92. JAMES A. MICHENER, *Sports in America* (New York: Random House), 1976, pp. 105–106.

93. TARA K. SCANLAN, "Social Evaluation: A Key Developmental Element in the Competitive Process," in *Children in Sport: Contemporary Anthology,* eds. Richard Magill, Michael J. Ash, & Frank L. Smoll (Champaign, IL: Human Kinetics, 1978), p. 140.

94. ORLICK, cited in *op. cit.,*[69] p. 148.

95. *Op. cit.,*[93] p. 141.

96. CHARLES HORTON COOLEY, *Human Nature and the Social Order* (New York: Scribner, 1902).

97. *Op. cit.,*[60] pp. 95–96.

98. MARTIN RALBOVSKY, "Destiny's Forgotten Darlings" in *Sport Sociology: Contemporary Themes,* eds. A. Yiannakis, T.D. McIntyre, M.J. Melnick, & D.P. Hart. (Dubuque, IA: Kendall/Hunt, 1979), p. 134.

99. *Op. cit.,*[92] p. 107.

100. *Op. cit.,*[98] p. 135.

6

Sport and Social Deviance

Sports is no longer the dilettante thing it once was, an hour-a-day thing. It's an all-out approach that practically demands cheating.   JACK KELLY

The only way of preventing civilized man from kicking and beating their wives is to organize games in which they can kick and beat balls.

GEORGE BERNARD SHAW

Sporting events are not a safety valve but create even more aggression.

RICHARD LEAKY

For when the One Great Scorer comes
To write against your name
He writes—not that you won or lost—
But how you played the game   GRANTLAND RICE

The goal of socialization is to produce individuals who internalize and abide by society's rules, scripts, or norms. When this is accomplished, the social order is relatively stable and a homeostatic balance is achieved. In any society, however, there are persons who stray from the expected guidelines. When this occurs, sociologists talk about deviant behavior. The concept of deviance is a slippery one. When Simmons, in 1969, asked people of different backgrounds, "Who is deviant?", many of the responses were predictable.[1] For example, sexual deviants (e.g., homosexuals, child molesters, prostitutes); substance abusers (e.g., drug addicts, alcoholics); and criminals were mentioned. Unpredictably, bearded men, artists, divorcees, pompous professors, and smart-aleck students were also indicated. Hence, the range of reactions to the query included some expected and some unexpected responses and, furthermore, highlights the *relativity* of what is judged to be deviant. While deviance is any behavior deviating from the social norms, sociologists typically limit their focus on those norm violations that are considered sufficiently offensive by so many people that the violator or violation carries a stigma.

Deviance is any thought, action, or feeling that runs contrary to social standards or expectations. It is rule-breaking behavior, although there is a continuum of tolerable behaviors. Social deviance is a broad concept encompassing cheating, criminality, chemical dependency, sexual immorality (e.g., prostitution and child pornography), deceit, genius, and godliness. *Deviance* can refer to either positive departures from some norm such as the innovative and eponymous "Fosbury Flop" (a high jumper goes over the bar backward and headfirst and lands on his or her back) or to negative departures from the norms, although emphasis is placed traditionally on the negative side. **Deviants** are individuals who engage in rule-breaking action. Consider the following reports of sport deviance:

- Nate Colbert, a former All-Star and minor-league coach for the San Diego Padres, pleaded guilty (February 1991) to a federal bank-fraud charge.
- Boxer Greg Haugen tested positive for marijuana after beating Hector "Macho" Camacho (February 29, 1991). The World Boxing Organization stripped Haugen of his title and reinstated his challenger, Camacho.
- National Collegiate Athletic Association (NCAA) officials restored the eligibility of four University of Nevada, Las Vegas, players who violated regulations by leaving unpaid a total of $129 in incidental hotel bills during recruiting visits.
- Reggie Rogers, three weeks after being released from prison for negligent homicide, signed a contract with the Buffalo Bills in February 1991.
- Professional football Hall of Famer Johnny Unitas filed for bankruptcy, under Chapter 11, after the city of Baltimore reneged on a portion of a loan it had guaranteed.
- Seton Hall basketball player Marco Lokar chose not to wear the American flag on his jersey during the Persian Gulf War. Boos on the part of fans and threatening phone calls influenced his decision to quit the team and return to his native Italy.
- Ben Johnson, after a superlative performance in the 1988 Olympics, was stripped of his medals after he was discovered to have been ingesting anabolic steroids.

- All-star catcher Benito Santiago was arrested in December 1990 for drunken driving and resisting police arrest in Coronado, California.
- Baseball Hall-of-Famer Don Drysdale pleaded no contest to a misdemeanor charge of drunken driving in February 1991. He was fined $2,350 and ordered to attend a three-month alcohol education program and perform 200 hours of community service.
- Jose Canseco received a speeding ticket for driving his red Porsche in Miami (February 1991) at a speed of 104 mph.
- Soccer star Diego Maradona was interrogated by Naples, Italy, prosecutors for suspicion about his involvement in a drug and prostitution ring.
- San Antonio Spurs player David Wingate had his rape trial (in which a 17-year-old girl claimed he raped her on September 16, 1990) postponed and was expected to rejoin the team in January 1991.
- Arkansas wide-receiver Brendan Cook died January 15, 1991, of an apparent self-inflicted gunshot wound to the head. He was found dead in the apartment complex where his ex-girlfriend lived.
- Denver Bronco running back Blake Ezor was being sought by the police for failing to complete his sentence in an October 1990 conviction of retail fraud. Ezor had pleaded guilty for changing the price tags on a compact disc player at a discount store.
- High school basketball coach Carl Owens (Harlingen, Texas) was arrested and charged with inciting a riot after his team's victory on February 15, 1991.
- Three Northern Illinois football players had a court date set for January 18, 1991, in Dekalb for criminal trespassing.
- A Cleveland State University basketball player was charged with the rape of a female student on November 3, 1990. The athlete in question had previously served nearly five years in a California youth institution after a 1981 murder conviction. The athlete was also being questioned in the death of a 19-year-old whose body was found in the trunk of a car in July 1989.
- Muskegon-High—Muskegon Heights (Michigan) basketball teams were forced to suspend their games, the oldest in the area's basketball rivalry, because of serious disturbances surrounding their recent games.
- The Track and Field Federation of Germany announced that top athletes would begin semimonthly drug testing in January 1991. This announcement followed allegations that many German athletes, particularly those from East Germany, routinely used performance-enhancing drugs.
- Hernell "Jeep" Jackson, a Texas-El Paso Player who died of a heart attack in 1987, was among those the NCAA alleged had free use of cars provided by the school's athletic department.
- Tulane University's President Eamon Kelly terminated the Blue Wave basketball program in 1985 after several players were accused of taking $23,000 from gamblers in a point-shaving scam. Seven students were eventually arrested and charged with drug trafficking, bribery, and conspiracy. Tulane coach Ned Fowler admitted

that star center John ("Hot Rod") Williams had received a $10,000 signing bonus plus weekly payments of $100.

- In the 1976 Montreal Olympics, a Russian fencer was discovered to have ingeniously wired his épée—the scoring being recorded by electronic means—so he could score points at his own volition.

The select acts described in these press releases are deviant, although their degree of deviance (i.e., severity) varies. Deviance in sports, like deviance in other realms of social life, stems from several sources. Sometimes deviance emerges unintentionally, or innocently, as when position incumbents lack knowledge of the rules, when the rules themselves are ambiguous or contradictory, or when rules are misinterpreted or misunderstood. However, when the norms are known, deviation from them is often a reflection of strains and pressures experienced by the actors in various social settings.

STRUCTURAL SOURCES OF SPORT DEVIANCE

Eitzen[2] proposes that the very structure of sport in America promotes deviance by encouraging rule infractions. Sociologists have identified several structural roots of social deviance in sport.[3] Consider Sage's[4] lucid account of the *structural* props contributing to deviance in intercollegiate athletics:

> The *structure* of big-time, commercial college athletics—a structure that is largely responsible for the pervasive corruption and abuses—has been left intact, with no substantive changes. . . .
>
> By the structure I mean the rigidly authoritarian system in which rules and policies affecting student-athletes are enacted and imposed without any input from the largest group in college sports—the student-athletes themselves. I am also referring to the now-common practice of keeping athletes involved in one way or another with their sport during the season for 40–60 hours per week—practicing, watching films, traveling to games, and being away from campus and missing classes.
>
> I'm referring to the weight training programs, film analysis, and "informal" practice sessions in the "off-season"; indeed athletes are expected to remain in training year-round. I am referring to the pressures brought to bear by mass media attention and the expectations of alumni and boosters who demand championship teams. I'm referring to universities who use athletes as public relations. This is the essential structure of major university football and basketball programs.

Incompatible Value Orientations

The overriding value atmosphere of sport is ironic (see Vignette 3.2). On the one hand, notions of sportsmanship and fair play (e.g., Grantland Rice's aphorism, "It's not whether you win or lose but how you play the game") are given homage but, on the other, the notion of winning at any cost (e.g., Vince Lombardi's declaration that "Winning isn't the most important thing, it's the only thing") has gained ascendancy. Often, both values cannot be realized, since they contain antagonistic claims. Just the same, these paradoxes are not unique to sport, as Williams's delineation of American value orientations vividly denoted (in Chapter 3). Consider the following "Ten Commandments of Sport" mentioned by Brasch:[5]

1. Thou shalt not quit.
2. Thou shalt not alibi.
3. Thou shalt not gloat over winning.
4. Thou shalt not sulk over losing.
5. Thou shalt not take unfair advantage.
6. Thou shalt not ask odds thou art unwilling to give.
7. Thou shalt always be willing to give thine opponent the benefit of the doubt.
8. Thou shalt not underestimate an opponent or overestimate thyself.
9. Remember that the game is the thing and he who thinks otherwise is no true sportsman [sic].
10. Honor the game thou playest, for he who plays the game straight and hard wins even when he loses.

The "structural" realities of sport, and not just those pertaining to big-time college or professional sport, make obedience to "commandments" such as these most difficult, because winning has become a preoccupation and an obsession at some levels of sport competition.

Inconsistency between Values, Norms, and Structural Constraints

Given the priority of winning and the restrictions placed on the amount of practice time allowed, especially for high school and collegiate teams (e.g., in 1991 the NCAA set a ceiling of twenty hours per week of practice time for athletes), it is not surprising that subterfuge is used to gain advantage over the opposition. Many high school or college teams conduct unofficial practices, sometimes called informal pick-up games, before the official practice date. On this matter, sport columnist Jim Murray related the following comment sent to him by an embittered ex-high school teacher:

> I was disgusted by the deceit practiced in the athletic department—men to whom our boys look for leadership. For example, our league had a rule against having more than a certain number of practices during the summer months preparatory to the beginning of the football season. But—by pure coincidence—the whole football team would show up in full uniform on unscheduled days. Also, the coaching staff would miraculously appear. I would say that, in some cases, the coaches and team did not come in direct contact, that is, they were separated by, probably, 200 yards, but this infuriated me as an educator. As far as I was concerned, the only thing we were teaching those kids was how to cheat. And what seemed even more ridiculous was that these coaches were breaking their own rules—rules they themselves had made.[6]

Role Conflict and Role Strain

Coaches are expected to cultivate discipline, yet they are expected to be sensitive to their players as both individuals and as representatives of different ethnic, racial, and social class backgrounds. Years ago, Sandy Koufax refused to pitch a World Series game because the date conflicted with a traditional Jewish holiday. Similarly, Muhammad Ali had to resolve inconsistencies between his roles of preacher (of the Black Muslim faith) and prize-fighter. When Ali refused military conscription, he was stripped of his World Heavyweight title by the World Boxing Association.

Although the triad described—(a) **incompatible value orientations;** (b) **inconsistencies between values, norms, and structural constraints;** and (c) **role conflict** and **role strain**—does not exhaust all of the structural sources of deviance, it does account for the more sociologically relevant causes of sport deviance.

In studying deviance in sport as well as in other social institutions, one must consider what and whose norms are being broken. For example, many tactics among football players (e.g., holding, spear blocking, tripping, clipping) are not only condoned but also encouraged under certain circumstances, despite the fact that the official rules explicitly forbid them. In basketball, defensive players will often place their hand on a dribbler's lower body, because it is annoying and breaks the latter's concentration. Similarly, basketball players often feign being fouled or deliberately commit an infraction as a strategy ploy. Finally, even the dubious recruiting practices of university personnel are justified on the grounds that "everybody does it" or that "we must do it to remain competitive."

☐ THE RELATIVITY OF SOCIAL DEVIANCE

Examination of the general deviance literature reveals several important qualifying and provocative observations. A highly significant one is that deviance is a *relative* phenomenon; that is, it can often be fully understood only within the sociocultural parameters in which it occurs. Deviance is neither absolutistic nor invariant, it is *situated behavior.* Consider these queries: Is a person without a swimming suit deviant at a nudist beach? Is a seven-foot-tall basketball player deviant when standing beside other centers in professional and collegiate basketball? Is killing deviant in the context of military invasion? Obviously, the answers to these questions underscore the importance of the social context in which the incident takes place.

Sport deviance varies by *time.* When the first Olympic games were held in the alluvial plains of Mt. Olympus, the runners ran in the nude. Then, nudity was perfectly acceptable; today it would be deviant.

Sport deviance varies by *place.* The Zuni Indian runners would not consistently try to outperform their competitors. Although this is entirely acceptable and appropriate in that geographical region, in general such behavior would be labeled deviant.

Sport deviance varies by *situation.* A boxer or hockey player trying to annihilate or "put away" another player is perfectly proper. On the other hand, a golfer trying to extinguish another golfer on the links through physical force would be booked for assault.

Sport deviance varies by *social status.* Within various sports, some superstar athletes have become such celebrities that authoritative personnel appear to "look the other way" or "bend over backward" to avoid having to negatively sanction them. Tennis players John McEnroe and Jimmy Connors have developed notorious reputations by pushing their sometimes despicable actions to the limit (and sometimes beyond).

In sum, deviance is relative, not absolute in nature. What and who is deviant often varies across time, place, situation, and social status.

☐ EUFUNCTIONS AND DYSFUNCTIONS OF SPORT DEVIANCE

Deviance in sport, like deviance in the broader society, has a host of consequences. On the surface it intuitively appears to have various negative effects on both the individual and society. And it does. Interestingly, deviance also performs several positive functions. We will first summarize some of the more common negative effects of deviance and then consider some of the latent positive features of this universal social phenomenon as they relate to sport.

Some Negative Features of Deviance

First, widespread deviance creates conflict, tension, and unpredictability between conforming (rule-abiding) and deviant (non–rule-abiding) individuals and groups. Illustratively, coaches like Woody Hayes, Frank Kush, and Bobby Knight, to name a few, have reputations of short and volatile tempers and ill-descript behaviors that create untold problems for officials, athletic directors, university presidents, and alumni. Second, deviance may channel scarce and costly resources into social control concerns. For example, the apparently increasing "organizational deviance" on college campuses (see Chapter 10) has funneled yeoman NCAA efforts into this one avenue, albeit a vitally important one. Third, deviance may have the consequence of undermining support by members of an organization or the society at large. The "Knight Report" on the status of intercollegiate athletics exposed some of the corruption in college sports and produced a wave of pro and con sentiments from the general public.[7] Fourth, rampant deviance can disrupt the social organization of society or of an institution and create what Durkheim called *anomie*. In summary, some effects of deviance are dysfunctional or disruptive to the dynamic balance of the society. Perhaps surprisingly, deviance also produces some eufunctions.

Some Positive Features of Deviance

First, deviance can encourage unity and cohesiveness. This function is akin to the social consequences of a natural disaster—flood, tornado, hurricane—in a community. It sometimes has the effect of coalescing diverse individuals and groups. Second, the negative sanctions meted out to deviants serve to define what is socially proper, appropriate, and tolerable. As such, deviance clarifies the boundaries or limits of normative behavior. Deviant behavior, as noted earlier, is not rigidly defined but can be thought of as falling at different positions on a continuum. The punishment or censoring of deviant acts signals what is and isn't acceptable. Third, deviance can function as a "safety value." Frustration, disappointment, and anger are common reactions to one's goals being thwarted. Ewald and Jiobu[8] make an argument for long-distance running and bodybuilding as being examples of positive sport deviance. Certain types of deviance may permit people to express their discontentment without disrupting the entire social fabric. Kenneth Colburn, Jr., advances the thesis that the fist-fight is "functionally indispensable" for ice hockey because it accommodates two otherwise disruptive aspects of the sport: (a) the necessity to engage in intimidation and (b) the necessity of avoiding one's career being prematurely terminated because of illegal and unpredictable assaults from opponents.[9] Accordingly, then, the fist-fight becomes an adjustment mechanism—a latent positive feature—between these potentially more serious and undesirable acts. Fourth, deviant behavior may serve as a reminder of the kinks in the social armor. In college athletics, for example, the widespread prevalence of recruiting violations may reflect the overwhelming pressure to win so that virtually any measure—legal, illegal, rational, irrational—will be taken to enhance victory. In summary, deviance is neither all bad nor all good. Some of its effects are dysfunctional while others are functional.

☐ THEORIES OF SOCIAL DEVIANCE

A variety of theoretical explanations for deviance has been proposed. For simplicity's sake they will be categorized under three rubrics: (a) biological, (b) psychological, and (c) sociological theories of deviance. *Biological* approaches assume that defects or weaknesses in a person's physical constitution predispose one to deviance. Representatives of this viewpoint include Lombroso's atavistic types (individuals with physical stigmas), Sheldon's somatotypology (endo-, ecto-, and mesomorphs) and the XYY syndrome (individuals possessing two Y chromosomes). *Psychological* explanations of deviance tend to focus on psychological "sickness" manifesting itself in the form of mental illness, psychopathic disorders, personality aberrations, and the like. *Sociological* theories of deviance look beyond the individual at broader social forces. Under this heading are included anomie, conflict, differential association, and labeling theories (Table 6.1). Given this text's inherent sociological approach, the emphasis here

TABLE 6.1 Popular sociological theories of deviance: Their basic question(s) and answer(s)

Theory	Basic Query	Basic Answer
Anomie	What social conditions produce deviant behavior?	Blockage from or restricted access to culturally prescribed goals and/or the culturally prescribed means to those goals.
Conflict	Who determines the "official" societal definition of deviant behavior?	Definitions of deviance are made by and protect the vested interests of the powerful and wealthy society members.
Differential association	How or through what social processes are deviant attitudes, values, and behaviors learned?	The company one keeps influences the learning of deviance.
Labeling*	What are the consequences of being labeled deviant?	There are two stages: primary and secondary

*Labeling theory is divided into two phases: *primary deviance* occurs when one violates a social rule but is neither labeled deviant by others or oneself; *secondary deviance* occurs when constituted authorities label one as deviant and the labeled person incorporates that social definition into one's self-definition.

resides in these theories. Anomie theory emerges from the functionalist perspective and sees incongruencies between the cultural goals and the established means to these goals; in contradistinction, conflict theory sees the dominant group exploiting the weaker one(s) and defines the latter's acts as deviant. Differential association stresses the role of learning, and the social processes and environmental contexts that increase (or decrease) the probability of deviant activity. Control theorists focus on the internal and external social control mechanisms that encourage conformity among the citizenry. While these theories fail to exhaust the explanations of deviance, they are the most popular contemporary explanatory schemes, although it is important to remember that "There are as many ways of explaining misbehavior [deviance] as there are ways of misbehaving, and there are innumerable ways of misbehaving. Indeed, the task of creating theories to explain human deviance has stood as one of the most difficult challenges for all the sciences of human behavior."[10]

A SOCIOLOGICAL THEORY OF SOCIAL DEVIANCE: ANOMIE THEORY

Granting that there is a multiplicity of theories of deviance, one provocative and widely endorsed sociological explanation that is applicable to sport has been advanced by Robert K. Merton and is called **anomie theory.**[11] Merton says, The "aim is to discover how some social structures exert a definite pressure upon certain persons in the society to engage in non-conforming rather than conforming conduct."[12] According to this formulation, our society prescribes norms of success for all persons. (For many roles in sport—athlete, athletic director, coach, trainer—this success means winning.) Society also prescribes the channel or means by which these goals can be achieved. However, because virtually all sporting contests create both winners and losers, someone is bound to be thwarted in the quest for victory. Hence, individuals will employ various means—proscribed as well as prescribed—to achieve the goal of success. One form of sport deviance, **cheating**—the breaking or bending of rules to gain a competitive edge—exists in sport and is engaged in by various individuals (players and coaches), teams, and organizations. Table 6.2, which presents Merton's typology, highlights the various modes of behavior by which individuals adapt to the gap that separates culturally prescribed goals from the means of obtaining them. When the goals are not easily achieved, social pressure to engage in nonconforming rather than conforming behavior becomes compelling.

TABLE 6.2   Modes of individual adaptation

Mode of Adaptation	Cultural Goals*	Cultural Means*	
Conformity	+	+	nondeviance
Innovation	+	−	
Ritualism	−	+	types of deviance
Retreatism	−	−	
Rebellion	±	±	

SOURCE: Robert K. Merton, *Social Theory and Social Structure* (Glencoe, IL: Free Press, 1957).

☐ **VIGNETTE 6.1**

Deviant Behavior in Professional Baseball

A wide range of deviance occurs in sport. In baseball, these practices are euphemistically dubbed "tricks of the trade."[18] They involve doctoring balls and bats, conning runners, feigning double plays, and "baiting" officials. The severity of these practices is variable; they do, however, fall under the generic heading of deviance in sport.

Pitchers

Perhaps the oldest trick in baseball is the infamous spitball, which dates from 1902 and was declared illegal in 1920. Coincidental or not, Babe Ruth's home-run production nearly doubled when this change was introduced. The spitball has not become extinct like the dinosaur but has resurfaced as the "mudball," "shampooball," "pine tar ball," "sandpaper ball," "petroleum jelly ball," and the "puffball." When a baseball is defaced or lathered, the pitcher grips and throws it as a fastball but his movement is magnified, thereby throwing off the batter's timing. Such balls create a drag that alters their flow lines. Pitcher Rick Honeycutt was caught in 1980 nicking a baseball with a thumbtack that had been ingeniously taped on his finger with a bandage. Honeycutt was fined $25 and suspended for ten days.

Baseball personnel maintain that the doctoring of baseballs is a common practice among pitchers. Pitching coach Dave Duncan guesses that 50% of pitchers do something to the ball, and Gene Mauch claims that "more pitchers are doing it than at any time in the 40 years I've been associated with baseball." One pitching coach has said, "I can now conceive of the day when a pitcher will come out to the mound wearing a utility belt, complete with files, chisels, hammer, nails, and hacksaw." I can't help but think that his statement is fraught with literary excess!

Some pitchers even avoid touching the rubber. A Cubs pitcher built a trench in front of the mound and pushed off from it while in the stretch. He believes it gave an extra foot or so to his fastball. While pitchers are occasionally called for balks, some have developed extremely deceptive and sometimes officially questionable pick-off moves.

Batters

Batters, too, have their ploys. Former Detroit Tiger Norm Cash openly admitted to rebuilding his bats. During his career, Cash used a hollow bat that had a hole eight inches deep and one-half inch wide bored into the top. The hollow portion Cash filled with cork, sawdust, and glue. The hole was then carefully disguised with smoothly sanded plastic wood. The advantage of a hollow bat is that it combines the mass of a larger bat with the whip of a smaller one. Graig Nettles was also fond of tampering with his bat, and in the second game of a doubleheader between the Yankees and Tigers, he blooped a ball into left and the end of his bat flew off. The umpires disallowed that hit, but not his earlier home run, which provided the victory margin for the Yankees. Today, bats filled with cork continue to be available, although the extent of their use seems to have diminished. Another competitive trick performed by batters is to erase the back line of the batter's box when they would prefer to stand slightly farther back from home plate than the official rules allow.

Fielders

Fielders have sleight-of-hand (and foot) tactics. First basemen often lift their foot off the pad before the throw arrives, a practice that can trick an official into thinking that a throw has arrived earlier than it actually did.

The phantom double play, where the second baseman or shortstop cleverly avoids touching second, is widely used. Infielders may also fake fielding a ground ball to stymie the runner advancing to second on either a hit-and-run play or a steal. Infielders may successfully block the runners and thereby prevent them from reaching a base pad, or they might sneak up behind runners to complete a successful pick-off play. Even the hidden-ball trick, where the fielder hides the ball and tags out the runner when he takes his lead off the bag, has been used in the major leagues.

Catchers are not without their deceptive techniques. One common trick is to pull the catcher's mitt deftly into the strike zone on a pitch that narrowly misses the corner of the plate. Catchers may conspire with the pitcher by doctoring a ball. They may conceal thumbtacks in their shin guards to use for this purpose. Catchers have been known to smear mud on the seams of the ball, scratch the ball with their shin guards, or surreptitiously daub the ball with petroleum jelly. Catchers may try to break a batter's concentration by talking constantly.

The deceptive ploys used by outfielders are fewer in number. One widely used tactic is to "freeze" a base runner by pretending to field a ball

they had no chance of catching. Outfielders also short-hop a ball, which makes it appear that the ball was caught.

Sign stealing is another trick used in baseball, although authorities suggest it is nothing more than educated guessing. When Billy Martin was managing the Texas Rangers, it was alleged that he stole catchers' signs with the aid of a closed-circuit camera installed in center field. Signals received by a television set in Martin's office were relayed, supposedly, to the dugout via walkie-talkie. Even groundskeepers have gotten into the act. Visiting teams that have speed and run a lot will often be greeted with wet basepaths, particularly around the take-off areas, which effectively reduces the team's speed. Conversely, fast teams will keep their own basepaths dry and hard, which enhances their chances of victory. Furthermore, teams that bunt may bow the foul lines inward, and some clubs will extend, ever so slightly, the dimensions of the batter's box. Groundskeeping practices of this sport permit teams to maximize their own strengths and/or neutralize the strengths of their opposition.

Note that there are *five* adaptation modes: (a) conformity, (b) innovation, (c) ritualism, (d) retreatism, and (e) rebellion. The plus and minus signs in Table 6.2 refer to acceptance and rejection, respectively, of the goals and means. Although not all types of adaptation are widely practiced in sport, several are.

Conformity

Conformists accept both the culturally prescribed goals and the means for achieving those goals. This adaptation mode is the only one in the scheme that is nondeviant. Snyder's[13] study of dressing-room slogans uncovered two—"live by the code or get out" and "discipline"—that suggest that athletic personnel are immersed in a social environment encouraging obedience to rules. Undoubtedly, players, coaches, and others abide by these dictates; however, few persons who play for any period of time escape committing, knowingly or unknowingly, rule infractions. Rule breaking has even been incorporated into game strategies, such as the intentional pass interference that prevents a touchdown or long gain; the deliberate tripping that prevents a breakaway score (in football, roller derby, basketball, hockey, and soccer); the pummeling of the second baseman that breaks up a double play; or the jabbing of an opponent's eyes and shoving in basketball, which invite a technical foul and disrupt the game's momentum. Deviant acts that are not serious are referred to as *patterned evasions of the norms,* or *normal fakery.*[14]

Innovation

Innovators accept the goals but alter the means for obtaining them. This form of adaptation reflects most clearly the modal type of sport deviance, particularly that which is considered immoral and unethical. Recent NCAA recruiting scandals demonstrate this pattern and portray its roots (see Chapter 10). A perusal of Vignette 6.1 provides one with an understanding of deviance as portrayed through "innovation."

Ritualism

Ritualists reject the cultural goals—winning at any cost for example—but accept the means. The ritualistic approach emphasizes participation, rather than winning, and is aptly summarized by the adage popularized by the indubitable sportswriter Grantland Rice: "It's not whether you win or lose, but how you played the game." In *The Ultimate Athlete,* George Leonard evoked the ritualistic pattern in the New Games Tournament slogan: "Play hard, play fair, nobody hurt."[15] In projecting future sport scenarios, Leonard talked of athletic contests that eliminated dehumanization, emasculation, sexism, ruthless competition, and unconscionable violence. New games like Earth Ball, Le Mans Tug of War, Infinity Volleyball, Yogi Tag, New Frisbee, Boffing, and Slaughter emphasize transcendence of exercise and encourage players to communicate with self, others, and nature. The "New Games" concept aims at developing happier, healthier, and more useful persons and avoiding the scourge of cutthroat competition.

Retreatism

Retreatists reject both the means and goals of sport. Some athletes who initially fit the ritualistic pattern eventually adopt this orientation. Joe Don Looney, former college and professional football player, joined a religious sect in India that denounced worldliness. Many persons, horrified and disgusted with the direction athletics has taken, reject entirely the emphasis placed on competition, sexism, elitism, violence, commercialism, and dehumanization. Merton uses the term *retreatism* to describe giving up. Individuals who have had aversive or negative sport socialization experiences also represent this genre. Because sports are such a pervasive phenomenon, initial sport experiences that leave a foul taste in the participant's mouth cannot be judged as positive. Orlick and Botterill suggest:

> The most important thing you can do to insure that the child gets the right start is to see that the child's participation is fun and enjoyable over and above everything else. The simple fact is that if children are not receiving some sort of positive rewards for their participation, they will not continue. Having fun, playing, and being part of the action can be extremely rewarding for kids.[16]

Sociologists have referred to such aversive socialization experiences as "degradation ceremonies"—activities designed to "turn off" and destroy the motivation and sporting spirit of participants. Gary Shaw, former football player at Texas, described such "run-offs" at the University of Texas:

> Royal . . . had all injured (if below the first four teams) wear a jersey with a big red cross stenciled on both sides. And if at all able to walk, the injured were to continually jog around the practice field the complete workout. The red crosses were to be signs of humiliation. And throughout the spring, Royal would refer to the guys that would do anything to get out of a workout and "couldn't take it." It may sound silly, but it was really an embarrassing stigma to be on your jersey. . . . It was never explained to us why only those injuries below a certain team were "fake injuries." There were always several members on the first team who were injured, yet they wore only solid jerseys.[17]

Rebellion

Rebels reject the means–ends nexus and attempt to actively substitute new, different, and more humanistic forms of sport. The social movements known as *shamateur activism* and the *humanitarian counter creed* (see Chapter 14) illustrate this mode of adaptation.

❑ DRUGS IN SPORT

The creativity in drug usage has become nearly incredible. For example, imagine a sprinter loading a suppository with cocaine and using it before a 100-yard dash; a female gymnast taking a growth-retardant hormone to prolong her career; an archer ingesting a drug that reduces the pulse rate to a near indetectable rate; or a swimmer taking a megadose of a nasal decongestant to enhance air flow through the lungs. As unbelievable as these deviant activities are, they have been employed.

What Are Drugs?

Although the answer to this question may seem obvious, it is not. Pharmacologically, drugs are chemical substances that affect our body's psychological functioning (the so-called "head trip") or physiological functioning (the so-called "body trip"). Most people (correctly) equate drugs with hallucinogens (e.g., LSD and peyote), marijuana, stimulants, cocaine, heroin, depressants, narcotics, tranquilizers, and inhalants. However, many ordinary products such as coffee, tea, cocoa, tobacco, soft drinks, chocolate, and alcohol contain chemical substances that are technically classified as drugs.

To maximize the social and economic benefits that accrue from stellar athletic performance, athletes (both amateurs and professionals) feel pressure to perform at consistently high levels. Lyle Alzado, former National Football League (NFL) stellar player, admitted in the summer of 1991 that his use of anabolic steroids and human growth hormones was to enhance his performance and ability to remain competitive, particularly as he grew older. Because sport seasons are long, wearing, and often injurious, some athletes take drugs for assistance. Drug usage has become a widespread and questionable social practice from our culture's standpoint.

Two broad categories of drugs are used in sports. The first, **restorative,** are taken to alleviate injury, pain, hypertension, sickness, and dissipation. Drugs included in the restorative category include painkillers (e.g., aspirin and Darvon), tranquilizers (e.g., Valium and Serax), barbiturates, (e.g., Seconal and Quaaludes), antiinflammatory agents, enzymes, and muscle relaxants. These drugs are often found in household medicine cabinets. Drugs that are considered to be **additive** are more controversial because the chemical ingredients they contain are ingested primarily to influence performance. Additive substances include amphetamines (e.g., benzedrine, dexedrine, dexamyl, and methamphetamine, commonly called "speed"), human growth hormones (HGH), beta-blockers, and anabolic steroids. Amphetamines stimulate the central nervous system. Anabolic steroids are fat-soluble organic compounds (synthetic derivatives of the male hormone testosterone) that can increase muscle size, alter fat distribution, and stimulate secondary male sex characteristics (i.e., increase facial and body hair and lower voice pitch).

Both types of drugs can have negative side effects, and their use sometimes poses an ethical dilemma. The International Amateur Athletic Federation has banned over 90 chemical substances. Additive drugs, the more controversial of the two, artificially stimulate performance and can cause physical or psychological addiction as well as irreparable body damage. Prolonged or excessive use of amphetamines can produce ulcers, convulsions, cerebral hemorrhage, paranoia, weight loss, cardiovascular collapse, nutritional deficiencies, sleeplessness, aggressiveness, impaired judgment, depression, and irritability. Anabolic steroids and growth hormones have been causally linked to heart disease, prostate cancer, testicular atrophy, liver and kidney damage, and swelling (edema).

Use of Drugs in Select Sports

The University of Southern California (USC), in the aftermath of Todd Marinovich's arrest for cocaine and marijuana possession, launched a probe of the University's drug-testing program. When USC commenced their drug-testing in 1985, 10% of those taking it failed; today, 2% fail. One of their football starters claimed that the system was easily beaten by hiding "clean" urine under their arms and secretly pouring it into the testing vials.

In excess of fifty Soviet athletes were found to have used banned drugs in 1990, and the United States and Soviets agreed to stop doping in sports.

Maury Wills, a former base-stealing champ, describes in his sordid book how he became a desperate cocaine addict by snorting a few lines offered by a woman he picked up in a bar, graduated to free-basing, and spent the better part of the next four years in an incredible orgy of narcotic self-destruction. During this time, he spent more than $1 million on illicit drugs—about $1,000 a day.

The use of performance-enhancing drugs is widespread in track and field. As cases in point consider that in 1991

- Olympic silver medalist and world record-holder in the shot put, Randy Barnes, had his two-year suspension for steroid use upheld.
- Four-time U.S. Olympian in the steeplechase, Henry Marsh, had his two-year suspension for failure to report for a drug test overturned by an arbitrator.

- Olympic silver medalist and world record-holder in the 400 meters, Butch Reynolds, sued The Athletics Congress/USA for $10 million in an attempt to have his two-year suspension for steroid use overturned.

Fifteen U.S. athletes in track and field and distance running were suspended. Sociologically, there are some conflicts of interest represented by the parties. For example, drug companies desiring to hawk their products may be inclined to find new substances to disguise the ingestion of certain drugs. Because many laboratories have contracts for drug testing, their economic survival is linked to their verdicts. Finally, our adulation of winners may deter honesty, as illustrated by Ben Johnson's hero's welcome in indoor meets in Canada and Los Angeles following a two-year suspension for using prohibited performance-enhancing drugs.

- Kevin Wiley, University of Texas lineman, was identified as a player selling falsified prescriptions for steroids similar to the falsified prescriptions that led to the arrest of another Longhorn player, reserve punter Brent Beauchamp.

In recent history, it was the drugs and banned substances disclosures at the 1983 Pan-American Games in Venezuela that blew the lid off amateur drug use. Now it is common knowledge that Olympic athletes have been accused of and found guilty of ingesting illicit drugs. Amid an aura of nationalism, Western observers have implicated Eastern Bloc athletes, particularly. Formal Olympic policy forbids practically all drug use. However, athletes in swimming, gymnastics, weightlifting, and track and field have been accused of using both steroids and stimulants. Soviet female gymnasts are believed to use amphetamines as well as drugs that retard growth and development (by their action on the pituitary gland); and swimmers, cyclists, and runners are said to use other stimulants.[19]

The International Olympic Committee's medical division has spent millions to deter and curb the illegal use of drugs in Olympic competition. The Olympic Committee purchased sophisticated laboratory equipment (chromatographs and spectrometers) costing millions of dollars. This equipment is sensitive enough to detect one-trillionth of a gram of amphetamine in the urine. Investigators can detect if any stimulants or narcotic drugs have been ingested four days before the test, or if any steroids have been used seven weeks before the competition. Not surprisingly, to avoid detection, some drug users mix "masking" drugs with the banned drugs to "fool" the sophisticated technology. Tests are administered to randomly selected team sports participants and to all top finishers, as well as to a few randomly selected athletes in individual sports. In less than an hour after an event, a sample of an athlete's blood is collected. Half is immediately analyzed, the other half refrigerated. If the immediate test confirms the presence of a foreign substance, the refrigerated sample is subsequently processed. If the findings of the first exam are corroborated, the event is forfeited. The culpable athlete faces both the loss of his or her medal as well as Olympic disqualification. In 1976, Soviet weight lifter Valentin Christov was found to have an illicit drug in his blood system and was stripped of his medal.

How widespread is the use of illicit drugs in Olympic competition? In Montreal, during the 1976 Olympics, only 0.5% of over 200 tests proved positive; most of these were for use of anabolic steroids. Aside from the issue of illegality and disqualification, athletes face a much graver consequence: drug usage can be lethal. In the 1960 Olympics, Danish cyclist Knud Jensen collapsed and died during the 100-km race. It was later determined that he had ingested Ronicol, a drug that stimulates the circulatory system by dilating the blood vessels.

Jack Scott reported, when he covered the 1968 Olympics in Mexico City, that the track and field athletes were not questioning whether chemicals should be used but, rather, which were the most potent and which could be ingested without detection. Scott said, "It is widely recognized in track and field circles that it is next to impossible to get to the top in most weight events and the decathlon without the use of these drugs since most of the top athletes are using them."[20]

The pervasiveness of drug usage is further underscored by the following comments. Gilbert observed, "It is far from excessive to conclude that the increasing use of drugs by athletes poses a significant menace to sport, one that the athletic establishment is assiduously trying to ignore."[21] American Hal Connolly, hammer thrower on several Olympic teams, said, "My experience tells me that an athlete will use any aid to improve his performance short of killing himself."[22] In 1970, nine out of twelve medalists in the world weight-lifting championships were disqualified when urine analyses revealed the presence of amphetamines, and in the 1983 Pan-Am Games, there were massive defections because of apparent illicit drug ingestion.

Examples of Drug Use in College and Professional Sports

Evidence from drug testing at the collegiate level indicates that the use of drugs among these amateur athletes is *not* excessive. As of the fall of 1991, less than 1% of Division I football student-athletes ($n = 8$, $N = 526$) were declared ineligible as a result of positive drug tests. Of interest, of the nearly 50 football players who tested positive, the overwhelming majority tested positive for anabolic steroids and the remaining positive tests were from diuretics and a urine manipulator. Additionally, only 2 of 1,873 athletes in baseball, basketball, lacrosse, skiing, swimming, track and field, and wrestling were ruled ineligible for positive tests.

Drug usage in professional sport is commonplace. Sport columnists have reported that a drug epidemic exists in baseball clubhouses, and the 1985 drug trials in Pittsburgh suggest this may well have been the case. Such baseball greats as Jimmie Foxx, Hack Wilson, Babe Ruth, Harvey Kuenn, and Don Newcombe are well known for their abuse of alcohol. But according to sportswriter Bill Conlin, "drugs are an invisible problem since you don't see guys passed out in hotel lobbies after snorting cocaine, smoking dope or popping pills. The nature of the beast is different, far more subtle and with lethal physical and psychological consequences. Drug experiences are not openly discussed on the team bus the way drinking exploits are."[23] Is drug usage widespread? In Conlin's view, "The rising tide of drug abuse is . . . as much a problem in major league clubhouses as it is in the school system, the business world, newspaper offices, the government, and the Armed Forces." Athletes who have had substance-abuse problems include Bob Welch, Maury Wills, Otis Nixon, Steve Howe, and Dexter Manley.

When examining drug usage in sports, however, one must tread cautiously for the following reasons: (a) Drug usage among athletes may not be deviant from the standpoint of contemporary youth's cultural values and practices. As mentioned earlier, when studying deviance, it is important to ask whose norms—those of the official culture or those of some subculture—are being broken. (b) An important consideration is the focus on "nuts, sluts, and perverts"—individual deviants—while ignoring collectivities such as formal organizations, corporations, and bureaucracies (see discussion of "organization deviance" in Chapter 10.[24] When we consider such machinations as Watergate, "Korea-gate," and other similar cases of corporate deceit, we can expect such values—or the lack of them—to be reflected in sport as well.

Whether drug usage among athletes is more prevalent than among other groups (e.g., youth subcultures and deviant gangs) is debatable. So, too, is the question of whether or not drug arrests and convictions are proportionately greater among athletes than among other social groups in America. As we have seen, the use of both restorative and additive drugs is commonplace among athletes in many sports. Lefkowitz contends that athletes may become involved with drugs because they are narcissistic individuals: "Athletes are people who are very much into their bodies—their bodies earn them their keep. . . . The drug experience is a sensual experience—it magnifies or enhances the senses for a period of time—and being involved in sports is a sensual experience. Because of this, athletes may be prone to drug experiences."[25] The various professional leagues share similar policies concerning drug usage, gambling, and associating with known criminals; they have not, however, enforced them uniformly.

☐ CRIME AND THE ATHLETE

Crime is a major topic within the deviance purview. *Criminal behavior* is legislatively defined and punished by governmental functionaries. Until recently, athletes who ran afoul of the law seemed to escape the workings of the criminal justice system. For example, sportswriter Randy Youngman said, "Babe Ruth could have been charged with rape on any number of his escapades."[26] Whether there was a conspiracy of silence to protect athletes in earlier periods or not is a contested matter. Today, however, it appears that more athletes (although some sociologists contend that the proportion of athletes getting into scrapes with the law is not significantly greater than that of some other segments of society) are breaking the laws, and contemporary newspapers—unlike those of former times—are devoting more coverage and giving greater exposure to these social problems.

In a United Press International (UPI) news release captioned "Arrests Continue to Make News," it was revealed that at least ten Missouri athletes had been arrested in the previous six months (for felony burglary, felony theft, assault, and driving while intoxicated); over two-dozen Colorado football players were arrested for various crimes during the late 1980s; five Oklahoma players were arrested for very serious crimes (rape, shooting a teammate, and selling cocaine); and two Iowa State athletes were charged with robbing a fast-food restaurant.[27]

Jim Bouton's iconoclastic book, *Ball Four* (1970), was among the first tomes to break the so-called conspiracy of silence and expose athletes (baseball players in particular) for what they are: mortal human beings with frailties.[28] According to Youngman, deviant athletic behavior is characterized by three basic aspects: (a) Chemical abuse is often involved; (b) athletes who come into repeated contact with law enforcement officials often receive light sentences or acquittals; and (c) allegations, indictments, and convictions even involve homicide.[29]

Athletes who have been arrested are not always convicted; sometimes they are not even brought to trial. Leon Spinks, during his short reign as a heavyweight boxing champion, was charged with reckless driving and possession of drugs, but these charges were dropped. Similarly, Jim Brown, former running back for the Cleveland Browns, has at least four acquittals, three dropped charges, and no convictions on his record.

Some athletes—Sonny Liston, who was arrested for impersonating a police officer and resisting arrest in Philadelphia in 1961; Bernard King, who was arrested for second-degree burglary; and Mack Herron, who was charged on three different occasions for cocaine possession—have had brushes with the law that involved leniency before they were eventually convicted. There has been a tendency for the charges to be reduced before the athlete is brought to trial. Consider the following examples: Marvin Barnes was charged originally with carrying a concealed weapon, not attempting to conceal one; Bobby Lee Hunter had a murder charge reduced to manslaughter; Ron Lyle's second-degree murder charge was a reduction of an initial charge of first-degree murder; and Don Murdoch was arrested for cocaine trafficking but convicted of a lesser charge of possession.

Some athletes—Cesar Cedeno, Rubin "Hurricane" Carter—have been charged with some degree of murder. Cedeno was charged with manslaughter in the slaying of a 19-year-old woman, and spent 20 days in jail and eventually paid a $100 fine. Carter was convicted of a triple murder and received a life sentence.

Some of those who speculate on the causes of criminal behavior opt for the **catharsis theory**. In their view, aggression defuses further aggression; thus, individuals who vent hostilities, vengeances, and frustrations are less likely to commit violent acts. Consequently, adherents to the catharsis theory believe that athletes are less inclined to commit violent crimes, because sport provides them with a constructive outlet for pent-up feelings of frustration, hostility, and aggression.

Social Learning theorists disagree with the catharsis explanation. They maintain that if violence is rewarded (i.e., positively reinforced) it may become manifest outside the initial setting in which it was reinforced. In short, athletes who are conditioned to behave aggressively on the field may be more prone to aggressive behavior off the field.

No theories sufficiently explain why people in general or athletes in particular deviate from societal norms. Nevertheless, social scientists continue to collect empirical data and formulate theories to explain such behaviors. Perhaps when athletes are no longer lionized, we will no longer consider their behavior—deviant and otherwise—any more unique than that of those engaged in nonathletic pursuits.

❏ VIOLENCE IN SPORTS

One area of sport that has drawn increasing attention is violence. Sport **violence** falls under the heading of deviance in sport. According to John Underwood:

> Once there was a game that had practically everything. Fun to play and exciting to watch, it was beloved by a nation of sports-minded people. It was held up to the nation's youth

as an exemplary physical test and as a builder of character. . . . In time . . . the game became contaminated, but the process was so gradual and insidious that few took notice. From the kiddie leagues to the major colleges and professional league, the sport's image grew more robust even as it decayed within. The injury rate mounted, sportsmanship declined. Vicious acts became commonplace.[30]

Underwood, a sports journalist, was alluding to the increasing violence that appears to be running amok in football. Without exaggeration, his observations are applicable to several other popular sports in Western society. What is the nature of this cancer— violence—that is eating away at the very heart of our sports? The irony of sport violence is reflected in the fact that fans and players endorse it. Hockey All-Star Gordie Howe bemoaned the *lack* of aggression in hockey today. Before the 1991 Hockey All-Star game, he said that the prevailing philosophy seems to be "turn the other cheek— and try not to get that close again. . . . the attitude is skate as best you can and don't get anybody hurt. . . . For the most part, it's a skating exhibition. You see Wayne Gretzky . . . out there and nobody touches him." At the same time Gretzky was urging National Hockey League (NHL) officials to legislate fighting out of the game (for the purported reason to have the league enhance its chances of securing a national television contract in the United States).[31]

Conceptualizing Violence

Social psychologists have conceptualized violence (or aggression) in several different ways, and some of these definitions are relevant to the present discussion. One claims that violence is any action or behavior that inflicts injury or harm on another. According to this approach, it is the *consequence* of the act that is important. A second definition of violence focuses on the *intent* of the act rather than its consequences. These two viewpoints are not moot academic distinctions. For example, on the basis of the former definition, sometimes referred to as the *behavioral definition* of violence, if I accidentally slam a car door on your finger and cause injury, then I have performed a violent act. According to the *motivational definition* of violence, if I intend to harm you but fail to properly negotiate the slamming of the car door, my premeditated action is still construed as violent (in intent). In practical terms, sport violence often appears to be intentional and certainly behavioral; that is, the act is often contemplated, and the planning is successful insofar as producing harm is concerned.

Two others forms of aggression that occur in sport are (a) *reactive* and (b) *instrumental*. Although in practice they sometimes are difficult to differentiate, *reactive aggression* is that which has an underlying emotional component with harm intended. Illustratively, a stellar wide-receiver may be a constant source of frustration for a substitute defensive back; the latter overreacts at every opportunity, so the former is forever "hearing the footsteps." *Instrumental aggression* is a nonemotional, task-oriented form. Illustratively, a base-runner trying to prevent a double play will forcefully tumble into the shortstop or second-base man to minimize the likelihood of the hitter being doubled up. A thorny problem is that, in sports such as boxing, hockey, and football, the sport is violent by nature, and the source of the aggression may be impossible to untangle and, further, may well have elements of both forms of aggression.

Today, violence in sports appears to have reached epidemic proportions. Never before have the safety and well-being of so many people been affected or have so many observed such deeds. According to Edwards and Rackages, evidence suggests the following:[32]

1. Sport-related violence of all types appears to have increased in both seriousness and frequency.
2. Not only have injuries due to sport violence increased, but, due to the high status and prestige accorded the athlete, many of the violent tactics responsible for the on-the-field injuries and deaths are being imitated by the young.
3. Out of the athletic turmoil of the 1960s, there developed a burgeoning interest among many social scientists in the important role of sport in human affairs and the implications of its structure and functioning for society.
4. Mass communications technology has undoubtedly heightened the general level of awareness vis-à-vis sport-related violence and ironically, served the dual function of both provoking the imitation of violent behavior and stimulating increased efforts to control and to prevent its occurrence. . . .

Before focusing on violence in contemporary sport, a few historical statements are insightful as reminders of its origins in antiquity. Violence in sport is not unique to our culture. It can be traced (at least) to the days of the Roman Colosseum, where gladiators dueled in mortal combat. Atyeo sketches a chronology of violence in sports and notes that most societies have featured violent sporting activities.[33] The ancient Greeks even passed a law allowing men to kill each other, provided they did so for entertainment purposes. Atyeo demonstrates how such violent events as medieval jousts and tournaments and the pugilism of eighteenth-century England reflected the sociocultural ambience of society.

Some sport critics find themselves in consternation when violence in sport is discussed. These social observers wonder why we even worry about violence when, for all intents and purposes, violence is sport. Or, as comedian Rodney Dangerfield gingerly put it, "I went to a fight the other night and a hockey game broke out." During boxing events in ancient Greece and Rome, the contestants fought until one party couldn't or wouldn't continue. According to legend, Theogenes of Thasos won 1,400 championships during his two-decade career and killed more than 800 opponents. From the mid-1940s to 1980, some 350 boxers died, most from cerebral blood clots. Full-contact karate (KO karate) is another modern sport that combines boxing, wrestling, and kicking one's opponent into helpless submission. Asking why there is violence, mayhem, and destruction in some sports is as naive as asking why you get burnt when you play with fire . . . violence goes with the territory. When violence is sport, the few ways of reducing it are to eliminate the sport altogether or alter it to some unrecognizable form. Would you recognize (let alone enjoy) boxing without punching; football without tackling; full-contact karate without kicking? Modern sport is not a free-for-all mayhem. Instead, it is the controlled, rule-bound, limited violence called "aggro."

An Example of Violence in Sport

The example presented in this section illustrates player violence (crowd violence is covered in Chapter 14) in popular American sports. It conveys some of the intensity and the extent of the violence that permeates American sport.

The very nature of hockey is violent. A notorious hockey melee is graphically described:

> The butt end of Forbes' hockey stick struck Boucha just above the right eye. The force of the blow caused Boucha to drop to the ice, stunned and bleeding profusely. Forbes then dropped his stick and pounced on the helpless Boucha. He punched him in the back of his head with his clenched fist, then grabbed the back of Boucha's head by the hair and proceeded to pound his head into the ice until Forbes was restrained by another North Star player.[34]

Fans seem to have a thirst for the hostility hockey engenders, and mayhem may even be encouraged to promote gate receipts, as suggested by Tutko and Bruns:

> The pros and cons of on-ice violence were even debated in the courtroom in 1975, when Boston's Dave Forbes was charged with aggravated assault with a dangerous weapon— his hockey stick. His victim was Henry Boucha of the Minnesota North Stars, who almost lost an eye when Forbes attacked him with his stick after they had scuffled on the ice. Forbes testified that Boucha was the real culprit, claiming that Boucha hit him with a "sucker punch" from behind, and that he felt he had to retaliate or Boucha would think "he could walk all over me." Fighting back, Forbes said, is an integral part of the game, taught to players as youngsters, and a player who doesn't fight back is an easy mark. . . .
>
> Before the trial (which ended with no verdict), National Hockey League President Clarence Campbell defended fighting as "a well-established ingredient for the economic well-being of the game." If violence ceases to exist, it will not be the same game," he said. "Insofar as fighting is part of the show, certainly we sell it. We do not promote it. We tolerate it and we bring it under disciplinary control which we believe satisfies the public."[35]

The climax of the "hockey war" between the Bruins and North Stars occurred on 26 February 1981. The lack of firm leadership in dealing with violence helped bring about one of the ugliest nights in NHL history. A brawl broke out seven seconds into the game and was followed by a dozen fights, one of which spilled into the runway leading to the North Star's dressing room. The game produced an NHL record: 406 minutes in penalties and the ejection of twelve players.

Minnesota Coach Glen Sonmer later admitted he had ordered his players to "do something" to refute opponents' taunts that his team was "gutless" and admonished that when the two teams played in Minnesota a week later, Boston coach Gerry Cheevers had "better bring a basket to take his head home in."[36] Brad Maxwell, a North Star defenseman, backed up his coach when he said, "I don't think we really cared about the two points. Our first concern was to go in there and prove that we could stand up to them, and show them we weren't going to take any cheap shots. . . . Maybe tomorrow we'll look back on this and realize we lost the two points by not winning, but right now nobody's very unhappy about the way the night went."[37]

Since the National Hockey League merged with the World Hockey Association in 1978–1979, the number of fights leading to penalties jumped from 740 in the initial merger season to (estimated) 980 during the 1985–1986 season. High-sticking and fighting penalties were up 40% and 34%, respectively, in 1985–1986 over the 1984–1985 hockey season. What this means is that teams often carry players on their rosters, not because of their hockey skill per se, but because they are physical bullies; similarly, clubs often also carry "policemen"—players whose job it is to protect teammates from belligerent "goons."

Different Views on Violence

For athletes participating in contact sports, it is not surprising that they tend to endorse and support the norm of violence. One is not surprised that years of sport socialization produced the following responses:

- I dream about Merlin Olsen; I see myself breaking his leg or knocking him unconscious, and then I see myself knocking out a couple of other guys, and then I see myself as the hero.—Jerry Kramer (football)
- If you have to go for the interception or the hit, go for the hit, it makes the lasting impression.—Cliff Harris (football)
- I like to believe that my best hits border on felonious assault.—Jack Tatum (football)
- If you put the ball on line halfway between me and another player, I am going to get that ball. If I knock the other player to the floor in the process—that's not playing dirty, that's playing hard.—Jerry Sloan (basketball)
- If they cut down on violence too much, people won't come out to watch. It's a reflection of our society. People want to see violence.—Bobby Clarke (hockey)
- America was not built on going to church. It was built on violence. I express America in the ring.—Ron Lyle (boxing)
- I had a license to kill for sixty minutes a week.—Alex Karras (football)

How does the public feel about sport violence? Some survey data suggest a negative but ambivalent attitude. Sport violence is a paradoxical social phenomenon. Some people believe it has a negative influence, especially on impressionistic young children; others argue it has no effect per se; that is, its stimulus value depends on the personality predispositions of the witness. Some believe violence adds to the excitement value of contests; others think it detracts from and corrupts the true spirit of sport. *The Miller Lite Report* found 60% of Americans believing violence is a serious sport problem and over 50% indicating that fights between players detract from their enjoyment of the game.[38] Not surprisingly, sport fans (57%) versus their nonsport fan counterparts (68%) were less likely to see violence as a problem. No significant difference in perceptions of the seriousness of violence was found when the variables of race, gender, age, education, and income were examined. Coaches (54%) were less likely to see violence as a serious problem than either sport journalists (74%) or sport physicians (77%). Although there are perceptual differences among the general public, fans, nonfans, coaches, sport journalists, and physicians, violence in sport is still viewed as problematic.

Despite occasional counterclaims to the role of violence in competitive sports, we may ask: Why so much emphasis on aggression? Some psychologists and psychiatrists believe that high levels of hostility—in fact, the ability to define one's opponent as a deadly enemy—are crucial for success in some competitive sports.[39] One of Vince Lombardi's pithy sayings is relevant here: "To play this game [football] you must have fire in you, and there is nothing that stokes fire like hate." Bianchi explains sports violence by arguing that unbridled aggression occurs in sports because of the pervasive sexism in our society.[40] Accordingly, men are taught to be domineering. The way men compete and perform must be superior to that of women. By way of the toys and games denied girls through traditional sex-role socialization, the young lad is conditioned to muscular and psychic aggression. Even in youth football, toughness, aggressiveness, and winning are portrayed as ideal values. Risk of physical injury is ignored or minimized. This, Bianchi maintains, is the initial training for confrontations with others in which one's self-respect, self-identity, and public acceptance are at stake. One cannot afford to lose. Winning is everything, even if it means trampling on friends. Hostility and violence are tools for removing obstacles on the way to the top.

Theoretical Explanations for Violence in Society and Violence in Sports

Social scientists attempting to explain violence have resorted to *three* different explanatory schemes: (a) the biological theory, (b) the psychological theory, and (c) the social learning theory.

Biological Theory. The biological theory, also known as the **drive-discharge model,** of aggression claims that the intent to harm or injure others is inherent in our biological makeup; that is, humans are biologically programmed for aggression. According to Nobel prize-winning ethologist Konrad Lorenz, aggression in humans is traceable to our atavistic evolutionary ancestors. As descendants of primitive life forms, we, like lower animals, are wired for aggression. Those who favor the biological explanation see aggression as stemming from an innate drive to behave aggressively. This drive, it is claimed, has enjoyed a long evolutionary history in the species and has provided a host of species-maintaining and species-preserving functions. Lorenz wrote: "The most important function of sport lies in furnishing a healthy safety valve for that most indispensable and, at the same time, most dangerous form of aggression. . . . collective militant enthusiasm."[41]

In a similar vein, psychoanalyst Sigmund Freud saw human aggression as a manifestation of the death instinct, or *thanatos*. To Freud, such instinctive energies necessitated periodic release; otherwise, he believed, they would lead to more catastrophic consequences. NFL coach and former player Mike Ditka supports this theory: "I feel a lot of football players build up a lot of anxieties in the off-season because they have no outlets for them . . . I'm an overactive person anyway and if I don't get rid of this energy, it just builds up in me and then I blow it off in some other way which is not really the proper way."[42] One way aggressive impulses could be safely discharged is through sublimation into socially acceptable channels, as occurs typically in contact sports. The notion of substitute discharge was popularized in the movie *Rollerball.* In the film, the entire world community is controlled by a single corporation, which banned war because it was too politically and economically threatening to corporate goals. Because humans had innate aggressive tendencies, it is necessary to provide some outlet for them. The sport of "rollerball"—a combination of physical mayhem, motorcycle racing, bowling, and skating—was concocted as the socially acceptable method for purging human aggression. In sum, sport, namely rollerball, became this institutionalized substitute for war.

Psychological Theory. A psychological theory of aggression is illustrated in the **frustration-aggression hypothesis.** Frustration is the blocking or thwarting of one's efforts to achieve some goal. Therefore, whenever an obstacle stands in the way of potential goal achievement, a common consequence is aggression (produced by the psychic state of frustration). The earliest formulation of this theory was a bit extreme, assuming that aggression was always the result of frustration and that frustration inevitably led to aggression. Contemporary social psychological research has discovered that frustration is neither a necessary nor sufficient condition for aggression to occur.

Frustration surfaces in sports in sundry ways. It may stem from failing to play up to one's potential, from debilitating and nagging injuries, from questionable calls of game officials, from the baiting and heckling of fans, or from the taunts of coaches or management. Consider Cesar Cedeno. Cedeno was presented an indefinite suspension for going into the Atlanta Stadium stands and grabbing a heckler. The fan had been yelling "killer" and "boy" at him throughout the game (the epithet "killer" referred to his manslaughter conviction in Santo Domingo for shooting to death a teenage girl). Cedeno's family was attending the game and witnessed the heckling and the attack. The frustration apparently motivated him to go into the stands after the antagonizer. Another example of frustration involved shortstop Garry Templeton. Templeton was fined $5,000 and suspended indefinitely after being ejected from a game for clutching his genitals and raising his middle finger to the crowd. His actions stemmed from fans' boos after he struck out (the catcher dropped the ball), and then leisurely jogged toward first base before veering into the dugout. After undergoing emotional counseling, Templeton admitted experiencing severe acute frustration in both his personal life and his career. The same questionable behaviors, apparently emerging from frustration, applied to ace Reds relief pitcher Rob Dibble during the summer of 1991 and the penalty-filled football game between Cincinnati and Buffalo in October 1991.

Social Learning Theory. The third explanation for aggressiveness is social learning theory. The sport version of this theory is dubbed the **cultural pattern model** and maintains that aggressive behavior is learned, like other behaviors, through reward and punishment contingencies. Simply, if one is reinforced for engaging in violent activity, the rewarded behavior probably will occur with greater frequency in the future. Recall, too, that reinforcements may be material (e.g., money) and/or social (e.g., praise, recognition, or awards). Hockey player Derek Sanderson recalls how he learned at age eight to become aggressive on the ice rink and to savor the results of others' violent play toward him:

> During a practice session, a puck hit me in the head and the blood began to flow. I skated over to my father and shouted "I'm bleeding!" He gave me the once over and

snapped, "You're all right, for Christ's sake." So I bled the entire practice, and when it was over he took me to the hospital, where I had three stitches. My father saved every one of my first 100 stitches. Soon I became proud of them. I'd come home after a tough game and say, "Hi, Dad, eight more!"[43]

Various forms of social learning can occur as a result of the mere observation of another's behavior, particularly if the other's behavior is rewarded. The observer receives vicarious reinforcement. This seems to be what Edwards and Rackages had in mind when they expressed dismay over youth in organized sport programs attempting to imitate the aggressive playing style of professional athletes.[44] Similarly, former hockey player Bobby Hull staged a one-man work stoppage to protest the blood thirstiness of hockey players. Hull refused to play because of his concerns over the effect of hockey violence on children, including his own four sons.

An Empirical Investigation of Violence in Sport and Society

There have been relatively few empirical tests of the validity of the preceding three theories of sport violence. A noteworthy one was conducted by anthropologist Richard Sipes, who tested whether the drive-discharge or the cultural pattern model better accounted for the relationship between society's social structure and sport forms. He was interested in the correlation between the nature of society (warlike and nonwarlike) and the existence of combative sports. Sipes defined "combative sport" as one played by two opponents (individual or team) in which there was actual or potential body contact or there was warlike interaction even in the absence of body contact; he defined a "warlike" society as one in which there were frequent attacks on others. The drive-discharge model predicts less violent sporting activities in warlike societies, because war would produce a drain or catharsis of innate aggression. On the other hand, the cultural pattern model predicts a positive relationship between the nature of society and the existence of different sport patterns; that is, warlike societies would have a preponderance of violent sports and nonwarlike societies would have a preponderance of nonviolent sports. Sipes selected twenty societies—ten warlike and ten nonwarlike—and found that 90% of the warlike societies had combative sports, whereas only 20% of the nonwarlike societies had combative sports. These findings support the cultural pattern theory and suggest that combative sports do not operate as alternate channels for the discharge of built-up aggressive feelings such as the drive-discharge model predicts. In another phase, Sipes traced the popularity of combative sports over a 50-year period (1920–1970) in the United States. A direct correlation between the popularity of warlike sports (as measured by NFL attendance and the sale of hunting permits) and the country's involvement in war was found. Interest in noncombative sports, as measured by parimutuel betting and major-league baseball attendance, declined during wartime. Again, there was some support for the cultural pattern paradigm of sport violence.

Do sports events increase aggression and hostility in spectators? Theoretically, two contrasting explanations have been advanced by social scientists. Social learning theorists argue that when an individual views positively reinforced aggressive behavior, the individual may be prompted to imitate similar behavior through vicarious reinforcement. The catharsis position claims that the viewing of aggressive acts by others may reduce subsequent aggressive acts by the viewer. Empirically, the results of various studies are not clear-cut, although this is probably due to methodological issues. Pencil-and-paper tests assessing the degree of pre- and postgame indices of hostility have been administered. The researchers have chosen aggressive sports (e.g., football, wrestling, and hockey) and relatively nonaggressive sports (e.g., swimming and gymnastics). Goldstein and Arms[45] studied fans attending two sporting events: football and gymnastics. Obviously, football is an aggressive "game," whereas gymnastics is nonaggressive. In comparing the pre- and postgame feelings of the fans, the researchers found that football spectators were more hostile, resentful, and irritable than gymnastics spectators. The hostility level for football fans, however, actually increased, regardless of whether their team won or lost, while gymnastics fans showed no such escalation. There was a slight tendency for spectators of violent sports to score higher on hostility after the contest than spectators of nonviolent events; however, these outcomes were not pronounced. Leuck, Krahenbuhl, and Odenkirk[46] replicated Goldstein and Arms's study with basketball spectators and discovered aggression levels increased between pre- and postgame measurements. Additionally, men (vs. women), students (vs. nonstudents), season ticket holders (vs. non-season ticket holders), and those with varsity athletic experience (vs. those without varsity athletic experience) were more aggressive spectators.

One potentially confounding factor in these analyses is self-selection; that is, hostile spectators may gravitate toward aggressive games (e.g., football), whereas nonhostile spectators may gravitate toward nonaggressive contests (e.g., gymnastics). The bulk of the research evidence suggests, however, that sports do not produce a catharsis effect; rather, aggression tends to breed aggression. Michael Smith, a student of collective behavior, denies the saltpeter-like effect of sport:

> I believe that violence in sport contributes to violence in the crowd, as opposed to the notion of catharsis, that viewing violent acts results in draining away feelings of violence. I have looked at newspaper accounts of 68 episodes of collective violence or riots among spectators during or after sporting events, and in three-quarters of those the precipitating event was violence in the game. Yet for decades and decades eminent scholars wrote without a shred of evidence that acts of violence in sport are cathartic or therapeutic for spectators.[47]

Some clinical evidence indirectly negates the cathartic function of sport and thereby supports its stimulant quality: football players are two times more likely to suffer from hypertension as the general public and four times more likely than track athletes.[48]

Of the three theories of violence—biological, psychological, and social—the social learning formulation has received the greatest empirical verification in the context of sport. Regarding violence in ice hockey, Vaz wrote:

> A rule-violating normative system is a structural part of the larger hockey system. Illegitimate tactics (including various forms of violence) are considered technical skills for achieving team success, and are the standards for the evaluation and recruitment of players. Ironically there exists no formal instruction in the training of young (or old) hockey players to obey the normative rules. Learning of the normative rules occurs informally, but the forbidden aspect of such rules is considered irrelevant.[49]

These observations suggest that violence in sport is learned rather than innate. Smith corroborates this allegation.[50] He interviewed Toronto high school hockey players about their perceptions of significant others'—parents, teammates, coaches, and nonplaying peers—responses to their aggressive play. In general, he discovered that significant others were perceived as responding favorably to the players' legitimate and defensive assaults and unfavorably to illegitimate action. Smith concluded that sports violence is a socially acquired behavior, a finding consistent with social learning theory. That sport socialization may include learning violence is dramatically documented by Robert Vare in his book *Buckeye, A Study of Coach Woody Hayes and the Ohio State Football Machine:*

> An inordinate amount of folklore has sprung up . . . around . . . Harold Raymond Henson III. It begins with the story of how he got his nickname—how his father, then serving his country in Fort Eustis, Virginia, hitchhiked fifteen hours back to Ohio, eyed his newborn son, and proclaimed, "He's got to be a champ." Six months later, according to another story they tell around Columbus, the older Henson, his own football career rudely ended by an appendicitis attack, carried his Champ out to the fifty yard line of Ohio Stadium and set him down on the sod. "Someday you will punish people on this field. . . . Someday you will be a Buckeye."[51]

Causes of Sport Violence

What are the causes of sport violence? Obviously, like many social science issues, this is a gargantuan query to try to answer. Biological, psychological and sociological variables contribute to this phenomenon, as well as interact in different sport settings. Here we will consider several institutional features of sport that contribute to violence. Coakley addresses *four* major sociological causative agents contributing to sport mayhem:[52] (a) Sport violence is related to commercialization insofar as victory (the operational definition of sport success) has been found to be linked to financial success. To achieve victory, it may be necessary to minimize the competitive edge of one's opponent. Instrumental aggression as incorporated into the role of "enforcer," whereby one of my less valuable team members intimidates, harasses or injures one of your most valuable players, is illustrative. (b) Sport violence is related to the social organization of teams. The highly competitive nature of sport teams, the manner in which the club imposes threats to adult status (because of the coach's overwhelming control and influence), physical well-being, masculinity, and feelings of personal adequacy facilitate the emergence of violence. (c) The socialization into sport and via sport for young athletes has, in certain sports (e.g., hockey and football), encouraged and rewarded aggressive play; and the model of violent player behavior may serve as a catalyst to similar behavior among spectators.

What can be done to stem the rising tide of violence that is sweeping sport? Sport psychologist Thomas Tutko recommends the total reconstruction of penalties, with emphasis placed on reducing injuries. In at least three professional sports, rules have been instituted to curtail the extent of potential injury-causing acts. Baseball, a sport not known for player violence, has declared illegal deliberate brush-back pitches, vicious take-out slides, and fisticuffs. The commissioner of basketball has levied heavy fines against players involved in altercations and, in 1978, a third referee was added in hopes of reducing the escalation of violent acts in National Basketball Association (NBA) games. Hockey has also taken measures to reduce the erstwhile fighting. Gary Flakne—the Minneapolis attorney who prosecuted Dave Forbes after he injured

Henry Boucha in an on-the-ice fight—said that the law must take the lead in saying there must be strict guidelines to avoid serious injury or death. Severe penalties for violent acts seem possible, but total reconstruction of sport rules would change not only how the sport is played but also how people think a particular game should be played. At present, no one seems to want a change, at least not a change of this type. Furthermore, professional athletes have, historically, little influence on these matters.

Less emphasis from the media, especially television, on the violent aspects of sport could make violence in sports less important to the fan than the contest itself. The emphasis given to sport violence by the media—television, radio, and print—has become redundant and is of questionable social benefit. (See Vignette 13.2 to do your own analysis of the relationship between media reports and actual behavior.) Ask anybody associated with the production of television sports what the greatest technological advance (except for color) in the past 25 years has been, and most assuredly they will indicate that the advent of instant replay was one of them. Instant replay is not a bad thing in itself; it permits sport zealots to see over and over again a play. Not only are the mass media capable of visually replaying sports violence ad nauseum, they can present the visual message to more people more quickly than ever before.

Edwards and Rackages's provocative article suggests that the mere alteration of rules may attack the symptoms and not the cause of sport violence.[53] For example, social violence at all levels—international, national, and personal—runs rampant. Consider the high violent crime rates in the United States, or the assassinations and attempted assassinations during the past twenty-five years (J.F. Kennedy, R.F. Kennedy, George Wallace, Norman Rockwell, Medgar Evers, Pope John Paul II, Gerald Ford, Martin Luther King, Jr., Ronald Reagan, and Anwar Sadat), or the My Lai massacre, or Jonestown, or the race riots in the 1960s. Historically, the very freedom most Americans enjoy grew out of violence. Collective violence characterizes the United States, from the American Revolution to Vietnam, from the Boston Tea Party to the invasion of Grenada and the bombing of Libya, from the early American frontier to contemporary urban disturbances, terrorism, and the Persian Gulf War. America has a violent legacy, and violence has played a role in social mobility: "Professional sports in the late nineteenth century and early twentieth century became avenues of upward mobility for lower and middle-class youths who were aggressive, tough, and manly."[54] H. Rapp-Brown once said, "Violence is as American as cherry pie," or as Ashley Montague has written, "America sets before the child the most aggressive kinds of models and then we wonder why we have such high rates of violent crime."[55] The litany of violence goes on and on.

Edwards and Rackages argue that American society is conducive to the generation of violence in both society and sport:

> American sport is . . . structurally and ideologically conducive to the generation of violence. It is based not just upon the legitimacy of competition but upon the primacy of interindividual competitiveness, of one person competing in direct physical opposition to another. Sports in America are . . . structured as "zero-sum games" . . . a winner and a loser . . . while collective actions and outcomes are viewed as important and even critical, each individual is . . . under the constant pressures of an ideological blueprint that lays fundamental responsibility to the individual for his [sic] own rewards and liabilities.[56]

The exploits of sport project a microcosmic picture of the exploits of society, or as former NHL player Bobby Clarke said, "If they cut down on violence too much, people won't come out to watch. It's a reflection of our society. People want to see violence,"[57] and promoters appear to be all too willing to provide it. Many forms of entertainment—movies, children's cartoons, news reports—are heavily laced with violence. To make major adjustments in the structure and functioning of American sports may require that major adjustments be made in the structure and functioning of our society.

Violence in sports clearly has become a major problem. Something must be done to alleviate this problem or our sports and societies will suffer dire consequences. We cannot afford to let our sports degenerate into vicious spectacles and our sense of play deteriorate accordingly. As historians Graham and Gurr state, "Violent antagonisms expressed violently destroy peace and men [*sic*] and ultimately community."[58]

❏ SUMMARY

Deviance is thought, action, or feeling that is contrary to the standards of conduct or the social expectations of a given group or society, and *deviants* are individuals who engage in rule-breaking behavior. Deviance, in various forms, pervades sport and society at all levels. *Anomie theory*, a sociologically rooted explanation of deviance, was advanced because of its usefulness in explaining deviance in sport. According to this theory, our society prescribes norms of success for all persons and also prescribes the acceptable means by which success can be achieved. Not all individuals, groups, or organizations, however, subscribe to the accepted goals and means. Therefore, with the exception of *conformists*, there are *innovators*, *ritualists*, *retreatists*, and *rebels*, all of whom alter in some fashion the cultural goals and/or the cultural means. Innovation is a common form of sport deviance. The concept of innovation helps to explain the recurring rule violations and other scandalous behavior plaguing amateur and professional sport.

Three structural roots of social deviance were presented: (a) *incompatible goal orientations*, (b) *inconsistency among values and norms and built-in constraints*, and (c) *role conflict* and *role strain*. Special attention was paid to the use of drugs in sport. Of the two types of drugs used, namely, *restorative* and *additive*, the latter appears more controversial and of questionable long-term value. We illustrated deviance in sport by drawing on both historical and contemporary incidents that, in light of the values advanced in the dominant American sport creed, exhibited a somewhat paradoxical nature. We called attention to the fact that it is important in the study of deviance to ask whose norms are being broken. Drug usage in sport may be seen as deviant from the viewpoint of mainstream culture, but it may not be seen as deviant from the viewpoint of contemporary youth.

Sport violence seems to have reached epidemic proportions. It occurred in the distant past and continues to the present, particularly in hockey, basketball, and football. Three theoretical explanations for violence in society and sport were considered. For example, the *biological* explanation (*drive-discharge model*) presupposes that violence stems from innate tendencies. The *psychological* theory (*frustration-aggression hypothesis*) argues that aggression results from the experience of having one's goals thwarted or blocked. The *social learning* formulation *(cultural pattern model)* contends that violence is learned, like other behaviors, through reward and punishment contingencies. The preponderance of the research evidence suggests that the social learning formulation is a more empirically grounded position.

☐ KEY CONCEPTS

Deviance
Deviants
Role Conflict
Role Strain
Incompatible Value Orientations
Inconsistencies between Values, Norms, and Structural Constraints
Anomie Theory
Cheating
Conformists
Innovators
Ritualists
Retreatists

Rebels
Restorative Drugs
Additive Drugs
Crime
Catharsis Theory
Social Learning Theory
Violence
Drive-Discharge Model (Biological Explanation)
Frustration-Aggression Hypothesis (Psychological Explanation)
Cultural Pattern Model (Social Explanation)

☐ ENDNOTES

1. J.L. SIMMONS, *Deviants* (Berkeley, CA: Glendessary Press, 1969).

2. D. STANLEY EITZEN, "Sport and Deviance," *Handbook of Social Science of Sport*, eds. G. Luschen & G.H. Sage. (Champaign, IL: Stipes, 1981).

3. HOWARD L. NIXON, II, *Sport and Social Organization* (Indianapolis: Bobbs-Merrill, 1976), pp. 20–21.

4. GEORGE H. SAGE, *Power and Ideology in American Sport* (Champaign, IL: Human Kinetics, 1990), p. 183.

5. RUDOLPH BRASCH, *How Did Sports Begin?* (New York: David McKay, 1970), p. 7.

6. JIM MURRAY, syndicated columnist (10 March 1972).

7. *Keeping Faith with Student Athletes: A New Model for Intercollegiate Athletics.* (Charlotte, NC: Knight Commission, 1991).

8. EWALD JIOBU, cited in Timothy J. Curry & Robert N. Jiobu, *Sports* (Englewood Cliffs, NJ: Prentice-Hall, 1984), p. 213.

9. KENNETH J. COLBURN, JR., "Deviance and Legitimacy in Ice Hockey: A Microstructural Theory of Violence," *The Sociological Quarterly* 27, no. 1 (1986), pp. 63–74.

10. *Op. cit.,*[8] p. 213.

11. ROBERT R. MERTON, *Social Theory and Social Structure* (Glencoe, IL: Free Press, 1957).

12. *Ibid.*

13. ELDON E. SNYDER, "Athletic Dressing Room Slogans as Folklore: A Means of Socialization," *International Review of Sport Sociology* 7 (1972), pp. 89–102.

14. *Op. cit.*[3] p. 23.

15. GEORGE LEONARD, *The Ultimate Athlete* (New York: Avon Books, 1975).

16. TERRY ORLICK & CAL BOTTERILL, *Every Kid Can Win* (Chicago: Nelson-Hall, 1975), p. 7.

17. GARY SHAW, *Meat on the Hoof* (New York: St. Martin's Press, 1972), p. 166.

18. STEVE WULF, "Tricks of the Trade," *Sports Illustrated* 54, no. 16 (13 April 1981), pp. 92–96, 98, 100, 104–108. The discussion and examples in this section have been gleaned from this source.

19. *Time* (18 January 1980) p. 70.

20. JACK SCOTT, *The Athletic Revolution* (New York: Free Press, 1971), pp. 148–150.

21. BIL GILBERT, "Three-Part Series on Drugs in Sports," *Sports Illustrated* (7 July 1969), p. 30.

22. *Ibid.,* (23 July 1969), p. 70.

23. BILL CONLIN, "Detecting Drug Abuse Isn't Easy," *The Sporting News* (10 October 1981), p. 21.

24. ALEXANDER LIAZOS, "The Poverty of the Sociology of Deviance: Nuts, Sluts, and Perverts," *Social Problems* 20 (Summer 1972), pp. 103–120.

25. LEFKOWITZ, quoted in Randy Youngman, "Crime and the Athlete," *Chicago Tribune* (22–25 October 1978).

26. *Ibid.*

27. "Arrests Continue to Make News" (29 August 1991), United Press International.

28. JIM BOUTON, *Ball Four* (New York: World, 1970).

29. YOUNGMAN, *op. cit.*[25]

30. JOHN UNDERWOOD, "An Unfolding Tragedy: Brutality in Sports (Part 1)," *Sports Illustrated* (14 August 1978), pp. 69–92. Quoted in Stephen K. Figler, *Sport and Play in American Life* (Philadelphia: W.B. Saunders, 1981), p. 199.

31. *Chicago Tribune* (18 January 1991), Section 9, p. 5.

32. HARRY EDWARDS & VAN RACKAGES, "The Dynamics of Violence in American Sport: Some Promising Structural and Social Considerations," *Sport Sociology: Contemporary Themes*, eds. A. Yiannakis, T.D. McIntyre, M.J. Melnik, & D.P. Hart. (Dubuque, IA: Kendall/Hunt, 1979), pp. 221–227.

33. DON ATYEO, *Blood and Guts: Violence in Sport* (New York: Paddington Press Ltd., 1979).

34. ROBERT C. YEAGER. *Seasons of Shame: The New Violence in Sports* (New York: McGraw-Hill, 1979), p. 23.

35. THOMAS TUTKO & WILLIAM BRUNS, *Winning Is Everything and Other American Myths* (New York: Macmillan, 1976), p. 17.

36. *Sports Illustrated* (7 March 1981), p. 9.

37. *The Minneapolis Star* (27 February 1981), p. 10c.

38. *The Miller Lite Report on American Attitudes Toward Sports* (Milwaukee: Miller Brewing, 1983), pp. 93–101.

39. ROBERT C. YEAGER, "The Physician and Sports Medicine," *Readers Digest* (July 1977), p. 25.

40. EUGENE BIANCHI, "The Superbowl Culture of Male Violence," *Christian Century* (18 September 1975), p. 842.

41. KONRAD LORENZ, quoted in Figler, *op. cit.*,[30] p. 176.

42. JAY J. COAKLEY, *Sport in Society* (St. Louis: C.V. Mosby, 1982), p. 59.

43. TOM PINKA, "Violence in Sports: American Style," unpublished manuscript, Illinois State University (1981).

44. *Op. cit.*[32]

45. JEFFREY GOLDSTEIN & ROBERT ARMS, "Effects of Observing Athletic Contests on Hostility," *Sociometry* 34 (March 1971), pp. 83–90.

46. M.R. LEUCK, G.S. KRAHENBUHL, & J.E. ODENKIRK, "Assessment of Spectator Aggression at Intercollegiate Basketball Contests," *Review of Sport and Leisure* 4 (Summer) 1979, pp. 40–52.

47. MICHAEL SMITH, quoted in D. Stanley Eitzen, *Sport in Contemporary Society* (New York: St. Martin's Press, 1984), p. 113.

48. *Ibid.*, p. 92.

49. EDMUND W. VAZ, "Institutionalized Rule Violation in Professional Hockey: Perspectives and Control Systems," *Sport Sociology: Contemporary Themes*, eds. A. Yiannakis, T.D. McIntyre, M.J. Melnik, & D.P. Hart. (Dubuque, IA: Kendall/Hunt, 1979), pp. 235–241.

50. MICHAEL D. SMITH, "The Legitimation of Violence: Hockey Players' Perceptions of Their Reference Groups' Sanctions for Assault," *Sport Sociology: Contemporary Themes,* eds. A. Yiannakis, T.D. McIntyre, M.J. Melnik, & D.P. Hart. (Dubuque, IA: Kendall-Hunt, 1979), pp. 228–234.

51. ROBERT VARE, quoted in James A. Michener, *Sports in America* (New York: McGraw-Hill, 1976), p. 35.

52. *Op. cit.*,[42] pp. 98–111.

53. *Op. cit.*[32]

54. WILLIAM J. BAKER & JOHN M. CARROL, *Sports in Modern America* (St. Louis: River City Publishers, 1981), p. 129.

55. Quoted in S.K. Figler, *op. cit.*, [30], p. 176.

56. *Op. cit.*,[32] p. 223.

57. BOBBY CLARKE, quoted in S.K. Figler, *Op. cit.*, [30], p. 177.

58. GRAHAM AND GURR, quoted in Donald W. Ball & John W. Loy, *Sport and Social Order* (Boston: Addison Wesley, 1975).

7

Sport and Social Stratification

We hold these truths to be self-evident, that all men are created equal, that they are endowed by their Creator with certain inalienable rights, that among these are life, liberty, and the pursuit of happiness.

The *Declaration of Independence* was signed on July 4, 1776. Thomas Jefferson, the author of this famed document, was a slave owner, as were many others who signed their names affirming the document's precepts. Moreover, slavery as a social institution persisted for nearly one century after the *Declaration of Independence,* and de jure (i.e., legal) and/or de facto discrimination toward minorities continued well into the latter half of the present century. Furthermore, women were not enfranchised until 1920. A significant ingredient of the American belief tradition resides in the statement "all men are created equal." Not only is this statement false, because males and females differ, even at birth, in physical and mental traits, but males and females tend to become more unequal as they move through the life cycle.

Individuals in society are highly variegated. They differ on such biological, psychological, and social dimensions as age, weight, IQ, race, religion, political persuasion, personality, ethnicity, and gender. The process of categorizing people on the basis of such characteristics is known as *social differentiation.* When these same individuals are arranged on a hierarchy with implicit or explicit evaluations of worth or importance, the process is called **social stratification.**

Social stratification is the hierarchical arrangement of social groups (e.g., racial, age, gender or ethnic groups) or societies into strata (social classes) that are unequal in power, privilege, prestige, and wealth. The term *stratification* can be thought of as a euphemism for patterned inequality. Of the myriad variables used in sociological explanations, social class is predominant because many social attitudes and behaviors are correlated with it. On this matter Berger wrote:

> A sociologist worth his salt, if given two basic indices of class such as income and occupation, can make a long list of predictions about the individual in question even if no further information has been given. Like all sociological predictions, these will be statistical in character. That is, they will be probability statements and will have a margin of error. . . . Given these two items of information about a particular individual, the sociologist will be able to make intelligent guesses about the part of town in which the individual lives, as well as about the size and style of his house. He will also be able to give a general description of the interior decorating of the house and make a guess about the types of pictures on the wall and books or magazines likely to be found on the shelves of the living room. Moreover, he will be able to guess what kind of music the individual in question likes to listen to. . . . He can predict which voluntary associations the individual has joined and where he has church membership. He can estimate the individual's vocabulary, lay down some rough rules for his syntax and other uses of language. He can guess the individual's political affiliation and his views on a number of public issues. He can predict the number of children sired by his subject and also whether the latter has sexual relations with his wife with the lights turned on or off. He will be able to make some statements about the likelihood that his subject will come down with a number of diseases, physical as well as mental. . . . He will be able to place the man on the actuary's table of life expectancies.[1]

To Berger's list of sociological predictions two other sport-relevant considerations can be added: (a) an individual's preference for spectator or participation sports and (b) the particular types of spectator and participation sports preferred. Berger's statements, as well as these, serve to underscore the manner in which socioeconomic status conditions an individual's life-style.

CHARACTERISTICS OF SOCIAL STRATIFICATION

Sociologist Melvin Tumin[2] identified five key characteristics of social stratification systems: (a) social, (b) ancient, (c) ubiquitous, (d) diverse, and (e) consequential. These features of social stratification will be used to organize the subsequent discussion. Remember, however, social stratification is not a monolithic phenomenon; it is multifaceted. Individuals occupy different positions in different stratification hierarchies. In modern industrialized societies, the most salient hierarchies are those based on class, ethnicity, sex, and age. I, for example, am a middle-class, WASP man, age forty-eight. How would my life experience differ from that of a lower class, black woman, age twenty-five? The advantage of the multiple hierarchy approach is that sociologists can compare the effects of different combinations of stratification positions. Table 7.1 captures the notion of multiple hierarchies of social stratification. Finally, race, social class, gender, age, and ethnicity are key social and theoretical categories that should be incorporated into social analyses of sport.[3]

SPORT STRATIFICATION IS SOCIAL

The adjective *social* preceding the term *stratification* signifies the root of social inequality. Social stratification cannot be fully explained by biological, psychological, or physiological differences that exist among humans. While these inequities are sometimes informative, they do not, in themselves, provide a sufficient account of social inequality. Why then does social stratification exist? *Two* sociological interpretations have been forwarded: (a) the *functional* explanation and (b) the *conflict* explanation.

Functional Theory of Stratification

In a classic functional interpretation of social stratification, Davis and Moore claimed that in societies with a complex division of labor, stratification is necessary because

TABLE 7.1   Multiple hierarchies of social stratification

	Race/Ethnicity	*Sex*	*Age*	*Class*
High strata	"WASP"	Male	Middle-aged, young adults	"High" occupation, income, and education
Low strata	Black, Latino and Latina, Native American (Ethnic/Racial Minorities)	Female	Elderly and children	"Low" occupation, income, and education

SOURCE: Adapted from Vincent Jefferies and H. Edward Ransford, *Social Stratification: A Multiple Hierarchy Approach* (Boston: Allyn & Bacon), 1980.

certain roles must be performed, and society must provide mechanisms to encourage, entice, and motivate members to perform them.[4] Accordingly, all social positions are not equally important to a society (e.g., a surgeon is more important than an orderly and a quarterback—a "skill" position, in the sports vernacular—is more important than an interior lineman). To illustrate, when the World League of American Football (WLAF) debuted in the spring of 1991, there were three salary levels: $25,000 for quarterbacks, $20,000 for positions other than quarterback and kicker, and $15,000 for kickers. Society ensures that vitally important roles will be performed by differentially rewarding their occupants. The differential rewards may be economic (i.e., money), social (i.e., prestige), and/or political (i.e., power). In general, functionalists argue that those positions most important to a society require the greatest talent and training and thereby receive the most lucrative rewards.

Take football positions, for example. It is widely acknowledged that certain positions are more crucial than others. According to the functionalists, occupants are remunerated in terms of the position's importance. The following list of the ten top-paid NFL players, by position, in 1991 is instructive:

Joe Montana	Quarterback	$4,000,000
Jim Kelly	Quarterback	$3,300,000
Jeff George	Quarterback	$2,768,000
Warren Moon	Quarterback	$2,700,000
Jim Everett	Quarterback	$2,400,000
Herschel Walker	Running back	$2,225,000
Eric Dickerson	Running back	$2,066,667
Bernie Kosar	Quarterback	$1,942,857
John Elway	Quarterback	$1,878,541
Randall Cunningham	Quarterback	$1,703,571

Critics of the Davis-Moore explanation of stratification argue that their thesis is tautological. According to them, social roles differ in their functional importance to the society. Positions that are highly functional to society depend on the ease with which the position itself or the person occupying that position can be replaced. Illustratively, the position of gas station attendant is highly replaceable because virtually anyone can pump gas; on the other hand, the position of neurosurgeon is highly unreplaceable because relatively few possess the education and experience to perform that role. In short, the notion of positional replacement is the basis for functional importance. Stark writes:

> Given the replaceability notion, the functionalist theory can easily be shown as a supply-and-demand argument about the existence of stratification. . . . It is easier to find good 6' 7" power forwards than it is to find good 7' centers. Thus, centers have the highest average pay of any position in the National Basketball Association.[5]

Conflict Theory of Stratification

According to conflict theorists, social stratification exists because inequalities in power, privilege, prestige, and wealth permeate societies.[6] As long as private property exists, there will be social injustice because those in advantageous positions will jealously guard their domains and resist any change running counter to their vested interests. The concept of **cultural hegemony,** meaning that the norms, values and interests of the dominant group become imposed on all other social groups, is applicable here. When workers become conscious of their exploitation by the elite (as illustrated by the 1990 spring training holdout), dissension among the social classes becomes inevitable. Recent conflicts between union-like players' associations (the so-called "proletariat") and team owners (the so-called "bourgeoisie") have led to boycotts and strikes (e.g., the 1990, 1985, 1981, and 1972 baseball players' strikes; the 1974, 1982, and 1988 football players' strike; the first NHL (hockey) strike in 1992; and the 1978 and 1979 umpires' walkout.

Consider the case of professional baseball. From the late 1890s to the middle 1940s, blacks were barred from participation in major league (American and National League) baseball but did form their own leagues.[7] The first paid black ballplayer was John W. ("Bud") Fowler, who played for a white team in New Castle, Pennsylvania, in 1872. Before the turn of the century (ca. 1883), two blacks, Weldy and Moses Fleetwood Walker, were members of the professional Toledo baseball club. Some regard them as the first blacks in professional baseball. Moreover, a few weeks after the signing of Jackie Robinson, Rickey announced the signing of four more blacks: John Wright, Don Newcombe, Roy Campanella, and Roy Partlow. Although the policy against hiring blacks changed slowly, by 1953, the practice of hiring blacks had become firmly entrenched. This exclusion was not due to inferior physical motor skills, or weaker physiological makeup, or athletic ineptness. Any explanation based on these premises can be quickly dismissed by an examination of performances by black athletes after Jackie Robinson (the first black player in modern integrated professional baseball) broke (actually *rebroke,* as will be seen in Chapter 8) the color barrier by moving from a minor league club in Montreal to the Brooklyn Dodgers in 1947.[8]

Prohibition of blacks in professional sports was essentially the result of a racist ideology acquiesced to by the greater white society, in general, and by professional baseball executives, in particular. In December 1867, shortly after the Civil War, the National Association of Baseball Players convened in Philadelphia to decide whether or not to accept black players. This organization unanimously called for banning clubs that listed blacks on their rosters. According to Peterson,[9] simple racial prejudice created baseball's color barrier. Although the association's members were Northerners, most shared the Southerner's belief that "Negroes" were inferior and not proper company for white "gentlemen." In view of blacks' present-day domination of some sports (baseball, basketball, football, and boxing), physical ineptness is unlikely to have been the reason they were denied participatory roles.

Instead, the historical reasons for such inequality stemmed from social sources. The opportunities denied to blacks were enjoyed exclusively by whites, who occupied positions of power and influence, and blacks' initial sport ban reflected this sociopolitical fact. In short, racial prejudice (unfavorable attitudes) and discrimination (unfavorable behaviors)—two related social processes—thwarted black participation in sport. In Chapter 8, we will elaborate on this point, and in Chapter 9 we will consider some of the social reasons why females were prevented from widespread sport participation until recently.

❏ SPORT STRATIFICATION IS ANCIENT

Social inequality in sport participation and spectatorship has existed from the dawn of recorded history, and it probably existed even before the advent of written records. The ancient Olympic Games formally commenced (informally, in 1453 B.C.) in 776 B.C. Certain social groups were categorically denied the privileges of either taking part or spectating. Females, who were not permitted to participate, formed their own games (the Heraen Games) in honor of Zeus's wife, Hera. Similarly, only Greek citizens with no police records and no relatives with police records were permitted to take part. Slaves, who were numerous in the Greek city states, were also prohibited from participating.

Although our knowledge regarding ancient sport participation and spectatorship is sketchy, we know that sporting feats were so popular during the heyday of the Roman Empire that people worked only every other day so they could attend the events, and Rome's Circus Maximus had a seating capacity of 260,000. Jousts and other equestrian events were popular during the Middle Ages, which spanned the fifth to the sixteenth centuries, but these were restricted to the nobility. In addition, little time for sporting activities was permitted, and this undoubtedly stifled sport participation, particularly among the common folk. Court-tennis, the precursor of lawn-tennis, was a royal and aristocratic passion. Henry VIII barred all but noblemen and property-owners from tennis, and bowling was prohibited except for noblemen and those who owned land valued at a set amount.

Historically, participation in sport has covaried with social class. During the Middle Ages, only the citizens of noble birth were free to engage in sport activities. Similarly, during the Victorian Era (1837–1901) sport only became a mainstay of upper-class English society. Sports were incorporated into the elite public schools such as Oxford and Cambridge. In the United States, the genteel New York Athletic Club was composed of well-heeled professionals and business persons. Likewise, in Canada, sporting clubs comprised and were regulated by members of the aristocracy.[10]

In the United States, sport has been (and continues to be) correlated with social class. In Chapter 2, we noted that many of the early sport forms and clubs were exclusive, almost snobbish. For example, the esteemed Knickerbocker Base Ball Club, formed around 1842, was reserved, primarily, for professional men, merchants, and businessmen. Seymour's comments on this prestigious club are revealing: "Mere skill in playing was not the only requisite for admission; a certain social standing in the community was necessary as well."[11] Professional baseball in the mid-1850s was a preserve of the genteel, aristocratic and leisured social classes. Veblen, an incisive social critic, advanced the notion of "conspicuous consumption" to describe the frivolous leisure activities of the well-to-do.[12] Accordingly, those who had no need to work for a living could flaunt their social standing by engaging in ostentatious behavior signifying their economic and cultural distinctiveness.

Three observations regarding the historical character of sport stratification are worth noting:[13] (a) The status accorded to athletes has varied. In Greece and Rome of antiquity, in Eastern Europe, and in America today, the athlete is/was highly regarded; in the post-Greco-Roman period, as well as in China during the early twentieth century, athletes did not enjoy high social status. (b) The elites who initiated a sport discarded it when it was taken up by the masses, a phenomenon which occurred frequently during the Middle Ages. (c) Direct competition between social classes and ethnic groups was discouraged or prohibited until recently. In England, the working class soccer clubs did not compete against higher-class opponents until the 1880s. Dunning and Sheard[14] examined the schism within the Rugby Football Union in England around 1895. The core issue was amateurism versus professionalism but, as Guttmann says, "The amateur rule was an instrument of class warfare."[15] The only way to keep the sport pure, said one English authority, was to rid it of mechanics, artisans, and laborers. Similarly, ethnic groups in South Africa only recently began to engage in competition with each other, and not without squabbles.

Historically, then, two patterns of sport have prevailed. First, elite sports "such as riding to the hounds, polo, boar hunting, falconry," fencing, tennis, golf, and cricket were reserved for society's upper echelons, who had the wherewithal and available time; second, folk sports "such as footracing, fisticuffs, wrestling, and eye gouging," were participated in largely by the masses.[16] Rader reports that as the population and wealth of the United States grew, a gentry (i.e., elite) and hoi polloi (i.e., common people) style of recreation emerged.[17] The explanation for the elite–folk dichotomy reflects the socioeconomic overtones associated with sport participation and spectatorship.

☐ SPORT STRATIFICATION IS UBIQUITOUS

Ubiquitous means "existing everywhere." It refers to something—in this case, sport stratification—that is omnipresent. One way of conceptualizing the universality of sport is to consider it in an international perspective.

Like so many facets of cross-cultural comparisons, nations vary in their sport emphasis. Alastair Reid, a Scotsman, said:

> I have never felt that in United States there is the same total immersion on the part of sport fans as in other countries—they are more critics than followers. In Europe or South America, crucial games so dominate the public attention as to affect everybody; but only on extreme occasions does anything like that universal goggling occur in the United States. It may be because sport is more specialized, or it may be because the United States does not lock horns with other countries as frequently as do the European national teams.[18]

Stratification in sport and leisure is an everpresent sociocultural phenomenon. Observers have noted that sport is like fashion; its influence filters downward. Numerous sports were initiated by members of society's upper crust and then adopted by less socially valued people. School sports, for example, began in England and were anything but democratic. Schools were designed explicitly to educate children of the gentry and were private and exclusive.

Social stratification exists both *between* and *within* sports. Some sports are classified as major (e.g., basketball and football), while others are considered minor (e.g., lacrosse, gymnastics, and crew) (Vignette 7.1). Even within a given sport, there are status distinctions. Judo awards a hierarchy of belts, boxing is divided into levels based on weight classifications, and in football, offensive backs are generally more visible than lineman. Illustratively, the famed Heisman Trophy, named after John Heisman, football coach and athletic director of the New York Downtown Athletic Club, is

◻ **VIGNETTE 7.1**

Claims Football Getting More Than It Should

BY GLEN LATIMER, ASSISTANT SOCCER COACH

"All animals are equal—but some animals are more equal than others."

The above quotation from George Orwell's *Animal Farm* can be applied to Illinois State athletic programs.

Which sport is "more equal" than others? Which has the most expenses in terms of training equipment, players' personal equipment and uniforms? Which has the most coaches? Which has the highest costs for travelling and meals? Which receives the most scholarships?

Did you guess? Well done!

Football is part of the traditional American way of life. As a "foreigner," I do not share this tradition through heritage. However, I enjoy watching football on T.V. and have seen ISU play. (I thought the Marching Band was excellent!) What does mystify me is why so much money is poured into one sport, when it does not pay for itself. Gate receipts plus advertising do not equal expenditures.

You can work out your own figures and try to work out the cost of just one football player for one season. Scholarship, uniforms, training, facilities and equipment, travel, meals, coaches, tape, hospitalization, etc.

All animals are equal but football players are more equal than others. Why? Why should they receive the lion's share in preference to any other sport or in preference to the Women's Athletics program? Are they special by tradition? Or because of the entertainment they provide? Irrespective of results, one could still make a case for deficit spending on this one sport if people felt they derived pleasure, entertainment, a social occasion, tradition or whatever from the games.

It is a fact of life, though, that attitudes change when times are hard. I am reliably informed that this is not ISU's most successful season. "They are building for the future"; . . . "we are a young team"; . . . "we need to get our offense and defense to play well together"; . . . "the big plays really hurt us" (taken from the Coach's Manual of Excuses to be Given to the Press).

I find it strange to see football continuing to take the lion's share of available funds, when on a cost-benefit analysis using whatever variables you care to employ, it does not warrant it!

Each year in Men's Athletics there are 120 full-ride scholarships available to all sports. Football has 73 of these. The next highest sport is basketball, which receives 15. You do not need a Ph.D. in mathematics to see the difference! Basketball operates nearly on a balanced budget and has a successful schedule.

Without being at all facetious, what would happen to ISU football if we only allocated 30 full-rides and redistributed the other 43 full-ride scholarships to other sports like track and field, cross country, golf, tennis, wrestling, swimming, baseball, soccer, etc. I venture to suggest that the football results would approximate to this season's results. However, the improvements in the other sports would be very noticeable.

For example, with 11 free rides in soccer it would be possible to produce a team of truly "national" standing within two years. No doubt coaches in other "minority" sports could make similar claims. (I use the term "minority" only because that is how the allocation of funds treats them.) But if the regulations could be changed and we could give 200 football scholarships, do you think our football program would be equal to the top college teams nationally?

Of course, what I am leading to involves a "mini-revolution"—especially in thinking. Why not spend the money at present going to football on the "minority" sports and make them "major" sports here at ISU? Then students would be able to see high-class national level competition and ISU could quickly gain a national reputation for producing top sportsmen and sportswomen in a variety of sports.

It really is a feasible idea, but (there's always a "but," isn't there?) it would mean a big reduction in the football program, or no football at all here! (Okay, cut out the wails of anguish!)

Is that thought really too awful to contemplate? Or is it just an idea that would take a little bit of getting used to?

It could be the choice between mediocrity and high-class performance and entertainment.

SOURCE: *Daily Vidette,* Illinois State University (12 October 1978), p. 20. Reprinted by permission.

---

awarded to the most outstanding college athlete. Only twice since its inception in 1935 has the award been given to a nonback (Larry Kelley, Yale, end, 1936; Leon Hart, Notre Dame, end, 1949). The granting of the Outland Award, given to the outstanding interior lineman, was introduced in 1946 to give proper recognition to stellar linemen. Some athletic contests bestow symbolic awards on contestants in the order that they finish (e.g., the gold, silver, and bronze medals awarded in Olympic competition or the common blue, red, and white ribbons).

Even in the traditional classless Soviet society, stratification is manifest in sport. Athletes in Russia are classified into echelons, the highest being called the "Honored Master of Sport." Standards of performance have been established in numerous sporting events, and Soviet athletes who meet these standards are rewarded materially and nonmaterially (Vignette 7.2).

SOCIAL STRATIFICATION IS DIVERSE

Three ideal types of stratification patterns have been identified: (a) class, (b) caste, (c) estate. In the United States, the most familiar form is **class,** a system of social inequality based on social, economic, and political factors. **Caste,** in contradistinction, is an inflexible form of differential advantage based on traditional beliefs, particularly religious ones. In India, the Hindu religion has traditionally solidified one's social position in terms of birth, whereas South African apartheid (racial segregation) is founded on a racial basis. The third stratification pattern is that of **estate,** a feudal-like social arrangement that existed in Medieval Europe, ruled by a hereditary monarch, and based on one's relationship to land. There were three estates—(a) the nobility, (b) the clergy, and (c) the peasantry—and these social positions were largely ascribed by the accident of birth but permitted a modicum of mobility.

In class-based societies, one's **position** or lot in life is allegedly **achieved.** The Horatio Alger rags-to-riches stories mirror this ideology. Additionally, such social forms encourage upward social mobility. *Mobility* refers to movement across, **horizontal mobility,** or up or down, the social-class ladder, **vertical mobility.** Vertical mobility can be assessed **intragenerationally,** which means a comparison of one individual's job(s) and salaries over a lifetime, or **intergenerationally,** which means comparisons between individuals of different generations, such as between father and son, mother and daughter. Sorokin colorfully describes upward mobility as "social

☐ **VIGNETTE 7.2**

Athletes' Rewards in Communistic Countries

Confidential intelligence reports explain how the athletes from the communist bloc made such a spectacular showing at the . . . Olympics.

The documents claim that communist countries have been force-training athletes for the Olympics since at least 1960. The star performers not only are subsidized but are pampered with luxuries in flagrant violation of Olympic rules, the documents allege.

This supports the frequent charge that communist governments develop professional athletes to compete against amateurs. One intelligence report quotes a past defector from the Cuban gymnastics team, Zulema Bregado Gutierrez, as stating: "All the athletes are professionals since athletics is their main employment."

She explained that Cuban athletes draw no salary but "receive other privileges which are tantamount to salary." She cited "free room and board and clothing." They get "much better food," and clothing "of the best materials available in Cuba," she said. These special advantages, she told U.S. intelligence men, "are not available to the rest of the population."

Another Cuban defector, Hector-Rodriguez Cordoso, told about being sent to Russia to study physical education. Summarizes an intelligence report:

"For a classless society," Rodriguez said, "Soviet athletes not only enjoy special class privileges, but they are actually segregated into categories according to their performance in competition.

"Most Soviet athletes who have won medals in competition of world significance, such as the Olympic Games, rank as first class athletes and receive a monthly stipend of 400 rubles in addition to other privileges such as automobiles, housing and the opportunity to travel abroad. . . .

"For every new world record a Soviet athlete sets," continues the intelligence report, "he re-ceives a bonus of 1,000 rubles and other benefits." The document adds that lesser athletes also "receive considerable recognition, monetary and otherwise, above and beyond what an ordinary worker would receive in the Soviet Union."

According to the document, "Rodriguez was emphatic in stating that the Soviet athletes with whom he came in contact made no secret of the fact that their efforts to excel were spurred primarily by the promise of material gain."

For communist athletes, the political indoctrination is as intensive as the physical training. The Cuban gymnast, Zulema Bregado, reported that "at least 30 minutes of political indoctrination is mandatory before every daily training session." Thereafter, she was required to train for four hours "every day of the week except Sunday, year round."

The athletes are carefully coached on how to react at the Olympics. States an intelligence document: "The Cubans make a special effort to orient their athletes so that once they come in contact with foreigners, they have a preconceived party line which they are to use.

"Every effort made by the members of the team, individually and collectively, is oriented to put the communist regime of Cuba under the most favorable light. For this reason, the Cuban athletes are considered one of the best means of conveying that message."

Some of these confidential documents date back to the 1960s. Yet they accurately forecast the behavior of the Cuban athletes who performed at the 1976 Olympics in Montreal.

The indefatigable Cuban runner, Albert Juantorena, dutifully dedicated his racing triumphs to Fidel Castro and the revolution. The formidable Teofilo Stevenson, the gold-medal heavyweight boxer, also always said exactly what Castro would want to hear.

Indeed, all of Castro's athletes arrived in Montreal with a full repertoire of Cuban revolutionary slogans. Not one of them expressed a thought of his own.

There could be no denying, however, that the Cuban athletes put on a tremendous performance. Hector Rodriguez told in an intelligence interview how they were groomed for their triumph. Relates the report:

"Rodriguez revealed that every Cuban province had a training center for athletic initiation in the schools. The main purpose of these centers is to recruit promising youths as young as 11 years of age . . . [and] train them politically and technically until they reach the age and necessary capability to enter another similarly specialized school.

"The latter is at the university level and is known as Superior School of Athletic Preparation. . . . The school is located in the former Cubanacan Country Club, one of the most luxurious of Havana, and the students receive privileged treatment with regard to food, clothing and housing."

The athletic triumphs are used, according to the intelligence documents, to divert public attention from "other failures" and to demonstrate "the superiority of Marxist-Leninism ideology in sports."

The Castro regime also inflates its triumphs by counting separately all the medals awarded to team members instead of the single award to the team.

The Cubans also divided "the number of medals gained by the number of the population of each participating country," states an intelligence report. "The main purpose of this statistical manipulation is to show that percentage-wise, the Cubans can field better athletes than any other country."

SOURCE: *The Barnesboro Star* (18 August 1976). (Report by Jack Anderson.) Reprinted by permission.

☐

---

climbing" and downward mobility as "social sinking."[19] Social descent, or downward mobility in sport, is richly illustrated in Warren McVea's case:

> He never got the six-figure salaries of superstar contemporaries, but he lived like a star. . . . Julius Erving was best man at his wedding. And at parties in McVea's $250,000 Houston home, local big shots rubbed elbows with famous athletes. He had an Eldorado and a Mercedes in his garage and a 1969 Super Bowl ring on his finger.
>
> "The guy lived the life," says Elmo Wright, McVea's college and Chiefs teammate. "He didn't settle for second best."
>
> But, about five years ago, "it seemed like the roof caved in," says Norris [Warren's nephew]. McVea's mother, with whom he was very close, died. About the same time, he was going through a divorce and lost $40,000 in the stock market. Then, a year later, his father passed away and McVea's home was sold for back taxes.
>
> Business ventures, including a stab at agenting, fell through. Loans were called in; McVea's cars were repossessed. "That left him pretty much down and out," says Norris.
>
> McVea, . . . faces charges that he scammed a local Kentucky Fried Chicken out of $75 worth of food. On Wednesday, he failed for the third time to show up for a scheduled court appearance.[20]

On the other hand, the life biographies of Pelé, Willie Mays, Hank Aaron, Bob Feller, Roberto Clemente, Fernando Valenzuela, Bill Russell, Althea Gibson, Mickey Mantle, Bob Cousey, Johnny Unitas, Joe Louis, Sugar Ray Leonard, Larry Holmes, Muhammad Ali, Jackie Robinson, Steve Cauthen, Willie Shoemaker, and Eddie

☐ **VIGNETTE 7.3**

Larry Holmes's "Rags-to-Riches" Biography

The idea that success in sports provides a pipeline to worldly pleasures continues to circulate. Although there are such auspicious cases they must be understood as individual occasions. Larry Holmes pummeled his former sparring mate, Muhammad Ali, on October 1, 1980, to retain his heavyweight crown. Holmes earned millions of dollars in that fight and today is worth around $3 million. As it so often turns out with boxers, times have not always been so good. Holmes was the seventh of twelve children. His father deserted the family when Larry was in seventh grade. At that time he dropped out of school and performed a variety of menial tasks—shined shoes, worked at a car wash and in the steel mills, and drove a truck. Despite Holmes's monetary and social mo-

bility he cautions: "You're getting X million to fight this guy. They forget the $65 paycheck for my first fight or the $100 for my second. I made $900 one year. Everything I got, I earned." Today matters are different. In 1980 he paid over $1 million in taxes and recently built a half-million dollar mansion on 2.5 acres of land outside his life-long home in Easton, Pennsylvania. He says, "The interest alone on my money will take care of my family, their family and then their family, too." Holmes's biography is a rags-to-riches story that, unfortunately, is considerably less common than many believe.

SOURCE: "Larry Holmes: Shadowboxing The Legend of Ali," Eliot Kaplan, *Family Weekly* (17 May 1981), pp. 39, 41.

☐

Arcaro evidence the social and economic success—"social climbing"—afforded to persons of humble origins in the world of sports (Vignette 7.3). Havighurst and Neugarten wrote, "athletic prowess combined with education often provides a very good base for mobility in a lower class boy,"[21] and Hodges reports, "college football has functioned as a highly effective status elevator for thousands of boys from blue-collar ethnic backgrounds."[22] Other means of fostering mobility, besides sports, include education, aggressiveness, intelligence, hard work, and sheer luck.

In caste-based societies, an individual's position is allegedly **ascribed,** which implies that little or no mobility is possible and that individuals remain in the same social stratum from the cradle to the grave. Although thousands of castes and subcastes exist in India, in theory there were four major castes: (a) the Brahmans (priests and teachers); (b) Kshatriyas (princes and warriors); (c) Sudras (manual workers); and (d) outcastes, or untouchables. The contemporary influence of the caste system has waned, particularly in the urban areas, but historically, great efforts were taken in the preparation and serving of food by different castes as well as the avoidance of the bottom caste. In practice, however, even in India, through sanskritization, some degree of social mobility has occurred in caste-based societies. Similarly, an individual's position in the estate system was also ascribed, although some mobility was possible, such as when a knight became an earl.

☐ SPORT AS A SOCIAL MOBILITY MECHANISM

The archetypical rags-to-riches story is that of Abraham Lincoln. "Honest Abe" ascended from a log cabin to the White House; in a similar vein, industrial magnates like Andrew Carnegie, John D. Rockefeller, and J.P. Morgan began life in poverty and later became millionaires. These tales stir the spirit but distort the fact that countless others failed to become successful despite lofty ambitions and tireless efforts. Research on social mobility cautions us on becoming overly optimistic about hard work and grandiose dreams producing major alterations in ascribed social realities.

According to Blau and Duncan, there is a pattern of moderate social mobility in the United States, but very few scenarios of the log cabin-to-White House variety.[23] Most of the social mobility can be accounted for by three factors: (a) an increase in white-collar positions necessitating someone to fill them, (b) the differential birth rate and increase in the number of slots available, and (c) migration of large numbers of unskilled workers who force existing urban groups into higher status occupations. Note that these explanatory variables are *social,* not individual, factors.

In what ways can sport be an escalator of upward social mobility? After reviewing the literature on sport and mobility, Loy proposed the following four channels through which involvement in athletics could facilitate social climbing:

1. Sport participation may foster the development of athletic prowess permitting a direct entry into professional sports with minimal formal education. Historically, boxers, jockeys, and professional baseball players fit this mold.
2. Sport participation may directly or indirectly enhance educational achievement. Participation in school sports may: (a) foster better grades, either because of the "spill-over" of desirable traits from athletics or the need to maintain minimum eligibility requirements; (b) increase the probability of graduation; and (c) lead to the granting of a tender from an institution of higher learning. Numerous sport participants have received these benefits in a wide range of sports.
3. Sport participation may lead to occupational sponsorship. Boxers have frequently been supported by wealthy persons and summer jobs often have been provided to college athletes. Major U.S. corporations have also provided facilities, time, and money for athletes to train for the Olympics and other international sporting events.
4. Sport involvement may nurture attitudes and behaviors conducive to success in other occupations. Some ex-athletes, upon retirement, have been able to channel their abilities into other occupational fields such as sports broadcasting and acting.[24]

There are two opposing camps with respect to the role sport plays in fostering vertical mobility for blacks, although the positions do not apply only to that minority group (Vignette 7.4). One position, the *sports-enhances-mobility* hypothesis, views sport as an effective avenue through which higher social status can be obtained. The second position, the *sports-impedes-mobility* hypothesis, sees sport as a dead end for the overwhelming majority of individuals who ultimately waste their precious time and energy honing sport skills. Braddock's[25] critical review of the race, sports, social mobility literature leads to the general conclusion that "sport does not inhibit social

Harry Edwards on the Role of Sport to Blacks

Harry Edwards has been a leader in raising blacks' consciousnesses to the pros and cons of sports. In the following excerpts (the first from his 1980 book *The Struggle That Must Be*), does he seem to have altered his views or mellowed a bit?

Outspoken sport sociologist Harry Edwards eloquently states:

> Because Black society has not yet learned to deal with it intellectually, sport has loomed like a fog-shrouded minefield for the overwhelming majority of Black athletes. It has been a treadmill to oblivion rather than an escalator to wealth and glory it was believed to be. There is today disturbingly consistent evidence that the Black athlete who blindly sets out to fill the shoes of Dr. J., Reggie J., Kareem Abdul-J., or OJ is destined to end up with no J—no job whatsoever that he is qualified to do in our modern, technologically sophisticated society. At the end of his sports career, he is not running or flying through airports like O.J. He is much more likely to be sweeping up airports—if he has the good fortune to land the job.

Despite the muckraking role Edwards often takes regarding the role of sports to blacks, his following statements temper some features of his more critical stance:

> . . . I do not advocate that Black society discourage its youths from . . . sport participation. To the con-

trary, I am thoroughly convinced that Black achievements in sports have benefited Afro-American society in many ways. On a spiritual level, the performances of outstanding Black athletes have bolstered Black pride and self-esteem. On a practical level, sports have been means to higher-education opportunities for many Black youths . . . who have moved on to establish productive careers in other fields. Further, by virtue of their enormous accomplishments in sports, Black athletes have demonstrated that the greatest obstacle to Black achievement in *all* areas of American life has not been lack of capability or competitiveness, but a lack of opportunity. By every measure, therefore, I believe that Black involvement in sport is as legitimate as Black pursuit of career opportunities in any other field—law, medicine, science, education, . . . and therefore is to be encouraged. But as with all careers, Blacks pursuing a sports career must approach the task intelligently. And first, foremost, and above all else, *this means recognizing that sport inevitably recapitulates society and that, therefore, it would be as impossible for a substantially racist society to have a substantially non-racist sports institution as it would be for a chicken to lay a duck egg.*

SOURCE: Harry Edwards, "Race in Contemporary American Sports," *National Forum* LXII, no. 1 (Winter 1982), pp. 19–22.

▢

mobility" but the methodological issues intrinsic to the two-dozen studies he reviewed necessitate the need for quality inquiries with adequate research designs and analyses. (Of interest, Oliver found that black families, vis-à-vis their white counterparts, are more in agreement with the sports-enhances-mobility theme.[26]

An important nuance when discussing mobility is the distinction between direct and indirect forms. *Direct mobility* focuses on the pecuniary benefits of having attained the status of professional athlete. Scoville's[27] data provide testimony to the economic advantage of being an athlete: The average income for all male athletes is considerably higher than the average income for nonathletes in the labor force. On the negative side of the ledger, the absolute number of positions in professional sport is very limited; the probability of becoming a professional athlete is slim (Table 7.2). Braddock[28] notes that nonplayer sport-related professions such as sportscaster, coach, and personal director also fall under the direct-mobility path, and when these are added to the professional athlete position, a more auspicious picture results.

Indirect mobility focuses on the byproducts of athletic participation: for example, the high school athlete who graduates because of the encouragement and social support others who recognized his athletic prowess extended; the college athlete who, without the benefit of a scholarship, would not have gone beyond high school. Indices of indirect mobility "include academic achievement, educational aspirations, and income and occupational attainments in non-sport occupations."[29]

While many persons have undoubtedly profited from sport in one or more of the previously mentioned ways suggested by Loy,[30] some crucial questions remain unanswered. How much mobility via sports is generally achieved? Is it long-lived or merely short term? The English poet A.E. Housman poignantly and humanistically, not empirically, captures the ephemeral nature of the sports limelight in the following stanzas:

> Smart lad, to slip betimes away
> from fields where glory does not stay
> And early though the laurel grows
> It withers quicker than the rose
> and finally, Runners whom renown outran
> And the name died before the man.[31]

Is sport a more effective mobility escalator than other occupational areas such as entertainment, the military, or education? In what ways does sport participation enhance mobility? Which sports are the most effective agents of upward mobility? Are team sports more effective than individual sports? Finally, assuming mobility is achieved via sports, how long does it last after a sports career has terminated?[32] Arthur Ashe addressed these provocative queries in an open letter to black parents, because blacks

TABLE 7.2 Probabilities of advancing from one level of sport to another, circa 1990

Approximate Number of Players in:	Football		Basketball		Baseball	
High School	750,000		550,000		400,000	
		$p = .05$*		$p = .025$		$p = .05$
College	40,000		14,000		21,000	
	$p = .003$	$p = .06$	$p = .0005$	$p = .02$	$p = .0016$	$p = .03$
Pros	2,300		280		625	
Rookies (annually)	250		55		100	

*The "p" represents the proportion of athletes at one level that continue to participate at another. For example, in football, .05 (40,000/750,000 = .05) of the pool of high schoolers play in college. These figures are approximations and probably conservative.

have frequently "bought" the insidious myth of the ease of upward social mobility achieved via sports:

> There must be some way to assure that the 999 who try but don't make it to pro sports don't wind up on the street corners or in the unemployment lines. Unfortunately, our most widely recognized role models are athletes and entertainers—"runnin" and "jumpin" and "singin" and "dancin."
>
> Our greatest heroes of the century have been athletes—Jack Johnson, Joe Louis, and Muhammad Ali. Racial and economic discrimination forced us to channel our energies into athletics and entertainment. These were the ways out of the ghetto, the ways to get that Cadillac, those alligator shoes, and cashmere sport coat.
>
> Somehow, parents must instill a desire for learning alongside the desire to be Walt Frazier. Why not start by sending black professional athletes into high schools to explain the facts of life.
>
> I have often addressed high school audiences and my message is always the same. For every hour you spend on the athletic field, spend two in the library. Even if you make it as a pro athlete, your career will be over by the time you are thirty-five. So you will need that diploma. . . .[33]

A sobering statistic is revealed in the answer to the question: How many blacks are professional athletes today? The answer, about 1,200! In 1991 there were fifteen times more black doctors, twelve times more black lawyers, and two and one-half times more black dentists than black professional athletes in the United States. The likelihood of a professional athletic career is an elusive dream for all but an infinitesimal few. The statistics bear this out. In 1990 there were approximately 400,000 high school baseball players, 21,000 college baseball players, and 625 major league baseball players, and each year approximately 100 rookies are added. Using these data, the probability of a high school baseball player being a major league baseball player is 625/400,000, or .0016. Consider football. In 1990, about 750,000 high schoolers played the game, 40,000 collegians, and about 2,300 major professionals, and each year about 250 rookies are added. The probability of a high school footballer playing professional ball is 2,300/750,000, or .003. Finally, the odds in basketball are slimmest of all. In 1990, approximately 550,000 played in high school, 14,000 in college, 280 in the National Basketball Association (NBA), and 55 rookies are added annually. The probability of a high schooler joining the NBA is 280/550,000, or .0005. Once major league status is obtained, the career duration is not great, because the average tenure is 7.5, 4.5, and 5 years in baseball, football, and basketball, respectively.

Two final sport trends are worth noting.[34] First, the sharp elite versus folk dichotomy that described social distinctions in sport is fading. We have begun to see a **democratization of sport** in the United States. With increasing affluence, leisure time, and mass-media exposure, we probably can anticipate further homogenization of the participant and spectator preferences of Americans, regardless of class. However, even when members of different social class positions enjoy the same sport, there may be revealing social differences:

> . . . while the upper classes purchase yachts and large cabin cruisers, the lower classes make do with small motor boats and row boats. The wealthy may own golf carts, the lower classes, if they can afford to golf at all, carry their clubs and walk. The wealthy wear expensive tennis, ski, golf, etc. sport clothing while the poor make do with the less

extravagant apparel. The wealthy go on expensive hunting safaris or follow their favorite collegiate or professional team across the country while the less affluent are content to watch these events on television. Wealthy sports fans purchase box seats costing, sometimes, thousands of dollars while the poor watch television or, if they attend the game, sit in the outfield or in the end zone.[35]

The **embourgeoisement** of professional athletes is another recent trend in American society. The occupational prestige accorded to athletes (Table 7.3) in America has approached and even surpassed the social and material rewards typically garnered by many professionals in American society. The salaries that some skilled athletes command at present are considerably greater than those received outside the sport realm. A public opinion survey showed that 27% of a random sample of Americans believed athletes enjoy great prestige.[36] Those occupations deemed "very prestigious" by large percentages of the sample (actual figures enclosed in parentheses) included: scientist (67%), physician (62%), minister (41%), lawyer (37%), engineer (34%), and teacher (30%). Those occupations perceived as having less prestige included artist (21%), businessperson (18%), entertainer (18%), politician (17%), journalist (17%), banker (17%), skilled worker (15%), and salesperson (6%).

Social Mobility Studies of Former Athletes

"Where does a young man go to get rich today? Wall Street? Law? Big Business?" When *Forbes* (1972) asked this query over 20 years ago the answer was "none of those listed." Instead, the correct response was "professional sports." On the surface one could argue that fame and fortune await one in professional sports. Average salaries in team sports are very high, and top money winners in individual sports enjoy envious prize monies. Even the *minimum* salaries in certain team sports place the typical athlete in the upper percentile rankings in terms of income.

Is sport an effective agent of social mobility? Sanoff and Schrof present a striking contrast to some earlier studies.[37] These writers followed up the 1980 University of Georgia football team, who earned the number one ranking in postseason polls. A decade later, the starting offense was interviewed. The findings were less than auspicious—nine out of twelve failed to receive their degrees, and none of the blacks received degrees.

A statistical study by the U.S. Department of Education of 8,100 college students, including athletes, from selected years between 1972 and 1986, found that by age 32, former football and basketball players had the highest rate of home ownership (77%) and earnings 10% above the mean of all former students who attended four-year schools. Once in the work force, the study reports, the former athlete likely will hold a job as a manager, salesman, or teacher at an average annual income of $26,000.[38]

McIntyre investigated the educational backgrounds of white male varsity athletes at Penn State.[39] His study was confined to individuals who participated in football, basketball, gymnastics, and wrestling during the 1958–1959 school year. He discovered that 69% of the football players' fathers had not completed high school, which compared with 35%, 31%, and 31%, respectively, for the fathers of baseball, wrestling, and gymnastic participants. The problem of making inferences about social mobility from this study is the reverse of the previous one; namely, we do not know—socioeconomically speaking—where these athletes are today.

TABLE 7.3 Occupational Prestige Ratings in the United States

Occupation	Score*	Occupation	Score*
Cabinet member, federal govt.	89	Social worker	50
		Newspaper columnist	50
U.S. rep. in Congress	86	Electrician	49
State governor	85	Airline stewardess	48
U.S. Supreme Court Justice	85	Trained machinist	48
		Policeman	48
Scientist	80	Bookkeeper	48
Physician	78	Insurance agent	47
College professor	78	Reporter on daily paper	47
Lawyer	76	Secretary	46
Diplomat, U.S. Foreign Service	75	Radio announcer	45
		Tax collector	44
Mayor of large city	75	Ballet dancer	43
Dentist	73	Post office clerk	43
Priest	73	Stenographer	43
Minister	72	Carpenter	43
Banker	72	Local official of labor union	41
Member, board of directors of large corporation	72	Railroad conductor	41
		Telephone operator	40
Psychologist	71	Mail carrier	40
Architect	70	Plumber	40
Airline pilot	70	Barber	38
Rabbi	68	Automobile repairman	37
Chemist	68	Garage mechanic	35
Civil engineer	67	Corporal in regular army	35
Sociologist	65	Beauty parlor operator	33
TV star	63	Cashier in supermarket	31
Captain in regular army	63	Taxi driver	30
Public school teacher	62	Clerk in a store	28
Osteopath	62	Housekeeper, private home	25
Optometrist	62		
Registered nurse	61	Coal miner	25
Druggist	61	Midwife	23
Owner of factory that employs about 100 people	60	Filling station attendant	22
		Waitress	20
Author of novels	60	Bartender	20
Building contractor	59	Soda fountain clerk	17
Economist	57	Janitor	16
Official of an international labor union	55	Share-cropper—one who owns no livestock or equipment and does not manage farm	15
Peace Corps member	53		
Journalist	52		
Undertaker	51	Garbage collector	13
Computer programmer	51	Street sweeper	11
Professional athlete	51	Shoe shiner	9

*The occupation score is based on a scale from 0 to 100.

SOURCE: Donald J. Treiman, *Occupational Prestige in Comparative Perspective* (New York: Academic Press, 1977), pp. 318–329.

Loy faulted social mobility studies of athletes for not simultaneously considering beginning and ending points, a methodological criticism that applied to earlier studies.[40] Loy tried to remedy this omission by examining the original social backgrounds and the subsequent occupations of an elite group of athletes from the University of California at Los Angeles (UCLA). All athletes had received at least three varsity letters during four years of sport competition. Of the approximately 1,386 "Life Pass Holders" that were sent Loy's questionnaire, 83% returned it. Loy discovered that college athletes, regardless of sport, were generally upwardly mobile by comparing father's occupational prestige with that of his son's first job (i.e., by studying intergenerational mobility).

Sack and Thiel compared mobility patterns of Notre Dame football players (the experimental group) with a random sample of university students who were not varsity athletes (the control group).[41] Individuals in both groups had graduated between 1946 and 1965. From this study, Sack and Thiel concluded the following: (a) Both groups had achieved upward social mobility. (b) Athletes, as opposed to nonathletes, were less likely to obtain professional or graduate degrees. (c) Athletes tended to come from lower socioeconomic origins than nonathletes. (d) Both groups had achieved income mobility (as determined by comparing father's income with their own). (e) There was a relationship between the player's status on the team during his senior year (e.g., starter, or second team, etc.) and present income. Starters earned substantially more than reserves. The researchers concluded that both football players and nonathletes from Notre Dame had experienced upward social mobility. However, there were differences favoring nonathletes in the attainment of advanced degrees.

Bend also compared a control group of nonathletes with an experimental group of athletes (subdivided into "casual," "active," and "superior" athletes) to determine the relationship between sport participation and social mobility.[42] He discovered a direct association between athletes' performance levels (casual, active, and superior) and income, education, and future expectations. Specifically, athletes vis-à-vis their nonathlete counterparts made more money, achieved higher levels of education, and anticipated making more money in the future. Acknowledging that this correlation could be spurious, Bend compared athletes and nonathletes, after controlling for parental socioeconomic status and the subject's intelligence level, and found the relationship to be genuine. Athletes were likely to earn more money and were more likely to graduate from college than nonathletes, and these differences could not be attributed to intelligence or social-class differences.

Several former athletes have been recipients of the coveted Rhodes Scholarship. This accolade, named after the British financier Cecil Rhodes, is an award enabling academically superior students to attend Oxford University in England. The following is a partial list of former college athletes who have received this meritorious recognition: J.W. Fulbright, 1925 (football, Arkansas); Howard K. Smith, 1937 (track, Tulane); Byron "Whizzer" White, 1938 (football, Colorado); Frank "Sandy" Tatum, 1947 (golf, Stanford); Hamilton Richardson, 1955 (tennis, Tulane); Kris Kristofferson, 1958 (football, Pomona); Pete Dawkins, 1959 (football, United States Military Academy, West Point); Bill Bradley, 1965 (basketball, Princeton); Misha Petkevich, 1973 (figure skating, Harvard); Tom McMillen, 1974 (basketball, Maryland); Pat

Haden, 1975 (football, University of Southern California [USC]); and Caroline Alexander, 1977 (pentathlon, Florida State).[43]

Former athletes have had stints at professional acting careers. Among the most prominent are Joe Namath (football, Alabama); Burt Reynolds (football, Florida State); O.J. Simpson (football, USC); Robert Shaw (rugby, England); Jim Brown (football, Syracuse); Robert Ryan (boxing, Dartmouth); Bruce Dern (track, Pennsylvania); Mike Connor (basketball, UCLA); Vince Edwards (swimming, Ohio State); Kirk Douglas (wrestling, St. Lawrence); Chuck Connors (baseball, Dodgers and Cubs); James Garner (football, Oklahoma); John Wayne (football, USC); Paul Robeson (football, Rutgers); Alex Karras (football, Iowa); Joe Greene (football, North Texas); Rosy Grier (football, Penn State); Bubba Smith (football, Michigan State); and Fred Dryer (football, Rams).[44]

Talamini's investigation of the retirement patterns of major league baseball players paints an auspicious picture.[45] Focusing on the occupational prestige of the jobs filled by ex-baseball players, he discovered that nearly three fourths were working in high-prestige occupations. Only 42% of the ex-players were in positions completely separated from the sports world because nearly 60% were within the social world of sport (e.g., within baseball itself, teacher-coach, athletic director, recreational director, sports information director). He reports that "contrary to the tragic theme in drama and literature, most ex-ballplayers are working in comfortable occupations with a middle class lifestyle."

❏ DISENGAGEMENT FROM SPORT

The transition from the glamour and glitter of the sport world to the "real" world can pose significant psychological and social adjustments. Retirement from professional sport can be an extremely difficult experience. One of the more poignant and sorrowful illustrations of this is the fate of former Kansas City Chiefs star, Jim Tyrer. After retirement from professional football, Tyrer experienced a series of personal and business failures that drove him to murder his wife and himself. Athletes who retire do not typically resort to this extreme type of destructive behavior, but sinking into social and psychological oblivion is not, unfortunately, an uncommon pattern. In the late 1970s, a program under the auspices of the National Football League Players' Association (NFLPA) was designed to help athletes cope with retirement. A career-counseling program was established in 1979 and financed through the NFL Management Council. This program included workshops focusing on those values, interests, and abilities of ex-players that are not football related. The program succeeded in placing former athletes in business organizations as well as in civic and children's groups. While career-counseling programs continue to exist, problems with financial backing have reduced the number of workshops over the past few years.

❏ SOCIAL STRATIFICATION HAS SPORT CONSEQUENCES

When sociologists talk of the consequences of social stratification, they have in mind the myriad ramifications affected by one's position on the social-class ladder. These consequences fall under *two* broad categories: (a) life chances and (b) life-styles. The term *life chances* refers to how long one can anticipate living (longevity), the nature of that living, and the extent to which one can enjoy the "good life," and all of these have been found to covary with one's social class moorings. The term *life-styles* refers to how one lives; it includes hobbies, organizational affiliations, sexual and social behavior, avocational pursuits, use of language, and leisure-time activities. Life-styles, like life chances, are also correlated with social class and are lucidly depicted in Berger's quote at the beginning of the chapter. We now examine some sport consequences, particularly spectatorship and participation, of social class.

FAVORITE SPORTS BY SOCIAL CLASS

Like many aspects of the social world, sport preferences are affected by social class. Curry and Jiobu[46] list characteristics of sports enjoyed by different segments of the social class ladder (Table 7.4). The pattern of responses reveals that upper-class persons prefer participation sports, whereas the modal response for both middle- and lower-class persons indicates a preference for spectator sports.

TABLE 7.4 Characteristics emphasized by certain sports and social stratification

Sport	Speed	Aggression-Hitting	Team Competition	Fine Skill, Long Formal Training	High Technology
Upper class sports					
Polo	yes	?	yes	yes	no
Yachting	no	no	no	yes	yes
Equestrian	yes	no	?	yes	no
Middle-upper middle class sports					
Golf	no	no	no	yes	no
Tennis	yes	no	?	yes	no
Football	yes	yes	yes	no	no
Middle-working class sports					
Basketball	yes	yes	yes	no	no
Baseball	yes	no	yes	no	no
Hockey	yes	yes	yes	no	no
Boxing	yes	yes	no	no	no
Competitive wrestling	yes	yes	yes	no	no
Working class sports					
Commercial wrestling	?	?	?	?	no
Roller derby	yes	?	?	?	no
Auto and motorcycle racing	yes	no	no	yes	yes

SOURCE: Timothy J. Curry and Robert M. Jiobu, *Sports: A Social Perspective* (Englewood Cliffs, NJ: Prentice-Hall), 1984, p. 68.

Despite the general popularity of sports, the list of favorite sports is relatively small and is specified by age, sex, residence, and socioeconomic variables. Among an adult sample ($n > 500$) of Minneapolis residents, Stone discovered only ten sports mentioned as favorites by 3% or more of the sample.[47] The last column in Table 7.5 presents the percentage of the sample that mentioned each particular sport, as well as their implicit rank ordering. Notice that football and, to some extent, baseball stand out. Notice, too, that age, sex, residence, and socioeconomic status influence the choice of favorite sports.

Because social stratification is our present concern, look at the socioeconomic strata column in Table 7.5. The designations in the table—L, M, and U—are statistically significant (i.e., unlikely to result from chance) and suggest a pattern to the differences. For example, the favorite sports of lower-class persons are baseball, bowling, and boxing; the favorites for middle-class individuals are football, swimming, and basketball; golf and tennis occupy the attention of upper-class individuals. (No social class differences were revealed for fishing and hunting.) Such generalizations appear logical in view of the fact that, historically, access to facilities for golf and tennis has

TABLE 7.5 Social differences in sports designated as favorites by metropolitan residents

Favorite Sports	Selected Social Characteristics				Percent of Respondents Selecting a Favorite Sport ($n = 540$)
	Age	Sex	Residence	Socioeconomic Strata	
Football			U-S	M-U-L	24.4
Baseball		M-F		L-M-U	15.4
Golf				U-M-L	11.3
Fishing		M-F			9.6
Swimming	Y-O	F-M	U-S	M-U-L	7.6
Basketball				M-L-U	6.8
Bowling		F-M		L-M-U	6.3
Tennis				U-M-L	3.7
Hunting		M-F			3.7
Boxing		M-F		L-M-U	3.3
Others too diverse to analyze					7.8

SOURCE: Gregory P. Stone, "Some Meanings of American Sport: An Extended View," *Sociology of Sport: Proceedings of the C.I.C. Symposium on the Sociology of Sport,* ed. Gerald S. Kenyon (Chicago: Athletic Institute, 1969), p. 11. Reprinted by permission.

*Categories of informants making most mentions of any specified activity are listed first, those making fewest mentions are listed last, reading from left to right. In the age category those less than forty years of age are designated "Y," those forty years of age or more are designated "O." In the sex category, men are designated "M" and women "F." In the residence category, "U" designates respondents living in the Minneapolis city limits; "S" those living in the suburbs. In the socioeconomic category those in the highest category are designated "U," those in the middle, "M," and those in the lowest, "L." Only significant associations ($p < 0.05$) are presented.

been limited to the upper crust. The emphasis on physical aggression among lower-class persons may explain their preferences for boxing.[48] Sports preference differences might also be explained by differential cultural values, with upper-class persons leaning toward participation sports and middle- and lower-class individuals leaning toward spectator sports.

Television Preferences by Various Social Structural Categories

Simmons Market Research Bureau compiled the data in Figure 7.1. The number of viewers of particular sports is shown, and for each sport, an indication of the most likely viewers. Because socioeconomic status is our present concern, examine the indicators of social class, namely, education, income, and occupation. To illustrate, using the hypothetical "average adult" as a baseline, note that for professional basketball, professionals, college graduates, and those earning incomes of $30,000 or more, are 34%, 33%, and 17% more likely to watch televised professional basketball than the average adult. What is sociologically revealing is that television sport preferences tend to be correlated with measures of social class.

Despite the reported differences, sports qualify as dominant preoccupations in American culture. In Stone's study, 75% of the men and almost 50% of the women reported discussing sports frequently or very frequently.[49] According to *The Miller Lite Report*, sports "is an element of American life so pervasive that virtually no individual is untouched by it."[50] At the extremes, the *Report* indicates that about 19% of the population are avid sport fans and 4% are unaffected by sport. The *Report* found a positive association between social class and both attendance at sporting events and participation in various participatory activities.

☐ ACTIVE PARTICIPATION IN SPORTS

Zelman advances the thesis that differences in sport participation of upper- and lower-class persons transcend the sheer cost of participating.[51] Most provocative is his claim that sports differ in the kinds of social experiences, personal needs, opportunities, and environment. To illustrate, upper-class sports, while often expensive, tend not to involve physical contact, and the competitive component may be subservient to the social experience the sport provides. Contrarily, lower-class sports tend to be less expensive, entail physical contact, and contain a high degree of competitiveness. Gender and age considerations of upper- and lower-class sport are also significant. Upper-class sports frequently attract young and old as well as men and women, whereas lower-class sports are often played considerably more by the young (vs. old) and men (vs. women). Sociologically, when the sports participated in by members of these two social classes are examined in depth, there are indeed meaningful differences that would otherwise go unnoticed.

The extent of active participation in sport can be documented in various ways. About 50% of the adult American population participates in one or more sports, when the term sports is broadly defined. But does this participation apply equally across the social-class spectrum, or is socioeconomic status related to it? Evidence suggests that social class and sport participation are correlated. The highly acclaimed physical fitness boom has a nonobvious side when scrutinized sociologically. Accord-

FIGURE 7.1 Most-watched sports on TV

The top televised sports, by number of viewers. For each sport, there is an index on most-likely viewers—for example, a baseball-watching index of 123 for men indicates men are 23% more likely to watch TV baseball than the average adult.

1. PRO FOOTBALL
63.2 million viewers
37 percent of U.S. adults

	Index
Precision/craft	132
$50,000 + income*	131
Male	125
College graduate	124
West	115
35–44	110
Married	106
Suburban	105
White	104*

2. BASEBALL
62.7 million viewers
37 percent of U.S. adults

	Index
Male	123
Professional/manager	119
Midwest	119
College graduate	117
$50,000 + income*	116
45–54	112
Married	108
Suburban	105
White	104

3. COLLEGE FOOTBALL
48.9 million viewers
29 percent of U.S. adults

	Index
College graduate	135
Professional/manager	133
Male	128
$50,000 + income*	124
45–54	114
Midwest	111
Married	108
Non-metropolitan	105
White	104

4. BOXING
37.2 million viewers
22 percent of U.S. adults

	Index
Precision/craft	154
Male	142
$25,000 + income*	112
18–34	111
Black	111
Attended college	108
Single	108
Non-metropolitan	107
Northeast, Midwest	103

5. COLLEGE BASKETBALL
36.2 million viewers
21 percent of U.S. adults

	Index
College graduate	134
Professional/manager	137
Male	127
$50,000 + income*	127
Midwest	114
Single	112
45–54	109
Black	108
Non-metropolitan	103

6. PRO BASKETBALL
34.7 million viewers
21 percent of U.S. adults

	Index
Professional	134
College graduate	133
Male	129
Black	127
West	119
$30,000 + income*	117
Single	116
25–34	112
Central city	103

7. PRO WRESTLING
28.8 million viewers
17 percent of U.S. adults

	Index
Black	149
Other (job)	139
Male	130
18–24	130
South	120
Non-metropolitan	120
No high school degree	117
Single	116
$20,000 + income*	103

8. BOWLING
28.6 million viewers
17 percent of U.S. adults

	Index
Northeast	117
55–64	114
Male	113
Suburban	113
High school graduate	112
$20,000 + income*	110
Married	108
Precision/craft	107
White	104

9. TENNIS

26.3 million viewers
16 percent of U.S. adults

	Index
College graduate	163
Professional/manager	157
$50,000 + income*	149
Single	140
West	122
45–54	117
City/suburban	109
Male	108
White	103

10. AUTO RACING

25.8 million viewers
15 percent of U.S. adults

	Index
Precision/craft	153
Male	134
Attended college	120
18–24	118
Midwest	113
$25,000 + income*	113
Single	109
Non-metropolitan	109
White	106

SOURCE: Simmons Market Research Bureau, Inc. Adapted from materials summarized by Julie Stacey and appearing in *USA Today*, Jan. 23, 1987.

From Jay J. Coakley, *Sport in Society* (St. Louis: C.V. Mosby, 1990), p. 231. Reprinted with permission.

*Household income.

Note: Demographic groups include age group, occupation, race, sex, education, geographic location, household income, marital status, and household location.

Note that people from households with incomes well above the median household income in the United States (about $27,000 in 1987) are most likely to watch pro football and baseball, college football, college basketball, pro basketball, and tennis.

ing to *Sports Illustrated,* the boom in physical fitness is "in large part illusory".[52] First, look at the demographics. Some societal segments, namely, rich rather than poor, executives rather than blue-collar workers, college graduates rather than high school graduates, and adults rather than children, are considerably more active. In other words, the increase in participation is not uniformly distributed across all social, economic, and age segments, and illustrates life-style consequences of stratification. According to *Sports Illustrated:*

> The much ballyhooed growth in the number of private health clubs and employee fitness programs has been paralleled by a less widely recognized decline in the availability of traditional fitness programs in parks, recreation departments and, above all, schools. . . . The myth that the boom is a demographic phenomenon has been nurtured in part by the gratifying increase in the number of women participating in it. But women have moved into fitness activities largely to the extent that they've advanced into the upper middle class, to which the boom is geared.[53]

Evidence also indicates that the physical fitness boom has not affected the nation's youth to the same extent as their adult parents! Exercise experts say that teens have a long way to go before they catch up with their elders. A comprehensive study of youth fitness published in the late 1980s revealed results that were not auspicious:[54]

- Only 2% of 18 million youth passed the President's Physical Fitness test, a series of exercises measuring strength, endurance, and flexibility.
- Slightly more than one-third of youth between 6 and 17 ($n = 18,000$) met physical standards established for an average healthy youngster (a mere 5% were accorded an "outstanding" label).
- According to a study conducted by the Department of Health and Human Services (DHHS), only 50% of some 8,800 students between grades 5 and 12 received enough exercise to develop healthy hearts and lungs.
- The DHHS discovered that slightly more than one third of fifth- through twelfth-graders had daily gym classes.
- Today's youth are more obese than those in the 1960s.

In short, social stratification considerations become meaningful when considering the much-talked about physical fitness boom. Young people, like those who are not middle class, do not seem to have jumped on the bandwagon. The sports fan and athlete indexes constructed by the *Miller Lite* research team provide a sense of the covariation between socioeconomic status and sport.[55]

☐ ATTENDANCE AT SPORTS EVENTS

The data in Tables 7.6 and 7.7 provide a major sociological observation apropos the link between social stratification and sport: Social class (as operationalized by education and income) is positively correlated with the number of sporting events attended: the higher the social class, the greater the attendance; the lower the social class, the less the attendance. To elaborate this contention, examine the "extreme" statistics in Table 7.6. For those with an eighth-grade or less education, note that 32% failed to

TABLE 7.6 Number of sporting events attended in the past year by level of education (%)

Number of Sporting Events Attended the Past Year (Y)	Educational Level (X)				
	Eighth Grade or Less	Some High School	High School Graduate	Some College	College Graduate
None	32	21	20	18	16
1–2	19	11	15	14	12
3–5	12	10	12	11	9
6–10	17	14	15	16	18
11–20	9	14	12	16	15
More than 20	11	30	26	25	30
	100%	100%	100%	100%	100%
	(n = 191)	(n = 154)	(n = 470)	(n = 187)	(n = 243)

$[G = .14 \quad C = .19 \quad V = .10 \quad \chi^2 = 47.07 \quad p < .001]$

SOURCE: Adapted from *The Miller Lite Report on American Attitudes Toward Sports,* Milwaukee, Wisconsin (1983), p. 23.

attend any sporting events in the past year, whereas 16% of the college graduates attended no sporting events. Similarly, 11% of those with an eighth-grade or less education attended more than 20 events, while 30% of the college graduates did the same.

Using income as the indicant of social class, notice that for those earning less than $10,000, 38% did not attend any sporting events, while for those with incomes of $40,000 or more, 13% responded similarly. For those earning below $10,000, 14% attended more than 20 events in contrast to 33% for those earning $40,000 or more.

TABLE 7.7 Number of sporting events attended in the past year by income (%)

Number of Sporting Events Attended the Past Year (Y)	Income Levels (X)						
	<$10,000	$10–14,999	$15–19,999	$20–24,999	$25–29,999	$30–39,999	$40 and over
More than 20	14	26	21	29	30	30	33
11–20	9	13	16	9	13	14	16
6–10	14	15	15	17	21	22	16
3–5	12	12	14	10	11	9	10
1–2	13	14	16	20	11	12	12
None	38	20	18	15	14	13	13
	100%	100%	100%	100%	100%	100%	100%
	(n = 231)	(n = 131)	(n = 164)	(n = 141)	(n = 134)	(n = 113)	(n = 166)

$[G = .20 \quad c = .27 \quad V = .13 \quad \chi^2 = 87.31 \quad p < .001]$

SOURCE: Adapted from *The Miller Lite Report on American Attitudes Toward Sports,* Milwaukee, WI (1983), p. 23.

❑ SPORTSFAN INDEX

The Sportsfan Index, whose construction is to be described, also demonstrates the linkages between social stratification and sport. The Sportsfan Index was created from responses to seven sport-related activities: (a) watch sports on TV, (b) listen to sports on the radio, (c) read the sports pages of the newspaper, (d) watch or listen to sports news on TV or radio, (e) read books on sports and athletes, (f) read magazines on sports and athletes, and (g) talk about sports. Respondents were asked how often they engaged in each of these activities and were assigned a point value. Finally, the Sportsfan Index was quarterized. The athlete index was constructed in a similar manner, with respondents being asked how often they engaged in various activities. In Table 7.8, notice that 16% of those with an eighth-grade or less education and 9% of college graduates fall in the "nonfans" category. At the other end, 7% of those with an eighth-grade or less education and 18% of college graduates fall in the highest (i.e., ardent fan) category.

Spectator preferences, like participation in sports, are correlated with social class. Gruneau indicated that the rich lean toward such sports as "polo, yachting, training race horses, and sports car racing;" middle-class persons enjoy watching "tennis, golf, sailing, and skiing," and, finally, lower-class persons prefer "bowling, pool, boxing, autoracing, arm wrestling, figure eight skating, motocross racing, demolition derbies, and pseudo-sports like professional wrestling and roller derby."[56] Eitzen and Sage suggest that the sports with working class appeal (dubbed *prole sports,* after *prole*tariat) have the following characteristics:

1. The necessary equipment (such as automobiles or muscles) and skills (driving, mechanical aptitude, or self-defense) are part of working class life.
2. The sports emphasize physical prowess and manhood (machismo).
3. They are exciting and, therefore, serve as an emotional outlet. Some focus on the danger of high speed and powerful machines. Others stress violence to machines or

TABLE 7.8   Sportsfan index by level of education (%)

Sports Fan Index (Y)	Eighth Grade or Less	Some High School	High School Graduate	Some College	College Graduate
			Level of Education (X)		
Fan (4)	7	24	23	18	18
3	33	34	30	35	40
2	44	35	36	35	33
Nonfan 1	16	7	11	12	9
	100%	100%	100%	100%	100%
	(*n* = 222)	(*n* = 158)	(*n* = 489)	(*n* = 194)	(*n* = 251)

$$[G = .09 \quad C = .17 \quad V = .10 \quad \chi^2 = 40.81 \quad p < .0001]$$

SOURCE: Adapted from *The Miller Lite Report on American Attitudes Toward Sports,* Milwaukee, WI (1983), p. 27.

human beings. Still others contrive events to excite the crowds (e.g., in wrestling events such as tag teams, Texas Death Matches, and the Battle Royales).

4. There is strong identification with heroes who are like the spectators in ethnicity, language, or behavior.
5. The sports are not school related.
6. With few exceptions, the sports they watch are individual rather than team-oriented (which is opposite their tendency to participate in team sports).[57]

No matter what the explanation, we find that persons of upper social strata are both the most frequent participators and spectators in various American sporting events. In sum, sport preferences, spectator, and participation are related to social class. Even today, sport and social class are linked. A person's social class is associated with spectator preferences and participation choices. Participation sports of the upper class include yachting in cabin cruisers, going on safari hunts, and polo; upper- and middle-class people enjoy tennis, golf, skiing; lower-class members bowl, wrestle, box, and play pool, baseball, and basketball. Spectator preferences are affected by social class, too. Upper-echelon individuals enjoy college sports (some traveling cross-country to see their team play), golf, and tennis; lower echelon individuals are attracted to sports of daring, courage, and even violence (e.g., motorcross, demolition derbies). Of course, the linkages between social class and sport are not invariant; just the same, patterned differences exist today just as in the past.

❑ LIFE CHANCES

How long one can expect to live on earth is correlated with social class. In one of the oldest studies of longevity patterns, Dublin found, after studying 4,976 graduates of Harvard, Yale, Cornell, and seven other colleges, that athletes lived about 4.5 years longer than age cohorts (life spans as found in actuarial tables).[58] His investigation was immediately attacked on methodological grounds; critics argued that it was inappropriate to compare college graduates (and at prestigious universities at that) with the "average" person. The two categories undoubtedly differ on such crucial variables as socioeconomic status with its correlates of social, financial, and even health service advantages. The real test, wagered the dissenters, should be between college athletes and college nonathletes. Apparently, Dublin recognized the limiting feature of his seminal investigation and, in anticipation, studied the longevity of 38,269 graduates of eight eastern colleges from 1870–1905 and concluded that nonathletes lived, on the average, about 2.17 years longer than athletes.

Montoye compared varsity athletes ($n = 628$) and nonathletes ($n = 563$) at Michigan State University and discovered that athletes died about two years earlier than nonathletes (62 vs. 64 years of age).[59]

One of the most significant studies of longevity was undertaken by Polednak and Damon.[60] They analyzed mortality data of 2,631 athletes who attended Harvard University between 1880 and 1912. The researchers advanced a tripartite conclusion: (a) Nonathletes lived longer than athletes, although the difference was not statistically significant; (b) participants in minor sports (e.g., fencing, golf, and swimming) lived significantly longer than major sports participants (e.g., baseball, football); and (c) mesomorphs died earlier than endomorphs, and the latter earlier than ectomorphs.

☐ SUMMARY

Social stratification is the hierarchical arrangement of social groups or societies into strata that are unequal in power, privilege, prestige, and wealth. Social class is a major explanatory variable in sociological analysis. Knowing people's social class enables us to make probability statements about their preference for spectator and participation sports and about the particular types of spectator and participation sports they enjoy. We considered five basic features of sport stratification:

1. *Social*. Stratification often results from prejudice and discrimination on the part of the dominant group.
2. *Ancient*. Stratification has existed since recorded history and probably before.
3. *Ubiquitous*. Stratification is omnipresent.
4. *Diverse*. Stratification may foster upward mobility as in a class-based society or stifle it as in a caste-based society.
5. *Consequential*. Stratification enables certain segments of society to enjoy scarce resources unavailable to other segments.

The exclusion of African-Americans from professional baseball between the late 1890s and the middle 1940s was due to prejudice and racial discrimination and not to any supposed biological inferiority. African-Americans' contemporary dominance in many major sports is indirect testimony to the social nature of stratification. Social stratification in sport existed in Greece as early as 776 B.C., when females and slaves were systematically denied the right to participate or, in some cases, to even spectate. Stratification in sport exists both between and within sports, as evidenced by classifications of sports into major and minor categories and by the differential prestige attached to weight classes, such as in boxing and wrestling. Sport has provided a channel of upward mobility for minority groups, as well as for individuals from the lower rungs of the social-class ladder. Within American society, there is evidence that persons from the higher social classes are the most frequent participators in and spectators at various sporting events.

☐ KEY CONCEPTS

Social Stratification
Social Class
    Sport Stratification Is Social
       Functional Theory of Stratification
       Conflict Theory of Stratification
        Cultural Hegemony
    Sport Stratification Is Ancient
    Sport Stratification Is Ubiquitous
    Sport Stratification Is Diverse
    Sport Stratification Is Consequential

Caste
Estate
Achieved Positions
Horizontal Mobility
Vertical Mobility
Intragenerational Mobility
Intergenerational Mobility
Ascribed Positions
Democratization of Sport
Embourgeoisement of Sport

◻ **ENDNOTES**

1. PETER L. BERGER, *Invitation to Sociology* (Garden City, NY: Doubleday, 1963), pp. 80–81.

2. MELVIN TUMIN, *Social Stratification* (Englewood Cliffs, NJ: Prentice-Hall, 1967).

3. M. ANN HALL, "The Discourse of Gender and Sport," *Sociology of Sport Journal* 5, no. 4, (1988), p. 330.

4. KINGSLEY DAVIS & WILBERT T. MOORE, "Some Principles of Stratification," *American Sociological Review* 10 (April 1945), pp. 242–249.

5. RODNEY STARK, *Sociology* (Belmont, CA: Wadsworth, 1985), p. 216.

6. R. BENDIX & S. LIPSET, "Karl Marx's Theory of Social Class," *Class, Status, and Power,* eds. R. Bendix & S. Lipset (New York: The Free Press, 1953), pp. 26–35.
   RALF DAHRENDORF, "Toward a Theory of Social Conflict," *Social Change,* eds. E. Etzioni-Halevy & A. Etzioni (New York: Basic Books, 1973).

7. ROBERT W. PETERSON, *Only the Ball Was White* (Englewood Cliffs, NJ: Prentice-Hall, 1970).

8. RAY KENNEDY & NANCY WILLIAMSON, "Money in Sports," *Sports Illustrated* 49 (17 June 1978), p. 51. See Leonard Broom & Philip Selznick, *Sociology* (New York: Harper & Row, 1963), and A.S. Young, *Negro Firsts in Sports* (Chicago, IL: Johnson Publishing, 1963).

9. *Op. cit.,*[7] p. 17.

10. JOHN W. LOY, BARRY D. McPHERSON, & GERALD KENYON, *Sport and Social Systems* (Reading, MA: Addison-Wesley, 1978), pp. 341–343.

11. HAROLD SEYMOUR, *Baseball* (New York: Oxford University Press, 1960), p. 16.

12. THORSTEIN VEBLEN, *The Theory of the Leisure Class* (New York: Penguin, 1899/1967).

13. *Op. cit.*[10]

14. ERIC DUNNING & KENNETH SHEARD, "The Bifurcation of Rugby Union and Rugby League," *International Review of Sport Sociology* 1 (1976), p. 54.

15. ALLEN GUTTMANN, *From Ritual to Record* (New York: Columbia University Press, 1978), p. 31.

16. JOHN T. TALAMINI & CHARLES H. PAGE, *Sport and Society: An Anthology* (Boston, MA: Little, Brown, 1973), p. 4.

17. BENJAMIN G. RADER, *American Sports* (Englewood Cliffs, NJ: Prentice-Hall, 1990), p. 2.

18. ALASTAIR REID, "The Sport Scene: Heavy Going," *The New Yorker* (21 February 1977), pp. 85–86.

19. PITIRIM A. SOROKIN, *Social and Cultural Mobility* (New York: Free Press, 1959).

20. *USA Today* (12 December 1985), Section C, pp. 1–2.

21. RICHARD HAVIGHURST & BERNICE NEUGARTEN, *Society and Education* (Boston: Allyn & Bacon, 1957), p. 45.

22. H.M. HODGES, *Social Stratification—Class in America* (Cambridge, MA: Schenkman, 1964), p. 167.

23. PETER BLAU & OTIS DUDLEY DUNCAN, *The American Occupational Structure* (New York: Wiley, 1967).

24. JOHN W. LOY, "The Study of Sport and Social Mobility," *Aspects of Contemporary Sport,* ed. Gerald S. Kenyon (Chicago, IL: The Athletic Institute, 1969), pp. 101–119.
    HOWARD L. NIXON, II, *Sport and Social Organization* (Indianapolis, IN: Bobbs-Merrill 1976), pp. 37–38.

25. JOMILLS HENRY BRADDOCK II, "Race, Sports, and Social Mobility: A Critical Review," *Sociological Symposium,* no. 30, Spring 1980, pp. 18–38.

26. MELVIN L. OLIVER, "Race, Class and the Family's Orientation to Mobility Through Sport," *Sociological Symposium* no. 30, (Spring 1980), pp. 62–86.

27. JAMES G. SCOVILLE, "Labor Relations in Sport," *Government and the Sports Business* ed. R. Noll (Washington, DC: Brookings Institute, 1974), pp. 185–220.

28. *Op. cit.*[25]

29. *Ibid.*

30. LOY, *op. cit.*[24]

31. A.E. HOUSMAN, quoted in James A. Michener, *Sports in America* (New York: Random House, 1976), p. 229. Reprinted with permission.

32. NIXON, *op. cit.*[24] p. 37.

33. ARTHUR ASHE, "An Open Letter to Black Parents: Send Your Children to the Libraries," *New York Times* (6 February 1977), Section 5, p. 2.

34. Nixon, *op. cit.*,[24] p. 36.
35. George H. Sage, *Sport and American Society* (Reading, MA: Addison-Wesley, 1980), p. 226.
36. "Occupational Prestige," *Public Opinion* (August/September 1981), p. 33.
37. Alvin P. Sanoff & Janice M. Schrof, "The Price of Victory", *U.S. News and World Report* (8 January 1990) pp. 44–52.
38. *Light and Shadows on College Athletics*, U. S. Office of Education, 1991. Reported in *USA Today* (3 January 1991), p. 8C.
39. T.D. McIntyre, "Socioeconomic Background of White Male Athletes in Four Select Sports at Pennsylvania State University," master's thesis, Pennsylvania State University (1959).
40. Loy, *op. cit.*[24].
41. Allen L. Sack & Robert Thiel, "College Football and Social Mobility: A Case Study of Notre Dame Football Players," *The Sociology of Education* 52 (January 1979), pp. 60–66.
42. Emil Bend, *The Impact of Athletic Participation on Academic and Career Aspiration and Achievement* (New Brunswick, NJ: The National Football Foundation Hall of Fame, 1968).
43. *Sports Illustrated* 50, no. 18 (30 April 1979), p. 84.
44. *Ibid.*, p. 78.
45. John T. Talamini, "After the Cheering Stopped: Retirement Patterns of Major League Baseball Players," *Free Inquiry in Sociology* 17, no. 2 (1989), pp. 175–178.
46. Timothy Curry & Robert Jiobu, *Sports* (Englewood Cliffs, NJ: Prentice-Hall, 1984).
47. Gregory P. Stone, "Some Meanings of American Sport: An Extended View," *Aspects of Contemporary Sport Sociology*, ed. G.S. Kenyon (Chicago: The Athletic Institute, 1969), pp. 5–27.
48. Ronald W. Smith & Frederick W. Preston, *Sociology: An Introduction* (New York: St. Martin's Press, 1977), p. 428.
49. *Op. cit.*[47]
50. *The Miller Lite Report on American Attitudes Toward Sport* (Milwaukee: Miller Brewing, 1983), p. 7.
51. Walter A. Zelman, "The Sports People Play," *Parks and Recreation Magazine*, 11 (February 1976), pp. 27–39.
52. Jerry Kirshenbaum & Robert Sullivan, "Hold on There, America," *Sports Illustrated* 58 no. 5, (1983), pp. 60–74.
53. *Ibid.*
54. *USA Today* (17 March 1986), p. C5.
55. *Op. cit.*[50]
56. Richard S. Gruneau, "Sport, Social Differentiation, and Social Inequality," *Sport and Social Order*, eds. D.W. Ball & J.W. Loy (Reading, MA: Addison-Wesley, 1975), pp. 121–184. *Op. cit.*,[35] pp. 213–214.
57. D.S. Eitzen & George H. Sage, *Sociology of North American Sport* (Dubuque, IA: William C. Brown, 1986), p. 246.
58. Dublin, cited in James A. Michener, *Sports in America* (New York: Random House, 1976).
59. Montoye, cited in *ibid*.
60. Polednak & Damon, cited in *ibid*.

8

Sport and Race

. . . sport inevitably recapitulates society and . . . it would be as impossible for a substantially racist society to have a substantially nonracist sports institution as it would be for a chicken to lay a duck egg. HARRY EDWARDS

Sport has long been comfortable in its pride at being one of the few areas of American society in which the Negro has found opportunity—and equality. But has sport in America deceived itself? Is its liberality a myth, its tolerance a deceit? WILLIAM OSCAR JOHNSON

The social significance of sport and its implications for race and sport is aptly captured in Doob's statement:

> Perhaps nowhere in the world are sports as important to cultural life as in the United States. . . . For many, sports provide a source of personal pleasure. For others, they also offer the possibility of public respect and admiration. And for some they hold the promise of the "American dream," a perceived way to advance from poverty and obscurity to fame and fortune. In our society, however, not all people have had the same chance to participate in sports, especially beyond the personal level. This is not just the result of obvious differences in skill, ability, or level of personal commitment. To some extent it has also been a reflection of prejudice and discrimination.[1]

Prejudice (literally means prejudging without knowledge), an unfavorable feeling or thought toward a person or group, and **discrimination,** the unfavorable treatment of a person or group, are not and have not been uncommon in sport settings. These social processes have existed in virtually all societies. In American society, *minority groups,* a term limited here to racial and ethnic groups (principally blacks and Spanish-speaking persons), have occupied socially, politically, and economically subordinate positions and have experienced second-class citizenship. Sport, being a microcosm of the larger society, tends to perpetuate these same patterns despite wishful thinking to the contrary. In this chapter, we consider the manner in which prejudice and discrimination have existed and continue to exist in the sport world. Our focus will be on blacks and Latinos and Latinas[2]—two of the most visible and most discriminated against minority groups in sport and society—although other ethnic minorities (e.g., Native Americans, Asian-Americans, Anglophones, and Francophones) also will be mentioned.

Minority groups are characterized by several outstanding features:[3]

1. Share common "visible" physical (e.g., skin color) and/or cultural (e.g., language, religion) characteristics.
2. Receive differential treatment from the majority group (e.g., as revealed in the social processes of segregation, assimilation, amalgamation, annihilation, expulsion).
3. Develop a "consciousness of kind" and/or self identity revolving around their uniquenesses.
4. Practice marital endogamy (i.e., marry within their social group).
5. Have a status (i.e., minority group) that is ascribed rather than achieved.

❑ THE MEANING OF RACE

Who Is Black?

The answer appears obvious. According to James Davis, "The answer is different for blacks than for any other racial, ethnic, or religious minority group in the country."[4] The definition stems from the unique nature of slavery in this country as well as Jim Crowism after the Emancipation Proclamation. Davis concludes that the American definition of "black" is anyone with any trace of African ancestry! The charismatic black leader Malcolm X, who was assassinated in 1965, understood this well when he said, "White society has always considered that one drop of black blood makes you black."[5] Of interest is the fact that many notorious black leaders have been essentially white! Of the 22 black senators and congressmen after the Reconstruction, 19 were mulattos and some were very light skinned. Walter White was 63/64 white and served as the National Association for the Advancement of Colored People (NAACP) president from the 1920s to after the Second World War.

There are *two* ways to classify races biologically: (a) a scheme based on observable physical characteristics (e.g., skin color, hair texture, eye shape, lip thickness) called *phenotypes,* and (b) a scheme based on unobservable genetic features (e.g., blood type) called *genotypes.* Neither system is exact. As a biological concept, "race" is virtually useless. Although anthropologists have attempted for years to unambiguously classify the genetically transmitted physical characteristics of human groups into categories, their ambitious efforts have been nearly futile. The typology that has gained the widest currency is a simple and nonprecise trichotomy: (a) *Caucasoids,* (b) *Mongoloids,* and (c) *Negroids.* Realize that many people cannot be neatly pigeon-holed into this conceptualization and that human races are probably best conceptualized as occupying different gradations along a continuum. Sociologists are concerned with the *social* significance—not the biological nature—of race. Regardless of the classificatory issues, humans attach, attribute, and define meanings to differential physical characteristics.

The focus on racial issues in sports raises a serious latent sociological concern. Laurel Davis argues that the preoccupation with race "itself is racist because it is founded on and naturalizes racial categories as fixed and unambiguous biological realities, thus obscuring the political processes of racial formation. The biological determinism underlying the preoccupation conceals both human agency and sociopolitical forces, including racism."[6] As you read this chapter, it is imperative that you be cognizant of this provocative argument.

❑ A BRIEF HISTORY OF BLACKS IN PROFESSIONAL AND AMATEUR SPORT

Professional Sport

On the professional level, boxing and horse racing were two of the earliest sports in which blacks participated and excelled. Tom Molyneux and Bill Richmond became the first recognized boxing champions around 1800; most of the riders in the inaugural Kentucky Derby in 1875 were black, and a black jockey, Isaac Murphy, won three Kentucky Derbies in the late 1800s. Preceding the dawn of the twentieth century (ca. 1883), two blacks, Weldy and Moses Fleetwood Walker, were members of the professional Toledo baseball club.[7] Toward the end of the nineteenth century, blacks were forced out of professional baseball and excluded from other sports as well and formed their own baseball league in the 1920s.[8] From the late 1800s to the mid-1940s, only a handful of black professional athletes were integrated in white professional sports. Henry McDonald became the first black football player in 1911, although it was not until 1946 that Marion Motley and William Willis became the first blacks in the All-American Football Conference, when they played for the Cleveland Browns.

☐ VIGNETTE 8.1

Latent Consequences of the Integration on Black Colleges

One of the *latent* consequences of integration is that black colleges have experienced a talent drain. When the NFL conducted its annual draft in 1970, twenty-nine players in the first six rounds came from predominately black schools located in the South. Black institutions such as Grambling, Jackson State, Southern, Alcorn, and Morgan State have supplied the NFL with superstar players. A decade later only twelve of the first 168 draftees came from black schools.

When Southern schools began to desegregate, black colleges could no longer depend on a steady supply of black athletic talent from segregated high schools. As a consequence, black colleges had to compete with large state-supported and private universities with considerably larger recruiting budgets. As the desegregation process continued, blacks from integrated secondary schools felt more comfortable attending schools of higher learning that had a large proportion of their student population white. Charles Henry, then the Big Ten's assistant commissioner, said:

> There was about a 16 year lag between the time of the Supreme Court desegregation decision in 1954 until there was meaningful integration of schools in the south. [In the 1978 Sugar Bowl, Henry commented] Ohio State had 31 blacks and Alabama . . . had 31. Not so many years ago, Alabama would have had none.

Sociologically, the manifest purpose of school integration would seem to have positive consequences; however, this sociolegal phenomenon has had some unintended and unpredicted negative ramifications.

SOURCE: Bill Jauss, "Black Colleges Hit by a Talent Drain," *Chicago Tribune* (4 May 1980), p. B2.

☐

In the 1950s, blacks (i.e., "Sweetwater" Clifton and Chuck Cooper) broke the racial barrier in the National Basketball Association (NBA). Other black "firsts":

- Althea Gibson became the first black to play in the U.S. championships in Forest Hills at age 22. She became, in 1957, the first black to win the U.S. title, to win Wimbledon, and to represent the United States in the Wrightman Cup matches.
- Bill Russell was the first black head professional basketball coach (for the Boston Celtics) in 1966.
- Emmit Ashford was the first black umpire (in the American League) in 1968.
- Wayne Embry was the first black NBA general manager in 1971.
- James Harris was the first black starting quarterback (for the season) in 1975.
- In the latter 1980s, Washington Redskin Doug Williams became the first black quarterback to win the Super Bowl.

Participation by blacks in white professional sport was virtually nonexistent during the first half of the present century.[9]

Amateur Sport

On the amateur level, blacks paralleled their professional involvement. A modicum of blacks attending Eastern schools (e.g., Amherst, Brown, Harvard, and Rutgers) early in this century participated in football, baseball, and track and field.[10] The emergence of black colleges provided greater sport opportunities. Blacks participated in U.S. Army athletics between 1890 and 1916 and won medals in the 1904 and 1908 Olympics.[11]

Paul Robeson, at Rutgers, one of the most celebrated black athletes in the first quarter of the twentieth century, was elected to Walter Camp's 1918 All-American team, and was subsequently withdrawn because of his political stance. Historically, blacks played almost exclusively at black colleges until fairly recently (Vignette 8.1). Among football conferences, the South East Conference (SEC) was the last to integrate, when Tennessee signed a black defensive back in 1966.[12] In summarizing the history of black involvement in sport, McPherson wrote:

> Black athletes were excluded from most professional sports until the "color bar" was broken by Jackie Robinson. From the early 1900s until 1947 the color line was prevalent in most other social institutions. Thus, except for the few amateur athletes who competed in track and field in the Olympics or who competed in college or in the Army, integrated organized sport was not available to most blacks until the late 1940s.[13]

In the latter 1980s Georgetown's John Thompson became the first black coach to win the National Collegiate Athletic Association (NCAA) basketball championship.

❏ STATISTICAL TRENDS DOCUMENTING BLACKS' INVOLVEMENT IN SPORT

The acceptance of minority players in the major team sports of baseball, basketball, and football is testimony to the changing social organization of collegiate and professional athletics. These are team sports where blacks are found in greatest abundance (boxing, too, could be added to this list, but it is an individual sport). In other team sports, there is a dearth of blacks (e.g., tennis, soccer, polo, auto racing, golf, swimming, and ice hockey, among others). In terms of their numerical contribution, black athletes in professional sports are a case study. Totally excluded at one time from several professional sports, they now comprise about 80% of professional basketball rosters, 22% of professional baseball rosters, and 55% of professional football rosters. These figures, which are significantly higher than the percentage of blacks in the American population (about 12%), say nothing of their record-breaking performances as measured by points scored, batting averages, yards gained, and All-Star nominations. For other ethnic minorities—Asian-Americans, Mexican-Americans, and Native Americans—there is relatively little college and professional participation. (However, recall the Leonard and Reyman study reported in Chapter 7, because they compared the participation patterns of several different racial and ethnic groups.[14])

A brief chronology, complemented by tabular representation of these trends, is instructive. Blacks have made substantial progress since World War II in select sports. Because sport is generally considered one of the first institutions to integrate, let us

---

◻ **VIGNETTE 8.2**

Branch Rickey's Strategy for Signing Jackie Robinson to a Professional Baseball Contract

Branch Rickey, former president of the Brooklyn Dodgers, consciously formulated a scheme to assure that the first contemporary black baseball player, Jackie Robinson (1919–1972), had special personal qualities as well as outstanding baseball ability. Rickey saw his task as a long-term campaign to:

1. "secure the backing and sympathy of the Dodger's directors and stockholders;
2. select a Negro who would be the right man *off* the field;
3. select a Negro who would be the right man *on* the field;
4. elicit good press and public reaction;
5. secure backing and understanding from Negroes in order to avoid misinterpretation and abuse of the project; and
6. gain acceptance of the player by his teammates."

Like any social action program this one met with friction. For example, ex-baseball star Rogers Hornsby stated flatly, "Ball players on the road live (close) together. It won't work . . ." Furthermore, the National League executives issued a report which included this statement: "However well-intentioned, the use of Negro players would hazard all the physical proprieties of baseball." (Seven club owners tacitly accepted this statement).

How did Robinson feel about his experience? "As I write this 20 years later, I cannot stand and sing the National Anthem. I cannot salute the flag; I know that I am a Black man in a White world. In 1972, in 1947, at my birth in 1919, I know that I Never Had It Made." (*I Never Had It Made* was Robinson's autobiography).

SOURCE: Leonard Broom and Philip Selznick, *Sociology* (New York: Harper and Row, 1963), pp. 529–530.

◻

---

examine the change in racial composition of players here, then in other arenas. One of the reasons sport is seen as a sphere of minimal segregation and discrimination stems from the fact that it was the first institution to integrate. Even the landmark 1954 Supreme Court decision *(Brown vs. Board of Education of Topeka)* declaring segregated educational facilities unconstitutional came later. After Jackie Robinson's debut in 1947 (see Vignette 8.2 for the strategy Branch Rickey employed in signing Robinson to a professional baseball contract), the hiring policy for blacks moved slowly, but by the mid-1950s, the trend toward hiring black baseball players was entrenched. Nevertheless, a decade after Robinson's entry, there were only about twelve blacks and six Latino players in all of professional baseball.[15] (As an aside, two Boston teams have had strikingly different experiences in hiring black players. The Red Sox have been very slow to do so, while the Celtics have been pioneers.) Figure 8.1 reveals the percentage of black players on professional baseball teams for eight different years. Notice, however, that blacks' percentage of the total has declined since 1970.

Figure 8.1 Line graphs representing blacks as a percentage of the total number of professional basketball, baseball, and football players, 1954–1990.

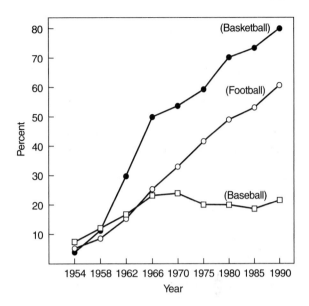

Blacks were excluded from professional basketball until about 1950, although black amateurs (in collegiate circles) were on rosters before then. When the NBA was founded in 1949, it was an all-white enclave. From the mid 1950s to the 1990s, the NBAs black composition has skyrocketed from under 10% to around 80%! There are more blacks, proportionately speaking, in this major professional team sport than in any other in the United States. The observation apparently attests to diminutive prejudice and discrimination. Karabel and Karen empirically explored several racially based questions in the NBA:[16] First, is there a correlation between the percentage of whites in a metropolitan statistical area (MSA) and the number of blacks on the team? Their answer was an unequivocal yes: in cities with black populations of less than 10%, 10% to 20%, and more than 20%, the percentages of blacks on the teams were 64%, 73%, and 87%, respectively. Further, the correlation (Pearson's r) between the number of black players on NBA teams and the percentage of blacks in the cities where these franchises are located tends to be positive.

In 1992, I discovered a correlation of +.04 between the percentage of blacks on NBA teams and the percentage of blacks in the MSA in which the teams were located. The magnitude of the association indicates a negligible relationship between the two variables.

Of all major sports (excluding boxing), professional basketball has made the greatest strides in fielding black players (Figure 8.1).

During the first quarter of the twentieth century, blacks played professional football, but they had been excluded from that sport domain from the early 1930s to the mid-1940s. Figure 8.1 lists the black percentage of total team makeup for football from 1954 to 1990.

Only since the late 1950s and early 1960s have blacks in professional baseball, basketball, and football surpassed the percentage figure (about 12%) for their makeup in the total U.S. population. The watershed years for these accomplishments were 1957–1958 for baseball, 1960 for football, and 1958 for basketball.

These statistical data seem auspicious for black athletes. However, within the sport milieu, we find subtle and even overt acts of **racism**—prejudice, segregation, discrimination—when we look deeper. In the next sections, we will more fully examine discrimination against minority groups.

☐ DISCRIMINATION IN SPORT

One of the persistent myths in North America is that organized athletics have escaped racism. Racism involves social, political, and economic discriminatory practices. The number of successful and marquee black athletes—Bo Jackson, Rickey Henderson, Muhammad Ali, Sugar Ray Leonard, O.J. Simpson, Hank Aaron, Frank Robinson, Kareem Abdul-Jabbar, Dave Parker, Willie Mays, Vida Blue, Michael Jordan, Dwight Gooden, Marcus Allen, and Calvin Peete—led many to infer that collegiate and professional sports have provided minorities an easy ladder for achieving social mobility. Sport, it is presumed, has "done something" for blacks. Much of this thinking has, unfortunately, been anecdotal, journalistic, and unsystematic. Sport sociology contains empirical evidence of the existence of institutionalized discriminatory practices (in the areas of recruitment, position assignment, performance expectation, reward and authority structures, and salary) in collegiate and/or professional circles.[17] Some of these racist practices are more or less directly demonstrable; others are more subtle, requiring inferential leaps.

Sports Illustrated's survey (reported in the 5 August 1991 issue) of professional athletes revealed that blacks still feel they are treated worse than whites in areas such as salary and contract negotiations, product endorsements, preferential treatment, and chances for becoming a manager.

One of the first blatant forms of overt discrimination in sport dates from the late 1800s. Boyle suggests that the feet-first slide was a deliberate ploy to injure black second basemen.[18] Similarly, newspaper editorials at the turn of the century warned of black supremacy in sports.[19] Racist incidents in sport are not antiquated historical events, however. In 1991, the *New York Times* reported charges of racism in tennis—charges including less desirable practice times, courts and balls, and the pairing of black opponents against each other in early tournament rounds. The *Times* quoted number 121-ranked Bryan Sheldon, "I entered a junior tournament at the Vestavia Country Club. . . . Going into the tournament, the officials here didn't know who I was. Then, I ended up winning it. The next year they changed it to an invitation-only tournament, and I didn't receive an invitation. Vestavia ended up losing their Southern Tennis Association sanction the following year. But they eventually got it back."[20] Such ugly prejudicial and discriminatory practices are not isolated events. One cannot help but think that such experiences reinforce segregation and may even dissuade blacks from taking up a game in which they could excel. Today, however, racism appears to take a less obvious form, and even sportscasters have been judged racially bigoted (Vignette 8.3). Three contemporary aspects of sport that appear to be racially biased are (a) position allocation, (b) performance differentials, and (c) rewards and authority structures.[21]

☐   **VIGNETTE 8.3**

Are White Announcers and White Owners Prejudiced against Blacks?

Howard Cosell is steaming at claims that white football announcers like himself are unconsciously prejudiced against black football players. The charges came from a blind psychologist, Raymond Rainville of the State University of New York. Rainville taped NFL games on all three TV networks, featuring sportscasters like Cosell, Don Meredith, Curt Gowdy, Frank Gifford, and Pat Summerall. Rainville compared their remarks about black and white players. He concluded blacks received much less praise than whites for doing the same thing. He feels the announcers are unaware of their biased attitudes. Here's Cosell's reaction: "It's garbage," said Cosell of Rainville's survey. "My whole life has been spent fighting for minority causes. I spent 3½ years fighting all alone for Muhammad Ali when he was stripped of his title. Who started the Jackie Robinson Foun-

dation in America? . . . I go out of my way the other way when it comes to black athletes because of my beliefs. And now some guy picks out a phrase here or there, which goes against the whole fabric of one's life."

Shortly before Cleveland Cavalier owner Ted Stepien purchased the franchise, he said: "This is not to sound prejudiced, but half the squad would be white. . . . White people have to have white heroes. I myself can't equate [sic] to black heroes. I'll be truthful—I respect them, but I need white people. It's in me. And I think the Cavs have too many blacks, 10 of 11. You need a blend of black and white. I think that draws, and I think that's a better team."

SOURCES: *Chicago Daily News* (11 November 1977). Jerome Karabel and David Karen, "Color on the Court," *In These Times* (February 1982), pp. 23–24.

☐

Position Allocation

One of the recurring patterns of discrimination in collegiate and professional athletics is **stacking,** a term coined by Harry Edwards in 1967. It is a common form of positional segregation underscoring the disproportionate concentration of ethnic minorities—particularly blacks—in specific team positions. Minority relations specialists talk of *two* types of segregation: (a) *de jure,* meaning supported by legislatively enacted laws, and (b) *de facto,* meaning supported by custom and tradition, but not by legal statutes. Stacking, then, may be conceptualized as a form of de facto segregation and the consequences of the two segregation patterns may not be too dissimilar. Stacking limits and restricts access to other team positions.[22] Consequently, intrateam competition is between members of the same ethnic and racial status. For example, in baseball, those who compete for pitching positions tend to be white, whereas those who vie for the outfield slots tend to be black; in football, the players who compete for quarterback positions tend to be white, whereas those who seek defensive back positions tend to be black. Before considering the empirical evidence of stacking in baseball, basketball, football, track and field, hockey, and soccer we will identify the theoretical underpinnings of position allocation.

Theoretically, stacking as a form of discrimination can be understood by combining the organizational principles of Grusky and Blalock. What is significant to Grusky is that: "All else being equal, the more central one's spatial location: (1) the greater the likelihood dependent or coordinative tasks will be performed, (2) the greater the rate of interaction with the occupants of other positions, . . . (3) performance of dependent tasks is positively related to frequency of interaction."[23]

Blalock maintained:

1. The lower the degree of purely social interaction on the job, . . . the lower the degree of racial discrimination.
2. To the extent that performance is relatively independent of skill in interpersonal relations, the lower the degree of racial discrimination.
3. To the extent that an individual's success depends primarily on his own performance, rather than on limiting or restricting the performance of specific other individuals, the lower the degree of discrimination by group members.[24]

The thrust of these formulations, according to sport sociologists Loy and McElvogue, is that those occupying central positions are more likely to engage in coordinative and dependent tasks and, consequently, will interact socially with other position incumbents. Loy and McElvogue forwarded the concept of centrality, which

designates how close a member is to the center of the group's interaction network and thus refers simultaneously to the frequency with which a member participates in interaction with other members and the number and range of other members with whom he interacts and the degree to which he must coordinate his tasks and activities with other members.[25]

They hypothesized that "racial segregation in professional team sports is positively related to centrality." Hence, one of the proposed forms of discrimination in organized athletics is spatial segregation, or what is called *stacking* in the sport literature.

Baseball.   Loy and McElvogue noted:

Baseball teams have a well-defined social structure consisting of the repetitive and regulated interaction among a set of nine positions combined into three major substructures or interaction units: (1) the battery, consisting of pitcher, and catcher; (2) the infield, consisting of 1st base, 2nd base, shortstop, and 3rd base; and (3) the outfield, consisting of leftfield, centerfield, and rightfield positions.[26]

Rosenblatt was among the first to observe stacking as a potential form of discrimination in major league baseball's social organization in noting that between 1953 and 1965 the distribution of positions on a team covaried by race. He pointed out that there were twice as many pitchers on a team as outfielders, but three times as many blacks were outfielders as pitchers.

A pictorial representation of the distributions of positions by race and ethnicity in major league baseball—depicting the phenomenon of stacking—appears in Figure 8.2. Note, particularly, that minorities are disproportionately positioned in the outfield and shortstop, whereas majority group members are disproportionately positioned at, particularly, pitcher and catcher. The position of outfield (right, left, and center) was 48% black in 1989.

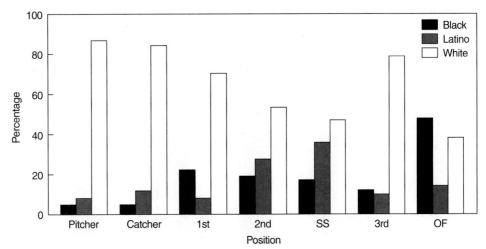

FIGURE 8.2 Position allocation in "big" league baseball, 1989
SOURCE: *USA Today* (10 August 1989), p. 110c.

Football.   Football, like baseball, also has a well-defined social structure. Whereas baseball's position alignments are defensive, football possesses both offensive and defensive lineups. The central positions for the offensive formation include center, guard, and quarterback (and sometimes punters and kickers); the central defensive positions include the linebacker slots. Figure 8.3 reveals that blacks are disproportionately positioned at running back and wide-receiver (offense) and defensive back (defense) and whites at quarterback, center, and guard. In the later 1980s, stacking in *professional* football continued to exist.

Even at the major *college* level, stacking is operative. Jones and colleagues studied the distribution of white and black players (*n* = 3,150) by position in the Big Ten, Atlantic Coast Conference (ACC) and Pacific Ten (Pac Eight at the earlier time frame) for 1972 and 1982.[27] Table 8.1 permits a detailed comparison of whites and blacks for 1982. The column labeled "Percentage Black by Position" indicates those playing positions where blacks are stacked. In using log linear analysis, Jones et al. statistically controlled several salient variables—football alignment, year, football letters earned in college, football conference, and conference school. This control procedure is significant because most studies of stacking have been primarily bivariate and thus raise the possibility of a spurious correlation between race and position. The researchers discovered that race was related to position allocation and that football alignment had an interaction effect on this relationship. The interaction effect can be easily seen by considering the odds ratios obtained in the inquiry: The odds of white offensive, white defensive, black offensive, and black defensive players occupying central positions were .714, .563, .119, and .304, respectively. The odds of whites being in central positions is greater on the offensive alignment but is reversed for blacks; that is, the odds of blacks occupying central positions is greater on the defensive alignment—such an outcome produces the interaction effect.

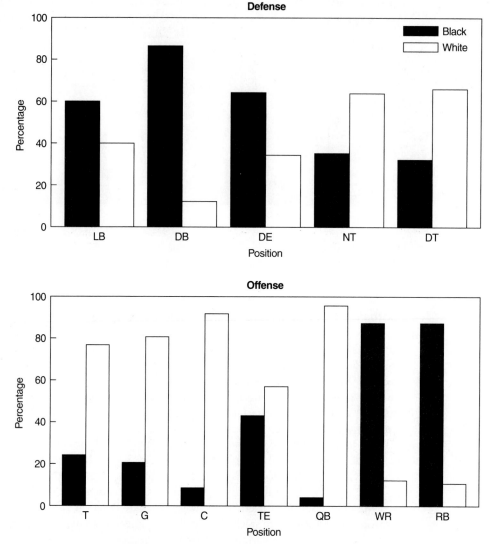

FIGURE 8.3 Position segregation in NFL defense and offense, 1989
SOURCE: *The CSSS Digest* 1, no. 2 (Summer 1989), p. 4.

Basketball. Research on stacking in basketball has been somewhat neglected, as a result, in part, of Edwards's declaration:

> In basketball there is no positional centrality as is the case in football and baseball, because there are no fixed zones of role responsibility attached to specific positions. . . . Nevertheless, one does find evidence of discrimination against black athletes on integrated basketball teams. Rather than stacking black athletes in positions involving relatively less control, since this is a logistical impossibility, the number of black athletes directly involved in the action at any one time is simply limited.[28]

TABLE 8.1   Distribution of white and black players by position in collegiate football (for the Big Ten, ACC, and Pacific Ten conferences) for 1982 (in percentages)

Playing Position	White	Black	Percentage Black by Position*
Quarterback	8.3	1.1	7.5
Running back	2.8	14.0	75.2
Fullback	2.8	6.3	57.7
Center	6.3	0.7	6.3
Left guard	8.8	1.5	9.6
Right guard	2.0	1.1	25.0
Right tackle	8.8	2.4	14.0
Left tackle	2.0	1.0	22.6
Kicker	3.4	0.1	2.4
Punter	2.1	0.1	3.8
Wide receiver	5.7	15.2	61.6
Tight end	6.0	3.9	28.3
Cornerback	5.6	19.2	67.5
Free safety	2.3	2.4	38.6
Strong safety	2.0	2.9	46.7
Middle linebacker	6.0	4.9	33.0
Right linebacker	3.8	3.1	32.8
Left linebacker	1.3	0.6	21.1
Outside linebacker	3.6	3.4	35.8
Middle guard	1.2	1.7	46.2
Nose guard	3.4	2.7	32.2
Left tackle	5.1	4.2	33.3
Right tackle	2.0	1.3	27.3
Right end	1.7	2.1	42.9
Left end	3.0	4.2	45.5
Totals	100.0	100.1	—
n =	(1,184)	(715)	37.7

*Since blacks made up 37.7% of the player population in 1982, those playing positions having less than 37.7% black were underrepresented, and the converse.

Former NBA great Bill Russell echoed Edwards's sentiments when he facetiously said: "The practice is to put two Black athletes in the basketball game at home, put three in on the road, and put five in when you get behind. . . ."[29] Ballinger has made an even stronger and more socially meaningful assertion:

> The NBA is segregated against blacks. Not just because so few black fans can afford to attend the games (black family income is . . . only 57 percent that of white families). Black players are kept out of the NBA solely on account of their color. There is a city-by-city quota system. The result is that the whiter the city the whiter the team. Phoenix has the smallest black population and the most white players. In Phoenix, Portland, San Antonio, San Diego, Denver, and Milwaukee the black population is less than 15 percent. The NBA teams in those cities have 13 percent more whites than the league average. The coaches don't pick the team; the market does.[30]

The astute basketball observer knows that basketball positions require different skills, strengths, and qualities. Characteristics like responsibility, leadership acumen, and cognitive traits such as keen judgment, decision making, and outcome control are also important. To substantiate this, Eitzen and Tessendorf content analyzed instructional manuals to determine the specific responsibilities, duties, and tasks associated with guard, forward, and center positions.[31] A general consensus regarding the requirements for these different positions was found. Guards were seen as the team's quarterback or floor general and were expected to possess leadership ability in addition to good judgment and dependability. Centers were believed to possess the greatest amount of outcome control because of their location near the basket and because they serve as their team's pivot. Desired traits in forwards included quickness, speed, physical strength, and jumping ability, the latter two characteristics giving credence to the notion of the forward as a "glass-eater." With this information, Eitzen and Tessendorf hypothesized that blacks would be overrepresented (i.e., stacked) at forward but underrepresented at center and guard.

I studied the relationship between race and position for *college* basketball players using a sample of 644 student-athletes at 47 NCAA affiliates.[32] Seven different operationalizations of position, the dependent variable, produced bivariate associations that were negligible and not statistically significant. The introduction of five control variables (NCAA division, playing and scholarship status, sex, and year in school) failed to alter the bivariate outcomes. My findings appear in Figure 8.4 and indicate that stacking in college basketball has declined, particularly at the center position, but continues to exist at forward and guard slots. Note that blacks are disproportionately positioned at forward and whites at guard.

Berghorn, Yetman, and Hanna conducted a longitudinal study (1958–1985) of men's and women's basketball teams on the variables of racial participation, degrees of equal opportunity for blacks and, of interest in the present context, racial stacking.[33] For their stacking analysis, they used data from 1970–1985 and examined position allocation in two different ways: (a) comparing guards, forwards, and centers and (b) comparing guards and forwards exclusively. When considering the first comparison—for *men* only—they write: ". . . distributions for men for each 5-year interval [1970,

FIGURE 8.4 Position allocation in NCAA basketball, 1987

SOURCE: Wilbert M. Leonard, II, "Stacking in College Basketball: A Neglected Analysis," *Sociology of Sport Journal* 4, no. 4 (1987), pp. 403–409.

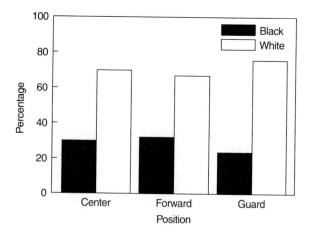

1975, 1980, and 1985] are significantly different from random, thus supporting the stacking interpretation. However, there was a substantial decrease in that difference from 1970 to 1975. Thereafter, the trend was reversed and the stacking phenomenon became more pronounced in 1980 and 1985." When considering the second comparison, Berghorn et al. found that the outcomes were *not* statistically significant and that the stacking phenomenon at guard and forward—so prominent in 1970—was eliminated five years later and had not reemerged. In short, as the participation rates of blacks soared an equal distribution of blacks and whites at guard and forward occurred; however, the center position continued to reveal white occupancy. When comparing the *women*, the researchers found a continuation of stacking as late as 1985 with the white imbalance greatest at the center position but also existing, to a lesser extent, at guard and forward.

Track and Field.   Historically, blacks have participated in track but not field events. The track events in which they have excelled include sprints and dashes, hurdles, and jumping (high, long, and triple jumps). Because blacks frequently participate in track events but not as frequently in field events, one may argue that stacking is extant here too. A moment's reflection may permit you to conclude, rightfully, that the events in which blacks participate and excel tend to be those requiring natural talent and less formalized coaching, instruction, and props.

These observations may be explained, at least in part, by institutionalized racism. There is a socioeconomic component to this phenomenon. The track events are inexpensive insofar as costs for equipment and facilities are concerned. Field events, like the pole vault, shotput, and discus, require additional cost outlays. But do most whites who participate in field events own their own equipment? We do not have data to answer this query directly, but shotputs and discusses are commensurate in price with quality basketballs. Another significant observation is that blacks have dominated the hurdles, yet it is doubtful that they own their own hurdles. Our contention is not to deny the role of socioeconomic factors; however, there also appear to be some pernicious prejudicial and discriminatory social processes operating.

Hockey.   Lavoie studied position occupancy in the National Hockey League (NHL) and concluded that stacking existed.[34] His stacking inquiry focused on the relationship between linguistic differences, specifically Francophones (French-speaking) and Anglophones (English-speaking) professional hockey players. In focusing on the position of goaltender, defense, and forward, he concluded that Francophones represent a substantial proportion of goaltenders, are rarely found in defense positions, and are intermediate in terms of position occupancy at forward. Hence, stacking apparently exists in the NHL when position and ethnicity are simultaneously examined.

Soccer.   Soccer in Britain has also been found to exhibit stacking patterns. Maguire compared position occupancy (goalkeeper, fullback, centerback, midfield, forwards) by race and discovered a disproportionate representation of blacks at certain positions.[35] Specifically, while blacks comprised nearly 8% of all players, only 1% were at the position of goalie but 14% at the forward positions. Additionally, 5%, 6%, and 8% occupied midfield, centerback, and fullback positions. When Maguire examined black and white occupancy of central and noncentral positions, he discovered that race and position were correlated. This can be observed in noting that whereas blacks comprised nearly 8% of all players, they made up 4.5% and 10.5% of central and noncentral positions, respectively.

A Provocative Observation

In 1990 blacks accounted for about 12% of the more than 250 million U.S. population. However, blacks comprised approximately 80% of professional basketball players, 70% of boxers, 55% of NFL players, 25% of track and field athletes (particularly those running in sprints, hurdles and jumping events), and 22% of professional baseball players. Obviously, their proportionate makeup in these sports well exceeds the proportion of blacks in the total population. Various explanations have been forwarded to account for this. One of the more provocative theses is elaborated by Phillips and Edwards,[36] who suggest that blacks are concentrated in relatively few sports (e.g., baseball, basketball, football, track, and boxing) and dismally represented in others (e.g., figure skating, gymnastics, sailing, horse and car racing, skiing, mountain climbing, polo, swimming, golf, tennis, and hockey) whereas white athletes are dispersed over a larger number of sports. Phillips contends that although blacks appear to be overrepresented, this would not be the case if "all sports were considered and the percentage of black participants in each were averaged, the overall proportion of top level black athletes . . . would come close to the proportion of blacks in the U.S. population."[37]

Consequences of Stacking

In the sports previously discussed (with the exception of professional basketball), stacking exists. There appear to be several significant consequences:[38]

- Because noncentral playing positions in baseball and football depend, considerably, on speed and quickness (skills that atrophy with age), playing careers are typically abbreviated for those occupying these positions.
- Truncated careers are a harbinger of less lifetime earnings.
- Shorter careers reduce players' pensions, because benefits from these programs depend on the duration of one's career.

In a study focusing on the relationships between position and experience and position and career duration, Best discovered that the occupancy of football positions by whites and blacks continues to exhibit stacking patterns.[39] Specifically, quarterback, center, and kicker were virtually all white, whereas linebacker and the traditional black positions continued to be dominated by blacks. Of central importance to the present consideration was the finding that whites vis-à-vis blacks had more experience and longer careers (median number of years played by blacks was around three, whereas the median number of years played by whites was around four), and these tend to accrue to those occupying the traditional white positions. According to Best, 75% of the black positions had shorter career durations than 75% of the white positions. Consequently, it *may* be that more whites than blacks will enjoy pension benefits and higher severance pay than their counterparts.

- The paucity of black coaches and managers may be traced to earlier position occupancy.

Another possible reason for the paucity of blacks in these circles could be overt discrimination among the owners, whereby competent blacks are eschewed because of owners' prejudices or because they fear the negative reaction of fans to having blacks in leadership positions.

Grusky's seminal investigation of the theoretical linkage between formal structure and organizational leadership, now a quarter of a century old, was replicated and extended by Leonard, Ostrosky, and Huchendorf.[40] All major league baseball managers between 1876 and 1984 ($N = 504$) as well as a random sample of players ($n = 504$) made up the units of analyses. The empirical results (Table 8.2) support Grusky's theory of formal structure and managerial recruitment. Managers were found to be recruited more heavily from the "high" interactive positions of catcher and infield than from the "low" interactive positions of pitcher, outfield, and designated hitter. This confirmation holds whether the operationalization of formal structure was the primary position, multiple positions, or the number of games played at each position.

Of the head coaches in the NFL in 1991, over half (sixteen of twenty-eight) did *not* play professional football, and of the twelve that did, nine were nonstarters. The professional playing positions of these nine included three tight ends, two linebackers, two quarterbacks, two defensive backs, two offensive linemen, and one running back.

Theoretical Explanations for Stacking. We have presented theoretical rationales advanced by Grusky, Blalock, and Loy and McElvogue to explain stacking. A host of other alternative explanations exist. For convenience's sake, we will subsume them

TABLE 8.2 Comparison of population of managers versus random sample of players by primary-position, multiple-response, and number-of-games-played operationalizations, 1876–1984 (%)

	Primary Position		Multiple Response		Games Played	
	All Managers (N = 504)	*Players Random Sample* (n = 504)	*All Managers†* (N = 504)	*Players Random Sample‡* (n = 504)	*All Managers* (N = 504)	*Players Random Sample§* (n = 504)
High inter. positions	69	41	73	57	73	48
Low inter. positions	31	59	27	43	27	52
Nonplayers*	(103)					
	N = 504	n = 504	N = 1,325	n = 1,019	N = 389,723	n = 153,852

*Nonplayers were excluded from high/low interactive calculations, hence base $n = 401$, not 504.

†Dummy variable = 1 for each position a player played at least one game, 0 otherwise.

‡Dummy variable = 1 for each position a player played at least one game, 0 otherwise; players not designating a playing position were excluded.

§Players not designating a playing position were excluded.

SOURCE: Wilbert M. Leonard, II, Anthony Ostrosky, and Steve Huchendorf, "Centrality of Position and Managerial Recruitment: The Case of Major League Baseball," *Sociology of Sport Journal*, 7, no. 3 (1990), p. 299. Reprinted with permission.

under three categories: (a) sociological or social psychological, (b) psychological, and (c) biological explanations. Importantly, these schemes overlap to some extent and hence are not mutually exclusive.

Sociological or Social Psychological Explanations.   According to **the stereotyping hypothesis,** stacking stems from management's *stereotypes* (concluding that what characterizes a few cases necessarily typifies all cases) of the physical, social, and personality attributes of minority and majority group athletes, coupled with their perceptions of the different physical, social, and personality skills required for occupants of different playing positions. Our earlier example—whereby coaching manuals indicated agreement regarding the skills of basketball guards, centers, and forwards—dovetails with this contention. In football, too, we have seen that central positions call for certain traits and skills and noncentral positions demand others; the fact that blacks and whites are unevenly distributed among these positions is testimony to this hypothesis. On the matter, Brower wrote:

> The combined function of centrality in terms of responsibility and interaction provides a frame for exclusion of blacks and constitutes a definition of the situation for coaches and management. People in the world of professional football believe that various football positions require specific types of physically- and intellectually-endowed athletes. When these beliefs are combined with the stereotypes of blacks and whites, blacks are excluded from certain positions. Normal organizational processes when interlaced with racist conceptions of the world spell out an important consequence, namely, the racial basis of the division of labor in professional football.[41]

Although Brower wrote exclusively about football, the same stereotyping process applies to other sports as well.

Tutko provided some evidence for the stereotyping hypothesis.[42] He presented 300 coaches (persons who should be able to identify objective characteristics of black and white athletes because of their direct personal experience with them) with a list of traits and characteristics and asked: Would you expect black or white athletes to score high or low on each of these items: (a) orderliness, (b) exhibitionism, (c) impulsivity, (d) understanding, and (e) abasement (humility)? The majority of the coaches expected blacks to be "low" on orderliness, understanding, and abasement and "high" on exhibitionism and impulsivity. The actual results from a scale of items measuring these traits found blacks scoring "high" on orderliness, understanding, and abasement and "low" on exhibitionism and impulsivity. Obviously, expectations and empirical results were polar opposites. The moral is simple: Coaches held conceptions of black athletes that were not scientifically verified. The pernicious side effect is that people think, feel, and behave toward social categories and their representatives in terms of preconceptions, even when their preconceptions are empirically fallacious. Such circumstances often create a self-fulfilling prophecy.

Williams and Youssef found that not only do coaches stereotype the mental, physical, and personality characteristics that are important to success at various football positions but coaches also stereotype players according to their race.[43] The results of the study supported the *matching hypothesis,* whereby coaches assign a disproportionate number of blacks, for example, to those positions where successful execution depends on those characteristics judged to be predominant in blacks; the same rationale applies to the allocation of whites to specific positions.

The **interaction and discrimination hypothesis** is premised on the notion that management and players define intimate transactions between minority and majority members negatively and, consequently, make decisions to exclude the minority members from central positions, which have high interaction potential. Underlying this hypothesis is the majority group's probable beliefs that minority group members possess undesirable characteristics and are not suitable associates.

The **outcome control hypothesis** claims that management and players exclude minorities from positions of control, leadership, responsibility, and authority because of prejudice or because they believe that ethnic minorities are not capable of adequately executing such behaviors. Edwards argued for this interpretation:

> Centrality of position is an incidental factor in the explanation of positional segregation of race in sports. The factors which really should be considered have to do with the degree of relative outcome control or leadership responsibilities institutionalized into the various positions. . . . Centrality . . . is significant only in so far as greater outcome control and leadership . . . are typically invested in centrally located positions since actors holding these positions have a better perspective on the total field of activity.[44]

To Edwards, this explanation, when interlaced with the myth of black intellectual incompetence, is the real culprit.

Medoff's **prohibitive cost hypothesis** is an economic explanation for stacking.[45] Accordingly, the high cost of training athletes for certain positions (from most to least expensive "occupational costs" in baseball are the positions of pitcher and catcher; shortstop, second and third base; first base; and outfield) coupled with the low socioeconomic standing of minorities, is responsible for differential position occupancy. As a result of blacks' inferior socioeconomic status, they are relegated to noncentral positions because training, instruction, equipment, and facilities tend to be inaccessible to them. Under such situational contingencies, blacks choose those positions where the occupational costs are minimal. Medoff provided a modicum of support for this notion by showing a positive correlation between the rising socioeconomic status of blacks and their increased share of central positions between 1960 and 1970. Such a conclusion assumes that all other conditions (e.g., prejudice and discrimination) have remained constant, an assumption that has not been empirically established and may be subject to the ecological fallacy (i.e., correlations for groups or aggregates do not necessarily apply to individuals).

Other researchers have questioned the validity of this interpretation. Lavoie argues that the prohibitive cost explanation is ambiguous and does not support the fact that Latinos from poor socioeconomic backgrounds are often found in the middle infield (i.e., particularly shortstop) central positions.[46] Yetman reanalyzed Medoff's data and argues that the latter's interpretation is not correct.[47]

The **differential attractiveness of positions hypothesis** assumes that minority members evaluate sport positions differently and choose positions on the basis of these perceptions. There are *two* branches to this hypothesis. First, minority group athletes choose to play those positions offering the greatest likelihood for individual success, recognition, achievement, popularity, prestige, and monetary reward. When former all-professional wide receiver Gene Washington was at Stanford, he played quarterback his first two years and switched to flanker as a junior. Washington, not his coaches, desired the change: "It was strictly a matter of economics. I knew a black quarterback would have little chance in professional ball unless he was absolutely superb."[48] Outfielders in baseball, and wide-receivers, cornerbacks, and running backs in football require independent task activity and receive much visibility and publicity; generally these positions are correlated with high salaries. This formulation does not, however, account for their underrepresentation in other lucrative and socially esteemed positions, such as quarterback, pitcher, or catcher, nor does it account for the virtual absence of blacks from sports such as swimming and diving, hockey, soccer, wrestling, polo, bowling, tennis, golf, yachting, auto racing, and horse racing.

The second variation of this hypothesis contends that blacks shy away from positions considered to be unattainable at higher levels of sport competition. Eitzen and Sanford found a significant departure by blacks from central to noncentral positions for a sample of 387 professional football players who had played in high school and college.[49] Yetman and Eitzen wrote,

> Given discrimination in the allocation of playing positions (or at least the belief in its existence), young blacks will consciously avoid those positions for which opportunities appear to be low (pitcher, quarterback), and will select instead those positions where they are more likely to succeed (the outfield, running and defensive back).[50]

According to the **role-modeling hypothesis,** young blacks emulate and seek to play positions in which black athletes have been successful. In other words, black youth model themselves after blacks who have attained notoriety, and often those visible blacks have played at noncentral positions. McPherson argued that the first black baseball players were predominately outfielders, and the first black football players occupied the offensive and defensive backfield and the defensive line.[51] It is precisely in these noncentral slots that blacks are overrepresented today (Figures 8.2 and 8.3).

Some indirect evidence supports the role-model theory. Brower interviewed twenty-three white and twenty black athletes and found that 90% of the black athletes had exclusively black role models (whereas white athletes had role models from both races) and that the majority of these role models played traditional black positions.[52] Castine and Roberts reported that, among black college players, 52% had a black idol and "played the same position as the idol when they were in high school," and 48% played "the same position as the idol while in college."[53]

The present hypothesis fails to explain blacks' selection of playing positions when the color bar was lifted and fails to explain blacks' shift from central positions in high school and college to noncentral ones in the professional leagues. This formulation implies the operation of irrationality, too. According to Eitzen and Yetman, "It assumes that as black athletes become older and are in keenly more competitive conditions, they will be more likely to seek positions because of their identification with a black star rather than because of a rational assessment of their own athletic skills."[54]

Psychological Explanations.   Worthy and Markle pose **the hypothesis that blacks excel at reactive tasks,** those in which athletes respond appropriately at the proper time to changes in the stimulus situation, and that whites excel at *self-paced* ones, those in which athletes respond at their discretion to a relatively constant and stationary stimulus.[55] These researchers reasoned that blacks should excel at hitting, a reactive task, whereas whites should excel at pitching, a self-paced task. They support this claim by demonstrating that whereas 7% of pitchers were black, 24% of nonpitchers were black. Another test of their contention applied to basketball. Free-throw shooting is self-paced, and field-goal shooting is reactive. Whites were found to excel at free-throw shooting and blacks at field-goal shooting.

Worthy and Markle's data were reanalyzed by Jones and Hochner.[56] The latter researchers found that blacks were superior at hitting and whites were superior at free-throw shooting, but they found no evidence of black superiority in field-goal shooting or of white superiority in pitching.

Dunn and Lupfer observed 55 white and 122 black fourth-grade boys playing a modification of soccer and discovered that whites appeared superior at self-paced activities and blacks appeared superior at reactive activities (findings consistent with Worthy and Markle's hypothesis).[57]

The present hypothesis may account for blacks' overrepresentation at reactive playing positions (e.g., outfielder in baseball and wide receiver, cornerback, and running back in football), and their underrepresentation in such self-paced sports as golf, bowling, and swimming. Just the same, the hypothesis does not explain their underrepresentation in the reactive individual sports such as fencing, auto racing, squash, skiing, and tennis.

Jones and Hocher *hypothesize that blacks and whites have personality differences:* "The manner in which an individual is socialized into sport activities will have a significant effect on his sports personality. . . . Further, this sports personality will have a significant effect on sports preference and performance."[58] Accordingly, black athletes in comparison to white (a) are individualistically rather than team oriented, (b) stress stylistic "or expressive performance over success or technical performance," and (c) "reflect a personalized power orientation associated with individual winning instead of a power orientation correlated with team winning." Although the researchers cite some evidence to support their hypothesis, the overall empirical evidence is quite meager.

Greenfield, however, exposits the characteristics of two styles of basketball: "White" ball, . . . is the basketball of patience and method. "Black" ball is the basketball of electric self-expression. One player has all the time in the world to perfect his skills, the other a need to prove himself. . . . A "black" player overcomes an obstacle with finesse and body control; a "white" player reacts by outrunning or outpowering the obstacle."[59]

Biological Explanations.   Several investigators have disclosed differences between select samples of white and black athletes on a variety of *anthropometric* (body measurements) indices.[60] These studies have shown that blacks have (a) longer arms and lower legs, (b) greater hand and forearm length, (c) less body fat, (d) shorter trunks, (e) narrower hips, (f) greater muscle mass, (g) greater skeletal weight, (h) wider bones in the upper arm, (i) more muscle tissue in the upper arm and thigh, (j) less muscle mass in the calf, (k) higher degrees of mesomorphy, (l) lower vital lung capacities, (m) different heel structures, (n) more of the muscle fibers needed for speed and power and less of those needed for endurance, and (o) higher specific gravities. Additionally, evidence suggests that blacks' bodies function differently than whites' bodies: They mature earlier, are more likely to have hyperextensibility (double-jointedness), dissipate heat more efficiently, become chilled easily in cold temperatures, and possess rhythmic abilities.[61]

These physiological racial differences have occasionally been used to explain blacks' dominance (in numbers and performance) in certain sports as well as their under-representation or overrepresentation in some sports and at particular playing positions. Illustratively, blacks' arm and leg lengths have been cited as explanations for outstanding performances in certain running and jumping events (track and field), and overrepresentation in some sport positions such as outfielder (baseball), and defensive back, running back, and wide-receiver (football). Their differential mesomorphy, vital lung capacity, and specific gravity have been advanced as reasons for their paucity in swimming and endurance events. Interestingly, three decades ago, it was common to hear that blacks excelled at sprints but were not particularly effective at long-distance running. Some felt this could be explained by anthropometric racial differences. However, all this thinking was eclipsed when East African runners won gold medals at the 1968 Mexico City Olympics. This was accomplished under the most dire circumstances in Africa; namely, few track clubs, few artificial tracks, and little enticement through scholarships at the university level and emphasis in higher education. In 1978 world records for the 3,000-, 5,000-, and 10,000-meter runs, in addition to the steeplechase, were set by Kenyan Henry Rono. Similarly, Ethiopian Miruts Yiffer won the 5- and 10,000-meter events in the 1979 World Cup.[62]

Several criticisms of these biophysiological explanations for racial variations in sport participation and performance demand our attention. First, most of these differences are central tendency (average) differences and neglect variations within particular racial stocks as well as the overlap among members of different races. Second, just how differences such as these affect athletic performance in interaction with each other is not fully known. For example, little evidence indicates that swimming savvy is influenced by buoyancy per se. Third, some of the traits of black athletes may offset one another. Malina wrote,

> The greater weight and density of the Negro skeleton, might possibly offset the advantage suggested by mechanical principles relative to body proportions; . . . further, since strength of muscle is physiologically related to its cross-sectional area, it is difficult to assume that the Negro calf musculature produces more power, enabling him to excel in the sprints and jumps.[63]

Fourth, the samples have not been randomly selected. Some studies have focused exclusively on top-level performers, thus making inferences to general racial populations risky.

❏ PERFORMANCE DIFFERENTIALS

On 25 April 1989 Tom Brokaw hosted a controversial telecast entitled "Black Athletes—Fact or Fiction." The aim of the program was to determine if black athletic superiority existed and, if it did, to offer explanations for it. Several years before the NBC news documentary, *Time* magazine reported, "Blacks have come to dominate major U.S. sports as no other minority group ever has. . . . Most of the records in major sports—rushing, slugging, and scoring marks once held by such legendary figures as Grange, Ruth and Pettit—have been bested by Tony Dorsett, Henry Aaron, and Wilt Chamberlain."[64] As we will see, the empirical data indicate that blacks and whites (as well as Latinos in baseball) neither perform equally nor receive equal treatment.

In the latter 1980s alone, the following records were set and/or shattered by black athletes: Dwight Gooden, twenty years old, became the youngest twenty-game winner in major league baseball. Vince Coleman's 100 stolen bases set a major league rookie record for base stealing. Walter Payton broke Jimmy Brown's all-time NFL record of 12,312 career rushing yards. Eric Dickerson gained 2,105 yards, breaking the NFL season rushing record. Mark Clayton caught eighteen touchdowns and broke the NFL record for touchdown receptions. Michael Spinks became the first light heavyweight champion to become the heavyweight champ. Isiah Thomas broke the NBA record (1,123) for assists. Kareem Abdul-Jabbar became the NBA's all-time scorer (41,420 points).

In addition to blacks' dominance, apparently their performance must surpass that of whites if they are to make the transition from the minor leagues to the majors or maintain their positions in a specific sport. This form of discrimination is called "unequal opportunity for equal ability." Let us consider performance differentials in several major sports. Because the evidence supplied here is selective and nonexhaustive, see the more comprehensive review of "Racial Differences in Sports Performance" by Samson and Yerles.[65]

Baseball

Rosenblatt observed that between 1953 and 1957 blacks' mean batting average was 20.6 points higher than whites'.[66] Between 1958 and 1961, this mean difference was 20.1, whereas between 1962 to 1965 it was 21.2. Other inquiries have discovered a continuation of this gap at around 21 percentage points.[67] According to Rosenblatt:

> Discriminatory hiring practices are still in effect in the major leagues. The superior Negro is not subject to discrimination because he is more likely to help win games than fair to poor players. Discrimination is aimed, whether by design or not, against the substar Negro ball player. The findings clearly indicate that the undistinguished Negro player is less likely to play regularly in the major leagues than the generally undistinguished white player.[68]

Pascal and Rapping studied whether black minor leaguers' credentials had to surpass whites' for them to be promoted to the majors.[69] Based on a sample of 784 major league players, divided into veterans ($n = 453$) and nonveterans ($n = 331$), they found that (regardless of position) blacks' mean lifetime batting average was higher than whites'. Furthermore, for pitchers who appeared in 10 or more games, blacks won 10.2 games in comparison to 7.5 for whites. These findings led Pascal and Rapping to conclude "On the average a black player must be better than a white player if he is to have an equal chance of transiting from the minor leagues to the major."

In baseball, some of the performance indicators that have been compared and contrasted among minority and majority group athletes include batting averages (lifetime and seasonal), slugging averages (lifetime and seasonal), home run averages, runs batted in, fielding, games won, earned run averages, number of strikeouts and walks, and fielding averages. In all instances blacks performed better than whites (or there was no statistically significant difference). Figures 8.5 and 8.6, drawn from a longitudinal study by Leonard, Pine, and Rice, illustrate the performance differentials among white, black, and Latino baseball players on two of the most significant offensive performance statistics in baseball, namely, batting and slugging averages.[70] The gap in performance differentials began to narrow in the 1975–1980 period, according to Phillips's data.[71]

Football

Demonstrating performance differentials in football is problematic because the game is heavily based on team performance and because offensive statistics are more extensive and more frequently tabulated than defensive ones. The most valid data for which comparisons between whites and blacks can be made are for running backs and wide-receivers. A significant performance factor in football is average yards gained. Black runners gained a little more than one-half yard per carry over their white counterparts, and wide-receivers gained nearly two more yards per pass reception. Black backs scored nearly twice as often as white backs, and black receivers scored more than whites by a factor of 1.78. Black players were also used more than white players. Scully wrote:

> Among running backs, blacks will have about 33 more rushing attempts per season, a differential of about 56 percent over white running backs, and they will have 4.4 more pass receptions per season, a 41 percent differential. Among wide receivers blacks will complete nearly eight more passes a season, a differential of some 50 percent in comparison to white wide receivers.[72]

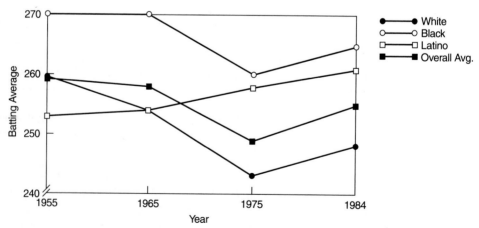

FIGURE 8.5 A trend line: Depicting White, Black, and Latino averages, 1955–1984
SOURCE: Wilbert M. Leonard, II, Jon Pine, & Connie Rice, "Performance Characteristics of White, Black and Hispanic Major League Baseball Players: 1955–1984," *The Journal of Sport and Social Issues* 12, no. 1 (1988), p. 38. Reprinted with permission.

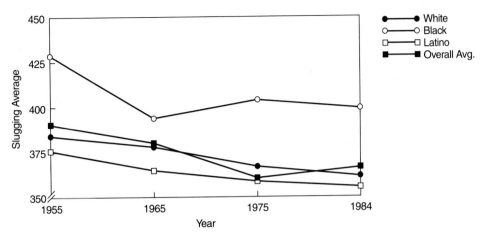

FIGURE 8.6 A trend line: Depicting White, Black, and Latino slugging averages, 1955–
1984

SOURCE: Wilbert M. Leonard, II, Jon Pine, & Connie Rice, "Performance Characteristics of
White, Black and Hispanic Major League Baseball Players: 1955–1984," *The Journal of Sport
and Social Issues* 12, no. 1 (1988), p. 38. Reprinted with permission.

Basketball

In an inquiry into the NBA salary structure in the middle 1980s, Koch and Vander
Hill provide data that, with one exception—free-throw percentage—indicate that
blacks excel at such phases of the game as games played, field goal percentage, points
per game, rebounds per game, blocks, assists, and steals per game.[73] The superiority
of the black basketball player existed at *both* the collegiate and professional level for
both the season and lifetime statistics.

Samson and Yerles conclude that on such performance measures as points (average,
season, per game, per minute); floor time (games played, minutes played); field goals
and free throws made; rebounds; assists; and the top five and top eight players, blacks
had superior statistics (although in some instances the differences were not statistically
significant).[74]

Do blacks have to be "better" than whites to make a professional team's roster? It
seems to be true insofar as whites are overrepresented among the nonstarters and are
underrepresented among the starters as a result of a survey using 1980–1981 data for
the NBA's twenty-three teams. However, there was no clear pattern that whites (measured in minutes played) occupied the most marginal positions (nine through eleven).
Karabel and Karen conclude:

> Our findings, . . . are more than sufficient to establish that the NBA is anything but
> color-blind. . . . [P]rofessional basketball is still a long way from meritocracy [*sic*]. And
> the economics of the box office suggest that the path to true color blindness may be a
> tortuous one indeed.[75]

Johnson and Marple also provide evidence that, in professional basketball, less-
productive black players appear to be released earlier than less-productive white players.[76] To test this hypothesis, they subdivided years of experience in professional bas-

ketball into three ranges: (a) rookies, (b) two to four years, and (c) five or more years. They found a reduction of white players from 46.5% to 37.7% between the first two ranges, whereas black players increased from 53.5% to 62.3% between the same ranges. This suggests that marginally skilled whites are provided more opportunities to make the team than less skilled blacks. For players with five or more years of experience, there was an increase (over the percentage in the two- to four-year range) from 37.7% to 46.3% for whites and a decline from 62.3% to 53.7% for blacks. This may mean that blacks are released more quickly than whites when their performances become suspect. To test this contention, Johnson and Marple checked for a correspondence between race and experience while holding points per game (ppg) constant. Points per game figures were grouped in three categories: less than 10 ppg, 10–19.9 ppg, and 20 or more ppg. Regardless of experience, blacks were in the majority. Of the marginal players who scored less than 10 ppg but were at least in their fifth year of experience, 43% were black, as opposed to 57% who were white and in the same category. This cannot be attributed to the unavailability of blacks, because they were in the majority among those who had five or more years of experience and who scored between 10 and 19.9 ppg (59%) or 20 or more ppg (63%). These data are consistent with other nonempirical suggestions that blacks must be better to be given a chance to play and to continue to play in professional sports.[77]

Track and Field

Samson and Yerles's comparison of black and white performances for both men and women in several track and field events is of interest.[78] They provide data from the 1960–1984 Olympic Games on the sprints (100, 200, and 400 meter), long-distance events (5,000 and 10,000 meters and marathon), jumping events (high, long, and pole vault), and throwing events (shotput, discus, and javelin). As with any data, these must be carefully examined, particularly in light of the boycotts (e.g., U.S. boycott of Moscow Olympics) and other socioeconomic and political concerns. With this caveat, in the various sprints, the overall percentage of black champions slightly exceeds 50%. In the various distance events, black athletes were champions in a little more than one third of the cases. (Of interest, though, is that all the black winners were from Africa, not the United States.) Black athletes do well in the sprints, whereas black Africans do well in the distance events. In the jumping events, white athletes dominate, except for the men's long jump, and this event can almost be categorized as a sprint (the black champions in this event were all Americans). White athletes have prevailed in the throwing events, with only one black champ between 1960 and 1984.

Professional Tennis

Among the top-ranked 150 men and women tennis players, one finds but a half-dozen blacks.

To summarize performance differentials in sport, we can repeat that indeed there are differences when athletes of different races and ethnicities are compared. Blacks and Latinos appear to be concentrated in relatively few sports, whereas whites are found in a wide range of sporting activities. However, when all sports are considered, the overrepresentation of blacks tends to disappear.

Explaining the Superiority of the Black Athlete

The data reported heretofore generally attest to the superlative performances of black athletes. Several "theories" suggest why this is so.

Matriarchal Explanation.   *Matriarchy* is a form of family organization investing power and authority in the female.[79] Superior black athletic performance, from one view, is the by-product of the black family structure that has been predominately matriarchal. Accordingly, black males reared in the absence of a father compensate for this social and emotional void by developing very positive, intimate, and intense relationships with the coach, who serves as a surrogate father. The upshot of this identification with the coach-as-father-figure motivates black male athletes to outperform white males, who have been socialized in the modal patriarchal (male-dominated) family system. As provocative as the matriarchal explanation seems, it does not correlate with other empirical findings. Although a larger percentage of black families are matriarchal, more whites (in absolute numbers) come from female-headed households. Further, past protests by black athletes against the dominant group—even white coaches—cast a dubious aspersion on the compensatory effect the coach-as-father-figure may have on the development of athletic prowess.

Race-Linked Characteristics Explanation.   Kane offered three major race-linked explanations of black athletic superiority, one of which claimed the existence of racially linked (genetically transmitted) *physical and physiological* characteristics.[80] This approach is limited by the scientific vagueness of the concept of race, because, as we've seen, races are not precise biological categories and racial categorizations vary culturally. Furthermore, "The preoccupation with the question of whether there are racially linked genetic differences that explain black success in sport is founded on and helps to naturalize the ideology of biological determinism. When the assumptions of biological determinism are called into question, the racism underlying the preoccupation is exposed."[81] Although the concept of race is biological, it is more meaningful in a social sense. Furthermore, the black population and the black athlete manifest significant variability in body physiques, body proportions, and other anatomical and biophysiological ("anthropometric") features. Curry and Jiobu wrote:

> Nobody proposes genetic factors, . . . to explain why East Germany has produced so many excellent swimmers, why Canadians do well at hockey, why Japanese-Americans are disproportionately represented in judo—or, for that matter, why British are hopeless at baseball, while white Americans are equally inept at cricket. In each case, it is easy to see cultural factors, not genetic ones, are at work.[82]

Kane's second explanation of black athletic superiority claims the existence of race-linked *psychological* traits.[83] Here, black athletes are conceived to be relaxed and tension free, particularly under pressure. This explanation is inconsistent with survey data reported by Edwards.[84] On the Institute of Personality and Ability Test, black athletes were found to be significantly more worried, concerned, and serious than white athletes. However, on another Institute for Personality and Ability Test (IPAT) item—casual-controlled—successful blacks scored significantly higher than whites. Because these data are attitudinal in nature, we must be alerted to possible discrepancies between paper-and-pencil test responses and actual behavior. Edwards raises the possibility that the myth of black athletes' "coolness" may become self-fulfilling.

Also difficult to reconcile with this stance is the higher incidence of hypertension among black Americans. In a recent study reported in the *Journal of the American Medical Association,* researchers attempted to discern whether high blood pressure in African-Americans is due to heredity or environment. An interaction effect was discovered. Blacks of low socioeconomic status and those without high school diplomas who had the darkest skin had higher blood pressure readings than those in the same categories but with the lightest skin. Among blacks with above-average incomes and who were well-educated, the blood pressure of those with the darkest skin was about the same as those in the same category with the lightest skin. The authors concluded, "The positive association between skin pigmentation and blood pressure in persons with low socioeconomic status may represent the interaction of an environmental factor, such as diet or socioeconomic stress [which is] present in persons of low socioeconomic status, with a susceptible gene that has a higher prevalence among blacks with darker skin color."

Kane's third formulation of black athletic superiority refers to unique, racially specific, *historical* experiences stemming from slavery. He contends that conditions on slave ships and plantations demanded an inordinate degree of physical and psychological stamina.[85] Calvin Hill, a black graduate of Yale and a former stalwart on the Dallas Cowboys, summed up the essence of this position: "I have a theory about why so many sports stars are Black. I think it boils down to the survival of the fittest. Think of what African slaves were forced to endure in this country merely to survive. Well, black athletes are their descendants. They are the offspring of those who are physically tough enough to survive."[86]

As a consequence of natural selection and the survival of the fittest, the potential for superior athletic performances was instilled in black athletes. As with other explanations, this one suffers from scientifically unacceptable assumptions. The implication that blacks are a "pure race" is not supported by demographic data regarding inbreeding and amalgamation among different racial groupings.

A Sociological Explanation.   Our own thinking leads to a respectful dismissal of Kane's race-linked explanations and the matriarchy theory. In their place, the ideas of Edwards and Eitzen and Sage[87] are judged to be more plausible. According to Edwards's sociological reasoning, the superiority of black athletes stems from blacks' social values differing from whites' and the reduced opportunities to participate in the spectrum of prestigious occupations in American society. This rationale also applies to the historical paucity of other ethnic minorities in American athletics. The fact that performance differentials exist does not mean, prima facie, that blacks are inherently superior but rather that the role models available for blacks and the closed occupational doors in other areas have prompted minority group members to channel themselves into one avenue—sports, an occupation from which they have not been barred.[88] Edwards said:

> With the channeling of black males disproportionately into sport, the outcome is the same as it would be at Berkeley if we taught and studied nothing but English. Suppose that everyone who got here arrived as a result of some ruthless recruitment process where

everyone who couldn't write well was eliminated at every level from age six all the way through junior college. It would only be a short time before the greatest prose—the greatest innovations in teaching, learning, and writing English—came out of Berkeley. It is the inevitable result of all this talent channeled into a single area. The white athlete who might be an O.J. Simpson is probably sitting somewhere behind a desk.[89]

Eitzen and Sage argue that black dominance in sport can be plausibly explained by structural constraints (social norms, values, and institutions) imposed on blacks in American society.[90] These constraints are twofold: (a) *occupational discrimination* and (b) the *sports opportunity structure*. Because blacks have historically been denied job opportunities in various sectors of American society, they have directed themselves into other socially acceptable nooks, one of which is sport. Occupational discrimination, however, does not explain why blacks have gravitated to some sports (e.g., football, basketball, baseball, boxing, and track) and not to others (e.g., swimming and diving, golf, tennis, soccer, gymnastics, skiing, and polo).

According to Phillips, the selectivity in blacks' sport preferences can be explained by the *sports opportunity structure*.[91] This is reminiscent of Medoff's prohibitive occupational cost hypothesis. Eitzen and Sage wrote:

> Blacks tend to excel in those sports where facilities, coaching, and competition are available to them (i.e., in the schools and community recreation programs). Those sports where blacks are rarely found have facilities, coaching, and competition provided in private clubs. There are few excellent black golfers, . . . and they had to overcome the disadvantages of being self-taught and being limited to play at municipal courses. Few blacks are competitive skiers for the obvious reasons that most blacks live far removed from snow and mountains, and because skiing is very expensive.[92]

A headline in the *Chicago Tribune* captured this notion: "Former Basketball Player Wants to Blaze Ski Trail for Blacks."[93] Bryan Wilson, former Houston college basketball player said: "I'm the only black person around, . . . It's a privilege and an opportunity for me to be on the U.S. Ski Team." On the same page, another headline read: "Chicago Group Backing 'Best Black Skier in the U.S.'" The article reports that no black athlete has ever made the U.S. team. In a similar vein, Calvin Peete established his own foundation to try to promote golf to black urban youths. According to the National Golf Foundation, there were about 23.5 million golfers in the United States in 1991. This figure represents about 9% of the population. About one-half million are blacks, and this figure represents only 2% of the black population. In 1991, there were only two black golfers on the Professional Golf Association (PGA) Tour—Calvin Peete and Jim Thorpe—and none on the Ladies' Professional Golf Association (LPGA) tour.

Ironically, racist ideologies and practices in the larger society appear to be partially responsible for black athletic superiority in some sports and their significant absence in other sports. The continuation of specific ethnic group athletic superiority may be an unobtrusive barometer of the dearth of equal opportunities in other work-related realms in American society. As these barriers are broken—and informal norms and legislation appear to have moved in that direction—we may witness an equalization of ethnic performances in the sport world as well as in the occupational world at large.

❏ REWARDS AND AUTHORITY STRUCTURES

We have seen that the athletic performances of blacks are frequently superior to those of whites in the sports in which they both participate. Is this fact a harbinger of greater financial remuneration or are blacks also discriminated against economically? In the early 1990s, blacks were among the highest paid professional athletes, particularly in boxing, baseball, basketball, and football. Listed are the names and salaries of highly paid black athletes in 1991:

1.	Buster Douglas, boxing	$19,558,000
2.	Mike Tyson, boxing	$14,800,000
3.	Evander Holyfield, boxing	$ 7,400,000
4.	John Williams, basketball	$ 5,000,000
5.	Patrick Ewing, basketball	$ 4,600,000
6.	Hakeem Olajuwon, basketball	$ 4,062,451
7.	Darryl Strawberry, baseball	$ 3,800,000
8.	Kevin Mitchell, baseball	$ 3,750,000
9.	Joe Carter, baseball	$ 3,666,667
10.	Eric Davis, baseball	$ 3,600,000
11.	Willie McGee, baseball	$ 3,562,500
12.	Tim Raines, baseball	$ 3,500,000
13.	Dave Stewart, baseball	$ 3,500,000

In fact, not only are blacks among the highest paid athletes, their arithmetic average salary at certain positions exceeds that of whites. Scully found that white and black athletes in pro baseball, basketball, and football were remunerated about equally.[94]

When average baseball salaries (arithmetic means) of whites and blacks are compared, there is little or no evidence to support the charge of economic discrimination. Since data for sports other than baseball are not readily available, the comments regarding financial rewards apply only to this sport.

Baseball

Scully writes that blacks have made dramatic improvements since Jackie Robinson's debut and that the salaries of black baseball players are equal to their level of ability.[95] When salary and performance differentials simultaneously exist, it is not easy to establish racial discrimination. To systematically tap this dimension, it is necessary to examine the interrelationships among race, performance, and salary. Some of the recent research supporting Scully's contention is in order. Christiano, using salary data from 212 nonpitchers in major league baseball, found a single indicator of salary discrimination against blacks. White infielders were more highly remunerated than their black counterparts. I refined and extended Christiano's inquiry by trichotomizing the independent variable (race/ethnicity) into white, black, and Latino categories.[96] Using nonpitchers, I developed and tested a salary model (using race and ethnicity, position, and free-agency status) and concluded that there were several instances of salary inequities but no systematic patterning. In short, the salaries of baseball players varying in race and ethnicity did not differ consistently even while holding other theoretically relevant variables constant. In another investigation of baseball players, I examined the relationship between salaries and race and ethnicity for pitchers.[97] I tested and specified a salary model for pitchers and concluded that there were several instances of salary inequities but small sample sizes precluded drawing a valid conclusion. Lavoie and I distinguished between starting and relief pitchers but found no trend in salary discrimination.[98]

Jiobu employed the technique of survival analysis in analyzing baseball data from 1971 to 1985.[99] He found that, in general, performance was the most influential determinant on career length; that is, players who perform the best tend to have the longest careers. However, when race and ethnicity was introduced into the analysis, Jiobu discovered that for Latinos their ethnicity had no effect on their career duration, whereas for blacks, their race had a negative impact on career duration.

Data on salary differentials for sports other than baseball are meager. Nevertheless, Mogrell reported no significant differences in the bonuses and starting salaries of black and white professional football players.[100] He did, however, find that salaries were higher for white veterans than for blacks, but this difference was not significant. We must, again, bear an important caveat in mind: Little can be inferred from the data unless adjustments for position, race, and performance are simultaneously considered. Because Scully demonstrated performance differentials favoring blacks, equal black and white salaries could be viewed as proof of salary discrimination, all other things being equal.

Another area of unequal opportunity is the lucrative business of making personal appearances and endorsing or promoting commercial products. Despite the athletic prowess of black athletes, in 1992 only one black—Michael Jordan—was among the top ten in receiving endorsement monies. Jordan was behind two other black nonathletes: Jaleel White, of "Family Matters," and Bill Cosby, of "The Cosby Show." Economists explain the dearth of black endorsements with the concept of "customer discrimination." Doug Williams, the first black quarterback to start in the (1988) Super Bowl earned $127,500 nine months after the Redskins had beaten the Broncos. Compare this with Jim McMahon's $1 million and Phil Simms's $750,000 windfall a few years earlier. Sport sociologist Harry Edwards said, "When advertisers decide to use an athlete in an ad they will almost immediately go to a white athlete. . . . These aren't people who consider this kind of thing to be racist. It just never crosses their minds."[101]

Basketball

Koch and Vander Hill studied the NBA salary structure in the mid-1980s and uncovered evidence that "equal pay for equal work" did not exist.[102] Holding constant performance and experience, they concluded that black NBA players (as a group) receive between $17,000 and $26,000 less than white players (as a group).

Football

In 1988 an income differential of $19,000 existed between the average white ($204,232) and black ($185,157) NFL players' salaries. Interestingly, the income

☐ VIGNETTE 8.4

Blacks in Sports

Success for few, disappointment for many

Blacks should forget about sports for their own good. So say two Ohio State University sociologists in a book, *Sports, A Social Perspective.* Robert Jiobu and Timothy Curry, professors of sociology, doubt their advice will be heeded.

They also dispute as myth the notion that sports are free of prejudice and predict that subtle racism in athletics will persist.

As a culture, black Americans obstruct the path to economic equality by overemphasizing sports. That overemphasis keeps young blacks from seeking success through other occupations, the sociologists say.

Both writers hope that virtually all blacks will abandon the dream of success through sports and aspire instead to the crafts, the trades, business, and the professions.

Overemphasis on sports leads to many disappointments, the researchers suggest, since only about 3,000 jobs exist for professional athletes.

At some point, after years spent on playgrounds instead of in libraries, most young blacks run headfirst into reality: They can't make a living in sports.

"There's no doubt that sports are relatively open compared to a lot of other desirable occupations. But still, it's just too difficult to become a professional athlete," Curry says.

Thwarted attempts by blacks to enter other fields have led to young blacks' picking athletes and entertainers as their role models, the sociologists say.

Athletics does a better job at reaching racial equality than does the rest of society, but it is still far from colorblind, the sociologists say. Subtle segregation still exists.

"You can't expect sports to disassociate from society," Curry says. Through a process called stacking, blacks and whites are channeled into specific positions from the time they are old enough to wear a football helmet or baseball cleats.

This stacking of black and white athletes starts early and is more apparent as the level of competition and the expectations of coaches increase—from Little League, to high school, to college, and finally to professional sports.

Few blacks play quarterback, center, or middle linebacker in football even though blacks make up about half of the National Football League rosters. Few blacks are pitchers or catchers or play any of the infield positions even though blacks make up more than 20 percent of major league baseball rosters.

Blacks are more apt to play the peripheral positions, away from the decisions of play, such as running back, wide receiver, defensive back, or outfielder, the sociologists say.

Those positions generally don't give blacks much of a chance to be team leaders and to communicate with their teammates during a game.

As a result, black athletes don't develop leadership and communication skills that could some day lead to coaching jobs, the sociologists say. Three out of four major league managers are former infielders and catchers.

An athlete unconsciously participates in the process of stacking before ever entering organized sports, Curry says. That's because a youngster will often pattern himself after a particular player—usually of the same race—and will want to play the same position as his hero.

Blacks have as much ability as whites to play quarterback, Jiobu says. "Is there any difference in the abilities of whites and blacks to throw a football? Of course not."

"Only exceptional black athletes are allowed to play positions traditionally given to whites," Curry adds. "The black player who plays that position has to be much better than a white player would have to be." Stacking also can hurt a white player trying to play a position usually held by blacks, he said.

"Stacking is something that people don't even notice is going on. It's just a natural pattern. I don't think anyone consciously discourages a certain race from certain positions," Curry says.

Stacking occurs in basketball to a lesser extent since blacks have dominated that sport more than any other, Curry says. NBA rosters are about 63 percent black. Still, through all levels, there is a disproportionately high percentage of white players who fill the play-making guard position, which is a leadership and communication position on the court.

Stacking isn't likely to disappear soon, Jiobu and Curry say. The tremendous salaries that both black and white athletes earn—even with stacking—make it unlikely that any of them would speak out against stacking, Curry says.

A belief that blacks are superior athletes also hurts in the long term, Jiobu and Curry say.

"Why are the British better cricket players? Why are the East Germans better at swimming or the Bulgarians better at weightlifting?," Curry asks. "It's because those are sports that their societies emphasize."

Since white Americans have roads other than sports open to them, they tend to emphasize gaining a career in professional sports far less than do blacks, Jiobu and Curry say.

Blacks actually are shorter, on the average, than whites, Jiobu notes, refuting the notion that a natural height advantage explains black domination of basketball.

"It was also thought that white athletes were better long-distance runners, but then in the '60s a number of black Africans emerged as great long-distance runners," Jiobu said.

The sociologists point to recent history to show that certain minorities have turned to sports when other ways of earning a place in society seemed impossible.

For instance, Irish boxers dominated from 1909 to 1928; Jewish boxers from 1929 to 1937; and black boxers have dominated ever since Joe Louis captured the heavyweight crown in 1937. The authors predict another minority, Hispanics, may challenge for dominance in the ring in years ahead.

One of the reasons few blacks are champion swimmers is simply that "there aren't that many swimming pools in the ghetto," Jiobu says. Also, whites dominate golf and tennis because athletes in these sports generally need individualized coaching by "pros" at country clubs to be successful. These clubs are much more open to the wealthy, who are most often white.

Blacks are also more interested in sports that are played professionally, rather than the minor sports, Jiobu and Curry say. That's because the pro sports are seen as a way to move up the economic ladder.

SOURCE: James Leickly, *OSU Quest,* Columbus, Ohio (Fall 1984), p. 4.

❏

---

hiatus was even larger than it was when the first study (1982) was conducted by the National Football League Players Association. In 1982 whites averaged $100,730 and blacks $91,980.[103]

Black athletes appear to have made little progress outside their athletic role (Vignette 8.4). Once their direct athletic involvement has terminated, there is evidence that discrimination continues to exist. This observation is reflected in areas discussed in the following sections.[104]

Managers, Coaches, and Owners

Black ownership of professional sport franchises is virtually nonexistent. In 1987, there were no black managers or coaches in professional baseball or professional football, and only 17% of head NBA coaches, a sport dominated by blacks, were black. The percentage of assistant coaches in baseball, football, and basketball was 9, 11, and 10, respectively. For minor league baseball, the situation is similar. The paucity of minority managers in 1989 is underscored by the fact that there were seventeen Latinos, nine blacks, and one Asian-American on more than 100 minor-league teams (Table 8.3).

Frank Robinson broke the major league baseball management "color bar" when he became the field general of the Cleveland Indians in 1974. In 1974, only three coaches in major league baseball (less than 3% of the total) were black. He guided the Indians to their best two-year record in ten years but was fired. Frank Robinson once said: "You hardly see any black third base or pitching coaches. And those are the most important coaching jobs. The only place you see blacks coaching is at first base, where most anybody can do the job."[105] In the summer of 1978, Larry Doby (the first black baseball player in the American League) became the second black baseball manager when he assumed management of the Chicago White Sox.

TABLE 8.3 Percentage of minority group hiring in professional baseball, excluding players

	1988 (%)	1989 (%)
Front office		
Black	6	9
Latino	3	5
Asian-American	1	1
Total	1,495	1,854
On-field personel		
Black	5	6
Latino	10	13
Asian-American	.3	.3
Total	1,306	1,588
Major league managers		
Black	NR	8
Latino	NR	4
Asian-American	NR	0
Total		26
Minor league managers		
Black	NR	9*
Latino	NR	17*
Asian-American	NR	1*
Total		

*These figures represent the actual *number,* not the percentage.

NR = not reported.

SOURCE: *New York Times* (3 December 1990), p. B12. Data supplied by Major League Baseball Commissioner's Office.

According to Spink, there are two primary reasons why there are not more black managers in major league baseball: (1) Former black ballplayers are not particularly intrigued with remaining in baseball after their careers have ended, and (2) ex-ballplayers are not excited about starting at the bottom of the ladder (i.e., back in the minor leagues) and working their way up.[106] Spink also says that black players are not fond of accepting the (often) radical salary reduction and the change of life-style that frequently accompany this career change. Although there are white managers who have not managed in the minors, most white managers have served their apprenticeships. Others argue that blacks are discriminated against and simply are not permitted to exercise this kind of leadership role.

In professional football, there is and has been only one "recent" black head coach (Art Shell, Oakland) and no black general managers. In 1987, 11% of NFL assistant coaches were black. According to *Sports Illustrated,* the NFL is interested in having more black players and coaches. The League has suggested that there are relatively few black head coaches in the college and university ranks, which is true, and that this is where they draw from, which is false. In 1980, seven of twenty-eight NFL coaches had been head college coaches; 54% of them, or fifteen of twenty-eight, had been ex-NFL players. As Braddock maintains, there is no shortage of blacks in the pool of players. The first black head coach in the history of professional football was Fritz Pollard, who coached the Hammond Pros between 1922 and 1925.

According to data compiled by the Black Coaches Association, in 1991, 29 (10% of 296) of Division I basketball teams had black head coaches, a figure that was down from a high of 38 in 1989. The 1991 *USA Today* survey found that of 3,083 key athletic department positions there were only 43 minority head coaches.

In the mid-1980s, there were 28 black NFL assistant coaches out of some 281 assistants. League statistics show that nearly three fourths of all professional coaches moved up from the college ranks (and that "pool is decidedly monochromatic"). At the time the article was published, the writer reported that only two Division I football coaches were black: Dennis Green (Northwestern) and Cleve Bryant (Ohio University). In March of 1986 Green announced his resignation from the college ranks to take a professional coaching position with the 49ers. While the modern-day NFL has finally hired its first black head coach—Art Shell of the Oakland Raiders—there has been a slight recent increase in the number of black assistant coaches. In 1983 there were twenty-seven black assistant coaches, up from twenty-one the previous year. Of the twenty-eight NFL teams, only five failed to have at least one black assistant. In the United States Football League (USFL), the same year, half of the twelve teams had black assistants. The increment in black assistants seems auspicious; however, "you still have to look at the positions they hold in the coaching hierarchy. Unfortunately, there doesn't seem to be much progression up the ladder. The majority are position coaches rather than unit coordinators or assistant head coaches—which are the major stepping stones to becoming a head coach."[107]

Sportscasting

Most blacks have had a job in radio or television sportscasting that has merely provided the "color."

Officiating

Game officials are overwhelmingly white. In the early 1980s, 19% (5 of 27), 8% (8 of 100), and 2% (1 of 60) of NBA, NFL, and major league baseball officials, respectively, were black. Evidence of stacking in officiating is supported by the fact that NFL officials are predominately head linesmen.

Executive Positions

College Sports. A *USA Today* survey reported that 12.5% of 3,083 key athletic department positions were held by minorities (blacks, Latinos, Native Americans, and Asian-Americans).[108] For comparative purposes, the 1990 census revealed that minorities comprised nearly 20% of the U.S. population. Of interest, of the 384 jobs held by minorities, 19% or 73 jobs, were positions of authority. In the 63 Division I programs surveyed, there were 2 athletic directors, 28 assistant athletic directors, and 43 head coaches (most jobs held by minorities, 236, or 62%, were at the assistant coach level). In addition, there were 44 minority academic advisors, 21 trainers, and 10 sports information directors. In summary form:

Position	Number of Minorities
Athletic director	2
Assistant athletic director	28
Head coach	43
Assistant coach	236
Trainer	21
Academic advisor	44
Sports information director	10

Professional Sports. In professional baseball in 1987, there were no high executive positions occupied by blacks and only one black assistant to then commissioner Peter Uberroth. Under Fay Vincent's administration, three areas—(a) central baseball (commissioner's and league offices), (b) front offices, and (c) on-field operations—have been targeted for improved minority hiring. In 1989, 15% (up from 9% in 1988) and 20% (up from 15% in 1988) of front office and on-field personnel (managers, trainers, scouts, and instructors), respectively, were minorities. The actual *number* of major league black and Latino managers in 1989 was two and one, respectively. Additionally, the actual numbers of minor league managers in 1989 were seventeen Latinos, nine blacks, and one Asian-American.

In professional basketball, Wayne Embry, a former NBA star, was the first black to occupy such a position in professional sports.

Sports critics have observed that relatively few former black athletes occupy positions of authority in sport. While it is true that few blacks occupy front office positions, let us consider some of their roles in professional baseball and advance reasons for their underrepresentation.[109] In 1980, home-run king Hank Aaron was vice-president and director of player development for the Atlanta Braves, and his ex-brother-in-law was vice-president for the Braves before his death in 1979. Then commissioner Kuhn had two black special assistants, Monte Irvin and Emmit Ashford. Ernie Banks, "Mr. Cub," was a member of the Cubs's board of Directors as well as the team manager of group sales. Former Brooklyn Dodgers Roy Campanella and Don Newcombe were directors of community relations for the Dodgers. Furthermore, Tommy Harper was the Boston Red Sox's assistant director of marketing and promotions; former Cincinnati Reds' pitcher Brooks Lawrence was an administrative assistant for his former club; and Elston Howard (the American League's first black Most Valuable Player, 1963) was in the front office with the New York Yankees.

Why have blacks been in short supply in executive sport positions? According to Bob Wirz, neither white nor black former players are excited about front office jobs: "If the players have achieved any degree of success, . . . they have been making so much money and they have established so many business connections outside of baseball that they're not interested in going to work for the kind of salaries that baseball jobs offer."[110] Another possibility is that universities are now offering sports administration programs, and professional clubs may be more interested in hiring those with recent academic training in such areas.

In summary, recent data indisputably lead to the bold conclusion that blacks' progress in sport's authority structures is very limited—few head coaches, few general managers, few owners, and few holding executive positions with teams, few offensive or defensive coordinators, and few working in the commissioner's office—in the NFL. In major league professional baseball, there have been no more than one-half dozen black managers in its 100-year history, few professional franchises are owned outright, a very small percentage of the coaches are black and, on one hand, you can count the third-base coaches—the person generally considered next to the manager in status and responsibility.

Baseball's Hall of Fame

Blacks have even been discriminated against in Baseball's Hall of Fame. In 1971, black stars of the former Negro Leagues became eligible for induction. Up until 1980, only nine blacks—Satchel Paige, Josh Gibson, Buck Leonard, Monte Irvin, Cool Papa Bell, Judy Johnson, Oscar Charlestown, Martin Dihigo, and John Henry Lloyd—had been inducted. In 1991, of some 120 inductees in Baseball's Hall of Fame, about 82%, 16%, and less than 2% were white, black, and Latino, respectively. Furthermore, only one display at Cooperstown was devoted to Negro baseball. Efforts are being made at present to establish a Negro Baseball Hall of History in Ashland, Kentucky. Unlike the Baseball Hall of Fame, there are to be no inductees; instead the museum is to feature memorabilia, cinema, and oral histories of black accomplishments in the Negro Leagues. This late-in-coming project is to be financed through the office of the baseball's commissioner, the Cooperstown Hall of Fame, and the state of Kentucky.

How good were the Negro teams in comparison to the major leagues? Between 1886 and 1948, there were 445 exhibition games between black teams and the white major league teams, and black teams were victorious in more than 60%.[111] Finally, only one Latino player, Roberto Clemente, is in the Hall of Fame. The first Latino to become a team captain was Manny Trillo in 1978.[112]

☐ SUMMARY

Prejudice and *discrimination*—racist social processes— continue to exist in sport. Three modern forms of racism are (a) *position allocation* ("stacking"); (b) *performance differentials* ("unequal opportunity for equal ability"); and (c) *rewards and authority structures*. *Stacking* refers to the disproportionate concentration of ethnic minorities, especially blacks, in specific team positions, and is a common form of spatial segregation (e.g., blacks tend to be overrepresented in baseball in the outfield positions, and whites tend to be overrepresented in the positions of pitcher, catcher, and infielder). Stacking has important consequences, because advertising offers tend to go to those players occupying central positions; black positions such as defensive back, running back, and wide-receiver are associated with truncated careers, life-time earnings, and pension benefits. Numerous sociological and social psychological, psychological, and biological reasons have been advanced for these differences. Empirical evidence suggests that blacks and whites do not perform at the same level. Generally speaking, black performance in the team sports of baseball, football, and basketball is superior as measured by many specific indices of performance. The superior performance of black athletes is probably due to occupational discrimination in the larger society, whereby blacks are channeled into a few socially acceptable outlets—such as sport—and to the sports opportunity structure, which permits blacks to gravitate to those sports from which they have not been barred. There is evidence that black superstars receive handsome salaries and other benefits, although they may have to outperform whites to receive them. Furthermore, blacks are not readily found in other sport-related occupations (e.g., sportscasting, officiating, management, or ownership and executive positions). In short, although strides toward equality have been made, racism in American sport continues to exist.

☐ KEY CONCEPTS

Prejudice
Discrimination
Racism
Stacking (Position Allocation)
The Stereotyping Hypothesis
The Interaction and Discrimination
  Hypothesis
The Outcome Control Hypothesis

The Prohibitive Cost Hypothesis
The Differential Attractiveness of Positions
  Hypothesis
The Role-Modeling Hypothesis
The Hypothesis that Blacks Excel at
  Reactive Tasks
The Hypothesis that Blacks and Whites
  Have Personality Differences

☐ ENDNOTES

1. CHRISTOPHER BATES DOOB, *Sociology: An Introduction* (New York: Holt, Rinehart, & Winston, 1985), p. 276.
2. *Latin, Latino, Latina,* and *Hispanic* refer to persons from those regions colonized by the Spanish and Portuguese and includes, geographically, Central and South America, Cuba,

Puerto Rico, the Dominican Republic, Southern California, Arizona, and Texas.
3. JAMES W. VANDER ZANDEN, *Sociology* (New York: John Wiley, 1979), pp. 293–294.
4. F. JAMES DAVIS, "Who Is Black?" *Illinois Quarterly* 43, no. 4 (Summer 1981), pp. 16–29.

5. MALCOLM X, *Playboy* (interview, May 1963).

6. LAUREL R. DAVIS, "The Articulation of Difference: White Preoccupation with the Question of Racially Linked Genetic Differences among Athletes," *Sociology of Sport Journal 7,* no. 2 (1990), pp. 179–187.

7. ROBERT BOYLE, *Sport: Mirror of American Life* (Boston: Little, Brown, 1963).
DAVID Q. VOIGHT, "Reflections on Diamonds: American Baseball and American Culture," *Journal of Sport History* 1 (May 1974), pp. 3–25.
ROBERT W. PETERSON, *Only the Ball Was White* (Englewood Cliffs, NJ: Prentice-Hall, 1970).
R. CLEMENT, "Racial Integration in the Field of Sports," *Journal of Negro Education* 23 (1954), pp. 222–230.
B. QUARIES, *The Negro in the Making of America* (New York: Collier, 1961).

8. PETERSON, *op. cit.*[7]

9. D. STANLEY EITZEN & GEORGE H. SAGE, *Sociology of American Sport* (Dubuque, IA: William C. Brown, 1978), p. 236.

10. E.B. HENDERSON, *The Black Athlete: Emergence Arrival* (New York: Publishers, 1968).

11. M.E. FLETCHER, "The Black Soldier Athlete in the United States Army, 1890–1916," *Canadian Journal of History and Sport Physical Education* 3 (December 1972), pp. 16–26.

12. *Op. cit.*,[9] p. 238.

13. BARRY D. MCPHERSON, "Minority Group Involvement in Sport: The Black Athlete," *Sport Sociology,* eds. A. Yiannakis, T.D. McIntyre, M.J. Melnick, & D.P. Hart. (Dubuque, IA: Kendall/Hunt, 1976), pp. 153–166.

14. W.M. LEONARD, II, & J.E. REYMAN, "The Odds of Attaining Professional Athlete Status: Refining the Computations," *Sociology of Sport Journal* 5, no. 2 (1988), pp. 162–169.

15. JOHN W. LOY & JOSEPH F. MCELVOGUE, "Racial Segregation in American Sport," *International Review of Sport Sociology* 5 (1970), pp. 5–23.

16. JEROME KARABEL & DAVID KAREN, "Color on the Court," *In These Times* 10–16 (February 1982), pp. 23–24.

17. PAUL HOCH, *Rip Off. The Big Game* (Garden City, NY: Anchor Books, 1972).
NORMAN R. YETMAN & D. STANLEY EITZEN, "Black Americans in Sports: Unequal Opportunity for Equal Ability," *Civil Rights Digest,* (August 1972), pp. 20–34.
LOY & MCELVOGUE, *op. cit.*[15]
NORRIS R. JOHNSON & DAVID P. MARPLE, "Racial Discrimination in Professional Basketball," *Sociological Focus* 6 (Fall 1973), pp. 6–18.
ANTHONY PASCAL & LEONARD A. RAPPING, "The Economics of Racial Discrimination in Organized Baseball," *Racial Discrimination in Economic Life* (Lexington, MA: D.C. Heath, 1972).
AARON ROSENBLATT, "Negroes in Baseball: The Failure of Success," *Transaction* 4 (September 1967), pp. 51–53.
GERALD SCULLY, "Economic Discrimination in Professional Sports," *Law and Contemporary Problems* 39 (Winter–Spring, 1973), pp. 67–84.

18. BOYLE, *op. cit.*,[7] pp. 103–105.

19. *Op. cit.*,[13] p. 158.

20. Cited in *The New York Times* (17 February 1991).

21. *Op. cit.*,[9] pp. 244–255.

22. One researcher defines stacking as the assignment "to a playing position, an achieved status, on the basis of an ascribed status." See Donald W. Ball, "Ascription and Position: A Comparative Analysis of 'Stacking' in Professional Football," *Canadian Review of Sociology and Anthropology* 10 (May 1973), pp. 97–113.

23. OSCAR GRUSKY, "The Effects of Formal Structure on Managerial Recruitment: Study of Baseball Organization," *Sociometry* 26 (1963), pp. 345–353.

24. HUBERT M. BLALOCK, JR., "Occupation Discrimination: Some Theoretical Propositions," *Social Problems* 9 (Winter 1962), pp. 240–247.

25. LOY & MCELVOGUE, *op. cit.*,[15] p. 6.

26. *Ibid.*, p. 8.

27. GREGG JONES, WILBERT M. LEONARD, II, RAYMOND L. SCHMITT, D. RANDALL SMITH, & WILLIAM L. TOLONE, "A Log-Linear Analysis of Stacking in College Football," *Social Science Quarterly* (March 1987), pp. 70–83.

28. HARRY EDWARDS, *Sociology of Sport* (Homewood, IL: Dorsey Press, 1973), p. 213.

29. *Ibid.*, p. 213.

30. LEE BALLINGER, *In Your Face! Sports for*

Love and Money (Chicago: Vanguard Books, 1981).

31. D. STANLEY EITZEN & IRL TESSENDORF, cited in Eitzen & Sage, *op. cit.*,[9], pp. 249–250.

32. WILBERT M. LEONARD, II, "Stacking in College Basketball: A Neglected Analysis," *Sociology of Sport Journal* 4, no. 4 (1987), pp. 403–409.

33. FORREST J. BERGHORN, NORMAL R. YETMAN, & WILLIAM E. HANNA, "Racial Participation and Integration in Men's and Women's Intercollegiate Basketball: Continuity and Change, 1958–1985," *Sociology of Sport Journal* 5, no. 2 (1988), pp. 87–106.

34. MARC LAVOIE, "The 'Economic' Hypothesis of Positional Segregation: Some Further Comments," *Sociology of Sport Journal* 6, no. 2 (1989), pp. 163–166.

35. JOE A. MAGUIRE, "Race and Position Assignment in English Soccer: A Preliminary Analysis of Ethnicity and Sport in Britain," *Sociology of Sport Journal* 5, no. 3 (1988), pp. 257–269.

36. J. PHILLIPS, "Toward an Explanation of Racial Variations in Top-Level Sports Participation," *International Review of Sport Sociology* 11, no. 3, (1976), pp. 39–56.

37. *Ibid.*

38. YETMAN & EITZEN, *op. cit.*[17]

39. CLAYTON BEST, "Experience and Career Length in Professional Football: The Effects of Positional Segregation," *Sociology of Sport Journal* 4, no. 4 (1987), pp. 410–420.

40. WILBERT M. LEONARD, II, ANTHONY OSTROSKY, & STEVE HUCHENDORF, "Centrality of Position and Managerial Recruitment: The Case of Major League Baseball," *Sociology of Sport Journal* 7, no. 3 (1990), pp. 294–301.

41. JONATHAN J. BROWER, "The Racial Basis of the Division of Labor Among Players in the National Football League as a Function of Stereotypes." Paper presented at the Annual Meeting of the Pacific Sociological Association, Portland, OR, 1972.

42. TUTKO, cited in Edwards, *op. cit.*[28] pp. 224–226.

43. R.L. WILLIAMS & Z.I. YOUSSEF, "Division of Labor in College Football Along Racial Lines," *International Review of Sport Sociology* 6, no. 1 (1975), pp. 3–10, 12–13.

44. *Op. cit.*,[28] p. 209.

45. M.H. MEDOFF, "Positional Segregation and Professional Baseball," *International Review of Sport Sociology* 12 (1977), pp. 49–54.

46. *Op. cit.*,[34]

47. NORMAN R. YETMAN, "Positional Segregation and the Economic Hypothesis: A Critique," *Sociology of Sport Journal* 4, no. 3 (1987), pp. 274–277.

48. JACK OLSEN, "The Black Athlete—A Shameful Story," Time 8 (August 1968).

49. D. STANLEY EITZEN & DAVID C. SANFORD, "The Segregation of Blacks by Playing Position in Football: Accident or Design?" *Social Science Quarterly* 55 (March 1975), pp. 948–959.

50. *Op. cit.*,[17]

51. *Op. cit.*,[13]

52. BROWER, cited in S. Castine & G.C. Roberts, "Modeling in the Socialization Process of the Black Athlete," *International Review of Sport Sociology* 3–4 (1974), pp. 59–73.

53. S. CASTINE & G. C. ROBERTS, *ibid.*

54. D. STANLEY EITZEN & NORMAN R. YETMAN, "Immune from Racism?" *Civil Rights Digest* 9 (Winter 1977), p. 6.

55. M. WORTHY & A. MARKLE, "Racial Differences in Reactive versus Self-Paced Sports Activities," *Journal of Personality and Social Psychology* 16 (1970), pp. 439–443.

56. J. JONES & A. HOCHNER, "Racial Differences in Sports Activities: A Look at the Self-paced versus Reactive Hypothesis," *Journal of Personality and Social Psychology* 27 (1973), pp. 86–95.

57. J. DUNN & M. LUPFER, "A Comparison of Black and White Boy's Performance in Self-Paced and Reactive Sports Activities, *Journal of Applied Social Psychology* 4 (1974), pp. 24–35.

58. *Op. cit.*[56] p. 92.

59. JEFF GREENFIELD, "The Black and White Truth About Basketball," *The Bedford Reader,* eds. X.J. Kennedy & Dorothy M. Kennedy (New York: St. Martin's Press, 1985), p. 197.

60. S.L. NORMAN, "Collation of Anthropometric Research Comparing American Males: Negro and Caucasian," Master's thesis, University of Oregon, 1968.

J. Jordon, "Physiological and Anthropometrical Comparisons of Negroes and Whites," *Journal of Health, Physical Education and Recreation* 40 (November/December 1969), pp. 93–99.

R.M. Malina, "Anthropology, Growth and Physical Education," *Physical Education: An Interdisciplinary Approach*, eds. R. Singer et al. (New York: Macmillan, 1972), pp. 237–309.

61. Jay J. Coakley, *Sport in Society: Issues and Controversies* (St. Louis, MO: C.V. Mosby, 1978), p. 304.

62. *Op. cit.*,[30] pp. 58–60.

63. Malina, *op. cit.*,[60] p. 300.

64. "The Black Dominance," *Time* (9 May 1977), pp. 57–60.

65. Jacques Samson & Magdeleine Yerles, "Racial Differences in Sports Performance," *Canadian Journal of Sport Science* 13, no. 2 (1988), pp. 109–116.

66. *Op. cit.*[17]

67. *Op. cit.*[17]

68. *Op. cit.*,[17] p. 53.

69. Anthony Pascal & Leonard A. Rapping, *Racial Discrimination in Organized Baseball* (Santa Monica, CA: Rand Corporation, 1970). This study has been criticized on the grounds that other factors besides hitting (e.g., bunting ability and defensive skills) are important.

70. Wilbert M. Leonard, II, Jon Pine, & Connie Rice, "Performance Characteristics of White, Black and Hispanic Major League Baseball Players: 1955–1984," *The Journal of Sport and Social Issues* 12, no. 1 (1988), pp. 17–30.

71. John C. Phillips, "Race and Career Opportunities in Major League Baseball: 1960–1980," *Journal of Sport and Social Issues* 7 (Summer/Fall 1983), pp. 1–17.

72. Scully, *op. cit.*,[17] p. 73.

73. James V. Koch & C. Warren Vander Hill, "Is There Discrimination in the 'Black Man's Game'"? *Social Science Quarterly* 69, no. 1 (1988), pp. 83–94.

74. *Op. cit.*[65]

75. Karabel & Karen, *op. cit.*[16]

76. Johnson & Marple, op. cit.[17]

77. Boyle, *op. cit.*[7]

Jim Bouton, *Ball Four* (New York: World, 1970).

Harry Edwards, *The Revolt of the Black Athlete* (New York: Free Press, 1969).

D.C. Boulding, "Participation of the Negro in Selected Amateur and Professional Athletics from 1935 to 1955." Master's thesis, University of Wisconsin—Madison, 1957.

Johnny Sample, *Confessions of a Dirty Ballplayer* (New York: Dial, 1970).

Wilbert M. Leonard, II, & Susan Schmidt, "Observations on the Changing Social Organization of Collegiate and Professional Basketball," *Sport Sociology Bulletin* 4 (Fall 1975), pp. 13–35.

78. *Op. cit.*[65]

79. *Op. cit.*[28] pp. 190–193.

80. Martin Kane, "An Assessment of Black Is Best," *Sports Illustrated* 34 (18 January 1971), pp. 72–83.

81. *Op. cit.*[6]

82. Timothy Curry & Robert Jiobu, *Sports* (Englewood Cliffs, NJ: Prentice-Hall, 1984), p. 102.

83. *Op. cit.*[80]

84. *Op. cit.*[28]

85. *Op. cit.*[80]

86. *Op. cit.*[28] p. 197.

87. *Ibid.*, pp. 175–176.
Op. cit.,[9] pp. 241–243.

88. Terry Bledsoe, "Black Dominance in Sports: Strictly from Hunger," *The Progressive* 37 (June 1973), pp. 16–19.

89. Harry Edwards, quoted in "The Black Dominance," *Time* (9 May 1977), pp. 58–59.

90. *Op. cit.*,[9] pp. 241–243.

91. *Op. cit.*[36]

92. *Op. cit.*[9]
Dick Mackey, "Blacks Find Golf a Tough Game," *Kansas City Star* (28 May 1972).
"Larry Vinson, First Black on White," Associated Press Release (23 December 1973).

93. *The Chicago Tribune* (17 February 1991), p.15.

94. Scully, *op. cit.*,[17] p. 76.

95. Gerald Scully, *The Business of Major League Baseball* (Chicago: University of Chicago Press, 1989).

96. Wilbert M. Leonard, II, "Salaries and Race in Professional Baseball: The Hispanic Com-

ponent," *Sociology of Sport Journal* 5, no. 3 (1988), pp. 278–284.

97. WILBERT M. LEONARD, II, "Salaries and Race/Ethnicity in Major League Baseball: The Pitching Component," *Sociology of Sport Journal* 6, no. 2 (1989), pp. 152–162.

98. MARC LAVOIE & WILBERT M. LEONARD, II, "Salaries, Race/Ethnicity, and Pitchers in Major League Baseball: A Correction and Comment," *Sociology of Sport Journal* 7, no. 4 (1990), pp. 394–398.

99. ROBERT M. JIOBU, "Racial Inequality in a Public Arena: The Case of Professional Baseball," *Social Forces* 67, no. 2 (1988), pp. 524–534.

100. ROBERT MOGRELL, *Wall Street Journal* (1 May 1973). Pascal & Rapping, *op. cit.*,[17] found significant differences in bonuses for whites and blacks before 1958. This difference decreased over the years so that by 1965 through 1967 it was virtually eliminated.

101. DALE HOFFMAN & MARTIN J. GREENBERG, *Sport$biz* (Champaign, IL: Human Kinetics Publishers, 1989), p. 97.

102. *Op. cit.*[73]

103. RICHARD E. LAPCHICK, "Blacks in the NBA and NFL," *CSSS Digest* 1, no. 2 (1989), pp. 1, 4–5.

104. *Op. cit.*,[9] p. 8.
BILL SIMMONS, "We Shall Overcome (Eventually)," *Professional Sports Journal* (February 1980), pp. 47–52.

105. PETE AXTHELM, "Black Out," *Newsweek* (15 July 1974), p. 57.

106. C.C. JOHNSON SPINK, "Blacks off the Field," *The Sporting News* (23 February 1980), p. 12. "Scorecard," *Sports Illustrated* (26 November 1979), p. 28.

107. GARY MIHOCES, "NFL Still Lacks Black Head Coach," *USA Today* (24 May 1983), p. 36.

108. Cited in *USA Today* (19 March 1991).

109. SPINK, *op. cit.*[106]

110. BOB WIRZ, quoted in *ibid*.

111. "Scorecard," *Sports Illustrated* (12 January 1981), p. 8.
Op. cit.,[30] pp. 46–47.

112. *Op. cit.*[30]

9

Sport and Gender

PATRICIA J. MURPHY AND WILBERT M. LEONARD, II

The last two decades have seen great gains for girls and women in sports. As participation in fitness training and competition has soared, performance has improved so much that two researchers recently predicted that top women runners may someday overtake men. But the male-dominated world of athletics doesn't yet offer a level playing field. THE CONGRESSIONAL QUARTERLY RESEARCHER

Even casual observers can see that women and men's experiences in sport are different and that those experiences have and are changing. This chapter uses some concepts from sociology and sociological reasoning to describe and explain the relationships between sport and gender. While reading this chapter, keep in mind that *sex* is a biological concept with the categories of *male* and *female,* whereas *gender* is a cultural concept with the categories of *masculine* and *feminine.*

In the first section of the chapter, we discuss the manner in which social meaning is given to the biological differences between women and men. We also describe the traditional notions of what women and men were expected to be and examine contemporary positions of women and men in society.

In the middle section, we explain how the social organization of sport influences sport participation and how, in turn, the social organization of sport influences gender definitions and the relations between the sexes. We examine ways in which gender socialization and discrimination have historically limited athletic participation for women in America. Further, sport may also function as a masculinity rite or as a mechanism that maintains male dominance in society, and it probably has the latent function of limiting the options of men.

Finally, we inquire into current issues and trends. Rapidly increasing numbers of women are competing and participating in a wider variety of athletic activities than ever before. We also explore the meaning of that participation and the debates over the routes to full equality and over the future of women's sports.

Chapter 8 explored the *social forces* lying behind racism in society and sport; in this chapter, the social forces behind sexism in society and sport will be examined.

❏ THE SOCIAL ORGANIZATION OF GENDER IN SOCIETY

The participation of women and men in the sport institution of society and the very shape of that institution are partly determined by the definitions of what men and women ought to be. In this section, we focus on the process of assigning *social meanings* to the biological differences between men and women. We describe traditional images of men and women, paying particular attention to late nineteenth-century images. Finally, we discuss the current status of gender definitions and the lives of women and men.

The Social Construction of Gender

There are obvious *biological* differences between males and females of the species *Homo sapiens.* Internal and external reproductive organs and genitalia, types and levels of hormones, chromosomal structure (male = XY and female = XX), and secondary sex characteristics are among the biological characteristics used to identify the *sex* of a human being. The sociologist, however, is more concerned with the analysis of *gender:* the social meanings that are given to these biological differences. Members of societies attribute certain characteristics to the individuals of the different sexes; we assign tasks and ascribe behaviors and attitudes. This social construction of roles, norms, and values makes up what we call the **social organization of gender** in society. Through the process of socialization, individuals learn how to be "appropriate" members of their societies; thus, an important part of socialization (see Chapter 5) is **gender socialization**—learning how to be a socially acceptable male or female.

The social definition given to sex varies cross-culturally and over time. Mead's classic study of three New Guinea tribes demonstrated that the organization of gender in society is social, not biological, in origin.[1] She detailed how the expectations concerning what is male and what is female could take very different forms, depending on the culture studied. The Arapesh women and men were gentle and unaggressive in their actions; the Mundugumor women disliked children and displayed anger and fierceness to the same extent as men, and finally, the Tchambuli men were given to artistic personal expression while the women efficiently conducted the institutional tasks of their society.

Traits defined as masculine in one society may be defined as feminine by another, or a third may not define them as more appropriate to one sex than to the other. These gender definitions are no less real, however, just because they are socially constructed and not biologically ordained. A society's social organization of gender influences how its members see themselves, how they act, and how they interact. In addition, the social organization of gender interfaces other forms of social organization, such as the social organization of family, work, and sport.

Traditional Images of Women and Men

It is impossible to adequately describe in a few paragraphs the complex and varied history (Vignette 9.1) of the social organization of gender. Certain themes, however, that describe the cultural images of women and men warrant attention. In general, social definitions of gender have been characterized by *polarization* and *inequality*. Although males and females are biologically more similar than different, most cultures of the past (including those that shaped contemporary America) and most current cultures socially define men and women as polar opposites. We refer to the other sex as "the opposite sex."

Metheny discusses the polarized images of the Greek gods and the reflection of these images in the expected behaviors of the Greek people.[2] Zeus and the admirable male gods were strong, competitive, and physical; the admirable female gods, like Demeter, were supportive, passive, and earth-mother types. The active–passive dichotomy has often characterized the difference between masculine and feminine. Men were expected to "do" things; women watched. Chodorow describes traditional masculine gender roles as emphasizing "doing" and feminine ones as emphasizing "being."[3] Anthropologist Ortner suggests that early in human history, femininity and female persons were socially associated with nature because of their tie to biological reproduction (earth mother); masculinity and male persons, on the other hand, were associated with culture and with building civilization, the purpose of which came to be seen as overcoming nature.[4]

In the American experience, colonial men were viewed as closer to God (indeed, God himself was conceptualized as a male), and women more subject to sinful influences. Women's inferior morality was kept under social control through marriage to a righteous man, who had the social authority to keep his property (wife and children) in line through social control mechanisms such as the occasional witch-burning. There

☐ **VIGNETTE 9.1**

Sociologist's Theory: Female Athletes Slighted

BY SUSAN MARQUARDT

Although there are some people who may believe that the women's liberation movement brought equality for females, there is still one area—sports—that continues to be a man's world.

Since the beginning of organized athletics, men have dominated the world of sports. One explanation for this unfortunate circumstance stems from society's attitude toward the female athlete, and some of these views were formed as early as 776 B.C.

"In the ancient Greek Olympic games, females were forbidden from participating or even watching the events," [Dr.] Wilbert M. Leonard, II, a sociology teacher at ISU, explained.

Leonard, who teaches a class on the sociology of sport, said that Greek society maintained a rigid sex-role definition.

"Much of the Greek culture focused on gods that were seen as intellectual, rational and athletic," Leonard pointed out. "In contrast, the goddess was viewed as fragile and a thing of beauty."

These opinions of females continued into Roman culture, which gave birth to the legacy that women were to serve as the childbearer, the childrearer, homemaker, and to some extent, a sex symbol.

Although society attempted to keep women out of the sports arena by relying on these sexist views, women began to revolt and formed their own branch of Olympic competition.

"The Heraen games began because women could not participate in Olympic events," Leonard explained. "These games differed (from men's events) since there was no face-to-face combat or sports that required much physical strength and aggression."

The women who dared to compete in the games faced an additional enemy other than their opponents. Because society viewed the woman

athlete in a negative light, she also battled the general public as well. This fact became evident from the term the public used to describe female participants.

"Women who were active in athletics were named Amazons which meant 'without breasts,'" Leonard said. He noted that such a term reflected the belief that women who participated in sporting events were less of a woman.

"Historically, it was impossible to be a female and an athlete at the same time. The two were not supposed to coincide."

"Sports that stress grace, beauty, and aesthetics are seen as more acceptable for females," Leonard explained. Examples of such sports would be gymnastics, tennis, swimming and diving.

The fact that women tend to enter these realms of athletics stems directly from society and the socialization of females.

Leonard explained that this is evident throughout history since women have been steered away from sports and into traditional sex roles.

"Sports has been the stag party in history since women have been few and far between," Leonard reflected. "It has been one of the last 'male things' to go."

Because of recent women's movements, however, the female athlete has begun to make strides in an attempt to catch up with her male [counterpart].

During the mid-1960s, efforts on the part of the National Organization for Women, in addition to other women's action movements, led to major changes in the public's opinion of women's roles.

Legislators also became aware of the need to recognize the changing role of women, specifically in the area of sports.

In 1972, Congress passed Title IX, which required schools to distribute funds equally to men's and women's athletic programs.

Although this law made some improvements for women's athletics, there are still some hurdles that must be crossed. One such obstacle stems from the economy.

"The years ahead will be tough economically as schools face declining enrollments and smaller budgets," Leonard noted.

Although this tightening of funds will affect both male and female sports programs, the results will be more significant for women since negative views towards women's athletics could resurface.

This train of thought, which reflects back to the ancient attitude that sports is a man's world, proves that women have yet to conquer one major opponent—the public.

SOURCE: "Women in Sports," *Horizons* (3 February 1983), p. 4.

---

were many other differences between the images of men and women, but preindustrial America saw both men and women as productive workers. The household production of goods by women indicated that although they were different from men, they were still important "do-ers" in society with an economic function.

Demos, a historian, has examined the history of the American family.[5] He notes that early America was characterized by a fusion of many social institutions (i.e., family, economy, and education), but this fusion came to an end with industrialization. The traditional gender roles became even more pronounced in the United States with industrialization. The location of the production of goods necessary for society shifted from the household to the factory. The family institution lost a major function and became socially redefined as a place of love, emotion, warmth, and escape (from the cold, cruel world of production), or what Lasch calls the "haven in a heartless world."[6] Images of men and women changed simultaneously. Men were now seen as the productive members of society, the ones who "do" important things in the public arena; women were expected to watch over the home fires, to be good mothers, and to provide support and comfort to their productive and civilization-building husbands. According to Demos, "Rooted at the center of Home stood the highly sentimentalized figure of Woman. It was she who represented and maintained the tender virtues. Men, of course, had to be out in the world, getting their hands dirty in all sorts of ways."[7]

The sermons and essays of the times reflected what was called the **cult of true womanhood.** Women became revered and admired but locked into rigid social roles. Inside their homes, they could be "true women," but they were "invisible" in the world of commerce and culture building. Even the women who worked in the factories and offices were invisible, because the place for a proper woman was outside the public sphere. The real world was the public sphere, real "work" took place there and not at home. As Gornick described, women were half the population, but this half stood "outside" looking in.[8]

Biomedical thought of the mid-nineteenth century both reflected and encouraged women's passivity. Physicians' beliefs about the health and biological nature of middle-class women became the standard ideas of what all true women should be like. The middle-class woman was seen as inherently sickly, too weak and frail for any but the mildest endeavors. Her health and personality were controlled by her "debilitating" reproductive organs. The theory of the dictatorship of the ovaries came to be used to define a lady's normal state of health as "sick." Thus, she had to be confined and prevented from doing anything that might damage her delicate reproductive system; and that meant that she had to be prevented from doing virtually anything. Ehrenreich and English wrote: "Doctors and educators were quick to draw the obvious conclusion that, for women, higher education could be physically dangerous. Too much development of the brain, they counseled, would atrophy the uterus. Reproductive development was totally antagonistic to mental development."[9]

A lady's function was to do nothing and to depend on her economically productive husband. The more "nothing" she could do, the higher her husband's status with other men. A **cult of invalidism** developed, not only legitimating the doctors' theories but also providing them with plenty of patients. This illustrates the classic male **instrumental role** (i.e., capable of getting things done, achieving) and female **expressive role** (i.e., capable of emotions and feelings). A pale, white, fragile woman was the cultural and romantic ideal of the feminine woman.

There were, of course, other kinds of women in society besides those who were white and middle class. Women of color labored in agriculture, factory, and domestic sectors. The late 1800s also saw an increase in immigration from southern and eastern Europe and a concomitant rise in feelings of Anglo-superiority and the fear of "racial hordes." Most immigrant women were found among the working poor. They were certainly not "ladies" in the genteel sense and, in addition, biomedical thought had "discovered" that these women were not governed by the same biological rules as middle-class women. The working poor, who often were sick as a result of overwork and unhealthy slum conditions, were defined as robust and healthy enough to do constant labor (although, like Typhoid Mary, they might carry disease-causing germs, if they got into the middle-class neighborhoods).[10]

Men's task in life was to achieve in the productive, public arena. Both biomedical thought and religious beliefs of the times helped clarify men's roles. Men were expected to conquer nature and build civilization. Just as middle-class women were seen to have a limited amount of energy, so were men. Men had to be very judicious to spend their energy wisely to become successful. The major concern was spermatic economy; "spending" too much sperm would drain energy away from building the railroad. The chief threats to spermatic economy were masturbation and women. The first was to be avoided at all costs. Dr. Issac Ray and Reverend John Todd suggested that men "needed a 'course of suitable discipline,' in addition to the useful 'rivalry' and the 'pressure' of frightening competition which . . . we cannot get at home."[11] Working to the point of exhaustion would also save sperm, as would limited encounters with the wife and other women, who could sap one's strength (and impede the march of progress).

Contemporary Gender Stratification

Some of these images of men and women carried over into the twentieth century. More importantly, these images became part of the ideology of the social institutions that characterized the twentieth century. The theory of the dictatorship of the ovaries was replaced by a Freudian analysis of woman, which "scientifically" demonstrated that she was psychologically inferior to man because her lack of a penis made it impossible to resolve her Electra complex.[12]

Many, if not all, institutions and the social organization of American life were clearly **patriarchal**—male dominated (literally, "rule of the father")—and characterized by inequality. A system of **gender stratification** (see Chapter 7) placed men and women in different social planes and rewarded them differentially. By the mid-1900s, and certainly by the end of World War II, women had demonstrated that they, too, could be productive workers in the public sphere. Many "Rosie the Riverters" went home immediately following the war, but the shape of the labor force was irrevocably changed. Women had always been active workers at child care, homemaking and often at paid jobs as well, but now the increasing numbers of women in the labor force made them visible in the public sphere. Access to earned income also made many women less dependent on men for survival. The various movements for women's and men's liberation that emerged during the twentieth century have raised questions about the cultural images of men and women and have challenged institutionalized gender inequality.

Undoubtedly, the polarized images of men and women are slowly being modified, and gender roles and social institutions are gradually changing. (The extent of the changes and the possible chances for gender equality are a matter of much debate in feminist circles.) Studies have indicated that a woman who works full-time, year-round earns about 60% of what a man makes; that because of discrimination, women do not translate their educational attainments into occupational and income attainments to the same extent that men do; and that women are still primarily found in the secondary, low-pay, no-career-ladder segment of the labor force.[13] At the same time, some women are in the military, in the pulpit, in the board room, and in jail more than ever before. The last quarter of this century will not be a time for clear-cut gender definitions and descriptions in the United States.

Snodgrass surveyed over 700 students to determine if traditional sex role stereotyping existed in 1990.[14] She discovered that the labels "aggressive," "dominant," "competitive," "never gives up," "feels superior," and "stands up under pressure" were rated *masculine;* "emotional," "excitable in a crisis," "devoting themselves to others," "gentle," "kind," "feelings easily hurt," "not decisive," and "needs security" were considered *feminine.* A few labels—"independent," "active," "worldly," "self-confident," and "needs others' approval"—were neutral. To some extent, the findings suggest that the clock had been turned back a generation!

☐ THE DYNAMIC RELATIONSHIP BETWEEN SPORT AND GENDER

The social organization of sport and the social organization of gender are two important parts of human life. These spheres of human activity have a dynamic relationship with each other. This section focuses on a brief history of that relationship. The quotations in Vignette 9.2 illustrate various attitudes toward the linkages between sport and gender.[15]

The definitions of appropriate gender behavior influence the participation and performance of men and women in athletic activities. Historically, the socialization of women into "proper" feminine behavior and the stigma attached to being defined as

☐ VIGNETTE 9.2

Comments on Gender and Sport

It's important for an individual to excel some-where, wherever it is. I don't think there's any more "gayness" in sports than in many other areas of life. I think sports has been set aside as a "mas-culine" thing, where other things have not. What I'm saying is if you take almost any other field—business or medicine, for example—there's a place for women even though in some areas it's been small. But women haven't been labelled with a gay image simply because they are in that area. However, if you're an athlete, that's historically been the stereotype.

—Marty, an amateur softball player (1976)

I think women's events should be confined to those appropriate for women, swimming, tennis, figure skating and fencing, but certainly not shot-putting.

—Avery Brundage,
President IOC 1952–1972 (1949)

I have always loathed compulsory sports, no mat-ter what the sport and no matter what form the coercion took. . . . Initially I assumed my dislike of organized team sports and the fanaticism sparked by athletic competition was merely a matter of personal taste. . . . I noticed this obsession with sports crossed all age and class lines, as well as occupational and racial ones. Were all men this way? Had I missed out on something?

—John Mitzel (1973)

Except for war, there is nothing in American life—nothing—which trains a boy better for life than football.

—Robert Kennedy (during his tenure as
U.S. Attorney General)

Not to have confidence in one's body is to lose confidence in oneself. . . . It is precisely the female athletes, who being positively interested in their own game, feel themselves least handicapped in comparison with the male. Let her swim, climb mountain peaks, pilot an airplane, battle against the elements, take risks, go out for adventure, and she will not feel before the world that timidity.

—Simone de Beauvoir (1949)

I always wanted to be somebody. . . . It's why, ever since I was a wild, arrogant girl in my teens, play-ing stickball and basketball and baseball and pad-dle tennis and even football in the streets in the daytime and hanging around bowling alleys half the night, I've worshipped Sugar Ray Robinson. It wasn't just because he was a wonderful fellow, and good to me when there was no special reason for him to be; it was because he was somebody, and I was determined that I was going to be some-body, too—if it killed me.

—Althea Gibson (1958)

The Women's Division believes in the spirit of play for its own sake and works for the promotion of physical activity for the largest possible proportion of persons in any given group, in forms suitable to individual needs and capacities, under leadership and environmental conditions that foster health, physical efficiency, and the development of good citizenship.

—from the "Creed" of the Women's Division,
NAAF (1924)

SOURCES: See endnote 15.

☐

unfeminine have often led women to exclude themselves from sports activity. Further, such cultural images, stereotypes, and myths about women's physiological capabilities were translated into structural barriers that excluded women from certain kinds of participation and discriminated against them with regard to the evaluation of performance and the distribution of resources.

The organization of sport in society influences the organization of gender in society. As a **masculine rite of passage,** participation in sport was expected of males to prove their manhood and to learn to succeed. At the same time, the exclusionist policies of men's sport and the goals and values of that sport can be seen to have historically functioned to maintain the woman's position as a second-class citizen.

Gender and Sport Participation

The social organization of gender in a society, because it defines the proper spheres of social activity for men and women, significantly influences men and women's participation and performance in sport. In this section we describe the historical participation of women in sport and explain this chronology partially by the cultural images of women, the socialization of women into these images, and the structural limitations placed on women's participation and achievements. Vignette 9.3 chronicles some significant events in the history of women in sport. The experiences of all women were not the same; the particular position of women of color in American society is noted. Finally, we raise feminist questions concerning the nature and control of sport in society.

Women's Historical Participation in Sport

Women have always been physically active and have throughout the centuries shown an interest in participating in organized competition based on physical skill. Although they were forbidden to participate in or to even view the Olympic Games of ancient Greece, women established their own program of sports competition, which they named the *Heraen Games* after Hera, the wife of Zeus. It was considered tolerable for women (especially Spartan women) to keep healthy to be good "breeders." The glories of true athletic success, however, were reserved for the men of ancient Greece, and the winners became religious, political, and cultural heroes. Women were not part of what was considered to be real sport but were "sporting" nonetheless.

In the American colonial experience, we see a similar pattern of women's sport participation. Women were restricted by the patriarchs of their communities in the games they could play, but evidence from journals, diaries, letters, and newspapers of the times indicates that the "ladies" of some wealth included dancing, "spectatoring" of horse and boat races, skating, sleighing, and kolven (an early form of golf played on ice) among their activities. The regulations and informal norms that governed women's participation varied among the colonies and social classes. The physical activities of the women of leisure composed a significant part of their social lives, but these activities were socially defined as different from those of men. One activity shared by both sexes was horseback riding. The game of cricket for women emerged in the 1700s, and there is evidence that colonial women held foot races.

◻ **VIGNETTE 9.3**

Significant Events for Women and Sport

circa 776 B.C.	Ancient Olympic Games exclude women; Heraen games organized for women's separate athletic competition.
1896	First modern Olympic Games exclude women.
	First extramural college basketball game (Berkeley vs. Stanford).
1900	Women allowed to participate in Olympics in only golf and tennis.
1920	Women win right to vote in the United States.
	Female swimmers become the first American women to win full Olympic status.
1921	Federation Sportive Feminine Internationale organizes women's track and field competition in fourteen events.
1923	Women's Division of National Amateur Athletic Federation adopts a platform stressing athletic participation for all women and "play days" instead of varsity competition.
1925	*The Sportswoman* is published, focusing on field hockey.
1928	First track and field events permitted for women in the Olympics.
1932	Mildred Didrikson wins 3 track-and-field medals in the LA Olympics.
1949	Ladies' Professional Golf Association formed.
1950	Althea Gibson breaks the color bar in American tennis.
1966	International Athletic Federation requires women athletes to "prove" they are female.
1967	Kathy Switzer "crashes" the "male only" Boston marathon.
1968	Sex tests are given for the first time to women in international competition.
1971	Billie Jean King becomes the first woman athlete to win more than $100,000 per year.
	AIAW becomes the governing body for collegiate women athletes and for intercollegiate competition.
1972	Women's 1,500-meter event included in the Olympics.
	Title IX is passed by Congress prohibiting sex discrimination in schools.
1973	Billie Jean King defeats Bobby Riggs in the nationally televised "Battle of the Sexes" tennis match.
1974	Little League Baseball admits girls.
1976	NCAA sues the Department of Health, Education and Welfare in order to stop Title IX.
	International Women's Professional Softball League begins with 10 teams in 7 states.
1978	Women's Basketball League founded.
1980	More than 1 million American girls are playing soccer.
	Financial rewards for women athletes in 6 major sports tops $16 million.
	International Women's Professional Softball League folds.
1981	20% of AIAW schools switch to NCAA membership after NCAA votes to hold its own college championships for women.
	Women's Basketball League folds.
	Two women elected to the 90-member International Olympic Committee.
	North American Soccer League names the first woman professional official.
1982	AIAW ceased operations.
1984	Twelve "new" women's events included in the Olympics.

U.S. Supreme Court narrows the scope of Title IX (*Grove City v. Bell*) by ruling that the law applies only to programs that directly receive federal aid.

1985   Average women's intercollegiate budget at major schools exceeded $2 million.

1986   Martina Navratilova's (tennis) winnings exceed $1¼ million.

1987   Major League Volleyball (women's league) commences play.
        Women's basketball game between Texas and Tennessee draws 23,912 spectators.

1988   Congress enacts the Civil Rights Restoration Act and prohibits sex discrimination through-
        out educational institutions receiving federal funds.

1990   Reporter Lisa Olson in conflict with New England Patriots regarding sexual harassment.

1992   NCAA delays imposing a 10% cut in athletic scholarships for women until the release of
        its gender-equity study.

The mid-nineteenth-century Victorian image of the "true" woman as fragile, frail, weak, sickly, pale, and ruled by her hormones was an image antithetical to women's participation in any but the mildest of pastimes. Tight, rib- and organ-crushing corsets were fashionable; exercise seemed vaguely indecent, even if one could get breath enough to do it. Aggression and intense competition were not advised for women, according to the physicians in the mid-1800s, but were most important to men in the struggle to build society. Thus, acceptable activities for women, especially before the later years of the century, were few. Croquet, bowling, tennis, golf, and archery were permitted forms of coeducational recreation but were designed more for social contact than for competition. However, some women continued to exercise, in addition to participating in recreational swimming, skating, and riding.

By the late nineteenth century, the ideology that rigorous exercise was harmful to women was being challenged by a new view that exercise was beneficial for women. Signs of women's sports participation in bicycling, swimming, tennis, golf, and basketball were witnessed in the 1890s and early 1900s. According to Spears, the late 1800s produced a major sports breakthrough for women.[16] Although the pale and fragile woman remained a cultural ideal until the 1930s, the rosy-cheeked girl on her bicycle was providing evidence that exercise made a woman healthier for housework and childbearing. Amelia Bloomer's bloomers allowed women to move, but modesty in appearance was still an important consideration in sports participation.

American sport became institutionalized with industrialization. Rules, associations, professionalism, and sports journalism replaced less formally structured patterns of sports activities. In addition, the turn of the century brought the end to the dominance of informal, coeducational activities. Coeducational sports were replaced by separate sports, separate structures, and separate participation. Athletic clubs for "ladies" organized women's competitions in tennis, golf, biking, archery, bowling, and fencing, which were the common recreational sports for women of the times. Colleges began to offer programs in physical education, partly to maintain the health of students and partly to disprove beliefs about female frailty. Women's colleges offered experiences not only in the traditional women's sports but in team sports as well. In college, physical education programs in the early twentieth century taught basketball, volleyball, field hockey, golf, and track and field. This era saw many other firsts in the history of women's sport: A woman named Melopomene "crashed" the first modern Olympics in 1896 and ran the marathon; women were first allowed to participate in the 1900 Olympics in golf and tennis (archery was added in 1904 and figure skating in 1908).

Twin suggests, however, that whereas some women in this era began to break new ground, active women were still not the ideal in the culture.[17] Marriage and motherhood continued to be the prime goals for women, and college women's involvement in sports was still nominal. Moreover, it was still believed that even if women needed exercise, it had to be *moderate* exercise in order to avoid physical harm or "masculinization." Except for the traditional "ladies" sports, the new women's team sports were virtually unknown to the public. Just as women's productive labor in the household was invisible and their paid work ignored, these competitive team sport activities of women were invisible. Men's sports were in the public sphere, but most women's collegiate sports took place within the walls of women's colleges (often closed to the male public to avoid "indecent exposures"). Although the Berkeley women played the Stanford women in basketball in 1896, intercollegiate games were at a minimum until the 1920s. The women physical educators did not value extramural sports, largely because they thought that "the qualities of womanliness are less related to success in athletics than are the qualities of manhood."[18]

Some trends from the turn of the century continued into the 1920s. One by one, women's events were added to the Olympics (fencing in 1924, and limited track and field and gymnastics events in 1928). Women had won the vote (in 1920) and had demonstrated work potential during World War I. Women played sports on industrial league teams, although most of these were sex-segregated. The Amateur Athletic Union (AAU) continued to add women's events to its national sport organization. Women were being accepted into national sport organizations, although they were rarely found in leadership positions. Women's participation in the Olympic Games really began in earnest in the 1920s. It appeared that women were finally "making it" in the public world of sports. *The Sportswoman,* a monthly magazine, began publication in 1925. Amelia Earhart, Gertrude Ederle, and Babe Didrikson Zaharias became sports stars and national heroines.

College sports did *not* follow this trend. Partly because of the traditional concern over women's physical limitations and proper deportment, women physical educators—through their organization, The Women's Division of the National Amateur Athletic Federation (NAAF)—drastically reduced the number of intercollegiate games and substituted such events as *telegraphic meets* (in which teams played on their respective campuses and telegraphed the results to the opponent) and *play days* (a less formal competition, often with pick-up games). *Sport days* did sanction bona fide women's college teams to play against each other; however, rules were sometimes altered to keep the contest player-centered and, furthermore, winners were sometimes not even announced. The philosophy of sport of the Women's Division of the NAAF emphasized values for women that differed from those of men's sport: (a) The point of sports was for as many women to play as possible, and financial and other resources were not to go just to the "elite" athletes. (b) Women's sports should be modified versions of men's sports, otherwise women become mere mimics of men. (c) Sports were mainly for fun—not for profit—and the intent was "to avoid countenancing the sacrifice of an individual's health for the sake of her participation in athletic competition."[19]

As a consequence of this philosophy and practice, Olympic hopefuls received no help at the college level (except for a few black colleges that trained track and field hopefuls). This made such training difficult and expensive, often limiting Olympic participation to women of means who could pay for private equipment and lessons in the country club sports. At the collegiate level, the number of women's varsity teams began to decline as emphasis was placed on the many, not the few. It was clear that women's sports, now visible, were not only separate from men's, but also different from men's.

The Depression and World War II disrupted American life. The impact of having millions of women in the labor force was to be permanently felt. Not only could women do hard, physical labor, but they could do it well. The women's liberation movement emerged partly from this realization and from attempts in the 1950s to pretend it all hadn't happened. The images of women in the 1950s stressed beauty, traditional femininity, and that a woman's place was in the private sphere of her family. Industry-sponsored competition for women fell by the wayside, track and field programs for women in all but black colleges virtually disappeared, and American women had their poorest performance in Olympic history in 1952.

The organizing body of women's athletics in the 1950s, the Division of Girls' and Women's Sports, slowly began to drift toward supporting women's Olympic activity and encouraging varsity competition and national championships. The status of women in the contemporary sport scene will be discussed in a later section, but it is important to note here that the mid-1970s were a period of much growth in women's sports participation. More schoolgirls and more college women were playing, and more professional sports opportunities were available to women than ever before. Increasing participation by women in the public world of work seems to have encouraged participation in other public arenas as well. As traditional gender roles are being challenged by women and men and by the law, the traditional role of women in sport is also being challenged.

Gender Socialization. The social organization of gender in a society and the definitions of what men and women are supposed to be and do affect their sport participation. Throughout most of American history, men were expected to participate in athletic competition; cultural images of the male as instrumental, powerful, and a capable achiever in the public sphere encouraged (if not forced) men to participate. Recent research has indicated that athletic success and involvement is still more important to men than women and is a stronger part of men's self-images.[20] Goffman writes:

> In an important sense there is only one complete unblushing male in America: a young, married, white, urban, northern heterosexual Protestant father of college education, fully employed, of good complexion, weight, and height, and a recent record in *sports*. Every American male tends to look out upon the world from this perspective, this constituting one sense in which one can speak of a common value system in America. Any male who

fails to qualify in any one of these ways is likely to view himself—during moments at least—as unworthy, incomplete, and inferior.[21]

The orientations of male and female athletes toward sport is dissimilar. Sage asked men and women athletes to respond (from strongly agree to strongly disagree) to popular sport slogans such as "Winning isn't everything, it's the only thing," "Show me a good loser and I'll show you a loser," "Defeat is worse than death because you have to live with defeat," "It isn't the winning but in the taking part which is most important," and "It isn't whether you won or lost, but how you played the game."[22] Responses to these sport slogans clearly revealed that winning was more salient for men than women. Nearly 50% of the men agreed that "winning isn't everything, it's the only thing" compared to 16% of the women. The socialization of men (vs. women) in American society tends to encourage a more competitive, serious, and professionalized orientation toward sports participation.

Traditionally, sports have been a masculine area of activity. Felshin characterized the social dynamics of women in sport as an **anomaly.**[23] The anomaly results from the culture's conception of sport as masculine and women's involvement in it as inappropriate. The traditional feminine ideal generally did not stress aggression, competition, muscles, or sweat. If allowed, tough competition among women happened in private and not in the public arena. The exceptions included the genteel sports of golf, tennis, swimming, and skating, but contact sport competition and sports requiring great strength were always considered inappropriate for women. One way of capturing this discussion is to consider the following didactic 2 × 2 table:

		Sex	
		male	female
	masculine	OK	anomaly
Gender			
	feminine	effeminate	OK

When sex and gender coincide the individual in question is "OK." However, when sex and gender are inconsistent, pejorative labels such as *effeminate* and *anomaly* are attached.

Through gender socialization, the American woman generally learned that being an acceptable "feminine" woman did not involve proving oneself in competition and that women who did were certainly not the feminine ideal. Indeed, even American women swimmers in 1976 commented that their muscular East German counterparts did not really look like women.[24] Given the cultural images that become part of female socialization, women often select themselves out of certain sport activities or select "appropriate" ones. Research has demonstrated that reference groups and role models are especially important for women athletes, especially given the absence of general encouragement in the culture.[25] In an investigation of female athletic role models, Rintala and Birrell conclude that women tend to be underrepresented and, when represented, cast in traditional sport roles.[26]

The sportswoman's traditional position of anomaly has led many women to participate in the more "feminine" sports. Women who choose to participate in the less "acceptable" sports tend to experience more **role conflict** and stigma than those in the "approved" sports. In one study, female athletes were divided into two groups—(a) those participating in the "feminine" sports (tennis, golf, swimming, and gymnastics) and (b) those participating in the "masculine" sports (track and field, volleyball, softball, basketball, and field hockey), and subjective responses to role conflict were explored. The results indicated that women participating in "masculine" sports experienced more role conflict than those engaging in "feminine" sports (46% vs. 34%).[27] Althea Gibson wrote, "It used to hurt me real bad to hear the girls talking about me . . . and they looked at me like I was a freak."[28] The joy and satisfaction found in sports competition was always tempered by social stigma, and many women athletes tried to overcome this by proving their "femininity" in other areas. A track and field star wears "short dresses and lots of make-up" when she is not a sport participant.[29] Stereotypes of women athletes as lesbians (images often perpetuated by male coaches, male players, and the mass media) function to socialize women away from certain kinds of athletic participation in a society where nontraditional emotional and sexual forms of expression are not highly valued.

Many of the cultural images that have affected women's self-perceptions and sport participation and performance were based on medical beliefs about the physical limitations of the female body. The Victorian theory of the dictatorship of the ovaries continued into the twentieth century in modified form. Medical myths have included the notions that (a) strenuous activities lead to childbearing difficulties (the opposite is, in fact, true); (b) women's reproductive organs are subject to damage (women's internal organs are more protected than men's); (c) women's bone structure is more fragile (smaller, yes; but just as strong); and (d) women would get unattractive bulging muscles ("unattractive" is a social value; and women lack the hormones necessary for such development).[30]

Current physiological research indicates that rigorous physical activity, such as marathon running, affects both men's and women's hormone levels. Shangold indicates that "because a woman's cycle is based on such a careful balance of events, a woman's cycle is more likely to be disrupted."[31] Most studies of the physical impact or danger of sport have concerned themselves with women because women's cultural image was that of the weaker sex. That image is being challenged by recent medical findings, which raise questions about our knowledge of women's so-called "limitations."

Some physiological differences do exist between males and females, and Figure 9.1 details some of the biophysiological differences related to athletic performance. Males have more muscle fiber in their arms and legs and have bigger and stronger shoulders and legs, which give them an advantage in throwing, hitting, and sprinting. The average male heart and lungs are 10% larger than those of the average female. Women sweat less copiously than men; further, authorities believe that women sweat more efficiently because their sweat glands are more evenly distributed over their bodies. Women's body fat also provides insulation against the cold as well as an extra reserve of energy (women runners don't seem to "hit the wall"). The female's narrower shoulders are helpful in swimming, but wider pelvic bones can cause leg injuries in running.[32] In general, some of the significant physiological differences between men and women include the average male being about 20% stronger than his counterpart, the average male reaction time being about 25% faster than his counterpart, males have more muscle mass, and about 50% more maximum oxygen uptake.

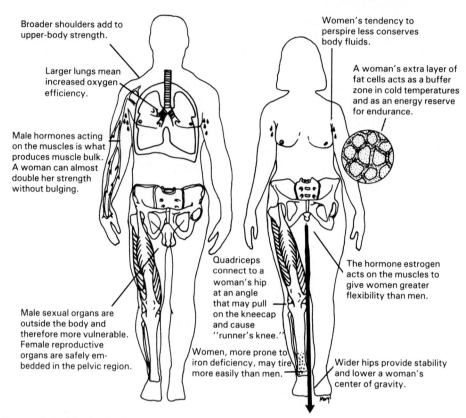

Broader shoulders add to upper-body strength.

Larger lungs mean increased oxygen efficiency.

Male hormones acting on the muscles is what produces muscle bulk. A woman can almost double her strength without bulging.

Male sexual organs are outside the body and therefore more vulnerable. Female reproductive organs are safely embedded in the pelvic region.

Quadriceps connect to a woman's hip at an angle that may pull on the kneecap and cause "runner's knee."

Women, more prone to iron deficiency, may tire more easily than men.

Women's tendency to perspire less conserves body fluids.

A woman's extra layer of fat cells acts as a buffer zone in cold temperatures and as an energy reserve for endurance.

The hormone estrogen acts on the muscles to give women greater flexibility than men.

Wider hips provide stability and lower a woman's center of gravity.

FIGURE 9.1   Biophysical differences related to athletic performance
SOURCE: *MS Magazine* (July 1981), p. 53. Illustration by Meryl Greene. Reproduced with permission.

Twin argues that it has been the *cultural* image of women rather than physical limitations that has made women's participation in sport limited and unequal. Women's limited and modified participation may have made it appear that women are not as capable as men.[33] Sparling studied sex differences in maximal oxygen uptake (aerobic capability), and Yandell and Sperduso studied sex differences in reaction and movement time.[34] Both studies concluded that cultural factors (goal orientation, motivation, and past history of physical activity), not biological factors, seemed to produce the sex differences.

Structural Discrimination.   Although feminine socialization led women to curtail their own activities and performances, another significant constraint on female sports participation has been **structural discrimination.** This concept refers to a situation in which the very structure and organization of sporting activities result in unequal treatment for a particular group.

Women have been structurally prohibited from participating in certain sport activities. The number of women participating in the Olympics has always been noticeably smaller than the number of men (5:1 in the 1976 and 1980 Olympics and 4:1 in the 1984 and 1988 Olympics), largely because there are fewer sports and events for women. The 1928 Olympics permitted five events for women and twenty-two for men; in the 1976 Summer Olympics, men still had twice as many sports and three times as many events.[35] Avery Brundage, President of the International Olympic Committee (IOC) between 1952 and 1972, used his position to limit the number and nature of women's events (see his comment in Vignette 9.2). The 1988 Seoul Olympics produced some major leaps in female events and participation.

Many other competitions were closed to women. The Boston Marathon banned women until 1968. The AAU forbade women to participate in long-distance running until 1972. Women's running events were permitted in the Olympics in 1928, but women were not allowed to compete in long-distance events. The 1972 Munich Olympics finally sanctioned women to run a 1,500-meter race. After considerable pressure, the 1984 Olympics included a 3,000-meter and a marathon race for women. Ironically, women may be more physically suited to long-distance running than to sprinting.

Limited opportunities (in many ways, virtual exclusion) for women was also the result of lesser funding for women's sports programs, inferior facilities, equipment, and training. Such inequality, which has been amply documented, provided the impetus for the emergence of Title IX to redress the inequality. **Title IX** is the 1972 amendment to the Civil Rights Act that prohibits sex discrimination in educational institutions receiving federal funds. Structural inequality sometimes operates very subtly. Lever studied the games children play and discovered that boys get much more exposure to playing complex team games, whereas girls are more likely to play without formal rules or structure, to use their imaginations, and to play indoors (i.e., their games are private, not public), which limits girls' early exposure to the world of sport.[36] Sex bias in subjective evaluations of male and female performance has been discovered in some research studies. Brawley et al. discovered that students (male and female) consistently underrated female and overrated male performance of exactly the same muscular task.[37]

Women of Color. The female experience in society is not the same for all categories of women. Gender stratification crosscuts systems of economic and racial stratification (see Chapter 7). Thus, the experience of the black woman in sport has differed from that of the white woman. Black colleges encouraged black women in track and field when white women's colleges were encouraging more "feminine" activities. Black women have excelled in the nontraditional fields but have rarely been seen in the country club sports. Why? The explanation partly lies in three social factors: (a) Black women have been disproportionately located at the lower end of the economic hierarchy and, therefore, have been unable to afford private golf, swimming, or tennis lessons. (b) Overt racial discrimination prevented black women from gaining access to the sports participated in by white women. (c) The cultural image of femininity has been defined by whites. A pale complexion might have been an approved image for the woman in America, but the referent was clearly the white woman. Black women could not be pale, rosy-cheeked, or really feminine, just as the Victorian medical definition of the innately fragile woman applied only to the middle class, not the immigrant "racial hordes." Black women often formed the vanguard of those pioneering new sports ground for women in general but only because a racist culture did not define them as "real" women.

Minority women athletes have faced limited opportunities, although gains have been made. In 1976–1977, minorities constituted 16% of female undergraduates but 8% of female athletes. In 1986–1987, the percentage of black women was about 10% of intercollegiate athletes, approximately the same as their enrollment rate.[38]

There's a dearth of minority women in sports leadership roles:[39]

- Five percent of college coaches and administrators are minority women.
- Of the 106 Division I schools that field women's basketball teams, only 11% are coached by black women.
- No executive directors of the fifty governing bodies for U.S. Olympic Sports are black women.
- There has never been a black woman on any U.S. Olympic basketball coaching staff.

The Paradox of Women's Sport.   Feminists often argue that the "history of sport has generally been one of male domination, resulting from cultural patterns which determine not only who participates but how sport is conducted and experienced."[40] Kathy Switzer, the woman who ran illegally in the 1967 Boston Marathon, argues that most of the sports we see take advantage of men's "strengths" and are organized to reflect men's physiology rather than women's, or some combination of both.[41] Studies of schoolchildren indicate that activities emphasizing strength, speed, and power are defined as "male" activities and that these activities are seen as more important than girl's games.[42] Kelly writes:

> Every standard of excellence of performance within sport is a male standard. . . . It is seldom noted, but is the case that all sports that have been invented to date (with the possible exception of sky diving) have been designed to magnify those particular aspects of physiology in which males excel. No sports have been designed to magnify the physiological aspects in which females excel.[43]

So, what is the **paradox?** Psychological studies find that the characteristics of masculinity are the most highly valued in the culture, but that women with such characteristics are not highly valued.[44] In sport, women who compete in masculine sports may not be highly valued; but even more importantly, if the sports are based on male standards and male physiology, most women cannot do what men do. Thus, women's athletic inferiority has been demonstrated. The increasing use of anabolic steroids (synthetic male hormones) by women indicates the desire to meet male standards and indirectly demonstrates that the criteria are male. What harm this does to women is yet unknown. We do know, however, that trying to obey the Army regulations of a 30-inch normal stride can cause stress fractures in short people; women in the Army who are generally shorter than men who obey the rules about the standard stride can cause harm to themselves and prove their inferiority at the same time.[45] If, however, female activities are based on female physiology, then female sport participation becomes one of who gets to decide the rules, organize the activities, and define the situation. Just what should the standards of sports be and whose bodies should they reflect? Even if women can occasionally beat men at their own games, who interprets the results? A study of fourth-grade sport competition indicated that boys attributed losing to another boy as an indication of the winner's skill and ability; a loss to a girl, however, was not explained by her ability.[46] Girls, rather, are thought to win through extralegal means: they do not play fairly.

Questions of who plays fairly and questions concerning the equality and control of women's sports loom as crucial contemporary issues. The meaning of women's greater participation in sport is open to debate.

Sport Influences Gender Stratification

The social organization of sport provides, through its images, ideologies, and structures, a mechanism for maintaining and legitimizing a particular organization of gender in society. What follows is a discussion of the way sport influences women's lives and women's gender roles, and the way sport influences the social definitions of men and masculinity in our culture.

Sport and Women as Second-Class Citizens. Simone de Beauvoir argued that sport is a way of expressing oneself in the world and of reaching toward perfection.[47] If women have continually been compared to males and their performances have been organized and judged according to male models, then the notions of women as second class or inferior are reproduced through sport institutions. What are imagined to be sex differences become institutionalized: Women's sporting events often stress grace, style, and beauty. The virtual lack of certain events (e.g., pole vault) suggests that women cannot really do what men do. Women's absence from the major professional team sports (e.g., football, ice hockey, and baseball) reinforces the notions that some matters are really a man's job and the woman's place is on the sidelines.

Successful sports competition can build confidence. Snyder, Kivlin, and Spreitzer discovered that female college athletes had more positive self-attitudes than did a control group of nonathletes.[48] Similarly, elite women swimmers who had competed between 1956 and 1970 and were studied ten years later by Ogilvie and McGuire reported having strong self-concepts, which they attributed to their sports participation.[49] *The Miller Lite/Women's Sports Foundation Report on Women in Sports* indicates that the "rewards of sports participation have been redefined." Girls who have participated in sports have higher self-esteem and leadership qualities and no longer regard sports participation as threatening to their femininity. When women are limited in their sports participation, either by stereotypes or structural barriers, then one mechanism for feeling good, powerful, or instrumental is unavailable.

Current data suggest that values and norms learned in sport participation can be translated into successful achievement in the public world of work. Hennig and Jardim suggest that successful women in organizations were often tomboys.[50] To the extent that we discourage sports participation, especially of a team nature, we may deny women the opportunity to learn skills useful to achievement in certain occupational situations.

Media images of women in sport have begun to reflect the increasing participation of women in a variety of activities. Following the 1952 film *Pat and Mike,* in which Katharine Hepburn portrays a character modeled after Babe Didrikson Zaharias, women athletes were virtually ignored until the 1970s. Television movies have depicted the lives of Babe Zaharias, Wilma Rudolph, and other track stars, skaters, and runners. The 1982 film *Personal Best* focuses on the relationship between two female track and field athletes and portrays athletic participation for women in a generally positive way. These women were unquestionably "attractive," which is contrary to the old stereotype of women athletes as unattractive "Amazons," but they were involved in a lesbian relationship, which is consistent with the old stereotype.

At the same time, the media continue to reflect some traditional cultural definitions of women. Article titles like "The Secret Scandal of Women's Tennis" reinforce the lesbian stereotype as well as suggest that the intimate lives of female athletes are just as important, if not more so, than their sporting lives.[51] Female athletes look to the mass media for identification objects. Former tennis star Billie Jean King had her contract endorsement discontinued with E.R. Squibb Company shorty after publicly acknowledging her lesbian relationship with her one-time secretary, Marilyn Barnett. Scholars have documented that sports magazines still stress men's activities significantly more than women's. Lumpkin and Williams's analysis of *Sports Illustrated* articles between 1954 and 1987 found a limited number of articles depicting female athletes (and articles that were shorter than those for the men) and found that women were most often featured in "their" traditional sports of swimming, golf, and tennis.[52] The beauty ideal for women that once limited their participation is now reason for participation. Women's sports magazines, in their ads and articles, reflect this new focus. Avon, Bonne Bell, and other cosmetic companies often sponsor tournaments for women. There is a new focus on clothing that is comfortable and attractive. There is another paradox here: The new cultural tie between beauty and sport encourages women to become participants, but men participate to achieve and to win, not to be pretty. *The New York Times* captions to pictures that accompanied a story on the New York Stars (of the now defunct Women's Basketball League) included the following: "Gail Marquis pats make-up on Althea Gwyn," and "in the locker room, the air is heavy with the smell of Halston perfume and there is talk of who will do the laundry and who last used the travel iron."[53]

Duncan conducted an insightful empirical analysis of the images of sports women and men (in the 1984 and 1988 Olympic Games).[54] The researcher focused on two categories of photographic features: (a) the content or discourse within the photographs (a category including physical appearances, poses and body positions, facial expressions, emotional displays, and camera angles) and (b) the context (a category including captions, surrounding written text, title, space in which the photo appears, and the substantive aspect of the article). Duncan concluded that both the content and context convey sexual differences:

> The implication is that they [women] can never be like men. In short, this study has demonstrated how sport photography as an ideological terrain of struggle may legitimate patriarchal relations. The issue . . . is one of power. Focusing on female differences is a political strategy that places women in a position of weakness. Sport photographs that emphasize the otherness of women enable patriarchal ends.[55]

In a study of the coverage of women's sports by sports departments, Theberge and Cronk argue that the restricted coverage of women in sports is not merely the result of journalists' biases against women in sport but, in part, is due to reliance on bureaucratic news sources and the standardization of the production process.[56]

Somewhat related to the Theberge study is a content analysis of the race and sex of persons portrayed on the covers of *Sports Illustrated*. As can be gleaned from Figure 9.2, females, both black and white, are considerably less represented than males. Note, too, that black females are even more underrepresented than white females.

Sport as a Masculinity Rite. If women who participated in nontraditional athletic activities were stigmatized as masculine or unnatural, woe to the boy who wasn't interested or wasn't good at sports. Coming of age for the American male often includes participation sports, and the ideas and concepts of sport are reflected in other activities (e.g., "Did you score last night?" does not refer just to sports). Sabo and Runfola suggest that "a primary function of sports is the dissemination of such traditional male values as male superiority, competition, work and success."[57] Sport is

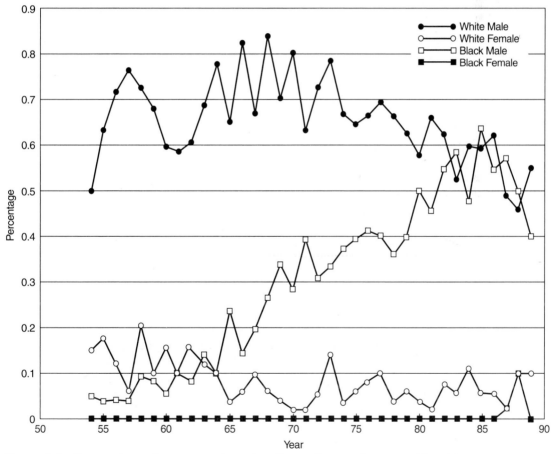

FIGURE 9.2   Race and sex of persons portrayed on *Sports Illustrated* covers, 1954–1989

☐ VIGNETTE 9.4

Out in Right Field

Throughout my entire school career, the time of day I dreaded most was Gym class. Whereas other kids seemed to look forward to Gym as some sort of relief from sitting at a desk and listening to a teacher, I dreaded the thought of sports.

The curse followed me throughout my entire life. In elementary school, part of the year we played baseball outdoors. The two best players (never me) were captains and they chose—one by one—players for their teams. The choosing went on and on, the better players getting picked first and me and my type last.

During the game I always played the outfield. Right field. Far right field. And there I would stand in the hot sun wishing I was anyplace else in the world. Every so often a ball looked like it was coming in my direction and I prayed to god that it wouldn't happen. If it did come, I promised god to be good for the next thirty-seven years if he let me catch it—especially if it was a flyball. The same thing occurred when it was my turn to bat. It was bad enough, but if there were any runners on base—or any outs—and it all depended on me—I knew we were lost.

The rest of the year in elementary school consisted of indoor Gym class, some of which were coed. The coed Gym classes consisted of things like dance lessons. The teachers would teach us essential dances like the fox trot, the mambo, and the merengue. These were always a chore because it was you and your girl partner—usually matched by height—and I of course was the shortest—and matched up with the shortest girl—who towered over me anyway. Dances like the Virginia Reel and square dancing, which were a group thing, I usually enjoyed a lot. A lot, that is, until it became clear from the actions of the rest of the guys in dance class that I was the only one having a good time. After that even that type of dancing was awful.

Junior high school was equally awful. For it was in junior high that real Gym classes started—Gym class with lockers and smelly locker rooms and gym uniforms and showers with eight million other guys.

I hated the sight of my gym uniform. The locker room stench almost knocked me out. And during Gym class I tried my best not to exert myself, so I wouldn't sweat too much, so I wouldn't have to take a shower with eight million other guys.

In junior high we still did things like play baseball. But things started to get rougher and rougher. We did things like wrestling. And gymnastics. To this day I can't climb a pole or a rope. Calisthenics were and are a bore.

High school was the same old stuff. However, in high school, sports started taking on new dimensions because the most highly prized girls looked to the best athletes. The football and basketball players. I was out of the competition from the beginning, but that didn't make it any the less awful.

There was absolutely no relief from sports in the early part of my life, for it happened not only in school, but also at home. My older brother was a good athlete. He went to ballgames and even tried out for and made some teams. He plastered our room with hateful pictures of the Dodgers at bat. Sports consumed his entire life, and he would get home from school, change his clothes and run out to play.

My father related to my brother completely in this way. They had a fine sports relationship, and would go off to ballgames together—or talk at the dinner table of the day's ballgames or the latest standings, which they both knew by heart. I was completely left out of this. After a while I grew resentful and wanted no part of it. Yet, every so often my father would try. He would take me out back for a while with a ball, bat, and glove and try to make a man out of me. Patiently he would throw a ball in my direction and I swung and missed it. After he quickly grew tired of that he would once again explain to me how to use the fielding glove he stuck on my hand and I would try my hand at catching. I soon grew tired of this—mainly because I missed so often and had to go chasing down the block after the ball. These sessions never lasted very long. Even Sundays were no relief—the television was usually on and blasting a ball game. I grew to hate the sound of Mel Allen's voice.

My father and brother seemed to have a great relationship. I didn't. Neither with my father, nor with my brother. I guess I was left to my mother. We seemed to get along fine.

SOURCE: Unbecoming Men: A Men's Consciousness-Raising Group Writes on Oppression and Themselves (Albion, CA: Times Change Press). Copyright © 1971. Reprinted by permission, pp. 36–38. Reprinted in *Men and Masculinity*, eds., Joseph H. Pleck & Jack Sawyer (Englewood Cliffs, NJ: Prentice-Hall, 1974), pp. 17–18.

---

an important means of socializing boys into their appropriate gender roles. Athletic success is seen by male adolescents as the best way to be popular with boys and girls.[58]

Fathers appear to be the most important significant other in socializing sons to be athletic and successful.[59] Fathers appear to attempt to reproduce traditional masculinity in their sons and to encourage them to learn through sports how to be successful men. Sports tell boys how to be instrumental—how to "do," how to "get" (the word *athlete* means "prize-getting"). One gets by winning, in the most popular sports, by defeating someone else in battle. Sage reports that male college athletes stress winning more than female athletes do.[60] Men are expected to succeed in the world of paid work; on the sports field, play is work, with productivity as a goal. Aggression leads to greater productivity in collegiate ice hockey,[61] thus, it is an important value in the male world of work.

Expression and emotion are not valued. Physical pain is denied and is a symbol of toughness. Feelings are not important in sport, and violence is normative. It is seen as normative by professional players, is taught to young ones, and increases gate receipts.[62]

Deegan and Stein characterize University of Nebraska football as a ritual reenactment of the American experience.[63] According to them, the big, tough, aggressive, and violent man "controlled by arbitrary, efficient, rational authority" abuses his body, while "the ideal, typical woman—the cheerleader—screams, jumps, and displays her body." Using Goffman's concept, they argue that this ritual "advertises" gender to the public and that sports reinforce and perpetuate the domination of women by teaching values reflecting male domination. Hoch calls sports a "school for sexism," where the structure encourages the exclusion of women, male bonding, and male leadership.[64] Some writers suggest that exclusionist male team sports teach men how to use physical power, and when linked to masculinity, violence, and male domination in the organization of sport, team sports may be partially responsible for male violence against women in general in the society.[65] In provocative articles, one entitled "Aggressiveness in Sports Has a Sorry Spinoff: Studies Show a Link to Wife-Beating," Capuzzo writes that battered women's advocates are alarmed by a correlation between the aggressions unleashed by sports viewing—especially pro football and basketball—and violence against women.[66] Importantly, those noting this relationship are *not* claiming that viewing or playing sports causes the battering but that the setting—betting, beer, and family—provides an environment conducive to violence. In another, entitled "Athletes and Rape: Alarming Link," Moore cites a report in *Mademoiselle* that at least fifteen gang rapes involving about fifty athletes were reported from June 1989 to June 1990.[67]

Just as women's roles have changed, so have men's roles, albeit more slowly. Some men argue that the male-only team sports are the last bastion of male supremacy. The questioning of traditional definitions of men and who is masculine has led sports scholars and others to ask new questions about men and sports. Males, too, can suffer role strain; ignoring the emotional, expressive, and feeling part of life and only focusing on winning can be psychologically unhealthy and stressful for men.[68] Some men are beginning to question the traditional assumption that manhood is to be proved by unemotional achievement in the public arenas.[69] See Vignette 9.4 for one male's poignant experience with scholastic sports.

❏ CURRENT ISSUES AND TRENDS

The social emphasis on equality for women and the changing definitions of appropriate female behavior have been accompanied by an increasing rate of female sport participation and monetary resources earmarked for women's athletics. Many issues remain, however, in the movement toward equality for women in sport. How should women's sports be organized, and who should control them?

Contemporary Women in Sport

Increasing Participation and Funding.   The number of women participating in athletics is rapidly increasing at all levels and in various types of activities. Women athletes are more visible in the culture, and many have become household names. The women's movement, increased participation of women in all areas of social life, and Title IX have been credited with the massive influx of women in sport from the mid-1970s to today.

According to the National Federation of State High School Associations' biennial surveys, between 1980 and 1982, young women accounted for 35% of high school athletes (the number amounted to about 1.75 million participants in 1984–1985), compared to 7% between 1970 and 1971. Basketball was the most popular girls' sport, with nearly 400,000 playing high school basketball and 17,047 schools sponsoring the sport during the mid-1980s.

The number of young women participating in interscholastic sports in 1990–1991—about 1.9 million—was virtually unchanged from the late 1970s. Further, nearly twice as many high school boys participated in athletics as girls.[70]

The ten most popular sports for American high school girls in 1990–1991 follow:[71]

Sport	Number of Participants
Basketball	387,802
Track-and-field (outdoor)	320,763
Volleyball	300,810
Softball (fast-pitch)	219,464
Tennis	132,607
Soccer	121,722
Cross-country	106,514
Swimming and diving	88,122
Field hockey	48,384
Golf	41,410

Before Title IX, there was no such thing as a women's athletic scholarship, in the mid-1980s, there were over 10,000 women's athletic scholarships and over 30 National Collegiate Athletic Association (NCAA) sponsored women's championships; in 1970 there were virtually none. By 1980, women accounted for over 30% of all participants in intercollegiate athletic programs (compared to 15% before Title IX) and 44% of intramural athletes. The American Council of Education had predicted that by 1990 women would be 50% of intercollegiate athletes, if their educational institutions could find the funding. In 1970, in excess of one-fourth million high school girls played on athletic teams; this figure soared to 2 million a decade later. Since 1970, the number of women tennis players has jumped from 3 to 11 million; and one third of America's 18 million joggers are women.[72] Unfortunately, under the Reagan administration, a "new" interpretation of Title IX resulted in fewer gains and even some "losses" for women in sport. The Supreme Court's ruling in **Grove City College v. Bell** is particularly important in this context. The focal point was on Title IX's meaning—specifically, whether an entire school should conform to Title IX dictates or merely the department within the school receiving federal funds. The former is a "broad" interpretation; the latter is a "narrow" one. In the Grove City College case, the court ruled in January 1984 that the language of Title IX was meant only for specific programs receiving federal monies, a declaration inconsistent with the original intent of the law. The consequences of this ruling for women's sports have been monumental.

Women are competing in an increasing number of events, at both the amateur and professional levels. The Colgate Women's Games of 1982 attracted 22,000 females between the ages of six and forty to track and field competition. There are now over 300 women's ice hockey teams. The 1988 Olympics in Seoul produced some major leaps in female participation. There were nearly twice as many women—about 2,500—than ever before. For comparative purposes, the number of female participants in the four previous Olympiads was 1,620 (Los Angeles, 1984); 1,088 (Moscow, 1980); 1,274 (Montreal, 1976); and 1,070 (Munich, 1972). Additionally, new events were debuted. In 1980 more than 1 million females under the age of 19 were playing soccer, according to the U.S. Soccer Federation; virtually none were playing in 1970. The year 1981 also saw two more firsts for women: (a) the election of two women to the 90-member International Olympic Committee, and (b) the naming of the first woman official to a major professional league (the North American Soccer League).

The funding status of women's athletics improved considerably during the 1970s. Corporations like Bonne Bell, Avon, Lily of France, Revlon, and Chesebrough-Ponds organized tournaments and donated money to the Development Fund of the Women's Sports Federation. In 1973, women received 1% of college athletic scholarships; in 1980, 22%.[73] The percentage of college athletic budgets allocated to women's programs has also increased; in NCAA Division I schools, 17% went to women's athletics in 1985, compared to 2% before Title IX.[74]

In 1989 the percentages of total expenses allocated to the women's programs were 18%, 24%, 32% in Divisions I-A, I-AA, and I-AAA, respectively. In Division II, the percentage was 28% (with men's football) and 37% (without men's football). In Division III, it was 32% (with football) and 46% (without football). In general, the women's programs receive considerably less money than the men's; the exceptions are those schools without football. The total sports budgets in the divisions follow:[75]

Division	Average Expenses (1989)
I-A	$9,687,000
I-AA	3,206,000
I-AAA	1,914,000
II (with football)	1,179,000
II (without football)	819,000
III (with football)	519,000
III (without football)	312,000

Financial rewards for female athletes in six sports federations (tennis, golf, bowling, skiing, racquetball, and basketball) topped $16 million in 1980, which compares with $1 million a decade earlier.[76]

The NCAA reported the results of a gender-equity study in Spring 1992.[77] The data indicated the following ratios of Division I schools:

	Ratio of Men/Women
Operating expenses	3.42:1
Scholarships	2.28:1
Overall participants	2.24:1
Recruiting budget	4.82:1

Inequality, more than twenty years after Title IX, continues to exist between men's and women's athletics. Many of these differences are in large part due to participation and spending levels for men's football and the lack of a comparable women's equivalent.

Changing Attitudes and Performances. Cultural images about women athletes appear to be changing. A study of seventh- and eighth-graders, in addition to college undergraduates, disclosed that the approval rating for female athletes was higher than that accorded to females in general, to male athletes, or to males in general. Male and female college students, in one survey, described female athletes as strong, strong-willed, brave, healthy, and leaders.[78] The stigma of female athletic participation is on the decline, according to Sage and Loudermilk,[79] but there are still some social costs, particularly to women in the more nontraditional fields. Sports participation may even be seen as a mechanism for status achievement by adolescent females.[80] In performance, women are gaining on men (Vignette 9.5). Although the gap in performance and standards between men and women continues, it has narrowed since the 1970s. To illustrate, in running (100-meter dash and marathon) and swimming (100-meter freestyle and butterfly) events, women athletes are within 90% of the men's records. Czech Emil Zatopek and Frenchman Alain Mimoun won the Olympic marathon in 1952 and 1956, respectively. Both would have lost to Joan Benoit in the 1984 Olympics. Since women have been doing long-distance running, their times have been consistently dropping, while men's times seem to have stabilized. Women's marathon times have dropped by nearly an hour in just 15 years. Grete Waitz shaved 5 minutes off her time between her 1978 and 1979 victories in the New York Marathon. Her times would have beaten men's times before 1970. Dyer compared male and female performances in track events and discovered that the differences, as measured by world records, is declining in all events and declining most rapidly in those events where the differences are the largest.[81] Dyer argues that social factors have held back women's performance, because the smallest differences between males and females are found in those countries that have strong training programs, encouragements, and rewards for female athletes.

Two conflicting theories propose to explain why the gap has narrowed and whether or not male and female parity will be achieved. Some advocate a *cultural* explanation and argue that the barrier women must overcome is psychological, a sport orientation that can be traced to differential sport socialization experiences. Others have rejected the cultural explanation in favor of a *physiological* one. The physiological position contends that male superiority is attributed to biophysiological differences—favoring males—in many types of sport competition.

Comparative survey data indicate that while men *participate* in a wider variety of physical activities, the gap between men and women is closing.[82] Illustratively, 58% of males versus 37% of females say they engage in five or more sporting activities on a regular basis. There are differences in male and female sport engagements. Few males participate in the popular female activity, aerobic dancing; on the other hand, few females engage in football or rugby, popular male activities. The discrepancies for other physical activities is less striking.

Additionally, the gap between men and women's sport *viewing* is even narrower than with active participation. Approximately 55% of the men versus 49% of the women indicate interest in watching five or more different sports. On a wide variety of sports, the differences are minimal; the differences are greatest in football and boxing (male choices) and in gymnastics and ice skating (female choices).

Professional Possibilities.   Some professional tournaments for women have increased their prize monies (e.g., LPGA Nabisco-Dinah Shore Open). Professional golf and tennis are well established, but few professional players can cover their expenses with their tournament winnings. Theberge notes that women professional golfers are more concerned with intrinsic rewards (i.e., self-satisfaction and love of the game) than with extrinsic financial rewards.[83] Professional women athletes still report that love of the game is an important factor, but they also describe the diffi-

☐ **VIGNETTE 9.5**

Sociology or Biology? Explaining Sex Differences in Sport

Researchers generally agree that, in many sports, if men and women competed against each other, the males would be victorious. This stems from the fact that men are generally larger than women, have more cardiovascular power, and have a larger proportion of lean muscle mass in their bodies. However, in running and swimming the gap between men and women has closed (see Tables A through C). According to *The Chronicle of Higher Education,* the reason women are competing close to men in certain events is because "more women are participating in those sports, they are more widely accepted, and they use better training techniques."

A controversial and intriguing consideration when comparing men and women's sport performances is the role played by biological vis-à-vis social and psychological factors. Stark contends that differential socialization may produce differences in levels of performance that appear to be biological but, in fact, are essentially sociological. He wagers that "A good way to explore the impact of socialization on sports performance is to compare male and female achievements *over time.* To the extent that there has been a decline in differential socialization for sports, there should be a decline in gender differences in performance." In effect, the argument is that since women have, historically, been socialized *away* from sports, the pool of talent has been much smaller than the pool of talent for males who have been socialized *into* sports. The probability of superior sport accomplishments reflects these pools, that is, the likelihood of male superiority over females would be great indeed because the sources from which the

TABLE A World records in the 100-meter dash

Year	Male	Female	% Difference*
1932	10.2	11.9	16.7
1961	10.0	11.2	12.0
1980	9.9	10.79	9.0
1989	9.92	10.49	5.7

two categories of athletes are drawn is so numerically imbalanced. To compare male and female records, historically, would be akin to comparing two nations' track records in which one of the nations had a million runners and the other a couple hundred.

Let us examine several data sets and derive some inferences. Table A lists men and women's world records in the 100-meter dash. In 1932 the female record was 11.9 seconds, and about 17% higher than the male's for the same year, or, in other words, females were 17% slower in this event than males. The differential drops to 12% in 1961, 9% in 1980, and 6% in 1989. Obviously, the gap is narrowing. Looking at the sex performance differentials in the 400-meter dash (Table B), we again note a convergence in male and female performances over time. Whereas women ran about

TABLE B World records in the 400-meter dash

Year	Male	Female	% Difference*
1921	47.0	65.0	38.3
1955	45.9	54.8	19.4
1980	43.9	48.15	9.7
1989	43.29	47.60	10.0

38% slower in 1921, by 1989 it had dropped to about 10%. Finally, the same general reduction in the differential over time is revealed when 100-meter freestyle swim times (Table C) are compared. Since women's swimming became institutionalized earlier than track, the earliest date for which their world record was found is 1905. Note that in 1905 women's record time was about 44% higher than men's but it was only 11% higher in 1980.

Stark says, "Many factors, better training and conditioning techniques, nutrition discoveries, bigger, healthier, and stronger athletes, and improved coaching, to name a few have caused records to be broken ... But only changes in participation rates caused by changes in differential socialization can have produced the very marked *declines in gender* differences in sports records. ... we can see that women have rapidly reduced the gap between the records until their performances plateaued at about 10 to 15 percent behind men. There the gap seems to have stabilized. This might reflect true biological differences. Or it might be a plateau awaiting a further surge in female participation rates."

TABLE C   World records in the 100-meter freestyle swim

Year	Male	Female	% Difference*
1905	65.8	95.0	44.4
1924	57.4	72.2	25.8
1936	56.4	64.6	14.5
1956	55.4	64.0	15.5
1972	51.22	58.5	14.2
1976	49.44	55.65	12.6
1980	49.44	54.79	10.8
1989	48.42	54.73	13.0

*The "% Difference" value is obtained using the following algorithm:

$$\% \text{ Difference} = \frac{\text{time for women} - \text{time for men}}{\text{time for men}} \times 100$$

For example, consider the men and women's 1932 100-meter dash records. The % Difference is:

$$\frac{11.9 - 10.2}{10.2} \times 100 = 16.7\%$$

SOURCES: Rodney Stark, *Demonstrating Sociology* (Belmont, CA: Wadsworth Publishing Co., 1984), pp. 46–49. *The Chronicle of Higher Education* (21 March 1984), p. 23.

culties of trying to enter a traditionally masculine domain. The Women's Sports Foundation lists about twenty professional organizations for women, most of which were founded in the 1970s, but women's professional team sports are not well established. If the Liberty Basketball League (for women) founded in 1991 is like the Women's Basketball League (WBL) founded in 1978, it will fold after three seasons. The International Women's Professional Softball League "died" in 1980 after just four seasons of play. According to Geils, it took approximately $.5 million to operate a WBL team, but the most successful team in the WBL probably only earned half of that amount in ticket sales.[84]

A growing concern to women looking for careers in sport is the declining number of coaching opportunities. At the college level, before Title IX, women accounted for over 90% of the head coaches for women's teams; today, less than 50% of these head coaching positions are held by women. According to the *Congressional Quarterly*, in 1992, the percentage of women coaches of college women's teams was 47 (vs. 90% in 1972 before Title IX), with a similar percentage for high school. In 1990, less than 16% of all college athletic directors were women.[85] Holman and Parkhouse discov-

☐ **VIGNETTE 9.6**

The Deathleticization of Women

In blatant and sometimes subtle ways the importance of women's athletics can be diminished, or what Eitzen and Zinn call the "de-athleticization of women." Colleges and universities are fond of publicizing their schools with nicknames, mascots, logos, and the like. The functions of these symbols are to create identity and unification. However, there is a seamier side to the naming of men and women's athletic teams. Data from nearly 1,200 institutions of higher learning demonstrate that in excess of 50% of these schools derogate and demean women's teams. Eight different categories— categories violating rules of gender neutrality— were identified: (a) physical markers, e.g., the use of "belle"; (b) *girl* or *gal* (just as the noun *boy* can be pejorative, *girl* or *gal* carries the same connotation); (c) feminine suffixes, for example, the suffixes of "ette" as in Tigerettes and "esse" as in Tigresses; (d) *lady* as in *Lady Redbirds*; (e) *male* as a false generic (e.g., just as the use of the terms *chairman* or *mankind* fails to consider other gender categories, counterparts in sports such as Rams, Stags, and Steers capture the generic notion; (6) male name with female modifier as in *Lady Rams, Lady Centaurs*; (7) double gender marking such as the men's team being referred to as the *Choctas* but the women's teams as *Lady Chocs*; and (8) male–female paired polarity, as when the men's team may be called the *Panthers* but the women's teams, the *Pink Panthers* or the men's team being called the *Bears* but the women's teams, the *Teddy Bears.*

Eitzen and Zinn discovered that when these discriminatory categories were used, over 50% fell into *male* being used as a false generic, followed in rank order by *Lady* (25%); feminine suffix (6.4%); male–female polarity (5.8%); male name with female modifier (4.7%); physical markers (.4%); and *girl* or *gal* (.2%). On further examination, Eitzen and Zinn found no significant differences in naming patterns by school type (public, independent, religious) but found significant differences by region of the country, with southern schools more prone to employ sexist names. The researchers conclude that the practices explored in the present research contributes to the maintenance of patriarchy and the diminution of women's collegiate athletic programs.

SOURCE: D. Stanley Eitzen & Maxine Baca Zinn, "The Deathleticization of Women: The Naming and Gender Marking of Collegiate Sport Teams," *Sociology of Sport Journal* 6, no. 4 (1989), pp. 362–370.

☐

ered that in 335 women's athletic departments the number of coaches for women athletes increased by 37% between 1974 and 1979, but the percentage of women in these positions declined.[86] Of the new coaches, 724 were male and 44 were female, and most of the head coaches were males. By 1990, the proportion of head female coaches of female sport programs had fallen to less than half and the decline has been greatest in the most popular intercollegiate sports for women. Defrantz, in a statement of the obstacles facing black women in sports reported that of 106 Division I schools that field women's basketball teams, a mere 11 are coached by black women; in only one of these 106 schools is there an African-American athletic director, there are no black female executive directors of the 50 governing bodies of U.S. Olympic sports, and the U.S. Olympic basketball coaching staff awaits its first black female coach.[87] Vignette 9.6 reports the results of a study focusing on the deathleticization of women athletes and women's sports.

Male vs. Female or Masculine vs. Feminine?

Most studies of the relationship between gender and sport have compared men and women and have asked how male and female attitudes and performances differ. Analyses using categories based on sex and sex differences, however, may be losing their usefulness. It appears that what makes a difference in attitudes and performance may well be the extent to which one personally accepts or rejects the stereotyped images of masculine and feminine. For example, the difference between female college athletes and nonathletes is that the former tend to be less "feminine" than the latter on sex-role inventories (not more masculine, but less feminine).[88] Public images of athletes also seem to depend on the perceived masculinity or femininity the athlete possesses, not on the sex of the athlete. As men and women continue to challenge stereotyped notions in their own personalities, masculine and feminine may become more important variables for sociologists to study than male and female.

Although it may make sense to focus on the masculine–feminine dimension rather than on sex, biological sex is still an important issue for women's sports. A woman still must prove she is a true biological female to compete in women's events in the Olympics. Parading nude in front of female physicians has been replaced by the more scientific Barr test of skin cells, which is used to check for chromosomal irregularities. Anabolic steroid tests are also used to weed out women trying to "take advantage" of the power of male hormones in female competition. Sports confusion over sex and gender may be illustrated by the ambiguous standards of women's body building. How do you judge muscles on a women? The only standard for muscles are male muscles. *Sports Illustrated* betrayed its own ambiguous attitudes when, in reporting on a 1980 event, half of the photos showed the women body builders on stage in competition while the other half showed them on the beach in muscular "cheesecake."[89]

Building Equality Into Sport

The 1970s demonstrated an increasing concern with the goal of equality for men and women in sports, and the 1980s and 1990s have reflected a continuing debate on how such equality can be established. Equal opportunity and equality can be interpreted in many ways, and diatribes and power struggles have emerged over differing conceptions of how women's and men's activities should be integrated or conducted as "separate but equal" activities. Arguments for separate sports include the notion that men's advantages in male-defined sports would lead to most women being outperformed. Some professional women's associations have left coeducational tournaments because the events for men paid so much more in prize money than those for women. The integration view suggests that male and female performance differences are mostly a matter of training and socialization and that such differences will disappear over time.[90]

Another form of the polemic of sex equality in sport is what Westkott and Coakley call the *critical verus the assimilationist perspectives*. The **critical perspective** asks "why should women want to participate in activities and organizations that have historically excluded them and operated on the assumption of female inferiority?"[91] This view suggests that real equality for women in sports requires rejecting the current patriarchal organization of sports and the values of winning at all cost, inexpressiveness, egotism, elitism, and aggression. Edwards, long an advocate of minority equality in sports, suggests that women should not accept the system of sports men have built but should build a new, more humane system.[92] Advocates of this perspective, citing psychological studies of mental health, wager that building sports on the basis of **androgyny** (a blending of traditional femininity and masculinity) would be more healthy for human beings than keeping a system based on mostly masculine values and male bodies.

The **assimilationist perspective** emphasizes women's assimilation into the existing sports structure. The emphasis here is on gaining access to the spheres of endeavor that are already valued, rather than changing those values, and on gaining access through culturally legitimate means. Title IX is an example of an assimilationist solution. Such access to sports is assumed to lead to access to other parts of the social order.

The less radical assimilationist approach still encounters opposition. Title IX was opposed by the NCAA from the outset. Lawsuits abounded, and much of current sport is being structured by the courts. Since the enactment of Title IX, the federal government has been stymied in explaining what it means and how it is to be implemented and enforced. Conflicting lower-court rulings and the proposed Hatch amendment to Title IX (Sen. Orrin Hatch, R-Utah), which drastically limits the scope of Title IX protections, indicate that gains for women may be in some jeopardy at the collegiate level and could have a domino effect through other levels.

The NCAA did not accept Title IX without a fight. To lobby against passage of the original legislation, the NCAA spent more than one-quarter million dollars, which is more money than the **Association of Intercollegiate Athletics for Women (AIAW)** spent on its seventeen national women's championships at that time.[93] When demands for equal rights for women began in the 1960s, they were basically ignored by the NCAA. The National Association for Girls and Women in Sports, however, formed the AIAW to organize women's national tournament competition. In 1981, however, the NCAA voted to hold women's championships in twelve sports, and what emerged appears to have been a power struggle between the two organizations over who would control women's collegiate sports.

In the aftermath of the 1991 NCAA convention of reform, there was but a dim memory of Title IX. There was such concern with cost-reduction measures that even those who wanted to make amendments for women were hushed because it wasn't protocol. As of 1991, about 28% of college scholarship monies were going to women, but the reform package was an across the board cut in the number of scholarships allotted. The effect of these measures on women's sports will not be progressive.

The NCAA–AIAW conflict seemed, in retrospect, to reflect the differences between the assimilation and critical perspectives. The AIAW was, in general, less oriented toward competition at any cost and had firm standards on eligibility and recruitment of athletes and thus, before folding, for the most part avoided many of the scandals that have plagued the NCAA. The advantages to women's programs in joining the NCAA were based largely on the NCAA's entrenchment in traditional sports: Its women's sports budget is already several times larger than that of AIAW; it already has an established and efficient bureaucratic structure, whereas the AIAW was just beginning to get established.

Some women sportswriters suggest that the NCAA wanted to take over women's sports from women. By October 1981, 20% of the AIAW schools had defected to the NCAA. The NCAA's offer to merge with AIAW was viewed skeptically by many women. Merger meant having four women on the 24-member NCAA executive committee. In June of 1982, the AIAW ceased operation. Some remember the merger of the Federation Sportive Feminine Internationale (a French-based women's alternative to the Olympics) with the International Amateur Athletic Federation in the mid-1920s. This merger resulted in a 64% reduction in the number of world championship events in which women were sanctioned to compete.[94]

There is no apparent consensus among people concerned with gender equality in sport regarding just what equality is and how it can be achieved. The future of women in sport and, consequently, the future of men in sport will likely bring the continuation of not only individual battles for athletic achievement but also struggles among groups for ideological and structural dominance in sport institutions themselves. This is, and will be, a "contested terrain."

❏ SUMMARY

Through *gender socialization,* we learn how to become "proper" boys and girls, men and women. Traditional images of American women stressed dependency, passivity, and expressiveness, while men were expected to be stoic and instrumental. With industrialization, the "women's place" came to be defined as the private sphere of the family, and men were expected to win in the public arena of work. The consequences of this gender stratification are seen in contemporary gender inequality in such areas as employment and income opportunities.

The limited participation of women in sport reflects the sociocultural definitions of gender, with some variation by race. The female athlete was an anomaly, and she was often taken less seriously than her male counterpart, if not structurally prohibited from certain forms of athletic participation. The social organization of sport itself affects our perceptions of men and women in society. In general, sport has functioned as a masculine rite of passage for boys and has been organized around activities suited for male bodies. This organization reinforces the cultural image of women as second-best, second-class citizens.

Changes in gender roles, changes in the position of women in the other institutional areas of social life, and Title IX have all served to increase interest in and funding of women's sports. The 1970s and 1980s were characterized by a massive influx of girls and women into sport participation at both the amateur and professional levels. Whether or not these changes will result in real equality in sport for women remains a matter of much debate.

☐ KEY CONCEPTS

Sex
Gender
Social Organization of Gender
Gender Socialization
Cult of True Womanhood
Cult of Invalidism
Instrumental and Expressive Roles
Patriarchy
Gender Stratification
Masculine Rite of Passage
Anomaly

Structural Discrimination
Title IX
Paradox
Role Conflict
Grove City College v. Bell
Critical Perspective
Androgyny
Assimilationist Perspective
Association of Intercollegiate Athletics for
  Women (AIAW)

☐ ENDNOTES

1. MARGARET MEAD, *Sex and Temperament in Three Primitive Societies* (New York: Dell, 1969, first published 1935).

2. ELEANOR METHENY, "Symbolic Forms of Movement: The Feminine Image in Sports," *Sport in the Socio-Cultural Process,* ed. Marie Hart (Dubuque, IA: William C. Brown, 1972), pp. 277–290.

3. NANCY CHODOROW, "Being and Doing: A Cross-Cultural Examination of the Socialization of Males and Females," *Women in Sexist Society: Studies in Power and Powerlessness,* eds. Vivian Gornick & Barbara K. Moran (New York: Basic Books, 1971), pp. 259–291.

4. SHERRY B. ORTNER, "Is Female to Male as Nature Is to Culture?" *Women in Sexist Society: Studies in Power and Powerlessness,* eds. Michelle Zimbalist Rosaldo & Louise Lamphere (Stanford, CA: Stanford University Press, 1974), pp. 67–88.

5. JOHN DEMOS, "The American Family in Past Time," *Family in Transition* (2nd ed.), eds. Arlene Skolnick & Jerome Skolnick (Boston: Little, Brown, 1977), pp. 59–77.
   ELI ZARETSKY, *Capitalism, The Family and Personal Life* (New York: Harper & Row, 1976).

6. CHRISTOPHER LASCH, *Haven in a Heartless World: The Family Besieged* (New York: Basic Books, 1977).

7. DEMOS, *op. cit.*[5]

8. VIVIAN GORNICK "Women as Outsiders," in Gornick & Moran, *op. cit.,*[3] pp. 126–144.

9. BARBARA EHRENREICH & DEIDRE ENGLISH, *Complaints and Disorders: The Sexual Politics of Sickness* (Old Westbury, NY: The Feminist Press, 1973), p. 28.

10. *Ibid.*

11. G.J. BARKER-BENFIELD, "The Spermatic Economy: A Nineteenth Century View of Sexuality," *The American Family in Social-Historical Perspective* (2nd ed.), ed. Michael Gordon (New York: St. Martin's Press, 1978), p. 375.

12. SIGMUND FREUD, "Three Contributions to the Theory of Sex," *The Basic Writings of Sigmund Freud,* ed. A.A. Brill (New York: Random House, 1938), pp. 553–632.

13. CYNTHIA B. LLOYD & BETH T. NIEMI, *The Economics of Sex Differentials* (New York: Columbia University Press, 1979).

14. SNODGRASS, cited in *The Chicago Tribune* (18 August 1990), Section 1, p. 1.

15. MARTY, quoted in "Slow Curve on the Outside Corner," *Women: A Journal of Liberation* 5 (1976), pp. 1, 12.
    AVERY BRUNDAGE, quoted in Mary Leigh, "The Enigma of Avery Brundage and Female Athletes," *Arena Review* 4 (1980), p. 16.
    JOHN MITZEL, *Sports and the Macho Male* (2nd ed.), (Boston: Fag Rag Books, 1976), p. 3.
    ROBERT KENNEDY, quoted in Nancy Gager Clinch, *The Kennedy Neurosis* (New York: Grosset & Dunlap, 1973), p. 266.
    SIMONE DE BEAUVOIR, *The Second Sex* (New York: Bantam books, 1952), p. 311.

Althea Gibson, "I Always Wanted to Be Somebody," *Out of the Bleachers: Writings on Women and Sport*, ed. Stephanie L. Twin (Old Westbury, NY: The Feminist Press, 1979), p. 131.

"Report of Progress, Women's Division, National Amateur Athletic Federation in America," AAPHERD 29 (June 1924), reprinted in *The American Woman in Sport*, eds. E.W. Gerber, J. Felshin, P. Berlin, & W. Wyrick (Reading MA: Addison-Wesley, 1974), p. 72.

16. Betty Spears, "The Emergency of Sport in Physical Education." Paper presented at the American Association for Health, Physical Education, and Recreation 88th Anniversary, Minneapolis, MN, 16 April 1973.

17. Twin, *op. cit.*[15]

18. Luther Halsey Gulick, in his presidential address before the Public School Physical Training Society, 1906, cited in Gerber et al., *op. cit.*,[15] p. 70.

19. Gerber, *op. cit.*,[15] pp. 71–74.

20. J.E. Stake, "The Ability–Performance Dimension of Self-Esteem Implications for Women's Achievement Behavior," *Psychology of Women Quarterly* 3 (1979), pp. 365–377.

21. Erving Goffman, *Stigma: Notes on the Management of a Spoiled Identity* (Englewood Cliffs, NJ: Prentice-Hall, 1963), p. 128.

22. George H. Sage, "Orientations Toward Sport of Male and Female Intercollegiate Athletes," *Journal of Sport Psychology* 2(4), 1980, pp. 355–362.

23. Jan Felshin, "The Dialectic of Woman and Sport," in Gerber et al., *op. cit.*,[15] pp. 179–210.

24. Michelle Kort, "Body Politics: A Chrysalis Sports Report," *Chrysalis* 7 (1979), pp. 84–86.

25. Michael D. Smith, "Getting Involved in Sport: Sex Differences," *International Review of Sport Sociology* 14 (1979), pp. 93–102.

26. Jan Rintala & Susan Birrell, "Fair Treatment for the Active Female: A Content Analysis of *Young Athlete* Magazine," *Sociology of Sport Journal* 1 (1984), pp. 231–250.

27. Eldon E. Snyder & Joseph E. Kivlin, "Perceptions of the Sex Role among Female Athletes and Nonathletes, *Adolescence* 12 (1977), pp. 23–29.
George H. Sage & Sheryl Loudermilk, "The Female and Role Conflict," *Research Quarterly* 50 (1979), pp. 88–96.
Mary M. Bell, "Role Conflict of Women as Athletes in the United States," *Arena Review* 4 (1980), pp. 22–31.

28. Gibson, *op. cit.*,[15] p. 141.

29. Willye B. White, quoted by Pat Jordan, "Sweet Home: Willye B. White," ed. Twin, *op. cit.*,[15] p. 93.

30. See Jay J. Coakley, *Sport in Society: Issues and Controversies* (St. Louis: C.V. Mosby, 1978), pp. 250–252.
Ann Crittenden, "Closing the Muscle Gap," in Twin, *op. cit.*,[15] pp. 5–10.
Thomas E. Shaffer, "Physiological Considerations of the Female Participant," ed. Twin, *op. cit.*,[15] pp. 11–23.
Waneen Wyrick, "Biophysical Perspectives," in Gerber et al., *op. cit.*,[15] pp. 403–515.

31. M. Shangold quoted in Deborah Larned-Romano & Jan Leavy, "Athletes and Fertility," *Ms* (October 1979), pp. 38–41.

32. Gary Selden, "Frailty, Thy Name's Been Changed: What Sports Medicine is Discovering About Women's Bodies," *Ms* (July 1981), pp. 51–53.
P.S. Wood, "Sex Differences in Sports," *The New York Times Magazine* (18 May 1980), pp. 31–38.

33. Twin, *op. cit.*,[15] pp. xv–xii.

34. Kathryn M. Yandell & Waneen Spirduso, "Sex and Athletic Status as Factors in Reaction Latency and Movement Time," *Research Quarterly for Exercise and Sport* 52 (1981), pp. 495–504.
Philip B. Sparling, "A Meta-Analysis of Studies Comparing Maximal Oxygen Uptake in Men and Women," *Research Quarterly for Exercise and Sport* 51 (1980), pp. 542–552.

35. Women's Sports Foundation, "Study Considers Women's Olympic Participation, Past and Present," *Women's Sports* (September 1980), p. 58.

36. Janet Lever, "Sex Differences in the Complexity of Children's Play and Games," *Sport and American Society: Selected Readings*, ed. George H. Sage, 3rd ed. (Reading, MA: Addison Wesley, 1980), pp. 281–290.

37. Lawrence R. Brawley et al., "Sex Bias in Evaluating Motor Performance," *Journal of Sport Psychology* 1 (1979), pp. 15–24.

38. "Women and Sports," *Congressional Quarterly* 2, no. 9 (6 March 1992), pp. 194–215.

39. *Ibid.*

40. ELEANOR METHENY, "Symbolic Forms of Movement: The Olympic Games," *op. cit.,*[36] pp. 269–276.
    MARY DUQUIN, "The Androgynous Advantage," ed. Sage, *op.cit.,*[36] pp. 263–280.

41. KATHERINE SWITZER, quoted in Christine Terp, "A Whole New Ball Game?" *Christian Science Monitor* (22 May 1981), p. 13.

42. CHARLES CORBIN & CHARLES NIX, "Sex-Typing of Physical Activities and Success Predictors Before and After Cross-Sex Competition," *Journal of Sport Psychology* 1 (1979), pp. 43–52.

43. DARLENE KELLY, "Women and Sports," *Women: A Journal of Liberation* 3 (1974), p. 16.

44. I.K. BROVERMAN, D.M. BROVERMAN, F. CLARKSON, P. ROSENKRANTZ, & S. VOGEL, "Sex-Role Stereotypes and Clinical Judgments of Mental Health," *Journal of Consulting and Clinical Psychology* 34 (1970), pp. 1–7.
    I.K. BROVERMAN et al., "Sex Role Stereotypes: A Current Appraisal," *Journal of Social Issues* 28 (1972), pp. 59–78.
    JOHN WILLIAMS & SUSAN BENNETT, "The Definition of Sex Stereotypes via the Objective Check List," *Sex Roles* (1975), pp. 327–337.
    JANET SALTZMAN CHAFETZ, *Masculine, Feminine or Human: An Overview of the Sociology of the Gender Roles* (2nd ed.), (Itasca, IL: F. E. Peacock, 1978), pp. 37–46.

45. JOAN ULLYOT, "Medical Miscellany," *Women's Sports* (January 1982), p. 52.

46. S.E. ISO-AHOLA, "Sex-Role Stereotypes and Causal Attribution for Success and Failure in Motor Performances," *Research Quarterly for Exercise and Sport* 59 (1979), pp. 630–640.

47. DE BEAUVOIR, *op. cit.*[15]

48. E.E. SNYDER, J.E. KIVLIN, & E. SPREITZER, "The Female Athlete: Analysis of Objective and Subjective Role Conflict, *Psychology of Sport and Motor Behavior,* ed. D. Landers (University Park: Pennsylvania State University, 1975), pp. 165–180.

49. BRUCE OGILVIE & LINDA GUSTAVSON McGUIRE, "How Competition Affects Elite Women Swimmers," *The Physician and Sports Medicine* 8 (1980), pp. 113–116.

50. MARGARET HENNIG & ANN JARDIM, *The Managerial Woman* (New York: Doubleday, 1977).

51. TOM SMITH, "The Secret Scandal of Women's Tennis," *National Enquirer* (19 May 1981), p. 28.

52. ANGELA LUMPKIN & LINDA D. WILLIAMS, "An Analysis of *Sports Illustrated* Feature Articles, 1954–1987," *Sociology of Sport Journal* 8, no. 1 (1991), pp. 16–32.

53. JANE GROSS, "First Place Stars: 2d Class Existence," *The New York Times* (24 December 1980), pp. 34–36.

54. MARGARET CARLISLE DUNCAN, "Sports Photographs and Sexual Difference: Images of Women and Men in the 1984 and 1988 Olympic Games," *Sociology of Sport Journal* 7, no. 1 (1990), pp. 22–43.

55. *Ibid.,* p. 50.

56. NANCY THEBERGE & ALAN CRONK, "Work Routines in Newspaper Sports Departments and the Coverage of Women's Sports:, *Sociology of Sport Journal* 3, no. 3 (1986), pp. 195–203.

57. DONALD F. SABO, JR., & ROSS RUNFOLA, *Jock: Sports and Male Identity* (Englewood Cliffs, NJ: Prentice-Hall, 1980), p. ix.

58. STANLEY EITZEN, "Athletics in the Status System of Male Adolescents: A Replication of Coleman's *The Adolescent Society,*" *Sport Sociology: Contemporary Themes,* eds. Andrew Yiannakis, T.D. McIntyre, M.J. Melnick, & D.P. Hart (Dubuque, IA: Kendall Hunt, 1979), pp. 150–154.

59. MARC FEIGEN FASTEAU, "Sports: The Training Ground," cited in *op. cit.,*[57] pp. 44–53.
    JOHN LEWKO & MARTHA EWING, "Sex Differences and Parental Influence in Sport Involvement of Children," *Journal of Sport Psychology* 2 (1980), pp. 62–68.

60. GEORGE H. SAGE, "Orientations Toward Sport of Male and Female Intercollegiate Athletes," *Journal of Sport Psychology* 2(4) (1980), pp. 355–362.

61. J.F. McCARTHY & B. KELLY, "Aggression, Performance Variables and Anger Self-Report in Ice Hockey Players," *Journal of Psychology* 99 (1978), pp. 97–101.

62. EDMUND W. VAZ, "The Culture of Young Hockey Players: Some Initial Observations," cited in *op. cit.,*[57] pp. 142–157.

63. MARY JO DEEGAN & MICHAEL STEIN, "American Drama and Ritual: Nebraska Football," *International Review of Sport Sociology* 13 (1978), pp. 31–44.

64. Paul Hoch, "School for Sexism," cited in *op. cit.*,[57] pp. 9–19.

65. Nancy Henley, "Changing the Body Power Structure," *Women: A Journal of Liberation* 6 (1978), pp. 34–38.

66. A. Capuzzo, "Aggressiveness in Sports Has a Sorry Spinoff: Studies Show a Link to Wife-Beating," *Chicago Tribune* (27 January 1991), p. 8.

67. David Leon Moore, "Athletes and Rape: Alarming Link," *USA Today* (27 August 1991), pp. C1–2.

68. Mark Naison, "Sports, Women and the Ideology of Domination," cited in *op. cit.*,[57] pp. 30–36.
Peter J. Stein & Steven Hoffman, "Sports and Male Role Strain," cited in *op.cit.*,[57] pp. 53–74.

69. Mitzel, *op. cit.*[15]
Mitzel, cited in *op. cit.*[57]

70. *Op. cit.*,[38] p. 198.

71. *Op. cit.*,[38] p. 210.

72. Christine Terp, "The Myths Come Tumbling Down," *Christian Science Monitor* (19 May 1981), pp. 12–13.
Frank Litsky, "Female Runners Vying," *The New York Times* (2 March 1982), p. 23.
Project on the Status and Education of Women 28 (1980), p. 4.
National Advisory Council on Women's Educational Programs of the Department of Health and Human Services, "From Title IX: The Half Full, Half Empty Glass," reprinted in *Graduate Woman* (January 1982), pp. 19–22.
Eitzen, *op. cit.*[58]

73. National Advisory Council on Women's Educational Programs, *op. cit.*,[72] p. 22.

74. *Ibid.*

75. *Op. cit.*,[38] p. 190.

76. *Op cit.*,[32] p. 32.

77. *The Chicago Tribune* (12 March 1992), Section 4, p. 1.

78. C. Atkins, C. Morse, & R. Zweigenhaft, "The Stereotype and Recognition of Female Athletes," *Journal of Psychology* 100 (1978), pp. 27–31.

79. *The Wilson Report: Moms, Dads, Daughters and Sports,* River Grove, IL: Wilson Sporting Goods, 1988.

Sage Loudermilk, "The Female Athlete and Role Conflict," *op. cit.*,[36] pp. 291–308.

80. Hans G. Buhrmann & Robert D. Bratton, "Athletic Participation and Status of Alberta (Canada) High School Girls," *International Review of Sport Sociology* 12 (1977), pp. 57–69.

81. K.F. Dyer, "Social Influences on Female Athletic Performance," *Journal of Biosocial Science* 8 (1976), pp. 123–129.

82. *The Miller Lite Report on American Attitudes Toward Sports* (Milwaukee: Miller Brewing, 1983), pp. 172–173.

83. Nancy Theberge, "The System of Rewards in Women's Professional Golf," *International Review of Sport Sociology* 15 (1980), pp. 27–42.

84. Donna Geils, "Requiem for the WBL," *Women's Sports* (January 1982), p. 8.

85. *Op. cit.*,[38] p. 204.

86. Milton Holman & Bonnie Parkhouse, "Trends in the Selection of Coaches for Female Athletes: A Demographic Inquiry," *Research Quarterly for Exercise and Sport* 52 (1981), pp. 9–18.

87. M. Defrantz, *Sports Illustrated* 75, no. 7 (12 August 1991), p. 77.

88. Ruth Colker & Cathy Spatz Widom, "Correlates of Female Athletic Participation: Masculinity, Femininity, Self-Esteem and Attitudes Toward Women," *Sex Roles* 6 (1980), pp. 47–58.

89. Dan Levin, "Here She Is, Miss, Well, What?" *Sports Illustrated* (17 March 1980), pp. 64–68.

90. Brenda Feigen Fasteau, "Giving Women a Sporting Chance," ed. Twin, *op. cit.*,[15] pp. 201–213.

91. Marcia Westkott & Jay J. Coakley, Women in Sport: Modalities of Feminist Social Change," *Journal of Sport and Social Issues* 5 (1981) pp. 32–45.

92. Harry Edwards, "Desegregating Sexist Sport," ed. Twin *op. cit.*,[15] pp. 188–191.

93. Bonnie L. Parkhouse & Jackie Lapin, *Women Who Win: Exercising Your Rights in Sport* (Englewood Cliffs, NJ: Prentice-Hall, 1980), p. 25.

94. Editorial, *Women's Sports* (May 1980), pp. 61–62.

10

Sport and Education

The focus on big money, the media pressure, drugs, gambling and betting are all part now of our national culture of intercollegiate athletics. That's when I thought it was time to say, "No more, we've had enough."

I don't believe it's a harsh action. We have to reassert that our primary values are academics and that academic integrity is vital to university life. Our raison d'être is teaching, it's learning, it's research. It's time for university presidents across the country to gain control of their institutions.

EAMON KELLY, President of Tulane University, explaining his decision to drop the men's basketball program (CBS, "Face the Nation" 7 April 1985)

In this chapter, *two* levels of sport are discussed: (a) **collegiate**, and (b) **interscholastic**. This discussion permits us to interface two pervasive social institutions—sport and education—in North American society. The extent to which sport and education are inexorably intertwined in the United States may contribute to an ethnocentric perspective. Chu writes: "when placed in cross-cultural perspective, the rise of sport at American institutions of higher education is utterly peculiar."[1] From a global viewpoint this arrangement is not typical. Loy, McPherson, and Kenyon report that the structure and functioning of collegiate sport in England, Australia, Germany, and Japan is on a "club" basis.[2] As a consequence, there tends to be no official athletic department or athletic director; instead, a club representative is responsible for scheduling. Additional differences include no athletic scholarships, no televising games, free admissions, volunteer coaches, participation is not viewed as anticipatory preprofessional training, and competition is available at several levels.

❑ COLLEGE ATHLETICS

In the review of the history of American sport (see Chapter 2), I reported that college athletics began in the latter half of the nineteenth century primarily as a diversion from the monotony and tedium of academic work. Initially, students controlled these extracurricular activities. Today, however, students have much less input, because coaches, college administrators, and others occupying specialized administrative sport positions make most of the major decisions. Intercollegiate sport programs have been criticized for primarily reflecting entertainment and public relations values rather than values in tune with the educational mission of institutions of higher learning. Today, intercollegiate athletic programs are an integral and socially prominent feature, albeit controversial, of higher education.

Diversification of Collegiate Sport

College sport programs are not homogeneous. Some are professional in everything but name; others genuinely approach their amateur billing. Intercollegiate athletics is a *diversified* phenomenon, a many-splintered thing.[3] Diversification is along numerous lines:[4] expenditures and revenues, scope of sports programs, primary source of funding, media coverage, social organization, and the role and status of sports at the institution, to name several significant factors. It is crucial to stress this variegation because the mass media routinely portray a nonrepresentative image of American "amateur" athletics. The teams ordinarily featured on national television are the top-flight ones; however, these are atypical of most sport teams and sport programs in the United States. In commenting on the different National Collegiate Athletic Association (NCAA) divisions, Coakley exhorts:

> The general level of athletic talent is higher in Division I schools than in the other two divisions, and the athletes are more likely to have the benefit of athletic scholarships. Additionally, the amount of team travel is greater, the national and regional media coverages is [sic] more extensive, and the consequences of winning and losing are usually greater. . . . The purpose of mentioning each of these associations [NCAA divisions] is not to create confusion but to emphasize that intercollegiate sport is a diversified phe-

nomenon. The extent of this diversity makes it difficult to generalize about the relationship between sport programs and higher education without specifying the type of
program being discussed.[5]

Others have also conceptualized these different echelons. Figler implicitly considers
different levels of performance:

> In many colleges . . . athletic programs exist . . . to provide an enriching experience. . . .
> This may be the case at many two year colleges, in some NAIA [National Association
> of Intercollegiate Athletics] institutions, and some four-year schools competing in Di-
> visions II and III of the NCAA and AIAW [Association of Intercollegiate Athletics for
> Women].[6]

Popular writer Michener, while urging us to acknowledge the tentacles of professionalization in amateur sports and reorganize accordingly, implicates different "hierarchies" of performance:

> It is quite obvious that intercollegiate football and basketball, as now played, are semi-
> professional sports in most schools and professional in others. This should be publicly
> acknowledged: I see nothing to be gained by denying it and much to be lost.[7]

It is important to be cognizant that the subsequent discussion pertains, primarily, to
"big-time" sports programs.

Intercollegiate Athletic Programs: Pros and Cons

The *pro* arguments concerning intercollegiate athletic programs, according to Coakley,[8] include the following:

1. Schools compete for students, and reputable sports programs help generate applications for admission—hence, sports serve as an *advertising* vehicle.

- Author James Michener once asked Don Canham, former athletic director at Michigan, "Isn't it really immaterial whether you go to the Rose Bowl or not? Don't you
get your share of the gate whether you play or not?" Canham replied, "Technically
correct, but you miss the . . . point. . . . it's not the money that counts. It's that
public exposure the visiting coach gets on television."[9]
- After successful football and basketball seasons, admission applications at Rutgers
increased by nearly one third, and alumni donations soared. Basketball coach (at
that time) Tom Young remarked, "Winning a championship is worth about $10
million in advertising."[10]

2. Because funding is variable, it is important to have the school recognized by
the state legislators, the business community, the foundation administrators, and the
alumni—sport is a *publicity* device. See Vignette 10.1 for the outcomes of an investigation of the relationship between sports success and financial success.

- Senior editor (*The Chronicle of Higher Education*) Douglas Lederman stated: "Proponents of big-time sports have long held that a visible, successful sports program
adds to an institution's financial well-being. They argue that a winning, big-time
program attracts students, fosters institutional name recognition and stimulates
state aid and voluntary giving. . . . But most of the fund-raisers and scholars who

☐ **VIGNETTE 10.1**

Sports Success Helps Schools?

(CPS)—Contrary to some campus sports boosters' claim that heavy investment in athletics helps the entire college, winning athletic teams do *not* help universities bring in more money from alumni or businesses, a researcher has concluded after combining 12 studies of the issue.

University of Nevada at Las Vegas professor James Frey said all the studies indicate successful athletic teams never increase—and often reduce—contributions to an institution.

Frey's conclusions . . . provide new ammunition for critics of intercollegiate athletic programs that argue that sports do not pay for themselves.

Frey, a sociology professor, acknowledges some winning teams help athletic departments raise money, but not other parts of the school.

"Most observers tacitly accept the belief that big-time athletic programs are partly justified because they boost fund raising," Frey noted. "It's time we realized that just isn't so."

The studies also show that "an institution that concentrates the bulk of its effort on raising money for athletics will probably not raise as much as it could for other programs," he wrote.

"By the same token, strategies that use athletics as a vehicle to raise monies for academic purposes are also unlikely to be successful," he added.

Most college administrators contacted by CPS seemed to agree.

University of Pennsylvania officials said their fund drive was no more successful in the two years before its football team won or shared two consecutive Ivy League championships than in the two after.

"I'd rather have the team winning because that's one less excuse for not giving," Steve Derby, the director of alumni giving, said. "But in terms of what prompts people to give, it just doesn't seem to make that much difference."

Contributions to the school's athletic department fund drive, however, have jumped substantially.

Notre Dame officials agreed. Notre Dame's flagging football fortunes—its team has won only five more games than it has lost over the past four seasons—haven't affected donations at all, development director Tom Bloom said.

And asking Notre Dame football fans who are not alumni for money has never worked out well, spokesman Richard Conklin added.

"Football may be the only thing they know about this place, but they treat us like a professional team," Conklin said. "You cheer for the Yankees, but you don't send them a check."

SOURCE: *Daily Vidette,* Illinois State University newspaper (14 February 1985), p. 12. Reprinted with permission.

☐

have studied the relationship between athletic success and fundraising are skeptical."[11]

- Budig's study of Big Eight faculty members' attitudes toward the functions of sports found that two thirds of those surveyed admitted that a successful athletic program helped the school's funding.[12]
- Oral Roberts, the president of the university bearing his name, admitted that one of the keenest ways to receive both public recognition and money was through sports.

- Rutgers ex-coach Tom Young turned a mediocre basketball program around by recording a thirty-one-game winning streak. During this time span (the late 1970s), the football team also went undefeated. Although the state legislature had contemplated declaring financial exigency (which would have affected the athletic program), it decided it could afford a little less austerity. Young said, "I would say that our budget situation has been markedly improved by athletics."[13]

3. Sport is a source of spirit and tradition that helps make the entire program of the school viable.

- According to the Board of Regents, the governing board for three major state universities in Illinois, "over the years participation either directly or indirectly in athletic events has become what can only be described as both a tradition and a national pastime. When the number of individuals taking advantage of the many opportunities for peripheral activities are added to the number of spectators and athletes, it is obvious that athletic programs at the universities serve many constituencies and can be quite important both as a morale booster and as a public service in many respects."[14]

The con arguments, according to Coakley, include the following:[15]

1. Maintaining the program is expensive.

- In the early 1990s, College Football Association (CFA) intercollegiate sports budgets averaged nearly $10.5 million annually (see Table 10.1 for a close look at the University of Michigan's revenues and expenses for 1991), and many sports programs were in deficit spending. Raiborn reported that in 1989 schools operating Division I-A football programs earned an average of $9,685,000 and spent $9,646,000.[16] (These figures can be contrasted with revenues and costs of $6,833,000 and $6,894,000 for the same programs in 1985.) Between 1985 and 1989 the general inflation rate was 15% whereas revenues and expenditures during this same time frame increased 42% and 40%, respectively. In 1986 Raiborn also reported that in 1985 average (arithmetic means) revenues for Division I institutions (that played football) were more than $4,800,000 and expenses were $4,609,000 (median revenues averaged $3.2 million). The difference between the mean and median figures suggests that the large revenues received by some schools had the effect of skewing the arithmetic average. Even at that, about half of all Division I programs were operating at a loss, and 40% of those earning money were earning $250,000 or less. Division II, Division III, and Division I (basketball programs but not football programs) revenues were $419,000, $71,000, and $598,000, respectively, while expenses were $719,000, $339,000, and $878,000, respectively. (In 1991 Executive Director Richard Schultz reported that 70% of Division I-A football programs were expected to operate at a loss; on average, about $600,000 per school.)

- Noting that only in Division I (with football programs) did revenues exceed expenses, Padilla concluded that

> athletics do not pay for themselves at most colleges and universities in America. Indeed, the average size of operating deficit at many . . . institutions obviously suggests that a substantial subsidy of institutional resources must be injected annually to keep intercol-

TABLE 10.1 Big Blue in the red: The University of Michigan athletic department's projected revenues and expenses for 1991

Income and Expenses	$ Millions
Operating revenues	
Football admissions	8.2
Other sports	1.6
TV and radio revenue	2.3
Concessions, parking, programs	1.9
Facilities revenues	.975
Postseason revenues	1.6
Utilities reimbursement	.140
Other income	2.5
Nonoperating revenues	
Fund raising	.700
Interest income on reserves	1.4
Total revenue	21.35
Expenses	
Salaries, wages, fringes	6.5
Sports programs	5.0
Scholarship costs	4.5
Facilities expenses	2.4
Administrative expenses	2.6
Debt service	1.0
Total operating expenses	22.1
Bottom line	
Deficit	.750

SOURCES: University of Michigan and *Chicago Tribune* (3 March 1991), Section 3, p. 12.

legiate athletics programs operating at the current level of inflated and ambitious expenditures.[17]

- Consider the University of Michigan in 1991. It fielded teams in twenty-one sports but made money on only two of these, football and basketball. It does not receive university monies but acquired a deficit of $.75 million! Table 10.2 contains the "balance sheet" for all Big-Ten schools in 1990.

- In 1991 the Big Ten went 2–4 in college bowl games and realized an $11 million profit! The largest single amount came from Iowa's appearance in the Rose Bowl. The check was divided up into eleven shares and distributed to the conference teams and the conference headquarters. In other games, the participating school receives everything up to $1 million, and the remainder is shared among conference teams.

- Postseason bowls are nonprofit organizations and are currently being audited to see if corporate sponsorship should be taxed. Despite some resistance, if such changes occurred, it could put some bowls out of business and tax the schools receiving money from their appearance.

See Figure 10.1 for the NCAA revenue-expenditure balance sheet.

TABLE 10.2   Big Ten balance sheet

School	Projected Expenses ($)	Bottom Line 1989–1990 ($)
Illinois	16,419,454	↑ $632,000
Indiana	14,140,000	↓ 75,000
Iowa	22,000,000	↓ 247,000
Michigan	22,100,000	↓ 320,000
Michigan State	13,606,000	↑ 2.8 million
Minnesota	11,838,287	↓ 490,000
Northwestern	Not available	Not available
Ohio State	23,970,800	↓ 790,015
Purdue	12,865,737	↑ 912,708
Wisconsin	15,239,230	↑ 150,000

Note.   While showing a surplus in 1989–1990, Illinois, Purdue, and Wisconsin still were operating under an overall deficit in 1991.

↑ , expenses increased; ↓ , expenses decreased.

SOURCE: *Chicago Tribune* (3 March 1991), Section 3, p. 12.

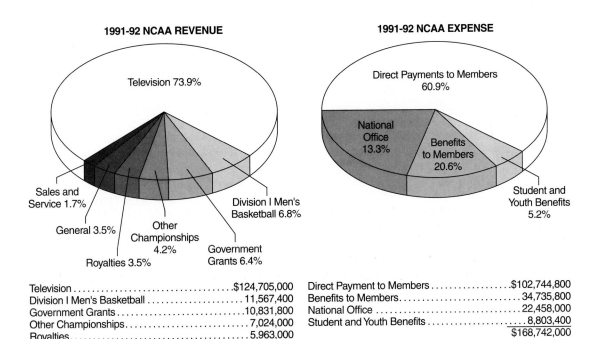

1991-92 NCAA REVENUE

Television 73.9%

Sales and Service 1.7%

General 3.5%

Royalties 3.5%

Other Championships 4.2%

Government Grants 6.4%

Division I Men's Basketball 6.8%

1991-92 NCAA EXPENSE

Direct Payments to Members 60.9%

National Office 13.3%

Benefits to Members 20.6%

Student and Youth Benefits 5.2%

Television	$124,705,000
Division I Men's Basketball	11,567,400
Government Grants	10,831,800
Other Championships	7,024,000
Royalties	5,963,000
General	5,848,700
Sales and Service	2,801,600
	$168,742,000

Direct Payment to Members	$102,744,800
Benefits to Members	34,735,800
National Office	22,458,000
Student and Youth Benefits	8,803,400
	$168,742,000

FIGURE 10.1   NCAA revenue sources and expense items

SOURCE: "Budget's Direct Payments Top $102 Million," *The NCAA News 28*, no. 32 (16 September 1991), p. 1.

☐ **VIGNETTE 10.2**

ISU Should Stop Using Tuition Dollars for Athletics

During the past two years, a *controversy* has developed over how much money ISU spends on intercollegiate athletics and whether such a practice is appropriate, especially at an institution that is severely underfunded.

In March 1989 [six] faculty Academic Senators introduced a resolution asking the administration to present a plan to the Academic Senate "phasing out the use of the income fund for intercollegiate athletics."

The resolution passed by a vote of 19 yes, 18 no, and four abstentions at the meeting of the Academic Senate. All 19 yes votes were cast by faculty members on the senate. Only three faculty members voted against the motion and three faculty members abstained. In other words, over three-fourths of the faculty members on the senate supported the resolution.

In the current fiscal year, ISU will spend over $1.1 million from the income fund for athletics. The income fund represents money raised through tuition; these dollars are used for academic programs. Since 1984, the amount of income fund dollars used for athletics has increased over 55 percent. In contrast, general revenue funds to the university have increased only 17 percent during this time period.

How does the administration justify using tuition dollars for athletics at ISU? It contends that a successful athletic program will increase alumni giving, that an athletic program is important in student life, that a successful athletic program will bring media attention to the university and that other institutions use tuition dollars for athletics. I will briefly discuss why I feel these arguments are invalid.

1. *A successful athletic program stimulates contributions to the university.*

On Jan. 14, 1988, *The Chronicle of Higher Education* published an article titled "Do Winning Teams Spur Contributions?" In this article,

Richard Conklin, assistant vice president for University Relations, stated, "There isn't any correlation between giving at Notre Dame and athletic success."

In this same article, Roger Olson, vice president of development at the University of Southern California, said, "The bulk of our fund-raising would be intact with or without athletics. The simple fact is that the person who wants to come in and give $8 million to build a new laboratory for our neuroscience research program is really interested in cutting-edge research."

In a more recent article (Jan. 8), *U.S. News and World Report* noted that all the revenue generated by the athletic program at the University of Michigan went back into athletics; none of the money went into academic programs.

Over the past two decades, several studies have been conducted to examine the relationship between the success of athletics, i.e., the football and basketball programs, and monetary contributions to a university. The best designed study on this topic showed that only a successful football program (Division IA) generated increased giving to an institution; however, this giving was to the athletic programs, not the academic programs of the universities (*Social Science Quarterly*). In fact, a negative correlation was found between giving to academic programs and the success of the football programs. Therefore, one could argue that giving to athletics might actually detract from giving to academic areas.

In a 1985 review of 12 separate studies, James Frey stated: "The overwhelming conclusion: There is no relation between athletic success and any measure of voluntary financial contributions" (*Journal of Advanced Support of Education*). At the present time, there is no hard evidence to support the argument that a successful athletic program at ISU will bring additional money into the university's academic programs. In fact, increased emphasis on athletics might actually result in decreased giving to academic programs.

2. *Athletic events are an important factor in student life and are highly valued by alumni.*

James Frey has published the only detailed study of alumni opinion on athletics in *Review of Sport and Leisure*. When alumni were asked to identify their most remembered experience in college, less than 3 percent mentioned athletics. Twenty percent identified social activities and over 15 percent identified faculty-student relations.

When alumni were asked for specific areas in which the university might spend additional funds, athletics ranked in the bottom one-fourth of responses. The top two responses were to maintain traditional academic programs and to increase faculty salaries.

Evidence suggests that student interest in athletics is limited at ISU, also. An unpublished survey conducted during the spring semester of 1989 by the *Daily Vidette* staff showed that 70 percent of the students interviewed were opposed to using tuition dollars for athletics. Recently, the *Daily Vidette* Marketing Department reported that three-fourths of the students at ISU have never attended a single sports event in Redbird Arena. Thus, the current data suggest that athletics are not a major factor in the life of most students at ISU and that alumni do not hold athletics in high priority.

3. *A successful athletic program will result in increased media exposure and will bring visibility to the university.*

It is undeniable that television exposure of intercollegiate athletic events, primarily football and basketball, results in a great deal of media exposure for a university. However, one should not be fooled into equating a university's visibility based on sporting events with its academic visibility and reputation.

In the Jan. 13, 1988 issue of *The Chronicle of Higher Education*, Richard Conklin of Notre Dame pointed out, "It took Father Hesburg 35 years to change the perception of the place from being a football school to being a serious university."

Universities such as Johns Hopkins, MIT, Cal Tech and the University of Chicago, which are recognized worldwide as premier undergraduate and graduate institutions, do not have major intercollegiate athletic programs. And yet, the academic reputation and visibility of these universities is well above that of almost all institutions participating in intercollegiate athletics. Athletic teams from the Ivy League are rarely seen on television; yet, their academic reputation is far superior to that of institutions such as the universities of Oklahoma, Louisville, Alabama, Kentucky and Nevada at Las Vegas, institutions that have a history of national athletic success.

As Vanden Dorpel of Northwestern University stated in *The Chronicle of Higher Education*, "Any institution that says it will somehow be transformed into a fine academic institution on the basis of sports is just wrong. Sports success will only build you a reputation for sports excellence."

Taking $1 million from ISU's academic programs for intercollegiate athletics will not enhance the university's visibility or reputation as an academic institution; it will only build its reputation as a "jock university," and then only if the football and basketball programs are extremely successful. Using the $1 million to fund innovative academic programs would do much more for ISU's academic visibility and reputation than spending these dollars for athletics.

4. *Other state universities use institutional funds for athletics.*

Data provided by the NCAA and Missouri Valley Conference indicated that other state universities also use institutional dollars, i.e., tuition or tax dollars, for athletics. However, this does not mean that the practice is academically sound nor that it enhances the academic image of an institution.

For example, in arguing last year against an increased state income tax, the Illinois State Chamber of Commerce pointed out that the "public perceives that many colleges and universities engage in an inordinate amount of time and money for developing and promoting intercollegiate athletics." Based on the data presented by the Athletic Department at ISU, this perception appears to be accurate.

Can we as academicians justify the use of $1.1 million in tuition dollars for athletics at ISU when our academic programs are woefully under-funded? In its January 1990 report, the Illinois Board of Higher Education Committee on Scope, Structure and Productivity of Illinois Higher Education reported that the public perception of higher education in Illinois was that "the price of higher education is rising at too fast a rate" and that "education should operate more efficiently or at lower costs and that the price charged to students should be controlled." In response, the committee recommended that higher education in Illinois should "improve the quality and cost effectiveness of its programs and services."

I would argue that it is *not* cost effective to spend $1.1 million from tuition dollars for athletics, particularly when the instructional budget per student at ISU ranks in the *bottom 3 percent* of the 204 national universities surveyed in "America's Best Colleges 1990," published by *U.S. News & World Report.*

The report from the Intercollegiate Athletics Strategic Planning Committee, which was ap-pointed and chaired by ISU President Thomas Wallace, stated that; "The Department of Intercollegiate Athletics supports and extends the university teaching and research functions." During my 19 years at ISU, I cannot think of one example in which intercollegiate athletics has supported or extended either teaching or research. Rather, *educational and research programs at ISU have been bled in order to support and extend intercollegiate athletics!*

I am not opposed to intercollegiate athletics at a university. Such programs are a source of entertainment for students, faculty/staff and community.

However, intercollegiate athletics *do not* contribute to our academic programs, and funds for intercollegiate athletics *should not* be taken from tuition dollars—dollars that students pay for classes in which they are enrolled.

SOURCE: Arlan Richardson, "ISU Should Stop Using Tuition Dollars for Athletics," *Daily Vidette* (27 February 1990), p. 5.

---

2. Sports are irrelevant to the academic mission of the school.

- To academic purists, it should be obvious that commercialized intercollegiate sport is inappropriate and inconsistent with the school's purported raison d'être. While there have been occasions when sport programs have been abolished, sometimes temporarily (e.g., San Francisco, Tulane, Southern Methodist), usually this has occurred when negligence and abuse have been disclosed. In the 1990s Northwestern eliminated men and women's track and cross-country; William and Mary trimmed women's basketball, wrestling, and swimming; the University of Maryland, facing a $3.5 million deficit, reduced the number of scholarships in several sports; and Wisconsin trimmed five of its sports offerings. On a more philosophical level, University of Chicago president Robert Maynard Hutchins persuaded the university's trustees to abolish football in 1939 on the grounds that intellectual development and pursuit of "truth" were the fundamental purposes of universities.

3. The opportunities of the student body for sports and recreation participation are restricted.

- The *Chicago Tribune* and Issacs wrote:

  Every time a student hands a tuition check to Illinois State University, he is making a contribution to the school's athletic department.

Each student is paying $95 a year as part of a student fee that goes directly toward funding intercollegiate sports. The money is Illinois State's largest source of revenue, accounting for $1.8 million of the department's $5.2 million budget.

The athletic fee [Issacs' school] entitles students to attend home games—if enough seats are available in the student section . . . the limited availability of intramural facilities clearly discourages extensive use of them by the student body. The result for many students is that they are, in effect, paying twice for the privilege of not participating in sports.[18]

4. The destructive public relations that result from a consistently mediocre or losing record.

• Michener, indirectly, addresses the destructive public relations function of a suspect athletic program, " . . . businessmen and legislators alike tended to agree that when the school stopped pouring money down the football rathole it gave evidence of managerial responsibility; its reputation was enhanced rather than damaged."[19]

5. The destruction of the university's purpose caused by commercialism.

• In a special issue of *Academe* devoted to the commercialization of college sport, the editor wrote, "Despite burgeoning scandal and growing evidence of runaway commercialization, the world of intercollegiate athletics shows little interest in reforming itself."[20]

Sage wrote:

Not only are big-time intercollegiate athletic programs a commercial business enterprise, functioning as part of a cartel, and employing athletes, but the programs are operated with employees (athletes) who are being paid slave wages. Whereas, even granting that collegiate football teams play only half the number of games as the pros, the collegiate players are vastly underpaid. A university that reports that its athletic program showed a million dollar profit need not be too proud; it was accomplished at the expense of exploiting its employees. . . . Another reaction I have to using sports to generate funds for academic purposes is related to the exploitation of student-athletes. I question the morality of using student-athletes to hustle money for the university—the university profits from the sweat of the athletes. At least the student-athlete should be paid a decent wage by the employers, if one of his functions is to produce capital, either directly or indirectly.[21]

Since our focus here is on the systemic connections between education and sport, let us turn to research data that pertain to the consequences of intercollegiate sport for student athletes. Scientific literature on college athletes is diversified and must be carefully scrutinized apropos the variables studied, the inferences drawn, the time periods covered, the institutions examined, the sampling procedures used, and the control group(s), if any, employed. The division (i.e., I, II, or III) in college athletics must also be considered, because collegiate sport is a variegated phenomenon. Some of these studies shed light on sport as a social and economic escalator. A synopsis of selective research on collegiate athletes will be discussed. Vignette 10.2 reports the views of a university professor regarding his school's use of tuition dollars for athletics.

☐ SOME ACADEMIC CONSIDERATIONS

ACT/SAT Scores

Numerous schools require standardized test scores, particularly the American College Test (ACT) or Scholastic Aptitude Test (SAT), as part of the admissions criteria. These scores are required because of their apparent predictive ability. A study undertaken by the highly respected American Institutes for Research (AIR) that surveyed over 4,000 students (athletes and those involved in extracurricular activities) at 42 Division I schools is of interest. The AIR study revealed that the lowest ACT and SAT scores were registered for football and basketball players (18.2 and 883.3, respectively), followed by participants in other sports (19.2 and 919.3, respectively), and, the highest, by students involved in other extracurricular activities (21.4 and 990.2, respectively). The findings apropos high school grade-point average (GPA) paralleled the standardized test findings. The use of standardized test scores is controversial, and Baumann and Henschen's study at the University of Utah provides ammunition for those critical of the use of these scores, particularly for minority athletes.[22] The researchers examined the correlation between ACT scores and actual GPAs for 753 male and female athletes at the university. They found that for white student athletes a combination of ACT scores and GPAs were the best predictors. However, for nonwhites, high school GPA was the best predictor. Baumann and Henschen argue that the Prop 48 minimum ACT requirement is suspect because, to the extent that their findings can be generalized, these standardized test scores lack validity in predicting college GPA for certain social categories.

Graduation Rates of College Athletes

Various reports of **graduation rates for athletes** and nonathletes exist. Colleges began to make public disclosures of such statistics in 1992, under pressure from Congress. While one must be wary of the public relations function of these statistics, the sports focused on, and the means for computing these rates, some select schools (Notre Dame and Northwestern among them) boast of impressive graduation rates for their athletes. On the other hand, some universities have notoriously low graduation rates and, understandably, have typically been reluctant to make them public. In 1991 *The Chicago Tribune* compiled data indicating that Minnesota graduated 36% of its athletes who had matriculated in 1984–1985, including graduation rates of 24% and 40% in football and basketball, respectively.[23] Other Big Ten schools' less than auspicious graduation rates can be gleaned from Table 10.3 and conference graduation rates for football and basketball players are revealing (Table 10.4).

Other salient graduation findings by the *Tribune* follow:

- Northwestern ranked at the top, with an 85% graduation rate; and Illinois, the second-ranked school, was more than 20 percentage points behind.
- Women Big Ten athletes graduated at a 67% rate in contrast to men's 54%.
- Notre Dame's athletes graduated at the exact same percentage as the student body— 93%.

TABLE 10.3 Overall graduation rates for Big Ten student-athletes in freshman class of 1984–1985, compared to all 1984–1985 freshmen

School	All Freshmen (%)	Student-Athletes (%)
Illinois	76.2	64.6
Indiana	57.6	53.8
Iowa	55.4	61.0
Michigan	76.5	60.6
Michigan State	59.7	60.8
Minnesota	27.0	35.9
Northwestern	85.7	85.0
Ohio State	46.2	52.9
Purdue	66.7	62.8
Wisconsin	59.8	56.5
NCAA Div. I	47.2	47.4

SOURCES: Big Ten Schools, NCAA report (May 1990); *Chicago Tribune* (12 February 1991), Section 4, p. 1.

- Ohio State, Iowa, Michigan State, and Minnesota saw their student-athletes graduate at a higher rate than the rest of the student body. (The average graduation rate for all student-athletes for NCAA Division I is 47%.)
- Graduation rates varied by school (Table 10.3), conference, sex, and sport (Table 10.5).

In our highly educated society, degrees are important mechanisms for achieving social mobility. Athletic grants provide the wherewithal—the means and financial incentives—for matriculation at institutions of higher learning. Without such inducements, individuals from certain social origins, particularly the lower and working classes, may find it virtually impossible to enroll in, let alone graduate from, college.

TABLE 10.4 Graduation rates for Big Ten football and men's basketball players for freshman class of 1984–1985 and incoming transfers for that year

School	Football (%)	Basketball (%)
Illinois	61	25
Indiana	52	63
Iowa	57	33
Michigan	59	0*
Michigan State	44	50
Minnesota	24	40
Northwestern	81	100
Ohio State	21	40
Purdue	39	60
Wisconsin	67	25
NCAA Division 1	38	33

*0 of 2 graduated.

SOURCE: *Chicago Tribune* (12 February 1991), Section 4, p. 1.

TABLE 10.5 Graduation rates for selected sports for Big Ten student-athletes in freshman class of 1984–1985 and incoming transfers for that year, in percentages

Men

School	Baseball	Golf	Gymnastics	Swimming	Tennis	Track/Cross-Country	Wrestling
Illinois	67	60	40	75	75	83	55
Indiana	37	100	—	67	50	80	20
Iowa	70	80	100	75	100	60	40
Michigan	14	—	80	78	100	40	57
Michigan State	50	100	100	100	100	80	33
Minnesota	19	0*	50	43	25	30	—
Northwestern	NA	NA	NA	NA	NA	NA	NA
Ohio State	86	75	50	17	67	60	73
Purdue	80	100	—	88	50	67	43
Wisconsin	45	33	66	75	66	57	33

Women

School	Basketball	Golf	Gymnastics	Softball	Swimming	Tennis	Track/Cross-Country	Volleyball
Illinois	100	50	50	—	88	100	25	83
Indiana	50	100	0†	100	60	100	40	25
Iowa	60	0*	50	50	86	67	60	50
Michigan	50	67	100	50	80	75	100	100
Michigan State	67	100	100	—	100	100	43	100
Minnesota	67	50	50	100	38	40	75	25
Northwestern	NA	NA	NA	NA	NA	NA	NA	NA
Ohio State	40	67	100	43	82	100	60	86
Purdue	100	100	—	—	100	100	43	67
Wisconsin	50	—	67	—	75	100	50	75

*0 of 2 graduated; † 0 of 1 graduated. NA, not available. *Note.* In instances where no percentage is listed (—), school had no freshmen in the sport in 1984–1985 or does not compete in the sport.

SOURCES: Big Ten Schools; *Chicago Tribune* (12 February 1991), Section 4, p. 1.

For a more representative perspective, a national survey that presents graduation rates for both athletes and nonathletes is needed; such a study has been completed. The dumb jock typecasting of college athletes is well-known (see Vignette 10.3 for James Thurber's rendition of this stereotype). A 1991 survey by *The Chronicle of Higher Education* reported that athletes actually graduated at a higher rate (56% vs. 48%) than the general student body. This survey, in which 262 of 295 Division I schools responded, charted recruits from the 1984–1985 class to see how many graduated in five years. On the national level, graduation rates of basketball players trailed in the diploma race. Because basketball and football comprise the major sports on most college campuses, we may conclude that the minor sports had the highest graduation rates.

VIGNETTE 10.3

James Thurber's Rendition of the Dumb Jock Stereotype

The folklore regarding the open society of the United States and the many talented youths who rise above poverty to "make it big" is not without its stereotypical counterparts. Indeed, many images exist of those not terrifically bright athletes who are unable to do much more than what is required by their particular athletic speciality. The "dumb jock" football player has never been more humorously presented than in this account of the mighty Bolenciecwcz in James Thurber's essay, "University Days."

Another course that I didn't like, but somehow managed to pass, was economics. I went to that class straight from the botany class, which didn't help me any in understanding either subject. I used to get them mixed up. But not as mixed up as another student in my economics class who came there direct from a physics laboratory. He was a tackle on the football team, named Bolenciecwcz. At that time Ohio State University had one of the best football teams in the country, and Bolenciecwcz was one of its outstanding stars. In order to be eligible to play it was necessary for him to keep up his studies, a very difficult matter, for while he was not dumber than an ox he was not any smarter. Most of his professors were lenient and helped him along. None gave him more hints, in answering questions, or asked him simpler ones than the economics professor, a thin, timid man named Bassum. One day when we were on the subject of transportation and distribution, it came to Bolenciecwcz's turn to answer a question. "Name one means of transportation," the professor said to him. No light came into the big tackle's eyes. "Just any means of transportation," said the professor. Bolenciecwcz sat staring at him. "That is," pursued the professor, "any medium, agency, or method of going from one place to another." Bolenciecwcz had the look of a man who is being led into a trap. "You may choose among steam, horse-drawn, or electrically propelled vehicles," said the instructor. "I might suggest that one which we commonly take in making long journeys across land." There was a profound silence in which everybody stirred uneasily, including Bolenciecwcz and Mr. Bassum. Mr. Bassum abruptly broke his silence in an amazing manner. "Choo-choo-choo," he said, in a low voice, and turned instantly scarlet. He glanced appealingly around the room. All of us, of course, shared Mr. Bassum's desire that Bolenciecwcz should stay abreast of the class in economics, for the Illinois game, one of the hardest and most important of the season, was only a week off. "Toot, toot, tootoooooot!" some student with a deep voice moaned, and we all looked encouragingly at Bolenciecwcz. Somebody else gave a fine imitation of a locomotive letting off steam. Mr. Bassum himself rounded off the little show. "Ding, dong, ding, dong," he said hopefully. Bolenciecwcz was staring at the floor now, trying to think, his great brow furrowed, his huge hands rubbing together, his face red.

"How did you come to college this year, Mr. Bolenciecwcz?" asked the professor.

"Chuffa chuffa, chuffa, chuffa."

"M'father sent me," said the football player.

"What on?" asked Bassum.

"I git an'allowance," said the tackle, in a low, husky voice, obviously embarrassed.

"No, no," said Bassum. "Name a means of transportation. What did you ride here on?"

"Train," said Bolenciecwcz.

"Quite right," said the professor. "Now, Mr. Nugent, will you tell us—"

The story of Bolenciecwcz is obviously an exaggeration, with a basis in fact only rarely.

SOURCE: Ronald W. Smith and Frederick W. Preston, *Sociology* (New York: St. Martin's Press, 1977), pp. 438–440. James Thurber, "University Days," Reprinted with permission.

Grade Point Average

A widespread belief about athletes is that they do not perform well in their studies. Although empirical data are in short supply, evidence suggests that it is equivocal.

Before noting additional specific academic achievement outcomes, the seriousness of the issue can be grasped by considering a heralded proposal regarding minimum GPAs at the 1991 NCAA convention. It was proposed that to be eligible to participate in intercollegiate athletics that, on an escalating scale, freshman should have a 1.6 average and seniors a 1.9 average (on a 4-point scale). Although the lowest possible C is 2.0, the proposal was opposed by a number of coaches.

In a comprehensive study of NCAA Division I schools commissioned by the President's Commission of the NCAA, it was found that, on a 4-point scale, football and basketball players had an average GPA of 2.46, compared to 2.61 for other college athletes, and 2.79 for students involved in extracurricular activities. When the schools were divided into "more successful" and "less successful" programs, GPAs of football and basketball players in "more successful" programs were lower than GPAs of other students (2.29 vs. 2.55).

Academic Orientation

Adler and Adler report the results of an inquiry of basketball players' academic experiences in a big-time college program.[24] The title of their investigation, "From Idealism to Pragmatic Detachment," suggests the fundamental finding—idealism and optimism tended to characterize the academic orientations of *male* university student-athletes (in basketball) early in their college careers; however, these auspicious goals and attitudes gave way to a progressive detachment from academic excellence. Given the case study methodology of the present research, one must be cautious of overgeneralizing, but, nevertheless, the process of college athletes' sport experience may well be one of initial excitement and optimism, followed by resignation and disengagement from more than minimal scholarly efforts. The authors suggest that the structure of top-level college programs—not the psychological characteristics of athletes—and the athletes' personal experiences within these social settings undermine the realization of the student-athletes' initial optimistic aspirations.

In a sequel to the Adlers' study, Meyer surveyed the attitudes, opinions, beliefs, and feelings of *female* athletes toward the student-athlete role.[25] Like the males in the Adlers' study, the females began college with idealistic views of education. Unlike the Adlers' findings, the positive view actually became strengthened over time. While male and female student athletes commenced college with similar views, they ended college with dissimilar views. Although the methodological differences between the studies must be carefully examined, other research arrives at similar conclusions regarding men and women's different orientations to sport.

Sage compared two groups of former high school students.[26] Members of one group continued their athletic participation in college, whereas members of the other did not. He found that nonparticipants had higher GPAs, were less likely to join a fraternity, and were more occupationally oriented (rather than socially oriented) than participants. His data suggest that athletes may be less academically oriented than nonathletes.

A caveat is in order. Just what academic achievement (when measured by GPAs and graduation rates) means is open to question. First, a GPA of 3.0 in physics means something different, undoubtedly, from the same GPA in physical education. Second, a GPA of 3.0 in physics probably means something different if we are comparing Podunk U. with Harvard students. Third, there is a semblance of evidence that athletes shop around for courses and because, at some schools, athletes' graduation rates are dismally low, we are dubious about what this augurs regarding academic achievement. Fourth, other considerations such as repeating courses, receiving incompletes, and being placed on academic probation are not reflected in these figures[27] (the AIR study did find, however, that a comparable number of student-athletes and extracurricular students fell into these areas[28]). Fifth, how these rates are reported can be a significant consideration. For example, Bobby Knight of Indiana has argued that several of his freshman recruits transferred to other schools and eventually graduated, but because they didn't graduate from Indiana (the school that recruited them), these were counted against him (Indiana). Additionally, some of his own recruits were only a course or two away from graduation when the statistics were compiled. In short, indices of academic achievement (graduation rates and GPAs) must be carefully examined for their validity. A variety of confounding factors may make them dubious indicators of scholastic performance.

A statistical study by the U.S. Department of Education of 8,100 college students, including athletes, from selected years between 1972 and 1986, found that by age 32, former football and basketball players had the highest rate of home ownership (77%) and had earnings 10% above the mean of all former students who attended four-year schools.[29] Once in the work force, the study reports, the former athlete likely will hold a job as a manager, salesman, or teacher at an average annual income of $26,000.

The empirical literature on college athletes is not systematic, representative, or consistent. We must remind ourselves of the pitfalls listed earlier. Take, for example, the high graduation rates of athletes at Northwestern, Notre Dame, and Stanford versus the considerably lower rates at Minnesota and Ohio State. The former are private schools with fairly high academic standards, whereas the latter are state universities with generally less stringent entrance requirements. Hence, the differences may be due, in part, to the academic admission requirements and prerequisites of the institutions studied. Although college athletes may have difficulties in taking their studies seriously and doing well, evidence suggests that some do well in their careers.[30] In fact, the NCAA periodically announces Silver Anniversary Award winners, accolades presented to former college athletes who have distinguished themselves in their chosen profession twenty-five years after their participation.

Exploitation of College Athletes

Numerous allegations that college athletes have been exploited have been voiced. Superficially, it seems puzzling how college athletes, especially full-scholarship recipients, are taken advantage of. Not only are all their basic expenses provided, but they frequently receive the positive social regard and status accompanying a visible and prestigious collegiate activity. When one peers beneath the surface, however, there is a seamier side. Patterns of institutionalized powerlessness,[31] mechanisms woven into the very structure of the sport institution (knowingly and/or unwittingly) that ultimately produce **exploitation** have been identified. Illustratively, the NCAA stipulates that scholarship athletes may legally receive monies to cover room, board, tuition, books; and fees and athletic grants-in-aid (this is what the NCAA officially calls what are popularly dubbed "athletic scholarships") are awarded on a yearly basis. A student must complete four years of eligibility in five years (exceptions include military service and religious work), and if the student transfers to another school, ordinarily, one sport season must be foregone. Finally, only under extenuating circumstances ("hardship") may athletes contract their services with professional sport franchises or agents before their class graduates.

Coakley declares these rules and regulations reasonable in facilitating an educational experience.[32] However, problems arise when commercial interests supersede educational ones. In schools, usually those with major football and/or basketball programs, the athlete's role in the academy has some parallels with rank-and-file workers in the labor force. Not only do athletes help generate revenues for their "sponsors," they also perform a public relations function without receiving any extra compensation. Further, the demands on the student-athlete appear to make it nearly impossible to be, simultaneously, a serious student and a serious athlete, and the former role is often short-changed. Allen Sack, a former Notre Dame football player, sees little difference between the demands of professional and elite college football programs except for the handsome material rewards garnished by professional athletes.[33]

Views on the Exploitation of the Student-Athlete.

Not everyone conceives the collegiate sport participant as a helpless, hapless, and hopeless soul akin to chattel and embedded in peonage. Consider, though, the perspective of several conflict-oriented former players and social scientists. Former all-pro National Football League (NFL) player Gene Upshaw provides a glimpse of the economic exploitation of college athletes:

> Once you receive financial aid based on your athletic ability, you are not much different from a Professional Athlete [sic]. A college is paying you to bring money and prestige to the school and to provide commercial entertainment for alumni, students, and the public at large. And the current NCAA battle over hundreds of millions of TV dollars means that the student-players whose time and sweat produce this money are being grossly underpaid.[34]

Sack's Marxist critique of big-time college football programs reinforces Upshaw's: "Given the inadequacy of the education received by the average athlete, his [sic] scholarship amounts essentially to room and board, i.e., subsistence. Like Marx's mid-nineteenth-century proletarians, college football players literally receive food and lodging while the surplus value they produce is expropriated by their employers."[35] Several insidious myths must be dispelled before fully comprehending the exploitation of college athletes, according to Sack.[36]

The first falsehood is perpetrated in the glib, albeit popular expression, "free ride." This phraseology intimates that full-scholarship athletes have the privilege of attending college for nothing. While such scholarship recipients are not directly paying for their schooling, indeed their physical labor and skills are being expended in exchange. On this score one college football player remarked, "My question is, after arriving early in August to three-a-day practices in 100-degree heat, and then into an 11-week season that takes a minimum of 60 hours a week in meetings, practice, and travel, and then into a conditioning program until spring practice starts, who's the guy that called a football scholarship a free ride?"[37] Using a dramaturgical metaphor,[38] many people are only familiar with the glamorous "front-stage region" of athletic contests, they are not privy to the "backstage" view, the near full-time commitment of sport participants (pre- and postseason activities and weight and conditioning training often occur year round). Although the athlete's college expenses are subsidized, a genuine educational experience is not easily secured. The number-one priority is ordinarily not academics, but sport. To use a familiar expression, one "eats, drinks, and sleeps" football. Although the aphorism hones in on football, other sports probably require a similar single-mindedness of purpose and focus.[39] When this all-encompassing mental centering is compounded by the typical physical fatigue factor, serious studying becomes tedious and burdensome, if not virtually impossible. In fact, it is so problematic that some would prefer not attending class at all; hence all one's time, energy, and effort could be concentrated on sport.

Some coaches have publicly admitted the duplicity and hypocrisy surrounding the student-athlete appellation. Former Alabama coach Paul "Bear" Bryant provided a candid and sobering remark:

> I used to go along with the idea that football players on scholarship were "student-athletes," which is what the NCAA calls them. Meaning a student first, and an athlete second. We were kidding ourselves, trying to make it more palatable to the academicians. We don't have to say that and we shouldn't. At the level we play, the boy is really an athlete first and a student second.[40]

Even a university president has been quoted: "Our athletes were recruited to be athletes, not students. There was never an expectation that they'd get their ass out of bed at eight o'clock to go to class and turn in their assignments."[41]

The exploitation of college student-athletes, especially black ones, is a dominant theme in the American sport literature. White athletes have not escaped being taken advantage of, but the black athlete is especially susceptible to such abuse or, as Penn State's Joe Paterno said, "We have raped a generation and a half of black athletes. We have taken kids and sold them on bouncing a ball or running with a football and that being able to do certain things athletically was going to be an end itself. We cannot afford to do this to another generation."[42] James Michener has also been less than laudatory: "They recruited blacks, used them, and tossed them aside when eligibility was over. They took 'Mickey Mouse' courses, none toward a degree, but maintained a B average. They were also discriminated against, and not accorded the same privileges as the white players."[43] I empirically examined this theme for college basketball players performing at NCAA Divisions I, II, and III.[44] In this survey black college basketball players experienced more "exploitation" than their white counterparts. Being an athlete had forced more blacks into taking a less demanding major, cheating academically, taking gut classes, hustling professors for grades, having others write their papers, and taking fewer courses during a term. Blacks felt more pressure to be an athlete first and a student second, felt less confident that they could handle college work, were more likely to have insufficient credits to graduate, were less likely to have been able to meet academic admission requirements without being an athlete, felt more threatened about the consequences of not abiding by the coach's philosophy, and felt inadequately rewarded for their efforts. Importantly, though the racial comparisons found blacks in a more disadvantageous position, the *absolute* values did not, categorically, present a consistently negative scenario for blacks. When division was introduced as a control variable, the results occasionally were modified. Hence, it is important to specify the NCAA Division when making statements apropos race and exploitation.

Sport sociologists Eitzen and Sage pinpoint the commercial infrastructure of intercollegiate athletics as the taproot of exploitation:

> The businesslike character of big-time college sport is more directly responsible for one additional problem. Young men . . . are paid slave wages (room, board, and tuition) to bring honor and dollars to their university. Thus, there are two questions of morality: (1) the use of student-athletes to hustle money for the university; (2) the exploitation of the athletes by paying them indecent wages.[45]

An Inquiry of College Student-Athlete Exploitation.   Having provided a sample of testimonials of the alleged exploitation of student-athletes, several questions come to mind: Are these accounts typical? Do most athletes experience exploitation and abuse? How representative and generalizable are these descriptions? I answered these queries by conducting an empirical investigation focusing on college basketball players' attitudes, opinions, beliefs, behaviors, and perceptions surrounding their college sport experiences.[46] Because of program diversification, I compared and contrasted the responses of athletes ($n = 505$) performing at different levels (NCAA Divisions I, II, and III) in several spheres.

Scholastic Activities.   My data did not support the contention that athletes take academic shortcuts. The potential benefits afforded by attending class surfaced, because almost three fourths disagreed that "I wish I could play my sport and not have to go to class at all"; and no divisional differences were produced. Eighty percent or more disagreed that they were coerced into taking a less demanding major, cheating on schoolwork, missing important exams, hustling professors for grades, having proxies write papers for them, and being cut off from the rest of the student body. More than 50% disagreed that they were forced to take easy courses, cut classes, take fewer courses a term, and miss taking courses they wanted; nearly 75% did not feel pressure to be an athlete first and a student second.

Because "pressure-cooker" sports are, intuitively, believed to be more characteristic of major programs, I examined cross-tabulations between division and the aforementioned variables. Generally, the higher the division, the more prone were athletes to feel forced into taking a less demanding major, taking gut courses, missing important exams, hustling professors for grades, taking fewer courses a term, miss taking courses they really wanted to, being cut off from the rest of the student body, and being an athlete first and a student second.

Attitudes Toward Present Sport Participation.   Two-thirds enjoyed playing as much now as in high school, although there was an inverse relationship between division and enjoyment (the "yes" percentages for Division I, II, and III athletes were 60%, 69%, and 78%, respectively). Nearly 60% felt adequately rewarded for the time and energy devoted to their sport (nonresponse percentage equaled 20%); although statistically significant differences failed to emerge, a smaller percentage of Division I (68%) than II (75%) and III (81%) student-athletes responded affirmatively.

Over four fifths (82%) felt that athletes in their sport made greater sacrifices than regular students to obtain an education, and nearly 60% disagreed that their education was "free." A direct association was found between division and "sacrifice," with nearly half of Division I versus Divisions II (34%) and III (29%) athletes responding affirmatively. More Division III participants felt their education was free than did those from the other two divisions. This correlation may be partially explained by considering that Division I scholarship athletes were nearly twice as likely to feel coaches made demands preventing them from being top students.

Perceptions of Admission, Academic, and Recruitment Policies. Despite the scuttlebutt surrounding accusations and evidence of shady admission criteria and dubious recruitment practices for athletes, over 80% felt confident of handling college-level work. Moreover, 85% felt they would have been able to meet the matriculation requirements even if they weren't an athlete. The fact that 43% frequented a counselor or tutor regarding academic difficulty muddles the apparent validity of the former item. Further, the higher the division, the greater the likelihood of a tutor being consulted; a more than 20-percentage-point difference existed between Divisions I and II. Respondents who used a tutor felt that the tutor's primary concern was ensuring that they really learned something; only 6% thought that the primary concern was to keep them eligible for their sport. I found no division differences, but, interestingly, 54% provided no response!

Accusations of transcript irregularities notwithstanding, 94% indicated that recruiters never offered to alter theirs. Surprisingly, nearly 8% of Division III athletes answered affirmatively in comparison to 2% and 4% of Division II and I athletes, respectively. Apropos accumulating credits toward graduation, nearly 70% noted that they will have amassed enough credits to graduate when their athletic eligibility expires. (The NCAA in 1981 voted to require athletes to complete 12 credit hours per term to remain eligible for varsity sports.) However, credit hours per se are insufficient in meeting graduation requirements. Most majors require a particular configuration of major and cognate courses; however, I found significant divisional differences, with 64% of Division I participants responding affirmatively versus 70% and 82% of Division II and III participants, respectively.

Subsidies, Pressures, Fears, and Threats. I found significant divisional differences in how student-athletes financed their schooling. Most Division I athletes were recipients of athletic tenders, whereas Division II and III individuals were subsidized by a combination of aids (the athletic scholarship was not the primary source). Because "strings" can be attached to financial aid, I pursued several probes. For example, although most (65%) did not fear having their aid withdrawn for failing to perform up to the coach's expectations, a significantly larger proportion of Division I (24%) than II (19%) and III (8%) athletes responded affirmatively. Similarly, while most (69%) were not threatened by having their financial aid withdrawn for not accepting their coach's philosophy, significantly more respondents from Division I (21%) than either II (9%) or III (7%) responded positively.

Insofar as athletic injuries are concerned, slightly more than one tenth felt pressured to return to action before healing completely (but one third of the respondents, in contrast to 15% and 12% of Division II and III respondents, respectively, felt pressure to return to action before their injury was satisfactorily restored).

In summary, using the bivariate associations, I found relationships between division and exploitation indicants in the anticipated direction. When controlling for race and sex, I found that the zero-order correlations tended to be upheld.

Observations.   The empirical findings left me with several pertinent cognitions. First, and consistent with popular opinion, Division I sport programs are more pressure-packed than their Division II and, particularly, Division III counterparts. At this level, athletes—regardless of race or gender—are more likely to be taking academic shortcuts, logging more sport-related hours but enjoying them less, visiting tutors for scholastic help, and thinking of professional careers. Former Oklahoma Heisman Trophy winner Steve Owens corroborates these outcomes in a statement made over twenty years ago: "In high school the game was almost entirely fun. Here it's a business. We're supposed to fill that stadium . . . I still love the game, but there's so much pressure, sometimes it makes me wonder."[47] Second, though I found differences among divisions in the predicted direction, the percentage differences were not always marked. Third, the data do not provide a scenario (from the participant's perspective) of a terribly abused and mistreated student—nor a pampered or coddled one—who is playing basketball in an exploitative milieu. Fourth, deviant activity is not particularly prevalent.

Several caveats warrant attention. The present sample consisted exclusively of basketball players, and the pressures from the general and specific sport ambiences are salient variables. For example, the basketball world at Duke or University of Nevada– Las Vegas (UNLV) is decidedly different from that at Albright College. Similarly, basketball at Bradley University strikingly contrasts with baseball. I examined and reported three different performance echelons. The fact that I analyzed a single sport is both advantageous and disadvantageous. A positive feature is that the sport scrutinized is held constant; had athletes from different sports been surveyed, another potentially confounding variable could have contaminated the results and necessitated additional analyses. A liability is that basketball, a major sport, may differ from minor sports (e.g., swimming, golf, tennis). Figler contends, however, that "While minor sports even at the highest competitive level may not generate wide public interest, they are probably as intense for the athletes and coaches as are the money sports at 'big-time' universities."[48] The truth of this statement awaits empirical confirmation, but it remains provocative. Further, participants in another sport or nonparticipants would provide a comparison group because I tallied only the responses of basketball players at a single point in time in a cross-sectional survey.

Social Desirability?   The responses portray neither an altarboy nor a greedy ringer image of the student-athlete. The subjective admissions of deviance appear to be less than that reported by the media, which raises several issues. Did the social desirability response set pervade their reactions? Although anonymity was guaranteed, past research has shown that items mirroring social undesirability are less often endorsed than those reflecting social desirability. The "social desirability" response set may have plagued the research because the marginal totals provide some evidence that "sensitive" areas received a relatively large percentage of "no response" (which could be analogous to taking the Fifth Amendment). According to Hanford, most violations reported to the NCAA are in the recruiting realm (because this is a more visible forum for other school representatives to peer and pry into); but it is generally believed that most infractions actually occur in the "academic and financial care and feeding of athletes once they are enrolled (and out from scrutiny by other institutions)."[49] Although the data do not prove that the responses are muffled or minimized, coaches and athletic directors believe that athletes tend to exaggerate and sensationalize.[50] If this happened here, then the sport critics' muckraking seems blown out of proportion.

   Coakley contends that it is difficult to obtain valid data verifying that athletes take less-than-demanding courses.[51] Nevertheless, various reports suggest that athletes take more than their share of easy classes.[52] The fact that the present data did not converge with this indictment may mean that time and distance must intervene before one can process, assimilate, appreciate, and objectively understand the nature of the sport experience. There is support from the actor that the time demands can be inordinate. Allen Brenner, former captain of the Michigan State football team, said in retrospect, "Playing college football is becoming a delusion. It takes too much of your time. There are fall meetings, fall practice, spring practice, weight programs. The plight of the player-student is almost impossible. He doesn't have enough time to study."[53]

Role Conflict?   Sociologically, the resolution of the incompatible demands and expectations on the "athlete-student" can be explained by invoking the mechanisms for coping with such incongruencies. Coakley identifies several social psychological processes for handling role conflict (e.g., integrating or synthesizing, withdrawing, compartmentalizing, and neglecting or de-emphasizing).[54] Although only indirect measures of role conflict were used, it did not appear to be a major problem and preoccupation because, illustratively, almost three quarters of the respondents did *not* feel pressure to be an athlete first and student second (although there were statistically significant divisional differences).

Pluralistic Ignorance?   Even twenty years ago, at the 1973 NCAA annual convention, a proposal to abolish "full-ride" grants-in-aid and, instead, award financial assistance on a need basis only, was rejected by the "major" athletic delegates (Division III schools did endorse the motion). The apparent reason college representatives voted against it stemmed from the alleged trepidation that it would open Pandora's box and lead to even more deception, duplicity, and illicit activity.[55] Assuming valid data, the fact that excessive duplicity did not exist may mean that perceptions of sport programs are plagued by a version of pluralistic ignorance in which "no one believes, but . . . everyone believes that everyone else believes."[56] The viability of this distorted perception exists because it is impossible for the NCAA's relatively small sleuth staff (but spending about $1 million annually) to monitor the practices of all institutions ($N \approx 800$) falling under its jurisdiction. With such conducive conditions, the stage is ripe for pluralistic ignorance to manifest itself.

False Consciousness versus Definition of the Situation.   These two familiar sociological concepts provide an intriguing point–counterpoint polemic. The concept of "alienation" occupies a dominant conceptual position in Marxian analysis. Accordingly, *alienation* is the sense of isolation and separation felt from work and/or meaningful social networks. Marx argued that although workers may be "objectively" alienated, they may not necessarily feel they are. This somewhat paradoxical situation leads to the notion of *false consciousness*, a belief actually counterproductive or destructive of one's own best self-interests.

Responses to several questions provide evidence that the college athletes I surveyed had a rather conservative and/or naive economic and political view of their potential rights and clout in the academy. More than half disagreed that they (a) deserve a share of the TV revenues they help generate (51%); (b) have the right to form labor unions (75%); and (c) have the right to the same kind of benefits other employees enjoy (52%). Further, when I cross-classified these items with division, no significant statistical differences surfaced. Some of these findings stand in stark contrast to those of Sack, who found that among active and retired NFL players, under-the-table payments were fairly common in major football conferences and that such payments had increased over the past twenty years.[57] Blacks vis-à-vis whites were more likely to have been offered and received such perks.

To W.I. Thomas, "if men define situations as real, they are real in their consequences." External (as well as internal) phenomena are endowed and ascribed meaning. The fact that perceptions of the same phenomenon can be variable supports the role of differential experiences and social forces in shaping our and others' behaviors. In short, if college athletes define their sport experiences as essentially nonexploitative, so it is. That comprises their definition of the situation, despite inconsistencies with others' definitions. Perspectives and viewpoints are often not universally similar. Truth and knowledge are not absolute but socially constructed!

It is paramount to underscore that the scientists' (sport sociologist for example) and actors' (actual participants) views are frequently not identical; but both are significant.[58] The data appear to corroborate Coakley's statement that "few athletes perceive themselves as . . . victims of exploitation."[59] If the sport muckrakers are correct, how can we explain the exploitative system? Former NFL player Bernie Parrish provides a thought-provoking argument for why college football players are willing to engage in a brutal and dehumanizing physical activity for which they well may be duped:

> [Players] feel part of something big and important, and that outweighs logic. . . . They're swept up in its exaggerated importance. . . . TV makes it glamorous. . . . Every action and reaction is subject to detailed analysis by the news media. Public awareness of the sport is acute. . . . The aura is intoxicating; for players, it is absolutely stupefying. They will endure practically anything to be part of the team.[60]

From this vantage point, the "inebriated" college athlete may have to wait years while the opiate runs its course before she or he can see the negative features of the sport experience. During one's actual engagement, the atmosphere may be too stupefying to produce critical and rational thought and judgment. Perhaps, too, during this latency period, the media are hyping and trumping up charges to sell their wares; hence, a plausible hypothesis for the apparent discrepancies. Finally, the media's attention is typically on the major schools, where there are more intense pressures and negative rumblings. However, these institutions represent only a fraction of all NCAA constituents, and we should not be misled into believing that this is the normal order of affairs. Collegiate sport is diversified; committing the fallacy of overgeneralizing is a serious faux pas, as is assuming a singular and monolithic definition of the situation by college athletes.

ORGANIZATIONAL DEVIANCE

> Athletics are taken seriously in most American colleges. . . . There is not much fun or freedom in the life of the candidate for the . . . team . . . intense rivalry smothers the spirit of fair play and leaves the game short of one of its greatest attractions. . . . The newspapers make capital of this in exaggerated paragraphs, and football [games] assume the appearance of a gladitorial show. . . . The money making value of the game is dragging sports down from its true place as a recreation, and, together with the rivalry before alluded to must tell against its best interests. But the evil does not stop here, for smaller colleges, like small boys, try to imitate their big brothers, and so offer distinguished players large salaries to coach their football teams that they may compete with some hope of success; and thus many of the men who become noted in college athletics have professionalism thrust upon them.
>
> R. TATE MCKENZIE, 1893[61]

The sociology of deviance literature has been preoccupied with the study of "nuts, sluts, and perverts"; that is, the focus has been on *individual* deviants as opposed to the nefarious behavior of *organizations*. Liazos wrote:

> As a result of the fascination with "nuts, sluts, and perverts," and their identities and subcultures, little attention has been paid to the unethical, illegal, and destructive actions of powerful individuals, groups, and institutions in our society. Because these actions are carried out quietly in the normal course of events, the sociology of deviance does not consider them as part of its subject matter. This bias is rooted in the very conception and definition of the field.[62]

The scandalous behavior involving infractions of NCAA regulations fall under the heading of "organizational deviance" or improprieties carried out by athletic departments, sports associations, and others.

Scandals in intercollegiate athletics are neither a recent (see McKenzie's quote at the beginning of this section) nor a unique social phenomenon. For example, "tramp athletes" or "ringers"—were not rare at the turn of the century. These were athletes who would play football for one school, baseball for another, and may not even be officially enrolled at the school they represented. Similarly, in 1929, the Carnegie Foundation[63] reported dismay with the illegal recruiting conduct of American institutions of higher learning. One conclusion was that "college sports have been developed from games played by boys for pleasure into systematic, professionalized contests." Iowa was expelled by Big Ten officials for improper financial assistance to athletes that year, and several Big Ten universities suggested it was time for the NCAA to become a regulatory rather than an advisory board. Finally, college basketball also had a scam, when point shaving and other irregularities surfaced at Manhattan College in 1951. Two players and three gamblers were arrested. However, more was to come. After probing the incidents, it was discovered that between 1947 and 1950, 86 games had been fixed at 23 cities in 17 states by 32 players. Seven colleges were found guilty of such infractions: Long Island University, New York University, Manhattan College, Kentucky, Toledo, Bradley, and City College of New York. Interestingly, in the year following the censure, Kentucky posted a 25–0 basketball season, and Bradley was runner-up in the NCAA tournament.[64]

Some believe, however, that the present-day disclosures of sport scandals are more serious and despicable, and strike at the heart of academia:

> The athletic world has been staggered . . . by a series of public disclosures revealing indiscretions by our colleges and universities. Transcript irregularities, illegal inducements for grants-in-aid, human rights violations against athletes and coaches alike, discrimination of opportunity against women, discrimination of opportunity against men under NCAA eligibility guidelines, economic mismanagement, and the absence of vision in athletic planning, development, and utilization of facilities. Suddenly "Watergate" has reached our institutions of higher learning and the list of casualties is mounting.[65]

In March 1991, UNLV legal counsel was assured by the NCAA that the Rebels basketball team would not have any of its players suspended for rules violations (there were allegations that incidental hotel bills incurred during recruiting visits were questionable).

The plight of college sport programs has been attacked by several sources. "NBC Sports Journal" charged, "The battle for control of college stars and the profits they bring their schools, continues between the NCAA, pros, the agents . . . and the student-athlete remains the pawn." Similarly, CBS's "60 Minutes" reported that "the games have become phony and so has the academics. It's just so much commerce. The athlete's been used. . . ." Coach Darryl Rogers, who replaced Frank Kush after his dismissal from Arizona State, proclaimed, "They'll fire you for losing before they'll fire you for cheating." John Underwood, sportswriter and commentator, wrote in his book *The Death of an American Game—The Crisis in Football:* "The rash of phony transcripts and academic cheating spells out the fact that athletics are now an abomination to the ideals of higher education. Victim: the student-athlete. Culprit: the system and those who run it." The litany of charges goes on and on.[66]

Intercollegiate athletics are in trouble. I have come across the following titles of exposé articles appearing in the popular press:

> It's Cleanup Time for College Sports[67]
>
> Out of Bounds[68]
>
> The Shame of College Sports[69]
>
> Foul Play in College Sports[70]
>
> Behind Scandals in Big-Time College Sports[71]
>
> Foul![72]
>
> College Sports' Real Scandal[73]

Academe, the official journal of the American Association of University professors, has written:

> College athletics in this country is in continuing crisis. Even after several years of proposals and discussions of reform, the gains achieved are quite modest. . . .

Despite the attention given to intercollegiate sports, reform in the media, and elsewhere, there is ample evidence that the problems in college sports are persistent, substantial, and fundamental. . . .

The time has come to recognize that intercollegiate athletics poses a major governance problem for American colleges and universities.[74]

Improprieties: Some Illustrations

The issue of impropriety in intercollegiate athletics has many sides—fiscal, educational, racial, social, and moral. To better understand why collegiate sports find themselves in this dubious situation, first consider a few documented mind-boggling cases.

In the spring of 1991, the University of Texas–El Paso was conducting its own investigation of alleged improprieties in its basketball program, as was Syracuse University for alleged wrongdoings of one of its basketball players.

Some key questions arise: Why have scandals such as these become so rampant? What lies behind the scandals in intercollegiate athletics? One source suggests that "hunger for the money and prestige of winning teams is emerging as the basic cause of abuses afflicting programs on many campuses."[75]

The manifest raison d'être of institutions of higher learning is to provide a public service that, in the long run, presumably benefits society. Unlike General Motors, their primary motive is not to make a profit. However, the present finds higher education financially strapped. Two interrelated variables help us understand the shaky industry of intercollegiate athletics. First, financial retrenchment has hit many academic institutions hard, and the future for their programs appears less rosy. Second, demographers predict that the traditional college-age population (persons between the ages of 18 and 22) is declining, and that this decline may continue until the year 2000 and beyond.

One of the pervasive rationales for intercollegiate athletic programs, notably those dubbed revenue-producing sports (usually football and basketball), is that they provide precious funding for the nonrevenue programs. Indeed, at some elite schools, the monies for football and basketball do perform this function. However, very few institutions can boast of this accomplishment. Sport programs as a rule are *not* money-making propositions.[76] Despite our knowledge that most sport programs do not turn a profit, it should not be construed that winning seasons, winning teams, and postseason play are unprofitable. Football teams appearing in major postseason bowl games (e.g., Rose Bowl) can garner as much as $6 million, although the money is typically split with conference schools. In the 1992 NCAA basketball tournament, each of the final four teams garnered about $1.25 million. A decade earlier, in the 1982 tournament, the four finalists received $530,000, the regional losers earned $340,000, and the first-round and second-round teams netted $125,000. In 1980, the final four—Indiana, North Carolina, Virginia, and Louisiana State—received $350,000; the regional losers, $237,000; and the losers in the first and second rounds of tournament play, $95,000. These recent figures take on special significance when one considers that 1952 NCAA finalists received a mere $7,800.[77]

Scandals might be a direct consequence of the severe *economic* pressures confronting schools and their athletic departments. The desire to end up in the black seems to have bred an emphasis on winning by any means, honest as well as dishonest. The corruption in intercollegiate athletics is related to the following premises: (a) winning is the goal, (b) fans do not flock to see losers play, and (c) there are more seats to fill today. All the reasons add up to a quest for the pot of gold that is measured by filled stadiums and lucrative bowl and television appearances. An NCAA survey revealed that in the past 20 years at least 82 colleges built new basketball arenas, 39 of which had seating facilities for more than 10,000. Similarly, seating capacities in the southeastern (SEC) and Big Eight conferences increased by 15% and 21%, respectively. This means that coaches (and other athletic personnel) frequently experience role strain because of the conflicting and incompatible social demands placed on those occupying these positions. The strain and tension coaches experience are rooted in their limited control of a game, which contrasts sharply with the complete responsibility they bear for a game's outcome. Hence, coaches (and others) frequently resort to unethical practices as a means of circumventing their problems.

Relative deprivation is another principle that may help explain deviant tactics. Relative deprivation is not a scarcity of valued cultural objects (e.g., money or prestige) in absolute terms but in comparison with others. It could be hypothesized that perennial "top" teams are less likely to cheat than those pursuing this elite category, because schools with successful programs attract aspiring athletes without having to offer anything but the potential of continued success.[78]

Others debunk the relative deprivation hypothesis and claim that, for various reasons, some high-powered schools appear to be beyond reach. For example, in July of 1990, shortly after UNLV had won the NCAA basketball championship, it was dealt a penalty for a 1977 rules infraction. The penalty issued prohibited it from 1991 postseason tournament play. This meant it would not be able to defend its national crown. In response, UNLV filed a suit over the 1991 postseason ban naming the NCAA as a defendant. The suit was structured in such a way that if the NCAA accepted one of the four alternative penalties, it would rescind the lawsuit. The NCAA changed the penalty banning the team from 1992 postseason play and thereby permitted the school to defend, albeit unsuccessfully, its basketball title.

A second rationale for successful athletics is a social rather than an economic one. Prestige is a social consideration with economic ramifications. Prestige refers to the public's image of a university, the university's relation with its alumni, and its ability to make dollars. It is believed that the ability to generate funds is linked to how well the team fares on the gridiron, in the fieldhouse, or on the rink (see Vignette 10.1 for a different view). In brief, big-time athletic programs are a business regardless of claims to the contrary. As support for this allegation, consider the following statement by Don Canham,[79] the former successful athletic director at the University of Michigan: "My job is poorly described by the term 'athletic director.' What I am is a sports promoter. . . . I promote our sports program . . . into the black or I'm out of a job. . . ." Bo Schembechler, the former football mentor at Michigan, said: "Don (Canham) gave me two orders. One, produce a winner and two, fill the stadium. I figure if I do the first, the second will happen automatically."[80] Finally, Tufts University head football coach is quoted as saying that "big-time football has become a business. It contains all aspects of the professional game except that the players are not paid."[81]

Manifest and Latent Consequences of Economic Success and Social Prestige

It is virtually axiomatic that financial success is contingent on winning—not guaranteed, but necessary. The question then becomes, What can be done to enhance victory? The logistics of recruitment is a good place to begin; it is also a niche where abuse has been widespread.

How valuable is a single recruit to a school's program? This is a difficult question to answer, but consider that the University of Oklahoma, before the arrival of Wayman Tisdale—three-time All-American and member of the U.S. gold-medal basketball team—the school grossed $285,000 in ticket sales and averaged 7,466 in attendance per game. In Tisdale's last season as a Sooner hoopster, ticket sales soared to $762,000 and average attendance to 11,510 (in an arena with a maximum seating capacity of 10,800). Further, this dollar figure indicates nothing of the social (prestige) capital a "Mr. T." brings to the school.

Recruitment Infractions. Larry Klein worked eight years in the NCAA Enforcement Department, and during that period, sixty-two colleges and universities, less than 10% of the total, were caught breaking its rules.[82] See Vignette 10.4 for a case study of the University of Illinois. The rule most often violated was the one regarding recruiting. This rule stipulates that recruits cannot be offered anything more than a scholarship before and after their matriculation. NCAA regulations also stipulate that a male college athlete may receive a grant-in-aid (i.e., the official name for a scholarship) in the form of books, tuition, board, and room.[83] NCAA Executive Director Richard Schultz insists that "99 percent of everything that is going on in intercollegiate athletics today is exceptionally positive."[84] The truth is that 10% to 20% of Division I athletic programs are in trouble with the NCAA's enforcement office at any given time.

Although recruitment authorities maintain that most is done according to the book, we cannot deny the recent wave of unethical and immoral public disclosures. Recruitment is vital, because talented athletes are the raw ingredients that increase the likelihood of winning programs. Several cases of illicit recruiting tactics have been revealed:[85]

Although some recruiting tactics are not illegal, they are controversial. In 1991 one Big East school (anonymous) described a technique used to woo a prospect. A film of its conference title game was taken, the name of the recruit was superimposed on the back of another player's jersey and then dubbed in an audio play-by-play that roared out the prospect's name each time he made an important basket. Jim Valvano employed a similar tactic when he coached North Carolina State. When a recruit visited the campus, he was taken to an easy chair, the lights would dim, and the championship game would begin. Valvano was shown in a team huddle, and then at the end with seconds remaining in a most crucial situation the coach would point at the camera and shout out the recruit's name while telling him he would hit the winning bucket.

Our cultural **values** admonish deceit, dishonesty, and exploitation. We've all heard the aphorism, "Honesty is the best policy." Is it? Does illicit recruiting pay? Sometimes it seems to, although this should not be construed to mean that a program

☐   **VIGNETTE 10.4**

The Case of the University of Illinois

The University of Illinois basketball program was under NCAA investigation for allegedly offering cash and cars to recruits. It was exonerated of these major accusations but placed on three-year probation for several self-reported infractions: an illegal recruiting contact at a restaurant during a prospect's unofficial visit to the campus, Illinois coaches and a player visiting a prospect more than once in a week, a coach making a recruiting contact off campus before the prospect completed his junior year in high school, misusing complimentary tickets, players given preferential treatment for a car loan, an assistant coach giving a small loan to a player, and so on. In addition to probation, the University was not permitted to recruit off-campus or to pay a prospect to come to campus during 1991, was barred from NCAA tournament play in 1991, was permitted only two scholarship awards in 1991–1992 and 1992–1993, and had to sever ties to the auto dealer where favoritism was apparently shown.

What is of interest is that the university—not the athletic department—paid $.85 million for the legal fees involved! The legal fees for head coach Lou Henson amounted to $41,000; for assistant coach Jimmy Collins, $148,000; and for player Deon Thomas, $147,000. The total tab for legal fees to ward off the school receiving the "death penalty" was about $850,000. Several days later, the *Chicago Tribune* ran an article entitled "Illini Stadium Needs Major Repair Work: Trustees May Face $40 Million Bill." Memorial Stadium, the home of the Fighting Illini, had its inaugural game in 1923. The team still uses the facility, and over the years it has fallen into disrepair and currently requires some major restoration. The anticipated tab for the stadium renovation highlights the costly business of running a major sports program. The potential price tag of $40 million came at a time when the newly elected governor was asking state universities to slash millions of dollars from their operating expenses. The University of Illinois' dilemma is simply a $1.6 million athletic department deficit, an $850,000 tab for legal fees, and a stadium requiring perhaps $40 million worth of repairs and upgrading. Such can be the fate of big-time collegiate sports.

☐

---

cannot be successful by running a "clean ship." For example, Edgar Jones (matriculated at the University of Nevada–Reno without proper academic credentials) was not suspended while litigation proceeded. Southwestern Louisiana was literally put on the map before it "lost" its program. Thompson and North Carolina State won the NCAA tournament in 1974. Centenary's sports information director said that Parish's basketball statistics, while not officially recognized by the NCAA, catapulted the small school into national prominence.

Other questionable recruiting tactics fall under the "dirty tricks" heading, for example, some recruiters have been known to derogate their competitors rather than to glamorize their own academy. The following illustrate such questionable recruiting practices:[86]

• One college is reported to have sent an anonymous letter to the parents of a prospect leaning toward another school. "Do you know that the assistant coach is a homosexual?" it asked.

- An assistant basketball coach at Purdue was censored because he mailed copies of an article criticizing Hoosier coach Bobby Knight for being inhuman and insensitive.
- A Chicago-area stalwart had agreed to sign a tender to an Illinois college on the morning of the national signing day. The coach of another Midwestern college got the prospect first and accused his rival of being schizophrenic. "Do you want your son to play for a madman?" he asked. The prospect changed his mind and signed for the other school the next day.
- A blue-chip basketball player from Kentucky was being recruited by DePaul. Other college recruiters were painting a sinister picture of life on the urban campus. Furthermore, the athlete's father was informed of the grisly details of the dormitory murder of a varsity tennis player by a team manager.

One may suspect that this writer is playing a muckraking role by disclosing the less-than-reputable behavior of higher education athletic personnel. One coach has said, "Sure, there are a lot of rumors that fly around about recruiting and dirty tricks. A lot of people say the whole thing is blown out of proportion. In this business, just an ugly rumor can lose a kid or hurt a program. But the more experience you get in the business, the more you realize that most of the rumors are true."[87]

Deviance in recruiting comes in a variety of forms. Monetary incentives are not the only illegal tactics used for luring athletes to schools. Athletes' transcripts have been altered; parents have been provided with jobs, housing, and money; athletes have been paid for nonexistent or nominal jobs; federal grant monies have been illegally used to subsidize student athletes; clandestine payments have been made; and athletes of marginal academic ability have had substitutes take tests for them. Whether or not these rule violations are deliberate and knowingly perpetrated by athletes or coaches, the fact remains that deviance is widespread and pervasive. Bobby Knight, Indiana University basketball coach, has said "Today's outstanding prospect completing his high school career may be offered all kinds of illegal inducements to attend college . . . clothes, travel, apartments at barely token rents, scholarships for girlfriends, free graduate school, guaranteed sales for gratis tickets, frequently at greatly increased prices."[88]

On the completion (or near-completion) of their college playing days, athletes often confront other hurdles, namely, the sometimes shady negotiations with agents. Professional scouts indicate that this is common among college football players, and one college coach thinks 50% of blue chippers (in basketball) are paid by agents to illegally sign a professional contract before their college careers have terminated. While this practice enhances the athlete's financial status, it clearly violates the NCAA rule that prohibits such transactions until a player's eligibility has ended.

If many players are taking illicit money or other gifts, who is giving them? The NCAA says "representatives of the University's athletic interests." These representatives include boosters' organizations, in addition to head and assistant coaches. Klein has also said, "The system works because every assistant coach, at least in basketball, wants to be a head coach, and he usually reaches his goal after making his boss look good."[89]

There is evidence that alumni and booster's clubs are a mixed blessing. Booster clubs have been responsible for many positive features of athletic programs, such as raising money for athletic scholarships, helping to pay for new or renovated sport complexes, and underwriting some of the inflationary costs of running a sport program. On the other hand, boosters are responsible for some questionable practices. Was it ethical for the University of Colorado's booster organization, the Flatirons Club, to solicit $200,000 so the school could hire Chuck Fairbanks to coach the football team? Fairbanks's salary was not $200,000; it was the cash needed for an out-of-court settlement with the New England Patriots, the professional team with whom he had broken his contract. This affair prompted a political science professor at the Big Eight school to say: "We have a professional football team here which bills itself as amateur—a professional team owned by several large contributors, administered on the campus of the University of Colorado."[90]

While coaches and overly zealous alumni and boosters have frequently been charged in recruiting violations, there has emerged still another perpetrator. Individuals called *scouts,* who are not connected with any school, have been known to roam the playgrounds and gymnasiums of major metropolitan areas seeking talented athletes to exploit. These self-appointed scouts contact coaches and athletic departments and offer to bring a particular athlete to the school for a fee. One former coach admitted that some scouts want $1,000 per inch for any player over six feet eight inches.[91]

Educational Duplicity.   Concerns over the seamier side of student athletes' academic preparation and progress led to the institutionalization of the controversial *Proposition 48.* Beginning in 1986, Proposition 48 required a 2.0 GPA in a core curriculum (math, English, social and natural sciences) of eleven courses and a minimum 700 SAT or 18 ACT score for college entry on an athletic scholarship. Individuals who met only one of these criteria were termed "partial qualifiers" and could accept an athletic scholarship but were banned from playing (for a minimum of one year) in order to improve their grades. The aim was to restore academic integrity to higher education by having athletes better prepared for college work and to enhance the chances for obtaining a college degree.

Although the purpose here is not to assess the validity of the standardized tests, a few comments help put the requirements into perspective. The national average is 20.6 on the ACT and 900 on the SAT. Under Proposition 48, the ACT and SAT minimums are 18 and 700, respectively. "Putting the SAT numbers in perspective, a student would need 14 of 85 correct on the verbal test, 17 of 60 in math to score 700." Turning to the ACT, a score of 18 would land the test taking individual at the 31st percentile (meaning that 69% of the test takers score above that cutoff). Among blacks who take core courses, the mean ACT score is 18.2. Among other minority groups members who take core courses, the mean ACT scores are 19.9 for American Indians and Mexicans, 20.9 for Puerto Ricans, and 22.8 for Asian Americans. On the verbal dimension of the SAT, blacks average 352, whites 442; on the math dimension blacks average 385, and whites 491. Finally, the average composite score for whites on the SAT is 925–930; for blacks between 710–715. These statistics become particularly important when considering the criticisms directed against these test standards.

What effect has Proposition 48 had? The data appear to indicate that the rate of athletes falling victim to Proposition 48 has *not* been reduced, although there appears to be increased awareness and concern from more persons. In 1989–1990, 85% of the proposition's casualties failed to meet the standardized test standard. This figure compares to 78%, 80%, and 82%, who failed to meet this standard in 1988–1989, 1987–1988, and 1986–1987, respectively. Although these figures reveal that the casualty rate hasn't changed, documentation indicates that the average SAT scores for blacks on the verbal and math test have increased 20 and 31 points, respectively, since 1976 (during the same time period, white scores declined by 9 points in the verbal and 2 points in math). Hence, we have somewhat of a mixed picture insofar as the test results are concerned.

On the heels of Proposition 48 came *Proposition 42* (submitted in 1988). Proposition 42 was even more stringent and stated that incoming freshmen must have a 2.0 GPA in a core curriculum *plus* a minimum score on the entrance tests to *qualify* for an athletic scholarship. The upshot is that *both* criteria must be met before a scholarship could be received. Athletes failing to meet both requirements would have to finance the first year of college themselves and would be denied one year of eligibility. Given that two thirds of the partial qualifiers are black and that blacks typically fail to meet the standardized test score requirement, it is obvious who will suffer most under this proposal. Sociologically, the concepts of manifest and latent functions are applicable. The manifest purpose of these propositions is to enhance the likelihood that athletes will be prepared for college and graduation. The latent function is that the burden falls disproportionately on black athletes.

The prime motivation of many student athletes at major universities may be to maintain eligibility. Grades, academic learning, social and cultural experiences, and progress toward a degree often become secondary considerations. It is on this point that there is some legitimacy to the allegation that athletes are active and/or passive victims of exploitation. Consider Bernard Madison, a basketball recruit at Montana State University majoring in business administration and apparently making progress toward a degree by taking basketball fundamentals and techniques, physical conditioning, wrestling theory, general biology (health), and safety with hand power tools.[92] Some athletes have even taken their grievances to court. A contingent of former basketball players at California State University, Los Angeles, filed a lawsuit charging that the school failed to provide meaningful education and had routed them into worthless physical education courses to keep them academically eligible. The ex-basketball players confessed that proxies were paid to take their entrance exams and that they had received credit for phantom courses. Mark Hall (see Chapter 6) also took his university to court and won.

Why do athletes allow themselves to be duped? One insidious myth that many of them believe is that their college apprenticeship will catapult them into a lucrative professional career. The media are replete with inflationary, and sometimes exaggerated, salary figures. Even some sport departments' press releases proudly proclaim their ability to promote players to the professional ranks. The University of Miami produced a recruiting brochure entitled "A Pipeline to the Pros," which featured former Hurricane athletes who had made it professionally. What are the odds of making the big time? Look at football first. Statistics compiled by the National Federation of State High School Associations indicate that about one million play the sport. According to the NCAA, about 41,551 played college football (4.6% of the high school players). Approximately 330 college draft choices go to professional football camps and 150 make team rosters. Statistically, football careers average around five years. Let us turn to basketball. About 600,000 high schoolers play basketball; this is reduced to 14,683 at college (2.4% of the high school basketball players). The professional basketball teams draft approximately 230 college players; 50 make the team. The average career in basketball is approximately five years.[93] It does not take a statistician to realize that the odds of making the big time are miniscule and that the attrition rate is staggering. Nevertheless, the dream of the professional pot of gold at the end of the college and high school rainbow persists.

Why do coaches engage in behavior they probably know is illegal, unacceptable, and exploitative? It seems that the relentless pursuit of victory by any means is used to enhance success. Basketball coach Tates Locke confessed: "I didn't do it [cheat] because the Joneses were doing it. I did it because I wanted to win. There were a tremendous number of people doing it then. And there are more now."[94]

One of the sobering and perplexing facts about the corruption plaguing college sports is that it has become almost normative (i.e., statistically typically). A decade or two ago, when practices within the sports establishment were beginning to be seriously questioned, athletes portrayed themselves as the victims of a pernicious system. Today, there are youngsters who openly admit to taking inducements that have been offered, but their gripe is that they are not getting their fair share of the enticements. Frank Lollino, former basketball coach at Chicago's Westinghouse High School, saw dozens of athletes make the transition to major college ranks.[95] When he was still permitting recruiters to attend practices, he recalled the following incident. Mark Aguire and Eddie Johnson were teammates on the squad. A recruiter pulled ten crisp thousand-dollar bills from his wallet and said that if Lollino brought him Eddie Johnson he could count on another $15,000!

❑ REFORMING THE COLLEGE SYSTEM

Who blows the whistle?[96] Reports of irregularities in the conduct of athletic programs are occasionally made by disgruntled coaches, recruits, players, alumni, and fans. Sometimes, the allegations are little more than vindictive charges made by parties seeking retribution or revenge. However, when the incidents seem to be valid, the NCAA sends the school a letter of official inquiry (OI) itemizing the charges and commences a formal investigation. More than a year often elapses before the NCAA delivers a verdict. One reason for the delay is that the NCAA currently has a small investigatory staff to police hundreds of colleges.

In 1986 Jan Kemp, a professor at the University of Georgia (UGA), blew the whistle on her school. Kemp, a true-blue Bulldog fan (she never missed a home football game from 1967 to 1982) legally protested (and won) the preferential treatment of athletes in the school's remedial studies program in which she taught. According to Kemp's testimony, nine football players who failed to pass UGA remedial studies courses were, nevertheless, transferred to the regular university curriculum to make them eligible for the 1982 Sugar Bowl. A federal jury awarded her $2.57 million for damages, suffering, and back pay. This verdict provides, it seems, a partial vindication for those desiring to raise the academic standards for college athletes.

Because the task is immense and the available resources (i.e., time, money, and personnel) are limited, it is probably more reasonable to assume that scandalous practices will have to be uncovered by the individual colleges rather than the NCAA investigation team. University personnel will have to become better sleuths if the corruption in intercollegiate athletics is to be significantly curtailed. At many schools, athletic program administrators have enjoyed nearly absolute autonomy, and this "free rein" atmosphere is conducive to questionable and unethical practices. Robert Atwell, vice president of the American Council on Education, said, "Athletics should be structured and financed like any other program at a university instead of receiving special treatment."[97] Penn State's football coach, Joe Paterno, offers this insightful sociologically relevant observation: "The excesses in sports are a microcosm of society. When society stops cheating, then we can expect the same of intercollegiate athletics."[98]

The evidence cited suggests a need for revamping the operative methods of intercollegiate sport. We may be talking about a small minority of institutions of higher education. Nevertheless, because these illegal tactics are being employed, some changes are necessary if athletic programs are to be run properly. Any reform effort will encounter an array of sticky political, financial, traditional, and administrative obstacles.

Shughart advocates three suggestions for resolving some of the issues plaguing college sports:[99]

1. Create degree programs in football and basketball. At many universities there are degree programs in other vocational areas—art, music, drama, industrial arts, and so on. Shughart rhetorically asks: "Why should academic credit be given for practicing the violin, but not for practicing a three-point shot?"
2. Extend the scholarship limit by two years. He argues that the inordinate time demands on athletes in particular sports, both in and out-of-season, may legitimately call for a time extension to their scholarship. The athlete, according to this suggestion, would still have four years of eligibility but an additional two years to complete schooling while on scholarship.
3. Allow the marketplace to determine the compensation for the athletes. Athletes in football and basketball can generate large revenues benefiting the school they represent. Because the NCAA sets guidelines for compensation, the rules are most restricting. He suggests that the athletes receive some of the monies their toil produces for the institution and believes this will counteract the temptation to accept illegal inducements.

In January 1991 the NCAA, under some pressure from college presidents, made several reforms bearing on athletes' rights, academic standards, and economics. A summary of key reforms included the following:

1. *Athletes' rights.* By August 1, 1996, athletic dorms are to be abolished. The athlete's work week is to be reduced to twenty hours, and the lengths of sport seasons and number of games reduced in many sports.
2. *Academics.* Athletes entering their fourth year must have completed at least 50% of their degree requirements. Division I schools are required to offer counseling and tutoring to recruited athletes.

3. *Economics.* There is to be a 10% reduction in the number of scholarships in men's and women's sports, staff reductions in all sports, cutbacks in the use of training tables, and a reduction in the number of paid visits for prospects.

Until the early 1970s, schools were not bound by scholarship restrictions. It was not uncommon, then, for major powers to stockpile blue-chip athletes. For example, in 1972, Pittsburgh brought in eighty-one freshmen, and one of them was Tony Dorsett. In the past several years, schools have operated under the "ninety-five-rule." Trimming five scholarships, on the surface, doesn't seem too consequential. However, consider that each year 100 players who normally would go to top teams now end up at some of the other schools. As an aside, scholarship limitations have been hypothesized for the increasing parity in college football.

In the summer of 1985, a consortium of schools, spearheaded by Boston's North-eastern University, launched an innovative scholastic program to abet former college athletes who failed to receive their degrees. Some eleven universities spanning from the East to the West Coast now offer a tuition-free education to scholarship athletes who have not graduated. As *Newsweek* aptly reported:

> That unfinished academic business underlies much of the integrity crisis in college sports. Potential for abuse can be limited when athletes are admitted and educated as students, when responsible adults place humane values above competitive pressures and when institutions do not succumb to a greedy pursuit of sport-generated dollars. It can be done; some schools still manage to play it straight— and win. But it seems to be getting harder all the time.[100]

The sociological import of this discussion can be summarized as follows. Deviance, individual and organizational, exists when parties attempt to achieve culturally valued goals and when the means for such achievement are diversified. Sometimes legitimate means will be employed; other times innovative schemes will be used. When the means chosen for goal achievement fall outside the culturally prescribed avenues, the sociological term *deviance* is applicable.

❏ INTERSCHOLASTIC ATHLETICS

The catalyst for interscholastic sports was athletic programs in the colleges. Intercollegiate sports programs began to flourish during the early part of this century and provided models for their high school counterparts. Cozens and Stumpf[101] report that school officials encouraged such extracurricular activities for two essential reasons: (a) to upgrade the physical fitness of American youth, because large numbers of high school students were found to be poorly conditioned when administered physical exams during World War I, and (b) educators believed that sports provided a medium through which positive traits (e.g., perseverance, esprit de corps, etc.) could be cultivated (see discussion of the dominant American sport creed, Chapter 3). Today, interscholastic sports are an important component of high school education. One author spoke to a high school principal who told him that he would probably receive more flak from the community by eliminating the sports program than by abolishing the English Department. While this personal experience may be somewhat atypical, it may not be too much of an exaggeration.[102]

What are the supposed consequences of interscholastic sport programs? On the one hand, they have been considered meaningful adjuncts and complements to traditional instruction; on the other, they have been criticized for being unnecessarily disruptive and misdirected. Coakley, Kniker, Schafer, and Armer[103] have summarized the traditional arguments for and against interscholastic sport programs. The *pro* arguments include the following:

1. Participation in sport and in other extracurricular activities increases students' interest in school in general and scholastic affairs in particular.
2. Sport prepares participants via anticipatory socialization to fill important positions in American society.
3. Sport stimulates interest in kinetic activities among the student body.
4. Sport generates school esprit de corps and cohesiveness, which makes the school a viable and meaningful social organization.
5. Sport evokes school support from teachers, administrators, parents, alumni, and the community.

The *con* arguments include the following:

1. Sport distracts attention from academic pursuits.
2. Sport focuses athletes on values that may no longer be functional in American society.
3. Sport relegates most students to a spectator rather than a participant role.
4. Sport creates an anti-intellectual spirit among students that is contrary to the manifest educational mission of the school.
5. Sport deprives academic programs of resources, facilities, personnel, and community awareness and support.

While both sides of the argument lack extensive empirical support, the pro position tends to hold sway over the con, certainly in terms of public sentiment. Because high school athletic programs are promoted or criticized on the basis of their consequences, the following discussion considers research regarding the consequences of interscholastic sport programs for the participants.

Popularity of Athletes and Nonathletes in Scholastic Settings

Coleman's work on adolescent society reached one bold sport conclusion: Athletic participation in high school was valued more than scholarship.[104] He reached this finding after studying ten Midwestern high schools of varying sizes, locations, and socioeconomic compositions during 1957 and 1958. This research, which has been replicated on several occasions (Vignette 10.5), is sufficiently significant that an analysis of his methodology is warranted. Coleman wished to determine why and with what effects this outcome was produced.

Coleman asked students at the high school to name the best student and the best athlete. He found that stellar athletes were easier to identify than good students. Students were queried as to whether they would prefer to be remembered as a brilliant student or a star athlete. Most preferred star athlete. Students were also asked to name members of the leading crowd, and they pegged participants in scholastic sports, particularly basketball and football, as the leading clique. When the students were

☐ VIGNETTE 10.5

The Importance of Sports to Male and Female High School Students

Girls rate intellect high; boys favor athletic ability.

Not many high school girls want to be remembered as athletic stars, but such a distinction is more important to boys, according to research.

Joel Thirer questioned 600 high school students for the study.

"Female athleticism has quite a way to go insofar as social acceptability to adolescent boys and girls," Thirer says.

Most girls in his study—43 percent—said they want to be remembered as "a brilliant student." Next down the list for girls was being remembered as "most popular," with 29 percent choosing that. And last, for 18 percent of the girls, was being remembered as an "athletic star."

The priorities were different for boys in Thirer and Wright's study. The greatest number—37 percent—picked "athletic star," 34 percent picked "brilliant student," and last, 29 percent chose "most popular."

Similar studies were conducted by other researchers in 1961 and 1976, showing then, also, boys valuing a reputation as an athlete much more than girls did. A difference, however, is that boys in the 1980s study rated their intellectual reputation more highly than they did in the '70s study.

Thirer and Wright looked at the same issue from another angle by asking both boys and girls "What is the basis for female adolescent popularity?"

The top answer from both groups was "being in the leading crowd." Boys ranked "leader in activities" next, and "being a cheerleader" third. Girls put "high grades, honor roll" second, and "coming from the right family" third.

"Being an athlete" was ranked fifth by the boys and fourth by the girls for what makes girls popular.

Thirer says the results apply to the issue of overemphasizing women's interscholastic sports, which he says serves "the elite few," and deemphasizing or eliminating physical education, which serves "the many."

Schools included in the survey are in Chicago; Carbondale; Jeffersonville, Ind.; Buckner and Morganfield, both in Kentucky; Indiana, Pa.: Worcester, N.Y.; and Seattle, Wash.

SOURCE: Mike Matulis, "Women's Sports Efforts Don't Mean Popularity," *The Pantagraph* (8 December 1985), p. A3. Courtesy of *The Pantagraph*.

☐

---

asked the criteria necessary to be a member of the leading crowd, the rank order of characteristics was personality, good reputation, athletic ability, good looks and success with girls, and brains and good grades. Finally, students were asked who they would like to be like. Not surprisingly, the athletes outdistanced the scholars.

Why are athletes accorded this social status? Coleman attributed it to the value system of the school and the community. Parents, teachers, peers, public relation and media personnel, and community-opinion leaders channeled males into sports through social rewards and reinforcements, so the social significance of sports to the high schools led to cohesion, esprit de corps, and identification. In summary, Coleman discovered that sports were of utmost importance in high schools, perhaps at the expense of scholarly pursuits. He contended that adolescents formed a subculture, a social system with distinct values and somewhat contradictory to the larger society and to the manifest goals of formal education.

Eitzen replicated Coleman's investigation fifteen years later.[105] Eitzen surveyed students at fourteen schools with different enrollments located in communities of varying populations. In regard to the question, "How would you like to be remembered?" Coleman had discovered 31%, 44%, and 25%, wishing to be remembered as a brilliant student, athletic star, and the most popular student, respectively. Eitzen found 25%, 45%, and 30%, respectively, indicating the same. Hence, the importance of athletic savvy appeared to persist over the interlude. Similarly, Eitzen found that being an athlete played a major role in being perceived as popular among one's fellow students. The original Coleman inquiry was replicated again in 1985, and the results were similar to those in Vignette 10.5.

Interscholastic Sports Participation and College Plans

Rehberg and Schafer explored the relationship between participation in interscholastic sports and college plans.[106] They sampled 785 male seniors from six urban Pennsylvania high schools. The dependent variable, the factor they were interested in studying, was educational expectations operationalized by "Do you or do you not expect to enroll in a four-year college?" Responses were trichotomized into (a) yes, (b) no, and (c) no response. The independent variable, the factor presumably accounting for variation in the dependent variable, was dichotomized into (a) athletic participation and (b) no athletic participation. Overall, 62% of the athletes and 45% of the nonathletes answered affirmatively to the query. The researchers then elaborated this relationship by asking, "Is this relationship causal or spurious?"[107] Three control variables—factors having a potential mediating effect on the original two—were introduced into the analysis. These control variables were (a) social status (b) academic performance, and (c) parental educational encouragement. For both athletes and nonathletes with high social status, grades, and parental encouragement Rehberg and Schafer found little difference in educational expectations. However, they did find an interaction effect among those in the low categories of the control variables. Athletes low in status, performance, and encouragement, had loftier collegiate expectations than nonathletes with those same characteristics. The results can be diagrammed as follows:

High status High GPA High encouragement	} For both athlete and nonathlete	→	High educational expectations
Low status Low GPA Low encouragement	} Athlete	→	High educational expectations
	Nonathlete	→	Low educational expectations

Rehberg and Schafer concluded:

Our data have shown that a greater proportion of athletes than nonathletes expect to enroll in a four-year college, even when the potentially confounding variables of status, academic performance, and parental encouragement are controlled. This relationship is especially marked among boys not otherwise disposed toward college, that is, those from working class homes, those in the lower half of their graduating class, and those with low parental encouragement to go to college.[108]

Before becoming overly optimistic about Rehberg and Schafer's conclusions, several qualifications are in order. Of the athletes sampled, only 16% were low in status, GPA, and encouragement; the remaining 84% had one or more characteristics favorably predisposing them to attend college. Coakley offered the following sobering comment:

> If we can estimate that about 30% of the males in any given high school participate in the interscholastic sport program, it is reasonable to use the Rehberg and Schafer study to conclude that sport participation has a significant impact on the educational aspirations of about 5% of the males in the student body and 2.5% of the total students in the high school. In other words, if we were talking about a school of 2200 students, 1000 of whom were males, there would be about 300 (at the very most) participants in the interscholastic sport program. Of these 300, only 16% or . . . 48 . . . students would have mediocre academic records and would come from families offering little academic encouragement. Those 50 students, constituting only 5% of the total students, are the ones most likely to experience increases in aspirations apparently resulting from sport participation.[109]

Spreitzer and Pugh discovered an intriguing sociological twist to the connection between athletic participation and educational aspirations.[110] Data they collected from 704 seniors in thirteen Connecticut high schools revealed that the positive correlation between athletic participation and postgraduation educational plans could not be accounted for by socioeconomic status, parental academic encouragement, grades, or intelligence. Hence, athletic participation appeared to have real positive effects. The significant mediating variables (between athletic participation and educational expectation) were the school "value climate" (wherein athletic achievement was more highly valued than scholarship) and perceived peer status (whereby the perception of high peer status facilitated and created a desire for continued recognition, perhaps through college attendance). In other words, a strong relationship between athletic participation and educational aspirations existed only in those schools emphasizing athletics as a source of rewards. In schools where athletics were not held in high regard, there was no such correspondence. In schools emphasizing scholarly versus athletic excellence, the relationship between athletic participation and educational aspirations was negligible.

Schafer and Armer compared the GPAs of senior high athletes with a matched sample of nonathletes in two Midwestern high schools.[111] Athletes who participated in either football or basketball, and for three or more years, had better academic records than nonathletes. A provocative result of their research was that sport participation did not guarantee academic success. Instead, it appeared to depend, in part, on the number of years played and the sport participated in.

In a comparative study of Canadian and American high school athletes, Jerome and Phillips discovered that Canadian participants were generally not accorded the same degree of prestige as American athletes.[112] Moreover, neither the academic achievement nor the goals of Canadian athletes were especially positive; in fact, the athletes had poorer academic records than nonathletes. Jerome and Phillips concluded: "In the absence of a differential reward structure favoring athletics, one cannot expect athletes, as a group, to excel in their school work to a greater degree than other students."

The following differences between high school athletes and nonathletes were advanced by Phillips and Schafer:[113]

1. Athletes attain slightly better grades and are more likely to desire and to obtain more education than nonathletes. This seems especially pronounced for athletes from blue-collar families.

2. A modicum of evidence suggests that athletes are less likely to become delinquent than nonathletes (the **deterrence hypothesis**). Research has not established whether this directly results from sport participation or from self-selection factors (e.g., individuals with delinquent tendencies may not go out for sports and, conversely, individuals with nondelinquent tendencies may go out for athletics) or a combination.

3. Athletes raised in blue-collar families are more prone to upward mobility than nonathletes from the same occupational category.

Why these differences exist has not been definitively established, but the differences may stem from several factors. For one, athletes often receive special attention and assistance from teachers and administrators, and these may boost their incentives for scholastic success. When this possibility is combined with mandatory minimum GPA requirements, one can logically speculate why grades may be slightly higher for athletes. Another reasonable explanation is that the positive habits cultivated in the sports realm (e.g., hard work, discipline, and perseverance) may transfer into academic circles. Finally, the self-selection factor must be considered. Perhaps conforming, talented, and ambitious persons engage in school sports, whereas those lacking these traits do not. Although these hypotheses are not exhaustive, they must be entertained because the relationship between sport participation and academic achievement is not simplistic.

Studies of the relationship between athletic participation and academic achievement fail to support a causal connection between the two variables.[114] Stevenson, among others, demonstrated that the differences between athletes and nonathletes are due to their initial dissimilarity (self-selection factors) rather than to the positive influence of sport socialization.[115]

When these data are synthesized to form a composite picture of the consequences of athletic participation, they appear to support the conclusion that only when athletes are held in high esteem are there positive academic aspiration and achievement effects. Moreover, the available evidence suggests that the United States, perhaps more than other countries such as Canada and England, bestows greater recognition on athletes and athletics. This prestige is likely to vary from nation to nation as well as from school to school and sport to sport.

❏ SUMMARY

College sport programs have been both chastized and glamorized, but the pro arguments for these programs tend to hold sway. Graduation rates for intercollegiate athletes are highly variable, although one national survey discovered that the graduation rate of college athletes is higher than that of college nonathletes. Academic achievement also varies. The validity of indices of academic achievement (i.e., grade-point averages and graduation rates) must be carefully assessed. Some evidence suggests that athletes earn more than nonathletes later in life. Conceptual and empirical concerns regarding the alleged exploitation of college athletes were given special consideration.

High school athletics, as with collegiate sport programs, has both pro and con positions. The empirical literature suggests that athletes frequently occupy the limelight, and many students prefer to be remembered as star jocks. Comparisons of the future educational plans of athletes and nonathletes have found loftier ambitions for the athletes, particularly those from less predisposing backgrounds. Some researchers found that athletes receive slightly higher grades and are more likely to aspire to obtain higher education than nonathletes, are less likely to become delinquent, and athletes from blue-collar backgrounds are likely to be upwardly mobile.

☐ KEY CONCEPTS

Collegiate Sport

Interscholastic Sport

Graduation Rates for Athletes

Exploitation

Values

Deterrence Hypothesis

☐ ENDNOTES

1. DONALD CHU, "The American Conception of Higher Education and the Formal Incorporation of Intercollegiate Sport," *Sport Sociology: Contemporary Themes* eds. A. Yiannakis, T.D. McIntyre, M.J. Melnick, & D.P. Hart (Dubuque, IA: Kendall/Hunt, 1987), pp. 146–156.

2. JOHN W. LOY, BARRY D. MCPHERSON, & GERALD KENYON, *Sport and Social Systems: A Guide to the Analysis, Problems, and Literature* (Reading, MA: Addison-Wesley, 1978), p. 258.

3. ELDON E. SNYDER & ELMER A. SPREITZER, *Social Aspects of Sport* (Englewood Cliffs, NJ: Prentice-Hall, 1989).

4. JAY J. COAKLEY, *Sport in Society: Issues and Controversies* (St. Louis: C.V. Mosby, 1990), pp. 328–329.

5. *Ibid.,* p. 139. Reprinted with permission.

6. STEPHEN K. FIGLER, *Sport and Play in American Life* (Philadelphia: W.B. Saunders, 1981), p. 128.

7. JAMES A. MICHENER, *Sports in America* (New York: Random House, 1976), p. 196.

8. JAY J. COAKLEY, *Sport in Society* (St. Louis: C.V. Mosby, 1978), p. 179.

9. *Op. cit.,*[7] p. 189.

10. JANICE KAPLAN, "What Price Victory?" *Nutshell* (August 1978), p. 57.

11. DOUGLAS LEDERMAN, quoted in *The Chronicle of Higher Education,* (13 January 1988).

12. GENE A. BUDIG, "Sports and Finances," unpublished manuscript, Illinois State University, 1972.

13. *Op. cit.,*[10] p. 57.

14. Illinois State University Report, "Cost of Athletic Program Minimal, Regent's Staff Concludes" (22 October 1982), p. 1.

15. *Op. cit.,*[8] p. 179.

16. MITCHELL RAIBORN, quoted in *The Chronicle of Higher Education* (28 November 1990), p. A38.

17. A. PADILLA, "On the Economics of Intercollegiate Athletic Programs." Paper prepared for the Amateur Athletic Foundation of Los Angeles and the Presidents' Commission of the NCAA, 1987.

18. "Student Fee Fair—Or a Hidden Tax," *Chi-

cago *Tribune* (4 March 1991), Section 3, p. 6. NEIL D. ISSACS, "The Losers in College Sports: Student-Athletes Are Pushed Aside by Hucksterism," *The Washington Post* (16 October 1977), p. Cl.

19. *Op. cit.,*[7] p. 216.

20. PAUL STROHM, "The Commercialization of College Sport," *Academe* (July–August 1987), p. 11.

21. GEORGE H. SAGE, "The Collegiate Dilemma of Sport and Leisure: A Sociological Perspective," *Sport in Contemporary Society* ed. D.S. Eitzen (New York: St. Martin's, 1979), pp. 190, 192.

22. STEVEN BAUMANN & KEITH HENSCHEN, "A Cross-Validation Study of Selected Performance Measures in Predicting Academic Success Among Collegiate Athletes," *Sociology of Sport Journal* 3, no. 4 (1986), pp. 366–371.

23. *The Chicago Tribune* (12 February 1991).

24. PETER ADLER & PATRICIA ADLER, "From Idealism to Pragmatic Detachment," *Sociology of Education,* 58 (October 1985), pp. 241–250.

25. BARBARA B. MEYER, "From Idealism to Actualization: The Academic Performance of Female Collegiate Athletes," *Sociology of Sport Journal* 7, no. 1 (1990), pp. 44–57.

26. JOHN J. SAGE, "Adolescent Values and the Non-participating College Athlete." Paper presented at the Southern Section of CAHPER Conference, San Fernando Valley State College, Los Angeles, 1967.

27. *Summary Results From the 1987–88 National Study of Intercollegiate Athletes,* American Institutes for Research (Washington, DC, 1988).

28. *Studies of Intercollegiate Athletics* (Washington, DC: American Institutes for Research, Center for Study of Athletes, 1988).

29. *USA Today* (3 January 1991), p. 8c.

30. Several books report that athletic preparation is so demanding of time and energy that it severely limits study time. Under such circumstances, maintaining the minimum average required for athletic eligibility would seem to be the basic academic orientation. See John Underwood, "Three-Part Series on the Desperate Coach," *Sports Illustrated* 36 (25 August 1969, 1 September 1969, 8 September 1969). Dave Meggyesy, *Out of Their League* (Berkeley, CA: Ramparts Press, 1971). Jack

Scott, *The Athletic Revolution* (New York: The Free Press, 1971). Gary Shaw, *Meat on the Hoof* (New York: St. Martin's Press, 1972).

31. HARRY EDWARDS, *Sociology of Sport* (Homewood, IL: Dorsey Press, 1973), pp. 176–178.

32. *Op. cit.,*[4]

33. ALLEN L. SACK, "Big Time College Football: Whose Free Ride?" *Sport Sociology: Contemporary Themes* (Dubuque, IA: Kendall-Hunt Publishing, 1979), pp. 96–100.

34. GENE UPSHAW, "Working Your Way through College on an Athletic Grant in Aid." Published by Center for Athletes' Rights and Education, Bronx, NY, no date.

35. *Op. cit.*[4]

36. *Ibid.*

37. GEORGE H. SAGE, *Power and Ideology in American Sport* (Champaign, IL: Human Kinetics, 1990), p. 175.

38. ERVING GOFFMAN, *The Presentation of Self in Everyday Life* (Philadelphia: W.B. Saunders, 1959).

39. *Op. cit.,*[6] p. 118.

40. *Op. cit.,*[7] p. 203.

41. RICHARD LAPCHICK, *Broken Promises* (New York: St. Martin's/Marek, 1984), p. 167.

42. HARRY EDWARDS, "Educating Black Athletes," *Current* (November 1983), pp. 25–36.

43. *Op. cit.,*[7]

44. WILBERT M. LEONARD, II, "The Sports Experience of the Black College Athlete: Exploitation in the Academy," *International Review for the Sociology of Sport* 21, no. 1 (1986), pp. 35–49.

45. D. STANLEY EITZEN & GEORGE H. SAGE, *Sociology of American Sport* (Dubuque, IA: William C. Brown, 1982), p. 131.

46. WILBERT M. LEONARD, II, "Exploitation in Collegiate Sport: The Views of Basketball Players in NCAA Divisions I, II, and III," *Journal of Sport Behavior* 9, no. 1 (1986), pp. 11–30.

47. STEVE OWENS, "Intercollegiate Athletics," *Sport* (November 1969), p. 94.

48. *Op. cit.,*[6] p. 118.

49. GEORGE H. HANFORD, "Commercialism, Entertainment, and Ethics in College Sports," *Sport in Contemporary Society,* ed. D.S. Eitzen (New York: St. Martin's, 1979), p. 187.

50. *Op. cit.,*[49] pp. 187–188.

51. *Op. cit.,*[4] p. 144.

52. J.H. Harrison, "Intercollegiate Football Participation and Academic Achievement." Paper presented at the Southwestern Sociological Association Meetings, Dallas, 1976.
P.F. Kluge, "Playing in a Different Court," *New West* 4, no. 24 (1979), pp. 65–75.
Dave Meggyesy, *Out of Their League* (Berkeley: Ramparts Press, 1971).
Jack Scott, *The Athletic Revolution* (New York: Macmillan, 1971).
Gary Shaw, *Meat on the Hoof* (New York: St. Martin's Press, 1972).
Charles Tolbert, "The Black Athlete in the Southwest Conference: A Study of Institutional Racism," unpublished doctoral dissertation, Baylor University, Waco, TX, 1975.
John Underwood, "Student-Athletes: The Sham, the Shame," *Sports Illustrated* 52, no. 21 (1980) pp. 36–72.

53. D. Stanley Eitzen, "Sport in Educational Setting," *Sport in Contemporary Society,* ed. D.S. Eitzen (New York: St. Martin's, 1979), pp. 169–172.

54. *Op. cit.,*[4] pp. 142–143.

55. *Op. cit.,*[49] pp. 184–185.

56. David Krech, Richard S. Crutchfield, & Egerton L. Ballachey, *Individual in Society* (New York: McGraw-Hill, 1962), p. 248.

57. Allen L. Sack, "The Underground Economy of College Football," *Sociology of Sport Journal* 8, no. 1 (1991), pp. 1–17.

58. Norman K. Denzin, *The Research Act* (New York: McGraw-Hill, 1978).

59. *Op. cit.,*[4] p. 149.

60. Bernie Parrish, *They Call It a Game* (Berkeley: Ramparts Press, 1971), p. 293.

61. R.T. McKenzie, quoted in D. Stanley Eitzen, ed., *Sport in Contemporary Society* (New York: St. Martin's, 1979), pp. 188–189.

62. Alexander Liazos, "The Poverty of the Sociology of Deviance: Nuts, Sluts, and Perverts," *Social Problems* 20, 1972, pp. 103–120.

63. Howard J. Savage, *American College Athletics* (New York: The Carnegie Foundation, 1929).

64. Min S. Yee & Donald K. Wright, *The Sports Book* (New York: Holt, Rinehart, & Winston, 1975), pp. 101–103.

65. "College Recruiting," *The Blue Chips* (Oklahoma City, OK: Football Enterprises, 1981), 3, no. 1, p. 106.

66. *Ibid.*

67. "It's Cleanup Time for College Sports," *US News and World Report* (1 July 1985), pp. 62–64.

68. "Out of Bounds," *Newsweek on Campus* (September 1985), pp. 8–14.

69. "The Shame of College Sports," *Newsweek* (22 September 1980), pp. 54–55, 57–59.

70. John Underwood, "Foul Play in College Sports," *Sports Illustrated* (19 May 1980), in *The Reader's Digest* 117, no. 7 (September 1980), pp. 81–87.

71. "Behind Scandals in Big-Time College Sports," *US News and World Report* (11 February 1980), pp. 61–63.

72. "Foul!" *Time,* 133, no. 14 (3 April 1989), pp. 54–60.

73. "College Sports' Real Scandal," *US News and World Report* (15 September 1986), pp. 62–63.

74. "The Role of Faculty in the Governance of College Athletics," *Academe* (January–February, 1990), pp. 43, 44.

75. *Op. cit.*[69]

76. S. Cady et al., "Costly Business of Sports Recruiting Escalates Toward Public Scandal," *The New York Times* (11 March 1974), p. 1.

77. Jim Barnhart, "Television Responsible for NCAA Tourney Growth," *The Daily Pantagraph* (8 May 1981), p. B1.

78. There are over 3,000 colleges and universities and branch campuses in the United States. Of these, about 18% are public four-year colleges, 44% are private four-year colleges, 30% are public two-year colleges, and 8% are private two-year colleges. Relatively few schools have self-supporting sport programs. The schools with successful football programs have the best potential for generating revenues, although at some schools basketball and ice hockey have also produced a profit. A survey by the Associated Press (AP) discovered that about fifteen teams since 1945 have consistently been "successful." These institutions include Notre Dame, Oklahoma, Texas, Ohio State, Michigan, Michigan State, Alabama, Tennessee, University of California at Los Angeles, University of Southern California, Louisiana State, Pennsylvania State, Mississippi, Nebraska, and Arkansas. See D. Crase, "The Inner Circles of Intercollegiate Football," *Sport Sociology Bulletin* 1 (1972), pp. 7–11.

79. Stephen K. Figler, *Sport and Play in Amer-*

ican Life (Philadelphia: W.B. Saunders, 1981), p. 140.

80. B. SCHEMBECHLER, quoted in James A. Michener, *Sports in America* (New York: Random House, 1976), p. 189.

81. *Ibid.*

82. LARRY KLEIN, "The NCAA Enforcement Sham," *Sport* (June 1977), pp. 42–48.

83. The AIAW (Association for Intercollegiate Athletics for Women), founded in 1972, and now defunct, was the women's counterpart to the NCAA. Their regulations regarding financial aid, recruiting, and transfers differed from those of the men's programs.

84. RICHARD SCHULTZ, quoted in *US News and World Report* (8 January 1991), p. 51.

85. "Dirty Tricks Included in College Recruiting," *Daily Vidette* (9 April 1980), p. 12.

86. FRED ROTHENBERG, "Failing Grades Omitted," *The Daily Pantagraph* (10 December 1978), p. B4.

87. *Ibid.*

88. *Op. cit.,*[69] p. 63.

89. *Op. cit.,*[82] p. 43.

90. *Op. cit.,*[71] p. 43.

91. *Ibid.,* p. 62.

92. *Op. cit.,*[68] p. 84.

93. *Op. cit.,*[68] pp. 85–86.

94. *Op. cit.*[82]

95. *Op. cit.*[67]

96. PETE AXTHELM, "How to Reform the System," *Newsweek* (22 September 1980), p. 59.

97. *Op. cit.,*[69] p. 63.

98. *Op. cit.,*[69] p. 63.

99. WILLIAM F. SHUGHART II, "Protect College Athletes, Not Athletics," *The Wall Street Journal* (26 December 1990).

100. *Op. cit.,*[68] p. 14.

101. FREDERICK W. COZENS & FLORENCE SCOVIL STUMPF, *Sports in American Life* (Chicago, IL: University of Chicago Press, 1953), Chapter 6.

102. *Op. cit.,*[4] p. 124.

103. C. R. KNIKER, "The Values of Athletics in Schools: A Continuing Debate," *Phi Delta Kappa* 56 (1974), pp. 116–120.
SCHAFER ARMER, "Athletes Are Not Inferior Students," *Transaction* 6, cited in Coakley, *op. cit.,*[4] p. 126.

104. JAMES S. COLEMAN, "Athletics in High School," *Annals of the American Academy of Political and Social Science* 338 (1961), pp. 33–43.

105. D. STANLEY EITZEN, "Athletics in the Status System of Male Adolescents: A Replication of Coleman's 'The Adolescent Society'," *Adolescence* 10 (1975), pp. 267–276.

106. RICHARD A. REHBERG & WALTER E. SCHAFER, "Participation in Interscholastic Athletics and College Expectations," *American Journal of Sociology* 73 (1968), pp. 732–740.

107. Elaboration is a statistical technique whereby an initial relationship between two variables is rigorously tested to see if it "holds up" when other variables, called *test factors,* or *control variables,* are systematically introduced into the analysis. See Wilbert M. Leonard, II, *Basic Social Statistics* (St. Paul: West Publishing, 1976).

108. *Op. cit.,*[106] p. 739.

109. *Op. cit.,*[4] p. 140. Reprinted with permission.

110. ELMER SPREITZER & MEREDITH PUGH, "Interscholastic Athletics and Educational Expectation," *Sociology of Education* 46 (1973), pp. 171–182.

111. SCHAFER ARMER, *op. cit.*[103]

112. WENDY C. JEROME & JOHN C. PHILLIPS, "The Relationship Between Academic Achievement and Interscholastic Participation: A Comparison of Canadian and American High Schools," *Journal of Canadian Association of Health, Physical Education, and Recreation* 37 (1971), pp. 18–21.

113. JOHN C. PHILLIPS & WALTER F. SCHAFER, "Consequences of Participation in Interscholastic Sports: A Review and Prospectus," *Pacific Sociological Review* 14 (1971), pp. 328–338.

114. LLOYD B. LUEPTOW & BRIAN D. KAYSER, "Athletic Involvement, Academic Achievement, and Aspirations," *Sociological Focus* 7 (1973), pp. 24–36.
WILLIAM J. HAUSER & LLOYD B. LUEPTOW, "Participation in Athletics and Academic Achievement: A Replication and Extension," *Sociological Quarterly* 19 (1975), pp. 304–309.

115. CHRISTOPHER L. STEVENSON, "Socialization Effects of Participation in Sport: A Critical Review of the Research," *Research Quarterly* 46 (1975), pp. 287–301.

11

Sport and Economics

Sports is too much of a game to be a business and too much of a business to be a game. ROGER KAHN

In this chapter the interrelationships between sport and the economy are demonstrated. Kahn's opening quote (taken from CBS Reports, "The Baseball Business," Bill Moyers, narr., 1977) captures the oxymoronic situation in which professional and top-level amateur sport finds itself today. To gain a perspective, it is useful to distinguish three levels of sport: (a) informal, (b) organized, and (c) corporate.[1] **Informal sport** is that which many of us engaged in during childhood and youth. Our primary motivation was to participate in spontaneous, playful activity from which we gained a sense of enjoyment, fulfillment, and satisfaction. These physical activities often included using makeshift bats, goals, balls, and boundaries and were played under somewhat ephemeral ad hoc rules.

Organized sport often accompanies extracurricular activities during grade school, high school, and college, but it may also include informal, interscholastic, amateur (e.g., YMCA and youth programs), and intercollegiate programs. The characteristics distinguishing organized sport include formal teams, leagues, codified rules, officials, standard equipment, and sponsors.

Corporate sport contains elements of informal and organized sport but adds other components, the salient ingredients of which are economics and politics—sport becomes big business and power politics. Corporate sport is identified by the commercial interests of owners, sponsors, and players and by the subordination of the players' participation for their own intrinsic interests to extrinsically motivated goals such as pleasing fans, owners, alumni, or powerful pressure groups. It is the cynosure for most of the discussion in this chapter. This level of sport has popularized the adage, "it's no longer a game, it's a business."

❏ EMERGENCE OF CORPORATE SPORT

Although no single event is responsible for the corporatization of American sport, both economic and political factors have contributed to its development. According to Hoch,[2] "The character and scale of sports today is the child of monopoly capitalism."[3] Sport began to take on its present appearance in the 1930s, when the economy began to recover from the Depression, and the bureaucratic nature of sport became well entrenched during the early 1950s. In elaborating on these points, Nixon wrote:

> This was a time when those in control of professional sport were forced to confront the dual dilemma of decreasing attendance and the unknown impact of television. In this context, a new sports entrepreneur stepped into the picture, one with less concern for the esthetic aspects of sports and more for sound business practices and the maximization of profits. These organization persons have fundamentally transformed the character of sports. . . .[4]

During the past 50 years, sports and industry have become intertwined. Hoch reported that, in 1927, boxing arena owners in major American cities were dismayed by the underuse of property and facilities between boxing matches and circuses.[5] To make their **capital** more cost-efficient, they persuaded Canadian hockey teams to play their games in the vacant arenas. Similarly, after World War II, owners realized that they could make even better use of their facilities if basketball games could be scheduled there as well. Hence, material conditions such as the availability of sports arenas that were used less than maximum created an impetus for sport production and consumption.

Ties Between Industry and Sport

Hoffman and Greenberg describe the symbiotic relationship between industry and sport by noting that there are three ways a company can use sport to sell a product: (a) An athlete or athletes can be paid to endorse its product(s). (b) A company can purchase television or radio time and advertise its wares. (c) It can sponsor an event and have its name linked to the event.[6] These three techniques are and have been used in sport. Let us consider more specific interconnections between business and sport. Auto racing was largely created by automobile manufacturers to promote, advertise, and sell their products. Today, companies that produce automobile accessories (e.g., tires, gasoline, oil, brake linings, shock absorbers, batteries, and the like) sponsor events and drivers because of the publicity gained by such endorsements. Father–son auto racers Richard and Kyle Petty are of interest in this context. Years ago STP paid Richard $1 million for putting its logo on his car's hood; Kyle signed a $1.5 million contract (over 3 years) for a similar arrangement.[7] In 1991 the U.S. Soccer Federation and Adidas agreed to a $21 million, four-year sponsorship contract that called for increased advertising and support by the company.

The Sponsorship of Sporting Events

In 1987 *Business Week* reported that nearly 3,500 U.S. companies spent $1.35 billion to sponsor sporting events.[8] The top corporate sponsors included Philip Morris, Anheuser-Busch, General Motors, RJR Nabisco, Ford and Chrysler, Moor Companies, U.S. Armed Forces, IBM, AT&T, and Gillette. As can be see in Table 11.1, these corporate sponsors pumped from $70 to $351 million into sport sponsorship. Some companies have even bought entire conferences. Phillips Petroleum and Goodyear once bought sponsorship for the entire Big Eight and Pac 10 conferences, respectively.

Another way in which corporations promote their products is to sponsor sporting events. Other examples of corporate sponsorship include the Mobile Cotton Bowl, the Federal Express Orange Bowl, and the Sunkist Fiesta Bowl. Additionally, Mercedes sponsors horse jumping championships; McDonald's, the high school All-America basketball game; Canon, the Sammy Davis, Jr., Greater Hartford Open; Schlitz Malt Liquor, professional boxing; and AT&T, the tennis challenge. Professional golf, tennis, bowling, and racquetball tournaments, as well as numerous amateur sporting events, have been underwritten by major U.S. corporations. This trend has been particularly evident during the past decade. For example, the corporations that merchandise Virginia Slims (they sponsored women's tennis tournaments until 1978), Coca-Cola, Marlboro cigarettes, and Old Spice after-shave (they sponsored hang gliding events), as well as other major corporations (Kemper Insurance, Colgate-Palmolive, and Avon, to name a few) have underwritten professional and amateur sport activities. In underwriting a sports event, the sponsor links, via the technique of classical conditioning, its product with a particular sporting spectacle.

TABLE 11.1   Top sponsors (1987)

Sponsors	Sports Advertising ($ millions)	Event Sponsorship, Licensing, and Related Promotion ($ millions)	Total ($ millions)
Philip Morris Cos.	260	91	351
Anheuser-Busch Cos.	290	60	350
General Motors Corp.	291	19	310
RJR Nabisco	92	82	174
Ford Motor Co.	130	15	145
Chrysler Corp.	115	16	131
U.S. Armed Forces	115	0	115
IBM Corp.	92	10	102
AT&T	72	10	82
Gillette Co.	45	25	70

SOURCE: Adapted from *Sports Marketing News* (15 February 1988) by Dale Hoffman & Martin J. Greenberg, *Sportsbiz* (Champaign, IL: Human Kinetics, 1989), p. 100. Reprinted with permission.

The idea behind such practices is to sponsor a product that in some way "fits" the corporate image.

Marathons.   Four of the United States's major marathons have corporate sponsors. The New York, Chicago, Marine Corps, Twin Cities, and Boston marathons are sponsored by Hanover Trust Company, Beatrice companies, no corporate sponsors, Pillsbury, and John Hancock Mutual Life Insurance, respectively. Major U.S. firms reportedly like the "yuppie-like" flavor of these events.

When a youngster, I thought that Gillette and "Friday Night Fights" were virtually one and the same (even though Gillette was only buying advertising time, like the sponsors of the Super Bowl and World Series). According to Ruby "The real boomlet in event or series sponsorship began about 1970 as the brainchild of a former athlete—tennis player turned promoter—Jack Kramer."[9] The top tennis tournaments were organized under one sponsor—first Pepsi, then Commercial Union (a British insurance company), and then Colgate-Palmolive—and participants earned points toward the Grand Prix Masters Championship. Volvo has also sponsored the Grand Prix and Masters.

Another substantial sum of money is provided by Anheuser-Busch for a variety of sporting events (e.g., a hydroplane named Miss Budweiser, the Budweiser rocket car, Paul Newman's Can-Am racing team, as well as national and local golden gloves tournaments). Their top of the line product, Michelob beer, sponsors golf tournaments and sailing regattas in addition to men's and women's ski races. Cigarette manufacturers are also in the limelight of sport sponsorship. NASCAR's Grand National race is christened the "Winston Cup," honoring an R.J. Reynolds corporation product, Winston cigarettes. This company also sponsors the Camel GT, The Winston Pro Motorcycle Series, and several other events.

Because there are risks in laying out large sums of money to sponsor sporting events, major corporations have enlisted the aid of firms that specialize in sports marketing. To illustrate, Citicorp, the nation's largest bank, decided to go into the credit card business. The corporation purchased Carte Blanche because the top two credit card companies, American Express and Diner's Club, were not for sale. After surveying its potential market, Citicorp concluded that its target customer was over age 35, was reasonably well off, and had an interest in participation sports such as tennis. Merchandising Consultants International suggested linking Citicorp's new product with tennis stars who were past their prime—players like Rod Laver, Ken Rosewall, and Marty Riessen—in what became known as the Carte Blanche Tennis Legends. Thus, an event was created for the purpose of selling Carte Blanche. Similarly, Coors actively sought to enhance its sales and in the early 1980s spent $3.5 million annually to sponsor bicycle, skiing, motorcross, rodeos, and tractor pulls in addition to sponsoring Lee Trevino (golfer) and Al Unser, Jr. (race car driver).

Such practices raise this important social question: "Is it actually news or is it free advertising when the press credits a sponsor who has attached its product name to an event?"[10] On the pro side are those who argue that commercialism is part of the very fabric of our capitalistic society; mentioning a sponsor is merely an instance of giving credit where credit is due. On the opposing side are those who argue that such acknowledgments provide the sponsor with free advertising. While both arguments have merit, it is not hard to see that such sponsorship serves a variety of functions, providing publicity as well as demonstrating good will.

Another way in which corporations merchandise their products is to underwrite the cost of constructing stadiums (e.g.., Schafer Stadium in Boston, Busch Stadium in St. Louis, and Rich Stadium in Buffalo).

Product Endorsements.   In 1990 *Sport* reported that companies in the United States and abroad spent $580 million to have professional athletes endorse their products.[11] The top ten endorsers included Arnold Palmer, Greg Norman, Jack Nicklaus, Boris Becker, Wayne Gretzky, Michael Jordan, Curtis Strange, Chris Evert, Bernhard Langer, and Ivan Lendl. What stands out among these top endorsers is that most are men in individual sports (particularly tennis and golf)—only Jordan and Gretsky and Evert fail to fit the pattern. Even college coaches reap benefits from endorsing certain commercial products. In basketball, Dale Brown, Louisiana State University (LSU) (LA Gear), Mike Krzyzeski, Duke (Adidas), and Bob Knight, Indiana (Adidas) have received $300,000, $260,000, and $200,000, respectively for donning the sponsors' shoes. In January 1991 a firm called Wizard Promotions contracted with several dozen coaches, including Gene Keady, Lefty Driesell, Jerry Tarkanian, Rick Pitano, Del Harris, and Don Nelson, in a pay-for-call service.

A few years ago, when Steffi Graf was ranked the number 1 women's tennis player, she was described as the "$4-million woman" because of her lucrative endorsement contracts including:

Jade, West German cosmetic firm, $390,000
GM/Opel Ag auto, $670,000
Hatex, West German clothing company, $420,000
Deutsche Granini, West German fruit juice company, $550,000

TABLE 11.2   Super Bowl income and expenses

	Super Bowl I (1967)	Super Bowl XXV (1991)
30-Second TV ad cost	$38,000	$850,000
TV viewers	75.4 million	120 million
NFL revenue from Super Bowl	$2.5 million	$25 million
Average regular season attendance	52,381	59,568
Average player salary	$22,000	$450,000

Adidas USA, off-the-track tennis clothes and shoes, $500,000
BASF, video and audio tapes, fee unavailable
Dunlop Slazenger, rackets, $600,000

Nike purchased 5,500 tickets to the January, 1991 Cincinnati–Oakland football game to be distributed to Los Angeles area Boys and Girls Clubs. A Nike spokesperson indicated that because of this magnanimous act needy children would have the benefit of attending the game. This purchase made the game a sellout. Had the game not sold out, the game would have been blacked out in LA. You don't suppose that Nike was concerned that a nonsellout meant that its commercials would not be aired in the second largest city in the country? Incidentally, the purchase was made 48 hours before kickoff time, making the ticket distribution problematic.

The Super Bowl and Corporate Connections.   The granddaddy of all sport spectacles—the Super Bowl—is the most lucrative annual event in America. It epitomizes the systemic relationship between sport and commerce. It has become a three-M industry: marketing, merchandising, and money! The economic aspects of the Super Bowl are awesome. How big has the Super Bowl with all its hype and panache become (Table 11.2)?

U.S. corporations use the Super Bowl to reward top personnel and court key clients. According to Jeff Provol, head of Total Sport/America of Chicago (a firm founded to stage lavish corporate parties), "This is where business is done—it's like playing golf with a client."[12]

Former presidents Nixon, Ford, and Carter (who invited both the Washington Bullets' 1978 championship basketball team and the U.S. Olympic team to the White House), as well as Reagan and Bush, typify how corporation managers feel about sports.

☐ THE PROFESSIONAL SPORTS OWNER

When typical sports fans sit in front of their televisions or in stadium stands, they can easily identify the players . . . the ones with the flashy uniforms that have the names Montana, Gooden, Jackson, Bird, Gretzky, and Jordan on the back. These individuals differ in terms of the specific tasks they perform, but they are identifiable, nevertheless, as the athletes, the performers. But ask those same fans to name the team owners and to describe the tasks that owners perform, and you are likely to draw blank stares.

Just how sports have evolved to the point where the sports page resembles either an accounting sheet or a court report poses a socially significant question. In many ways, the changing pattern of sport ownership is symbolic of the evolution of professional sport.[13] The earliest owners grew up with the game. Men such as George Halas (football), Eddie Gottlieb (basketball), and Clark Griffith, Connie Mack, and John McGraw (baseball) wrapped themselves up in the total operation of the franchise. Their whole business was sports, and they helped provide stability for young leagues. They made money by promoting the game and even barnstormed for the sake of exposure.

The second stage of ownership was initially viewed with great trepidation. These owners were business tycoons with large industrial holdings who sought both to contribute to the community and advertise their product(s). The beer barons, August Busch, Jr. (Cardinals), and Jacob Ruppert (Yankees), and Phil Wrigley (Cubs) with his chewing gum industry, were members of this genre. There was fear that they would overly commercialize sport by using it to market their products. This breed generally proved to be rich but public minded and showed compassion for the game. Some believe that the era of the true sports owner died when the Red Sox's Tom Yawkey and Cubs' Phil Wrigley passed away in the late 1970s and Bill Veeck in 1986.

The third stage in ownership witnessed the rise of the corporate manager who approached sport as a business proposition. Frequently an absentee owner, the corporate manager's interest often did not focus on town, team, or sport, but on the team up for sale that offers the best tax advantage. As explained later, such an owner, through the historic use of depreciation allowances and capital gains tax laws, seeks to use such a team for financial gain for a few years and then sells it. For instance, there were twenty-seven changes of ownership in the American Basketball Association in a decade, and from 1963 to 1975, the National Basketball Association added nine new teams and saw an overturn of forty-four owners and principals.[14]

Ownership Patterns

Who Are the Owners?   It is ironic that those who control sport are among the least known and least visible people in sport. While we cannot name and identify all of the owners, we can identify some typical contemporary ownership patterns.

One type of ownership is represented by the New York Knicks (basketball) and Rangers (hockey), Chicago Cubs and St. Louis Cardinals (baseball). These teams are subsidiaries (businesses whose controlling interests are owned by parent companies) of larger corporations, namely, Madison Square Garden Corporation (Knicks), *Chicago Tribune* (Cubs), and Anheuser-Busch (Cardinals). These teams, in effect, must share the same ground as the other interests of their parent corporation, such as cinema and oil with the Knicks, and beer and amusement parks with the Cardinals. Just because they are part of a corporation, however, doesn't mean these franchises can draw on the parent company's vast financial reserves. The Cardinals, for example, are fiscally autonomous—all of the money allocated for baseball operations must be generated by the team franchise. Table 11.3 demonstrates the nature of a conglomerate. Notice that five sport franchises represent subsidiaries of Gulf and Western.

In terms of the present free-agency market, there is some fear that the wealthiest teams will acquire the best players and dominate their sport. It is virtually impossible for an individual owner to compete for a player when a "corporate" team is also vying for him. John Bassett, when proprietor of the World Hockey Associations' (WHA)

TABLE 11.3   Gulf and Western Industries, Inc., as a conglomerate

I. Entertainment and Communication	II. Financial Services Association Corporation of North America	III. Consumer and Industrial Products

1. Paramount Pictures Corp.
  • Movies: *Flashdance, An Officer and a Gentleman, Staying Alive*
  • TV: "Winds of War," "Happy Days," "Cheers," "Taxi"
  • Cable TV: Made for cable TV entertainment packages, including Miss Universe, Miss USA, and Miss Teen USA Pageants; own ⅓ of USA network
2. Paramount Communications
  • Sports teams: New York Rangers and New York Knicks
3. Madison Square Garden In New York City, a sports and entertainment center attended by over 6 million annually: New York Rangers and New York Knicks, college basketball; track-and-field sports; professional tennis tournaments; horse shows; professional boxing; wrestling; Barnum and Bailey Circus; rock concerts
4. Simon & Schuster Trade books, Pocket Books, Silhouette Romance Novels, Washington Square Press, Webster's Dictionaries
	1. Corporate acquisitions in the U.S., U.K., Australia, and Japan
	2. Loans to about 100,000 persons in over 700 offices
	3. Credit cards services such as over 350,000 Execu-Charge Visa Cards
		1. Kaiser-Roth One of the U.S.'s largest apparel and hosiery companies, it includes Catalina Sportswear, Cole of California, Cheryl Tiegs Collection, No Nonsense Panty Hose
		2. Simmons Simmons Beauty Rest Mattresses, Fabrics, and Furniture
		3. Gulf and Western Food Products
		4. Gulf and Western Manufacturing Co. Network of BIG Autoparts stores

SOURCES: Beth B. Hess, Elizabeth W. Markson, and Peter J. Stein, *Sociology* (New York: Macmillan, 1985), p. 296. Anthony Baldo with Alexandra Biesada, Holt Hackney, Michael K. Ozanian, & Stephen Taub, "Secrets of the Front Office," *Financial Weekly* (9 July 1991), pp. 42, 43.

Birmingham Bulls, once said: "I lost two players . . . to the Rangers . . . I couldn't compete . . . so I called Madison Square Garden and told them if they sent me some dough, they could have them right away."[15]

A second ownership pattern is represented by Al Davis (Raiders) and the late Paul Brown (Bengals), Calvin Griffith (Minnesota Twins), and Walter O'Malley (Los Angeles Dodgers); throwbacks to the earliest days of ownership. Their major financial concern is their team. Griffith, for example, inherited the team from his father. Whereas the Twins experienced trouble with free-agent defections, the Dodgers are the envy of many team owners. The Dodgers own the team, stadium, concessions, parking lot, and even a service station on the grounds. Combine all these income sources with an annual draw of at least 2.5 million spectators and it is easy to understand why other franchise owners are envious.

A third type of ownership pattern is a public one. The Milwaukee Bucks basketball team and the Green Bay Packers (with several thousand shareholders) are two of less than a dozen publicly owned teams. This type of ownership is clearly the exception. Typically, these teams are housed in smaller metropolises and have experienced financial exigencies. The only way that some have survived has been to sell shares to the public to raise the necessary capital.

The fourth and most prevalent type of owner is the entrepreneur who has made megabucks in another business endeavor and channels some of it into the sport market. For example, Cleveland Cavaliers owners George and Gordon Gund own the Rusty Scupper Restaurants, Charles Bronfman (Expos) owns Seagrams Distilleries, George Argyos (Mariners) owns AirCal airlines, Ray Kroc, the deceased owner of the San Diego Padres, also owned McDonalds fast-food chain (now his wife Joan does), Nelson Doubleday (Mets) is the owner of Nelson Doubleday publishers, and Paul Snyder, former owner of the Buffalo Braves, owns a fast-food corporation and is the largest shareholder in Nabisco. George Steinbrenner, former Yankees owner, who built his shipping business into a $100-million-a-year operation, used some of his capital to buy the New York Yankees, and Kansas City Royals co-owner Arron Fogelman made his fortune in real estate. Finally, there is the National Football League (NFL) oil bloc represented by Lamar Hunt (Kansas City Chiefs), John Mecom (New Orleans Saints), Bud Adams (Houston Oilers), and Clint Murchison (Dallas Cowboys).

The fifth model is a combination of *public* and *private* ownership and is best exemplified by the Pittsburgh Pirates. The early 1980s were dismal years for the Pirates; after 40 years of ownership, the Galbreath family relinquished the team, hoping to sell it for $35 million. Eventually, a relatively unique arrangement was made: private investors put up $26 million for the team (thirteen firms and individuals, including U.S. Steel Corporation; Carnegie Mellon University; Harvey Walken, Chicago businessman; and Eugene Litman, Pittsburgh real estate dealer, each put up $2 million), and the city of Pittsburgh put up $24 million. The private investors own and control the club.

The problem fans have with identifying team owners is perhaps best represented by both former Philadelphia Phillies owner Ruly Carpenter and Tampa Bay Buccaneer owner Hugh Culverhouse. Carpenter, the grandson of R.R.M. Carpenter (the patriarch of Dupont, who purchased the Phils in 1943), grew up on an estate that had a full-sized baseball diamond in the front yard. As part of the family fortune, which was estimated at $100 million, Ruly inherited the team in 1972 at the age of 32.[16] A man who spent most of his time with the team, Carpenter was considered the prototype of the future owner. In 1981, Carpenter sold the franchise to Bill Giles, the club's executive vice-president, for a then major-league baseball purchase record of $30.175 million. The club was put on the market because of Carpenter's philosophical differences with other owners concerning the game's operation. His differences were characterized by a disdain for the free-agent draft, the escalating salaries that resulted from it, and the relentless battles with the Major League Players' Association. Hugh Culverhouse is not necessarily typical of all sports owners, and his lifestyle is undoubtedly light-years away from that of the typical fan. He and his spouse were described as ". . . nice people. They have a nice life. They skip off in their private jet (they're both pilots) or yacht to the Bahamas or some other foreign climate for long weekends of golf, gambling, and dancing. Out by the pool at Los Cedros, there is a patch of Astro-Turf. Drawing on a supply of 10,000 Japanese golf balls, the Culverhouses often while away a leisurely hour or so on the Astro-Turf, teeing up and driving one ball after another into the river."[17]

Flint and Eitzen identified the owners of 141 major league professional football, basketball, baseball, hockey, and soccer for 1982–1984.[18] The business holdings and the memberships of these owners were then determined. Nearly 50% of the owners made their money in four sectors: (a) communications and publishing, (b) oil and energy development, (c) real estate and land development (nearly one third of all owners fell into this category), and (d) transportation and distribution. Flint and Eitzen labeled these four areas as "entrepreneurial capital (private ownership)." Nearly 20% of the owners fell into the "monopoly capital (public corporation)" category and included the automotive industry, banking, finance, and insurance, brewing and liquor, industrialist and manufacturing, and sales and merchandising. Ten percent, 6%, and 17% of the owners were in franchise operations and management; the professions (law, e.g., Edward Bennett Williams, Orioles; Joe Robbie, Dolphins; Williams Davidson, Pistons; Hugh Culverhouse, Buccaneers; and medicine); and a residual category (inheritance unknown), respectively. Flint and Eitzen wrote:

> We had assumed that professional team owners, because they are wealthy business people and because their ownership makes them highly visible nationally, would be like the corporate elite. We found . . . that they tend to make their fortunes in business activities that do not require corporate innerlocks and social connections. Their businesses, for the most part, are local rather than national. Thus their social and business ties are more likely to be local.[19]

Sport owners are rich. In 1989 the average wealth of those listed in *Forbes* 400 wealthiest individuals was $672 million.[20] Between 20 and 30 sports owners have recently been on this roster. Ted Arison (Miami Heat), Edward DeBartolo (Pittsburgh Penguins and San Francisco 49ers), Ted Turner (Braves), and Jack Kent Cooke (Washington Redskins) had estimated worths of $2.86 billion, $1.4 billion, $1.76 billion, and $1.25 billion, respectively! In 1989 at least nine of the twenty-eight NFL owners had personal worths of at least $200 million.

Although it cannot be proven that owners are the cause of the problems in professional sports, sport franchise ownership has changed dramatically since its beginnings. Today, it is infiltrated by *syndicates* (groups of individuals or organizations that undertake some specific duty or carry out specific transactions or negotiations), *conglomerates* (a company consisting of many subsidiary companies or divisions that operate in a variety of unrelated industries, usually the result of mergers or acquisitions), and *shareholders* (holders or owners of shares of stock in a corporation).

What motivates someone to own a sport franchise? Sam Schulman said, "Owning a pro team is an ego trip."[21] Other reasons for ownership include "fun, excitement, ego fulfillment, power, visibility, personal satisfaction from knowing athletes ("jock sniffing"), vicarious identification as an athlete, another goal to conquer, and community service."[22] The reasons individuals choose to own a professional sport franchise can be subsumed under three general headings: (a) "psychic" income, (b) capital gain, and (c) tax shelter. Psychic income means the self-aggrandizement that stems from ownership; capital gain refers to the lucrative investment sport franchise purchasing can produce (e.g., Carrol Rosenbloom bought the Baltimore Colts for a few thousand dollars and sold it two decades later for $19 million); and tax shelter means the manner in which even financial losses in sport can be manipulated in conjunction with other business enterprises for a tax advantage (e.g., years ago, Charles O. Finley refused to sell the Oakland A's for between $10 and $12 million despite poor attendance and pitiful media packages because, apparently, it provided a tax shelter for other lucrative businesses).

❏ THE SIZE AND PROFITABILITY OF THE PROFESSIONAL SPORT INDUSTRY: DETERMINANTS AND MECHANISMS

How big is the sport industry? Sandomir compiled the gross national sports product (GNSP).[23] In 1986 the GNSP was estimated to be $47.2 billion (up from $44.1 billion in 1985), making sports the twenty-fifth largest industry in the United States. The GNSP includes a wide array of activities such as gate receipts, concessions and souvenirs, sporting goods, construction, tourism, TV revenues, endorsements and the like. As one example, consider the sporting goods industry. Acknowledging that the line between fashion and sports apparel is blurry, the sporting goods industry reported over $30 billion in sales in 1990 (and was expected to top $33 billion in 1991). An anticipated growth of 6% was predicted in 1991, but this was a slowdown from the 10% annual growth rate in the late 1980s. The "slowdown" was attributed to demographics (a decline in the number of young adults) and, particularly, the recession at the time. The breakdown in sporting goods sales in 1990 is of interest (Table 11.4).

Although billions are spent annually on sports and recreation, the professional sport industry accounts for a small slice of the total economic pie.

At the outset, it must be noted that the profits in professional sport are difficult to determine. Aside from this disclaimer, it is necessary to understand the political and economic climate in which American sports are embedded. Under capitalism, the ultimate goal is profit maximization. This can be accomplished through direct reve-

TABLE 11.4 Sporting goods
sales in 1990

Category of Sales	$ in Millions
Apparel	12,645
Footwear	7,665
Golf equipment	1,285
Exercise	975
Camping	865
Water sports	420
Bowling and billiards	405
Tennis	315
Baseball and softball	255
Soccer	110

SOURCE: John Helyar, "The Costs of Sports' Fashions"
The Wall Street Journal (20 February 1991), p. B1.

nues received from box office receipts, television and radio rights sales, or indirectly by using financial losses as tax deductions and the amortization of player contracts.

As a rule, professional sport franchises are not publicly owned corporations; consequently, they are not legally required to reveal the financial details of their operations. In fact, the finances of professional sport franchises are generally kept secret. Professional sport clubs have *two* major direct sources of revenue: (1) ticket sales and (2) the sale of media (television and radio) rights. Figure 11.1 presents diagrams that show the operating income of professional football, baseball, hockey, and basketball teams in the early 1990s. Although not all sports conform to this distribution pattern, it can be seen that about 90% of the revenue generated came from these two sources. Because ticket sales are a key component of a franchise's profitability picture, consider the determinants of live attendance.

Determinants of Attendance

Team Success.   Researchers have isolated a small number of variables that affect attendance variations at home games in professional team sports.[24] The most important factor is team success, measured by wins and losses. Almost without exception, winning teams generate higher ticket sales. However, economists maintain that a ceiling exists on how much a club can enhance its paid attendance by improving team quality, because of other variables that need to be considered (e.g., coaches, training methods, franchise location, stadium size, etc.).[25] Thomas says the professional sporting industry is like any other industry; the owner will acquire talented players up to the point where the value of the additional attendance just equals the cost of the additional athlete.[26] This being the case, there is little reason for an owner to even attempt to stockpile all of the superstar performers. Clearly, a league in which one team perennially dominates all others is not conducive to box office success.

Market Area.   Another critical variable that affects attendance figures is the market area in which games are played. All professional sport leagues assign clubs the exclusive right to operate in a restricted geographical territory. No other club within the league may perform in person or broadcast there without the home club's consent.

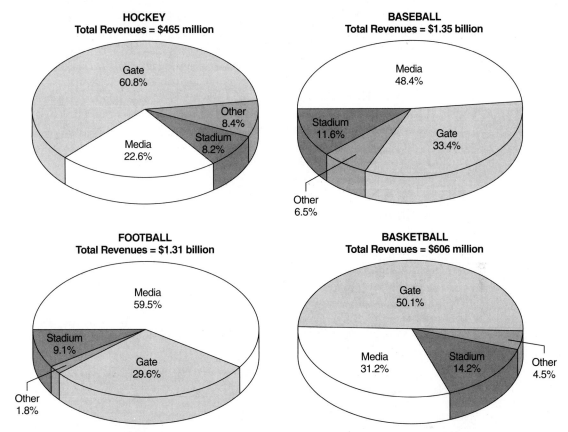

FIGURE 11.1 Operating income of hockey, baseball, football, and basketball teams in the early 1990s

This permits a club to monopolize a given market area. Because of variations in the size of market areas, as well as direct competition from other forms of entertainment and recreation, sport markets, from the start, vary with respect to potential revenues. Such market differences generally prove to be a potent force that affects the financial well-being of professional franchises.

There are several significant consequences of market areas. First, market areas possess differential revenue potential. This means that a super star is worth more in some market areas, such as New York or Los Angeles, than in other cities like Kansas City or Seattle. Quirk wrote: "Franchises in low drawing areas typically sell good players to franchises in highdrawing areas. . . ."[27]

In 1991 the Pittsburgh Pirates lost $7.6 million, despite winning the divisional championships, record attendance, and earning more TV monies than in their entire history. The Pirates' front office echoed Quirk by saying that the economic structure of baseball made it virtually impossible for them to pay their marquee names (Bonds, Bonilla) as much as they could make elsewhere. The Pirates, like other small-market franchises, can't command the megabuck broadcast deals enjoyed by teams in large market areas such as Chicago, Los Angeles, or New York. Because of the differential revenue potential, teams in certain territories are inclined to purchase highly sought players because they can defray the player costs in gate receipts. In strong market areas, as opposed to weaker ones, improvement in team quality enhances attendance. Therefore, owners in stronger markets are more inclined to invest (i.e., purchase players) because of the economic payoff, whereas, in weaker areas, owners will be less motivated to purchase quality players. In the long run, then, a competitive balance among league teams is not likely to be manifest. This is not to say that teams in weaker territories cannot win—like the Portland TrailBlazers in 1977—since the outcome of a contest is the result of numerous unpredictable factors: injuries, unexpected performances, or sheer luck.

Revenue Sharing

To compensate for market-area differences, some professional leagues practice **revenue sharing,** whereby home game receipts are divided with visiting teams. Consequently, in the course of a season, teams will share in the income generated by clubs in both strong and weak market areas. However, the extent of revenue sharing varies among the different sports. For example, visiting teams in the National League receive $.54 for every paid admission of more than $1, 40% in the NFL; but the visiting teams in the National Basketball Association (NBA) and National Hockey League (NHL) do not share ticket sales revenues.

Broadcast Rights and Sales

The other major source of revenue for professional teams is the sale of media rights. Historically, there has been dramatic change in this sphere. In the mid-1950s, only 15% of the revenues for a typical football and baseball club came from this source. Today, the modal football club depends on broadcast sales for almost 60% of its revenues, and the typical baseball, basketball, and hockey clubs depend on this source for nearly 50%, 31%, and 23%, respectively (see Figure 11.1).

Professional sports clubs receive media revenue from two sources: (a) Individual clubs negotiate their own broadcast packages with *local* radio and television stations, and (b) the league barters with *national* networks for all clubs within its jurisdiction. The former procedure produces major income differentials because of the previously mentioned differences in market strength; the latter leads to a more equitable distribution of income among teams within the league. In 1961, Congress passed legislation authorizing professional sport leagues to pool the sale of broadcast rights without violating antitrust laws, which meant that the league could negotiate national broadcast rights for all teams within its jurisdiction. The upshot of this monopolistic practice was that more money was generated from the sale of fewer games. According to Nader and Gruenstein, the real losers were the fans, because they ultimately had less access to sports programming and paid more for it.[28]

The established leagues have a sound combination of local and nationwide contracts. Consider, first, *national* contracts. The most recent four-year $3.6 billion NFL television pact (divided up among five broadcast and cable networks) guaranteed *each* team, for the next four years, about $32 million per year (this package was a 92% increase over 1987). The most recent four-year $1.48 billion major league baseball contract guaranteed each franchise about $14 million each year (this contract was up 102% from 1984). Finally, the most recent NBA contract of $875 million guaranteed each team about $9 million per year (a 250% increase from 1986). Two features of these monetary amounts are important to consider: (a) These are amounts guaranteed before a single ticket is sold, and (b) they implicate the amount of money that is due to revenue sharing in some professional sports. The NHL lost its national network contract in 1975, and the clubs must rely solely on local broadcast rights. This loss of television monies is one reason why the hockey "industry" is struggling. In general, the sport leagues that recently developed—the American Basketball Association (ABA; now merged with the NBA), the World Hockey Association (WHA), the North American Soccer League (NASL), the U.S. Football League (USFL), and the World Football League (WFL)—were not successful in selling their products to the networks because their franchises were generally located in smaller cities or in weaker markets that were less attractive to the national networks and advertisers.

Turning to the local level, we do find major revenue differentials. At the local level there are both cable and over-the-air television and radio sport packages. For example, the Cubs have a cable contract and an over-the-air contract with WGN. Pittsburgh had a cable contract with TCI and an over-the-air contract with KDKA. Because of market area differences, the Yankees made an estimated $69.4 million from media revenues in 1991 compared to $1.6 million for the New Jersey Devils.

Besides these two major revenue sources—gate receipts and the sale of broadcast rights—others include concessions, marketing rights to club emblems, and the sale of player contracts.

Noll conducted a comprehensive study of the finances of major sports teams and concluded that if one were to merely balance out revenues and costs, few franchises would show a profit.[29] Such a bleak financial picture stems from accounting losses (i.e., when expenses exceed revenues). Of utmost significance in the determination of profits are the less visible features of professional sport-like subsidies from local, state, and federal governments in the form of tax concessions, low rental fees for stadiums, amortization of contracts, and franchise appreciation.

When tax advantages and other benefits of ownership are considered, Noll found a pattern to these profits and losses: Clubs located in larger markets or fielding winning teams realized profits, whereas those in smaller markets or fielding losing teams were financially unsuccessful (i.e., showed smaller profits or even ended up in the red).[30] Also, the extent of both profits and losses is affected by the nature of revenue sharing. There is less discrepancy between profits and losses among teams in leagues that practice revenue sharing (NFL) than among teams in leagues that do not (NBA). Table 11.5 presents the most recent data regarding the financial character of the four major team sports.

Having considered the more obvious factors in the economics of professional sport, let us consider some of the lesser known features that affect the profitability of ownership.

TABLE 11.5   Revenues and operating income for major team sports, 1991

Sport	Revenues ($)						Operating Income ($)	
	Total	Gate Receipts	Media	Stadium	Other	Average per Team	Total	Average per Team
Baseball	1.35 B	450 M	652 M	156 M	7 M	51.8 M	183 M	7.1 M
Football	1.31 B	389 M	782 M	119 M	24 M	46.9 M	248 M	8.8 M
Basketball	606 M	304 M	189 M	86 M	27 M	22.5 M	129 M	4.8 M
Hockey	465 M	283 M	105 M	38 M	39 M	22.1 M	65.5 M	3.1 M

M, million; B, billion.

SOURCE: "Secrets of the Front Office," *Financial Weekly* (9 July 1991), pp. 28–43.

Franchise Appreciation

Despite owners' claims that players' demands for exorbitant salaries are driving them to the poorhouse, evidence suggests that these complaints are unfounded. First, the value of sport franchises has steadily increased.[31] A notable illustration is that the Seattle Mariners were bought for $13 million in 1981 and valued at $59 million seven years later, despite twelve straight losing seasons. Other examples follow:

> Sidney Schlenker purchased the Denver Nuggets in 1985 for $20 million and sold the franchise four years later for $65 million.
> In 1984 the Dallas Cowboys were bought for $60 million and sold five years later for $140 million.
> In 1979 the Baltimore Orioles were purchased for $12 million and sold nine years later for $70 million.
> In 1970 the expansion franchise Portland Trail Blazers was bought for $3.5 million and sold in 1988 for $70 million.
> The Denver Broncos were bought for $35 million in 1981 and sold in 1984 for $70 million.

Illustrations of capital appreciation can be found in Table 11.6.

Finally, the business magazine *Forbes* reported that the collective value of professional baseball franchises had increased $7.3 million for National League clubs since their inception.[32] Ten baseball teams have been sold since 1978, and the teams and their reported selling prices are listed in Table 11.6.[33] In early 1986 the media reported that George Steinbrenner refused an offer of $100 million by someone wanting to buy the Yankees.

In spite of these escalating franchise costs, one should not assume that sport ownership is a losing proposition for the buyer. There are pecuniary inducements—profit. Profit, however, is not automatic on acquisition. According to McPherson, "with few exceptions, the owner of a professional sport organization is an entrepreneur whose ultimate goal is to maximize profits directly from the sport franchise, or indirectly by using financial losses in the sport domain as a tax deduction for other interests."[34] In 1991 several big-money star players were released, among them Bo Jackson, Fernando Valenzuela, and Pete Incaviglia. The Royals and Dodgers (each) saved nearly

TABLE 11.6 Baseball teams' capital appreciation

	Latest Sale ($ Millions)	Year Sold	Buyer (Types of Owners)	Current Value ($ Millions): Franchise Appreciation
Mets	100	1986	Nelson Doubleday and Fred Wilpon	175
Rangers	85	1989	George W. Bush and Edward Rose	100
Mariners	80	1989	Jeff Smulyan and partners	90
Orioles	70	1988	Eli Jacobs	100
Tigers	54	1983	Thomas Monaghan	110
Indians	45	1986	Richard and David Jacobs	85
Twins	36	1984	Carl Pohlad	95
Phillies	30.2	1981	Bill Giles and partners	140
Pirates	21.8	1985	16 Partners	85
Mets	21.1	1980	Doubleday and Co.	175
Cubs	20.5	1981	Tribune Co.	135

SOURCE: Adapted from "The Sport 100 Salary Survey," *Sport* (June 1990), p. 70.

$2 million in releasing Jackson and Valenzuela, and the Rangers, about $1.25 million in releasing Incaviglia. Young players are clearly a fiscal bargain for the owners because a player's salary can skyrocket quickly, as Toronto's Kelly Gruber illustrates. He made $88,000, $96,000, $130,000, $462,000, $1,250,000, and $3,666,666 in 1986, 1987, 1988, 1989, 1990, and 1991, respectively. Despite owners' clamors that escalating salaries are driving them to the poor house, only one club in the last fifty years, the Seattle Pilots, filed Chapter 11 bankruptcy. Furthermore, twenty-two out of twenty-six baseball clubs were expected to show a profit in 1991.

The Law of Depreciation as Applied to Sport

Most owners do not purchase and maintain a sport franchise as a public service. Because of the sometimes uncertain profit outlook, there must be other monetary attractions for sports investment. One incentive is depreciation and its accompanying tax savings. The **law of depreciation** is a mainstay of American business practices. The value of tangible assets, like cars and office equipment, declines over a fixed period. Over the years, tools, equipment, and resources (and, uniquely, athletes in sport ever since the late Bill Veeck instituted the practice) wear out. The tax laws permit a portion of the value of a commodity to be deducted because it depreciates and becomes less valuable each year. This legal mandate, which is applicable to all businesses, takes an interesting and unprecedented twist when applied to sport.

Depreciation is a basic tax and business practice whereby one counts capital (the machines and tools used in production) as a deductible business expense. When owners acquire new players, they receive not only the legal right to their services but also the right to depreciate their players' values for several years. On the surface, this practice is sensible—athletes, much like cars, are generally less valuable after ten years—see Figures 11.2 (earned run average—ERA) and 11.3 (mean innings pitched) than when "new." But there is a peculiar factor in sports that makes depreciation so important in the present era of ownership.

Consider the purchase of a franchise. The cost of baseball's newest expansion franchises (Miami and Denver) was $95 million and the four newest NBA franchises (Orlando, Charlotte, Miami, and Minneapolis) had price tags of $32.5 million. The new owner buys basically two assets: (a) an "intangible" license to the franchise, which is really a monopoly right, permitting the team to engage in contests with other league clubs, to share in the broadcast revenues of the league, and to occupy an exclusive territory, and (b) a "tangible" batch of players (and contracts). Primarily, the franchise consists of a set of rights—the right to do business in a contrived monopoly situation and to share in league broadcast revenues, which can amount to $32 million annually (today in the NFL)—rather than some tangible product. The law of depreciation works this way. The license cannot be depreciated because, technically, it does not wear out (in fact, it typically appreciates, as demonstrated earlier). Players, on the other hand, do wear out, and their value diminishes. The law applies to this latter component of the franchise and is technically referred to as the amortization of player contracts.

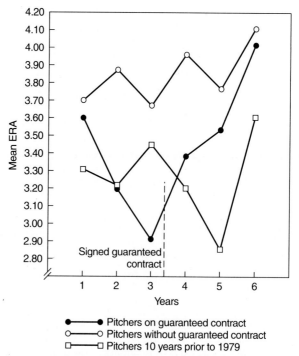

FIGURE 11.2 Example of decreased efficiency of pitchers with guaranteed pacts: Mean ERAs over six years

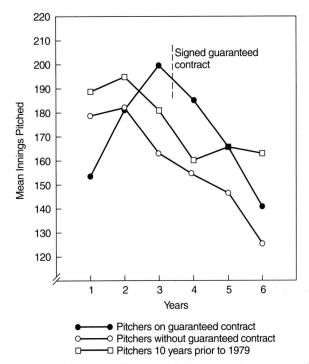

FIGURE 11.3 Example of decreased efficiency of pitchers with guaranteed pacts: Mean innings pitched over six years

Amortization of Player Contracts

Suppose the purchase price of an expansion franchise amounts to $80 million. The new owners allocate 50% of that amount ($40 million) to the value of player contracts, which is known in accounting as "capital assets of the enterprise," and the remaining 50% to the franchise license. The IRS allows the player costs to be amortized over a five-year period and treated as an annual indirect loss of $8 million (i.e., $40 million divided by five years equals $8 million per year). The value of amortization stems from it not being an out-of-pocket expense; it's purely on paper. Amortization can exceed the five-year period and commonly takes the form of writing off signing bonuses for the length of a player's contract. For example, in the early 1990s the Brewers gave Robin Yount a signing bonus of $1.5 million on a three-year contract. The Brewers were permitted to write off one half (per year) million over the three-year period.

In 1976 Congress passed the **Tax Reform Act.** It stipulated that the portion of the purchase price which the buyer allocated to player costs could not exceed the portion allocated by the seller and set a limit for player costs at 50%. Before some of the recent tax reform, the problem that arose was that the buyer and seller had diametrically opposed interests: The buyer wanted to allocate as much of the purchase price as possible to "tangibles" (the players' contracts) so as to depreciate their value, but the seller preferred to maximize the amount attributed to the "intangible" license and thereby treat the money as capital gains (profit from the sale of assets) and receive a tax break.

For years, the federal government allowed the buyer and seller to distribute monies in each of their best interests. This meant that as soon as a new buyer secured the title to a team, the buyer could begin the depreciation process again even though the seller had done the same before. The new buyer at a later date sells the club, and the new owner begins the amortization again. This process is called **depreciation recapture**. Aside from the economics of the matter, this procedure produced an important, un-anticipated consequence. Once a buyer had depreciated the cost of the contracts (a process taking about five years), it was no longer profitable to retain ownership of the club. In addition, other business tycoons saw the opportunity to purchase the club for their own financial gain. This helps to explain the turnover in sport club ownership and flurry of new franchises that have come and gone in recent years almost overnight. All owners have not been caught up in this merry-go-round; some have retained ownership for other reasons. However, the primary motive appears to be profit max-imization.

One final fiscal matter is important to any discussion of ownership and franchise purchases. If an owner amortizes the players' contracts but has no profits against which to offset them, no benefit is gained. At this juncture, the owner's other business operations become significant. If a team owner also owns a profitable brewery, chew-ing gum factory, or whatever, the amortization of contracts may be applied against the profits in the other business for appreciable tax savings. Suppose a franchise at the end of the year shows an operating loss (i.e., revenue minus direct costs) of $3 million per year for five years. If the **amortization of the players' contracts** over those five years amounted to $8 million per year, the owner can report annual losses of $11 million for tax purposes ($8 million for depreciation and $3 million for operating losses).

If the club is legally incorporated in a particular way (i.e., as part of a web of commercial industries) and if the new owner is in a high tax bracket, the owner can enjoy a sizable tax savings. For example, suppose the owner of a professional franchise also owns a large trucking firm that has earned $20 million during the same year that the owner has reported $11 million worth of losses. Instead of paying taxes on $20 million, the owner pays taxes on only $9 million ($20 − $11) Hence, an owner's loss in sport can be used to offset a profit in a nonsport business. In brief, the benefits of ownership stem from (a) the amortization of the players' contracts and (b) the tax bracket of the franchise owners. As Noll argues, there is "no evidence that the prime motivation of the vast majority of owners is any consideration other than profits."[35] Roone Arledge, president of ABC Sports, and lawyer Tom Evans echoed Noel's con-tention when they said, "Sports used to be run as a hobby by team owners. Now, it's a tax shelter for a lot of them or their corporations. . . . Of all the traditional tax-shelter deals, this is clearly the best.[36]"

In summarizing the benefits of ownership, it is crucial to recognize the amount of a franchise's cost that is distributed to players and the license itself. In the early 1960s, it was customary to estimate the worth of a franchise at $50,000 (the cost that could not be depreciated) and 98% as an expense item (player costs) that could be used for tax write-offs. Bill Veeck, deceased former baseball owner, gave an example.[37] When the Milwaukee Braves moved to Atlanta, the player costs were set at $6 million, and the cost of the franchise at $50,000. A ten-year depreciation on player contracts would yield an annual tax write-off of $600,000. Put differently, the Braves, according to Veeck, "would pay no taxes on their first $600,000 of profit and since corporate taxes ran about 50 percent," the club would save about $300,000 a year or $3 million over the ten years. Today, however, court decisions have established a precedent against the traditional allocation procedures.

Changes Affecting the Profitability of Franchise Ownership

A 1974 court decision disallowed clubs to allocate excessive amounts of money to players' contracts in order to reduce the tax advantages produced by amortization. E. Cody Laird, a minority owner of the Atlanta Falcons, sued for a $48,219 refund of 1967 and 1968 taxes. The Falcons were owned by a Subchapter S corporation called Five Smiths, Inc. The corporation was treated as a partnership, so the corporation itself did not pay taxes, but each partner paid a share of the taxes (if a profit accrued) or deducted a share of the losses (if a deficit accrued), which can offset taxes on a collateral business.[38] The franchise cost $8.5 million and, after various fees were paid, $50,000 was attributed to the franchise price and about $7.7 million to the player price. The IRS disallowed all but $1 million of this depreciation. While depreciating $1.5 million in both 1967 and 1968, the club reported losses of $506,329 and $551,047. Thus, the club cleared about $1 million each year before depreciation. The IRS slashed those depreciation figures to $200,000 for each year. Thus, the refund Laird was suing for was for income taxes on profits the IRS alleged the Falcons actually made.

Senior District Court Judge Frank Hooper placed the depreciable player value at slightly over $3 million. The unique item in Hooper's decision was an award of $4,227,043 for the value of television rights. The remaining $460,871 was ruled the value of the franchise. Also, the original contestant received a refund of less than half of the $48,219 he sought. The important consequence of this decision is not the amount awarded but the principles the award represents. Owners can no longer use a franchise for a quick tax write-off. This decision lends strength to the IRS rule of reasonable allocation apropos depreciation. Another important consequence is the judge's recognition of the importance of television rights. Today, professional sports are built on television money (see Chapter 14). Furthermore, Hooper's decision to disallow depreciation of television rights, because it was deemed impossible to determine the useful life of these rights, set an important precedent. While it will still take wealth to purchase a franchise, Hooper's decision may force owners to hold on to franchises longer, which may strengthen bonds between owner, fan, and team.

◻ THE FINANCING OF SPORT FACILITIES

The subsidization of sport facilities, write Snyder and Spreitzer, is one of the most controversial issues in the political economy of sports:

> The taxpayers subsidize professional sports through construction bonds, stadia rent below the market value, taxes foregone on the land, and appropriation of public services

to sports facilities in the form of water and sewage facilities, mass transit, law enforcement, and improvement of access roads. This use of public funds in support of private enterprise raises the critical question of "cui bono", who benefits?[39]

In February 1991 New York Mayor David Dinkins, a tennis buff, and the U.S. Tennis Association (USTA) announced a $150 million plan to expand and upgrade the National Tennis Center in an attempt to keep the U.S. Open in New York City. Although no revenue figures were disclosed, this bid was an attempt to keep the U.S. Open in New York City because it has been played there continuously since 1924.

Okner found that about 70% of all professional sport facilities (e.g., stadiums, arenas, and rinks) were publicly owned and financed (through revenue bonds issued by city, county, or state governments) and rented to sport associations at relatively low rates through so-called "sweetheart" leases.[40] In general, the average team pays less than 10% of its home gate receipts for stadium leasing.

What are the advantages of these cheap rentals? Okner contends that rentals are relatively inexpensive for the following reasons:[41]

1. To enhance the prestige of the community and thereby stimulate economic activity in nonsport enterprises.
2. To generate employment, consumer sales, and tax collections from sporting events.
3. To provide recreational opportunities to community residents.
4. To improve the morale of the citizens.

The Disadvantages of Typical Financing Arrangements

In the past two decades, numerous sport facilities have been built or renovated, ultimately, at the taxpayers' expense, which is due to the fact that the building projects often cannot pay for themselves and become public liabilities. The Superdome, for example is reported to have a yearly operating deficit of $3–$5 million. This also happened to the New Orleans Superdome ($163 million); Kansas City's Harry S Truman sports complex ($75 million); Philadelphia's Veterans' Stadium; Hackensack Meadowlands in East Rutherford, New Jersey ($340 million); Denver's Mile-High Stadium; and in the rehabilitation of Yankee Stadium ($100 million). When the revenue bonds cannot pay for the "public" projects, they become an open-ended general obligation that falls on the taxpayers. These projects, more often than not, do not pay for themselves; in fact, if they can pay half the operating expense—not even considering the bond payments—they are doing well. Despite these huge financial burdens, other U.S. cities—Columbus, Ohio, Atlanta, San Francisco, Chicago—are whistling the new sport facilities tune. Bud Selig, Milwaukee Brewers owner, was contriving a deal with civic officials to build a new stadium in 1991. Selig offered to build the stadium if the city provided the land and roads.

In addition to relatively low rental fees, other benefits are reaped by professional sport barons at the local level. For example, owners are relieved from paying property taxes, insurance, maintenance, as well as construction costs.

The location of a major sport franchise in a community is usually an economic boon because it increases the volume of business for hotels, restaurants, transportation, and other commercial enterprises in the community. Additionally, the city receives revenue from ticket taxes, concessions, employee taxes, and stadium rental fees.

For example, the Yankees add more than $50 million annually to their city, and the Pirates generate an extra $21 million or more. The Super Bowl adds over $100 million to the local economy. Other major sporting events like the World Series, Indianapolis 500, Kentucky Derby, NBA playoffs, and championship boxing matches create an economic windfall for a community.

Ethical Issues

Construction of new stadiums and the renovations of old ones raise two serious ethical issues. First, should public monies be used to finance such structures? Second, should public monies be channeled into sports, when many cities are suffering from dire housing shortages, inadequate school funding, insufficient medical facilities, and shrinking social welfare budgets?

In sum, professional sports occupy an envious position with respect to tax breaks and exemptions. Tax exempt stadium and arena bonds have typically been used to build sport complexes. Okner estimated that if stadium construction bonds were taxable, annual revenues in the tens of millions of dollars would fall into the federal government's coffers.[42] Moreover, local and state governments do not charge interest on construction bonds. Another financial loophole is that income derived from selling players, franchises, and equipment is not taxed as capital gain. Further, team owners are permitted to depreciate players' contracts.

☐ THE COSTS OF OWNERSHIP

On the cost side of the ledger are *three* primary expenses: (a) player compensation (e.g, salaries, bonuses, deferred payments, and fringe benefits); (b) game expenses (e.g., travel expenditures and stadium rentals), and (c) general and administrative costs (e.g., salaries for owners, executives, and concessionaires). Although the distribution of income varies from one sport and team to the next, the major percentage of expenses incurred are player costs.

The largest percentage of expenses incurred by owners is player costs. Not only are the average salaries high but the minimum salaries established by the respective players' unions are $110,000, $100,000, $50,000, and $25,000 for basketball, baseball, football, and hockey, respectively. Given that the average income in the United States in 1992 was less than $25,000, the minimum salaries would place many professional athletes in the ninetieth percentiles.

In 1991 the average salary of a major league baseball player was between $800,000 and $900,000, and Topps baseball cards paid each player approximately $22,000 for rights to picture him on the card. The distribution of salaries for the 1992 opening day rosters in major league baseball is revealing. Over 10% of the players ($N = 650$) made over $3 million (22 earned over $4 million), 17% made between $2 million and $3 million, 15% earned between $1 million and $1.9 million, and 58% earned less than $1 million. Of interest, player salaries went up over 30% between 1990 and 1992.[43]

Until recently (see Vignette 11.1), the salaries of professional athletes have been moderate (with the exception of Babe Ruth's $80,000 in 1932, which would be the equivalent of over $750,000 in today's dollars); however, recent studies have shown

Then and Now

A spring 1968 issue of *Sports Illustrated* featured nine St. Louis Cardinals baseball players beside their lockers under the headline, "The Highest-Paid Team in Baseball History." Among the highest paid players were: Bob Gibson ($85,000), Orlando Cepeda ($80,000), Roger Maris ($75,000), Curt Flood ($72,500), Lou Brock ($70,000), and Tim McCarver ($60,000). These salary figures are remarkable—then and now. Then because they were so huge; now because they are so small. Comparisons of the past with the present are often interesting. Below are listed some baseball im-

mortals with the salaries they earned then and in today's dollars; along with some contemporary superstars who currently play the same position. Using 1970 as a starting point, major league baseball players' annual average salary has risen from $29,303 (1970) to $44,676 (1975) to $143,756 (1980) to over $800,000 (1992). TV monies and inflated ticket prices have covaried with players' salaries, but since 1976 financial returns have increased threefold while players' average salaries have soared over sixfold.

Player	Position	Team	Salary Then	Salary in Dollars
Joe DiMaggio	LF	Yankees	$100,000 (1949)	$ 410,000 (1987)
Danny Tartabull	LF	Yankees		5,300,000 (1992)
Ted Williams	RF	Red Sox	125,000 (1959)	400,000
Bobby Bonilla	RF	Mets		6,100,000
Stan Musial	1B	Cardinals	100,000 (1958)	330,000
Will Clark	1B	Giants		4,250,000
Lou Boudreau	SS	Indians	65,000 (1950)	260,000
Barry Larkin	SS	Reds		4,300,000
Robin Roberts	P	Phillies	50,000 (1950)	200,000
Frank Viola	P	Red Sox		4,733,333
Yogi Berra	C	Yankees	65,000 (1961)	200,000
Mickey Tettleton	C	Tigers		3,333,333
Eddie Mathews	3B	Braves	65,000 (1966)	190,000
Kelly Gruber	3B	Blue Jays		3,633,333
Jackie Robinson	2B	Dodgers	35,000 (1950)	140,000
Steve Sax	2B	White Sox		3,575,000
Willie Mays	CF	Giants	80,000 (1959)	260,000
Ruben Sierra	CF	Rangers		5,000,000

SOURCE: "The Money Game," *U.S. News & World Report* (19 August 1985), p. 23. "Baseball Salaries '87," *Sports Illustrated* (20 April 1987), 66, no. 16, pp. 54–81. *The New York Times* (25 February 1992), p. B10.

☐

that the average income of professional male athletes is higher than that of most males in the labor force. According to Yee and Wright,[44] "The turning point came in 1960 when the upstart American Football League began bidding for rookies and veterans" from the entrenched National Football League. When Sonny Werblin of the New York Jets signed Joe Namath of Alabama in 1965, the salary escalation gained momentum. (According to Ballinger,[45] Namath's contract provided a base salary of $25,000 a year with the remainder spread out in deferred payments over many years.) Before then, salaries of $100,000 or more were rare. Following the loosening of the purse strings in professional football, the ABA began competing with the NBA for players, and the WHA began challenging the NHL. As Yee and Wright put it, "Money warfare since 1960 has resulted in salary increases in all professional sports, since pro athletes (and their players' associations and business managers) consider pay raises in sports other than their own as enhancing their own worth as well."[46]

In the past 20 years, average salaries in professional sport have skyrocketed. Salaries, particularly for superstars, are often misleading, however. When Warren Spahn pitched for the Milwaukee Braves, his salary was rumored to be $110,000; it was revealed later that his annual salary was $70,000. When the Oilers signed John Matuszak, their premiere draft pick, the press reported a four-year $300,000 contract. Later, in court, the truth was disclosed—a $25,000-yearly salary plus a bonus of $30,000. Remember, too, that most athletes have agents, business persons whose financial interests are best served by boasting of what they've garnered for their clients. Often, the deceptive figures that they broadcast serve to attract others to their fold.[47]

An Example of a Player's Contract

Leigh Steinberg, a leading contemporary sports agent, has detailed the contract of a rookie quarterback drafted in the first round in *Sport*.[48] Although the specifics vary from one contract to another, the patterning helps one grasp the nature of professional sports contracts. The present contract is for four years and $8 million with a $2 million signing bonus. The $2 million signing bonus is guaranteed before the player dons a uniform. The contract guarantees the player for the first two years even if he fails to make the team and for all four years even if injured. The structure of this contract means that nearly half of the value of the four-year contract—actually $3 million—is received the first year. The contract can be divided into four categories: (a) bonuses, (b) salary, (c) charities, and (d) incentive bonuses.

The Athletic Labor Market

Since salaries are the major expense item (in baseball alone in 1992, money paid out for salaries was in the hundreds of millions) and generate much discussion, let us ask "What variables affect salary determination?" To answer this query, we need to know something about the athletic labor market.[49] The pool of potential professional athletes consists of individuals whose skills make them sought-after commodities of production. There are two basic sources of training for aspiring professional athletes: (a) Hockey and baseball have farm systems whereby parent clubs own or have working agreements with minor-league teams and foot nearly all the training costs (in baseball costs, that amounted to between $2 and $4 million per team in the mid-1980s). (b) Football and basketball, on the other hand, sign players directly out of collegiate circles and bear virtually none of their prior training costs (costs that accrue to colleges and universities are one reason for the "four-year rule.")

Regardless of an athlete's source of training, a major predictor of future financial success is the perceived or actual indispensability (or replaceability) of the athlete as a factor of production. Today, an athlete's market value exceeds the value of his services (**opportunity cost**) in the best alternative employment (outside of sports), and the difference is termed **economic rent**. In a competitive market, players' salaries tend to equal their marginal revenue products.

Consider a company producing confectionery. For simplicity's sake, suppose a new worker produces fifty additional boxes of candy a day (the increase of fifty boxes of candy per day is the **marginal product**) and that each box sells for $1. As a result of employing the new worker, the company's output increases. If the firm sells the candy at $1 a box, the additional revenue—called the **marginal revenue product**—amounts to $50 (i.e., the marginal product of 50 multiplied by $1). Any knowledgeable person understands that if a new worker's wage surpasses $50 per diem, the added worker becomes a financial liability. Suppose this worker makes $20 per day. Assuming all other conditions equal, this figure is the worker's opportunity cost, and another firm would have to offer at least that amount to entice the worker there. In a competitive market, some company will pay close to the marginal revenue product.

While this hypothetical example focuses on an industry that produces goods rather than services, the factors in salary determination are, theoretically, the same. The athlete is producing a service, public entertainment, among others. Hiring professional athletes is supposed to increase outputs (i.e., wins and successful teams) that tend to attract more paying fans. As a consequence of increased attendance, the team's revenues will rise. If a team realizes $500,000 more per year for signing a player, then the athlete's salary is likely to approach this figure. Noll predicted that in a city of 3.5 million, a superstar may add 90,000 fans per season; hence, the athlete's salary will approach this added revenue.[50] Consider, too, a superstar pitcher who is well publicized and pitches frequently. Fernando Valenzuela earned $42,500 his rookie season and hoped for a $1-million contract the following year. Why? When he pitched, attendance rose 7,411 at home and 13,815 on the road. Performing a few arithmetical operations on your calculator will demonstrate that he brought in an additional $750,000 to $1 million in gate receipts alone! When the New York Knicks signed Patrick Ewing out of Georgetown for $1.5 million, season ticket sales nearly doubled from 5,700 to 11,000, meaning that his presence on the team accounted for nearly $3 million in increased revenues. Likewise, when the Buffalo Bills contracted with Jim Kelly for $1.5 million in 1986, average home attendance increased by more than 31,000. Because the average ticket was in the $25 range, the increased revenue amounted to nearly $800,000 per game and, with eight home games, to over $6 million for the season. Finally, when the Los Angeles Kings signed Wayne Gretzky to an eight-year, $20-million contract season, ticket sales grossed an extra $4 million or more, an amount attributed to his presence on the team.

☐ SPORT AS A MONOPOLY

The bugaboo in the discussion of salary determination is that sport labor markets have not been competitive historically (making professional sport unique among American industries) and that an athlete's marginal revenue product cannot be determined easily. Sport is virtually a self-regulating **monopoly.** Sport owners operate as a **cartel,** an economic body formed by a group of firms (teams) within the same industry (league) who deliberate on matters of common interest (e.g., rules, expansion, promotion, and scheduling). Such a socioeconomic arrangement is illegal in other American businesses. This monopolistic structure greatly contributes to sport's financial benefits.

To understand how this state of affairs evolved, it is necessary to momentarily regress in history. On 2 July 1890, President Cleveland, dismayed by the staggering impact of the Standard Oil Trust on American society, pressured Congress to pass the **Sherman Antitrust Law,** which made illegal "every contract, combination in the form of trust or otherwise, or conspiracy in restraint of trade or commerce among the several states or with foreign nations."[51] This declaration, while not directed at sport in particular, had profound implications for baseball for several reasons: (a) There was a group of twenty-five teams located in eight different states who engaged in interstate financial transactions. (b) Trade was restrained, because a team in one city could not directly hire a player in another city. (c) The owners conspired to keep a ceiling on players' salaries.

After Congress passed the Sherman Antitrust legislation, the courts began to adjudicate. In 1922, Supreme Court Justice Oliver Wendell Holmes handed down a venerable decree pronouncing that the transportation of players across state lines was purely coincidental and not interstate commerce and, hence, baseball was not violating federal antitrust laws. Although the courts tried other cases during the interim, professional baseball's extralegal status remained sacrosanct until the mid-1970s. Hence, Holmes's decision meant each baseball league (other professional team sports have also enjoyed this exemption by default) controlled three activities: (a) the competition for players, (b) the location of franchises, and (c) the sale of media rights. Our present concern is with the manner in which players were kept in bondage and the legal changes that have occurred in this modus operandi.

The Reserve Clause

Historically, the **player reserve system** eliminated interclub competition for players' services. Each club had the sole right to unilaterally negotiate with players whose services were reserved exclusively for that club. Under these circumstances, players' salaries were determined solely by the owner (Vignette 11.2). Economists term this a *monopsonist* relationship (whereas a *monopoly* means one seller, a *monopsony* means one buyer)—players have one buyer to whom they can sell their services, and the athlete "could take it or leave it." The monopsonist system applied to veterans as well as rookies. Dworkin said:

> The major impact of the reservation system was to cause an extreme imbalance in bargaining power between owners and players. . . . The owners prospered, while the players

▢   **VIGNETTE 11.2**

Ex-player Recalls His Contract Talks

BY ALEX THIEN

. . . much has been written and discussed about the merits of using agents during the negotiations of professional athletes' contracts.

"Back in 1946, when you negotiated a contract, it was a one-on-one affair and the athlete was at a distinct disadvantage," said [Donn] Lindgren, now the president of Donnell Steel Products Co.

He said he was in the process of trying to work out a contract with the late and one and only coach of this type, George Halas of the Chicago Bears.

"Like a lot of guys during that time, my football career was interrupted by World War II," Lindgren said, "and I went to great lengths to explain to Halas that I thought I was worth more than a mere $1,000 bonus for signing with his team."

Lindgren said he brought up everything he could—his college record, his time in the Marine Corps to work on Halas' patriotism, how well he got along with other people, the way he put his whole heart into whatever it was he did and how, of course, he loved professional football, the world's best game.

Halas listened patiently, appearing to hang on every word, then left the conference room for a couple of minutes. When he returned with what looked to be a contract, he looked Lindgren right in the eye. Then, in a stern but still fatherly way, Halas said:

"Kid, this is my final offer—10 hundred—take it or leave it."

Lindgren said that without one bit of hesitation he signed on the dotted line.

SOURCE: *Milwaukee Sentinel* (16 July 1981), p. 1, part 3.

▢

---

toiled for wages . . . below the level they would receive had they been bargaining in a more competitive environment.[52]

The player reserve clause, a standard feature of every player's contract, was most restrictive in professional baseball and hockey; it meant that players had no control over the team for which they played during their entire careers. Thus, the only way that players could change teams was if the owners chose to either release them outright or permitted another club to negotiate with them.

Consider how this restrictive practice operated in professional baseball. Once under contract with a particular organization, a player's destiny was at the owner's disposal. If the contract was sold or if the player was traded to another team, the player was obligated to the new organization. To become a **free agent**—an individual not under contract to any club—the baseball player had to secure an outright release from his present club; a practice rarely allowed. Furthermore, most players were first placed on **waivers,** thereby giving other organizations the option of purchasing their contracts at a nominal waiver fee. Professional sport organizations have a system of rules whereby other clubs in the league may claim a player before a club can drop a player from their roster "or trade that player or sell his contract to a club in another league. A club can pick up a player 'on waivers' by buying his contract for the stipulated waiver price. When a club places a player on waivers . . . it has the right to withdraw the player's name from the list a limited number of times even if a claim is made. If no other club claims the player, the player "clears waivers" and is subsequently dropped from the club or can then be traded to a club in another league.[53]

Social and legal changes have altered these traditionally restrictive procedures. Curt Flood's court battle set the precedent for change, but the most monumental change in the economics of professional sports, as applied to players, occurred a few years later. In 1976, arbitrator Peter Seitz, a U.S. District Court judge, upheld the free-agency status of Andy Messersmith and Dave McNally. Both pitchers played the 1975 season without a contract and claimed that in doing so were thus entitled to free-agent status. Management disagreed, citing their perpetual ownership of a player's services, but their pleas were denied and the reserve clause, which since the later 1800s had allowed owners to retain the players in perpetuity, was demolished. This court ruling set a precedent. A professional baseball player's legal status was judged similar to a football or basketball player who was required to play one year beyond a contract before being eligible for free agency. This new status permitted the athletes to negotiate with other clubs and freed them from virtual peonage. Scully's[54] analysis of baseball maintains that under the reserve clause the franchise that sells a player makes the profits, whereas under the free-agency system, the players receive the lion's share of the profits. However, he argues that neither system—reserve clause or free agency draft—has had much effect on the distribution of talent in the league because highly talented players tend to migrate to the large market areas.

The Option Clause

Professional football and basketball have not used the reserve clause; instead, they have employed the option system. The **option clause** gave the owners the exclusive right to invoke the terms of a player's contract for one year following its expiration. If a player wanted to enter the bidding market—and so become a free agent—he could be required to play one additional year for 90% of his previous year's salary. On the surface, the option system seems more just than the reserve system.

Until the 1974–1975 season, for example, the NHL had a perpetual reserve system akin to that of baseball. Today, however, it implements the one-year option system. The Commissioners in the NHL and WHA were not as adamant in the mandatory compensation procedure as football because of the direct economic competition between the WHA and NHL. The WHA and NHL negotiated a merger. In practice, however, labor conditions were not as auspicious as they might appear. For one thing, players who announced their intent to play out their option were subjected to an automatic 10% salary reduction during their option year. Furthermore, the Rozelle Rule (named after former NFL commissioner, Pete Rozelle) required that the new employer compensate the former (with either athletes or money of equal value) and, if the two bartering clubs could not agree, that the final transaction be determined solely by the commissioner.

The Free-Agent Draft

The reserve system, as applied to rookies, is called the **free-agent draft,** and it stipulates rules and regulations for signing players who have not previously negotiated contracts. Clubs select in the inverse order of their previous year's finish. Once a player has been chosen, the club retains exclusive bargaining rights and, as is the case with the reserve system for veterans, a rookie's contract can be traded or sold.

In baseball, the drafting club owns the draftee for six months. After that time, if the player has not signed, the name is returned to the pool of eligible draftees for possible selection by another club. In other sports, the drafting club retains perpetual option over the player, and the player could never expect to be returned to the pool of draftees—they had to either play for the selecting club or forego play. The legal status of the draft system (in football) has been debated in the courts. Although a 1976 court decision declared that the free-agent draft was an infraction of the federal antitrust laws, the draft is still used. The perpetuation of the free-agent draft is due to an agreement that clubs not meddle with another team's property. When tampering occurs, serious sanctions are leveled against the violator.

How Well Does the Free-Agent Draft System Work?   The manifest purpose of the player draft system is to provide competitive balance among the teams in a league. Hence, teams that finish at the bottom receive the first picks and teams that finish at the top receive the last. Evidence suggests that the draft's impact on team parity is limited.

To illustrate the argument, consider the New York Giants who won the Super Bowl in 1991 and the New England Patriots, who had the poorest record. When NFL clubs drafted college players, the "worst" team selected first and the "best" selected last. Because there are 28 NFL teams, the last-placed team picked first, twenty-ninth, fifty-seventh, and so on until the pool of eligibles was depleted. The Giants, on the other hand, picked twenty-eighth, fifty-sixth, and so on. The only real advantage to the last-place team lies in a single selection per year. It is reasonable to wager, in terms of a team sport like football, that a single first-choice player isn't likely to turn a franchise around, because there are offensive, defensive, and special teams. In basketball, however, it is more likely that the presence of a single superstar (e.g., Kareem Abdul-Jabbar, Michael Jordan, Patrick Ewing, Magic Johnson, David Robinson, Ralph Sampson, or Larry Bird) could (and can) have a significant impact on a team.

In summary, while the draft system may have some effect on achieving parity, its actual contribution is debatable. Despite owners' claims that the player draft and reserve system serve to equalize talent, evidence suggests this is not true. Dynasties have characterized all major professional team sports. For example, in baseball, the New York Yankees dominated the American League from 1921 to 1965 by winning six American League pennants between 1921 and 1928, seven between 1937 and 1943, and fourteen between 1949 and 1965. The St. Louis Cardinals, New York Giants, and Brooklyn Dodgers dominated the National League from 1940 to 1960. In similar fashion, the Boston Celtics reigned supreme in basketball during the 1950s and 1960s. Between 1947 and 1972, the Celtics won eleven championships, and the

Lakers six. The Minneapolis Lakers, led by George Mikan, won six basketball titles in three different leagues in seven years (1948–1954). Similarly, the Green Bay Packers dominated football during the 1960s; the Miami Dolphins, in the early 1970s; the Pittsburgh Steelers, in the middle to late 1970s; and the San Francisco 49ers, in the late 1980s. Two ice hockey teams that have dominated the sport are the Montreal Canadiens and the Toronto Maple Leafs. Up to 1975, twenty-eight Stanley Cups had been won by either the Canadiens (seventeen) or the Maple Leafs (eleven). Two other clubs, the Detroit Red Wings and the Boston Bruins, have won five or more Stanley Cups in the NHL. The first expansion team to win the Stanley Cup was the Philadelphia Flyers in 1974. Hence, whatever else is working, team championships have not been equalized over the last half century.

The Legal Status of Professional Athletes

We have seen that, historically, professional athletes, unlike other employees, have not been free to (a) offer their services to the highest bidder, (b) choose their employers, or (c) change jobs.[55] Although athletes did possess these freedoms in baseball's formative years, before the turn of the century, they were deprived of them. The legal prerogatives of the professional athlete are hotly contested matters, as evidenced by the first midseason baseball strikes in 1981 and 1985 as well as the labor tribulations during the 1990 spring training season, the first midseason football strike in 1982, and the first NHL strike in 1992.

In professional team sports, the owners argue that if players are permitted to freely negotiate contracts with various clubs, the richest clubs will end up with the best talent; as a consequence, the competitive balance of sports would be destroyed and would not be in the best interest of the game. A vicious cycle would ensue, in which the weakest teams would accumulate the poorest records, and their fans would desert them. Although the wealthiest teams may end up with many of the best players, there is no guarantee that they will win championships. In 1987, for example, money did not buy success in the NFL. The four teams with the highest average salaries were the Raiders, Jets, Patriots, and Giants—teams that had losing records. Super Bowl teams Washington and Denver ranked ninth and fourteenth, respectively. The average salary for the Super Bowl champions was $199,235; for the Raiders, $285,653. Basketball and baseball were similar.

Another example is the 1960 World Series, featuring the Yankees and the Pirates. The Yankees showcased such stars as Mickey Mantle, Yogi Berra, Bill Skowron, Roger Maris, Gil McDougald, Bobby Richardson, Clete Boyer, and Bob Turley. In this fifty-seventh "autumn classic," New York set several records: highest batting average (.338), most hits (91), most total bases (142), most runs (55), and most runs batted in, (RBIs), (54)—but lost to Pittsburgh four games to three.

Another argument advanced by the owners is that if players are allowed unrestricted negotiations they might experience conflicts of interest. For example, athletes might find themselves in situations where their actions could lead to victory for either their present club or for the club they were contracted to for the following season. To avoid this situation (regardless of whether or not it might occur), the system of rules we have been discussing was instituted to regulate interteam competition.

Some Recent Changes in Professional Athletes' Legal Status

Collective Bargaining in Professional Sport

Baseball. *Collective bargaining* is a term endemic to such industries as coal mining, steel production, the garment industry, and transportation. In the context of professional sport it has been less widely known, although strikes and lockouts catapulted this concept into the popular culture. *Collective bargaining*, by definition, is a process by which labor unions (e.g., Major League Baseball Players Association, NFL Players' Association [NFLPA], NBA Players Association) negotiate with owners and management regarding matters such as wages, pensions, free agency, working conditions and fringe benefits. The adjective "collective" denotes that the union bargains for all employees under its jurisdiction. In the baseball strike of 1981, for example, Marvin Miller, the players' representative, along with player representation—the "union"—negotiated for some 650 major league baseball players.

Theoretically, the purpose of the collective bargaining process is to ensure equitable conflict resolution between labor and management. Under ideal circumstances, different vested interests are "ironed out" "across the table" rather than in a strike. When the two parties fail to act in good faith or reach a stalemate, the National Labor Relations Act dictates some form of federal mediation to intervene. In the 1981 baseball players strike, the union felt that management was acting unfairly toward them and invoked the National Labor Relations Board (NLRB) to determine if their charges had merit. The NLRB deemed, among other things, that the owners had not bargained in good faith and should supply the financial data requested by the players association.[56]

What will this ultimately mean? Several significant questions come to mind: Do the exorbitant contracts set a precedent that endangers the basic structure of baseball? Can the game survive such economic pressures? Will the baseball fan, the last one in big-time sports who is able to enjoy moderately priced family entertainment, become disenchanted with escalating ticket prices, with the constant shifting of team heroes, and with the cold business aspects of the enterprise in general? Will baseball's competitive balance, necessary for fan appeal and gate receipts, be thrown out of kilter by the ability of wealthy franchises and free-spending owners to outbid their rivals for talent? The answers to these questions only time will provide.

Football. An agreement between NFL club owners and the NFLPA in 1977 included establishing minimum salary schedules for rookies and veterans, altering the player draft system, modifying Rozelle Rule changes in the option clause, voiding of arbitrary dress codes, and recognizing the union. Following the 1982 strike, a settlement included minimum rookie salaries of $30,000, increases $10,000 per annum increments up to a maximum of $200,000 for a player with 18 years of service, and provision for severance pay after two years.[57]

Basketball. David Stern, commissioner of the NBA, took over the helm in 1984 and was confronted with many serious problems. At that time, the NBA resembled a sinking ship, but he convinced the union's chief negotiator to accept a revolutionary collective bargaining agreement, namely, a salary cap of 53% for players' salaries from the league's gross revenues. This salary cap was the first instance of revenue sharing between owners and players in modern sports history. Of average gross revenues per team in 1989–1990 ($16.7 million), the players share—that is, the amount allotted for salaries—was $9.8 million with an average player salary of $750,000. Other changes in the player–ownership relationship have also occurred in professional basketball. These include (a) striking the option clause from standard player contracts, which means that basketball players do not have to play a year beyond their contract expiration date; (b) a player's owner has the right of "first refusal," that is, if the current owner equals the contract offered by another club, the owner retains the right to the player; (c) the compensation rule (much like football's former Rozelle Rule) was eliminated in 1980, and (d) the owners agreed to pay $4.5 million to about 500 players "damaged" by the old system.[58]

❏ SUMMARY

In discussing the economics of professional sport, attention was paid to the operational strategies of the sports owner. Several different types of owners have headed sport franchises, and many of today's owners are corporate managers, individuals who take advantage of federal tax laws. One federal statute that can be seen as a cause of the flurry of new franchises and the rapid turnover in sport ownership is the law of depreciation, which allows commodities to be deducted from taxes as their value depreciates with wear. When a new franchise is purchased, the new owner buys essentially two things: (a) the franchise license and (b) a batch of player contracts. The license cannot be depreciated, but the player contracts can (through the amortization of players' contracts).

If the depreciation of player contracts is combined with financial losses in the sport franchise, money can then be deducted from taxes owed by the owner on other profitable business endeavors for a considerable tax savings. Although many sport franchises may show accounting losses, one must be aware that these losses are only part of the picture, because they can be used to the owners' advantage in conjunction with other businesses. The financing of sports facilities frequently ends up in the public's lap, because stadium construction and renovation projects often do not pay for themselves. In addition, sport facilities are usually rented for nominal fees, and indirect tax benefits accrue to professional sport owners at the local level (publicly owned teams do not pay property taxes). Historically, players' salaries have been moderate, and a player's mobility was restricted by the reserve system, the option clause, and/or the free-agent draft. These standard operating procedures served to deny players the freedom to control their careers. Recent court cases have voided or modified many of these traditional procedures and, consequently, players' salaries have soared and team shifting has become more commonplace. Although the value of sport as an industry is difficult to determine, one thing is certain: It is vast. The gross national sports product is estimated to be in the $50 billion neighborhood. In general, professional sports are profitable (from the standpoint of tax benefits, depreciation, etc.), but they are perhaps less profitable today than a decade or two ago. Complexities aside, no one can deny that sport is big business in North America today.

☐ KEY CONCEPTS

Informal Sport
Organized Sport
Corporate Sport
Capital
Revenue Sharing
Law of Depreciation
Tax Reform Act
Depreciation Recapture
Amortization of Players' Contracts
Opportunity Cost
Economic Rent
Marginal Product

Marginal Revenue Product
Monopoly
Cartel
Sherman Antitrust Law
Player Reserve System
Monopsony
Free Agent
Waivers
Option Clause
Free-Agent Draft
Collective Bargaining

☐ ENDNOTES

1. BIL GILBERT, "Gleanings from a Troubled Time," *Sports Illustrated* 37 (25 December 1972) pp. 34–36.
   D. STANLEY EITZEN & GEORGE H. SAGE, *Sociology of American Sport* (Dubuque, IA: William C. Brown, 1978), p. 18.
2. PAUL HOCH, *Rip Off: The Big Game* (Garden City, NY: Anchor Books, 1972), p. 39.
3. *Capitalism* is an economic system in which investment in and ownership of the means of production, distribution, and exchange of goods and wealth are maintained chiefly by individuals or corporations.
4. HOWARD L. NIXON, II, *Sport and Social Organization* (Indianapolis, IN: Bobbs-Merrill, 1975), p. 56.
5. *Op. cit.,*[2] p. 30.
6. DALE HOFFMAN & MARTIN J. GREENBERG, *Sport$biz* (Champaign, IL: Human Kinetics Publishers, 1989), p. 98.
7. RUDY MARTZKE, "Riding Fans, Sponsors to Success," *USA Today* (7 April 1983), p. C1.
8. *Business Week*, cited in *op. cit.,*[6] p. 100.
9. MICHAEL RUBY, "TV Sponsors: You've Come a Long Way Baby," *Inside Sports* 3, no. 4 (April 1981), pp. 111–112.
10. JIM KAPLAN, "Viewpoint," *Sports Illustrated* (10 November 1980).
11. "The 1990 *Sport* 100 Salary Survey," *Sport* (June 1991).
12. *USA Today* (22 January 1986), p. 2A.
13. JAMES A. MICHENER, *Sports in America* (New York: Random House, 1976).
    RALPH NADER & PETER GRUENSTEIN, "Blessed Are the Fans for They Shall Inherit $12 Bleacher Seats, Indigestible Hot Dogs, $2 Bottles of Beer and 100 Overpaid Superstars," *Playboy* 25 (March 1978), pp. 98, 198, 200, 202, 204.
14. RAY KENNEDY, "Who Are These Guys?" *Sports Illustrated* (31 January 1977), pp. 50–58.
15. RAY KENNEDY & NANCY WILLIAMSON, "Money in Sports," *Sports Illustrated* 49 (17 July 1978), p. 88.
16. *Op. cit.,*[14]
17. *Ibid.,* p. 55.
18. WILLIAM C. FLINT & D. STANLEY EITZEN, "Professional Sports Team Ownership and Entrepreneurial Capitalism," *Sociology of Sport Journal* 4, no. 1 (1987), pp. 17–27.
19. *Ibid.,* p. 19.
20. *Op. cit.*[6]
21. "Trouble in the Sports World," *U.S. News and World Report* (12 August 1974), pp. 52–55.
22. D. STANLEY EITZEN, *Sport in American Society* (New York: St. Martin's, 1979), p. 325.
23. RICHARD SANDOMIR, "The Gross National Sports Product," *Sport in Contemporary Society* ed. D. Stanley Eitzen (New York: St. Martin's, 1989), pp. 190–196.
24. ROGER G. NOLL, "Attendance, Prices, and Profits in Professional Sports," *Government*

and the Sports Business (Washington, DC: The Brookings Institute, 1974).

25. HENRY DEMMERT, *The Economics of Professional Team Sports* (New York: Joint Council on Economic Education, 1976).

26. ROBERT THOMAS, "Demand for a Factor of Production: Will the Yankees Buy All the Best Players," *Readings in Labor Economics,* ed. Donald Coffin (Normal-Bloomington: Illinois State University, 1984), p. 65.

27. JAMES QUIRK, "An Economic Analysis of The Movements in Professional Sports," *Law and Contemporary Problems* 38 (1973), pp. 42–66.

28. NADER & GRUENSTEIN, *op. cit.,*[13]

29. *Op. cit.*[24]

30. *Ibid.*

31. EITZEN & SAGE, *op. cit.,*[1] p. 180.

32. "Who Says Baseball Is like Ballet?" *Forbes* (1 April 1971), p. 30.

33. *Chicago Tribune* (18 June 1981), Section 1, p. 14.

34. BARRY D. MCPHERSON, "Sport Consumption and the Economics of Consumerism," *Sport and Social Order,* eds. D.W. Ball & J.W. Loy (Reading, MA: Addison-Wesley, 1975), p. 262.

35. ROGER G. NOLL, *Government and the Sports Business* (Washington, DC: The Brookings Institute, 1974).

36. *Ibid.*

37. *Op. Cit.,*[2] pp. 51–52.

38. *Wall Street Journal* (27 February 1975), p. 16.

39. ELDON E. SNYDER & ELMER A. SPREITZER, *Social Aspects of Sport* (Englewood Cliffs, NJ: Prentice-Hall, 1989), p. 278.

40. BENJAMIN A. OKNER, "Direct and Indirect Subsidies to Professional Sports." Paper presented at the Brookings Conference on Government and Sport, Washington, DC, 6–7 December 1971.

41. *Op. cit.*[40]; *Op. Cit.,*[34] p. 264.

42. *Ibid.*

43. "The 1991 *Sport* 100 Salary Survey," *Sport* (June 1991).

44. MIN S. YEE & DONALD K. WRIGHT, *The Sports Book* (New York: Holt, Rinehart & Winston, 1975), p. 40.

45. LEE BALLINGER, *In Your Face! Sports for Love and Money* (Chicago: Vanguard Books, 1981), p. 14.

46. *Op. cit.*[44]

47. *Op. cit.*[45]

48. "The 1990 *Sport* 100 Salary Survey," *Sport* (June 1990).

49. *Op. cit.*[25]

50. ROGER G. NOLL. "Attendance Prices and Profits in Professional Sports." Paper presented at the Brookings Conference on Government and Sport, Washington, DC, 6–7 December 1971.

51. MICHENER, *op. cit.,*[13] p. 386.

52. J.B. DWORKIN, "Balancing the Rights of Professional Athletes and Team Owners: The Proper Role of Government," *Government and Sport: The Public Policy Issues* eds. A.T. Johnson & J.H. Frey (Totowa, NJ: Rowman & Allanheld, 1985), p. 25.

53. *Sports Dictionary* (Springfield, MA: G. & G. Merriam, 1976), p. 474.

54. GERALD SCULLY, *The Business of Major League Baseball* (Chicago: University of Chicago Press, 1989).

55. JAY J. COAKLEY, *Sport in Society* (St. Louis: C.V. Mosby, 1978), pp. 193–195.

56. PAUL D. STAVDOHAR, "Player Salary Issues in Major League Baseball," *Arbitration Journal* 33, no. 4 (December 1978), pp. 17–21.

57. "Behind Pro Football's Labor Peace," *New York Times* (6 March 1977), p. S9.
D. STANLEY EITZEN & GEORGE H. SAGE, *Sociology of North American Sport* (Dubuque, IA: William C. Brown, 1986), p. 206.

58. DOUGLAS S. LOONEY, "The Start of a Chain Reaction," *Sports Illustrated* 44 (16 February 1976), pp. 18–20.
EITZEN & SAGE, *op. cit.,*[1] pp. 206–207.

12

Sport and Politics

. . . sport and politics always have been institutional partners . . . particularly where [a] society's reputation or national pride are at stake. Although in the United States the separation of sport and politics may be viewed as the appropriate relationship, it is not the practiced one.

ARTHUR T. JOHNSON *and* JAMES H. FREY

In Chapter 1, we introduced the sociological concept of *social system,* a notion implying the interconnectedness of social institutions. In Chapter 5, the ties between the institutions of sport and the family via socialization processes were examined; in Chapter 11, the interfacing of sport and the economy were explored; in Chapter 10, the links between sport and education were considered; in this chapter, the interrelationships between **sport and politics** are analyzed; and in Chapter 13, the intersections of sport and religion.

The decade of the 1990s began with several sociopolitical incidents that highlight sports immunity from broader social currents:

- College basketball teams began wearing American flag patches on their jerseys when the Persian Gulf War broke out.
- Country clubs with exclusive membership were challenged to accept minorities.
- South Africa petitioned for readmittance to the Olympics.
- Female sportswriters fighting for equal access to athletes.
- The National Football League (NFL) threatening to rescind the decision to hold the 1993 Super Bowl in Phoenix after the Arizona voters rejected a paid state holiday for Martin Luther King, Jr.

Other examples of athletes or nations using sports to make political statements include:

- 1968—U.S. sprinters John Carlos and Tommie Smith gave the Black Power salute on the winners' podium and were subsequently suspended from the track team.
- 1976—Black African nations boycotted the summer Olympics because the International Olympic Committee (IOC) failed to ban New Zealand for permitting its rugby team to play in segregated South Africa.
- 1980—President Carter calls for the United States to ban the Moscow Olympics because the U.S.S.R. invaded Afghanistan.
- 1984—The U.S.S.R. boycotted the Los Angeles Olympics (in retaliation for the United States's action in 1980).
- 1990—Birmingham's Shoal Creek Country Club agreed to admit minorities under the threat of having golf's Professional Golf Association (PGA) championship canceled.
- The Annandale Golf Club in Pasadena, California, was to have been the site of the 1993 U.S. Women's Amateur. It withdrew its name apparently to avoid attracting attention to the fact that the Club has no minority members.
- The U.S. Tennis Association requested to have the U.S. Davis Cup team's first round match with Mexico on February 1–3, 1991, postponed because of the Persian Gulf crisis.
- Chicago Blackhawks owner Bill Wirtz decided to have the team wear United Nations flags on their helmets for the duration of the Persian Gulf crisis.

Sociologists Smith and Preston define **politics** as the "processes people use to resolve conflicts between private interests and the common good that occur within the institutional framework of government."[1] In the present context, the term *politics* is not used synonymously with, but in conjunction with, the term *government*. This discussion focuses on the process of *power*, a term denoting the ability of individuals or groups to affect others, even when these others oppose the goals or actions of the power holder. Weber defined power as "the probability that one actor within a social relationship will be in a position to carry out his own will despite resistance. . . ."[2] *Politics* and *power* are used in the Weberian sense in this discussion. As will be seen, sport is devoid of neither politics nor governmental intervention.

Even sports personalities have not been naive regarding sport–politics connections. Indiana University's basketball coach Bobby Knight[3] declared, "anyone who thinks we can compete internationally without politics being involved is either a complete moron or incredibly naive." Knight is correct, not only at the international level, but at other levels as well. "Behind the scenes [sports and politics], are as inextricably interwoven as any two issues can be. . . . It is unrealistic to say you shouldn't bring politics into sports," said Arthur Ashe.[4] Sugden and Yiannakis[5] have identified *four* levels to the politicization of international sport: (a) the quest for national prestige, by which nations seek to make their mark in the world community by achieving success in the Olympic Games; (b) the use of the Games by the host nation as a means of showcasing its political ideology and culture; (c) the use of athletic competition as a means for granting diplomatic recognition or nonrecognition to favored or delinquent nations; and (d) the manipulative use of the Games to coerce a nation to alter its internal or external political and/or military activities.

Sport sociologists Eitzen and Sage[6] consider politics endemic to sport for several reasons. (a) Athletes typically represent social organizations such as schools, communities, employers, states, regions, or even countries. Furthermore, some activities accompanying athletic events are symbolic of the athletes' allegiances. For example, schools have their fight songs, slogans, traditional music, and dress (with accompanying uniforms, mascots, insignias, and colors). (b) As sports become organized, a coterie of teams, sponsoring organizations, leagues, and regulative bodies emerge. The vested interests of one group are not necessarily those of another. Hence, competition and conflict—elements in the struggle for power—typically surface. At the professional level, there have been conflicts of interest between the National League and competing leagues in baseball's early evolution; the same holds true for the history of the American and the National Football Leagues (AFL and NFL), the American and the National Basketball Association (ABA and NBA), and the World Hockey Association and National Hockey League (WHA and NHL). Similarly, we have seen power struggles between players' associations and management (e.g., between professional baseball players and management during the summer of 1981; between the NFL players and management during the fall of 1982, 1985, and 1988; and between the NHL players' union and management in 1992) and between sport ruling bodies (the Amateur Athletic Union, AAU, and the National Collegiate Athletic Association, NCAA). (c) Systemic connections exist between the institution of sport and politics. Sport reinforces the larger social order in numerous ways. The national anthem accompanies most sporting events; clergy and politicians are fond of using sport as a metaphor for life's lessons, and hackneyed sports expressions are continually bantered about. In short, sport, like religion, tends to reinforce and legitimize the larger society and, as such, is a conservative laissez-faire mechanism. For these and other reasons, sport and politics are intricately entwined; they are not diametrically opposed.

There is a precedent for the belief that politics is power. Political scientist Morgenthau wrote: "All politics, domestic and international, reveals three basic patterns: . . . all political phenomena can be reduced to one of three basic types. A political policy seeks either to keep power, to increase power, or to demonstrate power."[7] This concept of power has relevance to sport. The Olympics have become a battleground for competing ideologies rather than friendly international competition. Following is an examination of the reciprocal connections between sport and politics using the modern-day Olympiads.

❑ THE OLYMPICS AS A CASE STUDY IN POWER POLITICS

In theory, the Olympic Games are above the rancor of international politics; in actuality, they are not. Avery Brundage, former International Olympic Committee (IOC) president, unmistakably captured what he believed the Olympics were and were not about:

> The Games are not, and must not become a contest between nations which would be entirely contrary to the spirit of the Olympic Movement and would surely lead to disaster. For this reason there is no official score of nations and tables of points are really misinformation because they are entirely inaccurate. To be correct they would have to be weighted since it is certainly unfair to give the winner of the marathon or decathlon, a winning gymnast, pistol shooter or yachtsman, and a winning football soccer or basketball team the same score. Moreover, the factor of population should be considered . . .
>
> Neither the Olympic Games nor any sport contest can be said to indicate the superiority of one political system over another, of one country over another. . . . The IOC resents attempts to use the Games as a political instrument or to pit one country against another. We trust that you will do everything in your power to discourage the publication of scoring tables, which are quite worthless. . . .[8]

Brundage's statement appears to be so much wishful thinking. Victories in international sport are functional equivalences of war victories of one country over another (Vignette 12.1).

In commenting on the Olympics, Espy wrote: "The modern games . . . have been utilized not so much for international fair play, peace, and understanding as for national self-interest, survival, and pride."[9]

To illustrate, let us briefly chronicle some significant political events since the inception of the modern Olympics.[10] During the 1896 Games, the first modern Olympiad, the pageantry of nationalism was apparent when Greece's Crown Prince Constantine escorted his compatriot marathoner across the finish line. In 1908, the U.S. team refused to dip the American flag to King Edward VIII of England. The Games were canceled in 1916 because of World War I. In 1936, there was pressure for the United States to boycott the "Nazi Olympics." Although the boycott failed to materialize, the nationalistic overtones were clearly evident (see Vignette 12.2). The Germans had already invaded Poland in early September 1939 so the Games were canceled in 1940 and again in 1944, during the war. In 1948, the new state of Israel was denied the right to participate because of the threat of an Arab boycott. In 1956,

⬛ VIGNETTE 12.1

Looking at the 1988 Olympic Games from a Different Perspective

Former IOC President Avery Brundage indicated that the Olympic Games should be individual competitions, not nation–state struggles. Furthermore, he suggests that for various reasons, it is invalid to compare countries in terms of the number of medals won. Brundage specifically alludes to the impact of differential populations and intimates the necessity of adjusting for these differences if one so desires to legitimately compare the medals garnered by different countries. The author has computed a "medal rate" for twelve countries participating in the 1988 (Seoul) Olympics.

The U.S.S.R. swept the field and gathered 132 medals. However, when the population of the various nations becomes a norming variable (see following formula for rate computation), a strikingly different picture emerges. When population size is adjusted, East Germany, Bulgaria, Hungary, and Romania were the top medal winners; the United States was down the list!

Country	Number of Medals (per Million Population)	Population in Millions	Medal Rate
USSR	132	291	0.45
East Germany	102	17	6.00
Romania	24	23	1.04
Bulgaria	35	9	3.89
South Korea	33	45	0.73
West Germany	40	61	0.66
United States	94	236	0.40
Great Britain	24	56	0.43
Hungary	23	11	2.09
France	16	55	0.29
Poland	16	39	0.41
China	28	1034	0.03

The medal rate was computed as follows: the criterion variable was the number of medals won; the norming variable was population (in millions). Hence, for Romania, $24/23 = 1.04$. This is interpreted to mean that 1.04 medals were won for every million people in the country.

Looking at the 1988 Olympics in this manner gives one an interestingly different perspective. Are there other variables that you think are necessary to take into account to arrive at a fair comparison?

SOURCE: Adapted from Leon F. Bouvier, "A Demographer Looks at the 1984 Olympic Games," *Population Today* 12 (October 1984), pp. 6–7.

⬛

☐ **VIGNETTE 12.2**

Sport as a Political Tool

The 1936 Olympic Games

When the National Socialists (Nazis), led by Adolf Hitler came to hegemony in 1933, the 1936 Games (sometimes called the "Nazi Olympics") had already been scheduled for Berlin. Hitler was reluctant to stage the games there but, on the urgings of his propaganda minister, was enticed to use them for showcasing purposes. In his preparation for war, he took this opportunity to show the world the nature of Aryan (a non-Jewish Caucasian) supremacy both in and outside the Olympic stadium. The city of Berlin was given a "face lift"—cleaned up, repainted, and primed for the series of sporting events. The stadium itself was built to seat 105,000, and the Olympic village was an architectural and aesthetic ideal. Reports circulated regarding the impressive nature of Berlin and the Olympic site. The final gold (33), silver (26), and bronze (30) medal tally was partial testimony to the superiority of the German athletes and their sport structure. But the real hero was a four-gold-medal winner African-American by the name of Jesse Owens. The one-time Ohio State student won the 100- and 200-meter races, long jump, and kicked off the victorious 400-meter U.S. relay team. Not being fond of blacks (or Jews), Hitler vacated his special box seat when Owens took the winner's stand. Although the Fuhrer's gestures were none-too-sportsmanlike, Germany garnered the lion's share of the medals, and the Third Reich's prestige soared both at home and abroad. Noteworthy is the statement made by Joseph Goebels, Minister of Propaganda and Enlightenment, that the Berlin Games were worth twenty divisions to Nazi Germany!

The 1972 Olympic Games

The modern Olympics reached their nadir during the 1972 Munich Games. It is a well-known political fact that the Middle East countries are constantly at each other's throats. On September 5, 1972, eight Arab terrorists (Commandos of the "Black September" organization) commandeered the Olympic Village and killed eleven Israeli athletes. Moreover, the German police eventually killed five of the eight Arabs. Meanwhile, athletes from Egypt, Kuwait, and Syria withdrew and returned home immediately in fear of retaliation.

The 1976 Olympic Games

Like many other Olympics, the 1976 Montreal Games were marred by political squabbles. Taiwan was ousted because the IOC recognized only mainland China—not to mention Canada's profitable commercial pact with Beijing. The political dispute escalated. Because both Chinas—mainland and Taiwan—could not compete, the United States threatened to boycott. A compromise was struck. Taiwan could fly its flag and play its national anthem (both of these had previously been forbidden) but could not call itself *China*. Despite Taiwanese athletes already being in Montreal, their government did not accept these terms and flew the athletes home. Additionally, two-dozen black African nations refused to participate because New Zealand did. Earlier, New Zealand sent a team to play rugby in South Africa, where apartheid reigned supreme. The black African nations did not condone this sporting occasion and registered their protest by withdrawing from the contest.

Sport-Based Diplomacy

A final example of the use of sport as a political tool concerns the restoration of diplomatic relations between the United States and China. In 1971, Ping-Pong matches fostered relations between the two countries. This "Ping-Pong diplomacy" stemmed from a team of table tennis players from the United States traveling to China and competing against the Chinese. For a period of nearly 20 years (early 1950s to early 1970s), China had remained isolated from international sporting events choosing to concentrate on domestic feats. International competition through table tennis was a catalyst to detente between the two countries. A similar goal was achieved by basketball matches between Cuba and the United States in the mid-1970s.

SOURCE: Richard Mandell, *The Nazi Olympics* (New York: Macmillan, 1970).

❑

---

as Olympic athletes from Hungary were en route to the Games, Soviet tanks invaded their country to quell the Hungarian revolt. Spain, the Netherlands, and Switzerland withdrew from participation to protest Soviet imperialism. During this Olympiad, the Soviet and Hungarian water polo teams played in what was described as a blood bath because of the violence, bloodshed, and mayhem that ensued. In fact, Hungarian spectators rioted when "their" swimmer was attacked by a Russian. In the same year, Iraq, Egypt, and Lebanon boycotted the Games because the Suez Canal had been seized by Anglo-French forces. Also, the Communist Chinese team walked out of the Games when the National Chinese flag was raised.

In 1952, East Germany refused to compete because it had been denied separate statehood. (East and West Germany did participate as a single team in 1956.) Of interest, the Soviet Union entered competition for the first time in 1952. The Argentine team was temporarily denied the right of participation, when the head of its Olympic committee was imprisoned as a Peronista in 1956. South Africa was prohibited from participating in the 1964 Olympics because of its Apartheid (racial segregationist and discriminatory) policies. The 1968 Games saw South Africa once again banned and the threat of a boycott by black American athletes. The boycott did not reach fruition, but the Black Power salutes of Tommie Smith and John Carlos during the playing of the national anthem is still vividly remembered by many. The 1972 Olympics displayed terrorism, and the 1976 Olympics witnessed the withdrawal of several nation states (see Vignette 12.2). In 1980, the United States boycotted the Moscow Olympics, and in 1984 the Soviets reciprocated. Although there were no major incidents in 1988, there was concern over the conflict between North and South Korea in the games held at Seoul.

The 1980 Olympics: A Case Study of International Power Politics

The 1980 Olympics are well remembered for the U.S. boycott and for the first time the Games were staged in a communist country. Before the 1980 Olympics, the *U.S. News and World Report* asked several politicians and the U.S. Olympic Committee (USOC) president for reactions to the mounting possibility of a U.S. boycott. These individuals' responses are enlightening insofar as they pertain to the relationship between sport and politics. When asked why he favored a boycott by the U.S. team, Robert F. Drinan, Democratic representative from Massachusetts, said:

> It seems very clear to me that we can anticipate dire consequences if we go forward with the Olympics in Moscow in 1980. First, the Soviet dissidents will be jailed or placed

incommunicado lest they get on television around the world and create an incident—
something that the Russians would obviously be embarrassed by. Second, will the Israelis
be allowed to participate? And if they are allowed to participate, will the Arab countries
not participate? Should the U.S. go forward without any questions when there could be
a confrontation in Moscow over the particular clash in the Middle East? . . . third, the
Soviets are violating the solemn promise they gave at Helsinki three years ago to observe
all of the international regulations about sports and . . . human conduct. They gave that
pledge in return for the legalization of all borders of the satellite nations.[11]

Edward J. Derwinski, Republican representative from Illinois, who also favored
the boycott, said:

The latest reason is the Soviet aggression in Afghanistan. It is a flagrant violation of the
basic precepts of the Olympics, which favor peaceful competition among the peoples of
the world. The Soviet Union has been in violation of many international standards in its
diplomatic, military, and economic activities for years, and there has been a tolerance in
the world about it. But this naked aggression may be the straw that breaks the camel's
back.

On top of the Afghanistan invasion, you have to look at the Soviets' propaganda role
against the U.S. in Iran and throughout the Middle East, the buildup of Soviet military
forces and the threat this poses to the North Atlantic Treaty Organization, the Soviet
military buildup in the islands north of Japan. You get a picture of an aggressive, belligerent, power. In these circumstances, I don't think the Soviet Union is the proper host
for the Olympics.[12]

In contrast to these affirmative boycott responses were two negative ones. Robert
J. Kane, president of the USOC, said:

I don't favor the concept of a boycott at all in Olympic Games. The Olympic Games
should be kept free of politics as much as possible, and it's up to those within the movement to protect it from politics.

And I don't think it would be conducive to the continuance of the games if boycotts
become common practice. There are always differences between nations, and if there
were a boycott every time this happened, there would never be Olympic Games.[13]

Leo J. Ryan, Democratic representative from California, had this to say:

The most important reason is that if we begin to use the Olympics for blatant and obvious political purposes, then we are as culpable as others—such as the Soviets, the
Chinese, and Adolf Hitler in 1936—who have treated the Games as simply and purely a
political platform. I just don't think that's good U.S. policy either public or private.[14]

With due respect to these individuals, the chronicle of Olympiads presented earlier
suggests that some of their statements are naive, uninformed, and unrealistic in light
of the sport–politics relationship. First, an apolitical sanctity of the Games permeates
their perspectives. This ideal has been eroded; in fact, it is dubious that it ever existed
in the modern Olympics (not to mention the ancient Olympiads). Second, there are
strong elements of groupthink.[15] **Groupthink,** a social psychological concept, is a
conformity-producing social process that incorporates several elements: (a) the illusion of invulnerability, (b) the illusion of morality, (c) stereotyped views of the enemy,
and (d) rationalizations, all of which appear to characterize their statements to some
degree.

Finally, Arthur Ashe responded to Representative Drinan's arguments this way: To Drinan's remarks that the Soviets may be forced to lock up political dissidents he replied, "What else is new?" Ashe maintained that such behavior on the part of the Soviet authorities is commonplace; the only difference he foresaw was in the potential numbers affected. As for Drinan's comments regarding who would and would not participate, Ashe pointed out that no-shows are typical among the invited. He paraphrased Abraham Lincoln's familiar expression by saying, "You can please some of the countries all of the time, buy you can't please all of the countries all of the time." To Drinan's third point, Ashe replied that the Soviets would probably break or at least bend the Helsinki rules, regardless of the situation. Moreover, he asked rhetorically, how many treaties has the United States broken with the Native American people.[16]

In a television interview in January of 1980, then President Jimmy Carter declared publicly that if the Soviet Union refused to remove its troops from Afghanistan, the United States would attempt to choose an alternative to the Moscow Olympic site. If neither of these occurred, he would invite other nations to follow the U.S. boycott. Although Carter did not have the authority to call off the United States' participation (the USOC did), he was obviously using the Olympics as a lever of foreign diplomacy. According to reports, Carter's decision was significantly influenced by a conversation with the Moscow ambassador. The former president asked the ambassador whether trade sanctions or a boycott would have the most punitive impact on the Soviets. The ambassador answered that, without a doubt, a boycott would. Carter proclaimed that evening, "Although the United States would prefer not to withdraw from the Olympic Games . . . the Soviet Union must realize that its continued aggressive actions will endanger both the participation of the athletes and the travel to Moscow by spectators."[17]

The political significance the Soviets (today, the former U.S.S.R. is the Commonwealth of Independent States) attached to the Olympics is demonstrated by the following passage from the *Book of the Party Activist* (the "Bible" of the Soviet Communist Party):

> The acute ideological struggle between (East and West) directly affects the choice of cities for the Olympic Games, the program of the competitions, the reporting of the preparations and the conduct of the Games. . . . The decision . . . to hold the Olympic Games [in Moscow] has become convincing evidence of the . . . correctness of the foreign policy course of our country.[18]

Public Reaction to the Potential U.S. Olympic Boycott. The reactions of the four statesmen previously quoted may not be representative of the general public's opinion on the matter. *Newsweek* commissioned a special Gallup poll to assess the general public's reaction. The following queries were asked in a nationwide survey ($n = 518$) several months before the scheduled Moscow Olympics:[19]

1. "Some people feel the U.S. should threaten to boycott the 1980 Moscow Olympics as a way of influencing Russian policy on Afghanistan. Others feel participation in the Olympics should not be involved in political controversies. Which opinion is yours?" Of those surveyed, 47% favored using a threat to influence policy, 42% said the Olympics should not be involved, and 11% said they did not know.

2. "If the Soviet Union refuses to withdraw its troops from Afghanistan, should or should not the U.S. try to get the Olympics moved from Moscow to another country?" Of those surveyed, 68% said should, 22% said should not, and 10% said they did not know.
3. "If the Olympic Games cannot be moved to another country, do you feel the U.S. should participate in the Moscow Olympic Games or boycott them?" Of those surveyed, 56% favored a boycott, 34% favored participation, and 10% said they did not know.
4. "If the Olympic Games are held in Moscow and the U.S. decided to participate, do you think this will have an impact on future Russian foreign policy?" Of those surveyed, 52% said yes, 36% said no, and 12% said they did not know.

In summary, the *Newsweek* poll showed that Americans (a) favored boycotting the Moscow Games, (b) believed that the United States should threaten a boycott to influence policy, (c) felt the United States should try to move the Games to another site, and (d) believed that U.S. action to boycott would influence Russian foreign policy.

Athletes' Reactions to the Potential U.S. Olympic Boycott.   Most athletes opposed the boycott. Bob Giordano, a weightlifter, expressed the following sentiments: "I've been training for ten years, always pointing to 1980. I don't believe the sports world is any place to voice political opinions. No one condones anything the Soviet Union is doing in Afghanistan, but that is not our realm. We don't want to get involved in it. If it came to a vote, I think the athletes would go against the President's wishes. I personally would. There are many other ways of protesting."[20]

Henry Marsh, a steeplechaser, said, "As a patriotic citizen, I realize a boycott would be a severe blow to the Russians. . . . But as an athlete, the very thought of a boycott breaks my heart."[21]

These remarks are understandable from their individual standpoints. Many of the athletes had trained for years, and disappointment penetrated their souls. In February of 1980, Congress overwhelmingly approved a resolution calling for a U.S. boycott of the Moscow Olympics. Within two months, American Olympic athletes filed suit seeking to block the USOC from boycotting the Games. The suit claimed that the USOC had violated their (the athletes') constitutional rights, because it had no authority under the Amateur Sports Act to prevent the United States from participating in the Games. In the end, of course, the United States did not participate in the Moscow Olympics.

The U.S. boycott of the 1980 Olympics was particularly hard on those athletes who had trained and dedicated their lives for years to participate. Those athletes sacrificed a great deal, but athletes in earlier days also paid a price for political decisions. Consider five baseball superstars of yesteryear: Ted Williams, Joe Dimaggio, Hank Greenberg, Bob Feller, and Willie Mays. These five had several things in common. They were superstars, and each lost the opportunity to break significant records standing in his day. The cost in terms of their winnings and careers is difficult to predict, but none apparently bemoaned the sacrifices they made. Williams sacrificed five years of baseball by putting in two hitches with the Marines as a pilot. Dimaggio enlisted in the Army for three years at the peak of his career. Bob Feller spent four years in the Navy (from age 23 to 27). Mays put in two years with the Army early in his career with the Giants. He wound up fifty-four home runs short of Babe Ruth's. It is conceivable that he, not Hank Aaron, would have been the first to surpass the "Sultan of Swat's" milestone. Greenberg was the highest paid player in the majors in 1941, when he became a private in the Armed Forces. After being discharged several months later and hearing of the bombing of Pearl Harbor, he reenlisted in the Air Force. Greenberg "rose to the rank of captain, earned four battle stars, and participated in the first land-based bombing of Japan in 1944."[22]

The 1984 Olympics were held in Los Angeles, the site of the only other Summer Games held in the United States (in 1932). Dubbed as the "Capitalist Olympics" in contrast to the Moscow Games (the first "Communist Olympics"), about 8,000 athletes representing 1,400 countries competed. The U.S.S.R. and its allies boycotted the LA Games. The 1984 Olympics, despite the political conflicts, will be remembered as economically successful. Nearly 7 million tickets were sold, and a profit tally of $15 million was recorded.

POLITICS AT THE STATE, NATIONAL, AND INTERNATIONAL LEVELS

While the sports–politics connection is most visible at the international level, it exists at the local or municipal and national levels as well.[23] Sport is without ideology. It is chameleon-like insofar as it can be "used" by any political–economic system (capitalism, communism, socialism, fascism, etc.). However, sport can be construed as a symbol to which individuals attach or attribute meaning. In short, sport can be used to convey ideological notions when individuals attribute such meaning to it.

Municipal and State Levels

Several illustrations highlight the reciprocal relationship between sport and politics at the **state** or **municipal level.** In 1991, the Nebraska Legislature passed a bill to block the National Collegiate Athletic Association (NCAA) rules limiting the amount of financial aid student athletes can receive, and in the 1980s, several states, notably Texas, introduced "No Pass No Play" (meaning, if you don't pass your courses you don't play sports) legislation. In the early 1970s, a budget reduction in Philadelphia lead to a preliminary decision to eliminate several hundred teaching positions and virtually all extracurricular activities. One of the extramural activities earmarked for cutting was the sport program. According to Coakley "Local officials and the general public seemed to accept the loss of teachers, but the pressure to reinstate athletics was so great that it became a campaign issue in city politics."[24] The polemic was alleviated when Philadelphia Eagles' owner Leonard Tose put up $79,000 to fund varsity football temporarily.

The Chicago Cub's management decided to consider the possibility of installing lights in lightless Wrigley Field in the early 1980s. Citizens of Chicago living within close proximity to the ballpark petitioned the city council. In 1982 a law took effect prohibiting night baseball at Wrigley Field, considering it a violation of Illinois' noise pollution laws. The Chicago City Council later concurred with this ruling by approving their own ordinance. But the profit motive won out, and Wrigley Field now has light facilities for night baseball.

In 1981, Illinois Governor James Thompson applied an amendatory veto to a bill that helped the beleaguered University of Illinois. The university was expected to suffer heavy financial losses after the Big Ten sanctioned the school for permitting Dave Wilson to play the 1980 season. The mechanics of the governor's veto permitted the Illinois Athletic Association to receive funding from state lottery receipts. This action was designed to compensate the university for the expected revenue loss (estimated to be between $750,000 and $1 million). The governor aptly signed the bill at the fighting Illini's Memorial Stadium and indicated that he thought the bill would help the financial condition of the state's only public land-grant institution.

During the summer of 1981, Kentucky governor John Y. Brown, Jr., publicly proclaimed that he wanted to have the Kentucky Wildcats' coach Fran Curci replaced by former professional coach George Allen. The university's president told confidants that he resented the governor's intrusion into the school's affairs. Allen withdrew his name from consideration and stated that "in view of the understandable concern and out of respect for the UK administration and athletics board regarding the timing of such speculation, at this time it is my decision in the best interest of all parties to withdraw my name from consideration at the University of Kentucky."[25]

The state of Alabama had a mandatory retirement age of 70 for public employees. In the spring of 1981, as the "Tide's" football coach Paul "Bear" Bryant prepared to surpass the all-time football victory record of Amos Alonzo Stagg (actually, Grambling's Eddie Robinson is the all-time winningest coach), Alabama governor "Fob" James signed a bill that exempted Bryant from the state's mandatory retirement age. The law allowed the University of Alabama to exempt any university employee from the statute; but critics asserted that the bill was intended for Bryant exclusively, despite the fact that the bill, as proposed, conveyed a more universalistic flavor.

Sports Facilities. Even the construction of sports facilities typically exhibits strong political underpinnings. Suppose a city decides to build a new sport complex. How will it be financed? According to Michener there are at least four options: (a) public taxation, (b) existing institutions, (c) group cooperation, and/or (d) individual initiative (e.g., Miami's Joe Robbie stadium).[26] Each of these options has, at one time or another, been exercised. Let us first consider public monies, which was the source of funding for the construction of Philadelphia's Veterans' Stadium, Kansas City's Harry S. Truman Sport Complex, Denver's additions to Mile-High Stadium, and the New Orleans Superdome.

Consider the outright chicanery involved in the Superdome's construction. In the early 1960s, the public voted to build the facility at an estimated cost of $35 million. As a result of escalating costs, labor–management disputes, and political maneuverings, the Superdome's final construction bill amounted to $163 million, and this figure excluded operating expenses (which amounted to $38,000 per day, including interest on revenue bonds in the late 1970s). Hence, the final cost exceeded by nearly five times the original expenditure estimate. Because the sports complex runs a deficit, the public ultimately bears the brunt of this financial albatross.

In the past 15 years, various sport facilities have been built or renovated, largely at the taxpayer's expense. Although this may not have been the original intent, the financial liabilities that develop frequently end up in the public's lap and are ultimately subsidized by the taxpayer. This raises a serious ethical, moral, and political dilemma: Should public monies be used for such purposes?

National Level

National governments recognize two major political roles sport can play in their homelands. First, sport is a mechanism that can encourage **social integration,** whereby national, religious, racial, or political rifts can be bridged and divisiveness can be circumvented. Institutionalization of sport at the **national level** facilitates the development of a national identity. Developing or emerging nations—Third World countries—have used sport as a political tool and as a means of accomplishing national objectives.

Major industrialized countries have also depended on sport to facilitate social cohesion. The linkage between sports and the aims of the former Soviet Union is clearly evidenced in a statement made by the chairperson of the Soviet Committee on Physical Culture and Sports:

> The principal aim and the major meaning of the development of physical culture and sports in our socialistic society lie in the active promotion of the comprehensive, harmonious development of the individual, in the preparation of every citizen in the U.S.S.R. for highly productive work and for the defense of socialism, and in the organization of a healthy way of life and recreation for the people.[27]

The People's Republic of China, like the Soviet Union, upholds the Marxist-Leninist philosophy. Kolatch has observed that physical culture in China serves multiple purposes—health, national defense, and productivity—and cultivates a spirit of national identity and unity.[28] Canada, too, has used sport to foster national unity and identity. Munro wrote: "The fact that we are all proud of our country regardless of what province we live in, or what language we speak, or what our political views are—shows another reason for strong federal effort in the sports field: National Unity."[29]

Although the United States does not have a cabinet position devoted to the administration of sport at the national level, it does have a President's Council on Physical Fitness and Sports, currently spearheaded by Arnold Schwartzenegger, and it has used athletes to promote a positive image of the country and its sports. For example, both Arthur Ashe and Muhammad Ali have conducted good-will tours in foreign countries. Under the sponsorship of the U.S. Information Agency, Ashe toured Africa for 2 1/2 weeks in 1971 giving exhibitions, interviews, and clinics (many of which were filmed for subsequent propaganda purposes). Historically, our federal government has not subsidized sports to the same extent as the governments of communist-bloc countries. A number of nations have cabinet positions for the purpose of administering the country's sports program. However, the United States has established Olympic training sites (e.g., Colorado Springs), and the motto "America doesn't send athletes to the Olympics, Americans do" is less true today than in the past. Sage lucidly conveys the amount of money allocated to the Olympics:

> . . . the overall financial investment in the American Olympic movement can be seen through the $250 million 1988–1992 quadrennial budget of the U.S. Olympic Com-

mittee (which does not include an expected $50 million from the sale of 1988 U.S. Olympic coins). This $250 million will come from many public and private sources: a projected $90 million to $100 million in sponsorships, a projected $60 million from the USOC's television rights for the 1992 Olympic Games, and anticipated federal legislation for an ongoing coin program and tax checkoffs.[30]

A second goal of national sports is to achieve some semblance of **social control** over the masses. This objective is best witnessed by the official policies of Russia, China, East Germany, and South Africa. In the Soviet Union, sport, or what is called *physical culture,* was based on the teachings and political ideologies of Marx and Lenin. The communist government in Russia took little interest in sports after the 1917 October Revolution. At that time, sports were snubbed because of their presumed links with bourgeois (i.e., materialistic and middle-class) ideology. By the mid-1920s, the merits of sport had been acknowledged, and sports and games in Russia became increasingly encouraged and accessible.

Sport is also used as a stepping-stone to official recognition from other nations and the resulting prestige. According to Reed, "Oil titans of the Persian Gulf hungry for clout of another kind, are pumping petro-dollars into athletics."[31] The Arab countries of Kuwait, Saudi Arabia, Iraq, Qatar, and the United Arab Emirates have made sports one of their top national priorities. Billions of dollars have been either spent or earmarked for the construction of various sports facilities: stadiums, swimming pools, golf courses, handball, tennis, squash, and basketball courts, sport-medicine centers, and the like. The Iraquis, before the Persian Gulf War, were said to spend more money per capita on athletics than any other country, including the United States and the former Soviet Union. Some of these countries have achieved political independence only a few years ago and are striving at present for two things: a seat in the United Nations and Olympic gold medals.

Sport and Politics in the United States

Those who think sport and politics are unrelated in the United States need to be cognizant of Congress' deliberations on nearly 300 legislative sport-related items. Johnson and Johnson and Frey have detailed the influence of government on the United States' professional and amateur sports.[32] The political process has impacted on sport in a variety of areas such as antitrust legislation, league mergers, collective bargaining (via National Labor Relations Board), reserve clauses, sports broadcasting, and the public's subsidization of sport facilities. Examples of the interfacing of these two social institutions—sport and politics—will be briefly considered.

Sport Telecasting. The revenues the tv networks and the sport franchises receive from sport telecasting are extremely lucrative. The courts and Congress have reviewed several issues and made rulings favorable, for the most part, to protect the vested interests of the franchises and networks. Television coverage of sport events has been restricted in two ways. First, the Sports Broadcasting Act of 1961 granted by Congress permits the leagues (e.g., NFL, NBA) to exclusively control national television coverage. The league typically offers a "package" of games, which the networks bid for, and then revenue sharing is practiced; that is, each league franchise receives a portion of the profit. Second, excluding games that are in the national "package," each home team has exclusive rights to telecast home contests and prevent coverage of games in its home territory (generally defined as a seventy-five-mile radius). The courts have interpreted this latter matter as falling within a reasonable restraint of trade, and authoritative opinion holds that such arrangements are particularly advantageous to the networks and franchises at the expense of the public.

Sport Television Blackouts. In 1973 Congress mandated that telecasting a professional game could not be forbidden if the contest was sold out three days before the event. Professional football is the only sport really affected by the law because the other professional sports do not typically sell out. Although the antiblackout policy does have some negative economic consequences—season ticket sales decrease and "no-shows" increase—for the franchise, the real beneficiary is the fan.

Cable Television. Cable television has begun to invade the sacred turf of the networks. Because sport contests are not copyrighted and cable owners need only register (not obtain a license) from the Federal Communications Commission, the cable companies can simply pass on sport telecasts they've received through the public air waves.

Public Subsidization of Sport. In a variety of ways, some of which are nonobvious, the taxpayer subsidizes various facets of the sport enterprise. These include "construction bonds, stadia rents below market value, taxes foregone on the land, and appropriation of public services to sport facilities in the form of water and sewage facilities and services, mass transit, law enforcement, and improvement of access roads."[33]

Professional and Amateur Sports Operate as a Cartel. Federal antitrust legislation forbids the formation of monopolies in any—other than sport—industrial sphere. The restraint of trade practices that professional sports enjoy include carving out a geographical area within which it operates unilaterally and, historically, has controlled entry and working conditions of the players via player reserve and option clauses.

International Level

As with the local and national levels, sports and politics are interconnected at the **international level** as well. International sport is aimed at bringing athletes together (sometimes from nations with divergent political ideologies) in hopes that friendly strife will encourage goodwill among the participating countries. The Olympics represent the quintessence of this philosophy, but a variety of other sports festivities share this goal. In addition to the quadrennial Olympics, there are the Asian Games (GANEFO), the Pan American Games, the British Commonwealth Games, the Third World Games, the Maccabiah Games, the CANUSA Games, the African Games, the University Games, the South Pacific Games, the Southeast Asia Peninsula Games, the Pan-Arab Games, the Mediterranean Games, the Far Eastern Games, the Bolivian Games, the Central American Games and the Goodwill Games, to name the most common ones.

Webster and Pooley advanced the thesis that "the intent of government politics is to demonstrate power through international sport."[34] International sport, as a political phenomenon, can be viewed in several different ways: (a) as **a political tool,** (b) as **a sociopolitical mirror** reflecting domestic problems, (c) as **a propaganda show-case,** (d) as **an outlet for national aggression,** (e) as **an economic showcase,** and (f) as **a cause of nationalism.**[35] These categories are neither exhaustive nor mutually exclusive; they do, however, suggest the political flavor of international sports.

The use of sports as a political tool is exemplified by the racial, ethnic and inter-national overtones of the Louis-Schmeling fight in 1938, the Olympics, ping-pong and basketball diplomacy, and the participation of Third World countries in interna-tional sport. The concept of sport as a mirror reflecting domestic social and political issues has been substantiated by victory stand demonstrations at the 1968 (Mexico City) and 1972 (Munich) Olympics, and by the fifty Hungarians who sought political refuge during the 1956 Olympics. Sport as an outlet for national aggression is epit-omized by the terrorism that swept the Munich Games, the antisoviet riots in Czechoslovakia in 1969, South Africa's apartheid policy, and the 1970 "Soccer War" between Honduras and El Salvador. The use of sport as a showcase for propaganda and economics is also highlighted by the Olympics. The amount of money spent on staging the Olympics is staggering, as are the social consequences. For example, the total costs of the Rome, Tokyo, Munich, Montreal, and Moscow Olympics were $30 million, $2.7 billion, $600 million, $1.5 billion, and $3 billion, respectively. The media rights alone to the Seoul Games (1988) were around $300 million and esti-mated to be $401 million for the Barcelona Games (1992). The strain placed by the Olympics on the Soviet economy necessitated a moratorium on all other construction (except for the Olympics) and produced shortages of produce, meat, and canned goods when these commodities were stockpiled for contestants, spectators, dignitar-ies, and the like.

Sports have stopped wars and wars have stopped sports. The staging of the ancient Olympic Games often invoked a truce between warring city states. The "Black Pearl," Pele, once halted an African war by merely showing up to be admired by both sides. On the other hand, the Olympic Games of 1916, 1940, 1944, and the boycotts of 1980 and 1984 provide sufficient evidence that sports are sometimes canceled or al-tered as a result of conflict and strife.

Even the Little League World Series has been subject to international political machinations. According to Michener, teams from Taiwan dominated the games dur-ing the 1970s. During a three-year period, Taiwan scored 120 runs and the United States only 2 runs in nine games. When the Taiwanese teams were suspected of cheat-ing, the Little League's board chairman subsequently announced that the World Series would be confined to four U.S. teams representing different regional cham-pions. It did appear, as one Taiwanese official declared, that Taiwan's teams were simply too good. Because of criticism, the ban forbidding competition with foreign teams was lifted a few years later. Interestingly, the Taiwanese teams won the World Series in 1979 and 1980 after the ban was lifted. In fact, teams from outside the United States have captured the world title most often in the past twenty-five years. In 1991, the Taiwan team won (again) the Little League World Series, their fifteenth title in eighteen appearances. Even the scoring of several Olympic events has been infused with political issues, as demonstrated by the 1991 rebuking of four judges at the World Gymnastics Championships. The action taken by the FIG (International

Gymnastics Federation) stemmed from the results of a computer program that tracked the judges' marks and assessed their fairness. One unnamed judge scored her country's team 10 places higher than it finished!

Sport Connections of Politicians

Several U.S. presidents have been sportsminded in one way or another, have credited athletics with being a very positive force in their careers, and have spoken appreciatively about the role played by the "friendly fields of strife."[36] Abraham Lincoln was an equestrian, swimmer, wrestler, runner, and jumper. As a youth, he was considered one of the strongest and most versatile athletes in Illinois. Theodore Roosevelt may have been the best athlete to become president, participating in baseball, lacrosse, polo, horseback riding, tennis, football, boxing, rowing, walking, and hunting. Woodrow Wilson combined the roles of coach and athlete. In addition to coaching his college football team, Wilson played golf, pool, and baseball. Franklin D. Roosevelt swam, rode horseback, and sailed, even after being confined to a wheelchair, and during his younger days, was known to ski, toboggan, and golf. Harry S Truman, who was known for his perpetual walks, umpired baseball games occasionally. When Dwight D. Eisenhower was a youth, he was a good baseball and football player; later in life he golfed and fished. John F. Kennedy swam, sailed, golfed, played tennis, and was fond of family games of touch football before he injured his back. Lyndon B. Johnson was a swimmer, equestrian, hunter, and fisherman. Richard M. Nixon played football at Whittier College but was better known as an avid fan. Gerald Ford played football at Michigan, captained the Wolverines, and was named the team's Most Valuable Player in 1934. Ford coached at Yale while working on his law degree and later in life became known for his interest and participation in golf and skiing. Jimmy Carter played basketball in high school and was a cross-country runner at Annapolis. He also played softball and tennis, jogged, and was a fond spectator of stockcar racing. Ronald Reagan played football at Eureka College and was also an accomplished equestrian. George Bush played baseball during his college days at Yale and jogged during his active presidency.

Some athletes have succeeded in transferring their athletic prowess to the political arena. During the past twenty years, there have been several prominent politicians with previous sport backgrounds. They included pitcher "Vinegar Bend" Mizell, ex-Olympian Bob Mathias, and track-and-field ace Ralph Metcalfe. Furthermore, "Whizzer" White, a former football player, sat on the Supreme Court bench. Former professional quarterback Jack Kemp has been touted for such positions as the President of the United States, U.S. Senator, and Governor of New York and now serves as Secretary of the Department of Housing and Urban Development. Tom Macmillan (D-MD), former basketball player at Maryland, is a legislator on the Knight Commission. Dick Butkus, former University of Illinois and Chicago Bear savvy linebacker, was the 1982 first-round draft choice for the Republican Party to run for Congress in a Chicago district.

Internationally, the media have informed us of Fidel Castro's pitching exploits and ex-dictator of Uganda Idi Amin's boxing accomplishments.

☐ SUMMARY

Contemporary sport sociologists maintain that *politics* is endemic to sport. A brief chronicle of the modern Olympics illustrated the interfacing of sport and politics and revealed that the Olympic Games have rarely been above the rancor of international politics. Special attention was paid to a case study of the U.S. boycott of the 1980 Moscow Olympics; the reactions of politicians, athletes, and the general public to the boycott were considered and analyzed. Politics penetrates sports at the local, national, and international levels. At the international level, governments use sport to demonstrate power. Further, international sport can be thought of in several different ways: as a *political tool*, as a *sociopolitical mirror* that reflects domestic problems, as a *propaganda showcase*, as an *outlet for national aggression*, as an *economic showcase*, and as a cause of *nationalism*.

☐ KEY CONCEPTS

Sport and Politics
Politics
Groupthink
State or Municipal Level
Social Integration
National Level
Social Control
International Level

Sport as:
   A Political Tool
   A Sociopolitical Mirror
   A Propaganda Showcase
   An Outlet of National Aggression
   An Economic Showcase
   A Cause of Nationalism

☐ ENDNOTES

1. RONALD W. SMITH & FREDERICK W. PRESTON, *Sociology* (New York: St. Martin's, 1977), p. 261.
2. MAX WEBER, *The Theory of Social and Economic Organization*, ed. Talcott Parsons, (New York: Free Press, 1964), p. 152.
3. NBC television Interview with Bobby Knight, quote, 1980.
4. ARTHUR ASHE, "Sports Boycotts Are against the Nature of Competition," *The Washington Post* (22 October 1978), p. 20.
5. J. SUGDEN & A. YIANNAKIS, "Politics and the Olympic$," *The North American Sociology of Sport Society Newsletter* 2, no. 1 (1980), p. 1.
6. D. STANLEY EITZEN & GEORGE H. SAGE, *Sociology of American Sport* (Dubuque, IA: William C. Brown, 1978), pp. 143–144.
7. HANS J. MORGENTHAU, *Politics among Nations* (New York: Borzoi Books, 1966), p. 36, cited in A. Yiannakis, T.D. McIntyre, M.J. Melnick,

   & D.P. Hart, *Sport Sociology: Contemporary Themes* (Dubuque, IA: Kendall/Hunt, 1976), p. 36.
8. AVERY BRUNDAGE, "President's Statement," *Bulletin du Comite International Olympique*, 55, quoted in Henry W. Morton, *Soviet Sport* (New York: Collier) 1963, p. 85.
9. RICHARD ESPY, *The Politics of the Olympic Games* (Los Angeles: University of California Press, 1979), p. vii.
10. "An Olympic Boycott?" *Newsweek* (28 January 1980), pp. 20–28.
11. "A U.S. Boycott of the Moscow Olympics?" *U.S. News & World Report* (28 August 1978), pp. 33–34.
12. "Should U.S. Boycott the Olympics?" *U.S. News & World Report* (21 January 1980), pp. 27–28.
13. *Ibid.*
14. *Op. cit.*[11]

15. IRVING L. JANIS, *Victims of Groupthink: A Psychological Study of Foreign Policy Decisions and Fiascoes* (Boston: Houghton Mifflin, 1972).

16. *Op. cit.*[4]

17. *Op. cit.*,[10] p. 23.

18. *Ibid.*

19. *Ibid.*, pp. 21–22.

20. *Ibid.*, p. 20.

21. *Ibid.*, p. 21.

22. MILTON RICHMAN, "Past Athletes Paid Price for Political Issues," *Daily Vidette* (13 February 1980), p. 11.

23. JOHN C.P. POOLEY & ARTHUR V. WEBSTER, "Sport and Politics: Power Play," *Sport Sociology: Contemporary Themes,* Yiannakis et al., (Dubuque, IA: Kendall/Hunt, 1976) pp. 35–42.

24. JAY J. COAKLEY, *Sport in Society: Issues and Controversies* (St. Louis: C.V. Mosby, 1978), p. 156.

25. JIM BARNHART, "Kentucky Governor Puts Foot to Football Coach," *The Daily Pantagraph* (15 July 1981), p. B1.

26. JAMES A. MICHENER, *Sports in America* (New York: Random House, 1976), pp. 343–344.

27. MARTHA M. SEBAN, "Political Ideology and Sport in the People's Republic of China and the Soviet Union," *Sport in the Sociocultural Process,* ed. Marie Hart (Dubuque, IA: William C. Brown, 1976), p. 308.

28. KOLATCH, cited in *ibid.*, pp. 313–314.

29. MUNRO, quoted in *op. cit.*,[23] p. 37.

30. GEORGE H. SAGE, *Power and Ideology in American Sport* (Champaign, IL: Human Kinetics, 1990), p. 84.

31. J.D. REED, "Building Sports Palaces in the Desert," condensed from *Sports Illustrated* (17 November 1980) by *Reader's Digest* p. 21.

32. ARTHUR JOHNSON, "Congress and Professional Sports," *Annals of the American Academy of Political and Social Science* 445 (September 1979), pp. 102–115.
ARTHUR T. JOHNSON & JAMES H. FREY, *Government and Sport: The Policy Issues* (Totowa: Rowman & Alanheld, 1985).

33. ELDON E. SNYDER & ELMER A. SPREITZER, *Social Aspects of Sport* (Englewood Cliffs, NJ: Prentice-Hall, 1983), p. 259.

34. *Op. cit.*,[23] Pooley & Webster, p. 38.

35. ROBERT KROPKE, "International Sports and the Social Sciences," *Sport in the Sociocultural Process,* ed. M. Hart, (Dubuque, IA: William C. Brown), pp. 317–325.

36. *Sports Illustrated* 50, no. 18 (30 April 1979), p. 78.

13

Sport and Religion

Anyone who will tear down sports will tear down America. Sports and religion made America what it is.   WOODY HAYES

Sport and religion—two universal social institutions—seem at first glance to have little in common. Many of us conceive of sports as interfacing with the secular and profane world and religion with the supernatural, transcendent, and sacred domain. Interestingly, and perhaps surprisingly, sport and religion manifest some significant interconnections. Annie in *Bull Durham* talks of the interconnections among baseball, religion, and life. Sport sociologist Harry Edwards has said that if America has a religion, it is sport.[1] This chapter provides a definition of religion, discusses some historical relationships between sport and religion, and demonstrates that, in some respects, sport has become the functional equivalent of religion in America today. The relationship between sport and religion is dialectical. Each influences the other; the connection is not unilateral.

❏ DEFINING RELIGION

Sociologists consider religion a cultural universal. Although religion takes a variety of forms, depending on the cultural context, it is found in virtually all human societies. What, then, is this erstwhile social institution? Definitions of religion abound. Durkheim defined **religion** as a "unified system of beliefs and practices relative to sacred things, uniting into a single moral community all those who adhere to those beliefs and practices."[2] A fascinating spinoff of Durkheim's conception of religion is found in the empirical investigation reported in Vignette 13.1. Similarly, contemporary sociologists Glock and Stark conceive of religion in terms of what a society considers sacred, that is, it "comprises an institutionalized system of symbols, beliefs, values and practices focused on questions of ultimate meaning."[3] Both of these definitions emphasize some notion of the sacred as well as beliefs and practices. Given the importance of the "sacred" vis-à-vis the "secular" in conceptions of religion, it is of interest that profane artifacts can become quasi-sacred, as Cuzzort and King lucidly illustrate with respect to the "Sultan of Swat's" bat:

> When Babe Ruth was a living idol to baseball fans, the bat he used to slug his home runs was definitely a profane object. It was Ruth's personal instrument and had little social value in itself. Today, however, one of Ruth's bats is enshrined in the Baseball Hall of Fame. It is no longer used by anyone. It stands, rather, as an object which in itself represents the values, sentiments, power, and beliefs of all members of the baseball community. What was formerly a profane object is now in the process of gaining some of the qualities of a sacred object.[4]

Ruth's bat underscores two important sociological observations: (1) profane objects can become sacred and vice-versa; and (2) consistent with the interactionist's perspective, the meaning of symbols is socially created, maintained, and altered; that is, symbols do not have fixed, immutable meanings. Before examining the interconnections between religion and sport, it is necessary to consider the functions served by religion as an institution.

❏ FUNCTIONS OF RELIGION

From a functionalist perspective, religion, as a social institution, meets a variety of "needs" for both the individual and society. First, consider the **individual or psychological functions** of religion. According to O'Dea,[5] the need for religion grows out

The "Home Advantage"

A common thread running through Emile Durkheim's sociological thinking is a concern with social order. In his treatise *The Elementary Forms of Religious Life,* he argues that the heart of religion is the sacred as opposed to the secular. In this same work he also wrote (1965:240): "In the midst of an assembly animated by a common passion, we become susceptible to acts and sentiments of which we are incapable when reduced to our own forces." This statement is similar to the social psychological concept of "social facilitation" and highlights the booster effect of others on task performance. In sport, Schwartz and Barsky studied whether performances in front of one's own crowd ("home" territory) was superior to that at "away" games. In sports it is commonly believed that teams do better at "home" than they do "away" or in a neutral setting. (This phenomenon is also reflected in the point spread in sport betting.) In their analysis of thousands of sporting contests in football, baseball, basketball, and hockey, they discovered that the "home advantage" does exist. However, it did not uniformly operate in these sports. Specifically, basketball and hockey (both indoor sports) found it more pronounced; less so in baseball and football (both outdoor sports for the most part). Specifically, the home team was victorious in 53% of professional baseball games, 58% of NFL games, 60% of college football games, 64% of professional hockey games, and 67% of professional basketball games. The researchers also discovered that offensive, not defensive, performances (e.g., points scored, td's, etc.) were facilitated. The "social" support provided by the home team crowd is apparently operating, although somewhat variable, in the most popular American team sports.

It is of interest, however, that the home court does *not* always give the edge to the hometown players. Baumeister (1985) concluded that the home team is more likely to lose a crucial game than to win. In professional baseball and basketball, the home team tends to win early games but lose in the finale. In the World Series, the home team has fared worse than 50–50 in terms of victory, and when the championship goes to seven games, the home team's win record collapses to .385. In NBA championship games the same pattern is revealed. When the series goes to seven games, the home team's percentage of victories is below 40.

Mizruchi considered that three variables—(a) provincialism and stability of the city, (b) uniqueness of the home arena, and (c) the tradition of the team—affect the home court advantage (HCA). More specifically, size of metropolis and suburb-located arenas were indirectly correlated with the HCA, whereas the franchise's age was directly related with the HCA.

My own investigation of the modern summer and winter Olympics supports a home advantage using gold, silver, and bronze medals won as measures of athletic success. This conclusion was arrived at by examining the number of gold, silver, bronze, and total medals won of host countries when comparing previous and subsequent performances.

Sociologically, the social significance of the content of this vignette—the home court advantage—is that human behavior is *situated,* that is, it varies from one social context to another. Such an interest in the contextual bases of human social behavior was a key concern of classical sociologists such as Durkheim, Weber, and Marx.

SOURCES: Barry Schwartz and Stephen F. Barsky, "The Home Advantage," *Social Forces* (1977), pp. 641–661. Emile Durkheim, *The Elementary Forms of Religious Life* (New York: Free Press, 1965, originally published in 1895). Roy Baumeister, "Hometown Fans a Mixed Blessing?" *Chicago Tribune* (28 April 1985), p. D2. Mark S. Mizruchi, "Local Sport Teams and Celebration of Community: A Comparative Analysis of the Home Advantage," *The Sociological Quarterly* (Winter 1985) 26, no. 4, pp. 507–518. Wilbert M. Leonard, II, "The 'Home Advantage': The Case of the Modern Olympiads," *Journal of Sport Behavior* 12, no. 4 (1989), pp. 227–241.

of three pandemic existential conditions: (1) contingency, (2) powerlessness, and (3) scarcity. *Contingency* refers to the multitude of uncertainties that humans face—uncertainties about jobs, education, families, children, money, health, death, and so on. Figuratively, our dependency is akin to a cork bobbing on a large body of water. Hence, religion offers solace and provides an oasis in a frightening and threatening world. To some, it provides a much needed psychological crutch to lean on for support during uncertain and unpredictable times. *Powerlessness* refers to our ultimate helplessness, particularly in regard to death. Our very mortality is the basis for feelings of powerlessness as O'Dea sees it. Religion facilitates people's acceptance of what is considered culturally undesirable (e.g., poverty, social inequality, and malevolent forces). Finally, *scarcity* refers to the finite nature of material goods and possessions. For the downtrodden, religion has historically provided hope for the future—in the hereafter; for those of substantial means, religion has justified their good fortune.

The **social functions** of religion—what religion contributes to the larger society—include: (a) social control and (b) social integration. The *social control* function of religion stems from the "scripts" of acceptable and unacceptable behaviors it provides. That is, religion provides both prescriptions and proscriptions. The "should nots" of religion are vividly illustrated by the Ten Commandments. These moral dictates inform Christians of what we should not (and should) do, feel, say, and think. The "shoulds" include such social responsibility exhortations as "being my brother's keeper," "doing unto others as you would have them do unto you," "helping those in need," and so forth. When these commands are internalized, they exert some degree of control that makes human actions predictable (and altruistic). Religion also binds together members of a community; in doing so, it performs a *social integration* or cohesiveness function (see Durkheim's definition of religion at the beginning of this section). Sociologically, subcultures within a society tend toward cohesiveness in direct proportion to their members' abidance by agreed-on social norms and values. Hence, an esprit de corps is created among the common believers.

☐ CHARACTERISTICS OF INSTITUTIONALIZED RELIGION

Most religions are characterized by one or more of the following elements: (a) beliefs, (b) hierarchy, (c) symbols, (d) rituals, (e) propitiation, and (f) magic.[6] Religious **beliefs** are manifested through sacred writings, articles of faith, and facsimiles. For example, Christian beliefs appear in the Bible, Hindus have their Vedas, Moslems have their Koran, and Mormons have their Book of Mormon. All religions have either an oral or written tradition codifying their statements of faith. Many religions are characterized by a **hierarchy of authority**. Catholics have popes, cardinals, archbishops, and priests, all of whom occupy different positions in the chain of command. Protestants have their elders, deacons, shepherds, and so on. Religions have their **symbols** (or icons), both concrete and abstract, which take on special sacred significance. For Christians, the cross symbolizes the death and resurrection of Christ; Jews have their phylactery (a small leather case containing verses of scripture). Other significant symbols include the fish (for Christians) and the Star of David and Menorah (for Jews). Another characteristic of religion is **ritual.** Rituals are activities prescribed or proscribed for believers. Catholics are familiar with confession, communion, the saying of rosaries, and (traditionally) abstaining from eating meat on Friday. Protestants are familiar with baptism, communion, and prayer. Closely aligned with ritual is the notion of **propitiation,** acts that place the doer in good standing with the supernatural power(s). Regular church attendance, prayer, baptism, confession, witnessing, tithing, and communion are positive behaviors. Negative propitiatory behaviors include eschewing pork for Jews and avoiding beef for Hindus. The last feature of religions is magic. **Magic** is a behavior one engages in to appease, cajole, or manipulate the supernatural forces. The line dividing magic and ritual is sometimes difficult to draw. In any event, the aim of such activity is to produce favorable responses from the supernatural power.

What has all this discussion to do with sport? For some observers of the sporting scene, sports constitute a secular or quasi-religion that evidences many of the trappings characteristic of religion. Consider how many of the formal features of religious systems discussed can be correlated with the dominant features of sport.

Beliefs

It is widely believed that participation in sports can be a redeeming force in personal and social affairs. Participation, it is claimed, cultivates personal discipline, prepares one for the competitiveness of life, contributes to physical fitness, fosters mental alertness, and reinforces religiosity and nationalism (see the discussion of Edwards's "Dominant American Sports Creed" in Chapter 3). At this point, we are concerned not with the veracity of these claims but with the parallels between sport and religion. Both have beliefs or ideologies. Sports, like religions, also have their scribes. The sport scribes include media personnel—radio and television broadcasters, magazine and newspaper reporters, and sports journalists—all of whom share the job of disseminating sport news.

Hierarchy

Sports have high councils and ruling bodies typical of bureaucratic structures. Walter Byers, former executive director of the National Collegiate Athletic Association (NCAA), more than once was alluded to as an autocrat insofar as collegiate athletic policy was concerned. Other ruling bodies include the International and the U.S. Olympic Committees (IOC and USOC) and Amateur Athletic Union (AAU). Within each of these structures, there exists a hierarchy of authority or, simply, a bureaucratic organization.

Symbols

Symbols of the faith include a wide assortment of items. Among these are bubble gum cards, autographs and photographs of athletes, game balls, official programs, remnants of synthetic turf, bats, clubs, pucks, chinstraps, and other such trophies.

Rituals

Guttmann has advanced the thesis that fertility rites of American Indians, the South African Zulus "soccer culture," and the ball games of the Mayans and Aztecs are examples of religious rituals and ceremonies that include physical activities in primitive societies.[7] He contends that although modern societies have a secular flavor to their sports, they are sometimes considered as a secular religion (see the discussion of sport as a civil religion later in this chapter). In a later section, we consider some of the rituals that sports participants engage in. Here, we consider rituals among the "worshippers." For avid sport fans, ritualistic behavior can include tailgate parties, pregame and postgame festivities, donning special jackets, caps, suits, pants, and the like (see Vignette 13.2 for a description of some fans' rituals). *Newsweek* described it this way: "A Football weekend is one of America's tribal rites. From great distances come clanspeople young and old to wear bright colors, eat strange aliments, drink strong liquids and shout incantations both wild and arcane."[8]

Propitiation

Sports' "disciples" find it expedient to make "pilgrimages" to shrines such as the Baseball Hall of Fame in Cooperstown, New York; the Pro Football Hall of Fame in Canton, Ohio; and the Naismith Memorial Basketball Hall of Fame (not to mention sport museums for hockey, soccer, softball, tennis, golf, bowling, swimming, lacrosse, skiing, wrestling, rodeo, roller skating, and fishing, among others); and to select stadiums (e.g., the Orange Bowl and the Superdome) and arenas (Hoosier Dome, Palaestra). The linkages between sport and religion can be inferred from the language used in an article on sports museums:[9] *honored, meccas, shrines, canonized, memorialized,* and *enshrined.*

Magic

Magic and religion share some similarities but are not synonymous. One major distinction lies in their different orientations. Simply put, magic is oriented to the here-and-now; its concern is with concrete matters such as controlling the weather, effecting victory in battle, or influencing the turn of the roulette wheel or the flip of the coin. Religion focuses on fundamental existence issues such as death, life's meaning, and salvation. A second major difference between magic and religion is characterized by the means employed to influence the powers that be. Religionists invoke means that have been successful in dealing with others—love, compassion, altruism, loyalty, dependability—in addition to prayer, sacrifice, and penance. Magic, on the other hand, employs mechanistic manipulation; that is, it entails the compulsion of superhuman spirits. To illustrate, carrying a rabbit's foot is sufficiently compelling that it may be thought to bring good fortune. In other words, the object—the rabbit's foot—is believed to possess the attribute of good luck in much the same way that it possesses a certain color and a certain length. You may recall the scene in *Bull Durham* in which a batter ran rosary beads across his bat for the purported magical power such an act could imbue. Given these differences between magic and religion, it is important to realize that both share some common features and may operate along the self-fulfilling prophecy lines. One of the important similarities is a faith in the potential consequences of such powers. Buhrmann and Zaugg empirically examined the relationship between church attendance and superstition and found the most superstitious behavior among the most frequent attenders and the least superstitious

☐ **VIGNETTE 13.2**

Rituals of Buckeye Fans

Two thousand years ago it would have been a loaf of bread, some meat, fruit, a jug of wine, and a long night on the stone seats of the Coliseum.

The idea's still the same, but you've come a long way, Buckeyes.

Today the pregame celebrations that dot the Ohio State campus feature motor homes, catered dinners, linen tablecloths, and sometimes even candelabra and crystal. Music is provided by expensive tape systems, a calliope, hired bands, or a wandering accordian player. And the toga look is replaced by more brilliant scarlet and gray—in everything from clothing and martini flags to cakes and cars.

But modern Buckeye tailgaters view their pre-pigskin parties as an art form, a serious means of self-expression.

Music and other special events also draw many to Martha Brian's prefootball festivities. The annual gathering sponsored by the associate professor of journalism has included a sing-along to calliope music, visits by Brutus Buckeye, and rounds of cheers led by Ohio State's and the opposition's cheerleaders.

Thorp Minister of the McElroy Minister Company sponsors his tailgate extravaganza before the final home game of the season. Complete with a catered dinner and a bartender to serve drinks, festivities were enlivened last year by the music of the Capital City Jazz Band and cheerleaders who danced and led the singing.

Some Clintonville residents are always fired-up for Ohio State football. Following a pregame party in the neighborhood, they travel to the game with Peter Souch III behind the wheel of his 1937 German-made Sacht fire engine.

While the all-night parties before Roman athletic events were often quieted by orders of local constables, Ohio State tailgaters are generally a fun-loving, law-abiding crowd, says Sharon Davis, an Athletic Department cashier who handles payments for football parking.

"Everybody's just here to have a very good time," Davis says of the party-goers at nearly 430 motor coaches and vans parked north of St. John Arena each Saturday.

The crowd is usually good-spirited and noisy both before and after the game, except for that rare occasion when victory eludes the Buckeyes.

SOURCE: Ginny Halloran, "Roman Revelry, Buckeye Style," *OSU Quest* (1981), p. 16. Reprinted with permission.

☐

---

behavior among the least frequent attenders. While a positive correlation existed, the magnitude was low (gamma = .16) despite its statistical significance.[10] Let us consider some popular magic-like practices that have been documented in the sports world.

Malinowski's "Gap Theory". George Gmelch, an anthropologist and former baseball player, conducted a fascinating study of the uses of magic in professional baseball.[11] Theoretically, he derived several testable propositions or hypotheses from the work of the esteemed British social anthropologist, Bronislaw Malinowski (1884–1942). Malinowski had embarked on an expedition to the Pacific Islands in 1915 when he was stranded after being declared an enemy alien at the start of the First World War. For three years, he conducted intensive participant observation studies in the Trobriand Islands in the South seas. He observed that the aborigines practiced magic in open-sea fishing pursuits but relied on their own skills when lagoon fishing. Malinowski proposed that the former fishing activities were fraught with doubt because of the unpredictability of the weather and danger and hypothesized that magic is more likely to occur in situations of unpredictability and uncertainty when chance or fate exist:

> We find magic wherever the elements of chance and accident and the emotional play between hope and fear have a wide and extensive range. We do not find magic wherever the pursuit is certain, reliable, and well under the control of rational methods.
>
> [In elaborating his "gap theory":] Thus magic supplies primitive man with a number of ready-made ritual acts and beliefs, with a definite mental and practical technique which serves to bridge over the dangerous gaps in every important pursuit or critical situation. It enables man to carry out with confidence his important tasks, to maintain his poise and his mental integrity in fits of anger, in the throes of hate, of unrequited love, of despair and anxiety. The function of magic is to ritualize man's optimism, to enhance his faith in the victory of hope over fear.[12]

Gmelch[13] maintained that professional baseball provided an excellent natural laboratory for testing Malinowski's hypothesis. Baseball is comprised of three primary psychomotor skills: (a) pitching, (b) hitting, and (c) fielding. Fielding is much less subject to the whims of chance (most fielders handle 90% of the balls hit or thrown to them without error) than is pitching (most fail to win two thirds of the games they start) or hitting (most batters fail to hit .333). For example, in 1991, the leading hitter in major league baseball registered a .341 batting average; the leading pitcher (minimum of sixteen decisions) had a 12–4 mark, and the leading fielder had over a .90 average. Because of the uncertainty and chance factors associated with hitting and pitching, Gmelch reasoned that these two aspects of baseball would be more subject to magical practices than fielding. The empirical results confirmed this notion; magical practices abounded among hitters and pitchers, but not among fielders. Moreover, the anthropologist classified magic into three categories: (a) rituals, (b) taboos, and (c) fetishes. Examples of each are informative.

Gmelch, during his own professional baseball career, recalled the *ritual* (behavior aimed at manipulating humans, supernatural forces, or natural phenomena to a desired end) he engaged in to maintain a hitting streak. He ate chicken every afternoon at 4:00, kept his eyes shut during the playing of the national anthem, and changed his sweatshirt at the end of the fourth inning. This was done for a week and discontinued when the streak ended. Athletic paraphernalia—jock straps, socks, sweatshirts, even the players' numbers—are often imbued with uncanny powers. *Taboos* (the avoidance of some activity) also abound in baseball. Three of the best known are not mentioning a nonhitter when it is in progress, not stepping on foul lines, and not crossing bats. *Fetishes* (objects endowed with special powers) are also popular among baseball players. Crucifixes, rosary beads, coins, bobby pins, and the proverbial rabbit's foot fall into this category. Many of these magical practices can be understood as having materialized through conditioning processes, in which particularly good or bad performance is associated with a particular phenomenon or event; then the phenomenon or event is repeated or avoided in hopes of eliciting the desired outcome. In summary, Gmelch observed that magical practices were more prevalent among

❏ VIGNETTE 13.3

Strange Practices of Professional Athletes

Fred Biletnikof, former wide receiver for the Oakland Raiders, downed three bottles of Maalox before every game, wore the same socks throughout a season (when they were dirty, he washed them himself by hand), and changed the flavor of the gum he was chewing if his team suffered a bad offensive series (the gum had to be opened by the Raiders' equipment manager, taken out of the package in proper order, and put in Biletnikoff's mouth while he stood facing the playing field).

Steve Preece, a safety who played for the Los Angeles Rams and Seattle Seahawks, dined on M&M's the night before every game; left for every game at precisely the same moment; augmented his vitamin-packed pregame meal every hour on the hour with bars of Hershey's chocolate or Nestle's Crunch; always dressed left to right, and always had the same player help him put on his game jersey; always kicked the end-zone pylon closest to his locker-room door twice with his left foot; and always stood on the 49-yard line for the national anthem. "I've been in a situation where I had to run back into the locker room at the last second and take care of some tiny part of the routine that I'd missed," he once said. "(But) if anybody were to ask me why I did this crazy ritual, I'd have a hard time answering."

Former Oakland A's pitching ace Vida Blue attributed a long string of victories to a baseball cap he began wearing in 1974. Still donning that hat in 1977, several umpires insisted it was too soiled to wear and threatened him with a fine and suspension if he didn't remove it. He finally yielded and ceremoniously burned the cap on the field before the game.

SOURCE: Skip Myslenski, "Altered States," *Chicago Tribune Magazine* (14 November 1982), p. 24.

❏

---

batters and pitchers (than fielders) because of the greater chance and uncertainty characterizing these activities. See Vignette 13.3 for a professional football player's superstitious behavior.

Athletes' superstitions may appear amusing and, at times, even incredible. However, they often perform an important psychological function. Sports psychologist Graham Neil says, "Superstition is a real coping strategy, a way to handle the anxiety that comes with competition."[14] Accordingly, ritualistic behavior provides the athlete with a sense of control over factors that, as important as they are to the game's outcome, lie beyond one's power. Additionally, such behavior can have a calming or soothing effect and therefore contributes to anxiety reduction, which can play a positive role in sport competition.

Do athletes employ much superstitious behavior? In one study,[15] one third of the athletes admitted to having superstitions. The superstitions tended to revolve around the specific characteristics of the sport—uniforms, equipment, and related paraphernalia. Zimmer notes that in hockey, because of the extensive use of equipment, superstitions abound; in basketball where equipment is minimal, superstitions surround the basketball and scoring; in swimming and gymnastics, lucky charms, magical numbers, and repetitive phrases were popular.[16] Gregory and Petrie concluded, "137 respondents endorsed 904 superstitions (with repetition) which could be grouped into 40 categories clearly indicating the strength of superstition in sport."[17]

The late psychologist B.F. Skinner noted similar "superstitious behavior" in his experiments with pigeons.[18] Frequently, hungry pigeons, after being fed, would apparently associate their activity immediately before receiving the food as somehow having "caused" such reinforcement. Hence, explaining athletes' superstitious behavior invokes at least two phenomena: (a) tension reduction via the "ritual" and (b) instrumental conditioning via Skinnerian principles.

In short, the similarities between sport and religion are numerous—so numerous, in fact, that some suggest that sport has become a functional equivalent of religion.

❏ CONNECTIONS BETWEEN RELIGION AND SPORT

Deford has argued that the twentieth century has witnessed a new liaison between sports and religion.[19] This new social movement he called **Sportianity;** others have dubbed it "Jocks for Jesus." The trend can be clearly documented by considering the religious organizations for athletes that have spawned since 1950. Organizations such as the Fellowship of Christian Athletes (FCA), Athletes-in-Action (AIA), Sports Ambassadors, Baseball Chapel, Hockey Ministries International, Pro Basketball Fellowship, SportsWorld Chaplaincies, Intersports Associates, The Institute for Athletic Perfection (IAP), and Professional Athletes Outreach (PAO) are nondenominational in character with the goal of recruiting new members to religion.

The FCA is one of the oldest members of this constellation. Its purpose is to challenge youth to accept Christ as their personal savior and to live their lives in accordance with His dictates. The scope, aim, and purpose of the FCA is revealed in the following quote:

> The Fellowship of Christian Athletes exists to present to athletes and coaches, and all whom they influence, the challenge and adventure of receiving Jesus Christ as Savior and Lord, serving Him in their relationships and in the fellowship of the church.
>
> The Fellowship of Christian Athletes applies muscle and action to the Christian Faith. It strives to strengthen the moral, mental, and spiritual fiber of the athletes and coaches in America.
>
> The Fellowship of Christian Athletes approach might well be termed "evangelism through fellowship"—centering on the person of Jesus Christ, the Bible, and the institution of the Church. In its ministry to the greats and unsung heroes of the sports world, FCA is a fellowship through which ordinary people help each other become better persons and better examples of what God can do with a yielded life.[20]

The FCA's ministry focuses on six program areas: (a) "Huddles" for junior and senior high school athletes, (b) "College Fellowships" for college and ex-college athletes, (c) "Adult Chapters" for adults desiring to advance and promote the Christian faith through sports, (d) a national conference held each summer, (e) coaches' clinics (ranging from junior high to the professional level), and (f) church involvement. In addition to these programs, the FCA sponsors other activities, including Bowl Breakfasts (preceding the Super Bowl and major college bowl games), Pro Bible Studies (in football, baseball, golf, basketball, and rodeo), Weekends of Champions, rallies, Golf Ministry, and "Pro" chapel services (baseball and football).

The FCA does not underwrite sport teams, but it does use older athletes and coaches to proselytize youth. Today, it boasts a multimillion-dollar budget and over 100,000 members. Among the most religious well-known activities engaged in by the FCA include huddle-fellowship programs. These programs consist of Bible study, prayer, and faith witnessing for high school and college athletes. The FCA also endorses social service programs such as visiting nursing homes and hospitals, being "big brothers" to needy children, and supervising community athletic programs.

What does the FCA mean to its participants? Tom Landry, former coach of the Dallas Cowboys, has said: "The star of athletic influence is shining brightly now. It may not always be so, but it is now. And I believe the Fellowship of Christian Athletes is the most effective group in America for passing along the influence of Christianity." The well-known evangelist Billy Graham has responded: "Our organization has worked hand in hand many times with the FCA. It's one of the most effective movements in this nation for the presentation of the Gospel to young people." One of the female conferees has said: "I can truly say it was the best week of my life (referring to the national conference in Indiana). It's beautiful here—and so are the people. I learned to be more loving, forgiving, and caring. It helped me have a good time in sports without fighting."[21]

Athletes-in-Action is a special unit of the Campus Crusade for Christ. Unlike the FCA, AIA does subsidize a variety of sport teams in basketball, gymnastics, track and field, wrestling, and weightlifting. These teams are composed of former college athletes who, in addition to competing with various college teams, make evangelical speeches and disseminate religious literature. Sport Ambassadors is the international counterpart of AIA. It has spread the Gospel by sending athletic teams to other continents to both play and pray.

Professional Athletes Outreach, another nondenominational religious organization, attempts to convert individuals to Christ through speaking blitzes. Professional athletes, former and contemporary, deliver the message at speaking engagements as well as participating in activities with secular and/or religious individuals in flag football games, tug-of-war, wrist-wrestling, and the like.

Baseball Chapel Inc. is a nonprofit Christian organization organized by major league baseball. It schedules Christian speakers for all major league baseball teams during Sundays of the regular season. The services take place in the hotels of the visiting team and in the locker room of the home team. One of the first chapel services for ball players was started by ex-Yankee Bobby Richardson, a second baseman from 1955 to 1966.

Biblical Exhortations

What does the Bible (King James version) have to say about sports? Several quotes capture it:

> Know ye not that they which run in a race run all, but one receiveth the prize? So run, that ye may obtain (I Corinthians 9:24).

> I have fought a good fight, I have finished my course, I have kept the faith (II Timothy 4:7).

But refuse profane and old wives' fables, and exercise thyself rather unto godliness. For bodily exercise profiteth little; but godliness is profitable unto all things, having promise of the life that now is and of that which is to come (I Timothy 4:7–8).

Interestingly, the first two scriptures are at apparent odds with the third. The first two endorse the familiar notion that when one gives one's all or one's best, the outcome (either victory or defeat) is immaterial. The third passage casts doubt on the relevance, both literally and figuratively, of physical exercise.

Religion and Sport: A Brief Contemporary History

Although sport and religion in contemporary America are intertwined, and some even consider American's true religion to be sport because of the parallels and functional equivalencies of the two social institutions, this was not always the case. Recall that our colonial Puritan forebears were incensed at sport, games, and recreation, particularly when engaged in on the Sabbath. As large waves of immigrants came to this country bringing along their cultural traditions (one of which was recreation on Sundays), coupled with the demise of the frontier, the church modified its antisport bias. With the advent of the new social order wrought by the Industrial Revolution, the church reneged on its opposition to sport and recreation. A new movement, "muscular Christianity," was used to attract converts. The rationale was that it was better to have individuals engaging in such physical recreation than to drink away one's leisure time. The "muscular Christianity" movement was a collective response to the waning spirituality and, at the same time, a ploy to convert members to the fold. Both the YMCA and YWCA spearheaded the movement's beginning in the second half of the nineteenth century. By the century's close, sport and recreational pursuits were widely accepted and increasingly adopted in all realms.

Sport has not always been welcome in religion. Up to 1880, "there was hardly a place in the country where a grown man could openly set about to play without doing violence to established prejudice and without a sense of personal shame."[22] But, by 1900, the idea of pleasure being intrinsically evil tended to have been eclipsed. Theological schools recognized the importance of play in the ministry. The philosophy of ministering to bodies and souls was adopted. One "minister was quoted by one of his flock as saying that good wholesome recreation was first cousin to religion and that the refreshing of the body went a long way toward giving the soul a chance."[23] This philosophy of combining recreation and religion triggered many sport–religion developments in the 1920s.

Experimentation was part of the cultural changes of the 1920s. Much effort was expended in applying the Gospel in the home, in the work area, and in recreation programs. Churches began including recreational facilities such as gymnasiums, swimming pools, and tennis courts. These facilities grew so rapidly that the trained personnel supply proved inadequate. More recreation leaders were needed to ensure quality recreation programs.

The greatest aid in providing leadership was the Young Men's Christian Association (YMCA). In 1922, this organization helped start church athletic leagues, and during this time, it helped churches enlarge their physical recreation programs. Today, the YMCA offers many recreational opportunities including softball, soccer, flag football, swimming, and gymnastics.

In addition to the YMCA, church recreation programs today are often directed by trained recreation professionals and/or youth directors. The *Church Recreation Magazine* reported, "recreation is a nice extra that churches can offer their members. It's a way of providing wholesome activities and allowing members to become better acquainted."[24] Activities include games, crafts, picnics, camping, retreats, special events, and sport leagues. The activities are designed to stimulate growth both physically and spiritually.

The future role of the church and physical recreation is auspicious. However, "religion is coming to a new appreciation of the importance of physical well-being as an aid to soul cultures. One hundred years ago churches were built on hillsides, surrounded by cemeteries; today they are built in settings of playgrounds, tennis courts, and swimming pools. Instead of preparing men for death, the new religion seeks to prepare men for life."[25] Preparation for life (i.e., eternal life) is a main theme in religion. Several analogies can be drawn between Christianity and sport:

First, both sport and Christianity have a central authority figure. The leader in sport is usually the coach; and the coach gives direction, guidance, encouragement, answers to questions, and acts as an example for the athlete. Similarly, God is the authority figure in Christianity. He is a perfect exemplar and gives His "team" (i.e., Christians) guidance, love, and answers to prayer (Peter 2:21). In both cases, the leader tends to be respected and admired. The athlete and Christian alike must be obedient to authority. "But as the church is subject to Christ" (Ephesians 5:24), so is the athlete subject to the coach.

Second, both institutions consist of a group of individuals who work together. In team sports, the group comprises the athletes, who combine their knowledge and skill to perform their best as a unit. In Christianity, the group is the "Church of Christ" (i.e., the group of believers) who join in fellowship to increase their knowledge of the *Bible*. The apostle Paul writes, "Therefore encourage one another, and build up one another . . ." (II Thessalonians 5:11). Christians as well as athletes need to "stick together" to learn the rules of the "game."

A third commonality that can be observed between Christianity and sport involves rules. Athletes must learn the rules of the sport before competing. Similarly, Christians have a "rulebook," namely, the *Bible,* which sets forth guidelines for Christian living. Knowledge of the rules without skill is useless for the competitive athlete. Athletes can use their knowledge to increase their skill, but skill wins the game most often. Christians need to know the Bible intellectually but will "lose the game" if it is not applied to their life. "But prove yourselves doers of the Word, and not merely hearers who delude themselves" (James 1:22). Putting the knowledge into action of living like Christ is the skill of the Christian.

Although rules are a necessity in both institutions, they are often violated. In sport, when a player breaks a rule, there is a penalty. In football, this may result in loss of yardage and/or down. When athletes break a rule at practice, they are often reprimanded. Evidence of inhumane sanctions is seen in collegiate sport. Trainer sessions, strenuous drills, and running the stadium steps have been used to physically and mentally abuse athletes. Christians also break rules, called *sinning,* and must deal with the consequences. One dissimilarity between sport and Christianity is seen regarding forgiveness. "The Lord tosses our sins away as far as the east is from the west and remembers them no more." Christians, then, can be compared to athletes; both are responsible for their own actions and can blame no one but themselves.

A fifth similarity is the evidence of hardship and pain in both Christianity and sport. Athletes must endure training and strenuous practice to improve and succeed at their sport.

Christians must also suffer (just as Christ suffered on the cross) and are not free from trials, tribulations, and temptations. "Consider it all joy, my brethren, when you encounter various trials, knowing that the testing of your faith produces endurance" (James 1:2,3). A track runner must suffer and run hard to build endurance. But for both the athlete and the Christian, the testing and training pays off by the rewards received.

A final similarity for both sport and Christianity is a goal. The goal for the competitive athlete is to win. Crossing the finish line first, ending the game with the most points, or surviving the longest are examples of winning in sport. The goal for Christians is eternal life in Heaven. Paul writes, "I press on toward the goal for the prize of the upward call of God in Christ Jesus" (Philippians 3:14). Christians must repent of their sins, accept Jesus as their Lord and Savior, and live for Christ daily to reach the goal of a life with Christ in Heaven. The road to success is narrow: In sports only one athlete or team typically wins. One difference between sport and Christianity is that athletes lose on account of their actions (i.e., lack of skill needed to win the game); the non-Christians, however, "lose" as a result of their own choices.

Another link between sport and Christianity can be seen in mass media productions. Books and films have been released that blend sport and religious themes. The book *Running for Jesus* is a personal account of the struggles of a female athlete as she chose to run for Jesus. Madeline Manning (Mims) Jackson says, "So much of my story is personal. I'm like anybody else. I have gone through some pretty rugged times, and I have spent years searching for myself and for my place in this crazy world."[26] Readers are inspired by her endurance, motivation, and devotion to God and running.

The film *Chariots of Fire* combined religion and sport as a motif. A male track athlete refuses to run on Sunday because of his religious convictions. The movie is inspirational and shows that sport can strengthen one's faith in God. Another film (and book), *Joni,* is the story of a former athlete who broke her neck and became paralyzed. The film and book describe travails with her handicap, acceptance of never walking or competing in sports again, and reliance on God.

Through the use of the history of sport in religion, analogies between sport and Christianity, and evidence of the relationship in organizations, ceremonies, sermons, and the media, we see that sport and religion are entwined.

Athletes who mix sport with religion are not in short supply. The esteemed evangelist Billy Sunday had professional baseball experience, as an outfielder, with Chicago and Pittsburgh. Sunday left baseball after being converted at a Christian mission in Chicago in 1886 following a weekend drinking binge. When he died in 1935, it was estimated that he had preached to over 100 million people. The inventor of basketball, James Naismith, was an unordained Protestant minister. Bob Richards, euphemistically called the "Vaulting Vicar," was an Olympic athlete. The House of David baseball team was known for playing against black baseball teams before integration, when the latter went on their barnstorming tours. Other professional athletes with ministerial connections include Calvin Hill, Albie Pearson, Donn Moomaw, Henry Carr, and Bill Glass.

Former maligned Notre Dame football coach Gerry Faust successfully blended Catholicism and football when he was a mentor at Cincinnati's Moeller High School. Not only did his teams live, play, and pray religiously, they also won more than 90% of their games (more than half of these victories were shutouts). When he took over the helm at the Golden Dome, there was some speculation that he'd have to tone down his spiritual zeal. According to Faust, "They did more at Notre Dame in the past than we did at Moeller. Each young man who wants to be blessed . . . is blessed. They bless them in the locker room. They kneel down in front of the priest, the priest puts his hand on each of their helmets and gives them a blessing. Almost all the kids do that . . . it is just a beautiful thing to see."[27] The cleavage between religion and sport is aptly expressed by Edwards, "The religious theme in the sports creed is clearly a Protestant emphasis. . . . The place of religion in sports is ill-defined but the emphasis is conspicuous enough to show that the creed recognized and appreciated traditional Protestant religious values."[28]

To understand the tie between Protestantism and sports, consider briefly Weber's classic treatise, *The **Protestant Ethic** and the Spirit of Capitalism.*[29] Weber did not say that Protestantism caused capitalism but that some of the core values of Protestantism were conducive to the development of the social, economic, and political system we know as capitalism. The value orientations embedded in Protestant ideology included:[30]

1. *Self-discipline and work.* John Calvin's (1509–1564) predestination doctrine claimed that humans were in a dichotomous situation—they were either condemned to hell or destined to live in the Lord's house forever. Psychologically, adherents to this tenet experienced doubt and anxiety about where they stood in relation to the afterlife. Asceticism or the denial of worldly pleasures, hard work, and self-discipline became symbolic of the chosen. Thus, one's anxiety about the hereafter was alleviated through hard work and self-discipline.
2. *Initiative and acquisition.* One who worked hard and avoided worldly pleasures and the evils of the flesh would be in an advantageous position insofar as the accumulation of goods was concerned. Since one never knew whether one was in the flock of the chosen, there was a relentless acquisition or stockpiling of worldly pleasures.
3. *Individualism and competition.* Puritan theology viewed each of us as alone before our Creator. Each individual thus sought evidence of God's favor and this often meant competing against and surpassing one's competitors.

The Protestant ideology influenced general cultural values; attitudes toward work and play were significantly affected. Therefore, it can be argued that the value orientations of sport are moderately consistent with the underlying values of traditional Protestantism. In short, sport values may be viewed as secularized versions of core Protestant values. Doesn't sport place such values as hard work, self-discipline, indi-

☐ VIGNETTE 13.4

Sport as Civil Religion

Michael Stein presents a provocative essay in which he argues that football at the University of Nebraska is a civil religion in the "Cornhusker" state. Let us consider his contentions.

The University of Nebraska football team, dubbed the "Big Red," has typically played before sellout crowds. Despite stadium expansion, the demand for tickets has perennially outdistanced the supply. In the latter 1970s, even the *suggestion* of an additional 8,000 seats resulted in an excess of 20,000 requests for tickets in less than a month.

According to Stein, students' purchasing of season tickets (about 90% of the student body) is virtually unprecedented. Further, Memorial Stadium, the home site of the Nebraska football games, is the third largest "city" in the state on a football Saturday. Pilgrimages to Memorial Stadium are regular social experiences for both in- and out-of-state football aficionados.

The media—both the electronic and print—provide extensive and frequent coverage of "Big Reg" football. From television and radio to newspaper coverage, Nebraska football is impressive. Stein writes: "The favorite gathering place of the faithful . . . is Memorial Stadium. . . . [f]or the football fan the stadium may be likened to a house of worship. . . . In addition to a large and faithful congregation, 'tithings' are offered which . . . assist in keeping Nebraska football . . . "in the black."

According to Slusher:

> The evolution of man has demonstrated a constant need for ritual. . . .
>
> With the reduction of ritual in religion, it is not surprising man turns to other "rites" to again see some form of quasi-order to his life. For many, sports fulfills this function. (p. 130)

Arguing the sport religion metaphor, Stein suggests that Nebraska football takes on the nature of a secular religion.

SOURCES: Michael Stein, "Cult and Sport: The Case of Big Red," *Mid-American Review of Sociology* 2, no. 2 (1977), pp. 29–42. H. S. Slusher, *Man, Sport and Existence: A Critical Analysis* (Philadelphia: Lea & Febiger, 1967).

☐

---

vidual initiative, and competition on a pedestal? Sport is often thought to be denomination-less, as conveyed in the notion of civil religion. On the other hand, Guttmann writes, "The emergence of modern sports represents neither the triumph of capitalism nor the rise of Protestantism but rather the slow development of an empirical, experimental, mathematical Weltanschaung."[31] *Weltanschaung*, a German word, means "world view." It refers to a particular perspective or point of view stemming from the perceived structural conditions of a society.

☐ SPORT AS CIVIL RELIGION

Unlike Great Britain, which has an official state church (the Anglican church), in the United States there is a separation between the two in custom and law. The range of religious expression—from obscure sects to mainstream denominations—is indeed enormous in this country. Given such diversity, one may wonder how such diversity produces a cultural consensus, a common belief system or overarching canopy. The

☐ VIGNETTE 13.5

Sport Is Not a Religion

Philosophers, sportswriters, and journalists have recently referred to sport as a religious experience or used religious terminology in analyzing sport. Yet sport fulfills none of the main functions of the Christian or Navajo religions, the former Western and monotheistic, with a theology developed through interpretation of written text, the latter non-Western, polytheistic, and transmitted orally.

Both the Christian and Navajo religions explain how and why human beings were created, and why human beings continue to experience insoluble problems. Both religions have developed procedures for the alleviation of unavoidable human distress, through sacramental recourse to supernatural, unchanging, and powerful deities. While these religions differ in their conception of life after death, both assume that life on earth can only be tolerable if human beings act on the beliefs their respective religions define for their adherents.

Sports fulfill none of the above functions. Sport can certainly tap emotions tapped by religion; it can also epitomize religious actions such as ritual death and sacrifice. But sport is organized and played for humans by humans, without supernatural sanction. We are now all aware that professional sports are organized as businesses; we should, however, also know that these business underpinnings have no more relevance to what happens on the field of play than ticket sales have on the performance of grand opera. Were we to distinguish the game itself from its necessary business correlates, we should not need false analogies, the use of which hinders our comprehension of both sport and religion.

SOURCE: Joan Chandler, "Sport Is Not a Religion," paper presented to *The North American Society for the Sociology of Sport,* Boston, 6–10 November, 1985.

☐

---

functional equivalent of a common belief system (e.g., common religion) is found in what Bellah calls **civil religion**—a shared public faith that raises secular phenomena to almost a religious level.[32] Manifestations of civil religion can be found in holiday celebration activities such as Thanksgiving, Memorial Day, New Year's Day, and the Fourth of July, mottoes such as "In God We Trust" on currency, the Pledge of Allegiance in which the phrase "under God" appears, formal public meetings, and even sport contests, inauguration speeches of Presidents, and facsimiles. See Vignette 13.4.

Prayers in and outside of sport are often exemplary of civil religion. Prayers are used as common forms of supplication at all levels of sport. The Sports World Ministry recruits Christian athletes to speak at schools across the country. Football player Norm Evan wrote, in *On God's Squad:*

> I guarantee you Christ would be the toughest guy who ever played this game. If he were alive today, I would picture a six-foot, six-inch, 260 pound defensive tackle who would always make the big plays and would be hard to keep out of the backfield for offensive linemen like myself. . . . The game is 90 percent desire, and His desire was perhaps His greatest attribute.[33]

While sport does exhibit some of the trappings of religion, at least one sport sociologist emphatically argues that "sport is not a religion" (Vignette 13.5).

☐ USES OF RELIGIOUS PRACTICES IN THE WORLD OF SPORT

The most direct uses of religion in sports can be appreciated by considering the extent of prayer, spiritual rituals, and or religious services before, during, and/or after sporting contests. Prayer is probably the most common religious practice, although little empirical data exist to confirm this speculation. A familiar religious expression is a Roman Catholic athlete making the sign of the cross before shooting a free throw. A former professional football player informed me that the team chanted the following prayer before each game:

> Lord, we thank you for this day
> Grant us guidance in our play
> Give us strength in our hands and hearts, to play the
> Fair and sportsmen's part. Courage, pride, and self-
> Esteem for the New York Giants football team.

Although this prayer is formal, casual observation of sport teams (e.g., football and basketball) reveals that a short form of supplication is common among athletic teams, particularly at the prep and collegiate levels. Marbeto surveyed California institutions of higher learning and established two facts:[34] (a) In excess of 80% of church-affiliated schools conducted team prayers in contrast to about 10% of public schools, and (b) over 50% of coaches and players repeated prayers related to the game (e.g., to win or to help them do their best). The time when the prayers were recited is revealing. Most took place before the game, the fewest at the end.

Pregame religious services are popular at the professional level, at least in football. According to one source, most professional football teams conduct brief pregame religious services, and numerous National Football League (NFL) teams carry their own chaplains. A noteworthy case is that of the 1975 Pittsburgh Steelers' Super Bowl appearance in which the team's management flew their "good luck priest" over from Ireland.[35]

The interfacing of sports, religion, and politics can readily be seen by considering that many sporting contests commence with two activities: (a) the playing of the national anthem and (b) a religious invocation. Several years ago, the Reverend Richard J. Bailer delivered the following controversial benediction before a football game between the Miami Dolphins and the Cincinnati Bengals:

> Creator God: Father and Mother of us all: We give you thanks for the joy and excitement occasioned by this game. We pray for the physical well-being of all the gladiators who run the gamut of gridiron battle tonight . . . but knowing that the tigers are voracious beasts of prey, we ask You to be especially watchful over our gentle dolphins. Limit if You will, the obfuscations of Cosell's acidulous tongue, so that he may describe this night truly and grammatically as it is. . . . A great game, in a great city, played before Your grateful children, on whom we ask peace and shalom. Amen.[36]

Before a World Hockey Association All-Star game, this classic invocation was delivered (note the figures of speech that emphasize the connections between sport and religion):

> Heavenly Father, Divine Goalie, we come before You this evening to seek Your blessing. . . . Keep us free from actions that would put us in the Sin Bin of Hell. . . . Help us

to stay within the blue line of Your commandments and the red line of Your grace. Protect us from being injured by the puck of pride. May we be ever delivered from the high stick of dishonesty. May the wings of Your angels play at the right and left of our teammates. May You always be the divine center of our team, and when our summons comes for eternal retirement to the heavenly grandstand, may we find You ready to give us the everlasting bonus of a permanent seat in Your coliseum. Finally, grant us the courage to skate without tripping, to run without icing, and to score the goal that really counts—the one that makes each of us a winner, a champion, and an all-star in the hectic Hockey Game of Life. Amen.[37]

Finally, an attempt to equate the game of football with the game of life was developed and expanded on by a Canadian pastor for the magazine *Christian Athlete:*

In a diagram of the "ultimate" play, the offensive line is made up of Love, Joy, Grace, Christ, Hope, Peace and Faith. The quarterback is Prayer. The blocking backs are Resurrection and Light. And the running back who will carry the ball is You, the Redeemed. On the other side, the defensive line is Fear, Sin, Satan, Despair, Worry and Separation. The linebackers are Sorrow, Tribulation and Unbelief. The deep backs are Darkness and Death.

The pastor describes the play: Jesus Christ is the center of this big play. He snaps the ball to Prayer and then brings down Satan. Prayer calls the signals, hands off to Redeemed and takes Worry out of the Play. Faith removes Unbelief; Peace overcomes Tribulation; Hope blocks Despair; Grace covers Sin; Joy erases Sorrow; Love casts out Fear; Light wipes out Darkness; Resurrection overcomes the last enemy, Death; and Redeemed scores. The end zone is marked "Eternal Life."[38]

Michael Novak,[39] philosopher and theologian, does not merely use the sport–religion connection metaphorically; rather, he argues that sports are natural religions and sees the following parallels between the two: (a) Both are characterized by an impulse toward asceticism, dedication to preparation, respect for one's body and soul, and an awe of competition. (b) Both feature ritualistic observances. (c) Both are organized social institutions. Novak wrote:

To have a religion, you need to have a way to exhilarate the human body, and desire, and will, and the sense of beauty, and a sense of oneness with the universe and other humans. You need chants and songs, the rhythm of bodies in unison, the indescribable feeling of many who together "will one thing" as if they were each members of a single body. All these things you have in sports . . . sports are a form of religion."[40]

☐ SUMMARY

Despite the seeming differences between sport and *religion,* the two are intricately interwoven; they are not diametrically opposed. Some, not all, even see sport as a functional equivalent of religion. Sport scribes—the media people—disseminate the sport news and provide testimony to the virtues of sport. Sport organizations—such as the National Collegiate Athletic Association (NCAA) the Amateur Athletic Union (AAU), and the International Olympic Committee (IOC)—like religions, are hierarchically arranged. Religious symbols include the cross, phylactery, and fish; and sport symbols include game balls, programs, pucks, chinstraps, and so forth. Sport adherents, like religious people, engage in a variety of rituals (e.g., tailgate parties and the wearing of special jackets, caps, suits, or pants). Finally, sport fans make periodic "pilgrimages" to places such as the Baseball Hall of Fame in Cooperstown, New York, or the Pro Football Hall of Fame in Canton, Ohio. The connections between religion and sports are also evidenced by organizations like the Fellowship of Christian Athletes, Athletes in Action, Sports Ambassadors, the Institute for Athletic Perfection, Sports Chapels, and Professional Athletes Outreach. Sport is linked with the tenets of the Protestant ethic; not to mention that sport is a form of *civil religion.* Religious practices—prayers, pregame religious services, and spiritual invocations—are found in a wide variety of sport contests.

❏ KEY CONCEPTS

Religion
Functions of Religion
    Individual or Psychological Functions
    Social Functions
Characteristics of Institutionalized
   Religion
    Beliefs
    Hierarchy of Authority

Symbols
Rituals
Propitiation
Magic
Sportianity
Protestant Ethic
Civil Religion

❏ ENDNOTES

1. HARRY EDWARDS, *Sociology of Sport* (Homewood, IL: Dorsey, 1973), p. 125.
2. EMILE DURKHEIM, *The Elementary Forms of Religious Life* (New York: Free Press, 1912), p. 47.
3. CHARLES GLOCK & RODNEY STARK, *Religion and Society in Tension* (Chicago: Rand McNally, 1965), p. 4.
4. R.P. CUZZORT & E.W. KING, *Humanity and Modern Social Thought* (Hinsdale, IL: Dryden, 1976), p. 27.
5. THOMAS F. O'DEA, *The Sociology of Religion* (Englewood Cliffs, NJ: Prentice-Hall, 1966), pp. 4–5.
6. DAVID DRESSLER with WILLIAM M. WILLIS, JR., *Sociology,* 3rd ed. (New York: Alfred A. Knopf, 1976), pp. 322–325.
7. ALLEN GUTTMANN, From *Ritual to Record: The Nature of Modern Sports* (New York, Columbia University Press, 1978), p. 85.
8. "Football Weekend," *Newsweek on Campus* (November 1985), p. 26.
9. PATRICIA HARRIS & DAVID LYON, "Sports Museums," *Adventure Road* September/October (1989), pp. 12, 14–15.

10. JAMES W. VANDER ZANDEN, *Sociology,* 4th ed. (New York: John Wiley & Sons, 1979), pp. 445–446.
    H.G. BUHRMANN & M.K. ZAUGG, "Religion and Superstition in the Sport of Basketball," *Journal of Sport Behavior* 6, no. 3 (October 1983), pp. 146–157.
11. GEORGE GMELCH, "Baseball Magic," *Transaction* 8 (June 1971), pp. 39–41, 54.
12. BRONISLAW MALINOWSKI, quoted in *ibid.*
13. *Op cit.*[11]
14. GRAHAM NEIL, quoted in *Psychology Today* (July 1984), p. 36.
15. *Ibid.*, pp. 36–39.
16. JUDITH ZIMMER, "Courting the Gods of Sport," *Psychology Today* 18 (July 1984), p. 30.
17. C. JANE GREGORY & BRIAN M. PETRIE, "Superstitions of Canadian Intercollegiate Athletes: An Inter-Sport Comparison," *International Review of Sport Sociology* 10, no. 2 (1975), p. 63.
18. B.F. SKINNER, *Science and Human Behavior* (New York: Macmillan, 1953).
19. FRANK DEFORD, "Religion in Sport," *Sport in Contemporary Society,* ed. D. Stanley Eitzen (New York: St. Martin's, 1979), pp. 341–347.

20. Fellowship of Christian Athletes Publication, 8701 Leeds Rd., Kansas City, MO, pp. 1–2.

21. *Ibid.*, p. 7.

22. Nancy Colton, "Religious Values in Sport," unpublished manuscript, Illinois State University, 15 April 1982.

Additional material in this section is drawn from Colton, *ibid.*, and Frederick Cozens and Florence Stumpf, *Sports in American Life* (Chicago: University of Chicago Press, 1953), p. 94.

23. *Ibid.*, p. 95.

24. Ann Gardner (ed.), "The Young and the Reckless," *Church Recreation Magazine*, 12 no. 2 (January, February, March 1982), p. 7.

25. *Op. cit.*,[22] p. 110.

26. Madeline Manning Jackson, *Running for Jesus* (Waco, TX: Word Books Publishers, 1977), p. 15.

27. Faust, cited in Loren Feldman, "A High-School Legend Leads the Irish," *Family Weekly* (18 October 1981), pp. 23–24.

28. *Op. cit.*[1]

29. Max Weber, *The Protestant Ethic and the Spirit of Capitalism*, trans. Talcott Parsons (New York: Charles Scribner's, 1930, original work published 1905).

30. Leonard Broom & Philip Selznick, Sociology, 4th ed.(New York: Harper & Row, 1968), pp. 464–465.

31. *Op cit.*[7]

32. Robert N. Bellah, "Civil Religion in America," *Daedalus* 96 (Winter 1967), pp. 1–21.

33. Norm Evan, quoted in Ira Berkow, "On Mixing Sports With Religion," *The New York Times,* (13 May 1982), p. D26.

34. Joseph A. Marbeto, Jr., "The Incidence of Prayer in Athletics as Indicated by Selected California Collegiate Athletes and Coaches," master's thesis, University of California, Santa Barbara (1967), cited in D. Stanley Eitzen & George H. Sage, *Sociology of American Sport* (Dubuque, IA: William C. Brown, 1978), pp. 130–131.

35. James A. Michener, *Sports in America* (New York: Random House, 1976).

36. *Ibid.*, p. 384.

37. Quoted in Frank Deford, "The Word According to Tom," *Sports Illustrated* 44 (26 April 1976), p. 69. Cited in D. Stanley Eitzen & George H. Sage, *Sociology of American Sport* (Dubuque, IA: William C. Brown, 1978), p. 130.

38. *Christian Athlete* May (1981), pp. 28–29.

39. Michael Novak, "The Natural Religion," in *Sport in Contemporary Society,* ed. D. Stanley Eitzen (New York: St. Martin's, 1979), pp. 335–341.

40. *Ibid.*, pp. 340–341.

14

Sport and the Mass Media

If all the year were playing holidays/To sport would be as tedious as to work. WILLIAM SHAKESPEARE

The **mass media** (plural of *mass medium*) are channels of communication that transmit messages through an electronic (TV, radio, recordings, films) or a print medium (e.g., newspapers, books, magazines, billboards) to a geographically dispersed audience. The media constitute one of the major social processes affecting and affected by sport, and the relationship between the media and sport is symbiotic, meaning that each needs the other for survival. Today, sport appears to depend on the media—on television and its money in particular—to remain viable. The evolution of the sport–media interdependency is described by Hoch:

> One factor that made a decisive difference was the tremendous coverage of sports by the press. About the same time the first sports leagues began, there developed (not by coincidence) the sort of mass-audience-oriented newspapers needed to sell mass consumption products. A symbiosis between sports and the new media was quickly established in which sports became the decisive promotional device for selling popular newspapers, and newspapers were the decisive promotional device for selling sports spectacles. This symbiotic relationship between sports and the media, now including radio and television, is a central feature of the political economy of both sports and the media to this day.[1]

Sociologically, the telecommunications revolution has been a basic determinant of **popular** (or mass) **culture.** According to the *Encyclopedia of Sociology*,[2] *pop culture* refers to the standardization of "material goods, art, life-styles, ideas, tastes, fashions, and values" and is partially "the homogenized product of the mass media." Sport has become one of the most visible and influential elements in contemporary mass culture.

POPULAR CULTURE AND SPORT
Leisure

What is *leisure?* Many think of leisure as time free from obligations, time to choose or not to choose to do certain things. Historically, however, its definition has not been consistent. Among the Greeks, leisure meant an activity pursued as an end in itself. During the medieval period, it implied contemplation of God. After the Renaissance, it took on a more contemporary meaning—time free from work and homemaking chores. According to Snyder and Spreitzer, "In sociological research, leisure has been studied as a type of time (interval of freedom from work), as a type of activity (freely chosen as an end in itself), and as a state of mind (relaxation or diversion)."[3]

Part of what people do in their leisure time, that is, what they engage in when not working or sleeping, is popular culture. Sociologists Denisoff and Wahrman use the concept "entertainment" to cover the products of mass culture.[4] Sociologically, popular culture provides us with glimpses of the values, attitudes, and behaviors extant in the general culture. In the United States during the past 150 years, the average work week in nonagricultural industries has been nearly cut in half—from an average of 66 hours in 1850 to about 37 in 1990. Consequently, Americans have more discretionary time today than in the past, more time free to pursue desired activities. What do Americans do in their leisure?

The Sport Consumer

A pervasive sport role is that of **sport consumer.** Two types of sport consumer roles demonstrate the relationship between popular culture and sport: (a) direct consumer and (b) indirect consumer.[5]

The **direct sport consumer** attends live sporting events (i.e., goes to the track, stadium, gridiron, rink, ballpark, arena, fieldhouse, or court). Table 1.1 (p. 4) reveals the extent of contemporary spectatorship.

The **indirect sport consumer** absorbs sport through the mass media of television, radio, books, films, magazines, newspapers, and everyday conversation. Although millions subscribe to sport magazines,[6] television far surpasses the others as a medium of sport consumption. The manner in which Americans' sport interests are whetted via the mass media can easily be inferred from various statistics reported in *The Miller Lite Report.*[7] A large percentage of Americans watch either sporting events on TV or the sport news; peruse the newspaper's sport section; read sport periodicals, and talk about sports. The data in Table 14.1 summarize these findings in more detail.

Table 14.2 permits a determination and comparison of household ratings and the percentages of men, women, and children that constitute the audiences for various sporting contests. In recent years, the World Cup (1 billion), Super Bowls (more than 100 million), World Series (more than 100 million), and the Summer Olympics have attracted the largest viewing audiences. College football rivalries (e.g., Texas vs. Oklahoma, Pitt vs. Penn State, USC vs. UCLA, and Ohio State vs. Michigan) and major postseason bowl games also typically draw huge audiences—live and via television—of sport buffs.

TABLE 14.1 The mass media as a source of sports consumption*

RESPONSES TO THE QUERY: How often do you do the following?	Daily or Almost Daily	1 or 2 Times a Week	2 or Fewer Times a Month	Never
Watch or listen to sports news on television or radio?	54%	21%	11%	10%
Read the sports pages of your newspapers?	39%	19%	13%	25%
Watch sports events on television?	17%	56%	21%	2%
Listen to sports on the radio?	9%	19%	27%	41%
Read magazines on sports and athletes?	4%	17%	39%	36%
Read books on sports and athletes?	4%	8%	35%	49%

*4% of the respondents indicated "don't know" for each question (n = 1,319).

SOURCE: *The Miller Lite Report on American Attitudes Toward Sports* (Milwaukee: Miller Brewing Co., 1983), p. 21.

TABLE 14.2   Sports on television

Sport	Household Rating %	% Viewing Audience			
		Men	Women	Teens	Children
Football					
NFL Super Bowl	43.5	47	36	7	10
ABC–NFL (Monday eves.)	16.9	57	33	5	5
CBS–NFL	15.1	57	32	5	6
NBC–NFL	12.8	57	31	6	6
College bowl games	9.2	52	35	5	8
College football, reg. season	6.9	56	32	5	7
Baseball					
World Series	23.9	51	39	4	6
All-Star game	20.4	51	34	5	10
Regular season	6.2	53	34	5	8
Horse racing					
Breeders Cup	4.0	40	43	5	12
Basketball					
NBA average	8.1	54	31	7	8
NCAA average	5.3	54	31	7	8
Bowling					
Pro tour	4.4	44	43	4	9
Golf					
Average, all	3.4	53	39	3	5
Tennis					
Wimbledon	3.6	43	42	8	7
Tournament average	3.1	44	42	7	7
Multisports					
"ABC Wide World of Sports"	5.0	45	40	6	9
CBS "Sports Saturday"	3.4	47	35	7	11
CBS "Sports Sunday"	4.8	50	34	7	9
"Sportsworld—Saturday"	3.2	48	39	4	9
"Sportsworld—Sunday"	3.5	47	35	8	10

SOURCE: Adapted from Nielsen Media Research, 1992.

☐ FUNCTIONS OF MEDIA SPORT

To Birrell and Loy,[8] media sport performs four functions. First, media sport performs an *information* function. It conveys knowledge of and about various sports, contest results, and voluminous statistics on players, teams, leagues, and so on. *Integration,* a second function, occurs to the extent that the sport audience is exposed to and internalizes common norms, values, rituals, and experiences. The third function, *arousal,* adds excitement to one's (perhaps) typical routine and predictable life pattern. The fourth, the *escape* function, underscores the role of media sport in taking us away from our humdrum existences.

Although the medium of television (Vignette 14.1) has radically altered the landscape of sport, historically, the press and radio have also been important. We first examine the influence of **the press** and radio, because they dominated the social scene before the birth of television.

☐ THE PRINT MEDIA

The Press

Newspapers. The **newspaper** was the first significant mass communication modality. Despite the invention of writing millennia ago, Johannes Guttenberg's (1400–1468) development of the printing press had to await certain technological advances. Even with the advent of the printing press, social conditions had to ripen before its effectiveness and utility could be realized. Before 1800, only isolated sport reports appeared in the press. A boxing match in England was the first sporting event reported in the *Boston Gazette* on 5 May 1733 and was followed by sporadic accounts of prizefights and horse and boat races in the 1700s and 1800s.[9] Not until the 1830s did two critical social conditions—urbanization and literacy—reach the point where the selling of the printed page was financially feasible and socially appreciated.

Cozens and Stumpf provide an insightful sociological analysis of the emergence of the newspaper in general and the sport page in particular.[10] In the middle 1800s, sports, for the most part, were covered by weekly newspapers devoted exclusively to them. As early as 1835, the *Sun,* the *Transcript,* and the *Herald*—three New York newspapers—were covering prizefights, horse and footraces, and a few other sport spectacles. Henry Chadwick, who some believe deserves to be called the "original sportswriter" and "father of baseball," was reporting on United States–Canada cricket matches but receiving no compensation, because the well-entrenched New York dailies—the *Times* and the *Tribune*—were not giving much attention to sport news. Chadwick was eventually hired by the *Herald* in 1862 to report regularly on baseball games.

William Randolph Hearst purchased the *New York Journal* in 1895 and made a concerted effort to surpass his competitors in sport reporting. His efforts culminated in the sport section of the newspaper as we know it today. Hearst also instituted the practice of having athletic celebrities write sport columns: Hobart in tennis, Bald in cycling, Heffelfinger in football, and Batchelder in wheeling.

To fully appreciate the emergence of both the newspaper and the sport page, one needs an understanding of the changing social environment. Cozens and Stumpf discuss three sociologically relevant features:[11]

"Expansion of space and extent of coverage:"[12] Before World War I, sport coverage was confined to a few athletic contests, notably baseball, college football, horse racing, and boxing. Today, the sports page of major metropolitan newspapers covers the gamut of sporting activities. The expansion of this coverage had a social basis. The illiteracy rate dropped nearly 50% between 1870 and 1900 (from 20% to 11%), and the percentage of children attending public schools grew from 57% to 72%. The number of newspapers increased from 2,226 in 1899 to 2,600 in 1909, and total daily circulation rose from 24 to 33 million between 1909 and 1919.[13]

During this formative period, and today as well, there was a marked improvement in the quality of sportswriting over the earlier "yellow" journalism. In addition to possessing a knowledge of sport and the vicarious enthusiasm of fans, the sportswriter

◻ VIGNETTE 14.1

TV Sports—The Tube as a Shrine

Since coast-to-coast television became common-place . . . the American public has demonstrated an insatiable thirst for sports.

It gives weekly testimony to the thesis that sports is another religion in America. Or, as Barry Frank . . . put it . . . "Religion we do on Sunday morning; sports we do on Sunday afternoon." The ratings are better on Sunday afternoon. . . .

Add local baseball, basketball, and hockey to that. We watch arm-wrestling from Petaluma, Calif., and we watch a man on a motorcycle try to fly across a pool filled with sharks in Chicago. We watch great basketball players trying to play tennis and television comedians playing touch football. We watch almost anything and we ask for more.

Whether the constant bombardment of the public with free sports events on television is causing sports to eat its young—taking the payoff today at the expense of tomorrow's health—is, the networks say, the responsibility of sports, not of television.

"Greed is a never-ending circle," Frank said. "Where does it start? It's almost a perfect circle. The players want more money, the owners want to be able to give it to them. They in turn want more money. They say expenses go up and prices are rising, so the owners want to sell their product for more money."

The money is in large amounts.

What has resulted is a change in the fabric of American life. There was a time when businesses operated with half-interest the first week in October because the World Series was being played on the radio in the stockroom. Office pools flourished on the number of runs scored in an inning. In order for the greats of tennis to meet, they had to earn their way to the finals of the big tournaments and the Grand Slam meant winning the U.S., British, French, and Australian tournaments.

Instead we now have the World Series being played at night with the fans chilled in Cincinnati's Riverfront Stadium while America watches in the comfort of home with the sponsor's beer within arm's reach. Instead, we have Jimmy Connors and Rod Laver meeting in a match for a king's ransom in Las Vegas, starting times and timeouts are stipulated by television with the acquiescence of one commissioner after another.

But is it evil? Is it immoral to depict the Tasmanian breath-holding championship as sport?

Has television no conscience? Have the programmers no fear for what oversaturation might do to the future? "I'm concerned with that," Roone Arledge . . . said. "On the other hand, it really doesn't work out that way. . . . there are 23 copies of successful television formats and they have a way of shaking themselves out. There were too many westerns, but "Bonanza" and "Gunsmoke" went along fine. The bad ones go and the good ones stay."

It's the view of Alvin Rush . . . that sports television isn't the great menace to the live gate. "It's the same as the movies," he said. "Put on a great show, you'll draw a great crowd. It's still tough to get a ticket for a good event."

The officials of professional football, basketball, baseball, and golf speak of television as the great promoter of interest in their sports. Tournament golf admittedly wouldn't exist on the same scale without television. According to Steve Reid, who negotiates television contracts for the PGA, television provides 38 percent of the purses of tournaments that are not even on television. Sponsors know that golf moves merchandise. The great growth in tennis interest can be directly attributed to television, which showed world-class competition to an audience that had never seen it before.

The public away from the big cities had never seen big-league baseball or football, either, before the advent of the coaxial cable and national telecasts in 1951.

Television made the public aware of professional football, which had been the exclusive province of a few large cities. There were 12 teams in 1951; there are now 28.

America had become aware of tennis as an intensely competitive and athletic game when it was viewed, not too long ago, as the effete pastime of the wealthy. The infusion of television money has put new life into long-moribund boxing. Television of the 1972 and '76 Olympics has made gymnastics—especially women's gymnastics—a significant aspect of physical education in this country, and made Olga Korbut and Nadia Comaneci household names.

Arledge, Frank, and Rush . . . contend that they didn't make those events and games popular; they merely gave them exposure and the games won their own popularity.

A more demonstrable criticism of television sports is that it does no social commentary or investigative reporting of any kind other than occasional editorial comment. . . .

There are issues in sports that affect the public—the evils of recruiting, of falsified college admissions, of drug use, the threat of the agent and the use of public funds for private gains in the business of sports. But television still portrays only the fun and games.

There has been some belated attention given to the language of the broadcasters. CBS has even sent a former great quarterback (no names, please) back to freshman English because he doesn't speak the language and doesn't realize it.

But attempts to lift the pretty rug of sports and uncover the dirt get only the clucking expressions of regret from network sports.

Arledge and Frank concede that television in general has been remiss in that area. Arledge says ABC may delve into it when it introduces a magazine program later in the year with a format similar to CBS's highly rated "60 Minutes," which occasionally gives a segment to critical examination of areas in sports. . . . But none of the networks give the time or money for a fully developed report.

All three executives present the same kind of reasoning for not probing the unsavory areas. "The public is not interested in it" Arledge said. "Look at the sales of books. Bob Lipsyte wrote a great book (*Sportsworld*) that hasn't sold at all." (Note: author Lipsyte said that *Sportsworld* has sold "nowhere near" the first printing of 15,000.)

But so far the public has bought television at whatever lowest common denominator and asked for more and more. But some slight softening has been felt. Television has backed off in its tennis programming—which often matched live action on one channel against taped performances of the same players on another—when ratings dropped. Now, Arledge said, ratings for fewer tennis events have improved.

In recent years baseball has been putting fewer home games on local television . . . That was the nature of the NFL's blackout of home games, which both Arledge and Frank think Congress should not have interrupted.

And some NCAA officials perceive another danger in the glamour television imparts to any school it blesses with its camera. The revenue is shared among conference schools . . . but the ability to promise national exposure is the most potent recruiting tool today.

"If people decide it's better to stay home and watch on television than it is to go to the games, I don't think anything happens to television," Arledge said. "It means the owners are in trouble."

SOURCE: Steve Jacobson, *Newsday*, Inc., copyright 1976. Reprinted by permission.

must be knowledgeable about law, politics, business, fashions, domestic relations, genealogy, dramatics, and war.[14] Howard Cosell says that to cover sports one needs to be widely versed, not a shill: "The fact is that to cover sports today you need to be a Renaissance man. Why? Because sports invades the law, the politics, the economics, the sociology, the education and the medical care of the society. The least important thing is what happens within the arena."[15]

The 1920s witnessed a boom in sport columns. Several factors were conducive to this bonanza: (a) War veterans, having been exposed in various ways to sport, returned from overseas. (b) Institutions of higher learning across the country were building stadiums to accommodate spectators. (c) A postwar economic transfusion was contributing to the populace's affluence. (d) Sport was coming of age, and the "Golden Era" blossomed with such colorful personalities as Babe Ruth, Johnny Weissmuller, Red Grange, Cliff Hagen, Knute Rockne, George Halas, Bill Tilden, Jack Dempsey, Bobby Jones, and Helen Wills, to name a few. While several sports profited from newspaper publicity, it was the national pastime of baseball that was the major beneficiary.

"Reader interest demands free sport publicity":[16] Once sport became a permanent fixture in the newspaper, logistical matters of space, time, and energy to gather sport facts and write reports became a serious issue. Newspapers were generous with the amount of space devoted to sport, because the owners believed this appealed to their readers and maximized circulation (i.e., "sport sells papers").

"Sports page reflects the social scene":[17] The thesis that the sport section mirrors or reflects the key social issues of the day has been advanced. Brillhart reported that sport columns devoted space to the following social concerns:[18]

"The Depression and economic retrenchment"[19] were evidenced by adjustments in admission prices to accommodate lower-income persons and by the staging of various benefit and charity sport events.

Public morality was at issue with respect to the sale of beer at games, athletic proselytizing, and gambling in sport. There was also discussion of the proper role of women in sport, as well as their "proper" attire (i.e., skirts vs. shorts).

Technological change prompted debate as to whether or not football games should be broadcast by radio and raised the issue of night baseball.

"The basic American trait to help the underdog"[20] was reflected in the "Alabama" Pitts case. Pitts, who had been convicted of second-degree murder in New York at the age of nineteen in 1930, was offered a professional baseball contract that led to battles between various judicial bodies regarding its appropriateness and legality. The parallels between scandals in sport and in the world at large are probably not coincidental. For example, the infamous "Black Sox" and Teapot Dome scandals were coinciding events—one in sport, the other in politics. Again, one notices the parallels between events in sport and in the larger society.

The sport page has been a target of controversy. It has been praised extravagantly and criticized unmercifully for its contents. Despite the spectacular growth television has made possible for sport, the financial success of teams, particularly professional ones, has been greatly enhanced by the gratuitous coverage they receive in the newspaper. A favorable press—toward a player or a team—is enormously beneficial. Lever and Wheeler[21] report that sportsnews today has grown to about 50% of all general news coverage in comparison to about 15% at the turn of the century. Further, they report that the sports page has about five times the readership as the average section of the newspaper and that baseball, basketball, and football account for approximately 50% of all sportsnews.

In 1989 the first modern daily national all-sports newspaper, *The National,* made its debut, and in April 1991 *USA Today's Baseball Weekly,* a baseball tabloid, made its maiden voyage. This latter publication confronted a market that included *USA Today's* own colorful sports section, *The National* (now out of circulation), a revamped *Sporting News, Sports Illustrated,* and increasingly sophisticated sports sections of local papers—in addition to the electronic media such as cable television's ESPN and CNN.

Magazines and Periodicals.   The first American periodical devoted to sport, *The American Farmer,* was published in 1819. It contained articles featuring fishing, hunting, shooting, bicycle racing, and the philosophy of sport. The magazine industry has undergone considerable change; many **magazines** aimed at general audiences have, with the exception of *TV Guide* and *Reader's Digest* (both with a circulation of approximately 18 million), proved to be financial disasters (e.g., large-circulation periodicals such as *Look* and *Life* folded in the early 1970s). Specialized magazines, however, have thrived because of the selected readership they can offer their advertisers and patrons.

One of the most successful periodicals devoted to sports—*Sport*—has a circulation of 1.25 million. On 16 August 1954, *Sports Illustrated* made its debut. Today, it is the most widely subscribed to sport magazine, with a weekly circulation of 2.6 million. Other sport-based magazines are popular *(Field and Stream, Sports Afield, Hot Rod, Golf Digest, Car and Driver, PRO, Basketball Weekly, Football Digest, NCAA News, The Sporting News,* and *Golf)* but *Sports Illustrated* and *The Sporting News* stand out because they frequently highlight articles embracing socially significant issues.

Sports magazines play an important role in legitimating certain sports and certain athletes. Lumpkin and Williams content analyzed feature articles in *Sports Illustrated* between 1954 and 1987.[22] They focused on the sport, gender, race, role of the person featured, length of article, author, number of pictures, individuals pictured, and other descriptive characteristics. Some of their findings are revealing. Of the more than 3,700 articles analyzed, 91% featured men (men also authored 92% of the articles). The sports most often featured were (in rank order): baseball, football, basketball, boxing, track and field, and golf. Blacks were highlighted in less than one fourth and whites in about 75% of the features. The number of articles featuring women was miniscule. The researchers report that *Sports Illustrated* reinforces sexist attitudes in two ways: (a) Relatively few articles (and short ones) proclaim women's accomplishments, and (b) sex-appropriate sports—tennis, swimming, and golf—tend to prevail. In summarizing their findings in which white men, black men, white women, and black women—in that order—are most often portrayed, the authors report that the media reinforce and perpetuate traditional stereotypes and images of blacks and women in sports. Of interest, a "typical" *Sports Illustrated* issue sells between 150,000 and 200,000 copies and garners $5 to $6 million. For its swimsuit issue, about 2.5 million copies go to the newstands and $12- to $13-million in revenue is generated.

❑ THE ELECTRONIC MEDIA: BROADCASTING

Radio broadcasting was pioneered in the 1920s by receiver manufacturers such as RCA and Westinghouse. The early years of radio broadcasting strongly affected modern broadcasting and governmental policies toward it.[23] Moreover, the radio corporations extended their purview to television and shaped this medium as well. By the 1920s, live sporting broadcasts were being carried, first locally, and then nationally. Pittsburgh's KDKA, generally recognized as the first commercial radio station, was broadcasting fights and baseball games in 1921.[24] Lee indicated that public broadcasting actually came after sport broadcasting.[25] On 20 August 1920, a radio station owned by the Detroit News aired the results of the World Series and, the same year, the first college football broadcast came from a station located in Texas.

A heavyweight boxing championship between Jack Dempsey and George Carpentier (21 July 1921) was the first fight to be broadcast over the air waves. Six years later, "department store sales of radio equipment soared in the two weeks" before the Dempsey and Gene Tuney championship bout.

Radio ownership grew steadily from the 1920s to the present, and it is now estimated that there are more than twice the number of radio receivers (over 500 million in the early 1990s) than people in the United States. After the advent of television (98% of all U.S. households own at least one), radio broadcasting altered its marketing approach. Instead of large audience and national network programming, radio now specializes in ethnic programming, news, sports, talk shows, local concerns, or specific types of music. Many stations purchase the broadcast rights to college and professional sporting activities, and radio stations in America broadcast nearly one-half million hours of sport annually. There are also 24-hour sport channels that feature scores, games, and sport talk.

❑ THE ELECTRONIC MEDIA: TELEVISION

In commenting on the role of **television** and the media's technology, Gumpert said:

> . . . the television viewers . . . see a game that is altered by electronic techniques . . . the home viewer's relationship with the game is altered because of the intimate and revealing nature of the medium. The television viewer has been transformed into a participating expert who sees every visible nuance of the game. . . . Nothing escapes the camera's eye.[26]

The United States was the first country to introduce television to a mass audience (credit for its invention is attributed to Farnsworth in 1927). This occurred shortly after World War II, and today there are relatively few households—about 2%—not plugged in to this technological medium. Television, as an agent of socialization, has a profound impact on American society's life-styles and leisure activities. According to the Federal Communications Commission, there are 1,194 television stations (904 commercial and 290 public) in the United States, most of them affiliated with one of the three major networks (NBC, CBS, or ABC). According to the A.C. Nielsen Company , "Most of the mass-audience media are supported by advertising revenues and are influenced at least indirectly by the dictates of the advertiser."[27] Not only does television buy sports, but it inevitably takes a controlling role. Schecter said it well:

> Television buys sports. Television supports sports. It moves in with its money and supports sports in a style to which they have become accustomed and then, like a bought lady, sports become so used to luxurious living they cannot extricate themselves. So, slowly at first, but inevitably, television tells sports what to do.[28]

In fact, several professional teams are or were owned in part or totally by media companies. These include the New York Knicks and Rangers (Paramount Communications); Braves (Turner Broadcasting); Cubs *(Chicago Tribune)*; Phillies (Taft Broadcasting); Pirates (before 1986, Warner Communications); and Reds (Multimedia). Program selection results from choosing the most marketable products as measured by the Nielsen ratings (see Table 14.2), a weekly survey of a program's audience size based on a national sample of households. The relative popularity of sport programs can be inferred from the ranking of the largest total audiences for all programming: (1) *M*A*S*H;* (2) *Dallas;* (3) *Roots,* Part VIII; (4) Super Bowl XVI; (5) Super Bowl XVII; (6) Super Bowl XX; (7) *Gone with the Wind,* Part I; (8) *Gone with the Wind,* Part II; (9) Super Bowl XII; (10) Super Bowl XIII. The largest television audience for a single event was the Apollo II moon flight on 20 July 1969.

Television, like no other medium, dominates sport today. America's sports have become the prodigal child of television that provides the hawkers on Madison Avenue with a bonanza opportunity for vast markets. Because of television markets, the exploits of the major leagues have extended into America's remotest hinterlands. Skylines and central cities have been altered by the spectacle of stadiums, arenas, auditoriums, and amphitheaters. According to Johnson, "The geography, the economics, the schedules, the aesthetics, and the very ethos of sport have come to depend upon TV's cameras and advertising monies."[29]

The first televised sporting event appeared on 17 May 1939. The well-known sports announcer Bill Stern handled the play-by-play for a baseball game between two Ivy League schools, Princeton and Columbia. At that time, there were only about 400 television sets, many of them owned by the New York City networks. Television screens were both small and expensive by today's standards. The screens ranged from 5 to 12 inches in diameter and cost, at that time, $600 (at today's dollar value, the cost would exceed $2,000). According to a *New York Times* reviewer, "The players were best described by observers as appearing 'like white flies' running across the screen. When the ball flashed across the grass it appeared as a cometlike white pinpoint. The commentator saved the day, otherwise there would be no way to follow the play or to tell where the ball went. . . ."[30] Out of this inauspicious beginning, a symbiotic relationship between sports and television was conceived.

Because of the role of television in the sports world, it is of interest to consider several milestones in the history of this relationship:

1 June 1939—the first televised prizefight, between Max Baer and Lou Nova
26 August 1939—the first televised major league baseball game, between Cincinnati and Brooklyn
30 September 1939—the first televised college football game, between Waynesburg and Fordham

22 October 1939—the first televised professional football game, between Philadelphia and Brooklyn

28 February 1940—the first televised basketball game, between Fordham and Pittsburgh

30 September 1947—the first televised World Series game, between Dodgers and Yankees

14 July 1951—the first televised sports event in color, the Molly Pitcher Handicap horse race

The three major networks program about 1,600 hours of televised sports, with ESPN, alone, broadcasting nearly 1,500 hours of live sports coverage per year. Further, there has been an expansion of regional cable sport channels which cater to millions of subscribers.

Types and Sources of Spectating Pleasure in Televised Sports

Duncan and Brummett raise the question: "What makes sport spectatorship appealing and pleasurable for the fan?"[31] Drawing on media theories of visual pleasure, the researchers identify three sources of pleasure found in televised sports. The first, *fetishism,* is created "by commodifying athletes and their actions, that is, by treating the material of sports as goods to be closely examined, appraised, and assessed." The second, *voyeurism,* stems from the fact that "sport offers many unexpected opportunities for uninvited, illicit, and . . . voyeuristic looking." The third, *narcissism,* emerges from viewers' identification with the feats of athletes. The researchers argue that three dimensions—the technology, the content, and the social context—of televised sport promote these visual pleasures.

Football. The "game" that has profited immensely from "cyclops"—the television camera—is football. According to Michener, "Starting with a spectacle which already had the ingredients—power, speed, varied movements, choice of plays, enough natural pause between plays to allow the person at home to decide what [strategy the quarterback might employ], plus an alluring violence—the rules' makers and Commissioner . . . have been uncanny in their ability to make the right decision at the right time."[32] According to Chandler,[33] football is a superb television sport because of its patterned and recurring succession of crises—four downs to traverse ten yards and time between plays to permit viewers to guess what the next call might be and to allow announcers to set the stage for subsequent action; replay and comment on the last episode via instant replay are squeezed in; and these are then followed by commercial messages.

Speaking of instant replay, first introduced in 1963, it is noteworthy to consider the way in which it can and has created sport heroes. Former Green Bay Packer Jerry Kramer described his lionization through television as follows:

Over and over, perhaps twenty times, the television cameras reran Bart's touchdown and my block on Jethro Pugh. Again and again, millions of people across the country saw the hole open up and saw Bart squeeze through. Millions of people who couldn't name a single offensive lineman if their lives depended on it heard my name repeated and repeated and repeated. All I could think was "thank God for instant replay."[34]

TABLE 14.3 Total value and annual share per team for television rights in 1988–1992

Sport	Number of Franchises	Total Value	Annual Share per Team
Football	28	$3.6 billion	$32 million
Baseball	26	$1.48 billion	$14 million
Basketball	27	$875 million	$9 million
NHL (hockey)*	22	$51 million	$2.32 million

*The NHL did not have a network contract.

The birth of televised professional football can be traced back to the early 1950s. Franklin Mieuli, an advertising salesman for a San Francisco brewery, contacted the owner of the 49'ers, Tony Morabito. Mieuli suggested to Morabito the telecasting of the 49'ers–Rams games (blacking out television audiences where the game was played), for which Morabito would be paid $10,000. Not only did Morabito accept the invitation, but he was so impressed with the idea that he returned $5,000.[35] In contrast to this paltry sum, today's professional football, baseball, and basketball teams receive millions of dollars for the sale of telecast rights. Only professional hockey has been denied its share of this financial cornucopia, because it lost a national television package. Table 14.3 lists the total value and annual share per team for the sale of broadcast rights into the 1990s.

How far football's television revenues have skyrocketed can best be appreciated if you consider that in 1952 there were 11 NFL teams and the average team revenue amounted to only $70,000. By 1960, the NFL expanded to 13 teams and the average revenue per team rose to $238,000. In 1970, after the two football leagues merged, professional football grew to 26 teams and average revenue amounted to $1,754,000. In the early 1980s, the 28 teams received average television revenues amounting to $5.86 million, enough to guarantee each franchise a profit even if no ducats were sold. The 1982–1986 NFL television pact totaled about $2 billion, and guaranteed $13 million per team before a single customer passed through the turnstiles. Today, each NFL team is assured of between $30 and $35 million from media rights alone.

Baseball.   Professional (major league) baseball, like professional football, has clearly profited from television monies. In 1952, each of the 16 teams earned $260,000, and by 1960, with the same number of franchises, the average share had risen to $783,000. In 1970, baseball expanded to 24 teams, with each team receiving $1,310,000. Today, each major league baseball team is assured of between $15 and $20 million from media pacts. The New York Yankees, for example, derives in excess of $69 million from media sources—national, local, and cable TV and radio—and the Seattle Mariners, about $17 million.

☐ HOW TELEVISION HAS AFFECTED SPORT

In what ways have the media, particularly television, encroached into sport? Television has affected the economy, the ownership and location of franchises, and the scheduling, staging, management, dynamics, and even aesthetics of sport. Although TV has pumped megadollars into sport, the bargain, as we will see, is a Faustian one. Usually, TV is cast in the role of villain and has been criticized on several grounds: (a) The avalanche of televised sports will glue the masses to their sets and turn the nation into passive spectators rather than active participants. (b) Television reshapes sport to satisfy its own needs, whims, and schedule. (c) Television is responsible for contriving artificial time-outs and excessive commercials. (d) At the collegiate level, television provides select schools with a recruiting edge. (e) Television coerces sports into altering rules. (f) Television distorts the nature of the games it covers. (g) It has created a new category of sports, derogatorily referred to as "trashsports."[36] Some even believe mass media sport violence promotes social violence (Vignette 14.2). The following discussion examines some of these criticisms more closely.

The Scheduling, Staging, Management, and Dynamics of Sport

The role of football linesman was established because sportscasters needed to know the yard line where the offensive team gained possession of the ball. The linesman enabled sportscasters to quickly determine the distance traversed by the offensive unit. Another "official" has been added, although this one is neither dressed in the traditional referee's black-and-white striped uniform nor listed in the official program. It is the television network person, frequently adorned in an iridescent-colored outfit, whose job is to signal the game officials when arbitrary time-outs are to be called for "a word from our sponsor." Ordinarily, no problem is encountered in finding time for advertising; however, on occasion, an untimely time-out was manufactured to broadcast a commercial. Michener recalled a contest between the Philadelphia Eagles and New York Jets in Veterans' Stadium that illustrates this travesty.[37] With three and one-half minutes to go, the Jets kicked a field goal, making the score 24–23 Eagles. Deep in their own territory, after the Jets' kickoff following a field goal, the Eagles began running plays to "eat up the clock." The Jets had no time-outs left. At this juncture, the orange-vested television man began frantically waving his hands; the network had three more commercials to squeeze in. The referee called an arbitrary network time-out to stop the clock. As any sport fan knows, this intervention could be enough—although the Eagles went on to win—to change a game's momentum and outcome. In fact, Peter Rhodes, soccer official, once wore an electronic beeper so he could signal time-outs at the television network's request.

On 3 October 1981, Pittsburgh and South Carolina were appearing on ABC's regional football telecast. Pitt was ahead 21–0 and driving for another score, when the network switched to the more competitive Missouri–Mississippi State contest. This bait-and-switch strategy was unprecedented in ABC's sixteen years of college football coverage. Why? The fee charged to the sponsors is determined by the ratings and there was trepidation that such a lopsided game would lose television viewers. An occurrence such as this may be prescient of the future, because the NCAA was expected to sign a network contract stipulating the use of "cutaways" when a team was winning by 18 or more points at the half.[38]

There are other ways that television dictates the course of a game. Notre Dame and Georgia were scheduled to "lock horns" on Saturday, 9 November 1974. ABC discovered that if the schools would agree to play Monday night, 9 September, the network could broadcast the opening game of the college football season to a nation-

VIGNETTE 14.2

Socialization to Aggression: The Role of Television

What role does television play, sports on television in particular, in socializing one into aggression? Studies (Comstock, 1977; Eisenhower, 1969; Phillips, 1983) have provided plenty of empirical evidence that children spend numerous hours watching television and that the contents of the programs they watch are replete with violence, aggression, shootings, murders, rapes, hijackings, shoving matches, and verbal vindictives. It is estimated that by the tender age of sixteen the typical child may see as many as 20,000 homicides.

Although violence on television may be fiction, can youngsters differentiate fact from fiction? Do children merely find such exposures entertaining, or do they model themselves after the characters portrayed? According to Comstock (1977), the portrayal of television violence is most likely to produce aggressive responses when the violence is (a) rewarded, (b) exciting, (c) real, and (d) justified, and when the perpetrator of the violence is (e) not negatively reinforced for such behavior and (f) intentionally injures his "victim."

True, much of the violence on television does *not* meet these requirements. Sports, however, particularly boxing and football, appear to be exceptions. Phillips (1983) examined the impact of mass media violence on aggression by tallying the number of homicides three days before several heavyweight boxing championship fights. For all heavyweight boxing championship fights from 1973 to 1978, the number of homicides increased from the "norm" three days after each fight, regardless of whether the fight was publicized (mentioned on the evening network news). One theory purporting to account for this phenomenon is that prizefights may trigger homicides through some type of modeling of aggression.

Investigations have not been consistent in their findings regarding the role of television violence in producing aggressive behavioral responses. Apparently, however, "violence on television encourages violent forms of behavior and fosters moral and social values about violence in daily life which are unacceptable in a civilized society" (Eisenhower, 1969, p. 5).

If television violence encourages behavioral aggression, what theoretical mechanisms may be operative? Three have been considered: (a) desensitization, (b) role modeling, and (c) apparent approval. *Desensitization* refers to the reduced stimulus value of a phenomenon that appears over and over. Simply put, the more one sees of violence, the more natural, matter-of-fact, ordinary, and routine the act may be perceived. Role modeling refers to the tendency of humans to imitate the behavior of others. When celebrities engage in such behavior, the lionization of these characters may encourage the viewer to emulate their idol. *Apparent approval* refers to the viewer's possible perception that an act repeated over and over again may take on a quality of acceptability— why else would it appear so frequently?

The issue of the effect of television violence on viewers' behaviors is still open to debate. Just the same, its possible negative effects force us to address the nature and content of our television programs, and that includes sports.

SOURCES: David B. Brinkerhoff & Lynn K. White, *Sociology* (St. Paul, MN: West Publishing 1991), pp. 160–161. George S. Comstock, "Types of Portrayal and Aggressive Behavior." *Journal of Communication* 27 (Summer 1977), pp. 189–190. M. Eisenhower, *Commission Statement on Violence in Television Entertainment Programs. National Commission on the Causes and Prevention of Violence* (Washington, DC: U.S. Government Printing Office, 1969). David P. Phillips, "The Impact of Mass Media Violence on U.S. Homicides," *American Sociological Review* 48 (August 1983), pp. 560–568.

wide prime-time audience. The contest was subsequently moved up. Such machinations are not necessarily all negative, because each school received handsome revenues from its television exposure. It did prompt the late Paul "Bear" Bryant to exclaim, "We think TV exposure is so important to our program and so important to this university that we will schedule ourselves to fit the medium, I'll play at midnight if that's what TV wants."[39]

More recently, Michigan State's basketball coach Jud Heathcoate said, "When you talk about the dollars and the exposure I think we have to make some sacrifices in our schedule." On the other hand, Indiana University's basketball coach Bobby Knight dissented, "To hell with damned ESPN," referring to the 9:30 P.M. starting time.[40]

On 19 December 1975, The Blue-Gray All-Star Game was played in Montgomery, Alabama. The Miz-Lou Television Network had blocked off a three-hour segment for the coverage. When confusion at the start of the game indicated it might run beyond the time allotted, the television moguls dictated that the first quarter would last 12 rather than 15 minutes. But, as the game progressed, it appeared that there would be time left over, because it was moving along extraordinarily quickly. So, extra minutes were added to the third and fourth quarters, and in the final 31 seconds, the Yankee squad scored a touchdown and won, 14–13. One Blue–Gray committeeman apologized to the Confederates, tacitly admitting that they had won the game but instead were robbed of their win by television.

Another controversial contest was the fourth game of the 1977 National League Playoffs between the Dodgers and the Phillies. The game was played during a steady rainfall, much to the chagrin of the Philadelphia team and fans, particularly when it became apparent that the wet conditions were (probably) insurmountable obstacles to victory. A major reason why the contest was played during such deplorable weather was to avoid rescheduling the opening day of the World Series.

The 1978 Grand Slam of tennis was held in Boca Raton, Florida. The published starting time was 1:00 P.M. but it was necessary to push it up to 12:30 P.M. to accommodate television. A near riot flared up when irate fans discovered the match well into the second set before many of them were seated. Several weeks following the Grand Slam, NBC refused to telecast a title fight between featherweight champion Cecilio Lastra and challenger Sean O'Grady because the World Boxing Association failed to sanction the bout.

Finally, the television networks paid the cost of installing temporary lights in Notre Dame's stadium so they could telecast a night contest between the Irish and Wolverines of Michigan early in the fall 1982 football schedule. Similarly, Ohio State played its first "night" game ever (against Pitt) in the fall of 1985 under similar circumstances.

Some Ways that Sport Rules Have Been Altered to Accommodate Television

Golf, a sport altered by the electronic limelight, has been tailored for television.[41] Originally, golf scoring was based on *match play;* the number of holes won, not the total number of strokes, determined the victor. The problem with televising golf was twofold: (a) No one could predict the game's duration, and (b) a match could be decided at a hole where no cameras were mounted. The result was *medal play,* where players' total scores, or strokes, are compared against all other tournament participants. If scores are deadlocked at the end of regulation play, the tied players tee-off at the fifteenth hole and continue until a player wins one hole outright (instead of playing 18 holes the next day, as golfers had before television entered the scene).

Tennis, says Chandler,[42] has been a good television sport because it contains a series of patterned "confrontations between server and receiver with so many points to win a game, set, and match." However, the game's indeterminate duration is still not ideal for television. In the wake of this dilemma, there has been talk of modifying televised tennis such that it consists of three sets, with the victor being determined by the number of games won. At present, there is a set-ending tie-breaker procedure. The hyped television match between Billie Jean King and Bobby Riggs in September of 1973 was watched by over 37 million people and, interestingly, was viewed by more women than men. An upsurge in the number of tennis buffs, particularly women, followed the event.[43]

Professional football has seen numerous rule changes; the aim being to make the sport more appealing to the TV viewers. These alterations include longer kickoffs, "sudden deaths," moving in sideline hash marks, forbidding excessive contact of defensive backs with receivers, and liberalizing offensive holding.

Soccer and hockey have been disappointing television sports for several reasons: (a) Because of the constant movement (in soccer there are no time-outs, and play is stopped only when the ball goes out of bounds, when a flagrant foul is committed, or when someone is injured), it is difficult for cameras to follow the ball or puck. (b) The games lack the crisis points characteristic of football. (c) There is typically little scoring. Perhaps these contests will be modified so that they become more palatable television sports. The NHL expanded the pause in play following certain penalties to more than one-half minute to allow time for commercials and has considered replacing its traditional three twenty-minute periods with four fifteen-minute periods and substituting shorter intermissions between periods. Apparently, hockey barons believe this alteration will make the game more appetizing to television's hockey viewers and sponsors alike. Hockey on TV just doesn't fly. Whether it's the miniscule puck, the white ice background, or the depersonalization brought by helmets, hockey officials aren't sure. They have talked about using an orange fluorescent puck, tinting the ice blue and reducing the rink size to increase scoring. On the other hand, officials acknowledge that improved lighting and telecast technology has helped to sell the game. The difficulty in following the puck has a sociological underpinning because Canadian fans apparently do not have the same difficulty; Russians apparently have a similar problem following a golf ball or baseball. Perhaps part of the problem is one stemming from sport socialization, one which increased education and exposure could facilitate. In the wake of the 1994 World Cup soccer matches, the first to be played in the United States, there has been a proposal to switch from the traditional two forty-five-minute halves to four twenty-five-minute quarters.

Basketball, while somewhat monotonous, has great fan appeal because it involves considerable scoring and movement. Furthermore, the ball is large enough to follow on the screen, and frequent time-outs provide opportunities for commentary and commercials. In both college and professional basketball, features such as the shot clock, slam dunk, and three-point shot have been adopted to increase spectator interest.

Baseball, a slow game, has numerous characteristics making it a good television sport: the personal challenges between pitcher and hitter and the periodic minicrises involving three strikes, four balls, three outs, and nine innings.[44] In addition, baseball permits sufficient time for advertisements, commentary, instant replay, anecdotes, and is considered the traditional U.S. national pastime. The lowering of the strike zone and the American League's use of the designated hitter was to whet spectators' viewing appetites. Finally, installation of lights in 1988 in Wrigley Field was a prime example of sport accommodating to television.

Gymnastics boomed after television made a celebrity of Olga Korbut. Before her television debut, there were about 100,000 gymnastics adherents, but today that figure has more than tripled. Don Ohlmeyer said, "They held [before the 1972 Munich Olympics] important gymnastics meets at high school gyms, and couldn't sell tickets. Now they hold important meets in Madison Square Garden, and scalpers stand outside getting their price."[45]

The Location of Franchises

One of the most far-reaching ways in which television affects sport resides in the determination of franchise sites.[46] In recent years, franchises have popped up almost as quickly as dandelions on a summer lawn. To understand the location and probable success of a franchise, one must first grasp the concept of **market area.** Two criteria are determining factors in the location of franchises (a) **area of dominant influence (ADI)** and (b) **designated market area (DMA).**

The Area of Dominant Influence.   The *ADI* allocates every county in the United States to the metropolis dominating its television preferences. For example, McLean County in central Illinois shares bipartisan Chicago and St. Louis sport fans. If the viewers look north for news, sports, and entertainment, then Chicago is the ADI for the county; if they turn south, St. Louis is the ADI.

The Designated Market Area.   The *DMA,* a more sophisticated index of television viewers' habits, assigns geographical districts to the dominant metropolitan area during prime time. This latter measure is an indicator of advertising potential that is used by program sponsors and is an important consideration in the financial state of franchises. For example, the Baltimore and Milwaukee franchises have experienced problems despite metropolitan statistical areas (MSAs) of over two million. Part of the explanation lies in their ADI and DMA ratings. Baltimore is located between two other major sport meccas—Washington, D.C., and Philadelphia—and some of its potential audience is siphoned off by those areas. Milwaukee suffers the same dilemma because it is located between Chicago and Minneapolis. Tampa's case is the reverse because of minimal competition with other franchise cities. Hence, Tampa's television potential exceeds that of Cincinnati, Buffalo, Denver, New Orleans, Kansas City, Milwaukee, and San Diego. The decision to expand baseball in the early 1990s, to the cities of Denver and Miami was, in part, a result of their TV potential.

Finally, consider San Francisco and Oakland. Several competing professional franchises existed in the metropolitan area (e.g., the 49'ers and the Raiders, now in Irindale, and the Giants and the Athletics). The Bay Area is wealthy, ranks high on the television indices, and has a large population, but it experienced difficulty supporting two football teams and two baseball teams. This helps explain rumors of the Giants' liquidating and Al Davis's relocation of the "Oakland" Raiders.

In part, because of the anticipated additional television-generated revenue, the Boston–Milwaukee Braves are now located in Atlanta, the Minneapolis Lakers are now in Los Angeles, the Philadelphia–Kansas City Athletics are in Oakland, the Brooklyn Dodgers are in Los Angeles, and the New York Giants are in San Francisco. The Baltimore Colts moved to Indianapolis and the Oakland, then LA Raiders, moved to Irindale.

❑ THE ECONOMIC IMPACT OF TELEVISION AND SPORTS

The sport–media symbiotic relationship is primarily monetary. Billion-dollar fees and ever expanding coverage are reshaping American sports.

- The three major commercial networks gross $500 million to $1 billion per year from commercials aired during sports programs.
- The cost of sixty-second commercials during the Super Bowl exceeds $1.6 million.

The established leagues have a sound combination of local and nationwide contracts. Consider, first, *national* contracts. The most recent four-year $3.6-billion NFL television pact (divided among five broadcast and cable networks) guaranteed *each* team, for the next four years, about $32 million per year (this package was a 92% increase over 1987). The most recent four-year $1.48-billion major league baseball contract guaranteed each franchise about $14 million each year (this contract was up 102% from 1984). Finally, the most recent NBA contract of $875 million guaranteed each team about $9 million per year (this was a 250% increase from 1986). Two features of these monetary amounts are important to consider: (a) These are amounts guaranteed before a single ticket is sold, and (b) they illustrate the nature of revenue sharing in some professional sports. The NHL lost its national network contract in 1975, and the clubs now must rely solely on other broadcast sources. This loss of television monies is one reason why the hockey "industry" is struggling. In general, the sport leagues that recently developed—the American Basketball Association (ABA), which has now merged with the National Basketball Association (NBA), World Hockey Association (WHA), North American Soccer League (NASL), U.S. Football League (USFL), and World Football League (WFL) (now defunct)—were not successful in selling their products to the networks, because their franchises were generally located in smaller cities or in weaker markets that were less attractive to the national networks and advertisers. The fate of the World League of American Football (WLAF) remains to be seen.

Turning to the local level, we do find major revenue differentials. At the local level, there are both cable and over-the- air television and radio sport packages. To illustrate, the Cubs have a cable contract and an over-the-air contract with WGN. Pittsburgh had a cable contract with TCI and an over-the-air contract with KDKA. Because of market area differences, some teams (e.g., the Yankees) make many times the amount of other teams (e.g., the Royals).

The overall annual television expenditures for sport exceed $1 billion. In an Olympic year, these dollar figures soar dramatically. The following list shows the telecast costs to recent Olympics:

1960	Rome	$660,000	
1972	Munich	$13,500,000	
1976	Montreal	$25,000,000	
1980	Moscow	$100,000,000	
1984	Los Angeles	$225,000,000	
1988	Seoul	$333,333,333	
1992	Barcelona	$401,000,000	
1996	Atlanta	$500,000,000	(estimate)

☐ SOME CONSEQUENCES OF TELEVISION SPORT COVERAGE

The marriage of athletics to the electronic media, which appears so precariously successful today, was not without its crisis periods.[47] In 1948, the first year of major commercial television, John Cameron Swayze, Howdy Doody, and Milton Berle were popular television personalities. As equipment and technology were perfected, the auspicious impact of television on sport began to be felt by the early 1950s. But several latent consequences began to emerge; the following discussion considers some of these unanticipated consequences for several sports.

College Football

How important is television's money to college sport programs? Television income can mean the difference between a financially successful and a financially unsuccessful season. The College Football Association signed a lucrative five-year television pact with ABC for $210 million in 1990 and, several weeks later, Notre Dame inked a controversial $30 million deal. When the Big Ten and Pac-10 teams played on national TV in the 1992 Rose Bowl, the two schools did not pocket $6 million each; instead, the money was split among all of the conference schools and the conference headquarters. On the other hand, an independent school such as Notre Dame or Miami might pocket the entire television rebate. Consider, too, that television sports income is tax exempt. The IRS has ruled that television revenues procured by colleges and universities for the sale of broadcast rights are not taxable because these revenues are related to the business of the college. Because institutions of higher learning have pleaded financial exigency, it is easy to comprehend the importance of these monies. In fact, the controversy surrounding the conflict of interests between the College Football Association (CFA) and the National Collegiate Athletic Association (NCAA) has its roots in this issue.

Is there too much college sport on television? There is some evidence that, although regular-season football and basketball TV ratings have remained steady, TV moguls have made decisions that will reduce certain sport coverages. For example, in 1986 the networks decided to quit televising the Peach, Gator, and Citrus Bowls. Additionally, Lorimar Productions, which has telecast the Bluebonnet, Freedom, and Holiday Bowls, has indicated it might stop televising sporting events altogether. Of interest, the NCAA stipulates that any postseason bowl must guarantee each team at least one-half million dollars.

Television is a two-sided sword for colleges. Media exposure brings nationwide attention to the schools featured, and money fills their coffers. Television also, however, extends seasons, plays havoc with scheduling, and contributes to stressing sports over academics.

Professional Football

Following the 1982 NFL strike, a significant reduction in the average viewing audience size was witnessed (for that year). Specifically, an ABC spokesperson lamented that nighttime pro football had lost an average of four million viewers from 1981 games. A 1982 Monday night football game between the 49ers and Falcons had the notorious distinction of attracting the smallest TV audience in professional football's history on ABC. Television-viewing professional football fans apparently made amends, because Nielsen ratings for NFL football in the early 1990s had substantially increased.

College Basketball

In 1986 the NCAA's Division I basketball tournament was expected to gross $34.5 million (most coming from TV revenues). The NCAA keeps about 40% of this figure, leaving the remaining (approximately) $21 million to be shared by the 64 teams invited to participate. (Of interest, NCAA football bowls grossed about $39 million in 1985—all shared by participating teams and their conferences. The NCAA received virtually nothing; the only "cut" the NCAA receives from football is a share of the regular-season TV revenues).

The 1986 college basketball monies were distributed as follows:

First-round losers received $167,060.
Second-round losers received $334,120.
Losers in the regional semifinals earned $501,180.
Losers in the regional finals earned $668,240.
Each of the Final Four teams made $835,300.

The revenues for NCAA tournament basketball have soared so rapidly (teams in the final four in 1986 received $127,300 more than their counterparts in 1985) that warning signs have begun to appear—overexposure, as when 16 college basketball games were available for viewing in some TV market areas during 1985–1986, and economic trouble in the telecasting industry. College sport on TV seems to be reaching a critical juncture, although, at present, it's harvesting in a financial cornucopia.

The financial bonanza alluded to can be appreciated by considering the $1 billion seven-year contract agreed to by CBS and the NCAA in November 1989 and running through 1997. By paying the NCAA this amount, CBS earned exclusive rights to televise Division I basketball championships. Under the terms of this new contract (the previous contract, which expired in the 1989–1990 academic year, paid about $55 million per year), CBS paid the NCAA about $143 million annually for the tenure of the contract. In the early 1990s, monies from the NCAA basketball tournament provided about three fourths of the association's total revenue. (Revenues from football bowl games, which are not controlled by the NCAA, are even greater than basketball's and amounted to nearly $60 million in the early 1990s.) Exactly how the revenue windfall will be distributed continues to be debated.

Boxing

Other sports, notably boxing, were not so perceptive. Between 1946 and 1964, the year when the last Friday Night Fight of the Week was telecast, there were numerous matches on television; in some areas, boxing matches could be viewed nearly nightly. One correlate of this overexposure was a radical decline in club boxing; 83% of the small fight clubs in the United States closed their doors between 1952 and 1959. The result was little development of new talent—although old, worn-out boxers remained in abundance—to provide lifeblood to the sport. The return of boxing to television has been slow and calculated, often via theater or cable television.[48]

Baseball

Baseball presents another interesting case study. In 1939, minor league attendance (15 million) exceeded the majors (9 million). A decade later, the minor leagues saw 42 million people pass through the turnstiles, but by this time baseball buffs could see their favorite athletes on television for nothing. According to Kowet, "Minor league attendance figures plummeted . . . to 13 million in 1959, and to 10 million in 1969."[49] Furthermore, the number of minor league clubs declined from 488 in 1949 to about 150 in the 1980s.

Initially, major league sport owners grabbed every opportunity to put their clubs on the tube. The results, in some cases, were fiascoes. From a 1948 high of almost 21 million, attendance dropped to slightly less than 14.5 million in 1953. One sobering example is the Cleveland Indians' precipitous attendance decline between 1948 and 1956. During that period, the Indians won a World Series and an American League pennant and showcased a string of superb baseball players (including pitchers Bob Feller, Bob Lemon, and Mike Garcia). The Indians televised many of their home games during that time, and their attendance plummeted a whopping 67%.[50]

The (then) Boston Braves also fell on hard times. In 1948, they won the National League pennant and drew nearly 1.5 million fans, setting a season's attendance record. The management sold rights to televise nearly all their home games between 1949 and 1952. Although the Braves finished in the first division three out of those four years, attendance dropped from 1,445,000 in 1948 to 281,278 in 1952. Lou Perini, owner of the Braves, moved the franchise to Milwaukee and banned television cameras from their games. Despite nearly one million paid attendance in 1964, Perini realized that the geographical location of Milwaukee—between Minneapolis and Chicago—was ill-suited and sold the franchise. The team made an exodus to Dixie, where it located in Atlanta, a virginal sports television market.[51]

In 1969, major league baseball attendance reached an all-time high—27 million—although there were 24 rather than 20 clubs. The number of television spectators watching the World Series averaged 23 million per game. Baseball attendance in 1976 also set a record—31.3 million; was approximately 38 million in 1977; and by 1980, passed 43 million (the minor leagues were also having a banner year, as some 13 million attended their contests). Total attendance for professional baseball (both minor and major league) in 1980 surpassed 51 million and, 10 years later, in 1990 exceeded 50 million.[52] A variety of explanations have been advanced for baseball's "comeback": close pennant races, more home runs, exciting World Series, a more stable social atmosphere following the turmoil of the 1960s, and a game not played against the clock. Weiss offered this comment: "For a long time, TV didn't know how to show the game. They showed only the pitcher and batter. Now they show the whole field and have instant replays. These make a great difference in fan interest."[53] Just as football ratings were damaged by the 1982 NFL strike, baseball, too, suffered significant declines in viewership after its 1981 strike. By the mid 1980s, the ratings had climbed, thereby intimating that fans had forgotten their disgruntlement during the abbreviated 1981 strike-ridden season.

The Future of Television Sports

The major television networks—CBS, NBC, and ABC—have historically constituted the primary source of support and exposure for sport although, increasingly, cable television is making its presence felt. The monies paid to sport franchises seem to be a harbinger of financial growth for the networks. Paradoxically, William MacPhail, then CBS's television sports director, said, "Sports is a bad investment, generally speaking. The network needs it for prestige, for image, to satisfy the demands and desires of our affiliated stations. The rights have gotten so costly that we do sports as a public service rather than a profit-maker. We're doing great if we break even."[54]

Although there is a certain incredibility surrounding MacPhail's statement, in 1991 professional baseball was paying out $.75 billion (in salaries, fringe benefits, and other union-based agreements) and receiving $.5 billion from the networks. There was genuine concern about the future because projected expenditures were $537 million in 1987, $603 million in 1988, $680 million in 1989, $767 million in 1990, and $867 million in 1991, based on approximately 15% annual increases.

Apparently, the television networks feel barricaded into a competitive situation over the privilege of televising sports. While the costs are becoming astronomical, the networks (and syndicates) are reluctant to relinquish their rights for fear of losing prestige and advertising dollars. (There are some tell-tale signs that this may be changing.) It is interesting to speculate on what would happen if the networks eliminated or significantly curtailed their sport coverage. Nixon, a sport sociologist, said, "If television were ever to withdraw its financial support from sport, the existing structure of highly professionalized, commercialized sport could very easily crumble."[55] Roone Arledge echoes Nixon, "So many sports organizations have built their entire budgets around network TV . . . that if we ever withdraw the money, the whole structure would collapse."[56] There is little doubt that if television contract monies were not available, the complexion of sport would be dramatically affected. The networks, however, would probably withdraw only if the ratings nose-dived. Of course, that would happen only if Americans lost their voracious appetites for sports.

Since we have dwelled on the negative consequences of television sports, let us balance the ledger by mentioning some qualifications and/or positive benefits. First, the decision to play the first (1975) World Series game at night was made by baseball's management, not by the television networks. In fact, the networks were hesitant to do this, because the World Series coincided with the new fall entertainment season. Former baseball commissioner Bowie Kuhn said: "NBC did not want nighttime television in the 1975 World Series. We did—because you may have a difference of 25 million people from afternoon to night. We're trying to promote baseball to the American public. How are we going to do that by playing these big games on a Wednesday afternoon?"[57] Baltimore Oriole former manager Earl Weaver remarked, "Not only does it provide big revenue . . . but it gives people all over the U.S. a chance to see all the great players."[58] Kowet reiterated:

> TV created a new appetite for big-league sports, and the major leagues—to nearly everyone's satisfaction—were willing and able (in the jet age) to supply a new diet of big-league franchises. And besides contributing to the expansion of existing leagues, TV helped create entire leagues out of whole cloth (the AFL, the ABA, etc.). It raised pro football to a par in popularity with baseball. It introduced millions to tennis and golf (particularly women). It turned pro sports into a socially acceptable profession, and a desirable one.[59]

☐ RECENT TELEVISION SPORT COVERAGE

The *Miller Lite Report*[60] contains survey data that provides us a glimpse into Americans' attitudes toward television sports. The most favorite spectator sports (with percentage choosing in parentheses) were football (28%), baseball (18%), and basketball (8%). With the exception of an "other" category, all other sports fell at 5% or below. Football, from this perspective, is the number-one sport and, not surprising, the Super Bowl is the single sports event most Americans would prefer to attend.

Television preferences vary by social structural categories. Simmons Market Research Bureau, Inc., compiled Figure 7.1, which contains the number of viewers of particular sports and, for each sport, an indication of the most-likely viewers. Since socioeconomic status is our present concern, your attention is directed to indicators of social class, namely, education, income, and occupation. To illustrate, using the hypothetical "average adult" as a baseline, for professional basketball, professionals, college graduates, and those with incomes exceeding $30,000 are 34%, 33%, and 17% more likely to watch televised professional basketball than the average adult. What is sociologically revealing is that television sport preferences tend to be correlated with measures of social class.

Americans appear to be satisfied with the amount of sport coverage, because about 60% said sport coverage was just right. On the other side, 30% said there was too much TV sport, and 10% said there was too little. Several sociological variables provide some additional insights. Women, whites, and those with more education vis-à-vis their counterparts were more prone to feel that sport on TV is excessive. Although Americans are reasonably satisfied with the amount of coverage, the specific sports highlighted are more controversial. Slightly more than 50% believed some sports receive too much coverage (particularly, football and baseball) and others too little.

Attitudes toward sports commentators are of interest.[61] Approximately 50% say they contribute to the game's enjoyment, 36% say they have no effect, and 13% believe commentators detract from the game. Over 75% of those surveyed indicated that the quality of the commentators was good, very good, or excellent. Less than half (47%), however, said they paid close attention to the commentators; 21% say they rarely or never do. Finally, the major disgruntlement revolves around the beliefs that sportswriters and sportscasters place too much emphasis on the athletes' personal lives and winning and losing.

☐ TELEVISION SPORTSCASTERS AND SPORTS JOURNALISM

Television Sportscasting

Television **sportscasting** is a relatively new and highly lucrative occupation. In fact, some media announcers are making more money per year than many professional athletes. Brent Musburger, for example, was the highest paid sports announcer and earned about $2 million per year (in 1984 he signed a $10 million, five-year contract with CBS) before he was forced to take a pay cut. Sports not only have become a profitable form of show business, but the announcers of sporting events also have become celebrities in their own right. Following is a partial list of sportscaster salaries in the early 1990s:[62]

John Madden	$2,200,000
Al Michaels	2,100,000
Brent Musburger	1,833,333
Tim McCarver	1,800,000
Pat Summerall	1,600,000
Bob Costas	1,400,000
Dick Enberg	1,350,000
Frank Gifford	1,300,000
Jim McKay	1,100,000
Dan Dierdorf	1,000,000

Sportscasting is a pressure-packed job. In 1986 Joe Namath was bought out of his $850,000 ABC Monday Night Football contract, O.J. Simpson was asked to switch to college football, Frank Broyles was released from providing the "color" to college football games, and Al Michaels was added to the Monday Night Football sportscaster roster.

Sports Journalism

Sports journalism has become a buzzword among the networks. When Freeman Sauter took over the helm of CBS sports in 1980, he heralded the dawn of aggressive sports journalism. Television brass from the other networks countered that sports journalism had been part of their menus. *TV Guide* conducted interviews to determine if Sauter's approach to sports was revolutionary or commonplace, and the verdict follows:

> Behind the TV cameras we found men and women of talent and admirable intentions. But on our TV screens (more than 35 segments from shows that routinely feature sports footage were monitored) scattered among superficial interviews, updates and profiles, we found only a handful of journalistic gems.[63]

☐   **VIGNETTE 14.3**

Announcer Fired for Telling Truth

Smack dab in the middle of the debate about the health hazards of boxing, an excellent prizefight commentator has lost a major chunk of his livelihood because he told the truth.

Randy Gordon, a no-nonsense announcer with the ESPN cable TV network, got fired because he smelled a rat, brought it to the immediate attention of his viewers, and then exposed the charlatans who provoked the shady deal. A former boxer himself, Gordon has been earning a respectable $250 a telecast as an ESPN fight analyst. But after his impromptu detective act, the network fired him.

And although ESPN officials insist that their dismissal of Gordon had nothing whatsoever to do with his controversial remarks, it's a fact that ESPN is partnered on its boxing telecasts with snakelike promoter Bob Arum; and it's a fact that Arum was the man who bore the brunt of Gordon's on-air criticism.

Here's the sorry tale: Gordon, who supplements his income by writing for *Ring* magazine, was preparing for an ESPN fight telecast from Charleston, S.C., when a last-minute substitute filled in for a missing fighter.

Gordon recognized the replacement. He was Ed Flanning, a New York stiff who had been knocked out in the second round of a Manhattan match just six days earlier. Gordon told the "tomato can" that he was violating accepted boxing procedure by fighting so soon after getting KO'd. But the fighter claimed that he actually was Ed Flanning's brother, Anthony Flanning. A few minutes later, he changed his mind and said his name really was Rahim Tahib.

There was no fooling Gordon, however, and the ESPN commentator quickly notified South Carolina boxing officials, executives of Arum's Top Rank promotion company and his own network bosses of the fraud. But rather than prevent Flan-

ning from fighting, the Top Rank folks simply begged Gordon to refrain from telling viewers about the fake.

Gordon declined their invitation, informing viewers at the very start of the telecast that the fight they were to witness was severely tainted. Flanning's face got transformed into a bloody mask by the time he was knocked out in the fourth round.

Did Gordon's ESPN superiors congratulate him on his excellent sleuth work and his dogged determination to tell viewers all they should know about the farcical charade they were watching? Guess again, good buddy.

Less than two weeks after his conscientious exposé, Gordon was dumped from ESPN's weekly boxing series because of what the network termed "inconsistent performances." He also was canned from his assignment as co-host of an ESPN Sunday sports program.

The ESPN honchos agree that promoter Arum often has been displeased with Gordon's on-air comments. But they contend their decision to fire the brash announcer wasn't related at all to Arum's financial connection to ESPN.

Anybody who swallows that line also believes in the Easter Bunny.

In the happy conclusion to this sorrowful chapter in TV sports history, it now looks like Gordon will continue sharing his insights with TV boxing fans on a regular basis. He's already lined up a few gigs on the Home Box Office pay-channel and is expecting more boxing assignments on the USA cable network.

He might not possess the stentorian affectations of boxing ignoramus Howard Cosell. But Randy Gordon truly does "tell it like it is."

SOURCE: Gary Deeb, "Announcer Fired for Telling Truth," *The Pantagraph* (2 January 1983). Courtesy of *The Pantagraph*.

☐

Considering their seventy-five-year content analysis of the *Chicago Tribune*'s sports page, Lever and Wheeler come to about the same conclusion—sport is an opiate—for the print media:

> Sport remains an escape, an enjoyment, a source of relief from the minor aggravations and the boredom of everyday life. Although socially responsible journalism may require more detailed investigative reporting and the bringing of a more subtle and knowledgeable appreciation of the world of sport to its readers, there is no evidence of a growing public clamor for such reporting. And at least so far as the *Chicago Tribune* goes, the vast bulk of coverage remains focused, as it always has, on the playing field and the athletes who inhabit it.[64]

Because television sport journalists are employed by the networks and because the networks, in turn, must purchase the telecast rights from the leagues (NFL, NBA, major league baseball) and associations (NCAA), a conflict of interests exists. Such inconsistencies undermine deeply penetrating muckraking. For illustration, when ABC telecast NCAA football games, although ABC chose the broadcasters, an NCAA television committee carefully reviewed every game telecast and provided ABC with a report card on the announcers' conduct. ABC forbid any reference to professional football, did not run commercials featuring professional football players, and disallowed announcers from even mentioning professional scouts' perspectives on college football players. However, ABC was contractually bound to promote the image—through half-time "commercials"—of the schools participating in intercollegiate contests. The NFL also has a film archive that provides the networks with footage for telecasting. However, NFL films are a subsidiary of the NFL and frequently provide segments, which often go unedited, for marketing the NFL and its players. Major league baseball also has a subsidiary that provides the networks with footage. But the crux of the matter is that it is not uncommon for the networks to merely provide voice-overs, if need be, for promotions packaged by the subsidiaries themselves.

The upshot of these practices runs against the grain of objective in-depth sport reporting. There are consequences for announcers who do not parrot the party line:[65]

- When Baltimore Sun's Doug Brown wrote that (then) Colt owner Carroll Rosenbloom had contacts with gamblers, he was summarily deleted from the club's list of approved sportswriters.
- When Hot Rod Hundley, announcer for the New Orleans Jazz, criticized their coach, Elgin Baylor, he was fined by a Jazz executive, not the radio station that employed him.
- When ex-Bengel tight end Bob Trumpy lambasted the team's management on his radio talk show, he was relieved as color person on Cincinnati's telecasts.

Vignette 14.3 reports the circumstances—which are of considerable interest—surrounding the firing of an ESPN sports announcer for telling the truth.

☐ THE FUTURE OF TELEVISION AND SPORTS

The future of television sports will undoubtedly be tied in with cable television. Cable is an acronym that stands for a**C**tual tr**A**nsmission **B**e**L**ow ground lev**E**l and refers to the transmission of television signals via special (coaxial) cables rather than via the standard airwaves. Cable television has been around since the late 1940s, although it was originally confined to rural and suburban areas where receptions were poor. Today, it has become significant, and its possibilities are frightening to the networks and their affiliates:

> Cable television was born as CATV or community antenna television in the late 1940's. Initially, it served the function of 'providing television where there wasn't any'—in communities unable to receive off-air signals because of terrain or distance from TV stations. Typically the earliest CATV systems served a few dozen to, at most, a few hundred rural households. During those infant years, cable TV was of relatively little interest or concern to stations or the government. Yet now, thirty years later it has become one of the most controversial issues ever to face the broadcasting industry. Rapid growth of cable and pay cable, the fast-changing 'rules of the game,' both in regulation and in technology, make it difficult for even industry professionals to stay up-to-date.[66]

The growth of cable television has been phenomenal. In 1968, only 5% of the homes in the United States were wired for it; by 1980, this figure had soared to 26%, and represented 21 million homes. By the mid 1980s, it reached the critical 30% level, the point at which it would become economically viable, and by the early 1990s, it was over 60%.[67] In 1988 network sport events numbered 453, and ESPN sporting events soared to 723. This skyrocketing becomes particularly striking, because a decade earlier, the numbers of these sporting events on television were 341 and 158, respectively. Similarly, the media have influenced such changes as night baseball, Monday and Thursday night football, and the relocation of franchises. The media even influence the timing, place, and manner of play.

What does cable television have to offer the viewing public? Nothing short of a smorgasbord of programming. According to *Newsweek,* "Today's subscribers can receive channels devoted exclusively to women, children, blacks, Jews, senior citizens, Christians, Hispanics, devotees of sports, news and culture, even fitness enthusiasts."[68] To sport devotees this sounds good. But there is a catch, a fee is charged for such privileges. Commercial television moguls, with good reason, find the consequences of cable television threatening, as does the NFL. Although the cable industry currently earns about one-fifth the annual $11.3 billion revenues of the commercial networks, when its penetration reaches 30%—the critical mass—it is predicted that it will approach $2 billion per year in ad revenues. Cable TV is also controversial because many communities in the early 1990s were served by unregulated monopolies operating with exclusive rights guaranteed by local governments; thus, no alternatives were available.

After a decade of red ink, the cable television industry turned some profits. Nickelodeon, MTV, and CNN Cable Network ended up in the black. Cable TV's major sport entities are ESPN (found in thirty-seven million homes) and WTBS (found in thirty-four million homes). Since the inception of ESPN in 1979, it had never turned a profit until 1985 (when it realized a $1 million largess). Two interrelated factors are responsible for the recent modest financial success of cable television: (a) an increase in the number of cable viewers (about 60% of all Americans have access to cable TV), and (b) a desire on the part of advertisers to reach these captive audiences. As cable television grows, it will undoubtedly force commercial television to work harder and more creatively for what has been taken for granted. The networks' monopoly on sport programming has already been eroded.

Several baseball teams (e.g., Yankees and Pirates) have sold telecast right to pay-cable operators. Significant, too, is the interest of present and past sport owners Jim Fitzgerald (Bucks); John Fetzer (Tigers); Ted Turner (Braves and Hawks); Jack Cooke (Redskins, Lakers, and Kings); in cable and pay television companies. Eddie Einhorn, owner of the Chicago White Sox, heralded the new modus operandi of the professional sport owner. Several years ago, he assembled a sports television package that featured four Chicago franchises: the White Sox (baseball), Sting (soccer), Bulls (basketball), and the Black Hawks (hockey). For $21.95 per month, subscribers could see 112 Sox games, 28 Sting games, 56 Bulls games, and 56 Black Hawks games. Hence, for a subscription fee of $263, sport fans could glimpse 252 professional contests.[69]

What, then, is the future of television sports? Many sport owners see it as an electromagnetic wave. Author Roger Kahn has said, "I have seen the future. It measures 19 inches diagonally."[70] Instead of a supplement, pay television may be the primary source of sport revenue in the future. The NHL, which lost its network contract in 1975, began using regional **cable television** in the early 1980s to increase exposure and decrease financial deficits.

❑ SUMMARY

The *mass media* are forms of communication that transmit messages to geographically dispersed audiences and include broadcasting, telecasting, the press (magazines, newspapers, books), and public films. Although isolated sport stories appeared in the press before the 1800s, it was not until the 1930s that two social conditions—urbanization and literacy—reached the point where the sale of the printed page could be financially feasible and socially appreciated. From the first sport magazine—*The American Farmer* (1819)—to the popular *Sports Illustrated* and *The Sporting News,* which began in 1954; magazines devoted to sport began to grow and prosper. Radio was pioneered in the 1920s with broadcasts of sporting events (e.g., the World Series, boxing matches, and college football games). Television was introduced on a mass commercial scale in the late 1940s and today dominates sport. Television has affected the economy, the ownership and location of franchises, as well as the scheduling, staging, management, dynamics, and even the aesthetics of sporting events. Television's role in sport has been extravagantly praised and unmercifully criticized. Cable television will undoubtedly play a significant role in the future of television sports.

❑ KEY CONCEPTS

Mass Media (Mass Communication)	Newspapers
Popular (Mass) Culture	Magazines
Sport Consumer	Radio Broadcasting
Direct Sport Consumer	Television
Indirect Sport Consumer	Market Area
The Press	Area of Dominant Influence (ADI)

Designated Market Area (DMA)
Sportscasting

Sports Journalism
Cable Television

☐ ENDNOTES

1. PAUL HOCH, *Rip Off: The Big Game* (Garden City, NY: Anchor Books, 1972), p. 36.
2. *Encyclopedia of Sociology* (Guilford, CT: Dushkin, 1991), p. 178.
3. ELDON E. SNYDER & ELMER SPREITZER, "Sport," *Sociology,* ed. Robert Hagedorn (Dubuque, IA: William C. Brown, 1983), p. 353.
4. SERGE DENISOFF & RALPH WAHRMAN, *An Introduction to Sociology* (New York: Macmillan, 1983).
5. BARRY D. MCPHERSON, "Sport Consumption and the Economics of Consumerism," *Sport and Social Order,* eds. D.W. Ball & J.W. Loy (Reading, MA: Addison-Wesley, 1975), pp. 239–275.
6. SERGE DENISOFF & RALPH WAHRMAN, *An Introduction to Sociology* (New York: Macmillan, 1983).
7. *The Miller Lite Report on American Attitudes Toward Sports,* (Milwaukee, WI: Miller Brewing, 1983).
8. SUSAN BIRRELL & JOHN W. LOY, JR., "Media Sport: Hot and Cool," *International Review of Sport Sociology* 14 (1979), pp. 5–19.
9. BARRY D. MCPHERSON, "Sport Consumption and the Economics of Consumerism," *Sport and Social Order,* ed. D.W. Ball & J.W. Loy (Reading, MA: Addison-Wesley, 1975), p. 304. *Op. cit.,*[2] p. 169.
10. FREDERICK W. COZENS & FLORENCE SCOVIL STUMPF, *Sports in American Life* (Chicago, IL: University of Chicago Press, 1953).
11. *Ibid.*
12. *Ibid.*
13. EDWIN EMERY, *History of the American Newspaper Publishers Association* (Minneapolis, MN: University of Minnesota Press, 1950).
14. Several famous persons—Walter Cronkite, Ring Lardner, Grantland Rice, Red Smith, Ernest Hemingway, Bob Considine, James Reston, Paul Gallico, Shirley Povich, Damon Runyon, Heywood Broun, and John O'Hara—began their illustrious careers as sportswriters.
15. "Sports Not the Answer to All of Society's Problems," *U.S. News & World Report* 16 September 1985, p. 74.
16. *Op. cit.*[10]
17. *Op. cit.*[10]
18. DONALD BRILLHART, "The Sports Page and the Social Scene, 1929–1935," unpublished manuscript, University of California, Berkeley (1951).
19. *Op. cit.*[10]
20. *Ibid.*
21. JANET LEVER & STANTON WHEELER, "The Chicago Tribune Sportspage: 1900–1975," *Sociology of Sport Journal* 1, no. 4 (1984), pp. 299–313.
22. ANGELA LUMPKIN & LINDA D. WILLIAMS, "An Analysis of *Sports Illustrated* Feature Articles, 1954–1987," *Sociology of Sport Journal* 8, no. 1 (1991), pp. 16–32.
23. *Op. cit.,*[2] p. 176.
24. *Op. cit.,*[5] pp. 305–307.
25. ALFRED M. LEE, *The Daily Newspaper in America* (New York: Macmillan, 1937).
26. GUMPERT, *Talking Tombstones* (New York: Oxford University Press, 1987), p. 64.
27. "Nielsen Television 1981," A.C. Nielson Company (Chicago: Media Research Services Group, 1981).
28. LEONARD SCHECTER, *The Jocks* (New York: Paperback Library, 1970), p. 79.
29. WILLIAM JOHNSON, "TV Made It All a New Game," *Sports Illustrated* (29 December 1969), pp. 86–90, 92, 97–98, 101–102.
30. *Ibid.*
31. MARGARET CARLISLE DUNCAN & BARRY BRUMMETT, "Types and Sources of Spectating Pleasure in Televised Sports," *Sociology of Sport Journal* 6, no. 3 (1989) pp. 195–211.
32. JAMES A. MICHENER, *Sports in America* (New York: Random House, 1976), p. 26.
33. JOAN M. CHANDLER, "TV and Sports," *Psychology Today* 10 (April 1977), pp. 64–76. ELDON E. SNYDER & ELMER SPREITZER, *Social Aspects of Sport* (Englewood Cliffs, NJ: Prentice-Hall, 1978).

34. JERRY KRAMER, *Instant Replay* (New York: World, 1968), p. 262.

35. RAY KENNEDY & NANCY WILLIAMSON, "Money in Sports," *Sports Illustrated* 49, no. 3 (17 July 1978), p. 75.

36. DON KOWET, "For Better or For Worse," *TV Guide* 26 (1 July 1978), pp. 2–4, 6.

37. *Op. cit.,*[32] p. 295.

38. JACK CRAIG, "NCAA Sells out TV Fans," *The Sporting News* (24 October 1981), p. 11.

39. *Op. cit.,*[32] p. 298.

40. RICHARD ZOGLIN, "The Great TV Takeover," *Time* (26 March 1990), pp. 66–68.

41. *Op. cit.* Chandler[33]
    Op. cit.[32]

42. *Op. cit.,* Chandler[33]
    SNYDER & SPREITZER, *op. cit.,*[33] p. 150.

43. *Op. cit.,*[36]
    Op. cit.,[32] p. 292.

44. CHANDLER, *op. cit.*[33]

45. *Op. cit.,*[36] p. 3.

46. *Op. cit.,*[32] pp. 305–309.

47. *Op. cit.*[30]

48. *Op. cit.*[23]

49. *Op. cit.,*[30] p. 6.

50. *Op. cit.*[29]

51. *Ibid.*

52. "Behind Baseball's Comeback: It's an Island of Stability," *U.S. News and World Report* (19 September 1977), pp. 56–57.

53. *Ibid.,* p. 57.

54. JOSEPH DURSO, *The All-American Dollar: The Big Business of Sports* (Boston, MA: Houghton Mifflin, 1971), p. 264.

55. HOWARD L. NIXON, II, *Sport and Social Organization* (Indianapolis, IN: Bobbs-Merrill, 1976), pp. 61–62.

56. *Op. cit.,*[30] p. 6.

57. *Ibid.,* p. 3.

58. *Ibid.,* p. 6.

59. *Ibid.*

60. *Op. cit.*[7]

61. *Op. cit.*[7]

62. "*Sports* Annual Salary Survey," *Sport* (June 1991), p. 58.

63. SALLY BEDELL & DON KOWETT, "See the Reluctant Investigators Tiptoe," *TV Guide* (5–11 December 1981), pp. 9–10, 12, 16–17.

64. JANET LEVER & STANTON WHEELER, "The *Chicago Tribune* Sportspage: 1900–1975," *Sociology of Sport Journal* 1, no. 4 (1984), pp. 299–313.

65. LEE BALLINGER, *In Your Face! Sports for Love and Money* (Chicago: Vanguard Books, 1981), pp. 10–11.

66. "Coping with the Complexity of Cable in the 80's" (Chicago: A.C. Nielson, 1981), p. 1.

67. *The 1992 World Almanac and Book of Facts* (New York: Pharos Books, 1992).

68. "Cable TV: Coming of Age," *Newsweek* (24 August 1981), pp. 44–49.

69. "Tapping a New Gusher?" *The Sporting News* (7 November 1981), p. 6.

70. *Op. cit.,*[29] p. 76.

15

Sport, Collective Behavior, and Social Change

Fans aren't just interested in winning games anymore . . . When people come into the stands, they begin to feel the power to affect the outcome of the game. Now there is the feeling that they can do something. America is a candidate for a new kind of violence—the fans' desire to achieve power vicariously.

IRVING GOLDABER

Collective behavior is a concept encompassing a wide range of group behaviors. Riots, manias, panics, lynchings, stampedes, revivals, social and religious movements, revolutions, fads, mass suicides, fashions, crazes, public opinion, propaganda, and rumor fall under this rubric.[1] Some forms of collective behavior are relatively extemporaneous and ephemeral (riots and fads); others are longer lasting and require organization, planning, and orchestration (social movements). The study of collective behavior is sociologically significant because it illuminates some of the dynamics—the social processes—of sociocultural change through which new norms, values, institutions, and traditions emerge. Figure 15.1 provides a model for conceptualizing collective behavior. Notice that whereas much behavior is structured and governed by reasonably clear-cut social norms, collective behavior is relatively unplanned, unstable, and unpredictable.

Episodes of collective behavior—generally spontaneous, unstructured, volatile, and short-lived activities—abound in sport, as the following account demonstrates:

❏ A CASE STUDY OF COLLECTIVE BEHAVIOR IN SPORT

Nearly 100 people were killed (by being accidentally crushed against a fence) and nearly 200 people were seriously injured at a British soccer match on 16 April 1989.[2] Liverpool was scheduled to play Nottingham Forest in Sheffield, England, in a stadium with a capacity of 54,000. Because of inadequate security and fences in disrepair, in excess of 1,000 unticketed Liverpool fans made their way to the standing room only section of the Liverpool end zone. The overcrowding led to shoving and pushing to get through the gate, and crowd panic lead to crushing those in the front. British soccer has been described as a slum sport played in slum stadiums. Fans are drawn from depressed areas, and one of the few sources of pride is "their" successful soccer team.

The structure of soccer stadiums is conducive to violence. Marx describes a "typical" soccer field in Argentina as being surrounded by a moat, a concrete wall topped by iron spikes, and snarling German shepherd guard dogs providing watch.[3] Barbed wire fences twenty-feet high provide a line of demarcation between gangs with opposing soccer allegiances. Police are armed, some even wear riot gear, and some patrol the arena on horseback. A water canon is mounted outside the stadium in the event that mayhem necessitates its use. Players enter the playing field through a rubber tunnel that protects them from various objects—coins, stones, and food—that spectators may hurl at them. End zones accommodate standing room only, and terraces enable those standing farther back to see over those standing in front. There is no reserved seating. This arrangement enables spectators to push forward and permits unticketed spectators to disguise themselves. End zone tickets are the cheapest, and of course, those with the least money are the ones prone to purchase them. Social control agents, mounted police in riot gear, fences separating opposing team fans, and spectators from the playing field provide the stimuli to excite mayhem.

Other examples of collective behavior in sport include the following:

- On 29 May 1985, the final day of the European Cup in Heysel Stadium, Brussels, rowdyism was responsible for 38 deaths and over 200 injuries.

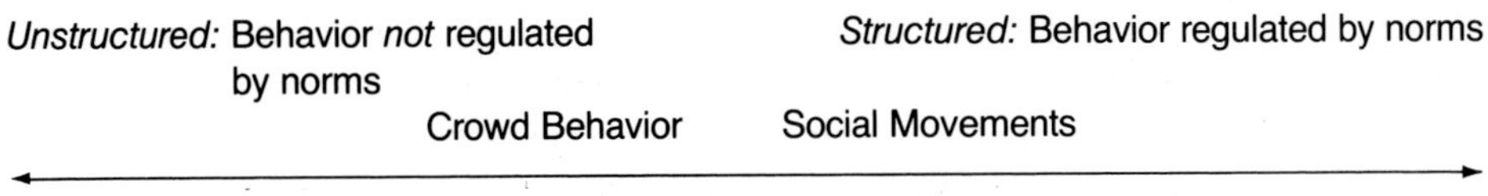

Unstructured: Behavior *not* regulated
by norms

Structured: Behavior regulated by norms

Crowd Behavior   Social Movements

FIGURE 15.1   A continuum for conceptualizing collective behavior

- On 24 May 1964, a soccer match between Peru and Argentina stimulated a brawl leading to the death of 300 spectators and 500 injuries. The fatalities resulted from a disputed referee's call.[4]
- In Glasgow, Scotland, 2 June 1971, 66 soccer fans were crushed after leaving the stadium but returned after their curiosity regarding the thunderous roar of the crowd motivated them to do so.
- On 4 June 1974, the Cleveland Indians played the Texas Rangers on (.10 a cup) "Beer Night" before a crowd of 25,134 in Cleveland's Municipal Stadium. While no deaths were reported, the Rangers right field bullpen was closed down because partisan Indians fans hurled firecrackers and beer cans at the relief pitchers. Streaking and other disruptive incidents necessitated irritating game delays. Fans climbed atop the Rangers' dugout threatening the players' lives, and eventually umpire Nestor Chylak, unable to control the melee, forfeited the game to Texas.[5]
- The Kentucky Derby has seen horses and jockeys jeopardized by fans who hurl paper cups and beer cans at them in the backstretch. In 1976, a smokebomb was thrown on to the track.[6]
- After Mike Quarry beat the likable Puerto Rican Pedro Soto in New York's Felt Forum, Soto's boxing adherents ripped out seats, tore down ceiling panels, wrenched toilets from their moorings, and set the room ablaze.[7]
- On 8 November 1963, at Roosevelt Raceway in Long Island, New York, fans protesting a horse race smashed the tote board, ignited a sulky on the homestretch, attacked a patrol judge inside his booth, overturned concession stands, and vandalized cars in the parking lot.[8]
- The U.S. Grand Prix at Watkins Glen, New York, has become so well-known for its uncontained hell-raising at a mud-sopped area inside the track known as "The Bog" that the auto race featuring the world's greatest drivers has almost become secondary. In one such incident, a bus chartered by touring Brazilians was hijacked and taken to "The Bog" to be burned, with all the Brazilians' personal belongings still aboard.[9]
- At the University of Kansas (KU) Jayhawks basketball fans pelted archrival Kansas State University (KSU) players with hot dogs. During the rematch, KSU fans retaliated by deluging KU players with bunches of ripe bananas, causing a 70-minute delay in the start of the game.[10]
- First in 1976 and then again in 1980, Schaefer Stadium in Foxboro, Massachusetts, was the scene of unconscionable fan behavior. In 1976, the Patriots demolished the Jets 41–7. The decimation extended beyond the gridiron. The toll included a stabbing of a spectator, an assault on a policeman, and the arrest of more than sixty people for drunkenness and brawling. Three dozen others were treated for various

injuries at a local hospital. In 1980, the Patriots beat the Broncos 23–14. The destruction included the death of a 69-year-old man hit by a car driven by a drunk teenager, periodic fistfights, broken automobile antennas in the adjacent parking lot, setting of bonfires, and car doors kicked in. One hundred people were evicted from the stadium, and fifty arrests were made. The increase in rowdyism at Schaefer Stadium has been attributed to the sale of beer (the stadium is named after a brewery) and traffic congestion, which virtually always exists when throngs enter and exit from U.S. Route 1.[11]

- The second game of a scheduled double-header between the Chicago White Sox and Detroit Tigers (12 July 1979) in Comisky stadium was canceled when 7,000 rampaging fans took the field. The ensuing melee, apparently stimulated (and approved by Bill Veeck as a zany crowd pleaser) by a planned antidisco demolition derby between games, found fans toting antidisco banners, igniting small fires, and demolishing the batting cage. Comiskey Park was in pandemonium. Thirty-nine persons (many of whom the police believed to be intoxicated) were arrested for disorderly conduct, although no serious injuries were reported.[12]

The entire spectrum of fandom is currently being studied intensively. Sport commissions and observers concur that a radical change has occurred in fans' behavior. It seems that the *"superfan"* has emerged, an individual who wants to be both a participant and a spectator. Arthur Fuss, security director for major league baseball, remarked: "Twenty years ago . . . professional sports were athlete-oriented. Now teams cater to the fan with jacket nights, bat days, beer nights, and the like. Fans feel they can get closer."[13] Sociologist Irving Goldaber asserted, "Fans aren't just interested in winning games anymore . . . they have to vanquish the other team. When people come into the stands, they begin to feel the power to affect the outcome of the game. Now there is the feeling they can do something. America is a candidate for a new kind of violence—the fans' desire to achieve power vicariously."[14] Goldaber labels this new form of violence "violence for vicarious power."

Psychiatrist Arnold Beisser has said, "We're seeing a new use of violence. It's being used not as a means to an end but for recreational purposes, for pleasure. It's an end in itself."[15] There is little doubt that both crowd and player violence in sport are increasing, and at what some consider an alarming rate. Collective violence has also marred sport in England, Europe, Asia, and Central and South America, and has accompanied a host of high school, collegiate, professional, and international events. The increasing incidents of violence have prompted the formation of special task forces to investigate the causes of such violence and to make policy decisions that will mitigate such occurrences.

❏ THEORIES OF CROWD BEHAVIOR

The study of *crowds,* temporary collections of people in close physical proximity, has a fairly long and rich history. Blumer's taxonomy of crowds distinguishes among *four* types:[16] First, *casual crowds* are the loosest structured of the four and are typified by groups of people gathered at the beach to "sun and surf," to observe an automobile accident or a fire, or to stroll through New Orleans' French Quarter or along Boston's

Freedom Trail. Second, *conventional crowds* are those that share a common purpose or interest such as an audience attending a theatrical performance, public lecture, sport contest, or show. *Expressive crowds,* the third type, are those in which physical movement as a form of release or expression are salient. Expressive crowds include those attending professional wrestling matches, roller derbies, music festivals, discos, evangelical religious revivals, dances, and parties. Fourth, *acting crowds*—mobs, rioters, and so on—are those bent on action, often destructive of person and/or property and are typified by a lynch mob. In sport, sixty thousand fans assembled for the European Soccer Finals in Brussels, Belgium. British fans began taunting Italian fans, who were situated behind a fence. The two sides began hurling objects at each other, and eventually the British fans stormed and broke down the fence. The result of the melee left thirty-eight dead and over four hundred injured. Crowds in sport tend to fall primarily under the expressive and/or conventional rubrics, but as the Brussels incident previously described reveals, one type of crowd can be transformed into another type.

The common denominators of crowds, according to Turner and Killian include:

1. Uncertainty as to what should be done.
2. A feeling that something should be done.
3. The creation of a mood among those in close physical proximity.
4. Heightened suggestibility arising from the anxiety created by the mood.
5. A suspension of normal behavioral restraints.[17]

The origins and dynamics of crowd behavior have been explained by *three* primary conceptual approaches: (1) contagion theory, (2) convergence theory, and (3) emergent norm theory.[18]

Contagion Theory

According to the French sociologist Gustave LeBon, the originator of **contagion theory,** a collective mind engulfs individuals in a crowd ("the law of the mental unity of crowds") through emotional contagion. To him, the rational individual can be transformed into a crazed animal when the individual becomes submerged in the crowd. The resulting submission by individuals to the crowd sufficiently alters their customary thoughts, feelings, and actions to produce a degree of collective uniformity. Allegorically, the crowd's influence on individuals is analogous to the spread of an infectious disease; that is, the crowd creates the motivation for behavior.

Three social psychological mechanisms are responsible for such action: (a) *suggestibility*—a psychological state leaving individuals vulnerable and susceptible to others' influence and acting as a catalyst to the commission of alien acts; (b) *imitation* and *contagion*—the tendency to emulate the behavior of persons already acting; and (c) *circular reaction*—wherein an individual's behavior is both a response to and a stimulus for others' behaviors.

For example, a number of years ago Ohio State and Minnesota met in the latter's gym for the Big-Ten basketball championship. Minnesota was expected to win, and pregame activities—reminiscent of the Harlem Globetrotters' basketball wizardry routine—were intended to motivate the players and entertain the standing room only crowd. The game was fiercely contested from the opening tip-off to the final buzzer. As the game drew to a close, however, it became apparent that the home team would not be victorious, and angry Gopher fans hurled objects onto the court. Stimulated by these events, a Minnesota player committed a flagrant foul, and a scuffle ensued on the court. The mayhem had a contagion effect and triggered a melee among team members and partisan fans.[19]

Convergence Theory

Whereas the contagion explanation highlights the temporary transformation of individuals' thoughts, feelings, and behaviors, **convergence theory's** thesis is that individual's real selves, ordinarily laminated by a veneer of social propriety, manifest themselves under anonymous and deindividuated circumstances. In effect, convergence theory stresses the underlying asocial or antisocial proclivities of individuals whose behavior is ordinarily held in check by internalized social norms. The convergence model underscores the similar predispositions people bring to social situations. A sense of alienation, economic despair, powerlessness, and/or meaninglessness are some of the common emotional concomitants. For example, unruly sport fans generally attack the foes—visiting teams—rather than the home team. The patients in a psychiatric ward provide a heuristic analog useful for comprehending convergence theory. Patients are not placed in a psychiatric ward because they have infected one another (as in the contagion approach) but, rather, because they share a similar weltanschauung ("outlook"). Accordingly, the preexisting motivation acts as a catalyst to the crowd's behavior.

Emergent Norm Theory

The *emergent norm* scheme challenges the first two. Rather than viewing a crowd as an amorphous mass characterized by unanimity, uniformity, oneness, and similarity, this approach helps to explain the development of the illusion of unanimity and uniformity, because crowds contain motley types (core activists, cautious activists, passive supporters, opportunists, passersby, curiosity seekers, and unsympathetic dissenters). It stresses the initial differences in individual thoughts, motives, attitudes, behaviors, and predispositions that emerge in atypical social contexts. The **emergent norm theory,** supported by the small-group research of social psychologists Muzafer Sherif[20] and Solomon Asch,[21] stipulates that norms—behavioral expectancies—emerge to guide behavior (Vignette 15.1). Two kinds of social influence processes are at the heart of the emergent norm theory: (a) **normative social influence** stems from the perception of the consequences of deviating from the majority's opinion, and (b) **informational social influence** stems from people looking to others for behavioral cues, particularly when they are unsure of their own interpretation of social situations or how to act. The emergent norm formulation maintains that cultural scripts (i.e., norms) emerge and channel behavior in various social contexts and is helpful in explaining why crowds take a variety of forms. It is not helpful, however, in explaining the initial occurrence of collective behavior.

In summary, while the three paradigms of crowd behavior—contagion, convergence, and emergent norm theories—differ, they are not mutually exclusive. Consider crowd behavior at a sporting contest, for instance. Contagion—the reciprocal influence wrought by excitement, anticipation, and anxiety among spectators and players—is obviously evidenced. Similarly, convergence is witnessed, insofar as the stands

Emergent Collective Behavior in the 1987 NFL Strike

The introduction of "replacement" teams for the first time in the NFL provided an opportunity to investigate how controversial social definitions are constructed, modified, and interpreted within a modern social world. The results were consistent with the "emergent norm theory" of collective behavior.

The varying definitions given to the new teams were situated and interpreted within the participants' social locations within the world of professional football. (a) Language and (b) power were two of the main processes that were used to generate and maintain these self-serving definitions.

The owners called the new teams "replacement teams" so that the teams would appear as similar as possible to the regular striking teams. The new Bears were called "Replacement Bears." The owners pressured television networks to champion this definition. The networks complied because of their interest in successful ratings. Conversely, the regular players and several unions used negative labels to underscore the lack of ability and the intrusiveness of the new players. The new Bear team became the Scab Bears, the Bogus Bears, and the Phony Bears.

Some fans, coaches, and oddsmakers "accepted" the new teams. The nonunion players were not interpreted as replacements, as the owners hoped, but as less talented substitutes who were a great deal of fun to watch. Affectionate labels were used to reflect this definition. The new Bears were called Spare Bears, Care Bears, Near Bears, and Mini-Bears. Some sportswriters, however, provided mocking definitions of the new teams. The new Bears were tagged the "New Monsters of the Midway" and the "Cookie Monsters." The Union Bears had a reputation for being the physical defensive team from Chicago.

The substitute players, themselves, provided yet another definition of the new teams. Some replacements were trying to earn a place on the regular team after the strike while others were living out a dream making the most of the moment. "I played" was the signature linguistic term for the substitute players. Consequently, they saw themselves as "real" players. A replacement quarterback remarked:

> The fans accepted us as being **football players**, not scabs or replacements or whatever else you've heard.

The varying definitions of the new teams interjected certain problematics into lives of the participants in the social world of professional football. Since the replacement games counted in the standings, the substitute players had to avoid negative definitions if they were to maintain their view that "they were football players." One way they did this was to wear their "Walkmans" so that the music would drown out the sound of persons in the picket lines. The regular players were also caught in a dilemma since the replacement games counted in the standings. While they defined the new players as scabs, sometimes the regular players secretly pulled for them to win the games.

There were three major reasons why the regular players eventually gave in to the owners and ended the strike: (a) Replacement games were televised. Television networks needed Sunday NFL games. (b) The public did not side with the union players. Fans were used to Sunday football, and they had difficulty identifying with the "plight" of highly paid football players. (c) The media inadvertently worked against the objectives of the striking players. Their attention to the legitimacy of the replacement games deflected attention away from the union players' grievances. The causes of the strike, as emergent norm theory suggests, does not explain what people did or the changing issues in the strike.

SOURCE: Raymond L. Schmitt, "Strikes, Frames, and Touchdowns: The Institutional Struggle for Meaning in the 1987 National Football League Season," *Symbolic Interaction* 14, no. 3 (1991), pp. 237–259.

☐

are generally infested with partisan fans—some for the home team and others for the visitors. Finally, a norm may emerge in the course of the event that defines appropriate and/or inappropriate behavior and response.

In an analysis of the case study of the British soccer tragedy, Brinkerhoff and White write:

> The British soccer tragedy is a classic case of a panic crowd, and it is precisely the sort of event that contagion theory is designed to explain. People in the back pushed, and soon everyone was rushing forward in a blind panic. The whole thing took only a few minutes—too short a time for new norms to emerge or for any deliberate behavior.
>
> At first glance, convergence theory appears to have merit for explaining this crowd: Violence resulted when crowd members of a particular sort were drawn together to watch rough play. A little reflection, however, suggests that convergence theory is not very plausible here. The killing of Liverpool fans by other Liverpool fans. Under similar circumstances, a crowd of middle-aged, upper-class patrons of a sinking cruise ship could demonstrate the same panic reaction. This appears to be a simple instance of contagion.[22]

☐ THEORIES EXPLAINING SPORT SPECTATOR VIOLENCE

Case and Boucher provide a synthesis of several psychological and sociological theories advanced to explain violence on the part of sport spectators. "Traditionally, sport psychologists have attempted to study spectator violence by focusing on the aggression levels of individual fans. . . . In turn, sport sociologists have used collective behavior theories . . . to identify possible determinants of crowd violence in sport."[23] Psychological approaches to explaining sport violence include the drive-discharge, catharsis, frustration–aggression, social learning, and personality "theories." Sociological approaches to explaining sport violence include various explanations for crowd behavior as well as the value-added approach. Social scientists attempting to explain violence have resorted to three different explanatory schemes: (a) the biological theory, (b) the psychological theory, and (c) the social learning theory.

Biological Theory

The *biological theory* (also known as the *drive–discharge model*) of aggression claims that the intent to harm or injure others is inherent in our biological makeup; that is, humans are biologically programmed for aggression. According to Nobel prize-winning ethologist Konrad Lorenz, aggression in humans is traceable to our atavistic evolutionary ancestors. As descendants of primitive life forms we, like lower animals, are wired for aggression. Those who favor the biological explanation see aggression stemming from an innate drive to behave aggressively and believe that it is natural for individuals to seek out situations in which they can discharge their aggressive tendencies. This drive, it is claimed, has enjoyed a long evolutionary history in the species and has provided a host of species-maintaining and -preserving functions. Lorenz wrote, "The most important function of sport lies in furnishing a healthy safety valve for that most indispensable and, at the same time, most dangerous form of aggression . . . collective militant enthusiasm."[24] This perspective is closely aligned with the catharsis notion—the actual or vicarious expression of aggression is believed to reduce or drain subsequent aggression.

In a similar vein, psychoanalyst Sigmund Freud saw human aggression as a manifestation of the death instinct, or thanatos. To Freud, such instinctive energies necessitated periodic release; otherwise, they would lead to more catastrophic consequences. NFL coach and former player Mike Ditka supports this theory: "I feel a lot of football players build up a lot of anxieties in the off-season because they have no outlets for them. . . . I'm an overactive person anyway and if I don't get rid of this energy, it just builds up in me and then I blow it off in some other way which is not really the proper way."[25] One way aggressive impulses could be safely discharged is through sublimation into socially acceptable channels, as occurs typically in contact sports. The notion of substitute discharge was popularized in the movie *Rollerball*. In the film, the entire world community is controlled by a single corporation that banned war because it was too politically and economically threatening to its corporate complex. Because of humans' innate aggressive tendencies, it was necessary to provide some outlet for them. The sport of "rollerball"—a combination of physical mayhem, motorcycle racing, bowling, and skating—is concocted as the socially acceptable method for purging human aggression. In sum, sport, namely rollerball, became an institutionalized substitute for war.

Psychological Theory

A *psychological theory* of aggression is illustrated in the *frustration–aggression hypothesis*. Frustration often results from the blocking or thwarting of one's efforts to achieve a goal. Therefore, whenever an obstacle stands in the way of potential goal achievement, a common consequence is aggression (produced by the psychic state of frustration). The earliest formulation of this theory was a bit extreme, assuming that aggression always resulted from frustration and that frustration inevitably led to aggression. Contemporary social psychological research has discovered that frustration is neither a necessary nor sufficient condition for aggression to occur,[26] but this criticism does not deny its explanatory power in sport.

Berkowitz, arguing that no direct link exists between frustration and aggression, proposes that for the two to be linked together, two other considerations are necessary:[27] (a) Frustration must produce an emotional readiness to respond, and (b) the emotional readiness must occur in a setting providing cues linked to aggressiveness. Geen and O'Neal conducted an experiment to empirically test Berkowitz's contentions.[28] Male subjects were requested to deliver shocks to an experimental accomplice. Half of the subjects viewed a boxing film interspersed with loud noises, and half the subjects viewed a nonaggressive sporting event. The results indicated that the greatest degree of aggression occurred in the former situation. Not only did the researchers claim an outcome consistent with Berkowitz's explanation but they suggested looking at the role played by other factors (e.g., alcohol, excitement, heat) that may increase the arousal levels of spectators in sport.

Frustration surfaces in sports in sundry ways. It may stem from failing to play up to one's potential, from debilitating and nagging injuries, from questionable calls of game officials, from the baiting and heckling of fans, or from the taunts of coaches or management. Consider Cesar Cedeno during the strike-ridden 1981 baseball season. Cedeno was presented an indefinite suspension for going into the Atlanta Stadium stands and grabbing a heckler. The fan had been yelling "killer" and "boy" at him throughout the game (the epithet "killer" referred to his manslaughter conviction in Santo Domingo for shooting to death a teenage girl). Cedeno's family was attending the game and witnessed the heckling and the attack. The frustration apparently motivated him to go into the stands after the antagonizer. Another example of frustration involved shortstop Garry Templeton during the same abbreviated baseball season. Templeton was fined $5,000 and suspended indefinitely after being ejected from a game for clutching his genitals and raising his middle finger to the crowd. His actions stemmed from fans' boos after he struck out (the catcher dropped the ball) and then leisurely jogged toward first base before veering into the dugout. After undergoing emotional counseling, Templeton admitted that he was experiencing severe acute frustration in both his personal life and his career. In the summer of 1991, Cincinnati's Rob Dibble, a "nasty" boy, admitted it was necessary to seek counseling to control his volatile temper and aggressive behavior—both of which apparently stemmed from frustration.

Social Learning Theory

The third explanation for aggressiveness is social learning theory. The sport version of this theory is dubbed the *cultural pattern model* and maintains that aggressive behavior is learned, like other behaviors, through reward and punishment contingencies. Simply, if one is reinforced for engaging in violent activity, it is probable that the rewarded behavior will occur with greater frequency in the future. Recall, too, that reinforcements may be material (e.g., money) and/or social (e.g., praise, recognition, or awards). Hockey player Derek Sanderson, for example, recalls how he learned at age eight to become aggressive on the ice rink and to savor the results of others' violent play toward him[29] (see Chapter 6).

Various forms of social learning can occur as a result of the mere observation of another's behavior, particularly if the other's behavior is rewarded. The observer receives vicarious reinforcement. This seems to be what Edwards and Rackages had in mind when they expressed dismay over youth in organized sport programs attempting to imitate the aggressive playing style of professional athletes.[30] Similarly, former hockey player Bobby Hull staged a one-man work stoppage to protest the blood thirstiness of hockey players. Hull refused to play because of his concerns over the effect of hockey violence on children, including his own four sons.[31]

❏ AN EMPIRICAL INVESTIGATION OF VIOLENCE IN SPORT AND SOCIETY

There have been relatively few empirical tests of the validity of these three theories of sport violence. One noteworthy one was conducted by anthropologist Richard Sipes,[32] who tested whether the drive–discharge or the cultural pattern model better accounted for the relationship between society's social structure and sport forms. He was interested in the correlation between the nature of society (warlike and nonwarlike) and the existence of combative sports. He defined a "combative sport" as one played by two opponents (individual or team) with actual or potential body contact or with warlike interaction even in the absence of body contact; in a "warlike" society, attacks on others were frequent. The drive–discharge model predicts less violent sporting activities in warlike societies, because war would produce a drain or catharsis of innate aggression. On the other hand, the cultural pattern model predicts a positive relationship between the nature of society and the existence of different sport patterns; that is, warlike societies would have a preponderance of violent sports, and nonwarlike societies would have a preponderance of nonviolent sports.

Sipes selected twenty societies—ten warlike and ten nonwarlike—and found that 90% of the warlike societies had combative sports, whereas only 20% of the nonwarlike societies had combative sports. These findings support the cultural pattern theory and suggest that combative sports do not operate as alternate channels for the discharge of built-up aggressive feelings as the drive–discharge model predicts. In another phase, Sipes traces the popularity of combative sports over a 50-year period (1920–1970) in the United States. Sipes found a direct correlation between the popularity of warlike sports (as measured by National Football League, NFL, attendance and the sale of hunting permits) and the country's involvement in war. Interest in noncombative sports, as measured by parimutuel betting and major league baseball attendance, declined during wartime. Again, there was some support for the cultural pattern paradigm of sport violence.

Do sports events increase aggression and hostility in spectators? Two contrasting theoretical explanations have been advanced by social scientists. Social learning theorists argue that when an individual views positively reinforced aggressive behavior, the individual may be prompted to imitate similar behavior through vicarious reinforcement. The catharsis position claims that the viewing of aggressive acts by others may reduce subsequent aggressive acts by the viewer. The results of various empirical studies are not clear-cut, although this is probably a result of methodological issues.

Pencil-and-paper tests assessing the degree of pre- and postgame indices of hostility have been administered. The researchers have chosen aggressive sports (e.g., football, wrestling, and hockey) and relatively nonaggressive sports (e.g., swimming and gymnastics). Goldstein and Arms[33] studied fans attending two sporting events: football and gymnastics. Obviously, football is an aggressive "game," whereas gymnastics is nonaggressive. In comparing the pre- and postgame feelings of the fans, the researchers found that football spectators were more hostile, resentful, and irritable than gymnastics spectators. The hostility level for football fans, however, actually increased, regardless of whether their team won or lost, while gymnastics fans showed no such escalation. There was a slight tendency for spectators of violent sports to score higher on hostility after the contest than spectators of nonviolent events; however, these outcomes were not pronounced. Leuck, Krahenbuhl, and Odenkirk[34] replicated Goldstein and Arms's study with basketball spectators and discovered aggression levels increased between pre- and postgame measurements. Additionally, men (vs. women) students (vs. nonstudents), season ticket holders (vs. non-season ticket holders), and those with varsity athletic experience (vs. those without varsity athletic experience) were more aggressive spectators.

One potentially confounding factor in these analyses was self-selection; that is, hostile spectators may gravitate toward aggressive games (e.g., football), whereas nonhostile spectators may gravitate toward nonaggressive contests (e.g., gymnastics). The bulk of the research evidence suggests, however, that sports do *not* produce a catharsis effect; rather, aggression tends to breed aggression. Michael Smith, a student of collective behavior, denies the saltpeter-like effect of sport:

> I believe that violence in sport contributes to violence in the crowd, as opposed to the notion of catharsis, that viewing violent acts results in draining away feelings of violence. I have looked at newspaper accounts of 68 episodes of collective violence or riots among spectators during or after sporting events, and in three-quarters of those the precipitating event was violence in the game. Yet for decades and decades eminent scholars wrote without a shred of evidence that acts of violence in sport are cathartic or therapeutic for spectators.[35]

Some circumstantial evidence indirectly negates the cathartic function of sport and thereby supports its stimulant quality: Football players are two times more likely to suffer from hypertension as the general public and four times more likely than track athletes.[36]

Of the three theories of violence—biological, psychological, and social—the social learning formulation has received the greatest empirical verification in the context of sport. Regarding violence in ice hockey, Vaz wrote:

> A rule-violating normative system is a structural part of the larger hockey system. Illegitimate tactics (including various forms of violence) are considered technical skills for achieving team success, and are the standards for the evaluation and recruitment of players. Ironically there exists no formal instruction in the training of young (or old) hockey players to obey the normative rules. Learning of the normative rules occurs informally, but the forbidden aspect of such rules is considered irrelevant.[37]

These observations suggest that violence in sport is learned rather than innate. Smith corroborates this allegation.[38] He interviewed Toronto high school hockey players about their perceptions of significant others'—parents, teammates, coaches, and nonplaying peers—responses to their aggressive play. In general, he discovered that significant others were perceived as responding favorably to the players' legitimate and defensive assaults and unfavorably to illegitimate actions. Smith concluded that sports violence is a socially acquired behavior, a finding consistent with social learning theory. That sport socialization may include learning violence is dramatically documented by Robert Vare in his book *Buckeye, A Study of Coach Woody Hayes and the Ohio State Football Machine:*

> An inordinate amount of folklore has sprung up . . . around . . . Harold Raymond Henson III. It begins with the story of how he got his nickname—how his father, then serving his country in Fort Eustis, Virginia, hitchhiked fifteen hours back to Ohio, eyed his newborn son, and proclaimed, "He's got to be a champ." Six months later, according to another story they tell around Columbus, the older Henson, his own football career rudely ended by an appendicitis attack, carried his Champ out to the fifty yard line of Ohio Stadium and set him down on the sod. "Someday you will punish people on this field. . . . Someday you will be a Buckeye."[39]

❑ A THEORY OF COLLECTIVE BEHAVIOR

Smelser's **value-added theory of collective behavior** has attracted considerable attention among social scientists for its elegance in isolating some critical ingredients of collective behavior.[40] The notion of "value-added" is borrowed from economics and means that each collective behavior ingredient adds its value to prior determinants and increasingly focuses and channels the nature and course of subsequent collective acts.[41] Smelser attempted to determine *why* collective behavior episodes occur *where*, *when*, and *in the ways* they do. Accordingly, *six* determinants of collective behavior have been itemized: (a) structural conduciveness, (b) structural strain, (c) growth of a generalized belief, (d) precipitating factor(s), (e) mobilization for action, and (f) operation of social control.

Structural Conduciveness

Structural conduciveness refers to social conditions that are opportune for collective behavior to occur. This determinant is like the National Weather Bureau's appellation "tornado watch." The conditions are ripe for the spawning of tornadoes, but they are not inevitable at this stage. Because sport stands are inhabited by partisan fans (Vignette 15.2), the social basis for potential conflict exists. If, on the other hand, fans were a homogeneous and disinterested mass, and physically segregated, the conditions for disruption would be minimal. Structural conduciveness in sport takes *four* basic forms.[42] The *first* includes social factors—ethnic, racial, political, religious, social class, national, regional, and other cleavages that often provide the tinder for hostile outbursts. So-called natural rivalries can exploit existing antagonisms, as is suggested in the following account:

> Helmets strapped to their chin, the 400-man special operations battalion fanned out along Commerce Street at dusk. The barricades were in place, 200 reinforcements stood by, the ambulances were positioned, and Deputy Police Chief Robert O. Dixon, cucumber-cool in his tent command post, pronounced his forces ready.
>
> Seven hours, several fights, three assaults (one with a deadly weapon), and 119 arrests later, a water truck gently hosed down the drunken, staggering remnants of a throng that had numbered 20,000 or so, including Cecil Samara, who has the words "Big Red" permanently enameled across his six front teeth.
>
> What it was was football—which is neither just a game nor a spectator sport around here. It is serious business. . . . And when it involves the University of Texas and the University of Oklahoma in Dallas each fall, it is what remains of the War Between the States.[43]

The *second* form of structural conduciveness in sport derives from the insufficiency of channels for protesting grievances or the absence of targets to which blame can be attributed. Smelser suggested that developing countries are generally deficient in institutionalized channels for expressing disgruntlement, and this may explain, in part, the rampant sport riots in South and Central American countries and in parts of Europe.[44] The *third* type takes into account the availability of objects on which crowd hostility can be projected and vented. When spectators have easy access to playing surfaces, acts of violence may be more frequent if something triggers an episode of collective action. Managing the ecology of the sport site has been advocated as a counterdeterminant to such outbreaks. The *fourth* form encompasses the existing communication channels that play a role in collective behavior. The mass media are highly significant in this process, particularly when disproportionate amounts of space, time, and attention are allotted to sporting events. Similarly, the congestion in

☐ VIGNETTE 15.2

Home and Visiting Team Fans' Perceptions of a Football Game

Americans are sports fanatics and every year millions attend sporting events. It is of social psychological and personal importance that a sport contest is perceived differently. The present study involves the spectacle of collegiate football and conveys the significance of individuals' personal characteristics, their needs, desires, motives, and particularly, group identification such as devotion to one's team.

Albert H. Hastorf and Hadley Cantril studied partisan fans' perceptions of the final game of the 1951 season between two Ivy League football teams, Dartmouth and Princeton. Princeton went into the finale undefeated and was led by All-American quarterback Dick Kazmaier. Shortly after the opening kickoff it became evident that the event was going to be rough. Kazmaier left the field in the second quarter with a broken nose and a Dartmouth player was carried off the field in the third quarter with a fractured leg. Tempers flared both during and after the game. Princeton won the fracas and was penalized 25 yards, and Dartmouth 70 yards.

Accusations as to who started the dirty play erupted immediately. Both campus and metropolitan news media added fuel to the already kindled fire. As one might probably predict, Princeton accused Dartmouth of instigating the behavior whereas Dartmouth singled out Princeton. At this juncture, Hastorf and Cantril intervened and collected data for subsequent analysis. First, they designed a questionnaire for the explicit purpose of determining how each side saw—perceived—the contest. Queries regarding how the game was played, "rough and clean," "rough and dirty," "clean and fair," who started the rough play, and the like, were asked of both Princeton (n = 161) and Dartmouth (n = 163) psychology undergrads one week following the game. Second, undergrad-

uates at both institutions were later shown a film of the game and asked to note and record the number and nature (i.e., mild or flagrant) of infractions as well as who started the violations. At this point, we should mention that the researchers were not concerned with the accuracy (veridicality) of perceptions; rather, they were focusing on the process of social perception.

Some of the empirical findings were these. Most important was the marked contrast in perceptions of what transpired that Saturday afternoon. Nearly all Princeton students described the game as "rough and dirty" and not one perceived it as clean and fair. Almost 90% of the Princeton undergrads claimed the Dartmouth team started the fracas, in contrast to 53% (modal response) of the Dartmouth students who claimed both teams were responsible. Interestingly, upon reviewing the game film, Princeton students saw Dartmouth players violate the rules twice as often as their own team, and, furthermore, saw the Dartmouth team make over twice as many infractions as did the Dartmouth students. When the severity of the infractions were judged, the ratio was about two "flagrant" to one "mild" on the Dartmouth team, and one "flagrant" to three "mild" on the Princeton team.

The Dartmouth students saw the game differently. Hastorf and Cantril observed that "While the plurality of answers fell in the 'rough and dirty' category ... [and] ... over one-tenth thought the game 'clean and fair,' over one-third introduced a new category, 'rough and fair,' to describe the action." Although a third of the Dartmouth students felt their team had instigated the rough play, the majority thought both sides were culpable.

While additional specific findings could be reported, the discussion is sufficient to convey the flavor of the research report. Let us now consider some interpretative dimensions advanced by Hastorf and Cantril. It should be obvious that the game was selectively perceived by the bipartisan groups. During an athletic event, a multitude of events are simultaneously happening (on and off the field), and an observer catches only part of what is taking place. According to the authors, a happening only has personal relevance when it reactivates something of significance in "a person's assumptive form-world"—that is, of the matrix of events occurring on the field only some will be experienced, and usually those events witnessed will be affected by one's unique personal and social characteristics.

In summary, the empirical data suggest that it is dubious to conceptualize a football game as "something out there" that is objectively reacted to by the spectators. Rather, the content exists and is experienced only when the occurrences taking place have some kind of egoistic significance. Out of the avalanche of stimuli, only those events imbued with personal significance will be abstracted and experienced. The next time you view an athletic event, it might be interesting to imagine what other spectators are actually seeing.

SOURCE: Albert H. Hastorf and Hadley Cantril, "They Saw a Game: A Case Study," *Journal of Abnormal and Social Psychology* 49 (1954), pp. 129–134.

sports stadia provides a forum for the rapid transmission of rumor and other unverified or unverifiable reports.

Structural Strain

Structural strain is social malaise—frustration, deprivation, dissatisfaction, disgruntlement, conflict, tension, and uncertainty—that people experience. The infamous "Soccer War" between Honduras and El Salvador demonstrates the multifaceted nature of collective violence. Before the 1969 World Cup soccer games, El Salvadoreans had illegally migrated to Honduras. Although El Salvador was overpopulated, it was industrialized and affluent, whereas Honduras was a sparsely populated and economically depressed, agrarian country. The migrations deepened the resentments of Hondurans toward El Salvadoreans because of the latter's economic prosperity and control of the Central American Common Market. The antagonisms were further kindled by periodic border disputes between the two countries. Rumors of the decimation of El Salvadoreans in Honduras prompted the former country to mobilize troops and cross the border. Following the games and subsequent incidents, the two countries severed diplomatic and commercial ties.

Hooliganism. The **hooliganism**—wherein spectators invade pitches and playing fields to challenge participants and officials, ransack soccer trains, and throw sundry objects at visiting team players—of British soccer fans has been scrutinized under the heading of structural strain.[45] For example, in a soccer game between Manchester City and Leeds United (both English teams), Leeds' fans tossed beer cans at City's goalie when their team fell behind 2–0. Fans poured onto the playing field when it became obvious they were going to be defeated. Order was not restored until constables riding horses forced the fans back into the stands. On the same day, but in a different city (Exeter), fans who had already invaded the playing surface carried their rowdiness into the streets and tossed a wide assortment of artillery—beer cans, bottles, and bricks—through windows. British fans are such fanatics that at least three English teams—Leeds United, Manchester United, and the Glasgow Rangers—have been barred from competing with European teams at one time or another because of the wantonly destructive behavior of their enthusiastic supporters. When Scotland defeated Wales in Liverpool in 1977, moblike behavior on the part of fans led to the death of one man, and fifty others were hospitalized for stabbings, bottle lacerations of the face, and other assorted injuries. Scots are reputed to be the rowdiest of the rowdy fans. The fact that twenty-five Scots were arrested for various misdemeanors—drunkenness and theft—substantiates this allegation. Scotland's victory over Wales entitled them to play in the World Cup tournament in Argentina. Was the behavior of Scot fans transferred to South America? One of the best-selling buttons—"Argentina, We'll Make You Cry"—suggested it was.[46] Taylor's provocative explanation for this collective activity is of social import:

> The subculture of soccer in a working class community refers to groups of working men bound together with a concern for the game in general [the soccer consciousness] and the local team in particular. . . . During the last quarter of the nineteenth century and throughout the Depression . . . players were very much subject to control by such local soccer subcultures; expected to receive advice, "tips," expected to conform to certain standards of behavior [as the subculture's "public representatives"], and [in return] given a wage for so long as they fulfilled these expectations.[47]

What happened? This quasiprimary fan–player relationship was usurped through bureaucratization, professionalization, internationalization, and alterations in the control of the game, and alienated the working-class fans. Taylor said:

> As structural change in the game threatened [the] central value [that the game is theirs] and . . . exposed it as an illusion, a reaction has occurred in the [working class] subculture, and in the process of reaction, other values have had to take a second place. In particular, where once the turf was sacred, now [working-class fans are] prepared periodically to take up occupation of that turf in the assertion of other values.[48]

In short, Taylor interprets English hooliganism as resulting from working class fans' efforts to redress what they perceive as injustices and to reassert personal control over the game.

Dunning, a leading British sociologist of soccer hooliganism, reports that the fans most often involved in violence are from the rough sections of the working class. They come from depressed neighborhoods where violence is part of their everyday life, where being streetsmart and the ability to drink and fight are necessary survival mechanisms. For many of these fans fighting is one of the few sources of excitement, meaning, and status available. There is a close identification with the community, and what you have is the equivalent of a New York, Los Angeles, or Chicago street gang transported to a football (soccer) contest.[49]

Growth of a Generalized Belief

A **generalized belief** provides a potential solution to people's woes; it is two-pronged and provides (a) a diagnosis and identification of the causes producing the strain and (b) a prescription for coping with (mitigating or eradicating) the strain. Frequently, the generalized belief takes the form of an ideology—shared beliefs and definitions regarding the cause or the solution to the dilemma. The "Soccer War" provides a good illustration. According to Smith, before and during the games, the press reported charges of abuse of Honduran fans by El Salvadoreans, "accusations of brutality" directed at players on both teams, and rumors of Honduran renegades "taking El Salvadorean property and lives." These equivocal reports, issued in an already charged atmosphere, provided further fuel, in Smith's view, "for the development of hostile beliefs which presumably played a part in the" violence that erupted at the games.[50]

Precipitating Factors

Collective behavior does not erupt in a social vacuum, something or someone must initiate or precipitate the mass action. Smith's analysis of seventeen soccer riots showed that many of the contests at which unruly crowd conduct occurred were inordinately rough.[51] Interestingly, in many soccer riots, the mob action of spectators seems to have been precipitated by violent episodes (rough player interaction, spectator aggression, or reactions by police to fan behavior). The events that precipitated spectator hostility most frequently were disputed referees' calls—invalidating a goal, removing a player, or acts of violence—(often) in the waning minutes of a closely contested game. Cheffers and Meehan have studied the influence of "unwarranted" player actions—for example, fights—on fans' behavior.[52] Interestingly, in soccer, football, baseball, and hockey, fisticuffs among the contestants have triggered violence in the stands on 57%, 49%, 34%, and 8 1/2%, respectively. Common sense is corroborated in Cheffers's statement that "If it [violence] is on the field it will be in the stands." Hockey appears to be an anomaly insofar as violent action is more common than in the other sports investigated but precipitated stand violence less than 10% of the time. The researchers hypothesize that fighting is so common in hockey that spectators have become inoculated against its catalytic effects.

Fans' hostile reactions sometimes appear to be attempts to redress perceived injustices. Consider the following incident in professional football:

> With less than a minute remaining in a game between the Vikings and Cowboys in Bloomington, Minn., Dallas takes the lead on a disputed touchdown pass . . . virtually assuring a Vikings' defeat, and disappointed fans to go bonkers. One end of the field becomes a rain of whiskey bottles, golf balls, beer cans, flasks; at the other, two police officers stop fights among drunks. A whiskey bottle, lofted from the stands, strikes [the] referee . . . in the head, knocking him semi-conscious and opening his forehead.[53]

Mobilization of Participants for Action

Once a precipitating event occurs, the **mobilization of participants for action** begins to fester. Leadership, directed or diffuse, plays an important role at this juncture. To illustrate, consider a soccer game between Argentina and Peru in Lima's national stadium.[54] The violence that ensued was triggered by a referee's disallowance of a Peru goal that would have tied the score with six minutes remaining on the clock. Following the referee's decision, Matias Rojas, known as "Bomba" (the Bomb) because of prior attacks on officials, scaled a 7-ft barbed-wire fence. Rojas was detained before he could confront the referee, but he apparently provided a role model for others; a second man climbing the fence was tripped by an officer and then struck with a club. This appeared to divert the crowd's wrath to the police rather than to the referee. Others rhythmically pushed and kicked large holes in the metal barricade and gained entrance to the playing field and began scrapping with the police. Fires were set in the stands. In the end, three policemen died and much property damage was suffered. Leaders, like "Bomba," may incite a crowd or, in other cases, may taunt the audience into action simply with derogatory chanting, challenges, and directives.

Operation of Social Control

Social control consists of counterdeterminants used to prevent, interrupt, deflect, or otherwise reduce the onset or escalation of collective violence. Social control measures fall into *two* generic categories: (a) techniques aimed at preventing or minimizing the onset of collective outbursts, and (b) techniques used to extinguish violence after it has erupted. Once a collective episode is in progress, quick and intelligent control on the part of authorities is necessary but must be handled judiciously. Premature action has, on occasion, provided a catalyst for continued and even escalated misbehavior. For example, the use of tear gas in the Lima riot appears to have been ill-advised. Even the display of physical force can be problematic. According to Smith, the 500 policemen assigned to Ibrox Stadium in Glasgow for a Ranger–Celtic game were not a sufficient counterdeterminant, as in excess of forty people were injured.[55]

Smelser proposed that in instances of collective violence, the ultimate determinant of the course of events is the behavior of those responsible for maintaining social control.[56] Given the fan's desire for victory and the reality (in most sports) that only one team (or individual) will win, fans' expectations for winning may be unrealistically inflated by officials, coaches, announcers, and sportswriters who banter a team's remotest hope for success. In short, unrealized expectations can be exacerbating. In an atmosphere pervaded by emphasis on winning, it is not surprising that frustrations build up, perhaps to be vented when some occasion provides the opportunity.

❑ SOCIAL MOVEMENTS IN SPORT

Another important manifestation of collective behavior relevant to sport is that of social movement. A **social movement** is a relatively persistent and orchestrated effort to either change a situation defined undesirable or to prevent the alteration of a situation deemed desirable. As such, social movements tend to either encourage or discourage some facet of social change. Unlike the more fleeting forms of collective behavior, social movements are generally more organized, are of longer duration, and exert a concerted effort to change society. Familiar illustrations of social movements include the American and French Revolutions, women's, gay, and gray liberation, antinuclear, civil rights, ecology, and temperance movements. The often-used word *liberation* in the names of these movements captures the perceived importance of freedom from oppressive conditions. Social movements—collectivities that act with some continuity to promote or resist change in society—come in different types, the most common of which are transformative, migratory, expressive, utopian, reform, redemptive, alternative, revolutionary, and resistance movements.[57] These social movements differ in their goals, tactics, duration, and objectives. For example, revolutionary movements advocate radical change in the existing social structure whereby the old order is replaced with a new (e.g., the American and Russian Revolutions). Reformist movements, on the other hand, advocate changing some feature(s) of the existing social order (e.g., the movement to change public policy on abortion). Redemptive social movements, such as the "born again" Christian's, attempt to change people's lives. Following is a discussion of several prominent theories of social movements.

Theories of Social Movements

Why and how social movements originate is a none-too-easy query to answer. Some social movements' emergences are easier to comprehend than others. Policies, circumstances, and/or conditions that negatively affect the vested interests of certain categories of people often produce social movements (e.g., antiabortion, women's, and antiwar movements). More difficult to explain are those collective actions that seek new rights, aims, and goals. According to Oberschall,[58] a quartet of conditions lie at the origin and growth of social movements:

1. Changes in the basic conditions of life most likely to produce dissatisfaction and in the usual way for providing relief and handling problems.
2. Changes in beliefs and values, aspirations and expectations used in reacting to life conditions;
3. Changes in the capacity to act collectively, such as increased group size, more freedom to organize, better communications, greater mutual support among group members; and
4. Changes in opportunity for successful action, such as weakness of the opposition, support from powerful allies, and the success of other social movements.

Psychological Explanations

The earliest formulations that attempted to account for the origin of social movements looked to the psychological characteristics of those involved. By definition, those opposing the status quo (those spearheading changes in social conditions), fell into the deviant category and were sometimes considered "unbalanced," "deficient," and, later, as individuals whose psychological needs were not satisfied through conventional structures.

Sociological Explanations

From looking to the individuals who orchestrated or followed social movements, attention turned to looking at "society" for the roots. The societal approach has been dominated by two major theories: (a) *strain theory* and (b) *resource-mobilization theory*.

Strain Theory.   The tension and pressure individuals feel toward some social matters produces a strain that reduces their interests, desires, and abilities to operate within normal preestablished limits. (Smelser's second step in the value-added approach is labeled "structural strain," and he originally intended his paradigm to apply to social movements as well as the more dynamic and volatile aspects of collective behavior.[59]) Illustratively, the frustration caused by restrictive rules and regulations for Olympic-aspiring athletes when they know that some athletes in some countries are essentially "professional," and that the rules requiring amateur status are ridiculous led to the emergence of the shamateur movement (see discussion later in this chapter).

Deprivation Theory. The deprivation theory argues that when individuals feel deprived of basics considered important to their welfare, social movements may emerge. When individuals feel their inalienable social, economic, and political rights are violated, they may organize to bring about a more just state of affairs. Deprivation need not be absolute, because individuals tend to evaluate their circumstances relative to a particular category of people. In sport, the absolute value of professional athletes' financial compensation is light years above the average worker. However, athletes' salaries, for example, relative to the monies owners garner, is perceived as unjust. Hence, the labor activism movements discussed later become salient. Another version of strain theory focuses on deprivation as the taproot of social movements. The deprivation may be relative (e.g., when athletes receive a small share of the sport pie—despite the fact that their share is still mightily handsome) or absolute (e.g., when, in real dollars, certain societal segments are totally lacking). Accordingly, professional athletes may spawn a social movement, such as conventional labor activism, to enhance their social, political, and economic standing.

Strain theory's appeal and acceptance has declined since it became popular in the 1960s. A major contribution is that it set the source of social movements with social—not psychological—factors. Its primary weakness resides in its tautological reasoning. How do we know that Olympic athletes felt strain? Because they formed the shamateur social movement. Why did the shamateur movement unfold? Because there was strain. In short, the circular argument has proved problematic.

Resource-Mobilization Theory. How members of a social movement acquire and use resources—the media, individuals' skills and talents, physical equipment, and financial aids—to accomplish their collective goal is the cynosure of resource-mobilization theory. Accordingly, despite frustrated, tense, and "strained" people or, for that matter, unstable "deviant" individuals, a social movement will not emerge until people organize, direct, orchestrate, and mobilize their resources. Successful social movements hinge not on numbers per se, but on initially attracting politically experienced, and/or powerful individuals to their fold. For example, blacks have been discriminated against (see Chapter 8) in sports ever since their "integration." However, the politically wise and articulate black leader Harry Edwards provided dynamic and powerful leadership. In various ways, he helped mobilize blacks to protest (as in the victory stand demonstrations) their treatment in American society.

Strain (or breakdown) theory accents conditions 1 and 2 in the preceding list, whereas resource-mobilization (or solidarity) theory focuses on conditions 3 and 4. Like other competing theories, both have some explanatory power. Notice that strain theory links up with structural functionalism while resource mobilization theory dovetails with the conflict perspective.

The NCAA as a Social Movement

The **National Collegiate Athletic Association (NCAA)** is the dominant organizational force in intercollegiate athletics today. Over 800 colleges and universities maintain membership in it. All universities operating big-time intercollegiate athletic programs are members of this voluntary association. The financial status of the NCAA is very comfortable. Hence, there is ample reason to examine the NCAA as a socioeconomic phenomenon.[60]

The NCAA, which originated as a reformist movement, has matured to the point where either its outright demise, or a substantial restructuring, may occur. The reform genre of social movements is characterized by an attempt to modify some component of society without radically transforming the entire social fabric. The part of society that the NCAA originally attempted to remedy was the unfashionable violence and other abuses that marred intercollegiate athletics, football in particular, during the late nineteenth and early twentieth centuries. It is not unreasonable to suggest that the mayhem associated with football's flying wedge, an obsolete offensive formation where blockers formed a wedge surrounding the ball carrier, was partly responsible for the formation of the NCAA in 1906.

The Life Cycle Hypothesis

Social movements have a life cycle. Although social movements rarely have identical natural histories, there are sufficient commonalities among them to advance a **life cycle hypothesis**. Many social movements progress through *five* stages: (a) unrest, (b) excitement, (c) formalization, (d) institutionalization, and (e) dissolution.[61] Notice that these phases parallel those in Smelser's value-added scheme. Movements, such as the NCAA, that pass through these formal stages become the formal organizations that constitute part of the institutional fabric of society.

Unrest. The incipiency stage of any social movement is the perception that something is grievously wrong and needs to be rectified. Social unrest is often the principal precipitating factor. In the early twentieth century, intercollegiate athletics were disreputable and struggling. The rugged, dubious, and violent nature of intercollegiate football, typified by mass formations, gang tackling, and woefully inadequate equipment, led to many injuries and deaths. In the 1905 season, eighteen football players were killed on the gridiron. Unfortunately, colleges and universities were not organized in such a way that they could easily change football's rules and regulations; therefore, some academic institutions simply chose to eliminate football as an intercollegiate sport. It is accurate to state that the general public was somewhat revolted by the violence that permeated intercollegiate football.

Midway through the 1905 football season, President Theodore Roosevelt became the catalyst for important changes. After viewing a picture of a badly mauled Swarthmore football player, he threatened to abolish the game if remedial steps were not taken to modify its most objectionable aspects.

Excitement. The transition of a social movement from the stage of unrest to the stage of excitement is characterized by a clearer identification of the problem(s) needing attention. Whereas, during the stage of unrest, conditions are vague and ill-defined, conditions are adequately pinpointed during the stage of excitement so that specific action can be taken. To convert the unrest into action, a skillful and powerful leader (like Roosevelt) is essential. Roosevelt's threat to discontinue intercollegiate football was taken seriously. As a result, an initial meeting of Ivy League schools to consider a course of action blossomed into a larger meeting attended by representatives of sixty-two colleges and universities.

Formalization.   On 28 December 1905, a task force sought merger with an existing Football Rules Committee, having no formal connection with academia. This resulted in the formation of the Intercollegiate Athletic Association, the forerunner of the NCAA. The formalization stage of the life cycle of a social movement is characterized by the delegation and clarification of authority over business matters and rules and the creation of a general statement outlining the organization's philosophy and goal(s); This is almost exactly what occurred during the formative years of the NCAA. One important product of these deliberations was the approval of a dramatic innovation, the forward pass, "perfected" by Notre Dame's Knute Rockne and Gus Dorais. The approval of the forward pass clarified an otherwise murky situation in terms of football rules and, more importantly, opened up the game of intercollegiate football. The forward pass ultimately rendered the mass physical mayhem of the flying wedge obsolete. It also tremendously increased spectator appeal and hastened the development of big-time commercialized intercollegiate football as we know it today.

Institutionalization.   When a social movement such as the NCAA becomes a part of the established social order, it ceases to be a social movement in the traditional sense. Instead, it takes on the trappings of a formal organization with characteristic bureaucratic structures. The maturation of a social movement seems almost inevitably to result in a formalization of the movement's rules and traditions. Efficient bureaucrats replace agitators, and formal structure replaces informal customs. This stage of social movements may last almost indefinitely; in the case of the NCAA, such activities commenced on the day of its founding and have continued unabated to the present. A thick book of NCAA regulations prescribes a multitude of activities that have barely entered the mind of many people. Further, the NCAA currently conducts over 70 championship tournaments in men's and women's sports.

The scope and complexity of intercollegiate athletics, as typified by athletic recruiting abuses, the multiplication of postseason games, and highly lucrative television revenues, have created (some say for the better), a full-time NCAA professional detective staff that investigates allegations of rule infractions. The NCAA is frequently in the sports pages of newspapers because of its vitriolic conventions and its status as a litigant in a host of lawsuits.

Dissolution.   Some social movements never reach this stage; there is evidence that the NCAA has developed intolerable internal pressures that may bring about its dissolution as an organization. It is not outlandish to suggest that the NCAA may fracture into numerous sectlike bands, each doggedly pursuing parochial goals considered unrealistic by the NCAA as a whole.

An athletic organization that attempted to write common rules for, and include under one administrative roof, the Cincinnati Redlegs baseball team and the Little

League baseball teams of Cincinnati, Ohio, would undoubtedly have problems. This is, in a real sense, the bind in which the NCAA finds itself today. Its membership, which includes universities that operate athletic programs that are professional in everything except name, also includes colleges that field club teams composed of amateurs in the purest sense.

It is not clear that the NCAA can, despite its amoeba-like tendency to create new divisions, survive the heterogeneity of its membership. Few such organizations have ever succeeded in similar situations.[62] Further, some affiliates are so well-heeled financially that they are able to delay and frustrate the NCAA with innumerable Lilliputian legal suits. The NCAA typically wins such legal battles in the end but only after the points of controversy have long since become moot.

As early as 1910, the NCAA adopted the following formal objective:

". . . the regulation and supervision of college athletics throughout the United States in order that the athletic activities of the colleges and universities of the United States may be maintained on an ethical plane in keeping with the dignity and high purpose of education."[63]

While it is tempting to argue that goal displacement has taken place, a more realistic assessment of the growth of the NCAA would question whether the original objective was ever realized.

The NCAA has evolved from the small, pressure organization comprised of members with similar interests that constituted it before 1947. Today, the NCAA is a large, unwieldy organization that seldom reaches a consensus on any topic of substance. The "Golden Years" of the NCAA have most probably passed, and the future is likely to bring the demise of the NCAA as we now know it. In its place, there may arise either a series of separate organizations with internally homogeneous memberships or an NCAA that redistributes nearly all of its important powers to constituent divisions.[64] The key to this development will be, as in the past, the financial character of modern-day, big-time intercollegiate athletics. The irony is that the same factors responsible for the growth of the NCAA—the commercialization, bureaucratization, and professionalization of collegiate sport—may bring about its disintegration.

❏ CONTEMPORARY SOCIAL MOVEMENTS IN SPORT

Our case study of the NCAA as a social movement provided a historical account of the life history hypothesis of a social movement. Now, let us turn to four social movements that have evolved more recently in sport: (a) *conventional labor activism*, (b) *egalitarian movement*, (c) *shamateur activism*, and (d) *the democratic movement*.[65]

Conventional Labor Activism

The **conventional labor activism** movement was spawned by the monopolistic and capitalistic practices of professional sport owners in which athletes have felt exploited. In an article appropriately titled "The Owners Are Destroying the Game," Wayne Embry, the first black general manager (appointed by the NBA's Milwaukee Bucks), said: "Once this [basketball] provided a lot of fun, and a lot of good things came out of this game. But now it's a multi-million-dollar business. And some of the owners, out of ignorance, have taken basketball away from the players and the public who know the game . . . and those owners are destroying it."[66]

As noted in Chapter 11, professional sports have historically operated under various confining practices that restricted athletes' mobility and salaries. Several cases highlight the manner in which individuals have felt denied and then retaliated in an attempt to redress these restrictive practices.

In 1969, St. Louis Cardinals outfielder Curt Flood was traded to the Philadelphia Phillies without having been consulted and without his consent. Such practices were perfectly proper under professional baseball's reserve clause. Flood fought the trade and took professional baseball to court, arguing that such business transactions amounted to baseball players' being treated as slaves and chattel. He argued that such action would force him to abandon his St. Louis business, uproot his family, and was in violation of federal antitrust laws, because the trade required him to either play for the team he had been traded to or quit. The Supreme Court ruled in favor of professional baseball's traditional modus operandi.

Another illustration of labor activism is the successful challenging of the "four-year college rule" by Spencer Haywood. Haywood, who enrolled at the University of Detroit but subsequently quit school to sign an alleged million-dollar contract with the Denver Rockets, had jumped to the Seattle Supersonics and then to the New York Knicks. During this sojourn, a rule—the four-year college rule—designed to protect the colleges, intruded. It stated, in essence, that no athlete could sign a professional contract until his college class graduated. In compliance with this rule, Haywood's contract with Seattle was voided. Later, however, a judge struck the ruling down on the grounds that it restrained Haywood's right to earn a living.[67] A more recent case involving similar litigation is that of Mark Hall of the University of Minnesota. Hall, a talented basketball player, was put on academic probation and thus became ineligible for the team. He took the university to court and was reinstated on the team after a federal judge declared the school had jeopardized his future as a professional athlete (see Vignette 15.3).

These cases are but a few highlighting the upsurge of conventional labor activism in sport. Moreover, professional players are increasingly turning to professional agents to help them negotiate and secure equitable contracts. Conventional labor activism can also be witnessed in such unprecedented occurrences as strikes—the football strikes of 1974, 1982, and 1988; the baseball strikes of 1972, 1981, and 1985; the umpire strikes of 1978, 1979, the short-lived one of 1991; the North American Soccer League (NASL) 1979 strike; and the 1992 NHL strike—holdouts, boycotts (particularly at the Olympic level), and collective bargaining pursuits of professional athletes and union-like players' associations. The labor movement in sport, like labor activism in general, has tried to secure more favorable salaries and fringe benefits (i.e., bonuses and retirement perks), better working conditions, more Social Security benefits, and improved financial situations for athletes.

Egalitarian Movement

The **egalitarian movement** has goals similar to those of the labor movement, but its principal aim is to improve the political, social, and economic status of *black* athletes.

☐ **VIGNETTE 15.3**

Do College Athletes Have the Right to Play Regardless of Their Academic Circumstances?

Mark Hall, one of the Big Ten's best basketball players in the early 1980s, ran into academic difficulty—became academically ineligible and took the university to court and was eventually reinstated. A Minneapolis judge, Miles W. Lord, declared the University of Minnesota had "improperly jeopardized Hall's future as a professional and ordered him reinstated to the team."

To stay eligible for intercollegiate athletics, Hall had to achieve three things: (1) maintain a passing grade point average, (2) accumulate the proper number of credits, and (3) be enrolled in a degree program. He accomplished two of the three, the first two by earnings D's in rudimentary courses in the Gopher's open-admission program. He failed to meet the third criterion when the university's University Without Walls program rejected him. He then tried to major in the school's general college program but again was refused admission. Finally,

he submitted an application for an independent studies program but, again, was rebuffed. All the denials stemmed from scholastic insufficiencies.

Hall eventually learned that some "irregularities" regarding the handling of his admissions application occurred. He then took his case to a U.S. district judge (a University of Minnesota graduate) who sided with Hall. The university "responded that the courts had no business interfering with a strictly academic decision." The judge exhorted "that Hall's protected interest was in playing college basketball so that he could be drafted by a professional team; rejecting Hall—making him ineligible to play—without letting him answer the charges against him therefore violated his due process rights." Lord ordered Hall admitted to a degree program and returned to the team.

SOURCE: "Do Athletes Have a Right to Play," *Newsweek* (25 January 1982), p. 91.

☐

This movement was ignited by alleged racist practices in amateur and professional sport.

Sport sociologist Harry Edwards has been a major proponent of this movement.[68] He organized the Olympic Project for Human Rights before the 1968 Mexico City Olympics. Although he failed to produce a black boycott of the Games, it had far-reaching effects on American athletics. His and others' sway was, according to Nixon, "seen in the wave of threatened and actual boycotts . . . by black athletes in response to" racist practices of academic institutions, athletic personnel, and others. Rebellions among black athletes declined from about 180 during the 1968–1969 academic year, to less than 30 during the first half of the 1971–1972 season, to practically none today.[69]

Edwards's efforts to enhance black pride and reject racist policies materialized in victory stand demonstrations of black athletes. For example, in the 1968 (Mexico City) Olympics, Tommie Smith and John Carlos, after placing in the 200-meter sprint, raised gloved hands and lowered their heads in a Black Power salute during the playing of the United States' national anthem. When asked why they had acted in this manner, they claimed they did so to call attention to racial strife in America. Similarly, Vince Matthews and Wayne Collett, after placing first and second in the 400-meter race in the 1972 (Munich) Olympics, stood casually chatting and joking with their backs turned to the American flag. When queried as to why they had done this, they proclaimed it was to personify the casual attitude of whites toward blacks in the United States.

Finally, the egalitarian movement led to the banning of South Africa from Olympic competition in 1968 and Zimbabwe in 1972 because of their **apartheid** policies.

According to Edwards, those active in the egalitarian movement are college and professional black athletes who wish to bring about equal opportunity and rewards for black athletes. The movement is reformist in nature and aimed at restructuring sports for the benefit of blacks.

Shamateur Activism

The term *shamateur* is a hybrid term that joins the words *sham* (something that is not what it is purported to be) with *amateur* (a participant who plays for the love of the activity). The World Sports Federation (WSF), founded by Suzy Chaffee and Jack Kelly, advanced a platform for eliminating exclusivity, duplicity, and guilt experienced by "shamateur" Olympic athletes.

Olympic Sham. The foundation for the **shamateur movement** can be appreciated if the present-day Olympic symbolism and ideology are compared with the historical realities of the Olympiads. The official Olympic symbol consists of five interlocking rings or circles meant to represent sporting friendship and networks among persons of different continents. The Olympic flag consists of the linked rings on a white background. Even the circles' colors—blue, yellow, black, green, and red—are symbolic, because at least one of these hues appears in every nation's flag. The Olympic motto—Citius, Altius, Fortius—means "faster, higher, stronger." The Olympic creed reads: "Not to win but to take part, Not to have conquered but to have fought well." All participants take the Olympic oath, vowing to respect and abide by the rules of good sportsmanship. Finally, the Olympic flame symbolizes continuity between the ancient and modern Games. This torch is lit by the sun's rays in Olympia, Greece, and then transported by relay runners to the host site.

Although the ideals claimed are virtuous, many pernicious realities undermine one's faith in them. Furthermore, it is difficult to ignore the jingoism incited by international sport. According to McMurty, "Nationalistic gestures permeate just about every phase of the games; flags, anthems, uniforms, and nation scores punctuate the action like a military exercise."[70] Lyman reports the following goals of the shamateur movement:[71]

1. The individual athlete must have the right to determine the extent of training time required instead of the present sixty-day limit.
2. The National Olympic Committee and sports associations shall be responsible for arranging for athletes to be paid expense money, broken time payments and insurance coverage in connection with training and competition, whether these sources be private, governmental or commercial.

3. Athletes may receive scholarships and financial assistance while fulfilling educational requirements and may receive remuneration for actual employment in the athlete's sport, including positions as coaches.

4. Athletes may accept remuneration for television and other public appearances not involving actual competition in the athlete's sport. Remuneration for endorsements of commercial products connected with the athlete's sport may be accepted, but a share of such remuneration is subject to the rules of the International Federations and must be given to National Associations and other participating athletes.

5. National and International Federations and Olympic organizations shall be required to have competing or recently retired athletes as voting and fully participating members of such bodies.

For the most part, these stipulations appear to be reformist in character. They simply make it easier for such athletes to reap rewards openly. Only the mandate that the athletes, not the customers, public, coaches, or mass media, be responsible for their practicing runs counter to the existing structure of sport. The condition that the Olympics be for the participants may, however, have broad revolutionary implications.

Democratic Movement

Jack Scott, a critic of contemporary sport, has spearheaded the **democratic movement.**[72] He explicitly chastises sport for its win-at-any-cost ethic and its dehumanizing practices. This social movement dovetails with what Edwards calls the "humanitarian countercreed." The movement has been called democratic because of its belief that sport and athletics should, as Nixon states, "be of the people (participants), for the pleasure of the people (participants), and run by the people (participants)." It is humanitarian insofar as it shuns the spirit of annihilating one's opponent and, instead, advocates genuine concern for, in Nixon's words, "the welfare of fellow competitors."[73]

Scott also denigrates many aspects of contemporary sport—the hyped commercialism, the authoritarianism, the win-at-any-cost philosophy, the chemical abuses, the recruiting scams, the elitist spectator orientation, the overemphasis on "proving" masculinity, the exclusion of women, and the general conservative orientation—all of which, the sport establishment appears to be bent on preserving. Consequently, it is not difficult to see the fundamental differences between the sport establishment as we know it today and the democratic movement.

Each of the four social movements—conventional labor activism, egalitarian activism, shamateur activism, and democratic activism—poses some threat to the contemporary organization and character of American sport. The conventional labor activism and egalitarian activism movements are more reformative than revolutionary and have had success, as witnessed by the outcomes of union–management negotiations.

The shamateur movement has had some success, as witnessed by Olympic athletes' membership in the U.S. Olympic Committee (USOC), the appointment of a former Olympic athlete to the position of vice-president of the U.S. Ski Association, and former International Olympic Committee (IOC) President Lord Killanin's concession to mitigate some of the inequalities in amateur sport.[74]

Scott's democratic movement is the most revolutionary and transformative of all because it calls for a radical restructuring of contemporary sport. It takes little imagination to see what profound changes would take place in sport as we know it today if his ideas were implemented. It is not likely, in the short run at least, that Scott's ideas will materialize, because sport's dominant values—winning at any cost, commercialism and competitiveness—are reinforced by the values in the larger society. Just the same, it is important to appreciate the kinds of sociocultural change these social movements aim to bring about.

F.A.N.S.: The Consumer Movement

Consumer advocate Ralph Nader launched an aborted campaign (recall from our earlier discussion that not all social movements pass through all the life-cycle phases) to defend the rights of sports fans in the summer of 1977. The new **consumer movement** was dubbed **F.A.N.S.**—the *Fight to Advance the Nation's Sports*. To better understand Nader's contention that fans are being exploited, we would have to delve again into some facets of the economics of sports, a topic sufficiently discussed previously in Chapter 11. Instead, we will briefly consider some of the factors that Nader and others believe contribute to fan disgruntlement. According to Nader and Gruenstein,[75] the current state of affairs is the result of the corporatizing of sport.

Nader and Gruenstein advanced the following "bill of rights" for F.A.N.S., which proposes that fans have the following rights:[76]

1. Participate in the formation of the rules and procedures that govern the play and operation of professional and amateur sports competition.
2. Be informed about the operations and practices of professional and amateur sports.
3. Purchase reasonably priced tickets to sporting events and receive fair value for their money. Tickets to sporting events should be made available to the greatest number of fans and should not be reserved only for the wealthy and well-connected.
4. Ensure that food sold at those events is reasonably priced and well prepared.
5. Have their interests represented before Congress and other Governmental bodies.
6. Have their interest in the broadcasting of sports events effectively represented to the electronic media.
7. Have their interest in the resolution of labor, contractual, and other disputes involving sports effectively expressed and represented. Additionally, fans have an interest in ensuring, to the maximum degree possible, the health and safety of athletes.
8. Have their interest in maintaining or establishing the integrity of a sport, team, or event effectively expressed and represented.
9. Have knowledge of relevant information concerning sports enterprises that receive special public benefits in the form of low-cost leases of publicly owned

facilities, tax benefits, and other subsidies and privileges. Those enterprises further have a special responsibility to serve the public interest.

10. Fans are also citizens, taxpayers, and consumers and, as such, have an interest in seeing that the proper role of sports in America—as an enrichment of the quality of life—does not become exaggerated or distorted and that those associated with sports do not receive special legal, tax or other privileges detrimental to the public interest.

Evidence from a survey by Yankelovich suggested (correctly) that Nader's effort to rally fans to F.A.N.S. would not materialize.[77] A nationwide poll of 839 fans asked: Would you be interested in joining a fans group formed by consumer advocates? Of those surveyed, 85% said "no," 14% said "yes," and 1% said "unsure." The sample's responses may, in part, be due to the fact that they can express dissatisfaction by simply staying home or tuning their television to another channel. According to Kennedy and Williamson, the fans' reaction is more complex:

> It seems as though nothing can deter American sports fans from their preoccupation with professional sports or from their enthusiasm for it—not even expressed complaints about the commercialization that has occurred, the big salaries paid to the players, the motivations of the owners or the increase in unnecessary violence. . . . Instead, sport fans . . . state unequivocally that . . . they are enjoying professional sports even more now, are rooting harder than ever for their favorite teams, and are more enthusiastic about the star players than they were in the past.[78]

In comparing the survey data from Yankelovich et al., with some of F.A.N.S.'s proposals, we note some discrepancies:[79]

1. Fans did not seem particularly interested in knowing the operations and practices of professional sport. Of those polled, 78% said "no" to the question: Are you interested in knowing the details of contract negotiations and player salaries?

2. Fans did not appear to be overly concerned about the present and future cost of tickets. The responses to three questions support this statement: (1) Compared to other entertainment prices, do you think tickets to big-time sports events are too high, pretty reasonable, or a "bargain." Of those responding, 50% said "reasonable," 44% said "high," and 3% said "bargain." (2) If prices for tickets to your favorite sports event increased by 10 percent, would you still go? Of those responding, 76% said "yes" and 24% said "no." (3) If prices increased by 25% would you still go? Of those responding, 56% said "yes" and 44% said "no."

3. Fans did not seem to be overly dismayed by the cost of food served at sporting events, judging from responses to the question: Compared to prices at restaurants, theaters, and movies, do you think concession prices at sports events are too high, reasonable, or a bargain? Of those responding, 56% said "high," 38% said "reasonable," and 1% said a "bargain."

In short, the public opinion survey indicated that although some fans may be disgruntled, they are "more in mood to revel than rebel." The level of fan interest is up, their fun in watching games is up, their loyalty to favorite teams is up, and their enthusiasm for star players is up. Peter Gruenstein, former executive director of

☐ **VIGNETTE 15.4**

The Public's View of Various Facets of the Business of Professional Sports

Query	% Agree	% Disagree	Don't Know
Are professional athletes over-paid?	76	20	4
Are professional athletes devoted to the game?	42	50	8
Have sports events turned into spectacles?	55	42	3
Too much attention has been placed on entertainment and not enough on athletics?	59	35	5
Are there too many professional teams?	39	57	4
Owners tend to be more reasonable in labor disputes than professional athletes?	37	48	15

When respondents were asked if the cost of tickets to sporting events was too high, too little, or just right, 50%, 1%, 41% fell into the respective categories. Interestingly, an equal split occurred when the sample was asked whether athletes should (48% concurred) or should not (45% concurred) be permitted to strike. Relatedly, 52%, 40%, and 5% said strikes by players have no effect, decrease, and increase their support for a particular sport.

SOURCE: *The Miller Lite Report on American Attitudes Toward Sports* (Milwaukee: Miller Brewing Co., 1983), pp. 71–85.

☐

F.A.N.S., may be correct when he said: "We're in the Stone Age of consumerism in sports. . . . There's little recognition of fans as consumers and little understanding of the business of sports."[80] F.A.N.S. folded a few years after its inception! As long as contemporary sport fans endure the "abuses" of sport and accept the status quo (see Vignette 15.4), they will continue to provide the lifeblood for sport's current structure and functioning.

☐ **SUMMARY**

Collective behavior encompasses a wide range of group phenomena, including mass suicides, riots, manias, panics, mobs, revolutions, fads, fashions, public opinion, and social movements. The study of collective behavior is significant because it illuminates the dynamics of sociocultural change. To understand this social phenomenon, we considered three explanations of crowd behavior: (a) *contagion theory* maintains that a collective "mind" engulfs individuals in a crowd by way of emotional contagion; (b) *convergence theory* holds that individuals' real selves are ordinarily layered with a veneer of social propriety and may be shed away under anonymous and deindividuated circumstances; and (c) *emergent norm theory* maintains that norms, or behavioral expectations, emerge and guide behavior in certain crowd situations. An explanation of collective behavior, known as *value-added theory,* sheds some light on past and contemporary episodes of collective violence. According to this theory, there are six determinants of collective behavior: (a) *structural conduciveness,* (b) *structural strain,* (c) *growth of a generalized belief,* (d) *precipitating factors,* (e) *mobilization of participants for action,* and (f) *operation of social control.* Each of these necessary conditions was illustrated with examples from the sport literature.

Several *social movements*—persistent and orchestrated efforts to change a situation defined as undesirable or to maintain a situation deemed desirable—in sport were considered: the NCAA as a social movement, *conventional labor activism,* the *egalitarian movement, shamateur activism,* the *democratic movement,* and the *consumer movement* (*F.A.N.S.*).

❏ KEY CONCEPTS

Collective Behavior
Theories of Crowd Behavior
    Contagion Theory
    Convergence Theory
    Emergent Norm Theory
Normative Social Influence
Informational Social Influence
Value-Added Theory of Collective
  Behavior
Hooliganism
Generalized Belief
Mobilization of Participants for Action

Social Control
Social Movement
National Collegiate Athletic Association
  (NCAA)
Life-Cycle Hypothesis
Conventional Labor Activism
Egalitarian Movement
Apartheid
Shamateur Movement
Democratic Movement
Consumer Movement (F.A.N.S.)

❏ ENDNOTES

1. MICHAEL D. SMITH, "Sport and Collective Violence," *Sport and Social Order,* eds. D.W. Ball & J.W. Loy (Reading, MA: Addison-Wesley, 1975), pp. 277–330.

2. DAVID BRINKERHOFF & LYNN WHITE, *Sociology* (St. Paul, MN: West, 1991), pp. 587–588.

3. GARY MARX, "Argentine Soccer—Way of Life, and Death", *Chicago Tribune* (21 March 1991) Section 4, pp. 1–2.
    Op. cit.[2]

4. MICHAEL D. SMITH, "Hostile Outbursts in Sports," *Sport Sociology Bulletin* 2 (1973), pp. 6–10.

5. RON FIMRITE, "Take Me out to the Brawl Game," *Sport Sociology,* eds. A. Yiannakis et al. (Dubuque, IA: Kendall/Hunt, 1976), pp. 202–205.

6. JIM BAUGH, "Rowdy Spectators—The 'Bad Apples' of Sports," *Family Weekly* (4 June 1978), pp. 7–8.

7. JAMES A. MICHENER, *Sports in America* (New York: Random House, 1976), p. 429.

8. *Ibid.*

9. *Op. cit.*[6]

10. *Ibid.*

11. ELDON E. SNYDER & ELMER SPREITZER, *Social*

Aspects of Sport (Englewood Cliffs, NJ: Prentice-Hall, 1978), p. 134.

12. "White Sox Fans Fiddle as Ball Park Burns," *The Daily Pantagraph,* [Bloomington-Normal, IL] (13 July 1979), p. B1.

13. *Op. cit.*[6]

14. *Ibid.,* p. 7.

15. ARNOLD BEISSER, quoted in Bil Gilbert & Lisa Twyman, "Violence: Out of Hand in the Stands," *Sports Illustrated* (31 January 1983), pp. 62–72.

16. HERBERT BLUMER, "Collective Behavior," *Principles of Sociology* ed. Alfred M. Lee (New York: Barnes & Noble, 1951), pp. 167–222.

17. RALPH H. TURNER & LEWIS M. KILLIAN, *Collective Behavior* (Englewood Cliffs, NJ: Prentice-Hall, 1972).

18. JAMES W. VANDER ZANDEN, *Social Psychology* (New York: Random House, 1977), pp. 394–398.

19. *Op. cit.,*[11] pp. 130–131.

20. M. SHERIF, *The Psychology of Social Norms* (New York: Harper & Row, 1936)

21. SOLOMON E. ASCH, "Effects of Group Pressure upon Modification and Distortion of Judgments," *Readings in Social Psychology,* eds. E. Maccoby, T. Newcomb, & E. Hartley (New York: Holt, 1958), pp. 174–183.

22. *Op. cit.,*[2] Brinkerhoff & White, p. 588.

23. ROBERT W. CASE & ROBERT L. BOUCHER, "Spectator Violence in Sport: A Selected Review," *Sport Sociology: Contemporary Themes,* eds. A. Yiannakis, T.D. McIntyre, M.J. Melnick, & D.D. Hart (Dubuque, IA: Kendall/Hunt, 1987), pp. 239–245.

24. KONRAD LORENZ, quoted in Stephen K. Figler, *Sport and Play in American Life* (Philadelphia: W.B. Saunders, 1981), p. 176.

25. JAY J. COAKLEY, *Sport in Society* (St. Louis: C.V. Mosby, 1982), p. 59.

26. A necessary condition is one that must be present if a certain effect is to be produced, although it doesn't guarantee the effect. For example, it is necessary to be a female to become pregnant, although not all females are or become pregnant. A sufficient condition is one that inevitably produces an effect in and of itself. For example, removing a person's heart is sufficient to produce death, although death can occur in other ways.

27. LEONARD BERKOWITZ. *Roots of Aggression: A Reexamination of the Frustration Aggression Hypothesis* (New York: Atherton, 1969).
R. GEEN & E. O'NEIL, "Activation of Cue-Elicited Aggression by General Arousal," *Journal of Personality and Social Psychology* 11, no. 3 (1969), pp. 289–292.

28. R. GEEN & E. O'NEIL, *op. cit.*[27]

29. TOM PINKA, "Violence in Sports: American Style," unpublished manuscript, Illinois State University (1981).

30. HARRY EDWARDS & VAN RACKAGES, "The Dynamics of Violence in American Sport: Some Promising Structural and Social Considerations," *Journal of Sport and Social Issues* 1 (Summer/Fall, 1977), pp. 3–32.

31. *Ibid.*

32. RICHARD G. SIPES, "War, Sports and Aggression: An Empirical Test of Two Rival Theories," *American Anthropologist* 75 (January 1973), pp. 64–68, 70–71, 80.

33. JEFFREY GOLDSTEIN & ROBERT ARMS, "Effects of Observing Athletic Contests on Hostility," *Sociometry* 34 (March 1971), pp. 83–90.

34. M.R. LEUCK, G.S. KRAHENBUHL, & J.E. ODENKIRK, "Assessment of Spectator Aggression at Intercollegiate Basketball Contests," *Review of Sport and Leisure* 4 (Summer, 1979), pp. 40–52.

35. MICHAEL SMITH, quoted in D. Stanley Eitzen, *Sport in Contemporary Society* (New York: St. Martin's, 1984), p. 114.

36. *Ibid.,* p. 92.

37. EDMUND W. VAZ, "Institutionalized Rule Violation in Professional Hockey: Perspectives and Control Systems," in *Sport Sociology: Contemporary Themes,* eds. A. Yiannakis et al., *op. cit.*[23] pp. 235–241.

38. MICHAEL D. SMITH, "The Legitimation of Violence: Hockey Players' Perceptions of Their Reference Groups' Sanctions for Assault," *Sport Sociology: Contemporary Themes,* eds. A. Yiannakis et al., *op. cit.*[23] pp. 228–234.

39. ROBERT VARE, quoted in James A. Michener, *Sports in America* (New York: Random House, 1976), p. 435.

40. NEIL J. SMELSER, *Theory of Collective Behavior* (New York: Free Press, 1962).

41. *Op. cit.*[1] A substantial number of ideas and illustrations in this section have been gleaned

from this source, copyright 1978 by Addison-Wesley.

42. *Op. cit.*[1]
    Op. cit.[4]

43. JAMES P. STERBA, "In Dallas Football Is Bruising for Fans as Well as Players," *The New York Times* (16 October 1976), p. 30.

44. *Op. cit.*[40]

45. IAN TAYLOR, "'Football Mad': A Speculative Sociology of Football Hooliganism," *Sport: Readings from a Sociological Perspective*, ed. Eric Dunning (Toronto: University of Toronto Press, 1972).
    HOWARD L. NIXON, II, *Sport and Social Organization* (Indianapolis, IN: Bobbs-Merrill, 1976), pp. 25–28.

46. "Scorecard," *Sports Illustrated* 48, no. 4 (23 January 1978), p. 14.

47. IAN TAYLOR, "Soccer Consciousness and Soccer Hooliganism," *Images of Deviance,* ed. Stanley Cohen (Middlesex, England: Penguin, 1971), pp. 142–143.

48. *Ibid.,* p. 156.

49. DUNNING, quoted in Jo Thomas, "British Soccer Fan: Why so Warlike?" *New York Times* (31 May 1991), p. 5.

50. *Op. cit.*[1]

51. *Op. cit.*[4]

52. CHEFFERS & MEEHAN, quoted in *op. cit.*[4]

53. "Spectator Violence Becoming Part of Sports Scene," *Toledo Blade* (12 December 1976), p. 3.

54. *Op. cit.*[1]

55. *Ibid.*

56. *Op. cit.*[40]
    Nixon, *op. cit.,*[45] p. 26.

57. HERBERT BLUMER, "Collective Behavior," *New Outline of the Principles of Sociology,* ed. A. Lee (New York: Barnes & Noble, 1951), pp. 167–222.

58. ANTHONY OBERSCHALL, "Collective Behavior and Social Movements," *Sociology,* ed. Robert Hagedorn (Dubuque, IA: William C. Brown, 1983), p. 516.
    CHRISTOPHER B. DOOB, *Sociology: An Introduction* (New York: Holt, Rinehart, & Winston, 1985).
    IAN ROBERTSON, *Sociology* (New York: Worth, 1981).

59. *Op. Cit.*[40]

60. Some of the following discussion has been

taken from James V. Koch & Wilbert M. Leonard, II, "The NCAA: A Socioeconomic Analysis," *The American Journal of Economics and Sociology* 37 (July 1978), pp. 225–239.

61. ARMAND MAUSS, *Social Problems as Social Movements* (Philadelphia: J.B. Lippincott, 1975), has identified similar phases in the natural history of a social movement: (a) incipiency, (b) coalescence, (c) institutionalization, (d) fragmentation, and (e) demise. Social movements work for change and change in the process of bringing about change.

62. Some have equated the operation of the NCAA to that of a cartel. A *cartel* is an agreement among firms in an industry—sport in the present—to regulate and monopolize transactions and entry barriers, and it usually consists of a relatively small number of members (although powerful) with similar interests, costs, and revenues. Both big-time collegiate and professional sport function in this manner. See James V. Koch, "Intercollegiate Athletics: An Economic Explanation," *Social Science Quarterly* 64, no. 2 (June 1983), pp. 360–374.

63. *Statement of Objectives* (Overland Park, KS: National Collegiate Athletic Association, 1910).

64. In January of 1978, the NCAA approved dividing its Division I football-playing schools into two divisions: (a) some 139 "elite" universities and (b) I-AA, consisting of 108 universities that did not have football programs but did have basketball programs. Division II (195 schools) and Division III (233 schools) remained unchanged. The College Football Association, which is composed of the major conferences (with the exception of the Big-Ten and Pac-Eight, which became the Pac-Ten on 1 July 1978, and independents in the sport), was dissatisfied with the reorganization. The association tried again to create a "super division" of major football powers.

65. NIXON, *op. cit.,*[45] pp. 64–70. Some of the following discussion and examples are gleaned from this source.
    JACK SCOTT, *The Athletic Revolution* (New York: Free Press, 1971).

66. "The Owners Are Destroying the Game," *Sport* (1977), p. 23.

67. MICHENER, *op. cit.,*[7] pp. 260–262.

68. Harry Edwards, *Sociology of Sport* (Homewood, IL: Dorsey, 1973).
Harry Edwards, "The Black Athlete on the College Campus," *Sport and Society,* ed. J. Talamini & C. Page (Boston, MA: Little, Brown, 1973), pp. 202–219.
Harry Edwards, *The Revolt of the Black Athlete* (New York: Free Press, 1969).
"The Black Athlete," *Sports Illustrated* 75, no. 6 (5 August 1991) pp. 38–77.

69. Edwards, *Sociology of Sport, op. cit.,*[68] p. 151.

70. Robert Kropke, "International Sports and the Social Sciences," *Sport in the Sociocultural Process,* ed. Marie Hart (Dubuque, IA: William C. Brown, 1976), pp. 317–325.
John McMurty, "A Case for Killing the Olympics," *Maclean's* (January 1973), p. 34.

71. David H. Lyman, "The Future of the Olympics," *The Student Skier Three* (Holiday 8–9), 1972, p. 8.
Nixon, *op. cit.,*[45] pp. 66–67.

72. Scott, *op. cit.*[65]

73. Nixon, *op. cit.*[45]

74. Nixon, *op. cit.,*[45] p. 69.

75. Ralph Nader & Peter Gruenstein, "Blessed Are the Fans, for They Shall Inherit $12 Bleacher Seats, Indigestible Hot Dogs, $2 Bottles of Beer and 100 Overpaid Superstars," *Playboy* 25 (March 1978), pp. 98, 198, 200, 202, 204. Some of the following data are gleaned from this source.

76. *Ibid.,* p. 198.

77. Yankelovitch, cited in Ray Kennedy & Nancy Williamson, "Money in Sports," *Sports Illustrated* 49 (31 July 1978), pp. 34–50.

78. *Ibid.,* p. 39.

79. These comparisons combine the research outcomes of Kennedy & Williamson, *ibid.,* and the proposals of Nader & Gruenstein, *op. cit.*[75]

80. Peter Gruenstein, quoted in *op. cit.,*[77] p. 41.

16

A Brief Summary and Discussion

In this final chapter, we reiterate several key themes addressed in this text, provide a context for past, present, and future considerations in the sociology of sport, and provide a sociological summary of some of the threads discussed in this book.

❏ SOCIAL CHANGE

Sources of Social Change

Social scientists have identified several sources of social change that are pertinent to sport in society. Some of these factors are internal to the society; others are external.

Technology.   As demonstrated in Chapter 2, the application of scientific knowledge to the production of goods and services is a widely accepted definition of *technology*. The role of technology in sports is briefly summarized in the section entitled "Technosports."

Ideology.   A system of ideas that justify or call for alterations in a given society or subsystem of society is a definition of *ideology*. In Chapter 15, a discussion of five sport ideologies—*conventional labor activism, egalitarian movement, shamateur movement, democratic movement*, and *consumer movement*—demonstrated the role of ideas, social change agents, and activities in the conduct of collective human activity.

Diffusion.   Whenever cultures come into contact, there is an inevitable "borrowing" and adaptation of elements from one cultural complex to another. In sports, a number of present activities were imported to this country. The "rudimentary" games of rugby, tennis, and handball are illustrative of the role of diffusion in social change.

Theories of Social Change

Theories, as we saw in Chapter 1, are attempts to explain or account for some phenomenon. Sociologists have proposed various theories to account for changes in a society's social organization, social structure, statuses, roles, and social institutions. Competing explanations exist because of the complexity of social life and because different theories make different assumptions and sometimes focus on different aspects of the same social phenomenon. Four of the more popular theories of social change are evolutionary theory, cyclical theory, and conflict and functionalist theory.

Evolutionary Theory.   Taking their lead from Charles Darwin, who viewed biological organisms as evolving from simple to complex, evolutionary theorists viewed society as "progressing" from a more simple arrangement to a more complex one. Durkheim's[1] concepts of mechanical solidarity (bonding in societies attributed to common norms, values, and outlooks) and organic solidarity (bonding in societies attributed to a clearly defined division of labor) and Tonnies's[2] concepts of *Gemeinschaft* (small social arrangements characterized by intimacy and cooperation) and *Gesellschaft* (large social arrangements characterized by urban society) emerge out of the evolutionary tradition.

Cyclical Theory.   Historians Oswald Spengler[3] and Arnold Toynbee[4] promote the view that societies tend to rise and fall and intimate that social change is not always socially desirable. Sorokin's identification of ideational cultures is rooted in cyclical theory.[5] Accordingly, some cultures emphasize ideational components (spiritual values); others emphasize sensate components (what is perceived through the senses).

Conflict Theory. Marx's classic statement that societies are in constant class conflict suggests that the struggles between groups that are unequal in power, privilege, and wealth is the bedrock of social change.[6] In Europe, the transition from a feudal to a capitalistic society reflected the exploitation, dominance, and hegemony of the powerful against those of lesser means. In this way an alteration in the social arrangements was brought about.

Functionalist Theory. According to the functionalist perspective, societies tend toward maintaining a balance, or social equilibrium. Because perfect equilibrium is not likely to be achieved, disruptive movement's *natures* are continuous in societies. These disruptive maneuvers elicit social change. Parsons' notion of "integration" implies that societies will tend toward achieving a balance, or equilibrium.[7] So precarious is this balance that alterations in the social structure are inevitable. As functionalist theories emerged, it became acknowledged that dissatisfaction among societal members was a catalyst of social change. Black athletes' dissatisfactions with the economic arrangements in professional sports, Olympic athletes' dissatisfaction with the hypocrisies of Olympic competition, and fan's dissatisfaction with the nature of professional sports could, arguably, be reasons for the spawning of the various social movements discussed in the previous chapter.

☐ TWO FUTURISTIC SPORT SCENARIOS

Technosports

It has been noted that a major source of social change is technology. Johnson has proposed that one scenario of future sports is aligned with technology.[8] One futuristic example of the role of technology was revealed in the movie *Golden Girl*. Susan Anton, the lead actress in the film, was portrayed as the model female athlete, who, through genetic engineering (i.e., breeding acceptable humans and sport psychology) was capable of accomplishing numerous only-dreamed-of sport feats. Although this was a fictional account, the biography of former USC quarterback Todd Marinovich indicates that the scientific production of superior athletes is not too far-fetched.[9]

Even in the Commonwealth of Independent States (formerly, the U.S.S.R.), today, athletes are deliberately selected for their potential physical prowess and then subjected to early systematic physical and psychological training. The success of these programs is witnessed by referencing the Olympic rankings of several eastern European countries.

The roles of scientific technology in the production of superior athletes is revealed in a wide variety of ways. For example, training regimens, diet, equipment, facilities, and performance-enhancing drugs fall under this rubric. Advancements in the field of biotechnology, such as muscle fiber typing, enable identifying whether an athlete is better suited for events requiring strength (e.g., fast-twitch fibers) or endurance (e.g., slow-twitch fibers). Advancements in the production of sport equipment are also noteworthy. Wooden tennis rackets have been replaced by metal rackets, and metal rackets by graphite composite. Each transition improved performances. Fiberglass vis-à-vis wooden poles are correlated with increased heights among pole vaulters. Specially designed shoes have enhanced performance and also reduced injuries. Artificial turfs have replaced natural grass, and domed stadiums vis-à-vis open stadiums have become increasingly prevalent.

The marriage of sport and technology, while not of recent vintage, seems to have skyrocketed in the present.[10] Balls, particularly those used in golf and baseball, are "livelier." They travel farther and longer. Protective gear, particularly in the contact sports, have tended to increase the intensity and impact of performance. Whether stopwatches, electronic starting blocks, electronic scoring mechanisms, and/or photo equipment, quantification tools in sports have become more accurate.

Blood doping is a practice whereby blood is withdrawn and later returned and is considered to increase stamina.

Technology contributes to role specialization in sports.[11] For example, two-platoon football, the designated hitter in baseball, and talk of a separate offensive and defensive alignments in baseball are partially the result of technology.

The role of computer technology in the major sports of baseball, basketball, and football is also widely used. The compilation of statistics of team tendencies in certain situations, or player tendencies, and the various charting that clubs engage in, nicely corroborates this stance. The analysis of data entered into the computer has been used to assist in the drafting of college players and to predict the outcome of sporting contests.

What is the outer limit of human sport performance? (See Vignette 16.1.) Can this outer limit be extended? Coakley argues that superhuman athletes may be developed in the future via chemical and mechanical means.[12] Is it too far-fetched to plant a computer chip in the appropriate niche of the brain to produce a particular type of biomechanical movement via brain stimulation? How about the use of replacement parts or prosthetic devices to enhance performance? Can that be done, and should that be done? The nature of modern technology also elicits a variety of ethical issues previously not of concern.

The Wellness Movement

The "fitness boom" in North America is controversial and dubious. On the one hand we are led to believe that participation rates have skyrocketed. On the other hand, many surveys show that no more than perhaps one fifth of the population actually routinely participate—with as many as four fifths of the population "inactive."

Ecosports

Ecosports highlight the interfacing of sporting expressions and the natural environment with an emphasis on spontaneity, not rigidly structured preexisting rules. In ecosports, the emphasis is on the process, not the end result, of physical activity. Popular ecosports include skydiving, hiking, walking, hopping, backpacking, sailing, orienteering, hang gliding, skiing, scuba diving, rafting, frisbee throwing, and the like. The martial arts—judo, ti-kwon-do, and aiikado—also fit into this niche. Perhaps the prototype ecosport is the "Never Never Game." It is described by Coakley as follows:

☐ VIGNETTE 16.1

What Has Happened to the .400 Hitter in Baseball?

Stephen Jay Gould, an evolutionary biologist, studies the evolution of systems. That is, he studies the nature of variation and change in various phenomena. One of the "systems" he studies is baseball. He addresses the query, "What has happened to the .400 hitter?" In 1897 Wee Willie Keeler batted .432; in 1924 Rogers Hornsby batted .424; and in 1941 Ted Williams batted .406. No baseball player since Williams—over a half century ago—has hit at a .400 or better clip.

Why has the .400 hitter become temporarily extinct? Baseball aficionados have argued that night baseball, grueling schedules, dilution of talent, and improved and specialty pitching have all contributed to this decline. Gould, while not denying that these factors may have had an impact, argues that such reasoning is based upon a false assumption. He says that the .400 hitter is not a thing or a phenomenon. Instead, it represents the extreme right hand tail of a normal distribution. To understand why the .400 hitter is nonexistent one needs to look at the entire distribution of batting averages over time.

For the past 100 years, the average (arithmetic mean) batting average has hovered around .260. What has happened is that the standard deviation (a measure of variability) has declined in almost law-like fashion. The standard deviations by decade are:

1870s	.0496
1880s	.0460
1890s	.0436
1900s	.0386
1910s	.0371
1920s	.0374
1930s	.0340
1940s	.0326
1950s	.0325
1960s	.0316
1970s	.0317

Importantly, the arithmetic mean has remained fairly constant but the standard deviation has gotten smaller.

Why has the standard deviation declined? According to Gould, it is because all athletes—pitchers and hitters—have gotten better. Unlike clock sports that have an absolute standard, batting in baseball reflects the limits of human performance; that is, there is only so much a body can do, and there is a dynamic balance between hitting and pitching. The batting feats of the greats of yesteryear, performed close to the limits of human performance and a wide gap existed between the poorest performers and the best ones at that time. Today that range in baseball hitting is less variable. As an aside, Gould maintains that a Wade Boggs is close to the limit of performance and could have batted well over .400 during the earlier days of baseball. The standard deviation has declined because the sport has gotten so much better. Paradoxically, the departure of the .400 hitter is a sign of better overall athletic performances.

Consider this. With statistics, through a standardization process, we can compare performances of top hitters at different times. The formula for such transformations is:

z = raw score - arithmetic mean/standard deviation

In the 1910s, 1940s and 1970s the means and standard deviations were .266 and .037, .267 and .033, and .261 and .032, respectively. As examples, Cobb batted .420 (1911), Williams batted .406 (1941), and Brett batted .390 (1980). The respective standard scores (z-scores) for these stellar performers were 4.16, 4.21, and 4.03. Since 99%+ of all batting averages fall within plus and minus three standard deviation units of the mean and since these three individuals are all at least four standard deviation units above the mean, there is indisputable statistical evidence that

Cobb, Williams, and Brett were spectacular hitters.

Gould says, "Paradoxically, this decline [variation] produces a decrease in the difference between average and stellar performance. Therefore, modern leaders don't stand so far above their contemporaries. The 'myth' of ancient heroes—

the greater distance between average and best in the past—actually records the improvement of play through time."

SOURCES: Stephen Jay Gould, "Entropic Homogeneity Isn't Why No One Hits .400 Any More", *Discover*, August, 1986, pp. 60–66. Stephen Jay Gould, "Losing the Edge", *Vanity Fair*, March, 1983, pp. 264–272.

It is a game created on the spot; it has never been played before and will never be played again. Coaches, performance statistics, specialists, player substitutions, and team standings are nonexistent. Since none of the participants has ever played before, neither involvement nor success depends on anything but general physical abilities. Any number of people can participate, and expensive and highly specialized equipment is not needed. The game action is initiated with the help of . . . a jar of beads. Participants are randomly divided into teams, with a member of each team designated to grab a handful of colored beads and throw them on the ground. The color combinations of the beads are used as a guide to consulting the game book. Each section in the game book outlines different aspects of the game experience, such as the specific items to be used in the game, action to be engaged in by the participants when they use those items, the game boundaries, the relationships among team members, and the goals of the game. Each phase of every Never Never Game is determined by chance (the colored beads). The game may be played as long as desired with no records kept, no scores, and no winners or losers.[13]

There appears to be an increasing predominance of physical activities that highlight spontaneity, loosely organized games, and natural play. In some respects, these may be thought of as reactive measures to our technologically sophisticated society.

❏ DEPARTMENT OF SPORTS?

Keeley (somewhat) facetiously writes that the United States needs a Department of Sports, headed by a Secretary of Cabinet rank position.[14] Under the Secretary's leadership, all sports activities in the country would be coordinated. Federal agencies could regulate and oversee such things as the manufacture of equipment, band instruments, souvenirs and stadia, parking and food, concessions, musical aggregations, and drum majorettes. Everyone engaged in sports would be licensed after examination and payment of appropriate fees and taxes.

Standards would be established concerning wages, working conditions, safety, and union representation. Fair employment practices would be mandated to ensure equal opportunity, and the present practice of barring participants because of sex, age, physical handicaps, would be ended.

Regulators recruited from consumer activist organization and public interest groups would be engaged to advise on such matters as safety belts for spectators, air bags for use by athletes engaged in contact sports, foam rubber baseballs, and hot dogs and mustard containing no carcinogenic ingredients.

Any involvement in international sports would require action by the Department of State, with reviews by the appropriate boards. American athletes would not be permitted to engage in sports with other nations unless a treaty permitted such participation. This would give the country greater leverage in foreign affairs and enable the President to inject human rights issues into sport.

Is the preceding scenario fact or fiction? At present, it is fiction; as for the future. . . .

☐ ENDNOTES

1. EMILE DURKHEIM, *The Division of Labor in Society,* trans. George Simpson (Glencoe, IL: Free Press, 1964, original work published 1893).

2. FERDINAND TONNIES, *Community and Society* (East Lansing, MI: Michigan State University Press, 1957, original work published 1887).

3. OSWALD SPENGLER, *The Decline of the West* (New York: Alfred A. Knopf, 1962, original work published 1918).

4. ARNOLD TOYNBEE, *A Study of History* (New York: Oxford University Press), 1946.

5. PITIRIM A. SOROKIN, *Social and Cultural Dynamics* (New York: American Books), 1957.

6. KARL MARX & FRIEDRICH ENGELS, *The Communist Manifesto* (New York: International Publishers, 1930).

7. TALCOTT PARSONS, *The Social System* (Glencoe, IL: Free Press), 1951.

8. WILLIAM O. JOHNSON, "From Here to 2000," *Sports Illustrated* 69, no. 26 (1974), pp. 73–83.

9. BRIAN HANLEY, "QB Marinovich Reared for Role," *Chicago Sun Times* (3 September 1989), p. 9.

10. JAY J. COAKLEY, *Sport in Society* (St. Louis: C.V. Mosby, 1990).
ADRIAN AVENI, "Man and Machine: Some Neglected Considerations on the Sociology of Sport," *Sport Sociology Bulletin* 5, no. 1 (1979), pp. 13–24.

11. ALAN GUTTMANN, *From Ritual to Record* (New York: Columbia University Press, 1978).

12. COAKLEY, *ibid.*[10]

13. COAKLEY, *op. cit.,*[10] p. 374.

14. JOSEPH C. KEELEY, "Why Not a U.S. Department of Sports?" *The American Legion* (August 1979), pp. 18–19.

Author Index

Subject Index

ISBN 0-02-369871-3

1939	Heisman Trophy, named after John Heisman, established.
	First televised sporting event, a baseball game between Columbia and Princeton announced by Bill Stern.
	Little League founded in Williamsport, PA.
1940	Olympics cancelled because of outbreak of World War II.
	Emergence of sport cartoons.
1942	All American Girls Baseball League formed by Philip Wrigley.
1944	Olympics cancelled because of continuation of World War II.
1945	AP sports wires established for major league baseball.
	Kenny Washington and Woody Strode become first blacks to play in NFL (LA Rams).
1946	All-American Football Conference (AAFC) formed as a rival to the NFL.
	Outland Trophy, an award for outstanding college linemen, established.
	First time every major league game scheduled for one day was played "under the lights."
	Marion Motley became first black in the All-American Conference (Cleveland Browns).
1947	Jackie Robinson became first black to play modern major league baseball.
	National Basketball Association (NBA) formed.
	First official motorcross race, held in Holland.
1948	First flying plastic disk — a frisbee — invented by Fred Morrison.
1949	Ladies' Professional Golf Association (LPGA) formed.
	Jackie Robinson (Brooklyn Dodgers) became first black to win MVP in professional baseball.
1950	Three blacks broke the "color bar" in the National Basketball Association.
	Congress created the United States Olympic Committee (USOC).
1951	College basketball scandal.
	National Association for Intercollegiate Athletics (NAIA) founded.
1952	PGA allowed blacks to enter competition under "approved entry" classification.
	U.S.S.R. competes in Olympics for first time.
1954	Debut of *Sports Illustrated*.
	Fellowship of Christian Athletes (FCA) founded.
1955	Roger Bannister ran in the first sub-four-minute mile.
1957	Althea Gibson became first black to win title at Wimbledon.
1958	Medal play in golf mandated in PGA.
1959	Althea Gibson became first black female professional tennis player.
1960	American Football League (AFL) formed.
	Charlie Sifford becomes first black golfer on PGA tour.
1961	First national paddleball tournament, held in Madison, Wisconsin.
1963	First sports "instant replay."
	Elston Howard (New York Yankees) became first black to win MVP in American League.
1965	Houston's Astrodome opened.
1966	Major League Baseball Players' Association founded.
	Bill Russell became first black head coach (Boston Celtics).
	The South East Conference (SEC) became last football conference to integrate.
	International Review of Sport Sociology became the first journal devoted to a sociology of sport.
	First Super Bowl.
1967	American Basketball Association (ABA) formed.
1968	Racquetball organized with first national championship, in Milwaukee.
	Emmit Ashford became first black umpire (American League).
1969	Denise Long became first female drafted by the NBA.
	Diane Crump became first woman jockey to ride on a major track.
1970	AFL and NFL merged under the title National Football League.
1971	Wayne Embry became first black general manager in basketball (Milwaukee Bucks).
	"Satchel" Paige became first black from black leagues to be inducted into Baseball's Hall of Fame.
	Association for Intercollegiate Athletics for Women (AIAW) founded.
	Billie Jean King (tennis player) became first female athlete to earn $100,000.
1972	Title IX program (of the Educational Amendments) passed by Congress.
	Professional baseball player's strike.
	World Hockey Association (WHA) started its first season of play.
	Mark Spitz's spectacular sports performances.
	National recommendation that sociology of sport be taught in universities with a major in physical education.